Recent Developments in Technology-Enhanced and Computer-Assisted Language Learning

Bin Zou
Xi'an Jiaotong-Liverpool University, China

Michael Thomas
University of Central Lancashire, UK

A volume in the Advances in Educational Technologies and Instructional Design (AETID) Book Series

IGI Global
DISSEMINATOR OF KNOWLEDGE

Published in the United States of America by
IGI Global
Information Science Reference (an imprint of IGI Global)
701 E. Chocolate Avenue
Hershey PA, USA 17033
Tel: 717-533-8845
Fax: 717-533-8661
E-mail: cust@igi-global.com
Web site: http://www.igi-global.com

Library of Congress Cataloging-in-Publication Data

Names: Zou, Bin, 1968- editor. | Thomas, Michael, 1969- editor.
Title: Recent developments in technology-enhanced and computer-assisted language learning / Bin Zou, Michael Thomas, editors.
Description: Hershey, PA : Information Science Reference, 2019. | Includes bibliographical references and index. | Summary: “”This book focuses on technological influences on language education and applications of technology in language learning courses including foreign and second language learning”-- Provided by publisher.
Identifiers: LCCN 2019027739 (print) | LCCN 2019027740 (ebook) | ISBN 9781799812821 (hardcover) | ISBN 9781799812838 (paperback) | ISBN 9781799812845 (ebook)
Subjects: LCSH: English language--Study and teaching--Computer-assisted instruction for foreign speakers. | English language--Study and teaching--Computer-assisted instruction. | Language and languages--Computer-assisted instruction.
Classification: LCC PE1128.3 .R43 2019 (print) | LCC PE1128.3 (ebook) | DDC 428.2/40825--dc2 3
LC record available at https://lccn.loc.gov/2019027739
LC ebook record available at https://lccn.loc.gov/2019027740

This book is published in the IGI Global book series Advances in Educational Technologies and Instructional Design (AE-TID) (ISSN: 2326-8905; eISSN: 2326-8913)

British Cataloguing in Publication Data
A Cataloguing in Publication record for this book is available from the British Library.

For electronic access to this publication, please contact: eresources@igi-global.com.

Advances in Educational Technologies and Instructional Design (AETID) Book Series

Lawrence A. Tomei
Robert Morris University, USA

ISSN:2326-8905
EISSN:2326-8913

Mission

Education has undergone, and continues to undergo, immense changes in the way it is enacted and distributed to both child and adult learners. In modern education, the traditional classroom learning experience has evolved to include technological resources and to provide online classroom opportunities to students of all ages regardless of their geographical locations. From distance education, Massive-Open-Online-Courses (MOOCs), and electronic tablets in the classroom, technology is now an integral part of learning and is also affecting the way educators communicate information to students.

The **Advances in Educational Technologies & Instructional Design (AETID) Book Series** explores new research and theories for facilitating learning and improving educational performance utilizing technological processes and resources. The series examines technologies that can be integrated into K-12 classrooms to improve skills and learning abilities in all subjects including STEM education and language learning. Additionally, it studies the emergence of fully online classrooms for young and adult learners alike, and the communication and accountability challenges that can arise. Trending topics that are covered include adaptive learning, game-based learning, virtual school environments, and social media effects. School administrators, educators, academicians, researchers, and students will find this series to be an excellent resource for the effective design and implementation of learning technologies in their classes.

Coverage

- Hybrid Learning
- Digital Divide in Education
- Higher Education Technologies
- Virtual School Environments
- Collaboration Tools
- Classroom Response Systems
- Bring-Your-Own-Device
- Educational Telecommunications
- Social Media Effects on Education
- Adaptive Learning

IGI Global is currently accepting manuscripts for publication within this series. To submit a proposal for a volume in this series, please contact our Acquisition Editors at Acquisitions@igi-global.com or visit: http://www.igi-global.com/publish/.

The Advances in Educational Technologies and Instructional Design (AETID) Book Series (ISSN 2326-8905) is published by IGI Global, 701 E. Chocolate Avenue, Hershey, PA 17033-1240, USA, www.igi-global.com. This series is composed of titles available for purchase individually; each title is edited to be contextually exclusive from any other title within the series. For pricing and ordering information please visit http://www.igi-global.com/book-series/advances-educational-technologies-instructional-design/73678. Postmaster: Send all address changes to above address.

Titles in this Series

For a list of additional titles in this series, please visit:
https://www.igi-global.com/book-series/advances-educational-technologies-instructional-design/73678

Advanced Technologies and Standards for Interactive Educational Television Emerging Research and Opportunities
Dionysios Politis (Aristotle University of Thessaloniki, Greece) Petros Stagiopoulos (Aristotle University of Thessaloniki, Greece) and Veljko Aleksić (University of Kragujevac, Serbia)
Information Science Reference • copyright 2020 • 200pp • H/C (ISBN: 9781799802532) • US $165.00 (our price)

Advanced Technology-Assisted Problem Solving in Engineering Education Emerging Research and Opportunities
Manjit Singh Sidhu (Universiti Tenaga Nasional (COIT), Malaysia)
Engineering Science Reference • copyright 2020 • 270pp • H/C (ISBN: 9781799804659) • US $195.00 (our price)

Recent Tools for Computer- and Mobile-Assisted Foreign Language Learning
Alberto Andujar (University of Almeria, Spain)
Information Science Reference • copyright 2020 • 378pp • H/C (ISBN: 9781799810971) • US $195.00 (our price)

Next Generation Digital Tools and Applications for Teaching and Learning Enhancement
Mary T. Grassetti (Framingham State University, USA) and Julie Zoino-Jeannetti (Framingham State University, USA)
Information Science Reference • copyright 2020 • 300pp • H/C (ISBN: 9781799817703) • US $195.00 (our price)

Handbook of Research on Digital Learning
Matthew Montebello (University of Malta, Malta)
Information Science Reference • copyright 2020 • 394pp • H/C (ISBN: 9781522593041) • US $245.00 (our price)

Handbook of Research on Fostering Student Engagement With Instructional Technology in Higher Education
Emtinan Alqurashi (Temple University, USA)
Information Science Reference • copyright 2020 • 567pp • H/C (ISBN: 9781799801191) • US $285.00 (our price)

Emerging Techniques and Applications for Blended Learning in K-20 Classrooms
Lydia Kyei-Blankson (Illinois State University, USA) Esther Ntuli (Idaho State University, USA) and Mohamed A. Nur-Awaleh (Illinois State University, USA)
Information Science Reference • copyright 2020 • 310pp • H/C (ISBN: 9781799802426) • US $195.00 (our price)

Profiling Target Learners for the Development of Effective Learning Strategies Emerging Research and Opportunities
Shalin Hai-Jew (Kansas State University, USA)
Information Science Reference • copyright 2020 • 183pp • H/C (ISBN: 9781799815730) • US $145.00 (our price)

IGI Global
DISSEMINATOR OF KNOWLEDGE

701 East Chocolate Avenue, Hershey, PA 17033, USA
Tel: 717-533-8845 x100 • Fax: 717-533-8661
E-Mail: cust@igi-global.com • www.igi-global.com

Table of Contents

Detailed Table of Contents

chapter investigates perceptions of 799 secondary-school Malaysian secondary school students of two age-groups, and three school-types (urban, suburban, and rural) towards the use of the SNSs for informal learning purposes. For this chapter, learning that takes place outside the classroom is classified as "informal learning". Data were analysed quantitatively and comparisons across age-groups and school-types were made. The findings revealed that there was a general acceptance of SNSs as an alternative learning mode and that difference in usage between age groups was not significant. However, the findings across school-types were significant. Suburban and rural students appeared to use the SNSs more frequently for informal learning than urban students. This strongly suggested the need for Government to intensify its efforts in improving ICT infrastructure and facilities in rural areas.

Although open educational resources (OERs) can help bridge high-school – university vocabulary gaps, optimal utilization of OERs requires effective self-directed learning. This bi-national two-year study adopted a design-based research paradigm to collect Chinese university students' (n = 358) perceptions regarding design factors that support self-directed vocabulary learning in mobile learning environments (MLEs). Results showed that additional scaffolding after Year One in the form of L1 translations of high-frequency academic words significantly correlated with improved performance on basic level vocabulary exercises and pop quizzes. However, results suggest that moving mobile learning into the mainstream will require (1) design features that provide additional scaffolding for more complex vocabulary learning, (2) clearer guidelines for students on integrating desktop and mobile devices and (3) ongoing guidance from teachers to develop students' capacity for self-directed learning to ensure optimal benefit from independent study of vocabulary OERs.

This chapter investigates the user experience of the language learning platform Busuu as a tool for learning Spanish as a Foreign Language (SFL). Social constructionism has been highlighted by previous research as the theory on which Busuu is based, however, Álvarez concluded that Busuu constitutes an ecological system of nested semiotic spaces where pedagogical elements and principles from different theories of language learning interweave in complementary ways. Following a review of existing research, the chapter analyses data arising from a study involving a mixed group of university students who used the premium version of Busuu for four weeks. Data were collected via pre- and post-tests, a user experience questionnaire, and individual interviews, and were analysed using descriptive statistics and thematic analysis. Findings suggest that Busuu did not fully satisfy the requirements of a social network in terms of ease of participation, communication, and collaboration. Further research is required to explore the implications of usability testing for the design of effective SNSLL.

This chapter reports two related studies involving experienced university teachers of English language and literature from China, who engaged in reflection on how to blend FutureLearn MOOCs (Massive Open Online Courses) into their existing English Language Teaching (ELT) curricula while attending courses at Coventry University (UK). The first study relates to 12 lecturers who enrolled on an 'upskilling' English for Academic Purposes (EAP) summer course in academic year 2016-2017. The second one relates to the experience of 5 visiting scholars who attended classes on module Theories, Methods, and Approaches to Language Learning and Teaching on a postgraduate course (Master's of Art) in English Language Teaching and Applied Linguistics in academic years 2017-2018 and 2018-2019. The MA integrates 'off-the-shelf' MOOCs into its curriculum. The chapter investigates the Chinese teachers' perspectives on the adoption of 'hMOOC' distributed flip blends in a Chinese ELT context.

This chapter investigates learner motivation in an English as a foreign language writing classroom in an Indonesian university. Its originality arises from the fact that no substantive studies have explored learner motivation in the digital classroom in Indonesian higher education. A mixed methods data collection process was conducted involving 144 students from three-year groups who responded to an online questionnaire. Two classes from Year 1 (47 students) were taken as a sample to observe the learning process between an existing group that was introduced to the learning of English writing through Edmodo. The other group used traditional materials for their writing tasks. The findings are significant in that the high levels of motivation reported by the students were not reflected in the way they completed their writing tasks as the use of technology affected their motivation in complex ways. In conclusion, the study encourages future research in Indonesia that measures English students' motivation and technology-mediated writing task performance through longitudinal studies.

Semi-direct speaking tests have become an increasingly favored method of assessing spoken performance in recent years. Underpinning evidence for their continued development and use has been largely contingent on language testing and assessment researchers' claim of their interchangeability with more traditional, direct face-to-face oral proficiency interviews through theoretical and empirical investigations from multiple perspectives. This chapter initially provides background and research synopses of four significant test facets that have formed the bases for semi-direct and direct speaking test comparison studies. These are followed by the inclusion of a recent case study comparing test taker output from a computer-based Aptis speaking test and a purposively developed identical face-to-face oral proficiency interview that found a slight register shift which may be viewed as advantageous for semi-direct speaking tests. Finally, future research directions are proposed in light of the recent developments in the semi-direct speaking testing research presented throughout this chapter.

Online English courses have been developing rapidly in the past few years. As instructional videos play a central role in such courses, what constitutes an effective instruction video becomes a critical question for online English course developers. This chapter offers perspectives of EFL learners on this issue via content analysis of their feedback on existing instructional videos used in online English courses. The data consisted of 51 learners' comments on three micro-courses and 3,510 learner reviews on 41 English MOOCs. Analysis of the data revealed the most favorable features of an instructional video, the means to actualize these features, and learners' perceptions of different aspects of the physical design of an instructional video. The findings provided video producers with suggestions on the design and production of instructional videos used in online English courses.

Not many studies have been present on the effects of blogging, particularly with respect to English as a Foreign Language (EFL) writing motivation. Those studies did not focus on the effect of the use of blogs on Turkish EFL learners' writing motivation. Thus, this chapter examines how the use of blogs affects EFL writing motivation among EFL learners in a Turkish EFL learning context. A questionnaire interrogating demographic information, a pre-test and a post-test measuring writing achievement were administered to a group of participants including 48 language learners. According to results, blogging on its own does not increase motivation; however, the process-based writing instruction mainly has positive influences on EFL learners' motivation in both traditional pen-paper and blog environments. Thus, EFL teachers need to know that the use of blogs does not increase motivation among Turkish EFL learners. To increase their motivation level, it is also recommended that teachers should use a writing environment where their students are encouraged to write in the target language.

This chapter is a review of a three-year journey into exploring the development, mobilisation, and enactment of Malaysian ESL teachers' technological pedagogical content knowledge through a professional learning community known as 'Going Digital'. The first part of the chapter summarises the investigation on the effectiveness of the TPACK-IDDIRR + PLC as a transformative model of professional development to

Preface

Despite the fact that computer-assisted language learning (CALL) has been developing as an area of research for more than four decades, there are still many unaddressed issues and challenges facing researchers and practitioners in the field. In recent decades, for example, CALL research has been challenged because of its perceived lack of a theoretical orientation (Hubbard, 2004, 2008) and several CALL researchers have highlighted relevant theories, concepts and gaps in CALL contexts which might have been ignored in the past (e.g., Chapelle, 2017; Stockwell, 2018; Hubbard, 2019). In addition, apart from the use of the acronym CALL, many others have been used over the years to describe research taking place in the dynamic area of language learning and technology, such as Mobile-Assisted Language Learning (MALL), blended language learning, Computer-Mediated Communication (CMC), Virtual reality (VR), Augmented reality (AR), Massive Open Online Courses (MOOCs), Social Network Sites (SNSs) and Artificial Intelligence (AI), to name but a few. All of these acronyms evidence how CALL is a rapidly changing field which has a tendency to be driven largely by technological developments rather than by changes in pedagogical theory (Thomas, Reinders & Warschauer, 2013).

Bearing in mind these latest developments in an ever-evolving field of practice and research, it is evident nevertheless that CALL has developed into a multi-faceted and diverse field of interest that spans several disciplines and now attracts researchers and practitioners from around the world. In responding to the changing landscape of CALL as we continue to explore new areas of learning technologies that are more mobile, flexible, inclusive and diverse (Stockwell, 2007), this book addresses a number of topics that are representative of the current state of play and aims to provide both coverage of the key trends in the research as well as address several of the emerging gaps related to empirical research on mobile learning, online integrated learning and virtual learning.

THE CURRENT STATE OF CALL

It is clear that as CALL educators we are now working in an era when many of the hopes of previous generations of researchers have been realised in terms of the technologies available to teachers and learners. There are opportunities like never before to remove the fourth wall of the classroom and communicate with teachers and learners all over the world (Son, 2002; Shrosbree, 2008). This presents learners with unrivalled opportunities to engage with users of foreign languages in very diverse contexts and across all levels of the educational spectrum from early years education to adult education and lifelong learning. For teachers, there are equally unparalleled opportunities to participate in communities of practice in order to improve their support structures, particularly in the area of digital literacies, as well as access to resources and tools (Hubbard & Levy, 2006; Thomas, 2015). While the number of resources has multiplied, teachers and learners need extra skills to navigate a new landscape shaped by social media, the use of big data for student analytics, and beyond these the promise and threats of artificial intelligence. It is therefore more important than ever before for teachers and learners of foreign languages to understand the implications of these new technologies for social interactions that have become normalised in our social and working lives. Above all, we need to consider how best to leverage the potential of the abundant information and resources that the World Wide Web brings to us, but in ways that can be meaningfully applied in our pedagogical contexts to aid intercultural learning and foreign language acquisition.

It is important then, in addressing the contemporary context of CALL to examine its history and to move towards an approach that recognises its diversity. Bax's (2000, 2003, 2011a, 2011b) research on CALL has been welcome in this respect as it sought highlight several inconsistencies and to adopt a more critical tone, rejecting the extreme forms of excitement and denial which often accompany the emergence of new digital technologies in the education domain. In order to understand the hype surrounding many CALL technologies we need to be aware of the uncritical approach which often distinguishes it. A more critical understanding of contemporary CALL is required if we are to move the field forwards and to resist the all too easy use of adjectives such as 'revolutionary' or 'transformative' which often distinguish the use of technologies. Indeed, in other areas of educational technology, a more critical approach has emerged that challenges the narratives of transformation, revolution, and positive disruption. It recognizes that the history of CALL is neither straightforward nor linear. It has been narrated from a particular standpoint, at a particular time and place, by a particular group of advocates. While many CALL technologies are continuously identified with learning, this obscures the fact that many if not all of these technologies were originally designed for other non-educational contexts, and therefore the technologies have had to go through a process of change, in ways that might have fundamentally altered their original intentions.

Indeed, although CALL is focused on learning, the theories of learning cited by many CALL researchers typically pre-date the advent of digital technologies, and these have been used in place of new theories of learning that might have been more appropriate in these new environments. The major theories that have emerged such as connectivism have done little to fully explain the dynamics of online learning environments or understand self-regulated learning. In addressing recent trends in CALL, we need therefore to refocus on the learning aspect and on the pedagogy rather than assume that the technology always already implies a certain in-built approach to learning which is unchallengeable. Likewise, the use of CALL technologies needs to be understood as more than a simplified approach to learning but one that is complex and framed by a series of sociocultural and personal behaviors and factors.

The historical narratives associated with CALL are often overwhelmingly positive and little acknowledgement has been made of how CALL technologies involve more than mere transmission of information. We need therefore to continue to ask key questions, such as to what extent technologies shape teachers and students' approach to learning and their moods and emotions? And what impact in turn might this have on how students' feel during learning? While there has been an increased focus on the social elements of digital technologies, they have also placed a significant emphasis on the importance of individuals in what is increasingly a learner-centered process in which gain will be achieved individually rather than collectively. Online learners in particular are seen as individual autodidacts who if well-resourced can achieve and it is more likely to privilege some than others in this respect.

The history of CALL has often taken little or no account of how educational technology has become a multi-billion-dollar industry promoted by commercial providers and vendors, as a trip to any large international or even national conference will evidence. Educational technology is therefore a direct development from these corporate pressures and influences which increasingly shape the types of learning taking place in educational organizations. Large tech firms are key supporters of approaches to educational technology that help support their products, from initiatives such as one laptop per child to flipped classrooms. In the wider context the increasing confluence of neoliberal policies and values and education is also evident in CALL developments related to the digitalization of resources and approaches to teaching. Digitalization is strongly connected to monetization strategies that are based on quantification and justified by the logic of markets. Learning analytics and learning gain are two examples of this. The role of technology has been central to the emergence of a new managerialist and corporatist idea of the international university in which access to learning and information is constant and a product to be purchased and consumed. Given this background more critical approaches of digital technologies have started to emerge, whose purpose is to offer alternative rather than superior perspectives, positioning themselves in a constructive critique rather than damaging way. The use of educational technology needs to be framed in more challenging ways rather than as purely celebratory or evangelical, and thus more critical skepticism needs to be brought to bear on their integration and use.

Arising from this perspective, critical digital pedagogy identifies how technology and pedagogy are not neutral (Stommel & Morris, 2018). Yet, educational technology is increasingly representing itself as inevitable, apolitical and based on positivist approaches, particularly due to the recent interest in learning analytics and big data. Pedagogy increasingly means learning management systems, summative assessment and a concentration on outcomes rather than process-oriented approaches and creativity.

Opposed to teaching, those involved in critical pedagogy do so in reflective ways aimed at actively investigating teaching and learning in which learners are at the center of the process. This process is aligned with Freire's (2007) *Pedagogy of the Oppressed*, in which he critiques the *banking model* or transmission mode of education. So much of CALL technologies rely on a similar logic. Critical pedagogy on the other hand advocates a critique of pre-packaged pedagogical content, in that content is co-constructed rather than decided in advance of learning. Opposed to the logic of knowing content, critical pedagogy is concerned with a pedagogy of "non-knowing". The banking model is replaced by "problem-posing education," a horizontal rather than vertical space for questioning and co-authoring. Given these broader concerns of critical pedagogy, it has also sought to address issues of age, race, culture, gender, ability and geography in the digital sphere (Stommel & Morris, 2018).

While CALL was defined by Levy (1997, p. 1) as "the search for and study of applications of the computer in language teaching and learning," the emergence of mobile and web-based devices over the last two decades has given them, rather than the traditional personal computer, a key role in the development of CALL in the intervening period. Although mobile technologies have overcome earlier challenges associated with lack of availability of expensive and/or large equipment, CALL is still plagued by its focus on proving the effectiveness of technology as opposed to pedagogical environments in which technologies are not used (Son, 2004). Indeed, the acronym appears to assume that technology can 'assist' the process of language learning in positive ways, in ways which align it with the 'victory narratives' which often distinguish the wider area of educational technology which purport to demonstrate deterministic enhancements.

The last decade has seen universities around the world increasingly embrace 'digital' technologies as a new 'common sense' as evidenced by numerous policy and strategy documents, as they have been used to enhance the 'student experience' and provide the information and communication technology infrastructure that their student-customers and future employers in the global economy all appear to demand. Though the wider debate about digital technologies has been highly polarized, the increasing 'normalization' of digital technologies in students' social lives has made them an integral part of the higher education landscape, providing a well-spring of ideas and excitement that fit with the entrepreneurial nature of contemporary education as a business and service. This one-sided approach to digital technology use in education has been evident in CALL over the last three decades. That technology 'assists' language learning, or in other versions of the acronym 'enhances' it (e.g., technology-enhanced language learning), is a taken-for-granted assumption that rarely leads to further consideration of its effects on teachers and learners or its sociocultural or socioeconomic support. In CALL studies, researchers often ask how more technology can help solve the problems they identify, or if technology is better than a low-tech or no-tech context, but rarely ask why technology is the solution. Computer-assisted language learning (CALL), as Pennycook (2018) has said of applied linguistics in general, is perceived "all too often [as] a rather rudderless domain of work that reacts to whatever new trend turns up on the radar" (p. 8). In addressing this current context of challenges and opportunities in the domain of CALL, this book brings together sixteen state of the art chapters to explore recent content and methodological trends in the field, and to adopt a questioning and critical stance that has been called for above.

AN OVERVIEW OF THE BOOK

In "Revisiting Gaps in the CALL Literature," Joy L. Egbert, Seyed Abdollah Shahrokni, Xue Zhang and Intissar Ahmed Yahia discuss some under-addressed areas in the CALL research and reinforce the key principles of CALL teaching and learning in order to explore several of the most important gaps in the literature in the CALL field. They argue that it is vital to look at these gaps in language teaching and learning in the CALL environment to address the rationale for the use of technology and to review the impact of CALL research. Arising from this basis, the authors then provide suggestions on how to research in the CALL context in an age of mobile devices. This chapter is crucial for establishing future directions in CALL research because some language researchers argue that there is a lack of rationale for CALL and ultimately challenge the role and use of CALL in language teaching and learning. Overall, this important chapter sets the scene for the book as a whole and provides a solid overview of the theoretical background of CALL research thus responding to these questions and criticisms of its role. Its argument is therefore consistent with previous CALL researchers' theories in the CALL field, such as Chapelle (2001, 2003) and Bax (2003, 2011), and provides further support and rationale to strengthen CALL research, teaching and learning as we move toward the second decade of the new century.

In Chapter 2, "Influence of Age-Groups and School-Types on Informal Learning Through the Use of Social Networking Sites," Siew Ming Thang and Lay Shi Ng explore the use of social networking sites for school students for informal language learning in Malaysia. The participants included 799 secondary school students aged from 14 to 16 years old who were from three types of school: urban, suburban and rural. Findings suggested that there was no difference among ages for students in terms of their use of several social networking sites for informal language learning. These sites included Facebook, WhatsApp, Twitter, Instagram, WeChat, and Line. All of the participants generally accepted that using social networking sites was a substitute learning method, however, there was a significant difference among school types. They found that students in suburban and rural areas seemed to use the SNSs more often for informal language learning than students in the urban area.

In Chapter 3, "Supporting Self-Directed Vocabulary Study Towards Effective Design of OERs for Mobile Learning Environments," Ingrid Barth, Bin Zou, Elana Spector-Cohen and Rosalie Sitman investigated vocabulary learning in the mobile environment using open educational resources (OERs) at two universities. More than 350 students participated in this study and they practiced vocabulary with various types of exercises on their mobile devices in an English language learning environment. Students generally held positive views on the use of mobile devices for vocabulary acquisition and completed several types of vocabulary exercises, but they also asserted that a quiet place and personalization should be taken into account when practicing vocabulary on their mobile phones. It was also evident from findings that extra guidance from teachers is also needed to facilitate students' learning and as a result the findings will help authors to reconsider the design of language learning and vocabulary acquisition using open educational resources.

In Chapter 4, "An Investigation of Social Networking Sites for Language Learning and the User Experience: The Case of Busuu and Learning Spanish as a Foreign Language," Miguel Saona-Vallejos and Michael Thomas explore the user experience of language learners who used Busuu as a tool for learning Spanish as a Foreign Language (SFL). They collected data including questionnaires and individual interviews from university students who learned Spanish on Busuu for four weeks and found that learners were not satisfied with Busuu's social network for communicating and collaborating. Findings suggest that curriculum designers should consider investigating usability in more depth in order to explore the effectiveness of social networking sites for language learning.

Chapter 5, "Enhancing Writing Skills via Mobile Learning and Wikis,"

Ruby Vurdien investigates a learning environment utilizing mobile phones and wikis with 21 advanced EFL students in a private language school in Spain. Learners worked together to edit peer reviewed writing tasks and gave feedback to each other to develop their writing skills on the wiki platform and smartphones. The results indicate that learners provided positive comments on the collaborative work with respect to peer editing and feedback on the smartphone and wiki and this in turn fostered a collaborative working environment for students to develop their writing skills through the use of negotiation of meaning and by sharing knowledge.

In Chapter 6, "The Need to Engage With Smartphones and Social Network Sites (SNSs) at Korean Universities," Thomas E. Webster discusses smartphone and social network site (SNSs) use in Korean Universities and in the broader educational context in general. The paper highlights the features and potential of smartphones and SNSs in language learning in Korea by exploring the technology infrastructure and maintenance issues, teacher training, teacher motivation, cultural complexity, critical thinking and student engagement. Webster argues that although smartphones and SNSs bring a number of benefits, there are also some shortcomings such as addiction, anxiety, insomnia and depression. Findings from the study suggest that in order to avoid risk, teachers should develop rigorous guidelines and pedagogical frameworks to help students use smartphones and SNSs appropriately for English language learning.

In Chapter 7, "An Exploratory Study of Using Personal Blogs for L2 Writing in Fully Online Language Courses," Lina Lee explores the use of personal blogs for the development of L2 writing skills in online language courses. Data collection included post-surveys, blog entries and comments, and interviews with 48 beginner level students who used blogs for writing their essays. The findings show that participants used blogging as an effective tool for building their writing skills. Peer feedback influenced learners' efforts to make improvements and thus Lee suggests that effective feedback interaction is crucial to develop online collaborative learning.

In Chapter 8, "Chinese English Teachers' Perspectives on 'MOOC Flipped Blends': Project BMELTE (Blending MOOCs Into ELT Education)," Marina Orsini-Jones and Bin Zou discuss the use of flipped-MOOC curricular integration in an ELT course at Coventry University in the UK. Participants were Chinese university teachers studying at Coventry and the paper examines participants' perceptions of using MOOCs in their ELT curricula. Findings suggested that participants all agreed that they had gained new insights into ELT theory and practice by using MOOCs although they may have several different ideas emerged about how to use MOOCs in different contexts.

In Chapter 9, "English Language Learner Motivation in the Digital Classroom: A Case Study of a Vocational University in Indonesia," Baetty and Michael Thomas analyse the integration of technology-mediated task-based learning (TBL) in an EFL context in an Indonesian university. In particular the paper explores the impact of technology in enhancing students' motivation and performance in TBL writing classes. Findings indicate that participants found that the technology did not always influence their motivation positively, but more longitudinal research is required to investigate students' learning outcomes related to writing in the TBL classroom in which CALL technologies are utilized.

In Chapter 10, "Toward the Future of Computer-Assisted Language Testing: Assessing Spoken Performance Through Semi-Direct Tests," Ethan Douglas Quaid and Alex Ballter investigated test taker output from a computer-based Aptis speaking test to compare semi-direct and direct speaking tests. They indicate that semi-direct speaking tests is an increasingly favored method of assessing spoken performance. Findings suggest that the computer-based Aptis speaking test could be an advantage for semi-direct speaking tests based on their research findings. In addition, the paper provides future research directions in light of the recent developments in the testing of semi-direct speaking.

Chapter 11, "What Constitutes an Effective Instructional Video? Perspectives From Chinese EFL Learners," Yan Ding explores the use of instructional videos in online English courses by investigating EFL learners' perspectives. Data collection included 51 learners' comments on three micro-courses and 3,510 learner reviews on 41 English MOOCs. The results show the most favored characters in instructional videos and revealed students' insights about the design of this medium. In conclusion, suggestions are provided on the design and production of instructional videos for online English courses.

In Chapter 12, "Using Blogs to Motivate English as a Foreign Language Writers," Emrah Özdemir and Selami Aydin discuss the use of Blogs in fostering Turkish English language learners' motivation in developing writing skills. Data consisted of a questionnaire, a pre-test and a post-test which measured the writing achievement of 48 language learners in Turkey. The findings suggest that blogging had positive impacts on EFL learners' motivation in both traditional pen-paper and blog environments. As a result, EFL teachers should be aware that the use of blogs on their own does not increase motivation among Turkish EFL learners. In conclusion the authors suggest that teachers need to create a writing environment that can motivate students to write in the target language.

In Chapter 13, "Mobilisation and Enactment of Malaysian ESL Teachers' Technological Pedagogical Content Knowledge: From Professional Learning to Professional Practice," Cynthia C. James and Kean Wah Lee investigated the development, mobilisation and enactment of Malaysian ESL teachers' technological and pedagogical content knowledge through a professional learning community. They firstly explored the effectiveness of the TPACK-IDDIRR + PLC as a transformative model of professional development, and then discuss how to understand the mobilisation and enactment of TPACK. Finally, they report on the affordances and constraints of technology integration in the classroom context. They found that the model shows positive implications in terms of fostering technology integration practices of ESL teachers and as a result they provide several recommendations for using the TPACK model in the CALL context.

Chapter 14, "Exploring Pre-Service Teachers' Developmental Trajectories of Digital Literacies," Le Wang, Yi Luo and Pengpeng Feng investigated pre-service teachers' digital literacies in a wiki-based collaborative writing context. Data consisted of semi-structured interviews and observation diaries with pre-service teachers. In analyzing the data, the researchers focused on participants' attitudes towards technology, task organization and feedback, modes and genres, teacher-student relations and roles and responsibilities. Results suggest that pre-service teachers liked utilizing digital technology to the extent that they were highly likely to use it in the future for writing instruction. However, in order to improve the writing skills of their students in this context, teachers will have to improve their digital literacy skills with technology.

In Chapter 15, "Avatar Teaching and Learning: Examining Language Teaching and Learning Practices in Virtual Reality Environments," Geoff Lawrence, Farhana Ahmed explore the instructive prospective of immersive social virtual reality in language teaching and learning. They discuss 'Karelia Kondor', an avatar-learner and teacher of languages in Second Life Environment. The results show the correlation between the use of a hyper-immersive and engaging theoretical model and suggest that language teaching should provide pedagogical support to increase the potential of these immersive methods and develop communities of practice and spaces for autonomous language learning by sharing target language experiences.

In Chapter 16, "Using a Complex Technology in a Language Course: Examining Second Life in Terms of Participation," Airong Wang also examined the effect of virtual learning environments in English language teaching and learning. Data collection included audio recordings and chat logs in a Second Life environment. She highlights three challenges: software complexity, unreliable functionality and hardware and connectivity issues in Second Life. She also addresses the importance of pedagogical organizations, technological support, and the use of peers review in immersive environments. Finally, she provides suggestions about how to use immersive environments such as Second Life in language teaching effectively.

In conclusion, this book has discussed a number of interesting and timely areas in the CALL field. It does not only provide an overview of the theoretical background that is shaping the current field but also a wide diversity of examples of CALL research and practice. It can help language teachers to use the theories to enhance their understanding of CALL and reproduce the CALL studies in their own language classroom teaching. Despite this, there are still some topics that need to be covered. For example, in the MALL context, how to integrate mobile devices into classroom teaching and the curriculum was not addressed in this book, but the integration of MALL with class materials is a key area for language teachers to investigate and discuss over the next five years (Zou, Li & Li, 2018). Another interesting topic which was not covered in this book is Artificial Intelligence (AI) which is certain to influence the field in unexpected ways over the next decade (Kim, Soyata & Behnagh, 2018). There are already many AI products for language learners to develop speaking skills on the market and its influence is growing rapidly (Zou, et al., 2019). We predict that in the near future AI technology will be another extremely fascinating area for CALL researchers and language teachers to use and explore in their language teaching and research.

Bin Zou, Michael Thomas

REFERENCES

Bax, S. (2000). Putting technology in its place: ICT in modern foreign language learning. In K. Field (Ed.), *Issues in modern foreign language teaching* (pp. 208–219). London, UK: Routledge.

Bax, S. (2003). CALL – past, present and future. *System, 31*(1), 13–28. doi:10.1016/S0346-251X(02)00071-4

Bax, S. (2011a). Beyond the 'wow' factor. In M. Thomas (Ed.), *Digital education and learning: Opportunities for social collaboration* (pp. 239–256). New York: Palgrave. doi:10.1057/9780230118003_12

Bax, S. (2011b). Normalisation revisited: The effective use of technology in language education. *International Journal of Computer-Assisted Language Learning and Teaching, 1*(2), 1–15. doi:10.4018/ijcallt.2011040101

Chapelle, C. (2017). *The handbook of technology and second language teaching and learning*. Oxford, UK: John Wiley & Sons. doi:10.1002/9781118914069

Freire, P. (2007). *Pedagogy of the oppressed*. New York: Continuum.

Hubbard, P. (2004). Learner training for effective use of CALL. In S. Fotos, & C. Browne (Eds.), *New perspectives on CALL for second language classrooms* (pp. 45–67). Mahwah, NJ: Lawrence Erlbaum.

Hubbard, P., & Levy. (2006). *Teacher education in CALL*. Amsterdam, The Netherlands: John Benjamins.

Hubbard, P. (2008). CALL and the future of language teacher education. *CALICO Journal, 25*(2), 175–188.

Hubbard, P. (2019). Five keys from the past to the future of CALL. *International Journal of Computer-Assisted Language Teaching and learning, 8*(3), 1-28.

Kim, Y., Soyata, T., & Behnagh, R. F. (2018). Towards emotionally aware AI smart classroom: Current issues and directions for engineering and education. *IEEE Access: Practical Innovations, Open Solutions, 6*, 5308–5331. doi:10.1109/ACCESS.2018.2791861

Levy, M. (1997). *Computer-assisted language learning: Content and conceptualization*. Oxford, UK: Oxford University Press.

Pennycook, A. (2018). *Posthumanist applied linguistics*. New York: Routledge.

Shrosbree, M. (2008). Digital video in the language classroom. *JALTCALL Journal, 4*(1), 75–84.

Son, J.-B. (2002). Online discussion in a CALL course for distance language teachers. *CALICO Journal, 20*(1), 127–144. doi:10.1558/cj.v20i1.127-144

Son, J.-B. (Ed.). (2004). *Computer-assisted language learning: Concepts, contexts and practices*. Lincoln, NE: APACALL.

Stockwell, G. (2007). A review of technology choice for teaching language skills in the CALL literature. *ReCALL, 19*(2), 105–120. doi:10.1017/S0958344007000225

Stockwell, G. (2018). *Mobile assisted language learning: concepts, contexts & challenges*. Cambridge, UK: Cambridge University Press.

Stommel, J., & Morris, S. (2018). *An urgency of teachers: The work of critical digital pedagogy*. Hybrid Pedagogy.

Thomas, M. (2015). Researching machinima in project-based language learning: Learner generated content in the CAMELOT Project. Researching language learner interactions online: From social media to MOOCs, 13, 129-148.

Thomas, M., Reinders, H., & Warschauer, M. (Eds.). (2013). *Contemporary computer-assisted language learning*. London, UK: Bloomsbury Academic.

Zou, B., Li, H., & Li, J. (2018). Exploring a curriculum app and a social Communication app for EFL learning. *Computer Assisted Language Learning*, *31*(7), 694–713. doi:10.1080/09588221.2018.1438474

Zou, B., Liviero, S., Hao, M. Y., & Wei, C. Y. (2019). Artificial intelligence technology for EAP speaking skills: Student perceptions of opportunities and challenges. In M. Freiermuth, & N. Zarrinabadi (Eds.), *Technology and the psychology of second language learners and users*. London, UK: Palgrave Macmillan.

Section 1
CALL Overview

Chapter 1
Revisiting Gaps in the CALL Literature

Joy Egbert
Washington State University, Pullman, USA

Seyed Abdollah Shahrokni
Washington State University, Pullman, USA

Xue Zhang
University of Hong Kong, Hong Kong

David Herman
English Language Fellow Program, Taiwan

Intissar Yahia
Washington State University, Pullman, USA

Adnan Mohamed
Washington State University, Pullman, USA

Faraj M. Aljarih
University of Benghazi, Libya

Chioma Ezeh
Washington State University, Pullman, USA

Nataliia Borysenko
Washington State University, Pullman, USA

Sonia Lopez-Lopez
Washington State University, Pullman, USA

ABSTRACT

The body of research on CALL tasks and topics grows daily; however, a number of areas remain under-represented in the literature. While there are many gaps in the CALL research to address, this chapter

DOI: 10.4018/978-1-7998-1282-1.ch001

updates an earlier focus on 8 gaps, chosen because of their perceived importance in language teaching and learning. In presenting the gaps, each section in this chapter: 1) provides a rationale for exploring the topic, 2) briefly reviews studies that typify the extant research in the focal area, and 3) provides recommendations for future research. This chapter encourages all stakeholders in CALL to join in the rigorous and multi-perspective exploration of these and other under-addressed areas and strengthen the use of CALL for language learning and teaching.

INTRODUCTION

As of 2018, the computer-assisted language learning (CALL) topic areas that are the focus of this chapter were those that the authors found meaningful but for which they previously found a lack of research (see Egbert, et al., 2018). Upon further review, this dearth has been substantiated. Although the research literature on CALL is growing quickly, still "the body of empirical evidence, compared to other subject areas, is small" (Leakey, 2011, p. 60). This is particularly true around some practices that are common in classrooms but which the research has yet to address in any depth. Gaps in the CALL literature do not only arise from unexamined topics, however; they may also be caused by methodological and other study limitations in the extant literature. The lack of research from different perspectives, for example, both theoretical and methodological, means that we do not know as much as we could about using CALL with English language learners (ELLs).

Effective pedagogy can be supported by sound evidence. While there are many gaps in the CALL research to address, this chapter specifically emphasizes eight foci chosen by the authors because of their perceived importance in language teaching and learning and the increased potential for student learning when supported with technology use. The authors, all CALL researchers, come from 7 different countries across 5 continents and from diverse educational backgrounds and contexts. Because no one topic is more important than the others, they are not presented in any specific order. In presenting the gaps, each section in this chapter: 1) provides a rationale for exploring the topic, 2) briefly reviews studies that typify the extant research in the focal area, and 3) provides recommendations for future research. The purpose of this chapter is to encourage researchers, teachers, and students to join in the rigorous and multi-perspective exploration of these and other under-addressed areas and strengthen the use of CALL for language learning and teaching.

MORPHOLOGY

The first focus of this chapter is the gap in the CALL research on the topic of morphology (the study of word parts and word formation).

Rationale

Morphology plays an important role in language learning. Published studies in areas other than CALL (see, for example, Foorman, Petscher, & Bishop, 2012; Goodwin, Huggins, Carlo, August, & Calderon, 2013; Kieffer & Lesaux, 2012) showed that if ELLs learn how to use morphological strategies, it is possible for them to comprehend the meaning and syntactic structures of new words by identifying the base, the meaning of any affixes, and the grammatical functions of suffixes. As Goodwin et al. (2013) note, "the more they know regarding the many functions of morphemes such as the lexical *(un + friendly)* or syntactic information *(ly)* communicated through roots *(friend)*, suffixes *(ly)*, and prefixes *(un)*, the more these English language learners can determine the meaning of unknown words and complicated syntactical structures within English text" (p. 1389). Including studies published between 1981 and 2010, Goodwin and Ahn's (2010) meta-analysis showed that morphological interventions had a statically significant effect on language learning. However, the morphology studies did not include CALL.

Non-CALL studies indicate the significance of morphology for language learning. They provide a strong argument in favor of incorporating morphology tasks in CALL settings due to the benefits of language learning. However, CALL research does not currently integrate morphology-based tasks among its topics; data on practices, effectiveness, and benefits is lacking in the CALL literature despite the wide availability of morphology software (e.g., *Root to Words*, http://www.taptolearn.com/; *Word Parts* https://www.wordparts.net/demo-videos/; and apps from Lumos Learning, http://www.lumoslearning.com/llwp/educational-app-listings-for-students/prefix-and-suffix.html).

Although morphology is a significant part of vocabulary (e.g., 60% of English words are derived words), it remains understudied in CALL research. This is quite obvious from meta-analyses of CALL studies. For example, Grgurovic, Chapelle, and Shelley (2013) summarized 37 CALL studies published from 1970 to 2006 in foreign and second language settings. The results showed that CALL has a positive impact on language learning; however, the analysis did not include studies about morphology.

CALL Literature on Morphology

There are several published studies that have mentioned, but not centralized, morphology. For example, Nerbonne, Dokter, and Smit's (1998) comparative study investigated whether natural language processing (NLP) can play a role in CALL through software called GLOSSER. Twenty-two adult Dutch students in a French language program were divided into groups and assigned to two reading tests: one on a computer using GLOSSER and the other on paper. The results indicated that NLP can play an effective role in helping students learn word meanings and structure. The study also reported that one of the significant components of GLOSSER was its morphological analyzer. While morphology was integrated in this study with other topics such as bilingual dictionaries and phonology, there is still a gap in the CALL research that looks solely at the role of computer-supported morphological tasks.

Beechler and Williams' (2012) pre-post study shows the impact of CALL on word recognition. This study examined whether a software application called *Dolch Basic Sight Words* (http://www.sightwords.com/sight-words/dolch/) can support vocabulary knowledge. The results showed that the use of the software improved English language learners' vocabulary recognition. However, the software in Beechler and Williams' (2012) study was restricted to giving learners the pronunciation of the words; it did not provide students with the meaning of the words. While useful in its own right, this study and others like it have not addressed the role of CALL morphology study.

There is one unpublished thesis devoted entirely to studying the effect of CALL on learning morphology. Mohamed (2017) conducted a pre-posttest study on adult ELLs' use of a software application (*Spelling: Prefixes and Suffixes*, https://www.topmarks.co.uk/Flash.aspx?b=english/spelling) for teaching morphology to ELLs. ANOVA results showed a statistically significant improvement, F (1.512, 7.562) = 44.716, $p < .05$), in learning aspects of morphology (i.e., prefixes, suffixes, and derived words). Interview findings indicated that learners benefited from the software application' immediate feedback. The study showed that the immediate feedback available in the app played a key role in assisting participants to learn about morphology. To date, Mohamed's thesis is the only study investigating the use of CALL for learning morphology.

Recommendations

Even though CALL research has examined the effects of multimedia and multimodal tools on vocabulary knowledge and text comprehension, there is not a single published CALL study that explores the specific role of using technology-based morphological software or other apps in supporting vocabulary learning. Morphology can be investigated in any aspect of CALL in which vocabulary learning is central, for example, computer-mediated communication, digital storytelling, and other types of writing, computer-adapted reading, and so on. Experimental studies of the impact of CALL-based morphology on vocabulary growth, descriptive studies of how learners use and perceive morphology software, and a combination of both could help to shed light on the classroom use of morphology tools. Even though it is a narrow area of language learning, it is an important one.

PARAPHRASING

A second focus of this chapter is gaps in the CALL literature on the topic of paraphrasing. Shi (2012) claims that the literature on paraphrasing has shown a lack of agreement on a definition of good paraphrasing, and this appears to be the case. In other words, what counts as "acceptable" paraphrasing is not well-defined in the literature because scholars and educational institutions view and word paraphrasing definitions differently. For example, Shi (2012) defines paraphrasing as "restating a source text in one's own words with a credit to the original author" (p.135). Other scholars define paraphrasing as rewriting the original text with new words (e.g., Hirvela & Du, 2013; Loh, 2013; Uemlianin, 2000) or as a technique for citing or giving credit to the original author (Loh, 2013). Synthesizing the disparate definitions from the literature, paraphrasing can more specifically be defined as creating a text through applying required changes on the syntactic, semantic, and lexical levels based on the ideas and the attitude of the original text while maintaining citation style guidelines. Although paraphrasing is a crucial skill in academics and life, there is little literature around the use of CALL for paraphrasing.

Rationale

Paraphrasing skills are required for students to avoid under-attributed sources in all types of communication. In addition, paraphrasing skills are essential for academic writing (Hirvela & Du, 2013; Keck, 2006; Sun, 2012). Paraphrasing skills are used in many ways, including writing summaries, academic essays, and publishable papers, avoiding plagiarism, and enhancing reading and writing skills. For example,

ELLs who want to publish scholarly papers in Western journals must learn how to paraphrase, or to restate what was said by the author of the original text, to avoid using too much quotation or committing plagiarism (Pecorari & Petric, 2014), because plagiarizing could make students fail a class or even get them rejected from an academic program. Further, Sedhu, Lee, and Choy (2013) note that a number of studies have provided evidence that paraphrasing skills play a role in enhancing ELLs students' reading and writing skills. In other words, ELLs need to learn how to paraphrase adequately in order to successfully accomplish many academic tasks.

CALL Literature on Paraphrasing

Despite the importance of paraphrasing, there is a little research that looks specifically at paraphrasing with English language learners (ELLs) in general and there are only a few CALL-based research studies on paraphrasing in particular. The extant studies are also fairly narrow in scope; much of the research is based on the relationship between language proficiency level and ELLs' ability to paraphrase adequately and little of it employs technology. For instance, Campbell (1987) conducted a study to compare native speakers and ELLs in how they incorporate external material in their papers. The results suggested that ELLs' paraphrases were less effective than their L1 peers' because language proficiency significantly affected paraphrasing competence. In another study, Johns and Mayes (1990) carried out a comparison between proficient and less proficient ELLs in performing paraphrasing tasks. They asked ELLs from both remedial and advanced non-native speaker classes to perform a paraphrasing task. The findings showed that, even though neither group could properly restate the main ideas of the original passage, the students with low proficiency in English tended to copy sentences directly from the text. Further, McLnnis (2009) compared native English speaker (NS) with ELL paraphrases and found that the paraphrasing tasks were more difficult for ELLs compared with their NS peers due to the ELLs' lower language proficiency. These findings demonstrate that students who do not have an adequate level of language proficiency may be significantly less able to paraphrase effectively compared with those who have higher language proficiency.

In other studies, Pecorari (2003) and Shi (2004) attempted to describe students' paraphrases. However, neither of these studies went beyond classifying student paraphrasing into one or two categories that did not reflect the complexity of paraphrasing. For example, Shi (2004) examined L1 and L2 textual borrowing strategies and he added another category "modified slightly" to refer to the words have been added or deleted. In fact, in her review of research on paraphrasing, Keck (2006) found that "a reliable method for describing different paraphrase's types has yet to be established" (p. 263); this idea still holds.

Based on this gap, Keck (2006) conducted one of the few studies that examines NS and ELL writers' use of paraphrasing strategies. The participants were 79 NS and 74 ELL university undergraduate student writers, who read a text of 1000 words in 45 minutes and summarized it in one paragraph. Keck developed a construct called *attempted paraphrases*, defined as "as an instance in which a writer selects a specific excerpt of a source text and makes at least one attempt to change the language of the selected excerpt" (p. 264). Based on Shi's (2004) categories, Keck then developed a Taxonomy of Paraphrase Types to classify the NS and ELL attempted paraphrases into "four linguistically-defined, mutually-exclusive categories," which are near copy, minimal revision, moderate revision, and substantial revision (Keck, 2006, p. 264). This classification introduced the concept of *unique links* and *general links* to code students' paraphrases. Unique links refer to words or phrases written only one time in the original text. General links refer to the words or phrases repeated more than one time in the original text. General links were seen acceptable because it makes more sense when they are repeated. According to the taxonomy, a near copy had 50% or more words contained within unique links, a minimal revision had 20–49% words contained within unique links, a moderate revision had 1–19% words, and substantial revision had no unique links. Trained coders inserted the participants' attempted paraphrases into a computer program developed by the researcher to highlight the repeated words or phrases, that is, unique and general links from the original text. The results revealed that NS and ELLs writers' one-paragraph summaries similarly included, on average, five sentences. The NS writers used moderate and substantial paraphrasing strategies more than near copy. Using these strategies, the NS writers changed major parts of the original text, and their paraphrases were adequate. However, ELLs writers mostly applied the near copy strategy, copying approximately half of the original text and making only a few changes. According to Keck, this study provides evidence that different levels of language can help or hinder students in performing paraphrasing tasks.

Milićević & Tsedryk (2011) conducted a study using both descriptive and statistical data in order to assess French-as-second language (FSL) learners' paraphrasing. The participants were 20 university students in first- and third-year French classes. The participants paraphrased 5 sentences, which were evaluated on four levels: extralinguistic, linguistic, semantic, and lexical-syntactic. Data analysis showed that the first year FSL learners used restructuring of sentences more than lexical substitution; they also performed fewer lexical-syntactic reformulations and used fewer complex lexical-syntactic substitutions than the third year FSL. The authors noted that the differences between student levels were because the first-year students were still developing their lexical knowledge. Further, the authors noted that limited vocabulary knowledge was a challenge for the FSL learners.

Another study by Keck (2014) reexamined the same NS and ELLs' paraphrasing data collected in Keck's (2006) study and included data from additional participants in order to analyze how NS and ELL writers use paraphrasing strategies to compose a written summary. The participants in this study were 127 NS writers and 103 ELL writers. This study identified the differences between novice writers and more experienced writers in their use of paraphrasing strategies using the same scheme from her first study. Keck found that, compared with more experienced writers, the NS and ELL novice writers who had not mastered academic writing skills tended to rely more on copying from the original text. According to the results of this study, language proficiency did not play a major role. In other words, both NS and ELL writers face difficulty in understanding how to paraphrase, and they were similar based on their paraphrasing experience.

Whereas the above-mentioned studies provide some guidelines for studying paraphrasing, a review of the literature demonstrates that there is a lack of research on whether technology use—for example, having access to an online thesaurus, instant feedback from peers or others, or other resources -- might help ELLs to overcome difficulties with paraphrasing. One study that clearly examined paraphrasing in a CALL context is Chen, Huang, Chang, and Liou (2013). The researchers developed an online corpus-based paraphrasing system called PREFER. Their study evaluated the effectiveness of this paraphrasing system. The system was used to offer different paraphrases to the participants. The findings of this study reveal that PREFER provided more support to the students compared with using an online dictionary and an online thesaurus.

In another CALL-based study, Tan (2017) investigated the effectiveness of an online discussion forum (ODF) as an interactive educational tool to help ELLs effectively perform paraphrasing tasks. Forty-three ELLs enrolled in a writing course were divided into four forum groups. They were given a lecture on paraphrasing and then had to complete a two-part assignment. The first part was to paraphrase a sentence posted by the lecturer, and the second part was to post a comment on another student's paraphrase. Those posts were analyzed, and the findings indicated that the students used "cognitive skills, evaluation, social cues, and invitation form to perform the paraphrasing task" (Tan, 2016, p.8); in addition, the ODF helped the students to interact, comment, and reflect their knowledge about paraphrasing. This study provides a useful foundation for further investigation of CALL-based paraphrasing.

Recently, one study explored two online paraphrasing websites. Rogerson and McCarthy (2017) conducted a study to compare the outcomes from two internet-based paraphrasing websites, www.paraphrasing-tool.com and www.goparaphrase.com, in order to examine their effectiveness. The results showed that students' paraphrases included many instances of plagiarism. One implication of this study is that teachers may want to raise student awareness of the dangers of using such online paraphrasing tools.

Recommendations

There is a variety of paraphrasing tools on the internet, such as paraphrasing websites, software, and apps (see, from example, Chen, 2019). Recently there has been some attention to the importance of CALL research studies that measure the effectiveness of online paraphrasing. However, these studies are still few and this indicates that there is a gap in the CALL literature on technology-supported paraphrasing. Due to the importance of paraphrasing to language learning, additional studies can: first, raise awareness that the available digital paraphrasing tools might increase the issue of plagiarism since their usefulness has not been sufficiently explored; second, find agreement among educational institutions on a definition of paraphrasing that looks at paraphrasing as both process and product, and; third, describe ways to evaluate students' paraphrasing fairly by developing a valid and reliable paraphrasing rubric. Studies from both quantitative and qualitative paradigms can be conducted to examine these issues.

TEACHERS' REGULAR USES OF CALL TASKS

A third focus of this paper is understanding actual uses of CALL tasks in language classrooms. Although there is a large number of anecdotes and studies that describe single technologies or single uses of technology, there is less information about what CALL teachers actually do throughout a session, semester, or other extended amount of time. "Actual" in the sense used here implies that technology is used as teachers and students would naturally use it for teaching and learning rather than as part of a research intervention or task imposed from outsiders that may never be repeated. Understanding how teachers want to and do use CALL tasks day in and day out can help not only to develop teacher education in authentic ways but also to uncover student outcomes from the long-term use of CALL.

CALL Research on Day-To-Day Uses

There are numerous studies that look at authentic uses of a specific technology; that is, in which students are provided with authentic contexts and activities, access to expert performances, and modeling, where knowledge is constructed and supported collaboratively, and assessment of learning is integrated into the task (see, e.g., overviews in Chapelle & Sauro, 2017; Farr & Murray, 2016). These studies generally provide excellent details about the tasks and technologies being explored, but it is unclear what happens in the same CALL classrooms on a day-to-day basis. Murthy, Warriem, and Iyer (2017) agree that "[I] ack of research on effective integration of technology, especially in higher education settings, has led to the problems such as ineffective use of technology and lack of dissemination of good pedagogical practices at a systemic level" (p. 55).

One example of the type of study that does not explore actual uses of CALL is Yang and Chen (2007), who conducted a qualitative study that explored participant views in relation to the integration of the Advanced Joint English Teaching (AJET) platform for one semester. In the study, 44 tenth graders from one high school participated in asynchronous and synchronous tasks created by the course instructor for the AJET platform. Results of the study indicated that the majority of the participants believed that the tasks provided them with learning opportunities and fit with their learning styles. However useful, the study was limited because AJET is not used on a daily basis by the instructor; the researchers were only exploring the benefits of the platform for the sake of research.

Another example of a study with a relatively narrow focus is Fidaoui, Bahous, & Bacha, 2010. The researchers conducted a qualitative study 48 fourth-grade Lebanese students that examined the effectiveness of technology use in second language writing. The methods included observations, student and teacher interviews, and questionnaires over a period of three months. The study found that the majority of students had positive attitudes toward CALL tasks. The authors emphasized the importance of careful planning and monitoring before integrating CALL in writing tasks. The study did not, however, look at the use of the class's CALL tasks holistically; evidence is still needed about how language teachers use CALL tasks in all areas and with whichever technologies they decide to use in the course of day-to-day instruction.

In another example of classroom research with a limited emphasis, Shih (2011) conducted a mixed-methods study that examined the use of Facebook in the English language classroom. The technology was integrated with peer assessment to help 23 Taiwanese first-year English majors learn writing skills. All the students were required to use Facebook to post their writing assignments and to give feedback to each other as well as to different groups. The study reported improvement of English writing skills and willingness of students to interact with others in English. Although the study showed positive results in the short term (8 weeks), it is unclear how technology use might impact the students and their learning if used by the teacher as an integrated part of the whole course. In fact, the author even pointed out the great amount of time it would take for an instructor actually to implement the study tasks. In other words, the study did not report on how the teacher really planned and implemented CALL tasks across language domains, discipline areas, and in and out of class work; this remains a gap in the literature.

Finally, in a study conducted by Ware and Kessler (2014), the authors examined adolescent interaction and pedagogical integration of telecollaboration in two schools, one in the United States and the other in Spain. Two classes of 7th and 8th graders were chosen at each school and the students communicated using five different prompts with an average of three weeks per prompt. Data were collected using online interactions, interviews from participating teachers, and written answers from students using an Intercultural Discourse Questionnaire (IDQ). Teachers reported that they observed benefits from having students interact online, but that time was a constraint. Other ways in which the teachers did or may have wanted to implement CALL in their classrooms was not reported on.

Recommendations

In order to fill in the gap in the research on the actual use of CALL tasks by language teachers, more studies need to be conducted that report on how technologies are being used throughout the semester.

Although such deep, longitudinal, all-day classroom research is challenging, the results could be profitable in suggesting how CALL teacher education might be conducted more effectively, what long-term goals CALL use can help both students and teachers reach, and all the other little details of CALL use in classrooms that might be getting lost on a day- to-day basis over time. Research can be conducted that investigates how teachers plan, implement, assess, and think about CALL tasks throughout the curriculum and school year and how this process affects student outcomes.

MULTIMODAL FEEDBACK

Multimodal feedback (MMF) refers to any combination of audio, video, haptic, graphical, or text feedback provided in the language learning process. Although CALL research on MMF is becoming more prevalent, there are still gaps in the literature.

Rationale

The multimodality offered in technology-mediated environments can enrich interactional opportunities in the language learning process (Guichon & Cohen, 2016) and facilitate individualized learning and attentive engagement (Huang, 2016). By definition, MMF enables the teacher and others to provide feedback to learners through two or more feedback modes, and students can be encouraged to choose their preferred feedback types and learn from new ones. In other words, MMF may foster and expand interaction from traditional, asynchronous, single-mode teacher-to-student feedback to more systemic feedback that is also synchronous, includes more modalities, and can be teacher-and-student, student-and-student, and student-and-other (Caruso, Faschini, & Kuuse, 2019). By providing multiple language models, MMF may be more comprehensible to learners (Egbert & Abobaker, 2018), and thus more effective for learning.

CALL Literature on MMF

In the last 10 years, there has been an increase in the number of studies across the disciplines that relate technology-mediated feedback (i.e., feedback supported by technology) to general academic engagement and performance (e.g., Borup, West, & Thomas, 2015; Morris & Chikwa, 2014, 2016). However, within CALL contexts, there is still only a small body of research on computer-mediated feedback (e.g., Elola & Oskoz, 2016; Tsutsui, 2004; Wik & Hjalmarsson, 2009). This research often addresses the use of audio software (e.g., Cappellini & Azaoui, 2017; Morris, & Chikwa, 2016) and screen-casting software (e.g., Ali, 2016; Elola & Oskoz, 2016; Séror, 2013) for the adaptive release of comments in feedback production and provision, along with feedback around assessment (Lamb, 2018). However, there is little research on the effectiveness of multimodal feedback; evidence is limited about the effectiveness of feedback mode (e.g., oral or written), media type (e.g., face-to-face, video, audio, text), feedback type (e.g., corrective, constructive), and feedback provider (e.g., teacher, peers, or self) in the language learning process, and no research exists that looks at these elements together.

To be useful, MMF research needs a solid theoretical framework for the investigation of the particular complexities of computer-mediated MMF practices. The effectiveness of a variety of elements/variables (e.g., feedback mode, type) within the particular discourse (e.g., feedback loops, interaction) need to be examined within such a framework. Although some researchers have proposed and used language learning task design principles to explore MMF tools, they did not examine the effectiveness of the tool on the language learning process or outcomes. For example, Tsutsui (2004) compared three feedback methods (i.e., interactive feedback, intrusive feedback, and delayed feedback) and argued that a multimedia tool could help enhance delayed feedback. He categorized 5 major types of errors in L2 oral performance, identified 8 guidelines for the development of an effective delayed feedback tool, and discussed how the multimedia tool met the guidelines, suggesting how the tool might enhance feedback and facilitate language learning. This study scaffolded knowledge of how language learning theories might be used to design MMF; however, how effectively the tools and techniques work in the learning process and their impact on outcomes is still unclear. Likewise, Cappellini and Azaoui (2017) explored multimodal feedback for language learning through desktop video conferencing (DVC) in two pedagogical settings. Drawing on the socio-interactionist approach, this study attempted to identify the interactional dynamics and multimodal density in the DVC environment; however, it did not test the effectiveness of the MMF in terms of linguistic and non-linguistic development.

The limited experimental research on MMF effectiveness is another gap in the literature. While non-experimental studies have used a small number of participants to explore and increase understanding of MMF, experimental methodologies used to determine cause-and-effect relationships are rare. For example, in a case study, Elola and Oskoz (2016) explored the use of MMF in the classroom; they investigated how the mode (i.e., oral versus written) and the medium (i.e., video software versus a word processor) influenced the manner in which instructors provide, and learners receive, feedback. Four college-level Spanish-as-a-second-language students in the U.S. completed questionnaires, wrote two narrative essays for the teacher's feedback, and participated in individual semi-structured interviews. Results indicate that both word processing and video software support effective feedback that could help learners improve their writing. In another study, Séror (2012) used descriptive methods to investigate the use of Jing screencast software for providing multimodal feedback on ELL writing and found it a powerful and interactive way to inform resource-rich feedback. Further, Huang (2016) investigated learner engagement through multimodal video feedback and identified strategies (cognitive and social) that learners employed to facilitate the construction of their oral feedback. While these studies help to explain the processes involved in and participants' perceptions of MMF, a balance of both descriptive and experimental evidence may have the best chance of providing a full picture of the use of MMF.

Finally, there is very limited research that has examined MMF types. One example is Sauro (2009). In a pretest/posttest and delayed posttest study, she examined and compared the immediate and sustained effects of two types of corrective MMF (metalinguistic and recasts) on the development of target form knowledge. Twenty-three Swedish first-year undergraduates at intermediate and advanced English proficiency levels completed two computer-mediated collaborative writing activities and computer- delivered acceptability judgment tests of the target form. A two-way repeated measure of variance was conducted to compare treatment conditions. Results indicated that both types of corrective feedback supported learning gains, but neither feedback type was significantly more effective than the other. Thus, there was no significant difference in the effects of the corrective MMF on the development of target form knowledge. Another recent study, Majlesi (2018), drawing on ethnomethodological conversation analysis, investigated grammar teaching when using two corrective feedback sequences (i.e., a collaborative activity between teachers and students involving verbal and other embodied practices) in Swedish as a second language classroom interaction. This study showed that the use of MMF made linguistic structures visible, noticeable, and thus learnable. It also pointed out that further investigation should look at teachers' embodied practices in providing MMF and responding to MMF in the conjoined activities of teaching and learning. More studies like these can help to fill the gap on the effectiveness of other MMF types, such as interactive and constructive feedback.

Recommendations

Emergent technologies are supporting opportunities for timely and meaningful feedback. The use of technology allows new forms of dialogue and interaction in language learning. To fill in the above research gaps, research can support the development of a solid theoretical framework that can help build future MMF effectiveness research; for example, how MMF-supported feedback loops can be translated into learning outcomes. Future studies can also examine the combination of feedback modes, types, and feedback providers. Additionally, deep understanding about the effectiveness of multimodal feedback in all its different iterations requires not only qualitative studies in natural settings, but also quantitative studies in controlled settings. Finally, studies pertaining to the effectiveness of MMF in terms of linguistic skills and non-linguistic skills would be useful. Questions for future research might include: How can MMF effectiveness be evaluated/ measured? How is MMF used by students? What do they attend to? How does the (type/ quantity/ quality/ mode/ provider) of feedback impact outcomes? How do outcomes differ across skill areas?

VIRTUAL ENVIRONMENTS

Schroeder (2008) used the term "virtual environment" to describe "a computer generated display that allows or compels the user (or users) to have a sense of being present in an environment other than the one they are actually in, and to interact with that environment" (p. 2). VEs such as *Second Life, Active Worlds, Minecraft, OpenSim, World of Warcraft*, and *Unity* are increasingly being used in language learning contexts (Chen, 2016; Jaska, 2015; Reisoğlu, Topu, Yılmaz, Karakuş Yılmaz, Göktaş, 2017). However, while these disparate environments have inspired a relatively large body of research, we lack studies on applicable and effective uses of these open-ended, sandbox tools because their affordances are different and they change regularly. Hence, there is a need to continuously investigate whether the use of such innovative technologies actually facilitates language learning (Chapelle, 2003; Dooly, 2018; Huang, Teo, & Zhou, 2019; Kessler, 2018). Such research could be a resource for language teachers when making decisions about whether it is worth jumping on the VE bandwagon.

Rationale

A range of virtual environments (VEs) has received attention in second language learning inquiry and have been explored by different researchers. Such technologies include online role-playing games, *Second Life,* (e.g., Chang, Sheldon, Si, & Hand, 2012; Dalton & Devit, 2016) and *Minecraft* (Bulkot, 2015; Swier, 2014). Because of the multimedia characteristics embedded in each VE, many researchers in the field emphasize that the use of VEs for language learning may support student engagement. Varidesk (2017), for instance, argues that *Minecraft* provides opportunities for language learning that can be limited only by what learners' imaginations are able to create.

Nevertheless, it is rare to find studies that have taken an in-depth look at the affordances of VEs. "Affordances" of virtual environments for CALL mean the opportunities they can support for increasing language learning gains (Chapelle, 2009), for example, supporting language acquisition principles including interaction, practice, feedback, comprehensible input and output, learner autonomy, noticing, motivation, culture and pragmatic learning, and learner interest. As Lin and Lan (2015) noted, interaction is the most-studied language learning principle in CALL VE studies (see, for example, Jauregi, & Banados, 2008); however, what might interest language teachers is how VEs could support language learning based on other language acquisition principles like comprehensible input and output, noticing, and feedback (Chapelle, 2009).

CALL Literature on Virtual Environments

As noted previously, a number of useful studies have investigated the affordances of VEs for language learning; however, there seems to be a paucity of research that provides results for some core aspects of CALL. These aspects include measured language learning outcomes and the affordances of VEs for specific domains of language learning (i.e., listening, reading, writing and speaking). For the former, research on VEs is more descriptive and exploratory; this means that there is not yet an understanding of the impact of VEs on students' language learning based on measured outcomes. Further, it is unclear under what circumstances the affordances of VEs could yield increased language learning outcomes. For instance, Wang (2015) explored how the discourse functions in the teacher's language output facilitated student participation in different task stages in *Second Life*. An English teacher and 17 students of mixed nationalities participated in group discussions and role-play activities in the VE. The results of the study indicated that first, the teacher positively influenced students' participation in *Second Life* through the use of discourse functions such as directives, questions, compliments, and apologies, and second, while the students' output was prominent in the during-task stage, the teacher played most of the technical and social roles during the pre-task phase. However, this study did not address how the affordances of VE use supported language learning outcomes and whether students' language learning outcomes increased from VE use. Although such descriptive studies are useful, other non-causal studies, including Chang et al. (2012), Dalton and Devitt (2016), Güzel and Aydin (2019), Lan (2019), and Liu (2009) also did not measure how the affordances of VEs impact language learning. Recently Lan, Hsiao, and Shih (2018) and Kessler (2018) outlined potential benefits of the use of VEs for educational purposes, which are flexibility, creativity, interactivity, collaboration, problem-solving skills, active knowledge construction, self-regulation, motivation, and concentration. However, we do not yet have studies that measure student learning outcomes based on these opportunities that VEs could provide.

Further, while communication and interaction are core principles of language learning (Egbert & Shahrokni, 2018), no research has addressed the link they have to student development of the specific language learning domains. For example, Shih and Yang (2008) investigated how learners employed different communication strategies during communication in virtual spaces and how they developed communicative competences in the target language through the use of 3D virtual reality technology. Taiwanese learners of English as a foreign language were immersed in a virtual scavenger hunt where they, in groups of two to five, were involved in text and voice chats with native speakers of English. Some functions of the technology, including slide-show control, real-time voice chat, virtual-object handling, and group management were added to the virtual activities to ensure that there was live and consistent interaction in the event. The results showed that students developed positive attitudes and communication strategies, but these were neither based on measurable language outcomes nor linked to any of the language learning domains. Likewise, Zheng, Young, Brewer and Wagner (2013) investigated how communication in a 3D virtual world might increase students' self-efficacy in communication in English. This pattern of exploring communication or interaction in VEs without tying it to the affordances of VEs for learning specific domains, as found in many other studies (e.g., Ibanez et al. 2011; Jauregi & Banados, 2008), is important with respect to the focus of individual studies, but additional research in other areas, such as how interaction in VEs could enhance a specific domain of language learning, would also benefit the field.

As discussed earlier, there is also a scarcity of research that measures the impact of the use of VEs on students' language learning and that investigates the affordances of VEs for specific aspects of language learning. Even when studies do measure students' language learning outcomes in VEs, the results are usually not tied to the affordances of the environment. For example, Berns, Gonzalez-Pardo, and Camacho (2013) conducted a study using an open VE. They created an application called *The Supermarket Game* in the *OpenSim* environment. The use of the VE and the app were aimed to motivate students toward language learning and help them to reinforce their comprehension skills by providing meaningful and motivating input. Language learning data were obtained from tests before and after the learners played the game in the target (German) language. The results showed that students' acquisition of new vocabulary was impacted positively. However, we do not know what affordances of the game supported students' vocabulary acquisition. In another study, Lan (2019) studied how Taiwanese students learn English within and beyond the classroom by means of VEs and suggested that VEs could enhance learners' performances in English as a foreign language. However, these studies did not clearly describe the affordances of the VEs and identify which affordances influenced the language learning outcomes. In other words, it was unclear whether it was the opportunity to interact that made the difference, engagement in the listening tasks, or something else.

Most recently, Wang, Lan, Tseng, Lin, and Gupta (2019) conducted a meta-analysis to study the effects of VEs used for language learning based on 13 primary studies published since 2008. The meta-analysis focused on two major issues, the role of interaction in VEs and the effects of the use of VEs claimed in findings of the analyzed papers. The meta-analysis showed that interaction supported by scaffolding and collaboration has a crucial role in promoting language learning. Further, the meta-analysis results indicated that the use of VEs integrated with a variety of teaching methods can highly enhance learners' communication and linguistic competences. Based on these results, the authors used the notion of "partnership" to interpret the relationship between VEs and language learners. The intermediate to high effect sizes of moderating variables and the patterns of interaction confirmed the impact on learners' cognition and affect. In terms of cognition, linguistic gains and creation are prominent achievements, while in the aspect of affect, 3D virtual worlds can enhance students' attitudes and self-efficacy, especially in collaborative learning conditions.

Recommendations

What research suggests thus far is that VEs are a promising technology for language learning. In the future, having a specific domain of language learning as a target while conducting research on the affordances of virtual environments is something to be considered. More research is needed to investigate how affordances of VEs could promote not only language learning in general, but also of deep acquisition of structural components (i.e., vocabulary, morphology, syntax, and discourse) and language domains (i.e., listening, speaking, reading, and writing). Further, causal studies and those that look for a relationship between VE affordances and learning outcomes can show how students' language learning is impacted by each affordance of VEs and what factors may have more impact on language learning outcomes. It might also be useful to study the relationship between each of the affordances and structural and pragmatic knowledge acquired while using VEs. Additionally, future research may focus on identifying the learning activities within VEs that may benefit language learning more than others.

USE OF THEORY FOR VIRTUAL ENVIRONMENT TASK DESIGN

Theory-driven CALL task design is another area in need of further investigation. Hubbard (2012) defines CALL theory as a set of perspectives, models, and frameworks explaining the phenomena related to the application of computer technology in second language acquisition (SLA). In addition to providing an evidence base for instruction, such theory can inform the process of CALL task design. A lack of SLA theory or model in much CALL research, and a lack of diversity in the theories and models used, signal important gaps in this literature.

Rationale

Task-based language teaching (TBLT) has been a successful model of task design in face-to-face classrooms (Benson, 2016; East, 2012); however, this model, which has been applied extensively to CALL environments, is seen as a restrictive model for VEs (Chapelle, 2009; González-Lloret & Ortega, 2014). The principles of TBLT, which include authenticity, learning by doing, input, inductive learning, and collaboration, make it suitable to support some aspects of VE use (e.g., Chen, 2016); however, the affordances of VEs require a more comprehensive approach to task design. In other words, what works in face-to-face settings might not be equally appropriate for virtual settings (Thomas & Reinders, 2010), and future research can help us to develop a more appropriate model of task design in VEs. For instance, task complexity, an issue which is often explained through Robinson's (2005) cognition hypothesis in face-to-face settings, may fail to be properly explained in VEs, as the medium provides unique opportunities for students' output processing (Adams & Nik, 2014). In addition, TBLT is a pedagogical model that is informed by a synthesis of theoretical underpinnings, rather than an SLA theory (Hubbard & Levy, 2016). Therefore, it is important that research questions around task design be explored through appropriate SLA and CALL theories and through a multiple-theory lens.

CALL Literature around Tasks

The rationale behind TBLT use is that it has been successful in language development in face-to-face classes, with results corroborating this claim (see Ziegler, 2016, for a review). For instance, Nielson (2014) showed that TBLT used in an online Chinese as a foreign language course helped sustain participation rates and improve learning outcomes, particularly the participants' speaking proficiency. Similarly, Yuksel and Inan (2014) found that participants communicating in face-to-face settings engaged in more negotiations for meaning, while participants in computer-mediated communication (CMC) conditions noticed significantly more language during task-based interactions.

While informing the online task design process with TBLT principles has been a move forward, the complex nature of VEs (see the section on VEs above) requires proper theorizing based on the characteristics of the medium and the nature of learner interactions required in each particular setting, an issue which has been emphasized in CALL research. For instance, Hampel (2010) conducted two case studies at Open University, assessing the experience and attitudes of two groups of 25 intermediate German learners about their online courses. Using Ellis' (2003) and Oxford's (2006) task frameworks, Hampel made a case for the incorporation of interaction, learner support, and computer mediation as crucial factors in the online task design process. The results of this study can be compared to those of Hampel (2006), in which he attempted to use Richards and Rodgers' (2001) framework, along with sociocultural and constructivist theories and concepts from multimodality and new literacies research, to create a model to investigate online synchronous interactions. These studies show that TBLT, alone, could not account for the unique characteristics of VEs, so the researcher strived to enrich the theoretical basis of the study.

Likewise, in a study on CMC task design for language learning, Rosell-Aguilar (2005) developed a model based on TBLT principles. After operationally testing the model using an in-house VE and a group of 10 testers, the results confirmed the potential of both the model and VE in supporting foreign language education. The researcher proposed additional pedagogical guidelines for the task design and implementation process in VEs, including the need for clear instructions, authentic materials, provision of a syllabus, and some procedural rules for online administration of distance learning classes. This study shows that using TBLT as the basis of task design, although it provides a structure, cannot capture all of the potential of the affordances of VEs.

There is also an imbalance in the use of SLA theories in CALL research, with a cognitivist view of language learning dominant in CALL studies (Chappelle, 2009; Palmer, 2010) and sociocultural (Lantolf, Thorne, & Poehner, 2015), functional (Halliday, 2003), and ecological (van Lier, 2004) theories receiving less attention. Of course, reliance on a specific theory, at the same time it structures the study, is limiting, and future studies could diversify the theoretical base of research by, for instance, relying on a theoretical framework that integrates salient aspects of different theories (e.g., Egbert, Hanson-Smith, & Chao, 2007; González-Lloret & Ortega, 2014).

Recommendations

As Chappelle (2009) argues, CALL materials based on one or a combination of SLA perspectives have "never been developed with much demonstrable success" (p. 750). The same could be said of CALL tasks. Indeed, the lack of a proper theoretical basis for the CALL task design process is a problem still needing attention. Developing a comprehensive framework for CALL task design requires an eclectic model which draws principles from available theories. This model, consisting of principles pertaining to specific phases in the second language learning process, may provide a basis for designing tasks in VEs. A new CALL paradigm that can support CALL task development might 1) be based on a scientific approach to non-linguistic aspects of language learning, 2) contextualize CALL in social and cultural settings, 3) allow researchers to employ both quantitative and qualitative methods, and 4) view computers as tools in service of language learning.

CONSIDERING CULTURE IN CALL ENVIRONMENTS

CALL research in general has not addressed the role of culture, perhaps in part because "culture" is not an easy term to define. The Cambridge Dictionary defines culture as "the way of life, especially the general customs and beliefs, of a particular group of people at a particular time" (http://dictionary.cambridge.org, 2019). In diverse classrooms where students come from different cultural backgrounds, cultural differences can play a major role in how students learn or perceive learning.

Rationale

The amount of published work that addresses culture in computer-assisted language learning environments is limited. While papers discussing how to teach culture with technology abound, those that focus on learners' cultural interactions with technology or the cultures imbedded in technologies are much fewer. Several recent studies have touched on this aspect, but there is currently more conceptual than empirical work. It is important for learning that CALL environments involve all learners and encourage them to approach learning in a way that aligns with their "culture, dispositions, attitudes, and approaches to learning that accommodate their own understanding of the world" (Brander, 2005, p. 146).

CALL Literature Focusing on Culture

The impact of individuals' cultural values on technology adoption in informal learning was examined by Lai, Wang, Li, and Hu (2016). The researchers conducted a study surveying 661 foreign language learners from Hong Kong, China, and the US. After analyzing the survey responses using structural equation modeling, the results showed a strong direct effect, but weak moderating effects, of cultural values on individuals' technology adoption in informal learning. These results confirm the significant role that students' cultural values play in the use of technology for educational purposes. Although the study does not specify exactly how that role actually impacts students' perceptions towards CALL tasks and their learning, it suggests considering students' cultural values and backgrounds when introducing and adapting educational technologies.

Another study that focused on culture and its role in CALL environments is Barak and Levenberg (2016). Their study focused on the concept of flexible thinking and producing an instrument for measuring what may drive individuals to think flexibly in technology-enhanced environments. The researchers point out that students, despite their cultural backgrounds, are expected to think flexibly to succeed in contemporary learning environments. The researchers, as a result, suggest a tool for measuring students' flexible thinking; however, measuring students' flexible thinking in this way is determined by the expectations in one learning environment. Students coming from other learning environments or cultures may fail to meet these expectations due to their different learning experiences. Without the awareness or consideration of students' differences, results from any measurement tool may provide adequate explanation of a phenomenon.

Furthermore, Balakrishnan and Lay (2016) investigated students' learning styles and preferences and their relation to the use of certain technologies. In this study, learners' intentions to use social media for learning based on their learning styles were investigated in terms of what factors may impact these intentions. After involving 300 Malaysian students, the study found that factors such as Self (social media efficacy, attitude, and enjoyment) and Performance (perceived usefulness and perceived flexibility) impact the intentions of students to use social media no matter what their learning styles are. These results also confirm the significance of understanding students' learning styles and preferences and how they can play a role in the use of technology for learning. However, the study only discussed the topic from the perspective of students' differences without addressing the nature of the technologies. The way technology tools are designed and whether they appear culturally biased may contribute to learners' motivations and intentions to use them.

When it comes to choosing appropriate mobile technologies for learning, culture may also play a central role. For example, in a study on mobile technologies in educational organizations, Chen and Zhang (2019) looked at the role of culture as well as context on the application of mobile technology "to facilitate learners' engagement and educational experiences" (Chen & Zhang, 2019, p. 142). The researchers conducted two sharply-contrasting case studies from a higher education institution in the UK and a state-owned enterprise in China and compared them in terms of "characteristics of learner groups, motivation mechanism of their learning journey, mobile functions, contents and learning culture" (Chen & Zhang, 2019, p. 143). Based on the comparison, Chen and Zhang found that consideration of culture and context in selecting appropriate mobile technologies has a positive impact on organizational learning and can lead to increased engagement in learning.

Culture may also have an important impact on how teachers use technology effectively. In a study by Warr, Mishra, and Scragg (2019), the researchers criticize the technological pedagogical content knowledge (TPACK) framework. They argue that despite the many studies on the role of technology in education, many teachers still encounter challenges in effectively employing it. Although the TPACK framework describes the type of knowledge teachers need to design effective utilization of education technologies, this framework has not significantly changed the extent to which teachers use technology in education. According to Warr et al. (2019), this is due in part to a lack of sufficient attention to the role of culture. In their study, Warr et al., (2019) suggest a new framework called the "Five Discourses of Design." The researchers believe that this framework can increase teachers' use of educational technology because it considers the two-way impacts of individual cultures and cultural systems on educational technology use (Warr et al., 2019).

Finally, in many studies (e.g., Warr et al., 2019; Balakrishnan & Lay, 2016; Rass, 2011; Lai et al., 2016) research on culture in CALL environments is generally conducted through self-report. For example, in a qualitative study, Rass (2011) studied the impact of Arab Muslim culture on the English writing of 18 first-year female Arab students. The study, focusing on the influence that Arabic first language and cultures have on ELL writing, investigated writing portfolios and sheets of error analysis. After analyzing the collected materials, Rass found that there is a strong impact of Arab Muslim culture on the students' writing in English. For instance, the writing had a great deal of repetition and exaggeration. Although this type of study is helpful in stressing the importance of considering students' cultures and cultural awareness, studies that use methods in addition to self-report are bound to uncover additional information.

Recommendations

According to Brander (2005), "software that is culturally biased can affect user achievement, motivation, and learning and thus determines the instructional usability of the program" (p. 147). Therefore, more attention might be paid to the culture, both explicit and implicit, of technologies and how it relates to students' and teachers' uses of those technologies. Another question is about what teaching practices teachers can adapt to consider students' cultural differences in CALL. Action research is one way to investigate culturally responsive CALL teaching (see, for example, Abolghasseminits, Jahromi, & Salimi, 2013) and can include all aspects of teaching (e.g., planning, assessment, etc.). Further, studying culture in CALL requires investigating the many variables that represent culture from a number of viewpoints, not only the students'; this can happen through the use of methods and data sources such as discourse analysis, non-participant observation, teacher journaling, and user tests of apps by experts. Tackling these issues is necessary in CALL research for an effective consideration of students' cultural backgrounds.

TRANSFER FROM CALL TEACHER EDUCATION

This section explores the gaps in research concerning the relationship between CALL teacher education (CTE) and language classroom environments.

Rationale

CTE exists for the purpose of equipping language teachers with the ability and confidence to effectively integrate CALL technologies into their classroom practice (Hong, 2010). As technologies become more readily available and integrated into language teachers' work and personal lives, interest in utilizing technology to support and enhance teaching and learning has also increased. Many language teacher education programs now address CALL in some form, at least as a topic in methods courses (American Council on the Teaching of Foreign Languages, 2011). Chao (2015) adds that "it is clear that interest in the effect of CTE is strong and that there has been a high expectation for teachers to use the knowledge and skills learned in a CTE class" (p. 103). Unfortunately, there remains a lack of research on teachers' transfer of knowledge and skills from CTE to the language classroom; in other words, insufficient evidence exists that supports the tangible impact of CTE on language classroom teachers' practice. Although CTE has been around for years, Kessler and Hubbard (2017) explain that "For the past two decades research has indicated a need to better understand the process and outcomes of CALL teacher education" (p. 282). Studies on CTE transfer have been conducted, but they often present a narrow perspective on the topic. Arnold and Ducate (2015) suggest that "to advance our understanding of CALL teacher education, [researchers must] move beyond research on teacher beliefs and attitudes to investigate actual practices and competencies, especially from a longitudinal perspective, that traces teachers' development" (p. 2).

CALL Research on Transfer

As Arnold and Ducate (2015) noted, one issue with the extant research on CTE transfer is an overreliance on self-reported data. Several researchers have noticed this limitation in their reviews of the literature with comments such as "many past studies [e.g., Bai & Ertmer, 2008; Egbert, Paulus, & Nakamichi, 2002] depended on survey or other self-reported data to identify the results of teacher education" (Chao, 2015, p. 104) and "... most previous studies were based on data collected from primarily self-reported sources, such as surveys and interviews" (Tai, 2015, p. 139). Despite the limitations using self-report as a solo data source, this method is still commonly being used to conduct research on the topic. Liu and Kleinsasser (2015), for example, used surveys and interviews to investigate knowledge and skills transfer from an a one-year in-service teacher CALL development series to EFL classroom technology integration. In addition, Wilson and Acheampong (2014) used focus-group discussions and questionnaires to collect data from language teacher trainees to explore transfer from CTE education to their own CALL environments. In yet another study, Hedayati, Reynolds, & Bown (2018) explored the impact of CALL training on Iranian EFL teachers' technology use through interviews and surveys. Participant perceptions can certainly provide important insights; however, an overreliance on self-reported data provides limitations on what we can learn about CTE transfer.

Another issue with the existing research involves researchers viewing CALL as a unitary construct. Hong (2010) notes "analytically, previous studies tend to regard L2 teachers' use of computer technology as a unitary construct – i.e., whether [or not] teachers use computer technology in the classroom" (p. 62). In other words, researchers who investigate teachers' classroom technology integration tend to focus on whether or not teachers are using some form of technology in their classrooms and not on *how* and *why*. In her review of the literature on CTE and classroom transfer, Chao (2015) found that "the underlying theoretical framework for most of the transfer studies in CTE can be considered as classic transfer, which aims for direct transfer of knowledge and skills between similar tasks or contexts" (p. 104). However, transfer can influence more than the specific tools or methods a teacher uses; it also has the potential to influence teachers' attitudes and positions toward technology in general. Hong (2010) points out that it is important to view CALL integration as multifaceted, with different computer technologies being used for different instructional purposes. Viewing technology use as a unitary construct can create analytical constraints in what we can learn from research when in reality some teachers "use computer technology to deliver their instruction, some to engage students in creating products, and some others to encourage students' use of computer technology during class time" (Hong, 2010, p. 62).

A third issue involves a reliance on studies involving small sample sizes. For example, Sharp (2017) examined what supports facilitated teachers' iPad use in second language classrooms, relying on data from four teachers. Further, Derbel (2017) explored the impact of an in-service initiative, designed to empower teachers of English as a foreign language to use technology in their classrooms, on teachers' classroom practices. In this study, questionnaires and semi-structured interviews were completed by five teachers. In addition, Liu and Kleinsasser's (2016) study involved six participants and Chao's (2015) study involved four participants. Hong (2010) notes that, while a focus on a small number of teachers in specific contexts can provide opportunities to provide meaningful insights into specifically designed CTE courses and identify context-specific issues regarding CALL integration, limited participant sample sizes and contexts do restrict the generalizability of the findings. Liu and Kleinsasser (2015) specifically note their small sample size as a limitation, suggesting that "future researchers may recruit a larger sample of participants to offer additional perspectives" (p. 132). Hong (2010) suggests that future research exploring transfer from CTE environments to classroom CALL integration should investigate the technology integration of language teachers working across schools and districts, and small-scale descriptive studies should be complemented with large-scale statistical studies.

A fourth issue is a limited understanding of the of the amount of CTE necessary to lead to transfer to language classroom practice. Hong (2010) points out that most studies on CTE focus on transfer from a single, specific CALL course. Little research has been conducted looking at greater quantities of CTE. Kessler and Hubbard (2017) note that "many language teachers are still graduating without having received sufficient formal preparation [in CALL integration]" (p. 285). There is little research, however, exploring how much CTE is considered sufficient. As a result of one such study, Hong (2009) suggests that, in order to increase the likelihood of language teachers integrating CALL practices in instruction at least once a week, "teachers appear to need at least 150 hours of technology education, which is equivalent to taking a 3 credit-hour technology course for 5 academic quarters in the teacher education program" (p. 92). Although one isolated study clearly cannot provide a definitive answer for how much CTE a teacher needs in order to effectively utilize CALL practices in their language classroom, this study can be seen as a starting point for further investigation.

Recommendations

A rich understanding of how language teachers are or are not integrating technologies in their classrooms is essential to providing effective CTE. In order to improve our understanding of the relationship between CTE and language teachers' classroom technology integration, there is a need for an increase in certain types of studies. For example, more studies are needed that do not rely solely on self-reported data; they can include strategies such as physical observations of teachers' actual classroom practice. When observing how teachers integrate technology, is it important to explore why and how they are doing so, moving beyond merely reporting on whether or not any technology is being used. Further, studies involving larger sample sizes are needed in order to increase generalizability. In addition, investigation into the quantity of CTE necessary to positively impact transfer is needed.

CONCLUSION

To ensure that CALL use reaches its potential, research on the effectiveness of CALL environments and the affordances of CALL use within them is central. Addressing the recommendations identified in each section of this paper can add both more information and more rigor to the CALL research and, hence, improve our understanding of language teaching and learning. However, the issues addressed here comprise only a small subset of CALL research topics, questions, and methodologies, and new theories of language, learning, and technology can fruitfully be applied to questions of CALL development. To this end, researchers, teachers, administrators, and students are encouraged to explore these and other gaps in the CALL literature.

REFERENCES

Abolghasseminits, S., Jahromi, F., & Salimi, F. (2013). Exploring the human element of computer-assisted language learning: An Iranian context. *Computer Assisted Language Learning*, *26*(2), 158–176. doi:10.1080/09588221.2011.643411

Adams, R., & Nik, A. N. (2014). Prior knowledge and second language task production in text chat. In M. González-Lloret, & L. Ortega (Eds.), *Technology-mediated TBLT: Researching technology and tasks* (pp. 51–78). Amsterdam, The Netherlands: John Benjamins. doi:10.1075/tblt.6.03ada

Ali, A. D. (2016). Effectiveness of using screencast feedback on EFL students' writing and perception. *English Language Teaching*, *9*(8), 106–121. doi:10.5539/elt.v9n8p106

American Council on the Teaching of Foreign Languages. (2011). *A decade of language standards: Influence, impact and future directions*. Retrieved from https://www.actfl.org/sites/default/files/publications/standards/StandardsImpactSurvey.pdf

Arnold, N., & Ducate, L. (2015). Contextualized views of practices and competencies in CALL teacher education research. *Language Learning & Technology, 19*(1), 1–9.

Bai, H., & Ertmer, P. (2008). Teacher educators' beliefs and technology uses as predictors of preservice teachers' beliefs and technology attitudes. *Journal of Technology and Teacher Education, 16*(1), 93–112.

Balakrishnan, V., & Lay, G. C. (2016). Students' learning styles and their effects on the use of social media technology for learning. *Telematics and Informatics, 33*(3), 808–821. doi:10.1016/j.tele.2015.12.004

Barak, M., & Levenberg, A. (2016). Flexible thinking in learning: An individual differences measure for learning in technology-enhanced environments. *Computers & Education, 99*, 39–52. doi:10.1016/j.compedu.2016.04.003

Beechler, S., & Williams, S. (2012). Computer assisted instruction and elementary ESL students in sight word recognition. *International Journal of Business and Social Science, 3*(4), 85–92.

Benson, S. D. (2016). Task-based language teaching: An empirical study of task transfer. *Language Teaching Research, 20*(3), 341–365. doi:10.1177/1362168815569829

Berns, A., Gonzalez-Pardo, A., & Camacho, D. (2013). Game-like language learning in 3D virtual environments. *Computers & Education, 60*(1), 210–220. doi:10.1016/j.compedu.2012.07.001

Borup, J., West, R. E., & Thomas, R. (2015). The impact of text versus video communication on instructor feedback in blended courses. *Educational Technology Research and Development, 63*(2), 161–184. doi:10.100711423-015-9367-8

Brander, B. G. (2005). Considering culture in CALL research. In J. L. Egbert, & G. M. Petrie (Eds.), *CALL research perspectives* (pp. 141–153). Mahwah, NJ: Routledge.

Bulkot, M. (2015). *Using Minecraftedu to establish common ground and increase collaboration in an American literature college course.* (Unpublished master's dissertation, State University of New York, Utica, NY).

Campbell, C. (1987). *Writing with others words: Native and non-native university students' use of information from a background reading text in academic compositions. (CLEAR Technical Report Series Publication No. TR4)*. Los Angeles, CA: Center for Language Education and Research.

Cappellini, M., & Azaoui, B. (2017). Sequences of normative evaluation in two telecollaboration projects: A comparative study of multimodal feedback through desktop videoconference. *Language Learning in Higher Education, 7*(1), 55–80. doi:10.1515/cercles-2017-0002

Caruso, M., Faschini, N., & Kuuse, S. (2019). Online tools for feedback engagement in second language learning. *International Journal of Computer-Assisted Language Learning and Teaching, 9*(1), 58–78. doi:10.4018/IJCALLT.2019010104

Chang, B., Sheldon, L., Si, M., & Hand, A. (2012). Foreign language learning in immersive virtual environments, In *Proceedings of the IS&T/SPIE Electronic Imaging* (pp. 2–9). Burlingame, CA: SPIE Digital Library. 10.1117/12.909835

Chao, C. C. (2015, February). Rethinking transfer: Learning from CALL teacher education as consequential transition. *Language Learning & Technology*, *19*(1), 102–118.

Chapelle, C. A. (2003). *English language learning and technology*. Amsterdam, The Netherlands: John Benjamins. doi:10.1075/lllt.7

Chapelle, C. A. (2009). The relationship between second language acquisition theory and computer-assisted language learning. *Modern Language Journal*, *93*(1), 741–753. doi:10.1111/j.1540-4781.2009.00970.x

Chapelle, C. A., & Sauro, S. (Eds.). (2017). The handbook of technology and second language teaching and learning. New York, NY: John Wiley & Sons.

Chen, J. C. (2016). The crossroads of English language learners, task-based instruction, and 3D multi-user virtual learning in Second Life. *Computers & Education*, *102*, 152–171. doi:10.1016/j.compedu.2016.08.004

Chen, M. H. (2019). Computer-assisted synonymous phrase learning: A feasible approach to lexical development. [IJCALLT]. *International Journal of Computer-Assisted Language Learning and Teaching*, *9*(2), 1–18. doi:10.4018/IJCALLT.2019040101

Chen, M. H., Huang, S. T., Chang, J. S., & Liou, H. C. (2013). Developing a corpus-based paraphrase tool to improve EFL learners' writing skills. *Computer Assisted Language Learning*, *28*(1), 22–40. doi:10.1080/09588221.2013.783873

Chen, Y., & Zhang, Y. (2019). Culture and context impact on mobile tech application in organizational learning: Case study of UK higher education institution and Chinese state-owned enterprise. In A. Forkish Baruch, & H. Meishar Tal (Eds.), *Mobile technologies in educational organizations* (pp. 142–169). Hershey, PA: IGI Global. doi:10.4018/978-1-5225-8106-2.ch008

Dalton, G., & Devitt, A. (2016). Irish in a 3D world: Engaging primary school children. *Language Learning & Technology*, *20*(1), 21–33.

Derbel, F. (2017). Technology-capable teachers transitioning to technology-challenged schools. *The Electronic Journal of E-Learning*, *15*(3), 269–280.

Dooly, M. (2018). "I do which the question": Students' innovative use of technology resources in the language classroom. *Language Learning & Technology*, *22*(1), 184–217.

East, M. (2012). *Task-based language teaching from the teachers' perspective: Insights from New Zealand* (Vol. 3). Amsterdam, The Netherlands: John Benjamins Publishing. doi:10.1075/tblt.3

Egbert, J., & Abobaker, R. (2018). Opportunities for engaging young English language learners through technology use. In N. Guler (Ed.), *Optimizing elementary education for English language learners* (pp. 158–176). Hershey, PA: IGI Global. doi:10.4018/978-1-5225-3123-4.ch009

Egbert, J., Hanson-Smith, E., & Chao, C. C. (2007). Introduction: Foundations for teaching and learning. In J. Egbert, & E. Hanson-Smith (Eds.), *CALL environments: Research, practice, and critical issues* (2nd ed., pp. 1–18). Alexandria, VA: TESOL.

Egbert, J., Paulus, T., & Nakamichi, Y. (2002, September). The impact of CALL instruction on language classroom computer use: A foundation for rethinking technology in teacher education. *Language Learning & Technology*, *6*(3), 108–126.

Egbert, J., Shahrokni, S., Zhang, X., Yahia, I., Borysenko, N., Mohamed, A., ... AlJarih, F. (2018). Planning for future inquiry: Gaps in the CALL research. *International Journal of Computer-Assisted Language Learning and Teaching*, *8*(2), 39–59. doi:10.4018/IJCALLT.2018040103

Egbert, J., & Shahrokni, S. A. (2018). CALL principles and practices. *OER.* Available at https://opentext.wsu.edu/call/chapter/principles-of-call/

Ellis, N. C. (2003). Constructions, chunking, and connectionism: The emergence of second language structure. In C. J. Doughty, & M. H. Long (Eds.), *The handbook of second language acquisition* (pp. 63–103). Malden, MA: Wiley-Blackwell. doi:10.1002/9780470756492.ch4

Elola, I., & Oskoz, A. (2016). Supporting second language writing using multimodal feedback. *Foreign Language Annals*, *49*(1), 58–74. doi:10.1111/flan.12183

Farr, F., & Murray, L. (2016). *The Routledge handbook of language learning and technology*. New York: Routledge. doi:10.4324/9781315657899

Fidaoui, D., Bahous, R., & Bacha, N. (2010). CALL in Lebanese elementary ESL writing classrooms. *Computer Assisted Language Learning*, *23*(2), 151–168. doi:10.1080/09588221003666248

Foorman, B. R., Petscher, Y., & Bishop, M. D. (2012). The incremental variance of morphological knowledge to reading comprehension in grades 3–10 beyond prior reading comprehension, spelling, and text reading efficiency. *Learning and Individual Differences*, *22*(6), 792–798. doi:10.1016/j.lindif.2012.07.009

González-Lloret, M., & Ortega, L. (2014). Towards technology-mediated TBLT: An introduction. In M. González-Lloret, & L. Ortega (Eds.), *Technology-mediated TBLT: Researching technology and tasks* (pp. 1–22). Amsterdam, The Netherlands: John Benjamins.

Goodwin, A., & Ahn, S. (2010). A meta-analysis of morphological interventions: Effects on literacy achievement of children with literacy difficulties. *Annals of Dyslexia*, *60*(2), 183–208. doi:10.100711881-010-0041-x PMID:20799003

Goodwin, A., Huggins, A., Carlo, M., August, D., & Calderon, M. (2013). Minding morphology: How morphological awareness relates to reading for English language learners. *Reading and Writing*, *26*(9), 1387–1415. doi:10.100711145-012-9412-5

Grgurovic, M., Chapelle, A., & Shelley, C. (2013). A meta-analysis of effectiveness studies on computer technology-supported language learning. *ReCALL*, *25*(2), 165–198. doi:10.1017/S0958344013000013

Guichon, N., & Cohen, C. (2016). Multimodality and CALL. In F. Farr & L. Murray (Eds.), *The Routledge handbook of language learning and technology* (pp. 509–521). London, UK: Routledge.

Güzel, S., & Aydin, S. (2019). The effect of Second Life as a virtual language learning environment on speaking anxiety: Second Life and anxiety. In M. Kruk (Ed.), *Assessing the effectiveness of virtual technologies in foreign and second language instruction* (pp. 115–146). Hershey, PA: IGI Global. doi:10.4018/978-1-5225-7286-2.ch005

Halliday, M. A. K. (2003). *On language and linguistics*. London, UK: Continuum.

Hampel, R. (2006). Rethinking task design for the digital age: A framework for language teaching and learning in a synchronous online environment. *ReCALL*, *18*(1), 105–121. doi:10.1017/S0958344006000711

Hampel, R. (2010). Task design for a virtual learning environment in a distance language course. In M. Thomas, & H. Reinders (Eds.), *Task-based language learning and teaching with technology* (pp. 131–153). London, UK: Continuum.

Hedayati, M., Reynolds, B., & Bown, A. (2018). The impact of computer-assisted language learning training on teachers' practices. *Journal of Language Teaching and Research*, *9*(6), 1127–1137. doi:10.17507/jltr.0906.02

Hirvela, A., & Du, Q. (2013). "Why am I paraphrasing?": Undergraduate ESL writers' engagement with source- based academic writing and reading. *Journal of English for Academic Purposes*, *12*(2), 87–98. doi:10.1016/j.jeap.2012.11.005

Hong, K. H. (2010). CALL teacher education as an impetus for L2 teachers in integrating technology. *ReCALL*, *22*(1), 53–69. doi:10.1017/S095834400999019X

Huang, F., Teo, T., & Zhou, M. (2019). Factors affecting Chinese English as a foreign language teachers' technology acceptance: A qualitative study. *Journal of Educational Computing Research*, *57*(1), 83–105. doi:10.1177/0735633117746168

Huang, S. A. (2016). Enhancing feedback provision through multimodal video technology. *Computers & Education*, *98*, 90–101. doi:10.1016/j.compedu.2016.03.009

Hubbard, P. (2012, August). Curation for systemization of authentic content for autonomous learning. From *EUROCALL Conference*, Gothenburg, Sweden.

Hubbard, P., & Levy, M. (2016). Theory in computer-assisted language learning research and practice. In F. Farr, & L. Murray (Eds.), *The Routledge handbook of language learning and technology* (pp. 24–38). London, UK: Routledge.

Ibáñez, M. B., García, J. J., Galán, S., Maroto, D., Morillo, D., & Kloos, C. D. (2011). Design and implementation of a 3D multi-user virtual world for language learning. *Journal of Educational Technology & Society*, *14*(4), 2–10.

Jaska, L. (2015). *Virtual worlds in pre-service teacher education: The introduction of virtual worlds in pre- service teacher education to foster innovative teaching-learning processes* (Doctoral dissertation). Retrieved from http://epubs.scu.edu.au/theses/428/

Jauregi, K., & Bañados, E. (2008). Virtual interaction through video-web communication: A step towards enriching and internationalizing language learning programs. *ReCALL*, *20*(2), 183–207. doi:10.1017/S0958344008000529

Johns, A. M., & Mayes, P. (1990). An analysis of summary protocols of university ESL students. *Applied Linguistics*, *11*(3), 253–271. doi:10.1093/applin/11.3.253

Keck, C. (2006). The use of paraphrase in summary writing: A comparison of L1 and L2 writers. *Journal of Second Language Writing*, *15*(4), 261–278. doi:10.1016/j.jslw.2006.09.006

Keck, C. (2014). Copying, paraphrasing, and academic writing development: A re-examination of L1 and L2 summarization practices. *Journal of Second Language Writing*, *25*, 4–22. doi:10.1016/j.jslw.2014.05.005

Kessler, G. (2018). Technology and the future of language teaching. *Foreign Language Annals*, *51*(1), 205–218. doi:10.1111/flan.12318

Kessler, G., & Hubbard, P. (2017). Language teacher education and technology. In C. Chapelle, & S. Sauro (Eds.), *Handbook of technology and second language teaching and learning* (pp. 278–292). New York: John Wiley & Sons. doi:10.1002/9781118914069.ch19

Kieffer, M. J., & Lesaux, N. K. (2012). Direct and indirect roles of morphological awareness in the English reading comprehension of native English, Spanish, Filipino, and Vietnamese speakers. *Language Learning*, *62*(4), 1170–1204. doi:10.1111/j.1467-9922.2012.00722.x

Lai, C., Wang, Q., Li, X., & Hu, X. (2016). The influence of individual espoused cultural values on self-directed use of technology for language learning beyond the classroom. *Computers in Human Behavior*, *63*, 676–688. doi:10.1016/j.chb.2016.04.039

Lamb, J. (2018). To boldly go: Feedback as digital, multimodal dialogue. *Multimodal Technologies and Interaction*, *2*(3), 49–65. doi:10.3390/mti2030049

Lan, Y. J. (2019). Contextual EFL learning in a 3D virtual environment. *Language Learning & Technology*, *19*(2), 16–31.

Lan, Y. J., Hsiao, I. Y., & Shih, M. F. (2018). Effective learning design of game-based 3d virtual language learning environments for special education students. *Journal of Educational Technology & Society*, *21*(3), 213–227.

Lantolf, J., Thorne, S. L., & Poehner, M. (2015). Sociocultural theory and second language development. In B. van Patten, & J. Williams (Eds.), *Theories in second language acquisition* (pp. 207–226). New York: Routledge.

Leakey, J. (2011). *Evaluating computer assisted language learning: an integrated approach to effectiveness research in CALL.* Bern, Switzerland: Peter Lang. doi:10.3726/978-3-0353-0131-1

Lin, T. J., & Lan, Y. J. (2015). Language learning in virtual reality environments: Past, present, and future. *Journal of Educational Technology & Society*, *18*(4), 486–497.

Liu, M. H., & Kleinsasser, R. C. (2015). Exploring EFL teachers' CALL knowledge and competencies: In-service program perspectives. *Language Learning & Technology*, *19*(1), 119–138.

Liu, T. Y. (2009). A context-aware ubiquitous learning environment for language listening and speaking. *Journal of Computer Assisted Learning*, *25*(6), 515–527. doi:10.1111/j.1365-2729.2009.00329.x

Loh, Y. L. (2013). Errors in paraphrasing and strategies in overcoming them. *Journal of Creative Practices in Language Learning and Teaching*, *1*(1), 4–17.

Majlesi, A. R. (2018). Instructed vision: Navigating grammatical rules by using landmarks for linguistic structures in corrective feedback sequences. *Modern Language Journal*, *102*, 11–29. doi:10.1111/modl.12452

McLnnis, L. (2009). *Analyzing English L1 and L2 paraphrasing strategies through concurrent verbal report and stimulated recall protocols.* (Unpublished master's thesis). University of Toronto, Toronto.

Milićević, J., & Tsedryk, A. (2011). Assessing and improving paraphrasing competence in FSL. In I. Boguslavsky, & L. Wanner (Eds.), *Proceedings of the 5th international conference on meaning-text theory* (pp. 175-184). Barcelona, Spain: Pompeu Fabra University.

Mohamed, A. F. S. (2017). *Immediate feedback in a morphology software application for English vocabulary learning.* (Unpublished master's thesis). Washington State University, Pullman, WA.

Morris, C., & Chikwa, G. (2014). Screencasts: How effective are they and how do students engage with them? *Active Learning in Higher Education*, *15*(1), 25–37. doi:10.1177/1469787413514654

Morris, C., & Chikwa, G. (2016). Audio versus written feedback: Exploring learners' preference and the impact of feedback format on students' academic performance. *Active Learning in Higher Education*, *17*(2), 125–137. doi:10.1177/1469787416637482

Murthy, S., Warriem, J., & Iyer, S. (2017). Technology integration for student-centered learning; A model for teacher professional development programs. In S. Kong, T. Wong, M. Yang, C. Chow, & K. Tse (Eds.), *Emerging practices in scholarship of learning and teaching in a digital era* (pp. 55–74). Singapore: Springer. doi:10.1007/978-981-10-3344-5_4

Nerbonne, J., Dokter, D., & Smit, P. (1998). Morphological processing and computer-assisted language learning. *Computer Assisted Language Learning*, *11*(5), 543–559. doi:10.1076/call.11.5.543.5660

Nielson, K. B. (2014). Evaluation of an online, task-based Chinese course. In M. González-Lloret, & L. Ortega (Eds.), *Technology-mediated TBLT: Researching technology and tasks* (pp. 295–322). Amsterdam, The Netherlands: John Benjamins.

Oxford, R. L. (2006). Task-based language teaching and learning: An overview. *Asian EFL Journal*, *8*(3), 94–121.

Palmer, S. D. (2010). *Second language pragmatic socialization in World of Warcraft.* (Unpublished doctoral dissertation, Office of Graduate Studies, University of California, Davis).

Pecorari, D. (2003). Good and original: Plagiarism and patchwriting in academic second-language writing. *Journal of Second Language Writing*, *12*(4), 317–345. doi:10.1016/j.jslw.2003.08.004

Pecorari, D., & Petrić, B. (2014). Plagiarism in second-language writing. *Language Teaching*, *47*(3), 269–302. doi:10.1017/S0261444814000056

Rass, R. A. (2011). Cultural transfer as an obstacle for writing well in English: The case of Arabic speakers writing in English. *English Language Teaching*, *4*(2), 206. doi:10.5539/elt.v4n2p206

Reisoğlu, I., Topu, F., Yılmaz, R., Yılmaz, T., & Göktaş, Y. (2017). 3D virtual learning environments in education: A meta-review. *Asia Pacific Education Review*, *18*(1), 81–100. doi:10.100712564-016-9467-0

Richards, J. C., & Rodgers, T. S. (2001). Communicative language teaching. *Approaches and methods in language teaching, 2*, 153-177.

Robinson, P. (2005). Cognitive complexity and task sequencing: Studies in a componential framework for second language task design. *International Journal of Applied Linguistics, 43*(1), 1–32. doi:10.1515/iral.2005.43.1.1

Rogerson, A. M., & McCarthy, G. (2017). Using Internet based paraphrasing tools: Original work, patchwriting or facilitated plagiarism? *International Journal for Educational Integrity, 13*(1), 2. doi:10.100740979-016-0013-y

Rosell-Aguilar, F. (2005). Task design for audiographic conferencing: Promoting beginner oral interaction in distance language learning. *Computer Assisted Language Learning, 18*(5), 417–442. doi:10.1080/09588220500442772

Sauro, S. (2009). Computer-mediated corrective feedback and the development of L2 grammar. *Language Learning & Technology, 13*, 96–120.

Schroeder, R. (2008, July). Defining virtual worlds and virtual environments. *Journal of Virtual Worlds Research: Past, Present, & Future, 1*(1), 2–3.

Sedhu, D., Lee, M., & Choy, S. (2013). The influence of teaching strategies on students' paraphrasing strategies: A case study. *International Journal of Independent Research and Studies, 2*(3), 130–137.

Séror, J. (2013). Show me! Enhanced feedback through screencasting technology. *TESL Canada Journal, 30*(1), 104–116. doi:10.18806/tesl.v30i1.1128

Sharp, S. K. (2017). *iPads in the second language classroom: An examination of iPad use by teachers through TPACK and teacher perception lenses* (Unpublished doctoral dissertation). University of Maryland, College Park.

Shi, L. (2004). Textual borrowing in second-language writing. *Written Communication, 21*(2), 171–200. doi:10.1177/0741088303262846

Shi, L. (2012). Rewriting and paraphrasing source texts in second language writing. *Journal of Second Language Writing, 21*(2), 134–148. doi:10.1016/j.jslw.2012.03.003

Shih, R. C. (2011). Can Web 2.0 technology assist college students in learning English writing? Integrating Facebook and peer assessment with blended learning. *Australasian Journal of Educational Technology, 27*(5), 829–845. doi:10.14742/ajet.934

Shih, Y. C., & Yang, M. T. (2008). A collaborative virtual environment for situated language learning using VEC3D. *Journal of Educational Technology & Society, 11*(1), 56–68.

Sun, Y. C. (2012). Does text readability matter? A study of paraphrasing and plagiarism in English as a foreign language writing context. [De La Salle University Manila]. *The Asia-Pacific Education Researcher, 21*(2), 296–306.

Swier, R. (2014). Tasks for easily modifiable virtual environments. *JALT CALL Journal, 10*(3), 203–219.

Tai, S.-J. D. (2015). From TPACK-in-action workshops to classrooms: CALL competency developed and integrated. *Language Learning & Technology*, *19*(1), 139–164.

Tan, K. E. (2017). Using online discussion forums to support learning of paraphrasing. *British Journal of Educational Technology*, *48*(6), 1239–1249. doi:10.1111/bjet.12491

Thomas, M., & Reinders, H. (Eds.). (2010). *Task-based language learning and teaching with technology*. London, UK: Continuum.

Tsutsui, M. (2004). Multimedia as a means to enhance feedback. *Computer Assisted Language Learning, 17*(3-4), 377–402.

Uemlianin, I. A. (2000). Engaging text: Assessing paraphrase and understanding. *Studies in Higher Education*, *25*(3), 347–358. doi:10.1080/713696160

Varidesk, (2017, Nov. 2). Minecraft can transform your world language classroom. *EdTech.* Retrieved from https://edtechmagazine.com/k12/article/2017/11/minecraft-can-transform-your-world-language-classroom

Wang, A. (2015). Facilitating participation: Teacher roles in a multiuser virtual learning environment. *Language Learning & Technology*, *19*(2), 156–176.

Wang, C. P., Lan, Y. J., Tseng, W. T., Lin, Y. T. R., & Gupta, K. C. L. (2019). On the effects of 3D virtual worlds in language learning–a meta-analysis. *Computer Assisted Language Learning*, *32*, 1–25.

Ware, P., & Kessler, G. (2016). Telecollaboration in the secondary language classroom: Case study of adolescent interaction and pedagogical integration. *Computer Assisted Language Learning*, *29*(3), 427–450. doi:10.1080/09588221.2014.961481

Warr, M., Mishra, P., & Scragg, B. (2019, March). Beyond TPACK: Expanding technology and teacher education to systems and culture. In K. Graziano (Ed.), *Society for Information Technology & Teacher Education International Conference* (pp. 2558-2562). Las Vegas, NV: Association for the Advancement of Computing in Education (AACE). Retrieved from https://www.learntechlib.org/primary/p/208009

Wik, P., & Hjalmarsson, A. (2009). Embodied conversational agents in computer assisted language learning. *Speech Communication*, *51*(10), 1024–1037. doi:10.1016/j.specom.2009.05.006

Wilson, K. B., & Acheampong, B. (2014). Implications of computer technology in language teaching: Accessing CALL in teacher education. *US-China Education Review*, *4*(9), 651–661.

Yang, S. C., & Chen, Y. J. (2007). Technology-enhanced language learning: A case study. *Computers in Human Behavior*, *23*(1), 860–879. doi:10.1016/j.chb.2006.02.015

Yuksel, D., & Inan, B. (2014). The effects of communication mode on negotiation of meaning and its noticing. *ReCALL*, *26*(3), 333–354. doi:10.1017/S0958344014000147

Zheng, D., Young, M. F., Brewer, R. A., & Wagner, M. (2013). Attitude and self-efficacy change: English language learning in virtual worlds. *CALICO Journal*, *27*(1), 205–231. doi:10.11139/cj.27.1.205-231

Ziegler, N. (2016). Taking technology to task: Technology-mediated TBLT, performance, and production. *Annual Review of Applied Linguistics*, *36*, 136–163. doi:10.1017/S0267190516000039

Section 2
Mobile Learning

Chapter 2
Influence of Age Groups and School Types on Informal Learning Through the Use of Social Networking Sites

Siew Ming Thang
HELP University, Malaysia

Lay Shi Ng
Universiti Kebangsaan Malaysia, Malaysia

ABSTRACT

The use of Social Networking Sites (SNSs) as a learning tool is increasingly popular nowadays. This chapter investigates perceptions of 799 secondary-school Malaysian secondary school students of two age-groups, and three school-types (urban, suburban, and rural) towards the use of the SNSs for informal learning purposes. For this chapter, learning that takes place outside the classroom is classified as "informal learning". Data were analysed quantitatively and comparisons across age-groups and school-types were made. The findings revealed that there was a general acceptance of SNSs as an alternative learning mode and that difference in usage between age groups was not significant. However, the findings across school-types were significant. Suburban and rural students appeared to use the SNSs more frequently for informal learning than urban students. This strongly suggested the need for Government to intensify its efforts in improving ICT infrastructure and facilities in rural areas.

INTRODUCTION

The popularity of social networking sites (SNSs) has rapidly increased over the past few years in Malaysia. GlobalWebIndex (2015) revealed that Malaysia has the second highest penetration of social networking usage among Internet users in Asia. It was further reported that on average a Malaysian with a social networking account spends 2.8 hours per day on SNSs. Now with the widespread use of smartphones, it

DOI: 10.4018/978-1-7998-1282-1.ch002

is believed that the time spent on SNSs will continue to rise. SNSs such as Facebook, Instagram, WhatsApp and WeChat are the most commonly used Internet-based social spaces in Malaysia, particularly among young individuals.

Boyd and Ellison (2007) defined a social networking system as a web-based service that allows individuals to do the following: i) build public or semi-public profile in a system, (ii) share a connection, and (iii) view and cross-list their relationship with others in the system. Such systems enable easy and rapid connection with friends, families, classmates, customers and clients. In addition, SNSs are also seen as media that allows people to come together around an idea or topic of interest. In fact, SNSs are increasingly being leveraged as a learning tool, especially for today's tech-savvy students. According to Lai et al. (2013), many students are immersed in out-of-school online activities. When using digital media, students engage in a new learning culture which is very different from what they have been enculturated in traditional schools. Many studies have indicated the potential of using social networking for learning purposes (Selwyn, 2009; Griffith & Liyanage, 2008). However, it is not possible to use it as a tool for learning in Malaysian secondary schools due to the constraint of not allowing students to bring their cell phones to schools. Thus, it would be interesting to find out to what extent students use SNSs for learning purposes outside the classroom which has been defined as "informal learning" in this study. This definition is in line with that of Livingstone (1999) and Marsick and Watkins (2001). Livingstone (1999) described informal learning as any activity involving the pursuit of understanding, knowledge or skill which occurs outside the curricula of educational institutions, or the courses or workshops offered by educational or social agencies. Marsick and Watkins (2001) further described it as intentional but unstructured, contextualized learning.

This study extends on these studies in its attempt to investigate how differences in age and school-types affect students' usage of SNSs for informal learning purposes. Findings of this study will add to the current body of research, conducted on the effects of social networking on Malaysian secondary school students.

The following research questions specifically seek to investigate whether there are differences in usage for the following categories of students: (a) between students of two different age-groups and (b) between students from three school-types (namely urban, suburban and rural):

1. What types of SNSs usage patterns are displayed among the different categories of Malaysian secondary school students?
2. How much time do these different categories of students spend on SNSs?
3. To what extent do these different categories of students use SNSs for learning and what types of learning do they focus on?
4. What are the differences in usage of SNSs for informal learning purposes of the different categories of students?

RELATED LITERATURE

Social Networking Sites

Social networking was introduced 15 to 20 years ago. Since then it has grown from a niche to a mass online activity, in which millions of Internet users (from different ages, cultures and education levels) are engaged in during their leisure time and at their workplace (Misra et al., 2015; Mazman and Usluel, 2011).Its impact cannot be overstated. Social networking is the most popular online activity worldwide accounting for nearly 1 in every 5 minutes spent online in October 2011, and reaches 82 percent of the world's Internet population, representing 1.2 billion users around the globe (ComScore, 2011). According to a study by Lenhart et al. (2010), young people were much more likely than older adults to use social networks. Several studies conducted in the U.S. found that 80% of online teens used social network sites, Facebook being the most popular, with 93% of those teens reporting its use (Manago et al., 2008). Likewise, it was reported that Malaysians were spending more than three hours on their smartphones each day, where 40% of users' time were spent on social networking and chatting (Vserv, 2015).

Differences in SNSs' Usage According to Age

Surveys have found substantial differences in social media use according to age. According to a report published by Pew Research Center, in 2018, 88% of the Americans between the ages of 18-29 used SNSs. However, the social media adoption rate of Americans between 30-49 was 78%, while older age group (50-64) was 64%. Women were more likely than men to use social media. The report also indicated that a majority of Americans used Facebook and YouTube, but young adults (especially those age 18-24) were especially heavy users of Snapchat and Instagram.

In USA, the age group between 35-44 displayed dominant use of SNSs across the social web (Briansolis.com, 2010). According to a survey by Sproutsocial (2017), more than 60% of Americans age above 34 preferred to use Facebook, while only 33% of Millennials preferred Facebook and 25% of younger Millennials (ages 18-24) identified Instagram as their favourite social media network. In Malaysia, over 90% of Internet users used SNSs. Older age group reported a lower rate of Internet use compared to younger group. Only 7.5% of Malaysians age 50-64 used Internet (MCMC, 2017). Hence, it is obvious that the usage of social media is higher among young Malaysians than the older age group.

Differences in SNSs' Usage According to the Urban-Rural Divide

Hosseini, Niknami, and Chizari (2009) reported that rural communities in Malaysia faced several challenges in the implementation and use of ICT. These include lack of interest and expertise in using ICT, concerns about the risks of using ICT, low quality of the services provided by the service centres, and the lack of interest by the private sector to participate in the rural development of ICT. According to Zulkhairi, Azizah, Abdul Razak, and Rafidah (2010), the rate of literacy and the rate of broadband penetration in rural areas still remained at a low level of less than one percent. Umar and Jalil (2012) further revealed that that there was a significant difference between urban school students and rural school students in terms of ICT skills. This clearly indicated that the ICT infrastructure in the rural areas had to be improved to rectify this situation. To overcome this the Government had assigned of RM12 billion to enhance ICT development strategy in rural areas through the National Broadband Initiative (NBI). Through this initiative, the Ministry of Information Communication and Culture aimed to increase broadband facilities and extend the coverage of internet access in rural areas, and hopefully this would lead to increase in ICT literacy rate.

Despite these efforts, Internet penetration in Malaysia is still very much an urban experience with ICT development in rural community lagging far behind (Wok and Mohamed, 2017). Government statistics compiled by Malaysian Communication and Multimedia Commission (2018) further confirmed this.

It indicated that majority of the Internet users were from the urban areas (70.0%) and only 30% were from the rural areas. Way back in 2008, Donner (2008) had proclaimed that the portability, simplicity and affordability of mobile devices would make them naturally suitable for educational activities and this statement proved to be true as mobile devices are widely used nowadays for education purposes in a variety of settings but its use in rural areas in Malaysia is still very limited due to poor internet coverage.

Regarding attitude towards ICT in rural areas, Halili and Sulaiman's (2018) study on 450 secondary school students from more than 10 rural districts in Malaysia revealed that on the whole the students had moderately positive attitudes toward ICT use for educational purposes. However, they further discovered that facilitating conditions were the most influential determinant of ICT use among rural students. In other words, the main contributing factor towards lack of ICT use was inadequate infrastructure and ICT facilities.

In January 2019, it was reported that 78% of the Malaysian population were active social media users (Statista.com, 2019) and majority of these users were teenagers. It was also earlier mentioned that those living in urban areas had better access to internet facilities than those living in rural areas. This seems to suggest that the use of SNSs for learning purposes would be higher among urban students than rural students. However, this cannot be confirmed without scientific inquiry and as far as I am aware of no study has explored this issue. Thus, to fill this gap in knowledge, one of the primary objectives of this study is to investigate to what extent students from different demographic background (urban vs rural) use SNS for learning informal learning purposes.

SNSs and Informal Learning

Many studies have dealt with the uses of SNSs in learning and learners' opinions toward the use of SNSs for learning. According to Pempek, Yermolayeva, and Calvert (2009), SNSs exposed students to an extensive range of discourse functions and online writing that enhanced critical literacy and language skills, and launched creative deployment of language play. Lai et al., (2013) stated that using technologies in informal settings could be more motivating and engaging than using technologies in school settings as informal learning often engaged students in real life problems and used community resources. Students with a collaborative learning preference had been found to use SNSs more frequently for informal learning (Vivian & Barnes, 2010). Boyd (2008) revealed that high school students used SNSs to connect with other students for homework and group projects. SNSs could also actively encourage online community building, hence, extending learning beyond the boundaries of the classroom (Smith, 2009; Brady, Holcomb and Smith, 2010). According to Tiene (2000), written communication on cyberspace enabled students to take part in discussions at a time convenient to them and articulate their ideas in more carefully thought-out and structured ways. Deng and Tavares (2013) added that web-based discussions could contribute to the development of students' reflective ability and critical thinking skills.

Learning online as well as through SNSs can be considered as an informal way of learning. According to Laskaris (2015) informal learning could give the highest level of learning with the deepest cognitive impact. In the Malaysian context, Hamat, Embi and Abu Hassan (2012) found that university students made use of social media for informal learning. Studies also revealed that students of different age-groups and school-types participate in informal learning activities for different personal reasons. According to Farrah and Melati (2013), Malaysian teenagers had the tendency to use SNSs to gather specific information for the purpose of completing assignments given by their teachers in schools. On the other hand, older age group used SNSs to access information and issues related to challenges associated with later life such as retirement, aging, and health, family and finances (Nimrod, 2013). They further found that when people of different age-groups were exposed to different types of knowledge they would decide on what to believe and practise in a systematic manner. There is still a lack of studies in the Malaysian context that explore the use of SNSs as an informal learning tool. Hence this study will add new knowledge to this area of research.

METHOD

Participants

A convenience sampling approach was used to recruit 799 students from three types of schools located in the Klang Valley and Selangor in Malaysia, i.e. an urban school, a sub-urban school and a rural school. The reason for choosing the three types of schools was to give a convincing representation of the different types of schools found in Malaysia. However, the choice of actual schools depended on the willingness of the principals to allow their students to participate in the study. A brief description of each type of school is given below:

The urban school is situated about 17 km from Kuala Lumpur. It is a secondary co-education school where the medium of instruction for all subjects except English and Bahasa Malaysia is in Mandarin. All of the students come from National Type Chinese School (with Mandarin as the medium of instruction). The performance of students in this school for the PT3/ UPSR (Primary Three/Primary Six) examinations is generally mixed with high and average performing students.

The suburban school is about 30 km from Kuala Lumpur. The students are Malay male and female students who come from national primary schools. The medium of instruction for all subjects except English is in Malay. The performance of students for the PT3/UPSR examinations in this school is mixed ranging from good to below average. Their proficiency in English is generally average. Students in this school generally speak Malay at home, come from middle income families where most of their parents are civil servants, and they live around Putrajaya.

The rural co-education school is about 30 km from Kuala Lumpur. It is a normal type of Malaysian school where students are drawn from the surrounding areas. The medium of instruction for all subjects except English is in Malay. However, the students in this school come from mixed primary school background. Some would have studied their primary education in a National Type Chinese school (with Mandarin as the medium of instruction, some in National Type Tamil schools (with Tamil as the medium of instruction) and some in National school (with Malay as the medium of instruction). The performance of students in this school for the PT3/UPSR examinations is mixed with more low performing students than high performing students.

In addition to that, only Form Two (14 years old) and Form Four (16 years old) students from the three different types of schools were utilised for this study. This was due to the fact that it was not possible to obtain permission from the Ministry of Education to conduct the research on examination classes (i.e. Form Three and Form Five students). Form Two students represented lower secondary school students who were generally assumed to be less exposed to technology than the Form 4 students who represented upper secondary school students. The truth of this assumption would also be investigated in this study.

The sample of this study consists of 50.9% female and 49.1% male, and they were secondary school students of age 14 and age 16 from the three different types of school mentioned above. Table 1 gives a breakdown of students according to the age-groups,, gender and school-types. As shown in the Table the number of suburban and rural students are almost equal for both age-groups whereas the number of urban students are almost one-third less for both age-groups. However, this difference will not affect the validity and reliability of the data since both descriptive and inferential statistical tools were utilised.

Instrument

In this study, the role of SNSs in teenagers' informal language learning experiences was measured through a questionnaire survey that consists of two sections:

1. Section A elicits demographic information of the students.
2. Section B elicits information from the students regarding their use of SNSs for informal language learning purposes This section consists of 14 items with a four-point likert scale comprising responses that varied from 1 (Never) to 4 (all the time).

Research Procedure

An e-mail was sent to the person-in-charge of each school to ask for permission to conduct the questionnaire survey during school hours. The participants were given approximately 15 minutes to complete the questionnaire survey. Participants were assured of their anonymity and were informed that participation was voluntary and that they would receive a small gift as a token of appreciation for participating in this study. The questionnaire was only distributed to Form Two (14 years old) and Form Four (16 years old) students from the three different types of schools.

Data Analysis

The questionnaire data were analysed using SPSS (Statistical Package for the Social Sciences) version 17. Descriptive and inferential statistical tools were used. The descriptive data analysis involved comparing of mean scores and ranking of items. Inferential statistics analysis involved the use of ANOVA to measure the significance of the difference in mean scores between the students from different school-types.

Table 1. Breakdown of students from the three different types of school

	Students Age 14						Students Age 16						Overall Total	Overall %
School	**F**	**%**	**M**	**%**	**Total**	**(%)**	**F**	**%**	**M**	**%**	**Total**	**(%)**		
Urban	42	21.8	48	24.7	90	23.3	53	24.8	60	30.3	113	27.4	203	25.4
Suburban	67	34.7	82	42.3	149	38.5	69	32.2	80	40.4	149	36.2	298	37.3
Rural	84	43.5	64	33.0	148	38.2	92	43.0	58	29.3	150	36.4	298	37.3
Total	193	100	194	100	387	100	214	100	198	100	412	100	799	100

Key: F=Female; M=Male

RESULTS

Analysis of Baseline Data According to Age-Groups and School-Types

Table 2 showed that the four most popular SNSs among the age 14 students are Facebook, WhatsApp, Instagram and WeChat with rankings that vary slightly with school-types.

As shown in Table 3, the SNSs that are most favoured by the age 16 students are WhatApps, Facebook, Instagram, WeChat and Twitter with some variation in ranking according to school-types. Thus, there seems to be not much difference between the preference of the age 14 and age 16 students except that Twitter features more highly in the age 16 group.

For this study, spending less than 5 hours on SNSs per day is considered as spending a reasonable amount of time on social networking and spending more than 5 hours on SNSs is considered as "excessive use". This is calculated based on the assumption that students need 8 hours of sleep per night and 7 hours to attend school leaving them with 9 hours for other activities. If more than 5 hours (i.e.55%) of this remaining time is used for SN, then they are left with only 4 hours (i.e. 45%) for important activities such as taking their meals, doing their homework, other recreational activities and relaxation.

Table 4 revealed that out of the three groups, rural students spend the least among of time on SNSs with 69.6% of them spending less than 5 hours on SNSs whereas the amount of time urban and suburban students spend on SNSs is almost the same (urban 57.3% and suburban 55.8%). We should be concerned with this pattern as we can expect higher usage in future particularly in the case of urban and suburban students where more than 40% of them are already spending more than 5 hours on SNSs.

With regard to the age 16 students, as shown in Table 5, the difference between the three groups of students are less apparent compared to the age 14 students. Between 69.8% to 65.8% spend less than 5 hours on SNSs which goes to show that for older students there is no rural-urban divide in the amount of time spent on SNSs. However, it noted that more than 30% of all three groups spend more than 5 hours

Table 2. SNSs that age 14 students are members to according to school-types

SNSs frequented by students	Age 14										
	Urban	%	R	Suburban	%	R	Rural	%	R	T	%
Facebook	86	22.7	1	108	17.9	3	125	23	1	319	20.9
WhatsApp	68	17.9	2	132	21.9	1	98	18	3	298	19.5
Twitter	24	6.3	7	64	10.6	5	39	7.2	5	127	8.3
Instagram	53	14	4	110	18.2	2	84	15.4	4	247	16.2
WeChat	68	17.9	2	96	15.9	4	113	21	2	277	18.1
Line	36	9.5	5	26	4.3	7	30	5.5	7	92	6
Tumblr	8	2.1	8	18	3	8	13	2.4	8	39	2.6
Pinterest	8	2.1	8	7	1.2	9	10	1.8	9	25	1.6
Skype	28	7.4	6	43	7.1	6	32	5.9	6	103	6.7
Total no. of respondents to Qs*	379			604			544			1527	

Key: R = Rank; T=Total; Qs=Questionnaires

Table 3. SNSs that age 16 students are members to according to school-types

SNSs frequented by students	Age 16										
	Urban	**%**	**R**	**Suburban**	**%**	**R**	**Rural**	**%**	**R**	**T**	**%**
Facebook	73	23.3	2	35	9	5	57	16.2	4	165	15.7
WhatsApp	86	27.5	1	99	25.6	2	100	28.5	1	285	27.1
Twitter	33	10.5	5	42	10.9	4	27	7.7	5	102	9.7
Instagram	39	12.5	3	102	26.4	1	74	21.1	2	215	20.5
WeChat	34	10.9	4	58	15	3	72	20.5	3	164	15.6
Line	13	4.2	6	6	1.6	9	6	1.7	7	25	2.4
Tumblr	7	2.2	8	17	4.4	7	2	0.6	8	26	2.5
Pinterest	10	3.2	7	8	2.1	8	2	0.6	8	20	1.9
Skype	18	5.8	5	20	5.2	6	11	3.1	6	49	4.7
Total no. of respondents to Qs*	313			387			351			1051	

Key: R = Rank; T=Total; Qs=Questionnaires

on SNSs which is still something to be concerned about. A comparison across indicated that the age 16 groups spend more time on SNSs then the age 14 groups.

Comparing the Differences in the Usage of SNSs for Informal Learning for Students of Different School-Types According to Age-Groups

Descriptive Statistics

For analysis of use of SNSs for the informal learning, both descriptive and inferential tools were used. For descriptive analysis, a mean score of 2.5 and above is taken as inclining to "often". The learning items showed in Table 6 demonstrated the different ways age 14 students use SNSs for informal learning. The Age 14 urban students have 3 out of 14 items (28.6%) that are inclined to "often". Out of these, only one of them (33.3.1%) are on learning of English. As for the suburban students, 9 out of 14 items (64.3%) are inclined to "often". Out of these items, 4 items (44.4%) are on the learning of English. Re-

Table 4. Time spent on SNSs per day by the age 14 students according to school-types

Time spent SN	Types of schools							
	Urban	**%**	**Suburban**	**%**	**Rural**	**%**	**Total**	**Total %**
Less than 2 hours	20	22.5	34	23.1	45	30.4	99	25.8
2 to 5 hours	31	34.8	48	32.7	58	39.2	137	35.7
5+ to 8 hours	12	13.5	28	19.0	26	17.6	66	17.2
More than 8 hours	26	29.2	37	25.2	19	12.8	82	21.3
Total	89	100	147	100	148	100	384	100

Table 5. Time spent on SNSs per day by the age 16 students according to school-types

Time spent SN	Types of schools							
	Urban	%	Suburban	%	Rural	%	Total	Total %
Less than 2 hours	23	20.5	36	24.2	31	21.1	90	22.1
2 to 5 hours	55	49.1	62	41.6	67	45.6	184	45.1
5+ to 8 hours	23	20.5	30	20.1	28	19.0	81	19.9
More than 8 hours	11	9.9	21	14.1	21	14.3	53	13
Total	112	100	149	100	147	100	408	100

garding the rural students, 8 out of 14 (57.1%) are inclined to "often" and 4 out of these (50%) are on the use SNSs for learning English.

Thus, the findings demonstrated that suburban and rural students are more inclined to use of SNSs for informal learning (around 60%) and out of these about 50% are inclined to use SNSs for learning English. The use of SNSs for informal learning in the case of urban students is rather low, only about 30%.

The learning items showed in Table 7 demonstrated the different ways age 16 students use SNSs for informal learning. The Age 16 urban students have 7 out of 14 items (50%) that are inclined to "often". Out of these, only 3 of them (33.3.1%) are on learning of English. As for the suburban students, 11 out of 14 items (78.6%) are inclined to "often". Out of these, five items (45.5%) are on the learning of English.

Table 6. The usage of SNSs for informal language learning purposes according to school-types (age 14) Key: 4 = "all the time", 3 = "often", 2 = "sometimes" and 1 = "never".

Student learning (age 14)	Urban			Suburban			Rural		
	N	Mean	R	N	Mean	R	N	Mean	R
1.Gain new knowledge	90	2.62	1	149	2.98	1	147	2.99	1
2.Learn from communicating with friends	90	2.31	5	149	2.87	2	147	2.63	3
3.Discuss lessons with friends	90	2.52	3	149	2.83	3	148	2.74	2
4.Give you a chance to communicate in English	90	2.57	2	149	2.82	4	147	2.67	4
5.Form a study group to discuss homework	90	1.89	10	149	2.72	5	146	1.85	14
6.Provide information related to your studies	90	2.28	7	149	2.70	6	148	2.57	6
7.Improve English through chatting with others	90	2.29	6	149	2.64	7	147	2.51	8
8.Improve English by reading articles or other people's writing	90	2.13	9	148	2.59	8	145	2.57	6
9.Learn new words in English	90	2.46	4	149	2.52	9	148	2.60	5
10.Use an online dictionary to find new words in English	90	2.24	8	149	2.18	10	147	2.37	9
11.Learn from communicating with teachers	90	1.82	11	149	2.07	11	146	2.03	11
12.Learn how to pronounce English words from an online dictionary	90	1.77	12	148	2.03	12	148	2.03	11
13.Form a group to chat in English	90	1.58	13	148	2.03	12	147	2.37	9
14.Learn words in foreign language	90	2.14	7	149	1.96	14	148	2.03	11

Table 7. The usage of SNSs for informal language learning purposes according to school-types (age 14) Key: 4 = "all the time", 3 = "often", 2 = "sometimes" and 1 = "never".

Student learning (age 16)	Urban			Suburban			Rural		
	N	Mean	R	N	Mean	R	N	Mean	R
1.Gain new knowledge	113	2.91	1	147	3.15	1	150	3.15	1
2.Learn from communicating with friends	112	2.66	4	147	3.10	2	149	2.81	4
3.Discuss lessons with friends	113	2.80	3	147	3.08	3	149	2.85	3
4.Give you a chance to communicate in English	112	2.88	2	147	3.07	4	150	2.88	2
5.Form a study group to discuss homework	112	2.23	10	147	3.03	5	150	2.68	6
6.Provide information related to your studies	112	2.56	6	147	3.03	5	148	2.66	8
7.Improve English through chatting with others	112	2.50	7	147	2.88	7	149	2.68	6
8.Improve English by reading articles or other people's writing	112	2.46	8	145	2.76	8	145	2.59	9
9.Learn new words in English	112	2.65	5	147	2.71	9	149	2.72	5
10.Use an online dictionary to find new words in English	112	2.34	9	147	2.63	10	149	2.56	10
11.Learn from communicating with teachers	112	2.05	12	147	2.51	11	148	2.24	12
12.Learn how to pronounce English words from an online dictionary	112	1.96	13	145	2.38	12	149	2.36	11
13.Form a group to chat in English	112	1.74	14	147	2.27	13	147	2.03	14
14.Learn words in foreign language	112	2.09	11	145	2.17	14	149	2.05	13

With regard to the rural students, 10 out of 14 (71.4%) are inclined to "often" and 5 out of these (50%) are on the use SNSs for learning English.

The findings clearly demonstrated that over 70% suburban and rural students use SNSs for informal learning and about 50% are inclined to use SNSs for learning English, even higher than the age 14 groups. The use of SNSs for learning in the case of urban students is much lower, only about 50% for informal learning and about 30% for learning English. However, the percentage is much higher than for the age 14 group.

Inferential Statistics

Inferential statistics were used to support or refute the findings from the descriptive analysis. Inferential statistical data analysis was undertaken using ANOVA to identify the statistically significant results. Most research studies use a cut-off of 5% (that is the p-value is less than 0.05). This is the p-value that is used for this research study. In view of that only significant findings were displayed and school-types with significantly higher mean scores were underlined.

The inferential analysis for the Age 14 students as shown in Table 8 revealed that 8 items out of the 14 items displayed significant differences. 3 of these items are specifically on the learning of English. The mean scores of age 14 suburban students are significantly higher than the urban students for all 8 items and the mean scores of age 14 rural students are significantly higher than the urban students for 6

Table 8. Comparison of mean scores across school-types for age 14 students

Students age 14	Urban			Suburban			Rural					
	N	Mean	SD	N	Mean	SD	N	Mean	SD	df	F	P-value
1.Gain new knowledge	90	2.62	.787	149	2.98	.881	147	2.99	.721	2	6.70	.001
2.Learn from communicating with friends	90	2.31	.956	149	2.87	.905	147	2.63	.907	2	10.27	.000
3.Discuss lessons with friends	90	2.52	.838	149	2.83	.926	148	2.74	.786	2	3.73	.025
5.Form a study group to discuss homework	90	1.89	.953	149	2.72	.959	147	2.37	.861	2	22.80	.000
6.Provide information related to your studies	90	2.28	.765	149	2.70	.794	148	2.57	.793	2	8.06	.000
7.Improve English through chatting with others	90	2.29	.902	149	2.64	.953	146	2.51	.832	2	4.24	.015
8. Improve English by reading articles and other's people writing	89	2.13	.894	148	2.59	.946	145	2.57	.941	2	7.82	.000
13. Form a group to chat in English	90	1.56	.823	148	2.03	.954	146	1.85	.897	2	7.63	.001

items. These findings confirmed that of the descriptive analysis in demonstrating that the use of SNSs for informal learning is clearly less in age 14 urban students compared to the other two groups.

The inferential analysis for the Age 16 students is more complex than the age 14 students. As shown in Table 9. 10 items out of the 14 items displayed significant differences. 5 of them are specifically on the learning of English. The mean scores of age 16 suburban students are significantly higher than the urban students for all 10 items. 5 of these items are on the learning of English. However, the mean scores of age 16 rural students are significantly higher than the urban students for only 3 items and two of these items are on the learning of English. The findings further revealed that the mean scores of the suburban students are significantly higher than the rural students for 4 items – all not on the learning of English. These findings supported the findings of the descriptive data in confirming that the use SNSs for informal learning is higher among suburban students and rural students than the urban students. Besides, it further revealed that rural students used SNSs for informal learning less than suburban students.

Ranking

With regard to the top five rankings, as shown in Table 6, the "gain new knowledge" item has the highest ranking for all age 14 groups suggesting that students see this as the most important thing they can gain from the SNSs. The next four items for the suburban group are all inclined towards learning through interaction with others suggesting that they view the social interaction online as very beneficial. With regard to the rural and urban students, their items 2 to 5 are also inclined to learning through interaction though not in the same order as the suburban students, except for one item i.e. item 9 which suggests that these two groups believe that using SNSs help them to learn new English words too.

Table 9. Comparison of mean scores across school-types for age 16 students

Students age 16	Urban			Suburban			Rural					
	N	Mean	SD	N	Mean	SD	N	Mean	SD	df	F	P-value
2. Learn from communicating with friends	112	2.66	.855	147	3.10	.894	149	2.81	.852	2	8.62	.000
3. Discuss lessons with friends	113	2.80	.888	147	3.07	.892	149	2.85	.833	2	3.92	.021
5. Form a study group to discuss homework	112	2.23	.958	147	3.03*	.925	150	2.68	.936	2	23.22	.000
6. Provide information related to your studies	112	2.56	.720	147	3.08	.848	148	2.66	.822	2	16.16	.000
7. Improve English through chatting with others	112	2.50	.794	147	2.88	.872	149	2.68	.894	2	6.43	.002
8. Improve English by reading articles and other's people writing	112	2.46	.879	145	2.76	.907	145	2.59	.961	2	3.50	.031
10. Use an online dictionary to find new words in English	112	2.34	.812	147	2.63	.838	149	2.56	.954	2	3.59	.028
11. Learn from communicating with teachers	112	2.05	.858	147	2.51	.932	148	2.24	.770	2	9.37	.000
12. Learn how to pronounce English words from an online dictionary	112	1.96	.859	145	2.38	.958	149	2.36	.901	2	7.97	.000
13 Form a group to chat in English	112	1.74	.791	145	2.17	.986	147	2.03	.883	2	7.18	.001

* For item 5, mean scores of suburban students also significantly higher than that of rural students.

With regard to the bottom five items, the three common items are items 11,12 and 13 with some slight variation in rankings. The overall pattern shows less preference for learning with teachers, group learning and also learning languages alone.

The pattern for age 16 students are somewhat similar to that of the age 14 students. The "gain new knowledge" item also has the highest ranking and the next four items for the suburban group are all also inclined towards learning through interaction. In addition to that items 2 to 5 items for the rural and urban students are also inclined to learning through interaction except for item 9.

With regard to the bottom five items, there are five common items for all age 16 groups except for one item in the case of urban students. On the whole the pattern indicates less preference for learning with teachers, group learning and also learning languages alone like in the case of age 14 students.

OVERALL DISCUSSION

This study investigated the use of SNSs for learning purposes by Malaysian secondary students of two different age-groups and three school-types. Four research questions were addressed in the study. First question looked into the SNSs patterns that Malaysian secondary school students preferred. The findings revealed that there is not much difference between the types of SNSs that are popular among students age 14 and students age 16 except for some variation in rankings. Generally, all students chose Facebook, WhatsApp, Instagram and WeChat as the first four choices except twitter features more prominently in the age 16 students. This is in line with the findings of GlobalWebIndex (2015) which suggests that there is no apparent difference in patterns of use between between students of different age-groups.

The second research question explored the amount of time the different categories of students spent on SNSs to get an idea of the extent of use. The study revealed that about 70% of the age 14 rural students spent less than 5 hours on SNSs whereas the percentage is between 55 to 58% in the case of the urban and suburban students. With regard to the age 16 students, the difference between the three groups of students are less apparent. This suggests that although accessibility to internet is less in the case of rural areas as pointed out by Wok and Mohamed (2017), older students in rural have more opportunity to access to internet. Despite lower usage among age 14 rural students, this pattern of usage in general is something to observe as it will lead to higher usage in future and this may have detrimental effects.

The third research question investigated to what extent the different categories of students use SNSs for informal learning and the types of learning they focus on. The findings revealed the used of SNSs for learning for informal learning is much higher in suburban students and rural students than urban students. In the case of age 14 the use of SNS for informal learning is highest among suburban students followed by rural students and the lowest among urban students. The pattern is somewhat similar in the case of age 16 students. In the case of learning of English it would also appear that suburban and rural students used the SNSs for that purpose more than urban students. These findings are very interesting and it is only possible to make some postulations regarding this at this stage. It is my conjecture that urban students are exposed to many opportunities to enhance their learning including attending tuition classes and out of the class learning activities. Hence, they do not utilise the SNSs much for learning and use it more for social communication purposes. In the case of the suburban students they are less exposed to learning opportunities and hence they depend on the SNSs to help them to learn. Likewise in the case of rural students but in this case to a lesser extent because they have less access to the internet. However further research needs to be undertaken to investigate the truth of this conjecture.

The last research question investigated whether there were any differences in usage of SNSs for informal learning between the students from the three school-types. The findings revealed almost similar findings. Generally all groups felt that using SNSs to gain new knowledge was most important followed by learning through interactions and learning new words in English. The least preferred types of learning for all groups were learning alone, learning through the help of a teacher and learning through a group chat. However, there seem to be less preference for activities that have to be performed alone or with the support of the teachers. These findings corroborated previous findings (Boyd, 2008; Smith, 2009; Brady, Holcomb and Smith, 2010) that show SNSs can be used for informal learning for a variety of purposes.

IMPLICATIONS AND CONCLUSION

In conclusion it is possible to say that Malaysian students age 14 and 16 from three school-types have used SNSs for informal learning to a reasonable extent and that their involvement in SNSs has beneficial effects. This study has identified the types of learning these students are involved in and they encompass a variety of learning activities: gaining new knowledge seem to be considered most important followed by search for knowledge and learning through interactions and learning new English words. However, the students show lower preference for activities that involve self-learning and teacher involvement. The differences between students from different school-types seem not be obvious in terms of learning types and preferences

Social networking has become an essential part of life for most Malaysian secondary school students and that it serves not only as a primary tool for communication and socialization but also a tool in assisting students' education development outside the classroom. The findings of this research can help teachers and parents understand how lower secondary and upper secondary students from different types of schools learn after classes. The fact that suburban and rural students seem to use the SNSs more frequently for informal learning is encouraging. This strongly suggests that the government should intensify its efforts in improving ICT infrastructure in rural areas so that their opportunities to learn through ICT including SNSs can increase and help rural students improve their ICT skills which were found to be lacking (Umar and Jalil, 2012).

Findings from this research study can also help school teachers design meaningful activities involving the use of SNSs for learning purposes knowing what learning activities the students preferred. Apart from that, this research may also help to expand methods for teaching languages in classroom contexts since the findings show that informal online engagement leads to successful language learning. According to the Global Information Technology Report 2015 by Dutta et al. (2015), Malaysia was ranked 32nd out of 143 countries listed in the Networked Readiness Index 2015, and it is the only country in Asia that was featured in the top 60. The report also revealed that the internet access in schools was ranked 34th out of 143. This clearly indicates that it will not be difficult for Malaysian schools to harness social networking as an educational tool.

Although this research has successfully achieved its objectives, there are unavoidable limitations that need to be mentioned here. It has to be admitted that there is a possibility of sample selection bias in this study. The study has targeted a fairly narrow demographic segment, namely, secondary school students (age 14 and 16) from three schools located in the Klang Valley and Selangor. An earlier study (Ng et al. 2018) which explored patterns of use of SNSs for informal learning between male and female students of the same sample population did provide insights into their patterns of use but exploring other variables such as different ethnic origins and different social economic status will further enrich the findings. However, it is not possible to explore all of them within the scope of this study. It is possible that this narrow focus may have limited the generalisability of the results to Malaysian school population as a whole. Hence, for future research, it is recommended that a more extensive study covering more variables and wider demographic segments be undertaken.

ACKNOWLEDGMENT

This paper was part of a research project (Code SK-2015-003) funded by the Malaysian Communications and Multimedia Commission (MCMC).

REFERENCES

Bond, B. J. (2009). He posted, she posted: Gender differences in self-disclosure on social networking sites. *Rocky Mountain Communication Review*, *6*(2), 29–37.

Boyd, D. M. (2008). *Taken out of context: American teen sociality in networked publics. (Ph.D. Dissertation)*. Berkeley, CA: School of Information, University of California-Berkeley; Retrieved from https://www.danah.org/papers/TakenOutOfContext.pdf

Boyd, D. M., & Ellison, N. B. (2007). Social network sites: Definition, history, and scholarship. *Journal of Computer-Mediated Communication*, *13*(1), 210–230. doi:10.1111/j.1083-6101.2007.00393.x

Brady, K., Holcomb, L., & Smith, B. (2010). The use of alternative social networking sites in higher educational settings: A case study of the e-learning benefits of Ning in education. *Journal of Interactive Online Learning*, *9*(2), 151–170.

Briansolis. (2010). The age of social networks. Retrieved from https://www.briansolis.com/2010/03/the-age-of-social-networks/

Bruestle, P., Haubner, D., Schinzel, B., Holthaus, M., Remmele, B., Schirmer, D., & Reips, U. D. (2009). Doing E-learning/doing gender? Examining the relationship between students' gender concepts and E-learning technology. *Proceedings of the 5th European Symposium on Gender & ICT Digital Cultures: Participation - Empowerment – Diversity, University of Bremen.*

Chun, W. S. M. (2013). An exploration of gender differences in the use of social networking and knowledge management tools. *Journal of Information Technology Management*, *24*(2), 20–31.

ComScore. (2011). It's a social world: Social networking leads as top online activity globally, accounting for 1 in every 5 online minutes. Retrieved from https://www.comscore.com/Insights/Press-Releases/2011/12/Social-Networking-Leads-as-Top-Online-Activity-Globally

Cuadrado-García, M., Ruiz-Molina, M. E., & Montoro-Pons, J. D. (2010). Are there gender differences in e-learning use and assessment? Evidence from an interuniversity online project in Europe. *Procedia: Social and Behavioral Sciences*, *2*(2), 367–371. doi:10.1016/j.sbspro.2010.03.027

Deng, L., & Tavares, N. (2013). From moodle to Facebook: Exploring students' motivation and experiences in online communities. *Computer Educ*, *68*, 167–176. doi:10.1016/j.compedu.2013.04.028

Donner, J. (2008). Research approaches to mobile use in the developing world: a review of the literature. *The Information Society*, *24*(3), 140–159. doi:10.1080/01972240802019970

Dutta, S., Geiger, T., & Lanvin, B. (2015). The global information technology report 2015. Retrieved from http://www3.weforum.org/docs/WEF_Global_IT_Report_2015.pdf

Yusop, F. D., & Sumari, M. (2013). The use of social media technologies among Malaysian youth. *Procedia: Social and Behavioral Sciences*, *103*, 1204–1209.

GlobalWebIndex. (2015). Quarterly report on the latest trends in social networking. Retrieved March 2018 from https://www.globalwebindex.net/hs-fs/hub/304927/file-2812772150 pdf/Reports/ GWI_Social_Summary_Report_Q1_2015.pdf

Griffith, S., & Liyanage, L. (2008). An introduction to the potential of social networking sitesin education. *Proceedings of the Second Emerging Technologies Conference 2008. Australia: Wollongong.*

Halili, S. H., & Sulaiman, H. (2018). (article in press). Factors influencing the rural students' acceptance of using ICT for educational purposes. *Kasetsart Journal of Social Sciences*, 1–6.

Hamat, A., Embi, M. A., & Abu Hassan, H. (2012). The use of social networking sites among Malaysian university students. *International Education Studies*, *5*(3), 56–66. doi:10.5539/ies.v5n3p56

Hosseini, S. J. F., Niknami, M., & Chizari, M. (2009). To determine the challenges in the application of ICTs by the agricultural extension service in Iran. *Journal of Agricultural Extension and Rural Development, 1*(1), 292e299.

Joiner, R., Gavin, J., Brosnan, M., Cromby, J., Gregory, H., Guiller, J., ... Moon, A. (2012). Gender, internet experience, internet identification and internet anxiety: A ten year follow-up. *Cyberpsychology, Behavior, and Social Networking*, *15*(7), 370–372. doi:10.1089/cyber.2012.0033 PMID:22690795

Kirkup, G. (2010). Academic blogging: Academic practice and academic identity. *London Review of Education*, *8*(1), 75–84. doi:10.1080/14748460903557803

Kirkup, G., & von Prümmer, C. (1997). Distance education for European women: The treats and opportunities of new educational forms and media. *European Journal of Women's Studies*, *4*(1), 39–62. doi:10.1177/135050689700400104

Lai, K.-W., Khaddage, F., & Knezek, G. (2013). Student technology experiences in formal and informal learning in WCCE 2013: Learning while we are connected. *Proceedings of the IFIP Computers in Education 2013 World Conference,* 290-290. Torun, Poland: Nicolaus Copernicus University Press.

Laskaris, J. (2015). 6 Benefits of informal learning. *Talentslms.com.* Retrieved from https://www.talentlms.com/blog/6-benefits-of-informal-learning/

Lenhart, A., Madden, M., & Hitlin, P. (2010). Social media and mobile internet use among teens and young adults. *Washington, D.C.: Pew Internet & American Life Project.* Retrieved from https://files.eric.ed.gov/fulltext/ED525056.pdf

Liu, C. Y., & Yu, C. P. (2013). Can Facebook use induce well-being? *Cyberpsychology, Behavior, and Social Networking*, *16*(9), 674–678. doi:10.1089/cyber.2012.0301 PMID:24028138

Livingstone, D. W. (1999). Exploring the icebergs of adult learning: Findings of the first Canadian survey of informal learning practices. *Nall Working Paper No:10.* Centre for the Study of Education and Work, OISE/UT, Toronto. Retrieved from https://tspace.library.utoronto.ca/bitstream/1807/2724/2/10

Malaysian Communications and Multimedia Commission. (2017). Internet users survey 2017. Retrieved from https://www.mcmc.gov.my/skmmgovmy/media/General/pdf/MCMC-Internet-Users-Survey-2017.pdf

Malaysian Communications and Multimedia Commission. (2018). Internet users survey 2018. Retrieved from https://www.mcmc.gov.my/skmmgovmy/media/General/pdf/Internet-Users-Survey-2018.pdf

Manago, A. M., Taylor, T., & Greenfield, P. M. (2012). Me and my 400 friends: the anatomy of college students' Facebook networks, their communication patterns, and well-being. *Developmental Psychology, 48*(2), 369–380. doi:10.1037/a0026338 PMID:22288367

Marsick, V. J., & Watkins, K. E. (2001). Informal and incidental learning. *New Directions for Adult and Continuing Education, 89*(89), 25–34. doi:10.1002/ace.5

Mazman, S. G., & Usluel, Y. K. (2011). Gender differences in using social networks. *The Turkish Online Journal of Educational Technology, 10*(2), 133–139.

Misra, N., Dangi, S., & Patel, S. (2015). Gender differences in usage of social networking sites and perceived online social support on psychological well-being of youth. *The International Journal of Indian Psychology, 3*(1), 63–74.

Ng, L. S., Thang, S. M., & Mohd, N. N. (2018). The usage of social networking sites for informal learning: a comparative study between Malaysia students of different gender and age group. [IJCALLT]. *International Journal of Computer-Assisted Language Learning and Teaching, 8*(4), 76–88. doi:10.4018/IJCALLT.2018100106

Nimrod, G. (2013). Applying gerontographics in the study of older Internet users. *Journal of Audience & Perception Study, 10*(2), 46–64.

Pempek, T. A., Yermolayeva, Y. A., & Calvert, S. L. (2009). College students'social networking experiences on Facebook. *Journal of Applied Developmental Psychology, 30*(3), 227–238. doi:10.1016/j.appdev.2008.12.010

Pew Research Center. (2018). Social media use in 2018. Retrieved from http://www.pewinternet.org/2018/03/01/social-media-use-in-2018/

Selwyn, N. (2007). An investigation in undergraduates' academic use of the Internet. *Active Learning in Higher Education, 9*(1), 11–22. doi:10.1177/1469787407086744

Selwyn, N. (2009). Faceworking: Exploring students' education-related use of "Facebook". *Learning, Media, and Technology, 34*(2), 157–174. doi:10.1080/17439880902923622

Smith, B. V. (2009). *Use of online educational social networking in a school environment.* (Unpublished master's thesis). North Carolina State University, Raleigh, NC. Retrieved from http://www.ncolr.org/jiol/issues/pdf/9.2.4.pdf

Social Media Today. (2016). Gender-specific behaviors on social media and what they mean for online communications. Retrieved from https://www.socialmediatoday.com/social-networks/gender-specific-behaviors-social-media-and-what-they-mean-online-communications

Sproutsocial. (2017). The Q1 2017 Sprout social index-The social generations: Millennials ask, Gen X buys & Baby Boomers observe. Retrieved from https://sproutsocial.com/insights/data/q1-2017/

Statista.com. (2019) Retrieved from https://www.statista.com/statistics/883712/malaysia-social-media-penetration/

Tiene, C. D. (2000). Online discussions: A survey of advantages and disadvantages compared to face-to-face discussions. *Journal of Educational Multimedia and Hypermedia*, *9*(4), 371–384.

Umar, I. N., & Jalil, N. A. (2012). ICT skills, practices, and barriers of its use among secondary school students. *Procedia: Social and Behavioral Sciences*, *46*, 5672–5676. doi:10.1016/j.sbspro.2012.06.494

Vivian, R., & Barnes, A. (2010). Social networking: From living technology to learning technology? In C.H. Steel, M. J. Keppell, P. Gerbic, & S. Housego (Eds.), Curriculum, Technology, & Transformation for an unknown Future. Proceedings of Ascilite Sydney 2010, 1007–1019.

Vserv. (2015). Smartphone user Persona report (SUPR) 2015. Retrieved from https://www.vserv.com/vserv-unveils-first-smartphone-user-persona-report-supr-malaysia/

Wok, S., & Mohamed, S. (2017). Internet and social media in Malaysia: Development, challenges and potentials. *The Evolution of Media Communication*, 45-64.

Yusop, F. D., & Sumari, M. (2013). The use of social media technologies among Malaysian youth. *Procedia: Social and Behavioral Sciences*, *103*, 1204–1209. doi:10.1016/j.sbspro.2013.10.448

Zulkhairi, M. D., Azizah, A., Abdul Razak, A., & Rafidah, A. R. (2010, November). Community informatics: Success factors at a rural community telecentre. *Proceedings of rural ICT development 3rd national conference on rural ICT development,* UUM Sintok, Malaysia. Retrieved from http:// www.moe.gov.my/userfiles/file/PPP/Preliminary-Blueprint-Eng.pdf

Chapter 3
Supporting Self-Directed Vocabulary Study: Towards Effective Design of OERs for Mobile Learning Environments

Ingrid Barth
Tel Aviv University, Israel

Bin Zou
https://orcid.org/0000-0002-4863-0998
Xi'an Jiaotong-Liverpool University, China

Elana Spector-Cohen
Tel Aviv University, Israel

Rosalie Sitman
Tel Aviv University, Israel

ABSTRACT

Although open educational resources (OERs) can help bridge high-school – university vocabulary gaps, optimal utilization of OERs requires effective self-directed learning. This bi-national two-year study adopted a design-based research paradigm to collect Chinese university students' (n = 358) perceptions regarding design factors that support self-directed vocabulary learning in mobile learning environments (MLEs). Results showed that additional scaffolding after Year One in the form of L1 translations of high-frequency academic words significantly correlated with improved performance on basic level vocabulary exercises and pop quizzes. However, results suggest that moving mobile learning into the mainstream will require (1) design features that provide additional scaffolding for more complex vocabulary learning, (2) clearer guidelines for students on integrating desktop and mobile devices and (3) ongoing guidance from teachers to develop students' capacity for self-directed learning to ensure optimal benefit from independent study of vocabulary OERs.

DOI: 10.4018/978-1-7998-1282-1.ch003

INTRODUCTION

This chapter describes a design-based research study to identify factors that facilitate the migration of vocabulary open educational resources (OERs) for self-directed learning (SDL) across different settings, from desktop learning environments in EU and partner countries to students in China who prefer to use mobile phones rather than desktops to study vocabulary. According to Brown and Campione (1996), understanding how and why an innovation works across diverse settings is essential for sustainable innovation. Thus, our first goal in this study was to understand how participants perceive the constraints that typically characterize mobile learning environments (MLEs). Our main assumption in this study was that desktop computers and mobile phones represent significantly different learning environments, each with their own affordances and constraints that need to be carefully considered when deciding which learning environment to select in order to achieve different objectives. This premise is based on Moore (1973), who over forty years ago observed that there are specific functions for which each medium is best suited, and that the unique strengths of different media need to be combined to attain different educational goals. Based on this assumption, our second goal was to identify what participating students perceive as effective instructional scaffolding that would enable them to overcome these constraints and go beyond bite-sized chunks that all too often characterize vocabulary learning in MLEs.

This bi-national study was based on *Roads to Academic Reading (Roads),* a set of vocabulary OERs that were developed as part of an EU-funded TEMPUS project to align tertiary level EAP courses in project partner countries with the Common European Framework of Reference for Languages (CEFR). The CEFR for teaching, learning and assessing foreign languages is currently being implemented in over 120 countries, from Chile to China, and effective wide-scale dissemination of this framework in additional geographical regions may ultimately depend on the availability of robust OERs that are appropriate for learners in Europe and beyond. The OERs used in this two-year study were originally designed for use in PC desktop-based learning environments, and at the end of Year One we incorporated additional design features based on students' perceptions of what types of scaffolding represent effective support of SDL for vocabulary learning in MLEs. This enabled us to achieve the third and final goal in this study, which was examining whether instructional scaffolding added at the end of Year One correlated positively with student outcomes among a new cohort of students who used the improved website in Year Two.

Before the study began, technical adjustments were completed to make the website 'responsive' (i.e., web pages detect the user's mobile phone screen size and orientation and change the layout accordingly) to accommodate Chinese students' preference for MLEs. This preference has been well-documented in Zou & Yan (2014) as well as in Zou, Li, & Li (2018). No changes were made to website content, and the length of texts as well as the level of difficulty of advanced level exercises remained significantly different from the small chunks that often characterize vocabulary learning on mobile devices. In addition, the vocabulary website provided 'vocabulary netto' without animations, gamification and competitive social elements such as leader-boards and tournaments typically found in vocabulary apps for mobile phones. Wang and Hannafin (2005) point out that advancing design, research and practice concurrently, instead of separately, facilitates improvement of design by enabling design features to emerge from research participants' input. As will be described below, this study created a unique opportunity to iterate through analysis, design, development and implementation, based on collaboration among researchers and participants in a real-world context to make these OERs as effective as possible for self-directed vocabulary study in MLEs.

ROLE OF SELF-DIRECTED VOCABULARY STUDY

Well-designed, high quality OERs that support independent study of English academic vocabulary outside the classroom can play a crucial role in widening equity of access and enabling students to identify and bridge their vocabulary gaps on their own. The role of research-based OERs becomes even more significant in view of the current wide consensus that vocabulary represents an essential building block or 'enabler' that supports the development of all four basic language skills (e.g. Nation,2001; Folse, 2006; Staer, 2008; Gorjian, et al., 2011; Wang, Zou, & Xing, 2014). This key role contrasts sharply to earlier views of second language vocabulary acquisition (SLVA) as a difficult-to-manage 'add-on' and the 'Cinderella' of language learning (Beheyd, 1987).

Recent wide recognition of vocabulary as an integral part of language learning has raised key questions regarding how many English words students need to know at tertiary level. According to Laufer and Ravenhorst-Kalovski (2010), 4000-5000 words represent a minimum threshold level that students need to reach in order to understand academic texts. However, this estimate was subsequently increased to 98% of lexical coverage recommended for academic texts (Schmitt, Jiang & Grabe, 2011; Schmitt & Schmitt, 2014).

Although reaching lexical coverage of 98% may seem daunting, research on high-frequency words has consistently shown that the BNC 1 – 2000 wordlists identified by Nation (2006) comprise between 75-80% of words in most academic texts, with high-frequency general academic words and low-frequency words combined with content-related, discipline-specific words making up the remaining 20-25%. However, in many countries, research findings on high-frequency words have been slow to impact teaching and learning of English as a Foreign Language (EFL) curricula in high schools, and students often enter university with significant gaps between the 'ideal' and their 'real' English entry levels. These gaps are often more prevalent in peripheral and geographically isolated regions which are frequently characterized by shortages of highly qualified English teachers and opportunities for SDL based on high quality OERs that enable students to identify and bridge academic vocabulary gaps on their own, before they enter university.

Even if focusing on high-frequency words can help to prioritize the vocabulary learning process, the 'zero-sum' nature of classroom teaching means there will probably never be enough classroom time for direct instruction of all the academic words tertiary level students in EAP or ESP courses need to know in order to reach 95% to 98% lexical coverage of their academic texts. Consequently, self-directed study of high-frequency vocabulary is essential to supplement what students learn in their EAP and ESP courses in order to reach proficiency levels that support understanding of academic texts published in English. According to Gui, (2006), EFL students in China see English vocabulary learning as the most important part of their linguistic competence. However, this recognition does not necessarily help students cope with the magnitude of this task, which Crystal (2009) has referred to as the 'Everest' of language learning.

Part of the challenges of self-directed study of vocabulary may be explained by the complex mix of capabilities, skills, and beliefs that represent essential components of SDL. The multiple components that SDL seems to demand can be clearly seen in Guglielmino's (1977) definition of a self-directed learner as one who exhibits

'...initiative, independence, and persistence in learning; one who accepts responsibility for his or her own learning and views problems as challenges, not obstacles; one who is capable of self-discipline and has a high degree of curiosity; one who has a strong desire to learn or change and is self-confident; one

who is able to use basic study skills, organize his or her time and set an appropriate pace for learning, and to develop a plan for completing work; one who enjoys learning and has a tendency to be goal-oriented (p. 73).

This mix becomes even more complex due to the context-specific nature of SDL: More recent studies, for example Du (2013), indicate that SDL performance appears to be closely linked to students' perception of self-efficacy, which Bandura (1994) defined as a context-specific belief that one can accomplish a given task. This context-specific view was reinforced by Nunan (1997), who emphasized that learner autonomy is not a permanent state, and may differ at different times, regarding different areas of learning. Although Dickinson (1987) distinguishes between autonomy and SDL, which he sees as only one step on the way to autonomy, the range of learner-related variables such as personality, cultural context and prior educational experience, which Nunan views as factors that affect learner autonomy among language learners, may similarly affect SDL of vocabulary. Consequently, one of the most important challenges facing designers of vocabulary OERs for SDL may be to identify which task-related factors help or hinder SDL performance in MLEs.

According to researchers such as Burston (2014), Kukulska-Hulme, (2016) and more recently, Lai and Zheng (2017), the majority of studies on mobile-assisted language learning until now have been conducted in lab and classroom trials or experiments of mobile applications in classroom contexts. Consequently, not enough empirical data are available regarding design factors that correlate with positive student outcomes among self-directed vocabulary learners in MLEs. To address this need, the next stage of our programmatic research will systematically explore additional design factors or combinations of factors that correlate with positive SDL outcomes

The shortage of data regarding identification of design features that represent best practices for SDL of vocabulary in MLEs is further compounded by additional challenges faced by designers of evidence-based vocabulary for OERs. These challenges are described in the next section of this chapter, followed by a description of the OERs used in this study.

CHALLENGES REGARDING EFFECTIVE DESIGN OF VOCABULARY OERS

Instructional designers who develop OERs to support self-directed study of general academic English vocabulary currently face a number of challenges:

Lack of a Clear and Coherent Set of Design Guidelines

Designers of vocabulary OERs need to draw on findings fragmented across different research areas that include second language vocabulary acquisition (SLVA) and SDL, as well as insights into the relative affordances and potential constraints to learning in different digital learning environments.

A number of frameworks that were originally developed for evaluating mobile assisted language learning (MALL) - e.g., Sweeney & Moore (2012), Reinders & Pegrum (2015), Rosell-Aguilar (2017)- could also be useful for vocabulary OER designers. These three frameworks specifically relate to the importance of implementing second language vocabulary acquisition (SLVA) research findings in designing language learning for MLEs. However, SLVA principles are not always clear-cut; neither are they easily translatable into design decisions. For example, the Sweeney and Moore framework (p. 13) clearly lists "maximum exposure to target language (i.e., minimal translation)" as a criterion for evaluating mobile apps for language learning. In contrast, Laufer (2005, p. 4) recommends "not to ban the L1 translations", as research shows that L1 glosses are beneficial for text comprehension and vocabulary learning.

This challenge may partly explain why, as Kukulska-Hume and Bull (2009) noted over almost a decade ago, "much of the relevant theory and empirical findings that relate to the large body of research on second language learning are often overlooked" by developers of language learning technology (p. 12). Similarly, Sweeney and Moore (2012) have observed that there is "potentially a chasm between those interested in the potential of mobile language learning, including developers with insufficient knowledge of pedagogy, and language teachers who know about pedagogy, but have little interest in mobile learning" (p. 14).

Going Beyond a 'One-Size-Fits-All' Approach

Designing resources for self-directed study of vocabulary for a specific target population usually requires first-hand knowledge of the diverse levels of prior knowledge, motivation, cognitive ability, as well as what Wang and Baker (2018) refer to as levels of 'grit and intention' that characterize the target population. However, vocabulary OERs are accessible to anyone, anywhere, and providing sets of exercises that increase in length of texts as well as in degree of complexity is essential to avoid a 'one-size-fits all' approach that fails to differentiate between levels of cognitive resources required to successfully complete the exercises. Although differentiation and providing differing levels of difficulty that address varied levels of ability represent one of the pedagogical criteria in Rosell-Aguilar's (2017) framework for evaluating language learning apps, many vocabulary OERs do not offer different levels of learning tasks that increase in degree of difficulty for different levels of ability.

Making Informed Decisions About Which Words to Focus on First

Although there is now widespread agreement that focusing on high frequency vocabulary will give learners the highest 'returns' on the time and effort they invest in learning new words (Nation, 2001), consensus has not yet been reached regarding which high-frequency wordlists best prepare students for their tertiary-level studies. Vocabulary OER designers currently have access to multiple research-based high-frequency wordlists to help them ascertain which words should be focused on first at tertiary level. Examples of these research-based wordlists include Nation's 1-2000 lists (2006) as well as general academic high-frequency wordlists such as Coxhead's (2000) Academic Word List (AWL) and Gardner and Davies' (2013) Academic Vocabulary List (AVL). In addition, English Profile (http://www.englishprofile.org/wordlists) currently provides free access to CEFR vocabulary information that indicates which words learners typically know at each of the six CEFR proficiency levels. Clearly, high-frequency wordlists are potentially valuable tools for helping teachers and students to prioritize the vocabulary learning process. However, dealing with multiple wordlists often represents yet another challenge for vocabulary OER designers.

High Incidence of Academic Terms and Concepts at CEFR C Proficiency Levels

Many general academic words, for example 'bias', on Coxhead's (2000) AWL as well as on Gardner and Davies' (2013) AVL represent key concepts that are essential building blocks which lay the foundation for academic literacy and equip students with concepts crucial for the development of critical thinking skills. Yet, according to the English Profile, many of these words appear only at the highest levels of proficiency on the CEFR (C1 and C2) - for example, 'assumption' (C1) and 'hypothesis' (C2). Moreover, in some countries, CEFR B2 is the target English proficiency exit level in tertiary education. This means that unless OER designers specifically include key academic concepts from beyond B2 level as target words, students in EAP and ESP CEFR-aligned courses with B2 exit levels might not learn key academic terms and concepts.

Against the background of the four challenges described above, the next section will describe how we addressed these challenges in the development of *Roads to Academic Reading (Roads)* and how these OERs differ from the majority of vocabulary OERs currently available.

Roads to Academic Reading

*Roads (*http://roads2reading.tau.ac.il*)* is a unique set of vocabulary OERs based on the four well-known research-based, high-frequency lists described above. These OERs were based on an earlier version of the website, created in 2010, which contained only Nation's (2006) BNC 1-2000 and Coxhead's (2000) AWL. Google Analytics showed that these OERs were being used in over 127 countries, which clearly indicated a need in many countries for research-based resources that support self-directed study of academic vocabulary.

THREE DIFFERENT ROADS OR 'ROUTES' TO HIGH-FREQUENCY WORDS

One of the central differences between *Roads* and other vocabulary websites is that these OERs help students and teachers collate and connect information across four well-known high-frequency wordlists. As mentioned above, there is now widespread agreement that focusing on high frequency vocabulary will give learners the highest 'returns' on the time and effort they invest in learning new words (Nation, 2001). However, identifying high-frequency words can be challenging even for native-English speakers. As Schmitt (2008) points out, "Even native-English speaking teachers cannot always rely on their intuitions to identify more frequent (and thereby generally more useful) words" (p. 333).

Roads provides three different 'routes' or 'roads' to identifying and teaching or learning words that frequently appear in academic texts: (1) text profiling, (2) wordlists with translations and (3) a search box with an auto-complete feature that allows users to enter individual words.

Road #1: Text Profiling

Students can upload any digital text and select one or more of the following wordlists: Nation's (2006) 1- 2000 BNC, Coxhead's (2000) AWL, Gardner and Davies' (2013) AVL, and wordlists for each of the six CEFR levels. The *Roads* text-profiler will then highlight words from the selected wordlists that appear in the user's uploaded text and offer possible translations in Chinese, Arabic, Hebrew or Spanish for high-frequency words. This reduces the need for dictionary lookups and provides the option to print out translation tables for students who may prefer to read printed versions of complex texts.

Providing students with user-friendly tools for text profiling their texts enables them to analyze their own vocabulary needs and decide on priorities most relevant to them. According to Thornton (2010), needs analysis constitutes an essential prerequisite for effective SDL. In addition, automatic highlighting of high-frequency words in the student's texts represents a form of instructional scaffolding based on two SLVA principles: Importance of providing context in vocabulary learning and Importance of noticing the target word.

With regard to the first principle, providing context, the students' own texts provide relevant context for target words. Because the meaning of words is often context-dependent, the key role of context has been well-documented in the SLVA literature (e.g. Sternberg, 1987; Nagy, 1995). Although context is key for showing students how the word is used, according to Heil, Wu, Lee and Schmidt (2016), the majority of the vocabulary apps they reviewed focused on vocabulary items as isolated units, i.e., as individual words without context.

The second principle is based on Schmidt's (1990) noticing hypothesis, which states that noticing is the essential starting point for acquisition of a language, and that learners cannot learn the grammatical features of a language unless they notice them. Highlighting high-frequency words in the student's text increases orientation towards and paying attention to the target word, and although noticing is just the first step, Schmidt (1995) has argued that "what learners notice in input is what becomes intake for learning" (p. 20). According to Kukulsa-Holme and Bull (2009), who reviewed more recent work on noticing, there is ongoing interest in approaches to encourage noticing in order to facilitate language acquisition in a range of contexts.

Road #2: Well-Known High-Frequency Wordlists With Translations

These wordlists are provided as tools that enable students to track their progress and get a sense of the size of the task ahead – not merely as long lists of decontextualized words to be memorized by students. These lists enable students to break their vocabulary learning into manageable chunks that facilitate realistic goal setting, which is widely recognized as an essential condition for SDL (see Thornton, 2010; and Lowry, 1989).

Words on these lists that appear on additional high-frequency wordlists are hyperlinked to flashcards, which cross-reference high-frequency words across 4 different wordlists to help students make data-based decisions on how to prioritize their vocabulary learning. The flashcards also provide supplementary information, such as pronunciation and additional words in the same 'word family' sorted according to part of speech, in order to help 'anchor' target words in memory.

Road #3: A Search Box With an Auto-Complete Feature

This allows students to enter any word to check if this is a high-frequency word and to see how many of the four research-based wordlists described above contain the specific target word.

DESCRIPTION OF RATIONALE BEHIND ROADS EXERCISES

In addition to providing three 'routes' to help users identify high-frequency words, *Roads* provides sets of between three to six exercises for each of the 300 target words that overlap and appear on both CEFR and AWL wordlists. These exercises implement two additional SLVA principles that Nation (2005) ranks among the 'ten best ideas' for teaching and learning vocabulary: (1) encouraging depth of mental processing when learning vocabulary and (2) providing multiple exposures and spaced repetition.

Encouraging Depth of Mental Processing

Nearly fifty years ago, Craik and Lockhart (1972) identified the levels-of-processing effect, which hypothesizes that memory recall is a function of the depth of mental processing, with deeper levels of analysis resulting in stronger memory traces than shallow levels of analysis.

This principle translated into the need to provide sets of exercises that gradually increase in amount and complexity of information that needs to be processed. Each set of exercises contains two to three basic level exercises.

Three Types of Basic Level Exercises:

- **Understanding Meaning**: These exercises establish the link between form and meaning by requiring students to identify three synonyms for target words.
- **Examples:** Require students to differentiate between examples and non-examples of target words.
- **Explanations:** The length of text to be processed increases and students are required to identify three correct explanations of target words.

Features of these basic level exercises include:

Teaching, Not Testing

According to Rosell-Aguilar (2017), many language learning apps provide exercises that test the user without first providing instruction. In contrast, *Roads* exercises focus on teaching, not on testing. Basic level multiple-choice exercises require learners to identify three correct answers out of four possible answer options, with each correct answer providing a different facet of the target word in order to build a rich, multi-faceted concept of that word.

Corrective Feedback

Roads exercises provide textual explanations of why a wrong answer is incorrect to help students understand and learn from their mistakes. Detailed feedback that goes beyond a check mark or a cross constitutes an evaluation criterion in Reinders and Pegrum (2015), as well as in Rosell-Aguilar (2017). Despite the importance of corrective feedback for self-directed study of vocabulary, Heil, Wu, Lee and Schmidt (2016) found that only 3 out of 50 vocabulary apps (6%) provided any explanation as to why specific wrong answers selected by users were incorrect.

Providing Multiple Exposures and Spaced Repetition

Roads provides spaced repetition by automatically generating pop quizzes or self-tests that enable users to check whether they can correctly retrieve the last five words for which they completed exercises.

As Baddeley (1990) suggested nearly three decades ago, repeated opportunities to retrieve the target word in different contexts are essential for vocabulary learning, and multiple exposures represent an essential condition for effective acquisition. *Roads* enables students to recycle newly-acquired words by providing sets of between three to five exercises on each of 300 target words, to ensure multiple exposures.

All sets of exercises on the *Roads* website are designed to take students through a learning process that builds up the meaning of the target word, layer by layer, starting from the first basic level exercise, '*Understanding Meaning*', which asks students to identify which answer does not mean the same as the target word. As mentioned above, the second basic level exercise, '*Examples*', asks students to identify which answer is not an example of the target word, while the third basic level exercise, *Explanations*, requires students to select three answers that explain a specific aspect of the target word. All three basic level exercises require students to identify three correct answers out of four possible options in order to build rich, multi-faceted representations of the target word and 'anchor' the word in the student's memory.

Advanced Level Exercises

'Language in Use' and *'Towards Academic Reading'* represent advanced level exercises that include much longer texts (between 200 – 250 words). These exercises contain 'teaching points' – (explanations that experienced language teachers would usually give during a lesson) and provide a 'tutor in the text' to support self-directed study of academic vocabulary.

As explained previously, many high-frequency academic words, such as 'assumption' and 'evidence', represent powerful concepts which act as lenses for helping students to see when and how writers are trying to impose their opinions on the reader. For these target words, *Roads* includes learning objects or "mini-lessons" with teaching points related to academic literacy or metacognitive questions that effective readers ask themselves in order to implement critical and creative thinking skills. Considerably more reading and in-depth processing of information are required for these exercises compared with the short multiple-choice questions that characterize vocabulary 'drill-and-practice' sites. Inclusion of exercises that focus on developing 21st century skills such as critical thinking represents an important objective for language learners, as reflected in the criterion '21C skills: Critical learning' in Reinders and Pegrum's (2015) evaluation criteria framework (see http://roads2reading.tau.ac.il/Resources for a list of exercises that focuses on critical thinking and academic literacy).

In summary, the central issue we attempted to resolve in this study was how to provide effective scaffolding that would support self-directed study by enabling students to go beyond small chunks and cope successfully with complex vocabulary learning tasks. Because our primary goal was to identify practical solutions in a real-life setting, we chose a design-based paradigm that would enable us to iterate through two cycles of analysis, design, development, implementation and evaluation in order to answer two main questions that characterize design-based research studies:

- What must be done to make this innovation effective?
- What design principles can we learn from the process of making it work that can inform the work of others?

Specifically, we examined:

RQ 1: To what extent do students who are 'digital natives' (Prensky, 2001) regard the characteristic constraints of mobile learning environments (e.g., small screen and constant scrolling) as barriers to independent vocabulary learning?
RQ2: What do students perceive as effective scaffolding that can help them go overcome the typical constraints of MLEs and go beyond 'small chunks' of content usually associated with MLEs?
RQ3: To what extent does additional scaffolding in the form of mouseover translations correlate with improved student outcomes on vocabulary exercises?

CONTEXT AND OVERVIEW OF THE STUDY

This study examined self-directed study of academic vocabulary among EAP students at two Chinese universities, i.e. students who used *Roads* to study outside the classroom to supplement vocabulary they learn in class. According to Stockwell (2013), although mobile device use in the classroom has been well documented, much less research has examined how students engage in mobile learning outside the classroom, which represents a very different setting. In order to design OERs for this setting, we adopted a design-based research paradigm that enabled us to examine students' perceptions of constraints that typically characterize MLEs, and what they view as effective scaffolding to help them overcome these constraints. Based on participants' perceptions, additional instructional scaffolding was added to *Roads* between Year One and Year Two. The impact of added scaffolding was examined at the end of Year Two by comparing student outcomes in Year One and Year Two.

It is important to emphasize at the outset that this study was aimed at designing a practical solution to guide possible revisions in an ongoing design (Reeves & Hedberg, 2003; Reeves & McKenny, 2012), and not a media comparison study of the relative effectiveness of PC-based vs. mobile learning environments (MLEs) under controlled conditions. As many researchers have observed, these types of studies produce what Russell (1999) calls the 'no significant effect' phenomenon. In addition, media comparison studies fail to address more productive questions about how to help students leverage the strengths and overcome the constraints of different digital learning environments.

METHODS

Year One

Participants

In Year One, six classes of participants were recruited from EAP courses in two universities (one private and one public located on the east coast of China) in the fall semester of the 2017-2018 academic year (n = 222). Participation in the study was voluntary and students could choose whether or not to register and log in or remain anonymous. CEFR proficiency levels ranged from CEFR A2 to B1, and most participants (88%) were between 17-20 years of age. Ages of other participants ranged between 20 to 36.

Measures

Three measures were used to collect data: (1) an online pre-intervention survey, which examined background and demographic variables as well as students' perceptions of themselves as persistent, self-disciplined vocabulary learners capable of successful SDL; (2) online post-intervention surveys (Survey Monkey©) and (3) data reports reflecting student performance that were automatically generated on the *Roads* website.

Online Pre-Intervention Survey

The pre-intervention survey collected demographic data (age and English proficiency level) and background information (device used most often for vocabulary learning -- computer, tablet or mobile phone). In addition, the pre-intervention survey examined two student-related variables that could affect students' independent study of vocabulary in a mobile learning environment: a) level of comfort with learning vocabulary in digital learning environments - e.g. "*I can quickly learn how to use technology-based tools to improve my English academic vocabulary* (three items, using a 5-point Likert scale, ranging from 1 'don't agree at all' to 5 'agree completely')

b) students' perceptions of themselves as persistent, self-disciplined learners, capable of successful independent study of English academic vocabulary. Three items used a 5-point Likert scale from 1 'don't agree at all' to 5 'agree completely' to examine: *If I invest enough time and effort, my vocabulary will improve; I can motivate myself to improve my vocabulary, without a teacher and a classroom*; and *I have enough self-discipline to learn vocabulary on my own.*

Examination of students' self-reported self-efficacy was based on Thornton (2010), who emphasizes that students may hold beliefs about (1) language learning and (2) roles of the student and teacher that can contribute towards psychological resistance to autonomous learning.

Online Post-Intervention Survey

The survey included three sections: The first section examined participants' perceptions regarding constraints that typically characterize mobile learning environments which may pose barriers to their vocabulary learning (e.g., *I can study from my mobile device only when I am in a quiet place*). Six items were included in this section (see Appendix 1). Participants were requested to respond on a 5-point Likert scale, ranging from 1 'strongly disagree' to 5 'agree'. The second section of the post-intervention survey collected student feedback on the *Roads* website (e.g., *The vocabulary website in this project helped me learn words I did not know.*). This section included 3 items on a 5-point Likert scale, ranging from 1 'strongly disagree' to 5 'agree'.

The third and last section examined participants' perceptions regarding types of scaffolding that facilitate vocabulary learning in mobile learning environments (e.g., "*A games element that gives you points and badges and lets you play against yourself*"). Six items were included in this section (see Appendix 1), with responses on a 5-point Likert scale, ranging from 1 'will not help at all' to 5 'extremely helpful – must have'.

The survey also included three open-ended questions: "*If you don't intend to use the site again, which 2 things should change before you use this website again? What do you think is the biggest disadvantage of learning on your mobile phone? Which two additional features would help you to learn vocabulary from your mobile device?*"

Due to privacy constraints, pre- and post-intervention surveys were completed anonymously, which meant that we were not able to collate individual students' responses before and after interventions.

Data Reports Automatically Generated on the Roads Website

Three automatically generated reports on participants' performance were collected: 1) number and type of exercises attempted on the website, 2) number and type of exercises successfully completed, and 3) number of automatically-generated 'pop quizzes' successfully completed. Only data for logged-in users were analyzed.

Procedure

At the beginning of the semester, the teachers at the two participating universities introduced the vocabulary website to students registered for six EAP classes and encouraged them to use the website for SDL during the semester. Participants could choose whether or not to register and log in when they used the website and were told that the website would automatically track their performance on exercises and pop quizzes. Following Stockwell (2010), participants could use any combination of their PCs and MDs to complete the exercises. Students could consult online dictionaries at any time while they used the website. At the end of the semester, students were asked to complete the anonymous post-intervention online survey.

Between Year One and Year Two, survey data were analyzed and input from participants was used to add instructional scaffolding to the website in the form of Chinese mouseover translations for high-frequency words.

Year Two

Participants

In the second year of the study, a new cohort (n = 136) of students registered in eight EAP classes was recruited from the same universities to participate in the follow-up study which began in the Spring semester of the 2017-2018 academic year. Participants' English proficiency levels were similar to those of the cohort who participated in Year One and ranged from CEFR levels A2 to B1. Most participants (81%) were between 17-20 years of age. The remaining participants' ages ranged from 20 to 33.

Measures

In Year Two we repeated the same three measures as those used in Year One: (1) an online pre-intervention survey, which examined background and demographic variables as well as students' perceptions of themselves as persistent, self-disciplined learners capable of successful SDL, (2) online post-intervention surveys (Survey Monkey©) and (3) data reports reflecting student performance that were automatically generated on the *Roads* website.

Procedure

The procedure in Year Two as identical to procedure in Year One, with one difference: Participants in Year Two had access to mouseover Chinese translations of high-frequency words while using the flashcards or working on the exercises, which we hypothesized would reduce cognitive load and interruptions to reading caused by dictionary lookups.

RESULTS

A total of 350 students completed the pre-intervention surveys: 219 in Year 1 and 131 in Year 2, and no significant differences were found between the first and second cohorts with regard to perceptions of themselves as independent learners of vocabulary in MLEs.

RQ 1: To what extent do students who are 'digital natives' regard the characteristic constraints of mobile learning environments (e.g., small screen and constant scrolling) as barriers to independent vocabulary learning?

This question investigated students' perceptions regarding constraints that typically characterize mobile learning environments as potential barriers to self-directed vocabulary acquisition. A total of 125 students answered these questions in the post-intervention survey - 72 students in Year One and 53 in Year Two. Figure 1 shows the means relating to students' perceptions of constraints that typically characterize mobile learning environments.

ANOVA with repeated measures showed significant differences in the perception of barriers ($F_{(5,355)} = 9.88$, $p<.001$). As shown in Figure 1, the barriers rated the highest by students were distraction and the need for quiet places for study. A slow network connection was perceived as significantly less of a potential barrier compared to the other constraints, and scrolling was perceived as significantly less of a potential constraint than distractions from emails, etc.

In order to check for differences between the first- and second-year cohorts regarding the students' perceptions of constraints that typically characterize mobile learning environments, six t-tests for independent samples were calculated. Table 1 shows the means, standard deviations and the differences between first and second cohorts regarding constraints that typically characterize mobile learning environments. As can be seen from Table 1, no significant differences were found between the two groups.

RQ2: What do students perceive as effective scaffolding that can help them overcome the typical constraints of MLEs and go beyond 'small chunks' of content usually associated with MLEs?

Participants were asked to rate to what extent seven specific features would help them learn vocabulary on their mobile devices (see Appendix 1). ANOVA with repeated measures showed significant differences in the forms of scaffoldings perceived as effective ($F (6,372) = 2.30$, $p<.05$). As seen in Figure 2, using post-hoc analysis, it was found that the highest scaffolding is personalization and this was rated significantly higher than translations, read-alouds, motivational emails and gamification with competitive elements. A total of 113 students answered questions related to scaffolding.

Figure 1. Means of students' perceptions regarding constraints that typically characterize mobile learning environments

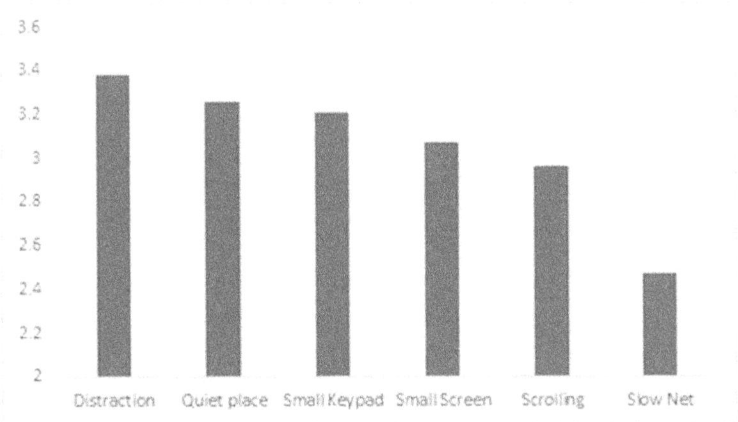

To check for differences between the first- and second-year cohorts regarding the forms of scaffolding perceived as effective, 7 t-tests for independent samples were calculated. Table 2 shows the means, standard deviations and the differences between the two cohorts. No significant differences were found between cohorts regarding their perceptions of scaffolding.

Table 1. Means and standard deviations for first and second cohorts regarding perceptions of constraints that typically characterize mobile learning environments

	First year Condition 1 (n=72)		Second year Condition 2 (n=53)		T
	Mean	St.d.	Mean	St.d.	(df=123)
Small screen	3.07	1.14	3.30	0.97	1.20
Small keypad slows input	3.21	1.16	3.00	1.04	1.04
Slow connectivity	2.47	1.26	2.55	1.15	3.41
Constant scrolling	2.96	1.17	2.83	1.09	0.62
Quiet place required	3.26	1.18	3.11	1.03	0.75
Distractions from emails, etc.	3.38	1.08	3.26	0.88	0.61

Figure 2. Perceptions of scaffolding in the post intervention survey

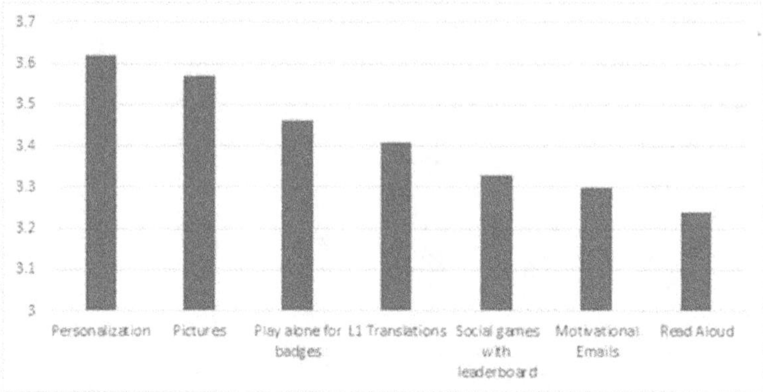

RQ 3: To what extent does additional scaffolding in the form of L1 mouseover translations correlate with improved outcomes on the vocabulary exercises?

We examined the extent to which the addition of L1 translations as instructional scaffolding correlated with improved student outcomes by comparing student outcomes in Year One (no access to mouseover L1 translations) with student outcomes in Year Two, after the addition of L1 translations.

Table 2. Means and standard deviations for first and second cohorts regarding perceptions of scaffolding

	First year Condition 1 (n=63)		Second year Condition 2 (n=50)		T
	Mean	St.d.	Mean	St.d.	(df=111)
Translation	3.41	0.82	3.40	0.81	0.08
Read aloud	3.24	0.84	3.14	0.88	0.61
Personalization	3.62	0.71	3.54	0.84	0.54
Emails	3.30	0.91	3.04	0.97	1.48
Pictures	3.57	0.88	3.56	0.93	0.07
Play alone with badges	3.46	0.84	3.28	0.86	1.10
Social game with leaderboard	3.33	0.86	3.28	0.97	0.31

Number of Exercises Successfully Completed Before and After Translations

In order to compare successful exercise completion rates before and after the addition of mouseover L1 translations, Chi square tests for independent samples were calculated across five types of vocabulary tasks increasing in complexity, as well as for automatically generated Pop Quizzes. As can be seen in Table 3, participants' performance improved significantly on three types of basic level exercise types: *Understanding Meaning*, *Examples,* and *Explanations,* after the addition of scaffolding in the form of mouseover L1 translations. Significant improvements were also found on the automatically generated Pop Quizzes. However, no significant improvements were found for the two advanced level exercise types - *Language in Use* and *Towards Academic Reading*. This progression in level of difficulty from basic to advanced level can be seen in the decreasing rates of successfully completed words between basic and advanced levels, as seen in Table 3 below.

DISCUSSION AND CONCLUSION

The central goal of this design-based research study was to identify, implement and evaluate design features that can help students who study vocabulary on their own to overcome the constraints of MLEs and go beyond the small chunks that typically characterize vocabulary learning in MLEs.

RQ1 explored the extent to which students who are 'digital natives' (Prensky, 2001) regard the characteristic constraints of mobile learning environments as barriers to independent vocabulary learning. Results showed that over 80% of students in both cohorts were aged between 17 – 20 years, which places them within the age-group of Prensky's digital natives, and over 70% of students reported that

Table 3. Percentage of correct exercises before and after adding translations and significant differences

Exercise Type	% of correct exercises BEFORE translations (First year)	% of correct exercises AFTER translations (Second year)	Chi (df=1)
Understanding Meaninç	61.6%	76.8%	24.37**
Examples	56.3%	63%	9.35*
Explanations	59.6%	71.5%	11.43**
Language in Use	54.7%	52.8%	N.S.
Towards Academic Reading	45.2%	50.7%	N.S.
Pop Quizzes (last 5 words studied)	7.1%	23.6%	35.64**

*p<.05, ***p<.001

they use mobile phones for vocabulary learning. Despite high levels of comfort with mobile phones, our post-intervention survey showed that students ranked four out of six MLE-related constraints above neutral. Distractibility (the temptation to switch to phone calls, emails, games and other distractions) was rated highest (3.38). This finding clearly reflects what Rosell-Aguilar (2017) refers to as the need for education apps to 'fight for users' attention, battling strong competition from other apps within the device, such as games, and from pop-up notifications from social media, messaging, or email" (p. 246).

The constraint which was rated second highest was the need for a quiet place when studying vocabulary. This seems to be somewhat at odds with one of the most-frequently cited strengths of learning with mobile learning environments; i.e., that mobile phones enable students to utilize small fragments of what would otherwise be 'down time.' As Sharples, Taylor and Vavoula (2007) have observed, one of the central characteristics of mobile learning is that it takes place while learners are 'on the move,' outside their classrooms, offices or homes (for example, commuting or standing in queues). However, these fragments of time often occur in noisy places, in contrast to the quiet required for vocabulary learning tasks that are more complex than the 'drill and practice' type questions that often characterize freely available vocabulary apps.

These findings reinforce Lai and Zheng's (2018) conclusions, according to which participants' perceived association of mobile phones with leisure and laptops with learning was directly related to the different levels of concentration that these two types of device afford. Their study also found that reduced concentration levels were further compounded by the noisiness of locations outside the home in which students typically use their mobile phones for studying vocabulary.

RQ2 investigated participants' perceptions of effective scaffolding that could help them go beyond 'small chunks' of content usually associated with mobile learning environments (MLEs). In both cohorts, students rated personalization highest – in other words, they perceived the capability to customize the website by adding their own words as the most effective type of support for improving independent study of vocabulary, followed next by the addition of translations and pictures. This is consistent with Steel (2012), who found the ability to personalize learning as one of the features that students liked best about using apps to support their learning. This focus on personalization is clearly reflected in Sweeney and Moore's (2012) evaluative framework, which defines "ability for a learner to personalize a list of items by choosing which items to practice, adding their own image or translation" (p. 8) as a key criterion for evaluating language learning apps. Similar perceptions regarding the importance of personalization were also established more recently by Lai and Zheng (2018). However, due to security concerns, the addition of personalization was not possible at this stage of the project.

Students in both cohorts reported very similar perceptions regarding the effectiveness of support features. Somewhat surprisingly, the two features that were rated least effective for improving self-study of vocabulary were those based on a social element: i.e., gamification with a leaderboard that lets students play against other students in their class, and motivational emails to remind students to learn vocabulary. The low ratings obtained for motivational emails raises the question of how EAP teachers can effectively incentivize students to engage in more independent learning of vocabulary. Although EAP teachers have attempted to integrate self-directed study into their courses, for example by setting specific vocabulary goals each week and providing students with a list of target words that may appear in high stakes evaluations, the effectiveness of these approaches has not been systematically examined. Consequently, the question of optimal ways in which teachers can effectively encourage and support OER-based self-directed study of vocabulary remains unanswered and reinforces Darasawang and Reinders'

(2010) observation that there is a need for extensive preparation, ongoing guidance, and follow-up support to ensure learners are able to derive optimal benefit from OERs.

As mentioned previously, the issues of 'transportability' of CEFR-aligned vocabulary OERs and effective ways of 'glocalizing' resources are becoming increasingly significant in view of the growing numbers of countries that have adopted the CEFR for teaching, learning and assessing foreign languages. Results showed that student perceptions regarding the effectiveness of the entire website to support learning of new words were reasonably positive, even though the site has no gamification elements or social elements. Only 13 out of 164 respondents reported that they would not use the site again, which suggests that *Roads* is sufficiently robust to meet the needs of populations that do not use Western alphabets, in regions beyond Europe and EU partner countries.

Finally, RQ3 examined whether additional scaffolding in the form of mouseover translations of other high-frequency academic words used in the exercises correlated with improved outcomes on these exercises. Mouseover translations were added to *Roads* after Year One, on the assumption that they provide effective instructional support by reducing cognitive load and interruptions due to dictionary lookups. The importance of 'perceived ease of use' was recognized by Davis (1989) in his Technology Acceptance Model (TAM), which refers to perceived ease-of-use (PEOU) as "the degree to which a person believes that using a particular system would be free from effort" (p. 320). As mentioned previously, Bandura (1986) emphasized that self-efficacy is context-specific, and L1 translations may increase students' perceptions that L1 translations of high-frequency words will help them cope more successfully with the exercises.

Although the role of learners' L1 has been somewhat controversial in EFL, with many advocating for maximum exposure only to L2, Laufer (2005), for example, has recommended against 'banning' the L1 translation of words and observes that reliable L1 glosses can be beneficial for text comprehension and word learning. While a summary of the advantages and disadvantages of the use of L1 translations is beyond the scope of this chapter, it is important to note that this issue, accurately described by Gabrielatos (2001) as a 'bone of contention', warrants broader consideration. One of the main contributions of study is that our results appear to reinforce a more constructive approach to the use of L1 in the EFL classroom, again, in line with Gabrielatos, who recommends focusing on more productive questions regarding L1 use, such as "what for", "when" and "to what extent" (p. 8).

To sum up, our results showed significant increases in successful completion for all three of the basic level exercises (*Understanding Meaning, Examples* and *Explanations)* after the addition of L1 Chinese translations. Moreover, and perhaps more importantly, students' performances on 'pop quizzes' (automatically generated self-tests that provide spaced repetition and test students' recall of the previous five target words for which they completed exercises) increased dramatically, from 7.1% to 23.6%. Taken together, significant improvements in basic level exercises and pop quizzes suggest that mouseover translations may represent a critical success factor that correlates with improved student outcomes in mobile learning environments.

However, for complex vocabulary learning tasks that required students to read much larger amounts of texts and process content that demanded more cognitive resources, the addition of instructional support in the form of L1 mouseover translations did not correlate with significantly improved outcomes. Clearly, instructional support does not operate in a vacuum, and it is important to bear in mind that participants' levels of English proficiency ranged from CEFR A2 to B1, which means that L1 translations may not have been sufficient scaffolding for them to cope successfully with advanced-level exercises. Consequently, future research should examine to what extent L1 mouseover translations correlate with the successful completion of advanced-level exercises among CEFR B2 students.

With regard to the lack of significant gains on advanced-level exercises, this raises an important question regarding what Goodhue and Thompson (1995) referred to as task-technology fit. Complex vocabulary learning tasks that go beyond 'small chunks' of content may be less suited to mobile learning environments that are typically characterized by the need for constant scrolling and distractibility, which could possibly raise questions regarding the future implementation of mobile devices in mainstream learning.

Clearly, moving mobile learning into the mainstream will require going beyond the 'bite-sized chunks' or vocabulary items as individual words, i.e. isolated units, without context, which characterized the majority of apps (42 of 50, 84%) reviewed by Heil, Wu, Lee and Schmidt (2016). Consequently, widespread adoption of mobile learning for vocabulary learning may ultimately depend on new and innovative solutions that instructional designers provide for effectively scaffolding successful performance of more complex vocabulary tasks in mobile learning environments. Until then, however, EAP students who learn vocabulary independently may require additional guidance from their teachers regarding technology-task fit, as we discuss below.

CONTRIBUTION

This bi-national study was unique in the opportunity it offered to test the robustness of OERs across different geographical regions as well as to obtain participants' input regarding prioritization of design features to support vocabulary learning in MLEs. In addition, the two-year time period enabled us to iterate through a cycle of analysis, design, development, implementation and evaluation. This study enabled us to begin 'mapping' different types of vocabulary learning tasks in order to identify the characteristics of tasks that may be better suited to desktop rather than mobile environments. Understanding which types of learning task correlate with positive student outcomes in different digital learning environments represents an integrative approach that will enable students to combine the relative strengths of different digital learning environments, instead of adopting an 'either-or' approach. This integrative approach was perhaps best summed up by Burston (2014), who concluded that the extent to which mobile assisted language learning will enter the mainstream of foreign language instruction will very much depend upon the degree to which "the hitherto narrow focus upon stand-alone MALL needs to give way to a seamless approach in which mobile devices and computers are used together to do what each does best in the fulfillment of task-based activities" (p. 116).

LIMITATIONS

Due to privacy considerations, use of the website did not require participants to register and login before using the site. This prevented identification of who used which digital learning environments for which tasks. Privacy considerations and constraints also applied to post-intervention surveys, which were also completed anonymously and therefore could not be collated with individual performance outcomes. In addition, very low response rates to open questions on the surveys did not allow for themes to emerge from content analysis of answers. Therefore, future surveys should be conducted in L1 to increase response rates.

FUTURE DIRECTIONS

Designing MLE-based vocabulary learning for inclusion into the mainstream in higher education institutions will require a more comprehensive understanding of how the complex weave of student-related, teacher-related and task-related variables can interact and how these interactions can change across different digital learning environments. In addition, instructional designers need to consider the multi-dimensional aspects of the cognitive-emotional-motivational matrix in which SDL takes place.

Specific directions for further research include the following:

1. Integration of OERs into classroom practice – investigating how tertiary level teachers can integrate OERs into their classroom practice to encourage and support students' self-directed vocabulary learning.

According to Thornton (2010), helping students develop the essential skills required for successful SDL represents a key aspect of the language teacher's role, and she provides a four-phase framework of concrete guidelines that outline how language teachers can help students overcome the challenges of SDL.

2. Integration with additional apps – exploring optimal ways of 'app-smashing' or combining vocabulary OERs with apps that focus on productive language skills e.g., speaking and writing via peer learning and collaboration. Combining productive as well as receptive skills and social interactions with peers in MLEs has the added value of contributing towards alleviating attrition. As Nielson (2011) observes, high attrition levels often characterize SDL language contexts, due to the difficulties of maintaining motivation levels when studying without a teacher or peers.

OERs for acquisition of English academic vocabulary can play a crucial role in helping tertiary level students in all geographical regions to bridge their vocabulary gaps. However, for OERs to fulfill this role, further research is required in order to identify critical success factors that go beyond access and focus on facilitating maximum benefits from self-directed vocabulary study.

ACKNOWLEDGMENT

This study was funded by the Israeli Ministry of Science, Technology and Space (Grant number 3-13682) and was based on a previous EU TEMPUS project (ECOSTAR: English as the Cornerstone of Sustainable Technology and Research, Project No. 543683-TEMPUS-1 2013-1-IL-TEMPUS-JPCR (2013-2017).

We would like to thank our Chinese colleagues Guhuai Jiang, Fang Liu, Yan Xu and their students, who helped to make this study possible.

REFERENCES

Baddeley, A. (1990). *Human memory*. London, UK: Lawrence Erlbaum Associates.

Bandura, A. (1986). *Social foundations of thought and action*. Englewood Cliffs, NJ: Prentice-Hall.

Bandura, A. (1994). Self-efficacy. In V. S. Ramachaudran (Ed.), *Encyclopedia of human behavior* (Vol. 4, pp. 71–81).

Beheydt, L. (1987). The semantization of vocabulary in foreign language learning. *System, 15*(1), 55–67. doi:10.1016/0346-251X(87)90048-0

Brown, A., & Campione, J. (1996). Psychological theory and the design of innovative learning environments: On procedures, principles, and systems. In L. Schauble, & R. Glaser (Eds.), *Innovations in learning: New environments for education* (pp. 289–325). Mahwah, NJ: Lawrence Erlbaum Associates.

Burston, J. (2014). The reality of MALL: Still on the fringes. *CALICO Journal, 31*(1), 103–125. doi:10.11139/cj.31.1.103-125

Coxhead, A. (2000). A new academic word list. *TESOL Quarterly, 34*(2), 213–238. doi:10.2307/3587951

Craik, F. I. M., & Lockhart, R. S. (1972). Levels of processing: A framework for memory research. *Journal of Verbal Learning and Verbal Behavior, 11*(6), 671–684. doi:10.1016/S0022-5371(72)80001-X

Crystal, D. (2009). *Just a phrase I'm going through.* London, UK: Routledge. doi:10.4324/9780203878491

Darasawang, P., & Reinders, H. (2010). Encouraging autonomy with an online language support system. *CALL-EJ Online, 11*(2). Retrieved from http://callej.org/journal/11-2/darasawang_reinders.html

Davis, F. D. (1989). Perceived usefulness, perceived ease of use, and user acceptance of information technology. *MIS Quarterly, 13*(3), 319–340. doi:, JSTOR 249008. doi:10.2307/249008

Dickinson, L. (1987). *Self-instruction in language learning.* Cambridge, UK: Cambridge University Press.

Du, F. (2013). Student perspectives of self-directed language learning: implications for teaching and research. International Journal for the Scholarship of Teaching and Learning, 7(2). *Article, 24,* 1–16. doi:10.20429/ijsotl.2013.070224

English Profile. Retrieved from (http://www.englishprofile.org/wordlists)

Folse, K. S. (2006). The effect of type of written exercise on l2 vocabulary retention. *TESOL Quarterly, 40*(2), 273–293. doi:10.2307/40264523

Gabrielatos, C. (2001). L1 use in ELT: Not a skeleton but a bone of contention. A response to Prodromou. *TESOL Greece Newsletter, 70,* 6–9.

Gardner, D., & Davies, M. (2014). A new academic vocabulary List. *Applied Linguistics, 35*(3), 305–327. doi:10.1093/applin/amt015

Goodhue, D. L., & Thompson, R. L. (1995). Task technology fit and educational purpose. *Management Information Systems Quarterly, 19*(2), 213–231. doi:10.2307/249689

Gorjian, B., Moosavinia, S. R., Kavari, K. E., Asgari, P., & Hydarei, A. (2011). The impact of asynchronous computer-assisted language learning approaches on English as a foreign language high and low achievers' vocabulary retention and recall. *Computer Assisted Language Learning, 24*(5), 383–391. do i:10.1080/09588221.2011.552186

Guglielmino, L. M. (1978). Development of the self-directed learning readiness scale. (Doctoral dissertation, University of Georgia, 1977). *Dissertation Abstracts International*, *38*, 6467A.

Gui, S. (2006). A holistic view of English vocabulary learning in China. *Foreign Language World* (1), 57-65.

Heil, C. R., Wu, J. S., Lee, J. J., & Schmidt, T. (2016). A review of mobile language learning applications: Trends, challenges and opportunities. *The EUROCALL Review*, *24*(2), 32–50. doi:10.4995/eurocall.2016.6402

Kukulska-Hulme, A. (2016). Mobile assistance in language learning: A critical appraisal. In A. Palalas, & M. Ally (Eds.), *The international handbook of mobile-assisted language learning* (pp. 138–160). Beijing, China: China Central Radio & TV University Press.

Kukulska-Hulme, A., & Bull, S. (2009). Theory-based support for mobile language learning: Noticing and recording. *International Journal of Interactive Mobile Technologies*, *3*(2), 12–18.

Lai, C., & Zheng, D. (2018). Self-directed use of mobile devices for language learning beyond the classroom. *ReCALL*, *30*(3), 299–318. doi:10.1017/S0958344017000258

Laufer, B. (2005). Ten best ideas for teaching vocabulary. *The Language Teacher. Special Issue: Vocabulary*, *29*(7), 3–4.

Laufer, B., & Ravenhorst-Kalovski, G. C. (2010). Lexical threshold revisited: Lexical text coverage, learner's vocabulary size and reading comprehension. *Reading in a Foreign Language*, *22*(1), 15–30.

Lowry, C. M. (1989). Supporting and facilitating self-directed learning. (ERIC Digest No. 93). Retrieved from ERIC database. (ED312457)

Moore, M. G. (1973). Toward a theory of independent learning and teaching. *The Journal of Higher Education*, *44*(9), 661–679. doi:10.2307/1980599

Nagy, W. E. (1995). The role of context in first- and second-language vocabulary learning. *Technical Report No. 627*, Center for the Study of Reading, Urbana, IL.

Nation, I. S. P. (2001). *Learning vocabulary in another language*. Cambridge, UK: Cambridge University Press. doi:10.1017/CBO9781139524759

Nation, I. S. P. (2005). Ten best ideas for teaching vocabulary. The Japan Association for Language Teaching, 29(7), 5-6.

Nation, I. S. P. (2006). How large a vocabulary is needed for reading and listening? *Canadian Modern Language Review*, *63*(1), 59–82. doi:10.3138/cmlr.63.1.59

Nielson, K. B. (2011). Self-study with language learning software in the workplace: What happens? *Language Learning & Technology*, *15*(3), 110–129.

Nunan, D. (1997). Designing and adapting materials to encourage learner autonomy. In P. Benson, & P. Voller (Eds.), *Autonomy and independence in language learning* (pp. 192–203). Harlow, UK: Longman.

Prensky, M. (2001). Digital natives, digital immigrants Part 1. *On the Horizon*, *9*(5), 1–6. doi:10.1108/10748120110424816

Reeves, T. C., & Hedberg, J. G. (2003). *Interactive learning systems evaluation*. Englewood Cliffs, NJ: Educational Technology Publications.

Reeves, T. C., & McKenney, S. (2012). 7 things you should know about educational design research. Web publication/site, EDUCAUSE. Retrieved from http://www.educause.edu/library/resources/7-things-you-should-know-about-educational-design-research

Reinders, H., & Pegrum, M. (2015). Supporting language learning on the move. An evaluative framework for mobile language learning resources. In B. Tomlinson (Ed.), *Second language acquisition research and materials development for language learning* (pp. 116–141). London, UK: Taylor & Francis.

Rosell-Aguilar, F. (2017). State of the app: A taxonomy and framework for evaluating language learning mobile applications. *CALICO Journal*, *34*(2), 243–258.

Russell, T. L. (1999). *The no significant difference phenomenon*. Raleigh, NC: North Carolina State University.

Schmidt, R. (1990). The role of consciousness in second language learning. *Applied Linguistics*, *11*(2), 129–158. doi:10.1093/applin/11.2.129

Schmidt, R. (1995). Consciousness and foreign language learning: A tutorial on the role of attention and awareness in learning. In R. Schmidt (Ed.), Attention and awareness in foreign language learning (Tech. Rep. No. 9, pp. 1–63). University of Hawaii at Manoa: Second Language Teaching and Curriculum Center.

Schmitt, N. (2008). Instructed second language vocabulary learning. *Language Teaching Research*, *12*(3), 329–363. doi:10.1177/1362168808089921

Schmitt, N., Jiang, X., & Grabe, W. (2011). The percentage of words known in a text and reading comprehension. *Modern Language Journal*, *95*(i), 26–43. doi:10.1111/j.1540-4781.2011.01146.x

Schmitt, N., & Schmitt, D. (2014). A reassessment of frequency and vocabulary size in L2 vocabulary teaching. *Language Teaching*, *47*(4), 484–503. doi:10.1017/S0261444812000018

Sharples, M., Taylor, J., & Vavoula, G. (2007). A theory of learning for the mobile age. In R. Andrews, & C. Haythornthwaite (Eds.), *The Sage handbook of e-learning research* (pp. 221–247). London, UK: Sage. doi:10.4135/9781848607859.n10

Staer, L. S. (2008). Vocabulary size and the skills of listening, reading and writing. *Language Learning Journal*, *36*(2), 139–152. doi:10.1080/09571730802389975

Steel, C. (2012). Fitting learning into life: Language students' perspectives on benefits of using mobile apps. In M. Brown, M. Hartnett, & T. Stewart (Eds.), *ASCILITE 2012 Conference Proceedings* (pp. 875–880). Wellington, New Zealand.

Sternberg, R. J. (1987). Most vocabulary is learned from context. In M. G. McKeown, & M. E. Curtis (Eds.), *The nature of vocabulary acquisition* (pp. 89–105). Hillsdale, NJ: Erlbaum.

Stockwell, G. (2010). Using mobile phones for vocabulary activities: Examining the effect of the platform. *Language Learning & Technology*, *14*(2), 95–110.

Stockwell, G. (2013). Tracking learner usage of mobile phones for language learning outside of the classroom. *CALICO Journal*, *30*, 118–136.

Sweeney, P., & Moore, C. (2012). Mobile apps for learning vocabulary: Categories, evaluation and design criteria for teachers and developers. *International Journal of Computer-Assisted Language Learning and Teaching*, *2*(2), 45–60.

Thornton, K. (2010). Supporting self-directed learning: A framework for teachers. *Language*.

Wang, D., Zou, B., & Xing, M. (2014). Vocabulary learning and consolidation with mobile application. *International Journal of Computer-Assisted Language Learning and Teaching*, *4*(31), 101–112. doi:10.4018/ijcallt.2014010106

Wang, F., & Hannafin, J. (2005). Design-based research and technology-enhanced learning environments. *ETR&D*, *53*(4), 5–23. doi:10.1007/BF02504682

Wang, Y., & Baker, R. (2018). Grit and intention: Why do learners complete MOOCs? *International Review of Research in Open and Distributed Learning*, *19*(3). doi:10.19173/irrodl.v19i3.3393

Zou, B., Li, H., & Li, J. (2018). Exploring a curriculum app and a social communication app for EFL learning. *Computer Assisted Language Learning*, *31*(7), 694–713. doi:10.1080/09588221.2018.1438474

Zou, B., & Yan, X. (2014). Chinese students' perceptions of using mobile devices for English learning. *International Journal of Computer-Assisted Language Learning and Teaching*, *4*(3), 20–33. doi:10.4018/ijcallt.2014070102

Chapter 4
An Investigation of Social Networking Sites for Language Learning and the User Experience:
The Case of Busuu and Spanish as a Foreign Language

Miguel Saona-Vallejos
https://orcid.org/0000-0002-1980-6042
University of Central Lancashire, UK

Michael Thomas
University of Central Lancashire, UK

ABSTRACT

This chapter investigates the user experience of the language learning platform Busuu as a tool for learning Spanish as a Foreign Language (SFL). Social constructionism has been highlighted by previous research as the theory on which Busuu is based, however, Álvarez concluded that Busuu constitutes an ecological system of nested semiotic spaces where pedagogical elements and principles from different theories of language learning interweave in complementary ways. Following a review of existing research, the chapter analyses data arising from a study involving a mixed group of university students who used the premium version of Busuu for four weeks. Data were collected via pre- and post-tests, a user experience questionnaire, and individual interviews, and were analysed using descriptive statistics and thematic analysis. Findings suggest that Busuu did not fully satisfy the requirements of a social network in terms of ease of participation, communication, and collaboration. Further research is required to explore the implications of usability testing for the design of effective SNSLL.

DOI: 10.4018/978-1-7998-1282-1.ch004

INTRODUCTION

Since the emergence of Web 2.0 applications strategies used by language learners to interact on social networking sites (SNS) have been a topic of growing interest to researchers in second language acquisition (SLA) and teacher education (Lamy & Zourou, 2013; Liu et al., 2015). Lee (2006), for example, argued that the frequency with which language learners use SNS may have a positive impact on their oral proficiency, vocabulary acquisition and syntactic complexity. Moreover, Blattner and Lomicka (2012) suggested that the social interaction that takes place in such environments may help students to develop their pragmatic competence. Lin, Warschauer and Blake (2016) inferred that dedicated social networking sites for language learning (SNSLL), rather than generic social networks such as Facebook, may enable language learners to have their first experience of using their L2 in meaningful conversations with others. While this potential seems promising, several challenges have also been identified in the research, including as Jones (2001) has pointed out, that it may be difficult for SNSLL platforms to engage language learners over a long period of time without teachers or peers to drive the process. Moreover, because the focus is often on social interaction, traditional areas that require in-depth knowledge, such as grammar instruction or pronunciation, may be under-represented in SNSLL course materials.

Founded in 2008 as a social network for language learning, Busuu defines itself as "the world's largest social network for language learning, providing courses in 12 different languages on web and mobile to more than 90 million learners worldwide" (https://www.busuu.com). Busuu promotes itself as a platform that enables learners to train their language skills through self-paced learning units following the Common Framework of Reference (CEFR) from A1 to B2 levels. In 2016, Busuu migrated to a mobile compatible platform and began to attract more research studies (Álvarez, 2016; Vesselinov & Grego, 2016), though its functionality remained quite limited in that language learners could only create a profile, upload content and receive feedback. While Busuu has a significant base of language users, it has attracted limited research to date. This chapter is significant in that it provides an extensive review of the growing body of research on social networks for language learning in order to contextualise Busuu, before investigating original data arising from an empirical study of the SNSLL through the lens of user-experience in order to explore the pedagogical principles underpinning the network's design.

BACKGROUND

In their history of SNS, boyd and Ellison (2008) explained that since 1997, at least 45 SNSs had been created. While some general SNS at that time were used by language learners to practise foreign languages, founded in 2007, Livemocha is commonly regarded as the first dedicated SNSLL of its kind (Brick, 2011a, 2013). This was later followed by Babbel in the same year, Busuu in 2008, and Wespeke in 2010. Table 1 lists social media that are commonly identified to be SNS.

While all of the social media listed in Table 1 are generally considered to be SNSLL, particularly Duolingo and Memrise, none of them offers the *sine qua non* pre-requisite of a social network, namely, the opportunity for learners to engage in full social interaction as defined by Boyd and Ellison (2008).

As Table 2 shows, there were already approximately five different language exchange sites before the creation of Livemocha in 2007. These SNSLL were based on the principle of key-palling (e.g., the use of email to conduct pen-friending relationships) as the concept of an online social network did not exist at the time. The most important SNSLL at the time, SharedTalk, does not exist anymore and the

Table 1. List of commonly identified SNSLL

No.	Website	Foundation	Skills	Levels	Model	Languages	Features
1	Conversation Exchange	2005	R/W/L/S	ND	Free	ND	- F2F exchange - Text, voice, video chat - Conversation topics - Foreign characters
2	Duolingo	2009	R/W/L/S	A1-B1	Free	33	- Written lessons - Gamified skill tree - Experience Points - Timed practice - Rewards - Class Platform - Not SNSLL
3	Lernu	2002	R/W/L/S	ND	Free	39	- Multilingual website - Text chat
4	Lingueo	2007	R/W/L/S	ND	Premium	ND	- Foreign language classes: kids, business, travel & leisure, specific subjects, tests - More a 1.2.1 teachers' platform than an SNSLL
5	Memrise	2010	R/W/L	ND	Freemium	200+	- Learn languages, other academic subjects and Trivia and Pop culture - Based on flashcards - Learners can be followed but no direct interaction with them
6	uTalk	1992	R/W/L/S	A1-B2 (CEFR)	Freemium	140+	- Extensive vocabulary - Measure achievements - Speaking games - Native voices - Educational platform - No chat

Table 2. Language communities: basic data and features

N	Community	Foundation	Skills	Levels	Model	Languages	Features	Users
1	Babbel	2007	R/W/L/S	A1-B2	Freemium	13	- Courses - Text chat - Message boards - Review manager -Certificates	20M
2	bili	2016	R/W/L/S	ND	Premium	ND	- Exchange - Parents' login - Teacher profile	ND
3	Busuu	2008	R/W/L/S	A1-B2	Freemium	12	- Level tests - Lessons - Feedback - Flashcards - Courses - 3 versions	70M
4	English Café	2008 – 04/2012	R/W/L/S	ND	Freemium	1	- Video and audio - Open forums - Create groups	ND
5	English, baby!	2008	R/W/L/S	ND	Free	1	- Text chat - Free lessons, TV - Forums, Quizzes - User comments	2M
6	HelloLingo	2015	R/W/L/S	ND	Free	ND	- Text chat - Mobile app - Language games	ND
7	HelloTalk	2012	R/W/L/S	ND	Free	100+	- Voice to text - Text to voice - Transliteration - Camera share - Doodle share - Translation - Counter - Free calls - Native chat - Save chat	8M
8	HiNative	2014	R/W/L/S	ND	Free	ND	- Q&A Platform - Pre-established forms - A Lang-8 subsidiary	ND
9	Interpals	1998	R/W	ND	Free	150+	- Text chat - Forums - Travel 'buddies'	3.8M
10	iTalki	2007	R/W/L/S	ND	Freemium	100+	- Teachers site - Discussion boards - Community blog - Notebook - No in-site chat - Mobile app	3M
11	Lang-8	2007	Writing	ND	Freemium	90	- Writing exchange	750K
12	Langademy	2016	R/W/L/S	ND	Freemium	ND	- Exchange time	ND
13	Language for exchange	2009	R/W/L/S	ND	Freemium	115	- Directory of schools - Travel abroad - Open forum -Text/audio/video chat	100K
14	LetsPal	2016	R/W	ND	Freemium?	ND	- Text chat - Blogs, photos	ND
15	LingQ	2007	R/W/L/S	ND	Freemium?	14	- Language library - Words tracking	600K

continued on following page

Table 2. Continued

N	Community	Foundation	Skills	Levels	Model	Languages	Features	Users
16	Livemocha	2007 – 04/2016 (Closed by Rosetta Stone)	R/W/L/S	A1-C1	Freemium	38	- Synchronous chat - Lessons - Virtual keyboard - Reward system - Weekly reports	18M
17	Mixxer (Dickinson University)	2005	R/W/L/S	ND	Free	9	- Skype - Group exchanges - Lessons - Blog - Writing correction	ND
18	MyLanguage Exchange	2000 Oct	R/W/L/S	ND	Free	115+	- Text chat - Translation - Homestay - Monitored pals - Notepad - Library - Bulletin board - Multi-dictionary -Lesson plan - Timer	3M
19	Palabea	2007 – 2013	R/W/L/S	ND	Freemium	ND	- Video/voice chat - Marketplace - Forums - Classrooms	ND
20	Pen4Pals	ND	R/W	ND	Free	ND	- Group chats - Open chat - Writing correction - Forums - Open participants	25.6K
21	Penpaland	2015	R/W	ND	Free	ND	- Language exchange - Online chat - Sharing media - Connect with people	ND
22	PlaySay	2008 –2013	R/W/L/S	ND	Freemium	ND	- iPhone game - Text chat - Pronunciation - Facebook practice	ND
23	Polyglotclub	2003	R/W/L/S	ND	Free	ND	- Exchange pals - Face2face events	745K
24	Smalltalk	2005 – 08/2015	R/W/L/S	ND	Free	ND	- Text chat - Mailbox - Public chat rooms - Language games	1.6M
25	Speaky	2015	R/W/L/S	ND	Free	110+	- Text /audio/video chat - Timed exchange - Calendar to set dates	1M
26	Tandem	2015	R/W/L/S	ND	Freemium	8	- Text /audio/video chat - Mobile app - Tutors	3M
27	Tongueout	2012	R/W/L/S	ND	Free	21	- Text /audio/ video chat - Public chatroom - Blogs, Photos - Videos, Events, Polls - Android App	ND
28	Triplingo	2011	R/W/L	ND	Premium	14	- Voice-life Translator -Dictionary -Flashcards - Cultural Guide - Calculator.	ND

continued on following page

Table 2. Continued

N	Community	Foundation	Skills	Levels	Model	Languages	Features	Users
29	Verbling	2011	R/W/L/S	ND	Freemium	38	- Video chat - Chat rooms by levels	ND
30	Wespeke (Carnegie Mellon University)	2010	R/W/L/S	ACTFL	Freemium	1	- Lessons - Text /audio/video chat - Say it again/slower - Record your voice - Upload pics in chat - Translator - Notepad	5K institutions

other four (i.e., Interpals, Mixxer, My Language Exchange, Polyglot Club) have not evolved to become recognisable SNSLL.

Table 2 indicates that after 2007, several new SNS appeared between 2008 and 2011. Four new SNS appeared between 2015 and 2016 to make a total of 30. These Web 2.0 communities, which were explicitly designed for language learning, were categorised into three types according to a typology outlined by Van Dixhoorn, Loiseau, Mangenot, Potolia and Zourou (2010), namely: structured Web 2.0 language learning communities (with lesson content), language exchange sites (without lessons contents), and marketplaces. As can be seen in Table 3, of the 19 communities currently existing only three (15%), Babbel, Bili, and Busuu, can be considered structured Web 2.0 language learning communities; 63% are merely language exchange sites; while 22% work primarily as marketplaces.

Recent empirical studies on SNSLL have been grounded in and supported by different theoretical frameworks. Most of that research has been framed along socio-cultural and socio-cognitive lines such as sociocultural theory (Álvarez, 2015, 2016; Brick, 2011a; Chwo et al., 2012; Gruba & Clark, 2013; Harrison & Thomas, 2009); activity theory (Malerba, 2015); socio-constructivism (De Azevedo, 2013; Brick, 2013); and social cognitive theory (Harrison & Thomas, 2009; Orsini-Jones et al., 2013). According to Wang and Vásquez (2012), this is due to the shift in CALL from a structural/cognitive approach to one that is more socio-cognitive, which views the computer as a tool that mediates interactions between language learners. This finding further corresponds to current developments of Web technology which has shifted from linking information to linking people, and aims to create more opportunities for greater interaction, in that interaction-based learning is a cornerstone of many socially- oriented approaches to L2 learning involving SNSLL. Most of the interaction on SNSLL takes place through their network functionality and therefore it is important to differentiate between social *network* sites and social *networking* sites, as they are frequently used interchangeably in the literature. For the purposes of this chapter, a *network* implies communicating with people who are already part of an extended social circle. *Networking* refers to relationship initiation, often between strangers.

Focusing on SNSLL, the research literature can be divided into three broad categories: descriptive studies, quantitative studies and qualitative studies (see Table 4).

A significant list of topics arises from our review of the research on SNSLL, the most significant being autonomy, collaboration and motivation. Descriptive research, primarily, tends to evaluate the main pedagogical features of the SNSLL studied and the role of the learners within the community.

From Table 5 it is evident that Livemocha was the first SNSLL created in the era of Web 2.0, and as a result, it has attracted the most research to date (42.3%). Busuu achieved second place (19.2%), while others such as Lang-8 and Wespeke have attracted fewer studies (3.8%).

Table 3. SNSLL fulfilling criteria

Communities	*Create profile*	*Add friends*	*Search for friends*	*Create a circle of friends*	*Communicate with friends*	*Exchange Feedback*	*Upload content*	*Peripheral awareness*	%
Babbel	✓	✓	×	×	×	×	×	×	25
Bili	✓	✓	✓	✓	✓	✓	×	×	75
Busuu	✓	×	×	×	×	✓	✓	×	37.5
English, baby!	✓	✓	×	×	✓	×	✓	×	50
HelloTalk	✓	✓	✓	×	✓	✓	✓	×	80
Interpals	✓	✓	✓	×	✓	✓	×	×	70
Lang-8	✓	✓	✓	✓	×	✓	✓	✓	90
Language for exchange	✓	✓	✓	×	✓	✓	×	×	70
LingQ	✓	✓	✓	×	✓	✓	×	×	70
LetsPal	✓	✓	✓	×	✓	✓	✓	×	80
Mixxer	✓	✓	×	×	✓	✓	×	×	60
MyLanguage Exchange	✓	✓	✓	×	✓	✓	×	×	70
Penpaland	✓	✓	✓	✓	✓	✓	✓	×	90
Pen4Pals	✓	✓	✓	×	✓	✓	✓	×	80
Polyglotclub	✓	✓	✓	✓	✓	✓	✓	×	90
Speaky	✓	✓	✓	✓	✓	✓	✓	×	90
Tandem	✓	✓	✓	✓	✓	✓	✓	×	90
Tongueout	✓	✓	✓	×	✓	✓	✓	×	80
Verbling	✓	✓	✓	✓	✓	✓	✓	×	90

Note: Adapted from boyd and Ilison (2008) and Duffy (2011).

Quantitative studies have primarily focused on developing the pedagogical design of SNS communities according to learners' needs. Qualitative studies, on the other hand, frequently combine mixed methods but can be considered mainly interpretive as they focus on topics such as students' perceptions of online communities for L2 learning; affordances and constraints of the platform in relation to pedagogical issues; the role played by learner autonomy; and the thematic analysis of learners' interactive discourse.

Table 6 shows that 30.4% of the empirical research in journals originated in conferences; 17.3% has been published in the Computer-Assisted Language Instruction Consortium (CALICO) journal, and at least 13% have been found on internet repositories.

Table 7 shows the target languages in empirical research on the subject. English (23.3%) is still the language mostly studied when doing research on SNSLL; followed by Spanish (16.7%), which has the same amount as other studies involving multiple languages (16.7%); while French and German share 10% of the research outputs each; Italian, Portuguese and Korean share 6.7% each; and Japanese, Dutch and Russian 3.3% each. Table 7 also shows that at least half of the researchers (50%) prefer to allow the

Table 4. Language learning related topics in empirical research on SNSLL

Research Focus	Study	Number	%
Autonomy	Andriani (2014); Brick (2012); Clark & Gruba (2010); Jee & Park (2009); Lamy & Mangenot (2013); Liaw (2011); Liu et al. (2013); Liu et al. (2015); Malerba (2011); Malerba (2012); Malerba (2015); Orsini-Jones et al. (2013)	12	40%
Collaboration	Andriani (2014); Brick (2011b); Harrison (2013); Lamy & Mangenot (2013); Liu et al. (2013); Liu et al. (2015); Malerba (2011); Stevenson & Liu (2010)	8	26.7%
Motivation	Brick (2011a); Brick (2013); Jee & Park (2009); Kétyi (2015); Liu et al. (2015); Malerba (2011); Malerba (2012); Orsini-Jones et al. (2013)	8	26.7%
Feedback	Andriani (2014); Brick (2011a); Brick (2012); Bündgens-Kosten (2011); De Azevedo (2013); Gruba & Clark (2013); Orsini-Jones et al. (2013)	7	23.3%
Interaction & discourse	Álvarez (2015); Gruba & Clark (2013); Jee & Park (2009); Liu et al. (2015); Malerba (2011); Malerba (2012); Zourou & Lamy (2013)	7	23.3%
Cultural exchange	Álvarez (2015); Harrison & Thomas (2009); Liu et al. (2015); Loiseau, Potolia, & Zourou (2011); Pettes Guikema (2013); Zourou & Loiseau (2013)	6	20%
Informal learning	Brick (2012); Chwo et al. (2012); Kétyi (2015); Lloyd (2012); Malerba (2011); Zourou & Lamy (2013)	6	20%
Community learning	Brick (2013); Bündgens-Kosten (2011); Jee & Park (2009); Liu et al. (2015); Pettes Guikema (2013)	5	16.7%
Exchange (Native / Non-native)	Brick (2011a); Brick (2012); Harrison & Thomas (2009); Jee & Park (2009); Pettes Guikema (2013)	5	16.7%
Formal learning	Brick (2011a); Brick (2012); Bündgens-Kosten (2011); Malerba (2011); Zourou & Lamy (2013)	5	16.7%
Identity	Álvarez (2015); Álvarez (2016); Harrison & Thomas (2009); Malerba (2011); Malerba (2012)	5	16.7%
Peers' assistance / scaffolding	Brick (2011a); Bündgens-Kosten (2011); Malerba (2011); Malerba (2012); Liu et al. (2015)	5	16.7%
Social-constructivist learning	Clark & Gruba (2010); De Azevedo (2013); Harrison (2013); Lloyd (2012); Malerba (2011)	5	16.7%
Authentic materials	Brick (2011a); Brick (2011b); Bündgens-Kosten (2011); Gruba & Clark (2013)	4	13.3%
Engagement	Bündgens-Kosten (2011); Malerba (2012); Liu et al. (2015); Pettes Guikema (2013)	4	13.3%
Negotiation of meaning	Harrison & Thomas (2009); Jee & Park (2009); Malerba (2011); Pettes Guikema (2013)	4	13.3%
Personal Learning Environment (PLE)	Brick (2011a); Brick (2012); Harrison & Thomas (2009); Malerba (2011)	4	13.3%
Real life contexts	Clark & Gruba (2010); Liaw (2011); Malerba (2011); Stevenson & Liu (2010)	4	13.3%
Virtual Learning Environment (VLE)	Brick (2011b); De Azevedo (2013); Harrison & Thomas (2009); Malerba (2011); Stevenson & Liu (2010)	4	13.3%
Active learning	Harrison (2013); Malerba (2011); Stevenson & Liu (2010)	3	10%
Basic skills	Andriani (2014); Brick (2011a); Bündgens-Kosten (2011)	3	10%
Communicative experience	Andriani (2014); Brick (2011a); Liaw (2011)	3	10%
Ecology of languages	Álvarez (2015; Álvarez (2016); Clark & Gruba (2010)	3	10%
Effective learning	Brick (2011a); De Azevedo (2013); Kétyi (2015)	3	10%
Grammar exercises	Brick (2011a); Jee & Park (2009); Orsini-Jones et al. (2013)	3	10%
Impression management	Harrison (2013); Harrison & Thomas (2009); Liaw (2011)	3	10%
Learner generated content	Malerba (2011); Loiseau, Potolia, & Zourou (2011); Stevenson & Liu (2010)	3	10%
Tandem learning	Brick (2011b); De Azevedo (2013); Lloyd (2012)	3	10%
TOTAL STUDIES		**30**	**100%**

Note: For space reasons, themes that were developed by one or two studies are not included in this table.

participants of their studies to choose the language they want to practise in SNSLL without indicating the language they have finally focused on.

Table 5. SNSLL investigated in empirical research

SNSLL	Research	Number	%
Livemocha	Andriani (2014); Brick (2011a); Brick (2011b); Chwo et al. (2012); Clark & Gruba (2010); De Azevedo (2013); Harrison (2013); Harrison & Thomas (2009); Jee & Park (2009); Lloyd (2012); Zourou & Loiseau (2013)	11	42.3%
Livemocha and others	Gruba & Clark (2013); Liu et al. (2013); Loiseau, Potolia, & Zourou (2011); Malerba (2012); Malerba (2015); Orsini-Jones et al. (2013); Stevenson & Liu (2010)	7	26.9%
Busuu and others	Gruba & Clark (2013); Liu et al. (2013); Loiseau, Potolia, & Zourou (2011); Malerba (2012); Malerba (2015); Orsini-Jones et al. (2013)	6	23%
Busuu	Álvarez (2015); Álvarez (2016); Brick (2012); Brick (2013); Kétyi (2015)	5	19.2%
Generic	Lamy & Mangenot (2013); Malerba (2011); Zourou & Lamy (2013)	3	11.5%
Babbel and others	Gruba & Clark (2013); Loiseau, Potolia, & Zourou (2011); Stevenson & Liu (2010)	3	11.5%
English café and others	Liu et al. (2013)	1	3.8%
Italki and others	Liu et al. (2015)	1	3.8%
Lang-8	Bündgens-Kosten (2011)	1	3.8%
Lang-8 and others	Liu et al. (2015)	1	3.8%
LingQ and others	Liu et al. (2015)	1	3.8%
Palabea and others	Stevenson & Liu (2010)	1	3.8%
Polyglotclub and others	Liu et al. (2015)	1	3.8%
Wespeke	Pettes Guikema (2013)	1	3.8%
Not specified	Orsini-Jones et al. (2013)	1	3.8%
TOTAL NUMBER OF SNSLL		**26**	**100%**

Table 8 shows the theoretical frameworks of sociocultural theory, socio-constructivism, and Vygotsky's (1978) Zone of Proximal Development as the most cited when researching SNSLL. At least 20% of other research papers in the field do not mention any theoretical framework at all.

Table 9 refers to methodological approaches used in empirical research about SNSLL. It shows that at least 40% of the research has been qualitative in orientation and based on case studies. Only 10% were quantitative studies, of which 6.7% were descriptive, and 3.3%, experimental. Approximately 26.7% followed a mixed-methods approach.

The participants in these studies involved mostly university students (43.3%), while 20% focused on teachers' opinions and 13.3% included the general public. 26.7% of these studies involved no participants. Concerning the duration of the studies, almost half (46.7%) did not define the period of the investigation. 23.3% lasted for at least three months, while 13.3% lasted between one and three months, and only 6.7% lasted for less than a month.

Table 6. Distribution of empirical research about SNSLL in journals

No.	Journal Title	Number	Empirical study
1	Conferences Proceedings	7	Chwo et al. (2012); Clark & Gruba (2010); Kétyi (2015); Loiseau, Potolia, & Zourou (2011); Malerba (2011); Malerba (2012); Malerba (2015)
2	CALICO Journal	4	Jee & Park (2009); Liu et al. (2015); Pettes Guikema (2013); Stevenson & Liu (2010)
3	Internet repositories	3	Andriani (2014); Brick (2013); De Azevedo (2013)
4	ALSIC, Apprentissage des langues est systemes d'information et de Communication.	1	Lloyd (2012)
5	Compass: The Journal of Learning and Teaching at the University of Greenwich	1	Brick (2011a)
6	Computer Assisted Language Learning	1	Álvarez (2015)
7	International Journal of Computer-Assisted Language Learning and Teaching (IJCALLT)	1	Brick (2012)
8	International Journal of Emerging Technologies & Society	1	Harrison & Thomas (2009)
9	International Journal of Virtual and Personal Learning Environments (IJVPLE)	1	Brick, B. (2011b)
10	Language Learning & Technology	1	Liaw (2011)
11	Signo y Pensamiento	1	Álvarez (2016)
12	Studies in Self-Access Learning Journal (SiSAL Journal)	1	Bündgens-Kosten (2011)
	TOTAL	**23**	

CRITICISMS OF SOCIAL NETWORKING SITES FOR LEARNING LANGUAGES

A frequent criticism of SNSLL relates to learning materials in that their one-size-fits-all approach has led to poor quality (Brick 2011a; Harrison, 2013; Liaw, 2011; Lloyd, 2012). Criticisms have also been levelled at their lack of contextualisation (Álvarez, 2016; Clark & Gruba, 2010; Orsini-Jones et al., 2013), as well as why their language exercises require high levels of memorisation rather than encouraging comprehension and students' critical and analytical skills (Liaw, 2011). Furthermore, SNSLL structured dialogues do not present learners with opportunities for negotiation of meaning, as their speaking exercises do little to help the development of spontaneous communicative skills (Jee & Park, 2009).

Similarly, as it has been argued with respect to some Web 2.0 applications, SNSLL are based primarily on a Web 1.0 pedagogy (Harrison & Thomas, 2009) as the materials revert to behaviourist principles (Álvarez, 2015; Chwo et al., 2012; Clark and Gruba, 2010; Malerba, 2015; Orsini-Jones et al. 2013; Zourou & Loiseau, 2013), leading their users first to motivation, then frustration, and finally demotivation (Brick, 2012; Clark & Gruba, 2010; Orsini-Jones et al., 2013). This cycle is reflected in high levels of user attrition (Lin, et al., 2016; Nielson, 2011; Stevenson & Liu, 2010).

Table 7. Target languages investigated in empirical research about SNSLL

Target Language	Study	Number of studies	%
No specified	Brick (2011a); Brick (2011b); Bündgens-Kosten (2011); Harrison (2013); Harrison & Thomas (2009); Lamy & Mangenot (2013); Liaw (2011); Loiseau, Potolia, & Zourou (2011); Malerba (2011); Malerba (2015); Orsini-Jones et al. (2013); Pettes Guikema (2013); Stevenson & Liu (2010); Zourou & Lamy (2013); Zourou & Loiseau (2013)	15	50%
EFL/ESL	Andriani (2013); Chwo et al. (2012); Jee & Park (2009); Kétyi (2015); Liu et al. (2013); Liu et al. (2015); Malerba (2012)	7	23.3%
Spanish/SFL	Gruba & Clark (2013); Kétyi (2015); Malerba (2012); Orsini-Jones et al. (2013); Lloyd (2012)	5	16.7%
Multiple languages	Gruba & Clark (2013); Kétyi (2015); Malerba (2012); Orsini-Jones et al. (2013); Lloyd (2012)	5	16.7%
German	Brick (2012); Brick (2013); Kétyi (2015)	3	10%
French	Álvarez (2015); Álvarez (2016); Lloyd (2012)	3	10%
Italian	Malerba (2012); Kétyi (2015)	2	6.7%
Portuguese	De Azevedo (2013); Lloyd (2012)	2	6.7%
Korean	Clark & Gruba (2010); Gruba & Clark (2013)	2	6.7%
Japanese	Gruba & Clark (2013)	1	3.3%
Dutch	Lloyd (2012)	1	3.3%
Russian	Lloyd (2012)	1	3.3%
TOTAL NUMBER OF STUDIES		**30**	**100%**

SNSLL also erase the boundaries between peer, co-learner and tutors (Gruba & Clark, 2013), and the value of feedback from peers with low proficiency is questionable (Brick, 2012; Jee & Park, 2009; Liu et al., 2015). Additionally, the artificiality of the sites (Gruba & Clark, 2013) has also been emphasised, in that it could lead to biased or stereotypical representations of culture and identities (Jee & Park, 2009). Other researchers have argued that SNSLL fail to determine clear learning goals (Harrison, 2013); that without a teacher, learners might feel at loss when trying to make sense of the language learned; and thus, experience what Harrison (2013) called "random language learning experiences". Moreover, there may be a tension between the 'formal' aspects of language learning and the 'informal' SNS model (Liaw, 2011), as well as a lack of clear boundaries between their educational and social dimension (Orsini-Jones et al., 2013).

In relation to the social aspect of SNSLL, it is evident that it may take time to develop a network of trusted partners and that such groups can only be built upon a trial and error basis (Brick 2011a; Brick, 2012; Harrison & Thomas, 2009). Consequently, without a level of intimacy between users, collaborative learning is likely to encounter difficulties (Gruba & Clark, 2013; Harrison & Thomas, 2009).

In addition to these pedagogical challenges, researchers have also identified a range of other potentially negative aspects of learning online, including cyber-flirting (Brick, 2011b; Harrison, 2013; Lloyd, 2012), Alpha socialisers (Lloyd, 2012), as well as cyberstalking and harassment (Orsini-Jones et al., 2013), which require more sophisticated impression management systems to enable users to set levels of exposure that would put their members at ease about self-disclosure (Cardon, 2008; Liaw, 2011).

Table 8. Theoretical frameworks of the empirical research about SNSLL

Theoretical framework	Study	Number	%
Sociocultural theory	Álvarez (2015); Álvarez (2016); Brick (2011b); Chwo et al. (2012); Gruba & Clark (2013); Harrison & Thomas (2009); Jee & Park (2009); Lamy & Mangenot (2013); Liu et al. (2013); Malerba (2011); Malerba (2012); Malerba (2015); Orsini-Jones et al. (2013); Zourou & Lamy (2013); Zourou & Loiseau (2013)	15	50%
Socio-constructivism	Álvarez (2015); Álvarez (2016); Brick (2012); Clark & Gruba (2010); De Azevedo (2013); Harrison (2013); Harrison & Thomas (2009); Liu et al. (2015); Lloyd (2012); Malerba (2011)	10	33.3%
Vygotsky's ZPD	Gruba & Clark (2013); Harrison (2013); Harrison & Thomas (2009); Jee & Park (2009); Lamy & Mangenot (2013); Malerba (2011); Malerba (2015);	7	23.3%
No identifiable theoretical framework	Andriani (2014); Brick (2011a); Bündgens-Kosten (2011); Kétyi (2015); Liaw (2011); Pettes Guikema (2013)	6	20%
Community of practice	Álvarez (2015); Brick (2013); Zourou & Lamy (2013)	3	10%
Ecologies of learning and teaching	Álvarez (2015); Álvarez (2016); Clark & Gruba (2010);	3	10%
Social interactionism	De Azevedo (2013); Harrison (2013); Harrison & Thomas (2009);	3	10%
More Knowledgeable Other (MKO)	Harrison & Thomas (2009); Jee & Park (2009);	2	6.7%
Social Cognitive Theory	Harrison & Thomas (2009); Orsini-Jones et al. (2013);	2	6.7%
Behaviourism	Álvarez (2016); Loiseau, Potolia, & Zourou (2011)	2	6.7%
Usability Testing	Liu et al. (2015); Stevenson & Liu (2010)	2	6.7%
TOTAL NUMBER OF STUDIES		**30**	**100%**

In response to these criticisms, Lloyd (2012) pointed out that SNSLL could be considered a convenient, ready-made 'bridge' between classroom-based language learning and the communicative use of L2s students are likely to encounter in real-life situations. Malerba (2011) added that SNS might enhance opportunities for active collaboration in formal L2 learning activities. Likewise, Jee and Park (2009), drew attention to how users need to cultivate learner autonomy, discipline and intrinsic motivation when learning in SNSLL, as there is no pressure brought to bear by the presence of an instructor. Moreover, Álvarez (2016) replied to previous criticisms about the reliance of behaviourist principles and cognitivism, arguing that they also provide other environments where users are required to interact and think of learning as emerging from interaction and co-construction. Then, he also mentioned how SNSLL use other features such as gamification to enliven specific repetitive and monotonous exercises, as well as promote competition through the use of ranking systems and 'friend challenges'. Malerba (2012, 2015)

Table 9. Methodological elements used in empirical research about SNSLL

Methodological Issues	Categories		Studies
Research Approach	Qualitative	Case study	Álvarez (2015); Brick (2011b); Brick (2013); Clark & Gruba (2010); De Azevedo (2013); Gruba & Clark (2013); Harrison (2013); Harrison & Thomas (2009); Malerba (2012); Malerba (2015); Orsini-Jones et al. (2013); Zourou & Loiseau (2013)
		Non-case study	Brick (2011a); Bündgens-Kosten (2011); Jee & Park (2009); Lamy & Mangenot (2013); Liaw (2011); Loiseau, Potolia, & Zourou (2011); Zourou & Lamy (2013)
	Quantitative	Descriptive	Brick (2012); Liu et al. (2013)
		Experimental	Kétyi (2015)
	Mixed methods		Andriani (2014); Brick (2012); Chwo et al. (2012); Liu et al. (2013); Liu et al. (2015); Lloyd (2012); Malerba (2011); Stevenson & Liu (2010)
Participants	No participants		Brick (2011a); Bündgens-Kosten (2011); Jee & Park (2009); Lamy & Mangenot (2013); Liaw (2011); Loiseau, Potolia, & Zourou (2011); Zourou & Lamy (2013); Zourou & Loiseau (2013)
	Not specified		Malerba (2011)
	Auto-ethnographic		Álvarez (2015); Clark & Gruba (2010); Gruba & Clark (2013)
	General public		De Azevedo (2013); Malerba (2012); Malerba (2015); Stevenson & Liu (2010)
	University students		Andriani (2014); Brick (2011b); Brick (2012); Brick (2013); Chwo et al. (2012); Harrison (2013); Harrison & Thomas (2009); Kétyi (2015); Liu et al. (2013); Liu et al. (2015); Lloyd (2012); Orsini-Jones et al. (2013); Stevenson & Liu (2010)
	Teachers		Álvarez (2015); Brick (2011a); Brick (2012); Clark & Gruba (2010); Gruba & Clark (2013); Liu et al. (2015)
Sampling	Inexistent. Theoretical Studies		Brick (2011a); Bündgens-Kosten (2011); Jee & Park (2009); Lamy & Mangenot (2013); Liaw (2011); Loiseau, Potolia, & Zourou (2011); Zourou & Lamy (2013); Zourou & Loiseau (2013)
	Not specified		Malerba (2011)
	Convenience sampling		Álvarez (2015); Andriani (2014); Brick (2011b); Brick (2012); Brick (2013); Chwo et al. (2012); Clark & Gruba (2010); Gruba & Clark (2013); Harrison (2013); Harrison & Thomas (2009); Kétyi (2015); Liu et al. (2013); Liu et al. (2015); Lloyd (2012); Orsini-Jones et al. (2013); Stevenson & Liu (2010)
	Purposeful sampling		Malerba (2012)
	Random sampling		De Azevedo (2013); Malerba (2012); Malerba (2015); Stevenson & Liu (2010);
Duration	Not specified		Brick (2011a); Bündgens-Kosten (2011); De Azevedo (2013); Gruba & Clark (2013); Jee & Park (2009); Lamy & Mangenot (2013); Liaw (2011); Liu et al. (2015); Loiseau, Potolia, & Zourou (2011); Malerba (2011); Malerba (2012); Malerba (2015); Zourou & Lamy (2013); Zourou & Loiseau (2013)
	≤ 1 month		Andriani (2014); Stevenson & Liu (2010);
	> 1 month < 3 months		Álvarez (2015); Brick (2013); Kétyi (2015); Lloyd (2012)
	≥ 3 months		Brick (2011b); Brick (2012); Chwo et al. (2012); Harrison (2013); Harrison & Thomas (2009); Liu et al. (2013); Orsini-Jones et al. (2013)

also concluded that formal and informal learning should be compatible and complementary and that the ultimate purpose of learners using SNSLL is to practise language skills, not just socialise (Liu et al., 2013).

In their favour, the use of SNSLL is generally considered easy and straightforward, and they work across a range of devices; they can be fun and engaging (Brick, 2013); and they allow learners to personalise learning and increase their autonomy and empowerment (Brick, 2012). Secondly, students may benefit from the authentic language use in a communicative context with native speakers (Brick 2011a; Jee & Park, 2009), something difficult to replicate in the language classroom (Brick, 2011b). Receiving instant feedback from other users, especially more proficient speakers of the target language, is a very important affordance that SNSLL can provide (Brick, 2011; Liu et al., 2013).

In summary, it is clear from the above review that there are still plenty of unanswered questions in the research on SNSLL, such as the proportion of users who have actually completed courses, what kinds of competencies users acquire (e.g., linguistic, pragmatic) and how much proficiency they develop (e.g., basic, intermediate, advanced knowledge), or even more challenging ones, such as the length of time required to achieve proficiency. It is evident that user experience is one of the most significant gaps in the research to date and this will form a central aspect of the research outlined in the next section.

METHODOLOGY

Context and Participants

The participants in this study had access to the premium version of Busuu and, following the platform's own study guide, they were asked to use it daily for a minimum of 10 minutes over four weeks. The participants were not given an upper limit for study time, as the research aimed to reflect the spontaneity that other users of the platform would normally experience. In total, 268 university students from a database of learners who had previously used the online learning platform Rosetta Stone at a language centre in a university in England were invited by email to take part in the study. A total of 14 students agreed to participate, of whom 7 (50%) had a Spanish language proficiency score of CEFR A1 level, 3 (21.42%) were at the A2 level, 2 (14.28%) were at B1, and a further 2 (14.28%) were B2. While the response rate was low, it was nevertheless viable in this context of this mixed methods study. 268 participants are registered with Rosetta Stone, however, the response rate may indicate that a much smaller group of core users interact with the application in a serious way.

As Table 10 shows, nine were female and five were male and their ages ranged from 18 to 54 years old. Seven participants were graduate students and seven were undergraduates, and nationalities included British (11), Belarusian (1), Italian (1) and Greek (1).

DATA COLLECTION

Based on previous evaluations of other SNSLL (Liu et al., 2015), the data collection tools are presented in Figure 1 and were designed to investigate the principles SNSLL adhere to and observe if there was an evolution in participants' learning performance as a result.

All of the participants were invited to take an online written proficiency test, so their language level could be determined before using the platform. This was important because the results were compared to

Table 10. Demographic data of the participants

Participant	Gender	Age	Nationality	Academic background	Spanish level
pa01	F	49	British	Graduate	B2
pa02	F	20	British	Undergraduate	A2
pa03	F	54	British	Graduate	A1
pa04	F	51	British	Graduate	A2
pa05	F	23	British	Undergraduate	A2
pa06	M	24	British	Undergraduate	A1
pa07	M	47	British	Graduate	B1
pa08	M	23	British	Undergraduate	A2
pa09	M	33	Belarusian	Graduate	A1
pa10	F	18	British	Undergraduate	A2
pa11	F	23	British	Undergraduate	A2
pa12	F	33	Italian	Graduate	B2
pa13	M	44	British	Graduate	B1
pa14	F	21	Greek	Undergraduate	A2

a post-test that was administered five weeks later, at the end of the main study to measure their learning outcomes. For this purpose, the Rosetta Stone examination, available at the *TellMeMore* campus was used. The participants took the written examination by themselves at home and the results were checked via the Rosetta Stone platform. While enabling the students to take the test at home may be viewed as compromising the efficacy of the test, it is now standard practice for online platforms and teachers and students are increasingly familiar with it. In the context of this research, the added flexibility provided by the online platform was required due to the time constraints placed on the researchers.

For the oral proficiency tests, a 10-item examination was prepared following the Curricular Plan of the *Instituto Cervantes*. An assessment criterion based on the CEFR and Cambridge Assessment Methods was utilised for the moderation of the participants' oral exams by a native Spanish speaking teacher to confirm the reliability of the results.

Based on Liu et al. (2015), participants completed a user experience questionnaire, which consisted of three different types of tasks: exploratory, specific, and open-ended (see Figure 2).

Figure 1. Data collection tools

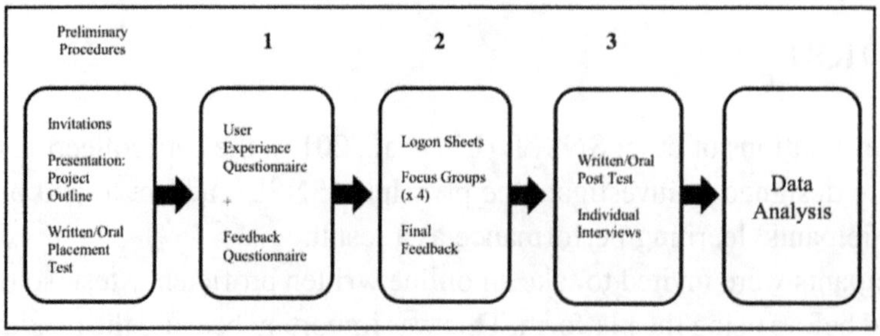

The site feedback questionnaire (based on Liu et al., 2015) was answered immediately after the user experience questionnaire. It offered a Likert scale, anchored in 1 (negative) and 5 (positive), and participants were also allowed to reply with open answers in some cases. The questionnaire was focused on skills, features, and future use and perceptions. The same questionnaire was applied after the participants used Busuu for four weeks to compare if their perceptions of the platform had changed. The participants were asked about the different language skills that could be improved through the use of Busuu to learn Spanish as a Foreign Language (SFL). Additionally, participants were asked if they thought the features present in the platform could help them in their learning of SFL.

The analysis of the data focused on the user experience questionnaire and the pre- and post- website feedback questionnaires. In addition, logon sheets, focus groups, and interviews applied in the research process were also analysed. Based on Brick (2011a), participants were requested to complete a logon sheet online every time they accessed Busuu, immediately after they had finished their practice session. An auto-ethnographic methodology was applied to these documents as participants were asked to describe and interpret their communicative behaviour while connected (Ellis, Adams & Bochner, 2011).

For each session, participants were invited to describe the specific theme practised; what they considered they learnt face-to-face; the means of communication used (message, text chat, voice chat, video chat, any other); a description of what they did and how they did it; mistakes made; what the participants enjoyed or did not enjoy during the session; difficulties during the session; their learning and practising plans for next time; and any specific problems with the platform.

The majority of the participants were able to participate in the four focus groups that took place. The objective of those meetings was to discuss specific topics elicited from the logon sheets as well as the user experience and feedback questionnaires. To further clarify the data from the website feedback questionnaires, logon sheets, and focus groups, participants were invited to participate in semi-structured interviews.

DATA ANALYSIS

The qualitative data collected were analysed through content analysis using NVivo 11. The quantitative data were analysed using IBM-SPSS-Statistics-23.0. As the sample research was small, and there were a limited number of response options, the data obtained were skewed. Hence, it was necessary to apply a nonparametric measure of rank correlation, specifically *Spearman's rho*, which measured the strength of association between two variables.

Figure 2. User experience questionnaire

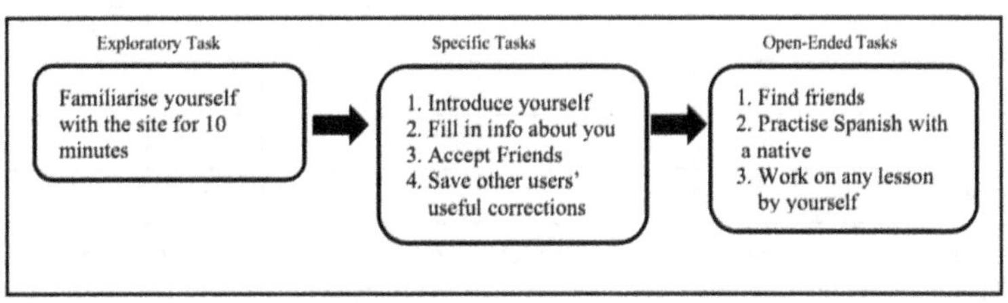

From the 28 original quantitative variables measured via the pre-site feedback questionnaire, these were doubled to 56 when adding the same number of variables corresponding to the post-site feedback questionnaire. Finally, the ten most relevant features were correlated, always taking pre- and post-written examination variation as a point of reference for all the correlations.

FINDINGS AND DISCUSSION

As the main focus of the analysis of Busuu related to participants' user experience, the five main variables reflecting this process were explored: 1) the features that were found in Busuu; 2) site design; 3) pre- and post-test results; 4) the social aspect of Busuu; and 5) participants' general perception of the Busuu platform.

Features of Busuu

The interview data showed that learning was not participatory in Busuu. On the contrary, while individual learning was encouraged by the platform's layout, it was organised in such a way that was counter to the principles of a community of practice in which learners share goals and are engaged in continuous collaborative and meaningful activity. As Table 11 indicates, the highest division of opinions was related to the usefulness of the learning features found in Busuu. When evaluating the 'friending' feature, 50% of participants agreed that it was not useful in the pre-test, and this increased to 60% in the post-test. Learning was not considered participatory as learners were not able to share their learning processes with other students.

Busuu suspended the friending feature when the platform was made compatible with mobile devices, and as a consequence, none of the participants were able to find or accept friends. Therefore, knowledge was individually rather than socially constructed, as there were no peers to create a meaningful learning environment.

Table 11. Features that can be found in Busuu

Measurable aspect	1		2		3		4		5	
	Pre	Post	Pre	Post	Pre	Post	Pre	Post	Pre	Post
1. Creating a profile	3	2	6	7	5	1	0	0	0	0
2. Friending	7	6	1	0	5	3	1	0	0	1
3. Vocabulary	6	0	2	0	4	2	2	5	0	2
4. Posting	2	2	2	0	3	2	7	5	0	1
5. Receiving feedback	4	0	2	1	3	3	3	4	2	2
6. Giving feedback	6	4	2	2	5	3	1	1	0	0
7. Images	4	2	3	0	4	2	3	4	0	1
8. Corrections and comments	4	2	3	1	3	1	3	3	0	1

Note: the horizontal numbers (1-5) refer to the five-point Likert Scale used in the questionnaire. The scores in each column refer to the raw scores (the numbers of participants choosing these scores in each case). This applies equally to Tables 12 and 14.

Accordingly, as Table 12 shows, the highest number of 'very dissatisfied' users related to the ease of finding contacts with 71.4% of participants. This increased to 85.7% when the dissatisfied replies were also included in the pre-test, and it was also the highest variable for dissatisfaction (70% of participants) for the post-test. Therefore, none of the users expressed being 'satisfied' or 'very satisfied' with this aspect of the site in both cases.

PRE- AND POST-TEST RESULTS

Busuu allowed users to create a profile, upload user-generated content, and give and/or receive feedback from peers on spelling, punctuation and grammar. Giving and receiving feedback were also related to learning development as they were shared activities; however, these characteristics meant that only 37.5% of the essential features every SNS should have were evident on the platform, according to the guidelines established by boyd and Ellison (2008) and Duffy (2011). The results in Table 13 show a comparison of the pre- and post-test results and confirms that Busuu favoured individual learning instead of social learning. Only 7.69% of participants, (participant 11) did not experience a positive outcome. 61.54% increased their results by one point. 15.38% increased by two points. 7.69% achieved 2.1 points, and the highest score was obtained by 7.69% of participants, who achieved 3.1 points.

In contrast, the results of the oral tests were not as positive as the increases in scores which were in all cases minimal. None of the participants were able to advance a complete level, and 66.6% remained at the same level of oral competency at the end of the entire process. One reason for this was the lack of native speakers to practise with.

Table 12. Feedback on site design

Measurable aspect	1		2		3		4		5	
	Pre	Post	Pre	Post	Pre	Post	Pre	Post	Pre	Post
1. Ease of finding information	1	0	4	1	5	4	3	4	1	1
2. Quality of learning activities	0	0	2	1	6	3	4	4	2	2
3. Ease of reading texts	0	0	0	1	5	2	4	3	5	4
4. Appearance	0	0	0	1	4	2	5	3	5	4
5. Displaying speed	2	0	1	1	2	1	5	1	4	7
6. Entertainment value	0	0	2	1	6	3	5	4	1	2
7. Overall learning experience	1	0	1	0	6	4	6	5	0	1
8. Instructions for activities	2	0	7	2	3	3	1	3	1	2
9. Ease of moving around	3	1	6	2	3	2	1	3	1	2
10. Ease of finding contacts	10	4	2	3	2	2	0	1	0	0

1= very dissatisfied … 5= very satisfied

Table 13. Pre- and post-tests results

Participant	Pre-written	Post-written	variation	Pre-oral	Post-oral
pa01	6.6 B2	6.8 B2	0.2	B2	B2
pa02	2.1 A2			A2	
pa03	1.6 A1	4.7 B1	3.1	A1	A1+
pa04	3.5 A2	4.9 B1	1.4	A2	A2+
pa05	2.0 A2	2.4 A2	0.4	A1-	A1
pa06	1.4 A1	2	0.6	A1-	A1-
pa07	5.3 B1	7.4	2.1	B1	B1
pa08	2.1 A2	2.9 A2	0.8	A1	A1
pa09	1.7 A1	2.2 A2	0.5	A1	A1+
pa10	3.9 A2	4.3 B1	0.4	A2+	A2+
pa11	2.7 A2	1.4 A1	-1.3	A1	A1
pa12	7.4 B2	9.2 C1	1.5	B2+	C1
pa13	4.4 B1	5.3 B1	0.9	B1	B1
pa14	3.7 A2	4.3 B1	0.6	A1+	A1+

BUSUU'S SOCIAL FEATURES

Participants did not have the opportunity to achieve useful knowledge by engaging in significant language learning activities, as Busuu did not provide opportunities to interact with other learners. When asked for the reasons why participants returned to the site or why they would or would not recommend it, the viewpoints varied between two extremes. One could be synthesised by what participant 14 said: "It is a great app. Although I can only see it as an additional feature. You still need to speak to people and use books". Additionally, participant 3 indicated: "This is supposed to be a social network site to help improve my Spanish. I never found anyone … that I could connect with".

When asked about what they disliked, 85.71% mentioned the difficulty of navigating the site, and 50% of those specifically identified that it was impossible to contact other language learners. In the post-trial questionnaire, participants were asked about what they liked least. 66.6% of participants mentioned not being able to find "friends"; 55.5% complained about the site not being user-friendly enough; and 33.3% about the grammar contents, which were "not sufficient", "not clear enough", or "difficult to go back to it when needed". Furthermore, 57.14% recommended improvements to its social dimension; participant 12, for example, specifically suggested that "the social aspect of the network should be implemented".

LEARNER PERCEPTIONS OF BUSUU

As learners did not have the opportunity to create a community of learning in Busuu, it was difficult for users to drive their own process of learning. When asked about the likelihood of returning to the site on their own in the pre-test (see Table 14), 71.4% declared they would, while 14.3% had some doubts, and a further 14.3% were neutral. It is important to highlight that none of the participants said that they would not do it; however, this was due to their commitment to take part in the research as some of them explained. In the post-test, the numbers decreased further to 70% who said that they would return, while 30% had some doubts.

Accordingly, when asked if they would recommend Busuu to other users to learn Spanish (Table 14), in the pre-test 42.9% participants expressed neutrality in their opinion. Interestingly, 35.7% said they would not do it, and 21.4% affirmed they would. Figures varied in the post-test: 60% still declared neutrality, 20% said they would not recommend it, and 20% agreed with supporting the site.

DISCUSSION

The study of Busuu outlined above indicates that the SNS satisfies only three of the eight social aspects expected by a social network for language learning (boyd & Ellison, 2008). The language learners in the study were able to create a profile, upload user-generated content, and receive feedback from other users. However, these features were not sufficient to enable them to network and practise the four main skills in Spanish. The backward shift from a social to cognitive approach was evident in the data and goes against the grain of Web 2.0 characteristics, such as ease of participation, communication, information sharing, and collaboration. Therefore, the pre- and post-test results of the study contradicted Vesselinov and Grego's (2016) stance, according to which Busuu users would need an estimated 22.5 hours of study to match the requirements for one college semester of SFL. In this sense, Busuu's language exercises appear to confirm the argument for lack of contextualisation identified by Clark and Gruba (2013) as it relied more on memorisation rather than comprehension (Liaw, 2013) and it was challenging for the learners to find others to learn with (Orsini-Jones et al., 2013).

Moreover, it was evident that there was a tension between the 'formal' aspects of language learning and the 'informal' SNS model (Liaw, 2011) related to Busuu, as well as no boundaries between the educational and social aspects inherent in all SNSLL (Orsini-Jones et al., 2013). Malerba (2012, 2015) focused her research on these aspects and concluded that formal and informal learning should be compatible and complementary and that the ultimate purpose of learners for using SNSLL is to practise language skills (Liu et al., 2013).

Lloyd (2012) had already pointed out this idea when saying that SNSLL could be considered a convenient, ready-made 'bridge' between classroom-based language learning and actual, communicative use of L2s in real-life situations; and Malerba (2011) had added that SNS might enhance opportunities for active collaboration in formal L2 learning activities. So, conversely, some of those very same authors who focused on the negative aspects of SNSLL have also mentioned some favourable options for users.

Table 14. General perception of the site

Possibilities	1		2		3		4		5	
	Pre	Post	Pre	Post	Pre	Post	Pre	Post	Pre	Post
1. Return to the site	0	0	2	0	2	3	7	6	3	1
2. Recommend the site	2	1	3	1	6	6	2	2	1	0

1= completely disagree … 5= completely agree

Arising from the findings on Busuu, course and materials designers may need to consider how the platform can incorporate more authentic language use in a communicative context with native speakers, even in the absence of a teacher's guidance (Brick 2011a; Brick, 2013; Jee & Park, 2009), as this approach may be useful in helping the students to learn foreign languages independently, anywhere and anytime (Andriani, 2014). SNSLL such as Busuu provide learners with the flexibility and variety needed for language learning (Orsini-Jones et al. 2013) but the learners may need more help in creating their own learning environment (Álvarez, 2016; Harrison & Thomas, 2009; Malerba, 2015).

CONCLUSION

Arising from the other studies reviewed above, SNSLL may be useful pedagogical tools for language learners who have different learning preferences (Chwo et al., 2012; Lloyd, 2012). The defining feature of SNSLL is that users with different skills can serve as a 'knowledgeable other' in building a distributed knowledge base for meeting their language needs (Liu et al., 2013). In this chapter we focused, however, on the overlooked area of user experience and SNSLL and found that learners were not able to improve their overall communicative competence in ways previously outlined. While the students' use of the site was relatively easy and straightforward, this was not enough to increase collaboration and collective knowledge-building experiences (Liu et al., 2015). Given the limitations of the study in terms of participants number and duration, it is evident that further longitudinal research is required to explore the pedagogical implications of usability testing for the design of effective SNSLL that are underpinned by constructivist pedagogies, particularly in the area of blended language learning.

REFERENCES

Álvarez, J. A. (2015). Language views on social networking sites for language learning: The case of Busuu. *Computer Assisted Language Learning, 29*(5), 1–15.

Álvarez, J. A. (2016). Social networking sites for language learning: Examining learning theories in nested semiotic spaces. *Signo y Pensamiento, 68*(68), 66–84. doi:10.11144/Javeriana.syp35-68.snsl

Andriani, G. (2014). Using Livemocha for independent language learning, a study of students' perception. Paper presented at Sriwijaya University Learning and Education-International Conference 2014, Sriwijaya University, Palembang, May 16-18.

Blattner, G., & Lomicka, L. (2012). Facebook-ing and the social generation: A new era of language learning. *ALSIC, 15*(1). Retrieved https://journals.openedition.org/alsic/2413

Boyd, D., & Ellison, N.B. (2008). Social network sites: Definition, history, and scholarship. *Journal of Computer-Mediated Communication, 13*, 210-230.

Brick, B. (2011a). How effective are web 2.0 language learning sites in facilitating language learning? *Compass: The Journal of Learning and Teaching at the University of Greenwich, 3*, 57–63.

Brick, B. (2011b). Social networking sites and language learning. *International Journal of Virtual and Personal Learning Environments, 2*(3), 18–31. doi:10.4018/jvple.2011070102

Brick, B. (2012). The role of social networking sites for language learning in UK higher education: The views of learners and practitioners. *International Journal of Computer-Assisted Language Learning and Teaching*, *2*(3), 35–53. doi:10.4018/ijcallt.2012070103

Brick, B. (2013). Evaluating social networking sites (SNSs) for language learning: An inquiry-based student project. Retrieved from http://coursefinder.coventry.ac.uk.public.freestyleinteractive.co.uk/Global/BES/Active%20Learning/Billy%20Brick.pdf

Bündgens-Kosten, J. (2011). Blogging in the target language: Review of the 'Lang-8' online community. *Studies in Self-Access Learning Journal*, *2*(2), 97–99.

Cardon, D. (2008). Le Design de la Visibilité: Un Essai de Typologie du Web 2.0. *Internet Actu*. Retrieved from http://www.internetactu.net/2008/02/01/le-Design-de-la-visibilite-un-essai-de-typologie-du-web-20/

Chwo, G. S.-M., Lin, Y.-S., Chen, P.-J., Lai, G.-W., Liu, H.-C., Ho, C.-C., & Wang, Y.-P. (2012) Engagement with Livemocha® as an informal learning resource - Initial findings from a technology university reading course in central Taiwan. *ICCE 2012. The 20th International Conference on Computers in Education. Proceedings*. 609-613.

Clark, C., & Gruba, P. (2010). The use of social networking sites for foreign language learning: An autoethnographic study of Livemocha. In C.H. Steel, M.J. Keppell, P. Gerbic, & S. Housego (Eds.), Curriculum, technology, & transformation for an unknown future. Proceedings Ascilite, 164-173.

De Azevedo, C. G. (2013). Livemocha: uma rede social de aprendizagem de línguas. Unpublished Masters' Dissertation, Universidade do Minho, Instituto de Educaçao. Retrieved from https://repositorium.sdum.uminho.pt/bitstream/1822/30231/1/Cristiana%20Gracinda%20de%20Azevedo%20Gon%C3%A7alves%20Cerdeira%20Lopes.pdf

Duffy, P. (2011). Facebook or faceblock. Cautionary tales exploring the rise of social networking within tertiary education. In M. Lee, & C. McLoughlin (Eds.), *Web 2.0-based e-learning: Applying social informatics for tertiary teaching* (pp. 284–300). Hershey, PA: IGI Global. doi:10.4018/978-1-60566-294-7.ch015

Gruba, P., & Clark, C. (2013). Formative assessment within social network sites for language learning. In M.-N. Lamy & K. Zourou (Eds.), *Social networking for language education* (pp. 177–193). Basingstoke, UK: Palgrave MacMillan. doi:10.1057/9781137023384_10

Harrison, R. (2013). Profiles in social networking sites for language learning – Livemocha R revisited. In M.-N. Lamy, & K. Zourou (Eds.), *Social networking for language education: New language learning and teaching environments* (pp. 100-116). Basingstoke, UK: Palgrave Macmillan.

Harrison, R., & Thomas, M. (2009). Identity in online communities: Social networking sites and language learning. *International Journal of Emerging Technologies & Society.*, *7*(2), 109–124.

Jee, M., & Park, M. (2009). Livemocha as an online language-learning community. *CALICO Journal*, *26*(2), 448–456. doi:10.1558/cj.v26i2.448-456

Jones, J. (2001). CALL and the responsibilities of teachers and administrators. *ELT Journal*, *55*(4), 360–367. doi:10.1093/elt/55.4.360

Kétyi, A. (2015). Practical evaluation of a mobile language learning tool in higher education. In F. Helm, L. Bradley, M. Guarda, & S. Thouësny (Eds), *Critical CALL – Proceedings of the 2015 EUROCALL Conference*, Padova, Italy (pp. 306-311). Dublin, Ireland: Research-publishing.net. 10.14705/rpnet.2015.000350

Lamy, M.-N., & Mangenot, F. (2013). Social media-based language learning: Insights from research and practice. In M.-N. Lamy, & K. Zourou (Eds.), *Social networking for language education: New language learning and teaching environments* (pp. 197–213). Basingstoke, UK: Palgrave MacMillan. doi:10.1057/9781137023384_11

Lamy, M.-N., & Zourou, K. (Eds.). *Social networking for language education: New language learning and teaching environments*. Basingstoke, UK: Palgrave MacMillan. doi:10.1057/9781137023384

Lee, J. S. (2006). Exploring the relationship between electronic literacy and heritage language maintenance. *Language Learning & Technology, 10*(2), 93–113.

Liaw, M.-L. (2011). Review of Livemocha. *Language Learning & Technology, 15*(1), 36–40.

Lin, C.-H., Warschauer, M., & Blake, R. (2016). Language learning through social networks: Perceptions and reality. *Language Learning & Technology, 20*(1), 124–147.

Lloyd, E. (2012). Language learners' 'willingness to communicate' through Livemocha.com. *ALSIC, Apprentissage des langues et systèmes d'information et de Communication*. 15(1): *Médias sociaux et apprentissage des langues: (R)évolution?* Retrieved from http://alsic.revues.org/2415

Malerba, M. L. (2011). Social networking in language learning. In M. Ciastellardi, C. Miranda de Almeida, & C.A. Scolari (Eds.), *McLuhan galaxy Conference. Understanding Media, Today. Conference Proceedings* (pp.142-153).

Malerba, M. L. (2012). L2 Learners' informal online interactions in social network communities. Conference paper. *CALL: Using, learning, knowing*. Gothenburg. Retrieved from http://www.researchgate.net/publication/269243503

Malerba, M. L. (2015). Learner's behaviours and autonomy in and Busuu online communities. Conference paper. Retrieved from http://www.researchgate.net/publication/280730772

Orsini-Jones, M., Brick, B., & Pibworth, L. (2013). Practising language interaction via social networking sites: The expert student's perspective on personalized language learning. In B. Zou, M. Xing, Y. Wang, M. Sun, & C. H. Xiang (Eds.), *Computer-assisted foreign language teaching and learning: Technological advances* (pp. 40–53). Hershey, PA: IGI Global. doi:10.4018/978-1-4666-2821-2.ch003

Pettes Guikema, J. (2013). Software review: WeSpeke. *CALICO Journal, 30*(3), 465–471. doi:10.11139/cj.30.3.465-471

Stevenson, M. P., & Liu, M. (2010). Learning a language with Web 2.0: Exploring the use of social networking features of foreign language learning websites. *CALICO Journal, 27*(2), 233–259. doi:10.11139/cj.27.2.233-259

Van Dixhoorn, L., Loiseau, M., Mangenot, F., Potolia, A., & Zourou, K. (2010). Language learning: Resources and networks. Study operated by the network 'language learning and social media'. Retrieved http://www.elearningeuropa.info/files/LS6/Language_learning-resources_and_networks.pdf

Vesselinov, R., & Grego, J. (2016). *The Busuu efficacy study.* Retrieved from https://www.busuu.com/en/it-works/university-study

Wang, S., & Vasquez, C. (2012). Web 2.0 and second language learning: What does the research tell us? *CALICO Journal, 29*(3), pp. 412-430.

Warschauer, M. (2000). The death of cyberspace and the rebirth of CALL. *English Teachers'. Journal, 53*, 61–67.

Zourou, K., & Loiseau, M. (2013). Bridging design and language interaction and reuse in Livemocha's culture section. In M.-N. Lamy, & K. Zourou (Eds.), *Social networking for language education* (pp. 77–99). Basingstoke, UK: Palgrave Macmillan. doi:10.1057/9781137023384_5

APPENDIX

1. Site Feedback Questionnaire

Please indicate your answers in the table below.

2. Skills

In your opinion, does this site help you improve the following Spanish skills? Indicate your answers in Table 16.

3. Features

Table 15. Feedback on site design

	VERY UNSATISFIED	NEUTRAL	VERY SATISFIED
1. Ease of finding the information/learning activities	1 2 3 4 5		
2. Quality of information/learning activities	1 2 3 4 5		
3. Ease of reading the text	1 2 3 4 5		
4. Appearance of site, including colours and graphics	1 2 3 4 5		
5. Speed of pages displaying	1 2 3 4 5		
6. Fun, entertainment value	1 2 3 4 5		
7. Overall learning experience	1 2 3 4 5		
8. Ease of understanding the instructions for activities on the site	1 2 3 4 5		
9. Ease of moving around the site without getting lost	1 2 3 4 5		
10.Ease of finding contacts to practise the language with	1 2 3 4 5		

	VERY UNSATISFIED	NEUTRAL	VERY SATISFIED
1. Speaking	1 2 3 4 5		
2. Listening	1 2 3 4 5		
3. Reading	1 2 3 4 5		
4. Writing	1 2 3 4 5		
5. Grammar	1 2 3 4 5		
6. Pronunciation	1 2 3 4 5		
7. Vocabulary	1 2 3 4 5		
8. Culture	1 2 3 4 5		

Were the following features helpful to you in learning Spanish? Please indicate your answers in the table below:
Did you use any other features during the test session? YES - NO
If yes, which one? What did you think about these features?

____
____
____

4. Future Use and Perception

1. How likely are you to return to this site on your own?

No way 1 2 3 4 5 I'll probably return the next time I sit down at my computer.
Explain why you are or are not likely to return to this site.

____
____
____

2. Would you recommend this site to your friends who are learning Spanish?

No way 1 2 3 4 5 I'll definitely recommend this site.
Explain why you would or you would not recommend this site.

____
____
____

3. What do you like best about this site?

____
____
____

	Used		**Not Useful at all**	**Neutral**	**Very Useful**
1. Creating/Editing a profile	Yes	No	1 2 3 4 5		
2. Friending Native Speakers			1 2 3 4 5		
3. Reviewing vocabulary			1 2 3 4 5		
4. Posting writings			1 2 3 4 5		
5. Getting feedback from other users			1 2 3 4 5		
6. Giving feedback to other learners			1 2 3 4 5		
7. Watching pictures/videos			1 2 3 4 5		
8. Reading comments other users' posts			1 2 3 4 5		

4. What do you like least about this site?

____
____
____

5. Do you have any recommendations or comments to improve this site?

____
____
____

Chapter 5
Enhancing Writing Skills via Mobile Learning and Wikis

Ruby Vurdien
White Rose Language School, Spain

ABSTRACT

This chapter reports on how a group of advanced EFL students in a private language school in Spain employed their smartphones and wikis to create a learning environment outside their classroom context to enhance their writing skills. Twenty-one participants of C1 level downloaded the Google application on their smartphones with a view to performing their reading and vocabulary tasks prior to writing their essays on a wiki learning platform, with subsequent peer editing and feedback. The findings suggest that the participants' general overview of this novel learning experience was positive and that collaborative work on the wiki fostered negotiation of meaning and sharing knowledge, which can benefit the writing process. The smartphone was deemed a convenient tool for reading and completing vocabulary exercises as its portability permits ubiquitous learning. Peer editing and feedback are crucial for developing linguistic proficiency, thereby improving writing skills.

INTRODUCTION

Writing is one of the skills that EFL learners have to develop since it is a medium for learning other subjects and for communicating with their tutors (Kassem, 2017). However, it is a challenging skill to master for both first and foreign language students (Umar & Rathakrishnan, 2012). To assist students in developing this crucial skill, social technologies such as wikis are becoming increasingly popular in the language classroom (Kurt, 2017). As a form of computer-mediated communication, wikis can support writing instruction (Lamb, 2004), bringing renewed attention to collaborative learning (Aydin & Yildiz, 2014; Bikowsky & Vithanage, 2016) and the joint construction of texts and meaning making (Li & Zhu, 2011; Kessler & Bikowski, 2010). Students work in pairs or small groups to construct written texts such as a narrative or a class wiki (Li, 2012) after going through various stages of drafting, revising, editing and publishing. Other wiki-based studies have concentrated on students' perception of teamwork (Elola & Oskoz, 2010; Li & Zhu, 2011) and its impact on their writing (Chao & Lo, 2009). Another advantage

DOI: 10.4018/978-1-7998-1282-1.ch005

of using wikis, as reported by Chen and Brown (2012), is that students can assess, comment on their peers' writing and provide feedback, which may not be possible in face-to-face classroom settings on account of time and space constraints (Matthew & Callaway, 2009). Recently, peer feedback has become an important pedagogical tool in EFL writing (Ai, 2017), and wikis allow students to provide feedback through peer interaction, thereby fostering communication and discussion.

Despite the vast amount of research conducted in the use of wikis in second language classes, further investigation to fully examine the affordances of wikis to develop language learning would be beneficial (Li, 2012). Research involving reviewing via wikis "has just begun to scratch the surface" (Ducate *et al.*, 2011, p. 515). Consequently, in an attempt to contribute to wiki-based research, this paper describes a cross-platform blended learning approach, that is, the application of smartphones and a wiki in an EFL class project in a private language school for a semester. The purpose of this research is to give some insight into the use of wikis to enhance students' learning in an EFL context by investigating students' perceptions of learning from smartphones and wikis, as well as considering whether peer editing and feedback can help towards grammar and vocabulary accuracy.

LITERATURE REVIEW

Mobile-Assisted Vocabulary Learning

Mobile phones are regarded as "particularly useful computers that fit in a (student's) pocket, are always with (students), and are nearly always on" (Prensky, 2005, p.2). Their portability (Chen & Desnoyelles, 2013; Kukulska-Hulme, 2013) and immediacy permit ubiquitous learning (Darmi & Albion, 2014; Dashtestani, 2015), that is, students can access, share and retrieve information at their preferred time and place (Chen & Desnoyelles, 2013), thus facilitating exposure to the target content (Thornton & Houser, 2005; Chinnery, 2006).

Thornton & Houser (2005) reported that their students' knowledge of vocabulary whilst learning via the mobile phone improved more notably than that of students using paper materials. The same authors concluded that sending regular messages by mobile phone could generate the spacing effect (studying is spread out over time) (Greene, 1989), which enabled vocabulary retrieval. Additionally, Lu (2008) who explored the effectiveness of SMS vocabulary lessons on mobile phones in an EFL class in Taiwan, remarked that generally, the students adopted positive attitudes to learning in that way. Correspondingly, Hsu (2013) claimed that the majority of his students from different cultures reacted positively towards MALL, whilst Qian and Tang (2018) stated that their students used mobile devices to support formal course learning. Additionally, a designed-based research study has reported that students in China prefer to learn vocabulary on their mobile phones rather than their computer (Barth *et al.*, 2019).

Mohd Asraf and Supian (2017) examined the benefits of mobile-assisted vocabulary learning outside the classroom. Their findings revealed that the students employed online dictionaries to assist with understanding the meaning of lexical items, and video features on their phones to practise speaking and the pronunciation of new words. The students noticed an enhancement in their metacognitive skills, leading to increased learner confidence and deeper gains in vocabulary learning. Further research (Ahmad, Armarego & Sudweeks, 2017) based on MALL found that a group of migrant women's acquisition of language learner vocabulary improved, thereby increasing their confidence in communication. Furthermore, Gürkan (2018) claimed that mobile assisted language learning techniques might enhance vocabulary learning not only through reading texts, but also by using annotations that can be in the form of text, graphics, audio or video, to help learners understand the lexical meaning. His students observed that their learning experience was motivating, and that video and graphic annotations were useful. Similarly, an empirical study (Çakmak & Erçetin, 2017) investigated the effectiveness of multimedia glosses on L2 listening comprehension and incidental vocabulary learning on mobile phones. It was seen that there were important effects of access to glosses on incidental vocabulary learning, with no differences among the types of glosses.

The smart features of the smartphone enable communicative language practice for language learning by giving access to authentic content and task completion (Chinnery, 2006). Tasks should be user-friendly, sensitive to the social and cultural setting, engaging and short. If built around such guidelines, tasks on mobile devices have a lot of potential for learning (Stockwell & Hubbard, 2013). According to Thornbury (2004), words that are learned over spaced reading sessions are better retained than those that are acquired in a more isolated context. When target words appear frequently in a text and students are sufficiently capable of understanding their meaning, this increased exposure can help with memory retention (Reynolds, Wu, Liu, Kuo & Yeh, 2015). Successful acquisition and retention of vocabulary via mobile game-based learning has also been reported in another study (Chen, Liu & Huang, 2019). Despite the overall effect of mobile devices in education being better than the use of desktop computers (Sung, Chang & Liu, 2016), one of the limitations of mobile technology is the reduced screen size of the mobile phone or the cost (Ally, 2013; Stockwell, 2007), and "the often distracting environments in which they are used" (Reinders & Hubbard, 2013, p. 366). The small screen size may pose problems for students since the texts downloaded on their mobile appear differently from conventional paper texts or others on a large computer screen (Chinnery, 2006). Based on the results of his study, Stockwell (2008) also suggests that some barriers such as pedagogical, psychological and environmental factors impede the implementation of mobile learning.

Wikis and Writing Skills

Wikis encourage students to participate, collaborate and engage in writing. Creating a wiki involves several users sharing a website; pages can be edited by members themselves via a web interface (Richardson, 2006). Both individual writing and shared collaborative construction of text (Li & Zhu, 2011; Nami & Marandi, 2013) are possible. To that end, users can add to the content, generate feedback and track the changes (Liou & Lee, 2011). A wiki is regarded as a teaching tool linked to collaboration and active student engagement, while also facilitating socio-constructivist learning (Karasavvidis, 2010). Student interaction to promote negotiation of meaning (Kessler & Bikowski, 2010), peer assessment and reflection are other useful features of wikis (Karasavvidis, 2010; Lundin, 2008). These can be fostered by means of specifically designed tasks. Moreover, instructional design and practice are deemed fundamental for achieving successful outcomes when wikis are implemented in the classroom (Warschauer, 2010).

Previous studies on wikis for enhancing writing skills have revealed increased student motivation and the production of longer and better quality contributions due to the simplicity of publishing and reorganising content (Mak & Coniam, 2008; Karasavvidis, 2010; Barton & Heiman, 2012), as well as a reduction in learners' writing anxiety (Kassem, 2017). In addition, wikis support writing development not only in the planning, modifying and revising of texts, but also in the socio-cultural aspects of writing. Texts produced on wikis are considered more 'real' since students are writing in an authentic environment for their peers, who can have immediate access to their contributions. They can view and monitor their progress in writing, go back and edit their texts or consult previous assignments (Mak & Coniam, 2008). Adding, reorganising, joint knowledge building and revising content on wikis (Ducate & Lomicka, 2008) have been found to facilitate text expansion, which can result in more complex writing (Mak & Coniam, 2008). In short, wikis "stretch the input and output limits of the FL classroom by … presenting further opportunities for interactive and meaningful practices" (Elola & Oskoz, 2010, p.53).

The affordance of wikis fosters collaboration, encourages interactions and develops students' writing skills (Lundin, 2008). Due to their being 'intensively collaborative' (Godwin-Jones, 2003, p. 15), wikis have been regarded as popular platforms in collaborative writing in language classes. Hudson (2018) employed Wikispaces, an educational platform, to engage L2 students in a task-based study. The findings suggest that the students appreciated the opportunity of using wikis to assist them with their writing task and of working collaboratively. Nevertheless, it was found that not all students felt comfortable with wiki technology and its features. Furthermore, Wichadee (2013) compared summary writing skills between students collaborating on wikis and those learning in a face-to-face class. The findings suggested that the students' summary writing skills improved considerably. Hsu and Lo (2018) analysed their students' written language production on pre- and post-tests, and noted a significant effect for wiki-mediated collaborative writing on the content quality and linguistic accuracy compared to that of those who wrote their essays alone. Nonetheless, there was no apparent effect on organisation and linguistic complexity. Another study (Khoii & Arabsarhangi, 2019) involving young EFL learners reported on greater progress in the development of writing skills by means of collaborative activities on wikis.

Wikis and Peer Feedback

Several studies have reported that a considerable amount of reviewing, directed mostly at content and meaning-developing changes, occurs during wiki writing activity (Qing, 2019; Aydin & Yildiz, 2014; Kessler, 2009; Kessler *et al.*, 2012; Mak & Comiam 2008; Arnold *et al.* 2009). Notwithstanding, research conducted on feedback and reviewing in writing tasks has pointed out that untrained writers are more inclined to check their texts less frequently and at surface level, and to do very little correction without peer or tutor support. Superficial checking, for example, punctuation and spelling, predominates regardless of the writer's competence (Fitzgerald, 1987). Studies on second language writers and corrective feedback focus mainly on research concerning the influence of feedback on writing (McGrath *et al.*, 2011; Ferris, 2012). Some scholars posit that corrective feedback generally assists students irrespective of the degree of explicitness in feedback (Ferris & Roberts, 2001). Still viewpoints seem to differ regarding what, how and when errors should be corrected (Krashen, 1982; Truscott, 1998; Hyland & Hyland, 2006). Pedagogically speaking, positive feedback is deemed significant in providing "affective support to the learners" and encouraging "motivation to continue learning" (Ellis, 2009a, p. 3).

What is more, Storch (2005) mentions that students are more receptive to feedback when writing on wikis, since they feel responsible for their collaborative writing task. It has also been found that incorporating wiki as a peer feedback tool can enhance critical thinking skills (Demirbilek, 2015). However, in the case of employing more than one Web 2.0 application, such as Google Docs and wikis to facilitate peer feedback, the applications' features can influence the comments made by students (Canham, 2017). Editing in wikis is transparent because all changes are archived, thereby enabling tutors and learners to observe the progress of the writing activity. Although research (Qing, 2019) has shown that peers attempt to be friendly and supportive when providing online feedback in an open learning environment, students may feel uncomfortable and reluctant to modify their peers' texts in an open source wiki environment

(Lee, 2010). As Nami and Marandi (2013) suggest, their students would rather leave their comments in separate postings instead of editing the content of their peers' essays. Likewise, in Lund's (2008) study students' concerns were raised about non-expert editing and abuse, whilst Kessler (2009) indicated that the participants in his study showed more willingness to edit their peers' contributions rather than their own.

Kaufman and Schunn (2010), however, stress the need for peer assessment research to discover more about students' perceptions and attitudes affecting their performance. Previous studies reported that students sometimes perceive peer assessment as unfair and question peers' qualifications to review their tasks (Kaufman & Schunn, 2010; Strijbos, Narciss & Dünnebier, 2010). Furthermore, Topping (1998) maintains that the quality of peer feedback is not comparable with that of the tutor feedback, but "its immediacy, frequency, and volume compensate for this (p. 255). Strijbos *et al.* (2010) state that more specific and elaborated feedback leads to better performance and outcomes. Despite the learning effects of providing feedback being relatively obvious, peer feedback does not automatically result in meaningful learning, since it depends on the feedback quality and assessor's expertise (Van der Pol, 2008).

Last but not least, lack of linguistic competence plays an important part in peer feedback. Whilst some students are able to identify and correct errors left unattended in their peers' writings, for the less proficient ones, recognising inaccurate structures may be much simpler than replacing them with the appropriate forms (Sotoudehnamah & Pilehvari, 2016). The same authors state that students cannot be expected to acquire target structures instantly after they have been highlighted through feedback. Therefore, time is needed for students to assimilate how errors that affect the quality of a text can be amended. Hyland and Hyland (2006) remark that less proficient learners need more explicit explanations to make the necessary changes.

THEORETICAL FRAMEWORK

Peer feedback is supported by several theoretical frameworks, for example, process writing (Hyland & Hyland, 2006), collaborative learning theory and Vygotsky's concept of the Zone of Proximal Development (ZPD) (1978). Vygotsky (1978) points out that learning takes place via social interaction among learners' ZDP. Social interaction is believed to facilitate learning by bridging the gap between the students' actual and potential levels of development. Further to this, Vygotsky (1978) adds that peer interaction assists students in developing their cognitive skills and fosters their full potential. Previous literature has suggested that a wiki is a good tool for constructive learning and collaborative work (West & West, 2009). Due to its collaborative nature, a wiki has "the potential to advance and realize a collective ZPD" (Lund, 2008, p. 40) with its characteristics and affordances that are socially performed. Scaffolding is another construct to explore how students interact in a wiki environment. Miyazoe and Anderson (2010) posit that " (…) collaborative learning fostered by scaffolding – provides a main support" (p. 185) for the use of wikis in education.

With the support of peer-to-peer scaffolding and collaborative learning, a wiki is therefore conceptualised as a tool for mediated actions that engender meaningful interaction. In this particular study, learning is influenced by the students' keen participation as they "do things together, negotiate meanings, and learn from each other" (Wenger, 1998, p. 102), rather than work independently (Leong & Bodrova, 2007). Various types of peer assistance are required to develop new skills and concepts within the learners' ZPD (Deborah & Brodova, 2001). As a consequence, on the basis of this theory and the fact that the participants in the present study interacted with each other when providing corrective feedback, a social constructivist approach was adopted.

The current study aims at contributing to the existing research base by exploring students' perceptions of their actual learning experiences via the smartphone and wikis, which is consistent with their attempt to edit their peers' tasks. Therefore, the study also demonstrates the extent to which students attend to peer editing and feedback to help towards grammar and vocabulary accuracy.

Hence the following questions guided the study:

- What are the students' perceptions regarding learning vocabulary from their smartphone followed by the use of wikis to improve their writing skills?
- How can peer editing and feedback help students towards grammar and vocabulary accuracy with a view to enhancing their writing skills?

METHODOLOGY

The Project

A wiki-based project, which lasted for a semester, was designed in an EFL advanced class enrolled for a C1 Cambridge examination course with a view to assisting the students in developing their writing skills. As additional tools, smartphones were employed to aid the participants in their learning process. The participants used a Google application on their smartphones to read their newspaper articles, downloaded from the BBC and The Guardian newspaper, for content knowledge and contextual vocabulary exercises. Google forms were employed to share with the students the web link to their reading materials and the vocabulary exercises. Each exercise comprised ten questions with either True/False or multiple choice answers to check for comprehension and learn new words and expressions that could be incorporated in their essays on the wiki, the aim being to enhance their writing skills. Tasks were set on a bi-weekly basis and the students were requested to post their essays individually on the wiki after having completed their reading and vocabulary work. The essays were of a discursive nature, the students having to support their stance on the different topics with their own arguments. In total eight essays of between 220 and 260 words each were written by every participant throughout the project. Subsequent to contributions being posted on the wiki, the tutor read the texts and highlighted all grammatical and lexical inaccuracies prior to the students editing the errors and providing feedback for their respective peers. Peer editing was conducted in groups of three and these were reassigned for each task, since Arnold *et al.*'s (2009) finding showed that students complained about their peers not participating equally and poor communication within the group. Finally, corrections were checked by the tutor. Figure 1 below shows the different steps followed in the project.

Participants

Twenty-one EFL Spanish participants, who were 20-25 year-old university students at a private language school in Spain, were studying different degrees, namely, Engineering, Economics, Languages, Law, Science and Medicine. They had all been successful in their Cambridge English First examination (B2 – Common European Framework of Reference) and their common target was to raise their level for

Figure 1. The steps followed in the project

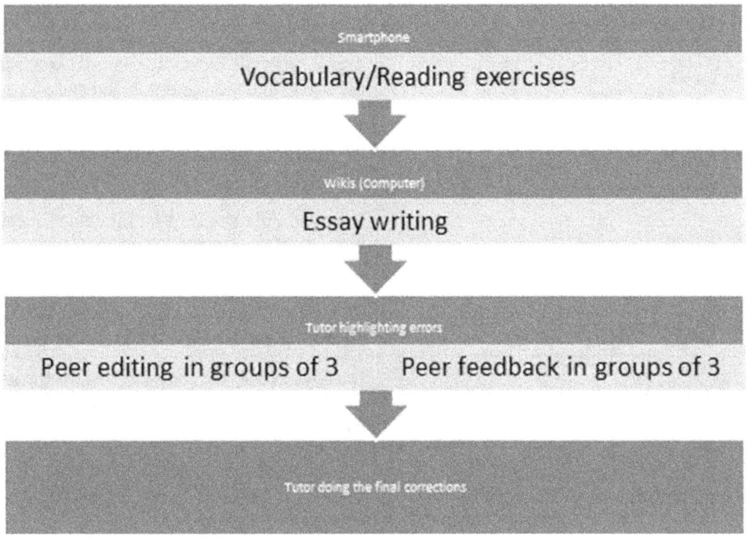

the Cambridge English Advanced examination (C1). Their writing proficiency ranged from average to good. All the participants owned a smartphone and were familiar with its use.

Online Tasks

Eight topical articles, which would rouse the students' interest, were selected from the BBC and The Guardian newspaper to prompt student engagement in the reading activity prior to posting their contributions on the wiki. Target vocabulary items were chosen in each article and exercises were devised to check comprehension so that the participants could attempt to incorporate such lexical resources in their writing tasks on the wiki. Table 1 shows the essays the students wrote upon completion of their reading and vocabulary exercises on their smartphone.

These tasks were intended to encourage the students to organise and express their views on the different subjects, which, hopefully, would be beneficial in terms of examination preparation and influential in their attaining a C1 level in the writing paper.

Figures 2 and 3 show examples of the exercises on smartphones and wikis.

DATA COLLECTION AND ANALYSIS

A qualitative and quantitative approach was adopted and data were collated from different sources; more specifically, these consisted of 168 essays published on the wiki, two questionnaires administered at the beginning and end of the project, and individual interviews conducted upon its completion. The initial questionnaire gathered information about the students' experience of using wikis and smartphones for various purposes and their expectations of the learning experience; the final questionnaire, sought to obtain additional data concerning their participation in and their perceptions of the project, as well as the benefits of learning by means of wikis and smartphones and recommendations for improvement.

Table 1. Online tasks

Newspaper articles	Essays
Pico Iyer on the art of slow travel.	Travel broadens the mind. Choose two ideas and explain which of the two is more important to you and give reasons.
Can technology identify China's top graduates?	Technology will soon replace face-to-face job interviews. Comment on the points made in the article and decide on the most important one.
Clever girls, stupid boys?	Boys and girls aim hard for the same educational goals. Discuss in terms of your own educational system. Give reasons for your answer.
How much of the world's fossil fuel can we burn?	Fossil fuel affects the global climate. Discuss the positive and negative points and what can be done to improve the situation.
Travel companies must focus on lifestyle to survive: Something to declare.	Designer brands are the best. Discuss the issue by considering the way young people dress today and how important fashion is to them.
Connecting with voters: Does being a 'normal bloke' work?	Politicians should project a different image from their normal self. Think of the way politicians behave in your country and how they can improve their image.
The philosophy of privacy: Why surveillance reduces us to objects.	The Internet has intruded on our privacy. Consider the different means that can be used to protect our privacy.
The future of learning and teaching in higher education.	How do you foresee the future of higher education in Spain? Discuss the possible changes that can take place and how they can benefit students.

Figure 2. Exercises performed on the smartphone

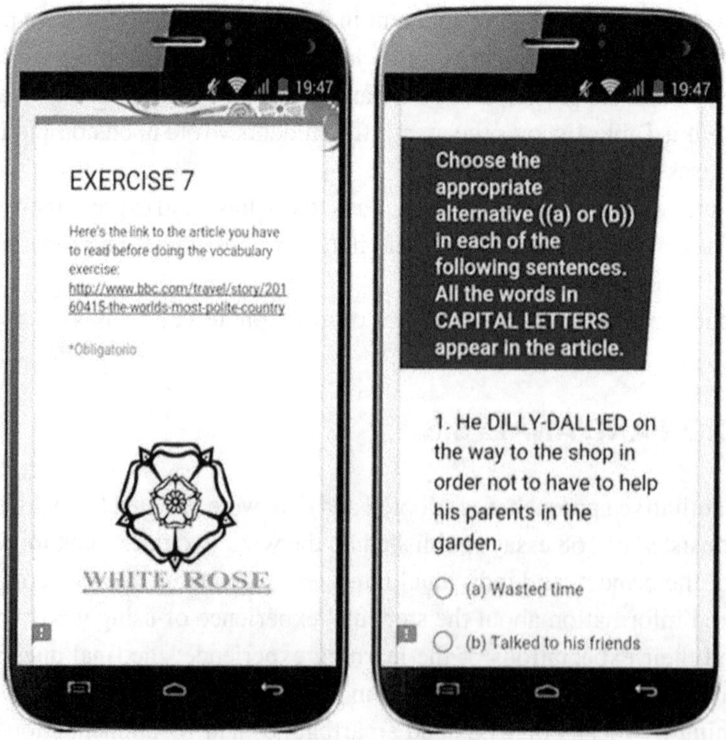

Figure 3. Essay writing on a wiki

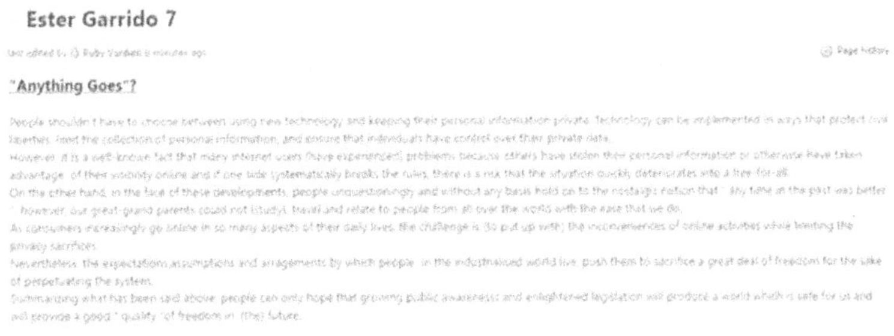

All twenty-one participants completed both questionnaires and were also interviewed. Furthermore, two separate tests (pre- and post-) were set to monitor the progress of the participants and these were graded by the teacher-researcher. The marking scale (1-5), as employed in the series of Cambridge English examinations, was based on the language criteria focusing on the use of a range of appropriate vocabulary and control and flexibility in terms of simple and complex grammatical forms.

Finally, a survey comprising twelve statements (illustrated in Tables 2 and 3) was completed by the participants for further data analysis. A five-point Likert scale ranging from 1 (strongly disagree) to 5 (strongly agree) was used to gauge the students' reactions to the project. The responses elicited from all twenty-one students corresponded to their perceptions of their learning experience and their attitudes to peer editing and feedback.

All the participants signed their consent form and were informed that they could withdraw at any time.

RESULTS AND DISCUSSION

Students' Perceptions Regarding Learning From Their Smartphones and Wikis

By analysing the students' responses in their interview, it was found that they tended to view the learning experience as positive due to their belief that they had enhanced their writing skills (Table 2, statement 6, mean = 4.25, SD = 0.70); this finding contrasts with that of Mak and Coniam's (2008), who noted that for some students writing accuracy had worsened when they participated in collaborative writing on a wiki. The students in the present research thought they had developed greater confidence in writing, which concurs with another finding (Khoii & Arabsarhangi, 2019); they had also become more proficient in linguistic accuracy, which tallies with other studies (Hsu & Lo, 2018; Wang, 2015). They admitted that the articles they read on their smartphones created the background for their writing tasks, thereby facilitating the development of arguments in their essays and the right choice of lexicon. Additionally, their confidence boosted through their interaction by sharing their individual knowledge of grammatical structures when managing text editing, a finding also apparent in another study (Hudson, 2018). Likewise, Nami and Marandi (2013) reported in their study that shared knowledge on a wiki helps students to learn beyond what they could achieve on their own. Furthermore, the results in the pre- and post- tests (Figures 4 and 5) support the students' claim. An improvement was noted in both grammatical and lexical accuracy. As shown in Figures 4 and 5, all participants had improved their scores, with a difference of 0.5-1.0 between the pre- and post- tests in both criteria, a finding which could be deemed positive. This progress could be attributed to the fact that the students had been writing for a period of time and would undoubtedly have improved to some extent. Nonetheless, the students might have paid more attention to grammatical correctness and appropriate use of the targeted vocabulary, suggesting a concern to enhance the quality of their writing. By the same token, and as pointed out in several studies (Nami & Marandi, 2013; Kuteeva, 2011; Hyland & Hyland, 2006; Elola & Oskoz, 2010), grammatical accuracy and lexical appropriateness seem to remain the main consideration for quality writing on wikis.

Reading different articles enabled the students to acquire new vocabulary (Table 2, statement 3, mean = 4.42, SD = 0.50) which, they all reported, they endeavoured to incorporate in their essays (Table 2, statement 4, mean = 3.93, SD = 0.83), their primary goal being to enhance their writing performance. Good writing requires the acquisition of different linguistic abilities including a wide range of lexical resource and syntactic expression (Aydin & Yildiz, 2014). It was, therefore, crucial for the students to gain knowledge of new vocabulary, and, in their view, contextual vocabulary acquisition via their smartphones was more meaningful than learning words out of context, which tallies with other findings (Thornbury 2004; Agca & Özdemir, 2013). In addition, apart from text-based definitions, another affordance of the mobile phone is to enable students to learn words from images, which can consolidate the learning process (Gürkan, 2018; Agca & Özdemir, 2013). Figure 6 below shows the percentage of the targeted vocabulary correctly used in the eight essays each student was requested to produce. Although, as illustrated in the figure, the percentages over the eight tasks vary, still the highest figures were observed in the last two tasks, suggesting that progress was more noticeable towards the end of the study. A possible explanation for this variation could be that they had gradually gained confidence in developing their writing skills and focusing on the target vocabulary. Nevertheless, some students commented in their interview that, despite their wider range of lexicon, using the targeted vocabulary in their writing was a challenge. This might be because they worked individually and could not discuss the pertinent choice of words with their partners. The benefits of collaborative writing on wikis, as perceived in a study (Nami & Marandi, 2013) can imply a student-centred learning context in which students become sources of orientation for each other, are responsible for their own learning and solve problems emerging throughout task completion. Conversely, another study has revealed that students preferred working on their own due to their freedom to manipulate their texts to suit their personal style (Elola & Oskoz, 2010).

In addition, they discerned this novel approach to learning as more dynamic, since they enjoyed task performance on their smartphones (Table 2, statement 1, mean = 4.04, SD = 0.64). Unlike texts in their course books, the articles were regarded as topical and more related to their area of interest. Four of them remarked in their interview that they were not accustomed to reading newspaper articles in English due to lack of motivation and time, and, therefore, appreciated this opportunity. Furthermore, the students believed that their smartphones played a pivotal role in their learning owing to their portability and ease of information sharing and retrieval, which is in line with a similar finding (Chen & Desnoyelles, 2013). Smartphones allowed for task performance outside the traditional classroom and at the students' preferred time, whilst the asynchronous nature of wikis permitted students to work at their own pace. This feature fostered by the wiki might have been a determining factor to explain why the students unanimously agreed that they spent time reading the task instructions and planning their tasks carefully (Table 2, statement 5, mean = 3.68, SD = 0.90) prior to publishing their essays; this meant drafting, editing and re-reading their work. The awareness that they were writing not only for their tutor but also for a public, their peers, stimulated them to follow this procedure. Therefore, they were capable of producing better quality work, rather than, for instance, adopting a somewhat cursory approach to completing homework tasks without checking for organisation, content or language. Correspondingly,

Goodwin-Jones (2003) posits that writing on wikis will only be successful if students are determined to earnestly follow the instructions and collaborate with each other.

Increased motivation in writing (Table 2, statement 2, mean = 3.68, SD = 0.85) was reported as they became familiarised with the subject through their reading, which was not in the event of the de-contextualised writing tasks assigned in their course book. This feeling of being motivated was also reflected in the questionnaire when the students concurred that they gradually became competent in expressing their views in their writing tasks, and were committed to their bi-weekly essay writing followed by peer revision. Accordingly, Brophy (2013) claims that students are motivated when they believe they can succeed in a given task. This finding runs counter with Lee (2010), who highlights that the choice of wiki tasks affects the student's level of engagement in collaborative writing. Wichadee (2013), however, states that knowledge sharing and collaboration are two prominent factors that help develop proficiency in essay writing on wikis.

Despite the perceived benefits of the use of the smartphone and wikis from the perspective of the students, certain challenges and limitations were revealed in the second questionnaire. Five students claimed they would rather have attended to task completion on their computer, since they complained that the smartphone screen size was not effective for such learning purposes; this constraint was identified in previous studies (Lu, 2008; Stockwell, 2007; Chinnery, 2006). Nevertheless, in Dashtestani's (2015) study, the students did not have consensus concerning such a challenge. They focused more on the high cost, lack of Internet-based facilities or the slow speed of the Internet as some of the main limitations. Another drawback students mentioned in the current research was that their smartphones did not permit them to open other windows on Google to check lexical meanings and they were compelled to guess the answers in their vocabulary exercises. This might suggest that students should not be limited to using only the smartphone technology when engaged in such activities, although portability, one of its features, allows learners to adapt learning to their own personal learning styles and preferences (Sole, Calic & Neijmann, 2010). Other mobile devices equipped with multimodal services could be recommended because these can provide effective learning (Sandberg, Maris & De Geus, 2011).

Table 2. Students' perception of their learning experience

	Mean	Median	SD
1. I liked reading the articles and performing vocabulary tasks on my Smartphone.	4.04	4	0.64
2. I was motivated to write my tasks on the wikis.	3.68	3.5	0.85
3. I learned new vocabulary in the articles I read.	4.42	4	0.50
4. I incorporated the new vocabulary in my writing tasks	3.93	4	0.83
5. I planned my writing tasks carefully because my peers read them .	3.68	4	0.90
6. I enhanced my writing skills.	4.25	4	0.70

Figure 4. Students' performance in pre- and post- tests

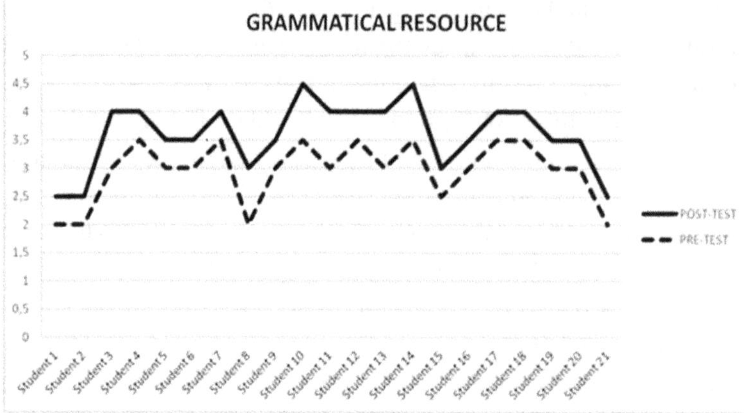

Figure 5. Students' performance in pre- and post- tests

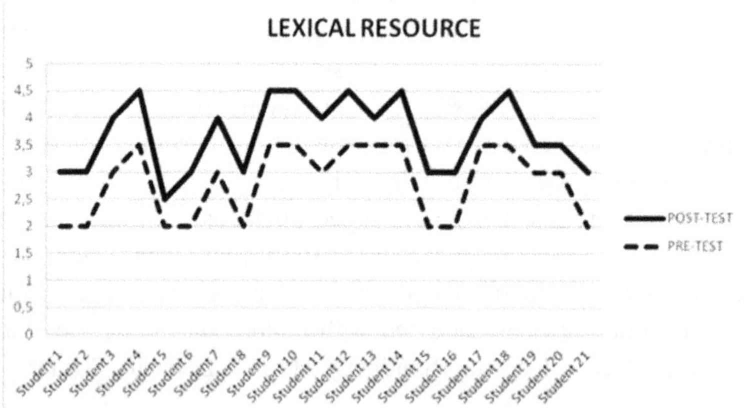

Figure 6. Percentage of vocabulary used correctly

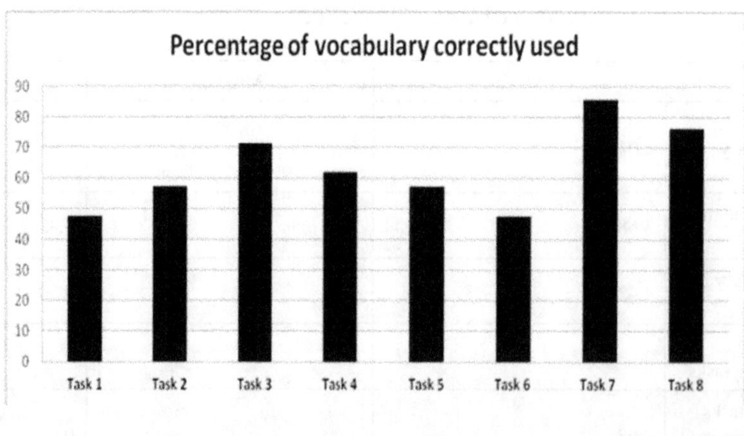

Peer Editing and Feedback for Vocabulary and Grammar Accuracy

Interestingly, the students acknowledged that they learned from correcting their peers' essays (Table 3, statement 4, mean = 4.38, SD = 0.74). By collaborating in small groups the students could discuss the errors already highlighted by their tutor and negotiate towards providing corrections. Helping students focus their attention on inaccuracies relates to the 'noticing the gap' hypothesis (Schmidt & Frota, 1986). In order that students can overcome errors, they must make conscious comparisons between their own output and the target language input. In this particular case, the students had to attend to the different types of errors made by their peers, which means that it was crucial for them to be aware of grammatical forms. Furthermore, Schmidt (1995) argued that attention is necessary for learning to take place. Consequently, focusing on their peers' corrections might enhance the students' competence in grammatical structures. Two-thirds of the errors were correctly amended in 158 essays, whilst in the remaining ten the students managed to perfectly attend to all the highlighted errors. Nevertheless, the same ungrammatical structures re-occurred in subsequent essays written by six of the students; thus suggesting that despite being engaged in the error correction task in their small groups, the students were not necessarily paying attention to the grammatical structures to be learnt, supporting Truscott's (1998) claim that students are aware of the task itself, however, this does not involve conscious attention to the details of what is to be learnt.

Task editing was considered a motivating activity (Table 3, statement 1, mean = 3.90, SD = 0.90) due to the students striving for the accuracy of their language. Their primary goal was not to repeat the mistakes in subsequent tasks. As an aid they resorted to online dictionaries, word reference and spell-checkers (Table 3, statement 5, mean = 4.15, SD = 0.91), illustrating their intention to check the mistakes thoroughly. Their engagement in collaboration to make decisions and solve problems related to editing can be regarded as a perfect medium for language development (Blake, 2008; Ortega, 2009). Likewise, Swain (2000) posits that students' engagement in helping each other deliberate on language usage during their interaction can lead to the acquisition of the target language. In the present study the students dealt with grammatical errors, such as verb tense form, prepositions, punctuation or spelling; consequently, they mentioned that they did not encounter great difficulty in editing such mistakes (Table 3, statement 3, mean =2.76, SD = 0.94), since they believed they were competent in such grammatical structures. In a different study (Kessler *et al.*, 2012) the participants corrected each other's spelling and punctuation mistakes. Nevertheless, they occasionally made changes in verb tense. According to the researchers, it is unclear why students chose to correct seemingly more simple errors in form as opposed to more complicated ones, such as verb tense. Other participants have been reported to be unconcerned about the accuracy of their partners' writing as long as the meaning was appropriately conveyed (Kessler, 2009). Likewise, students have also demonstrated a tendency to disregard grammar (Elola & Oskoz, 2010). In comparison, Kost (2011) found that students succeeded in amending grammatical errors, which is similar to the finding in the current research. The participants showed satisfaction with the way they exchanged views in their group before reaching an agreement. An important feature of employing wikis in collaborative work is that students are provided with the opportunity to notice their linguistic inaccuracies and endeavour to improve their language accuracy. In this particular study the students negotiated together to enhance their writing, a finding also emerging in other research (Hsu & Lo, 2018; Aydin and Yildiz's, 2014), which might not have been possible without the wiki technology.

Regarding meaning-related changes or content, the analysis of the students' contributions shows that the less proficient students paid less attention to meaning since they stated that they were either not skilled enough or had no knowledge of alternative answers. Contrary to this finding, previous research has revealed that students paid more heed to meaning in unstructured wiki-based and web-based collaborative writing tasks in which students focus more on content with a view to conveying a message (Aydin & Yildiz, 2014; Kessler, 2009, Arnold *et al.*, 2009; Kessler *et al.*, 2012). Aydin and Yildiz (2014) added that it was crucial for their students to negotiate meaning for task completion due to task design. Although learning via wikis promotes peer interaction and facilitates the sharing of knowledge (Hsu & Lo, 2018; Li & Zhou, 2011; Nami & Marandi, 2013), students in this study did not always possess the expertise to provide assistance in meaning-making in language accuracy. For instance, in the following phrases the inaccurate use of the targeted vocabulary was left uncorrected " … they used their bandwagon to attract their friends …; … gender stereotypes are built around by education and society …; to make the product appealing without a lot of non-fills …; there has been a deep shakeup in the working world …" In their feedback one student stated: "We couldn't correct the mistakes, because we didn´t understand the meaning of some words …", whilst another one remarked, "I thought my peer wouldn't like it if I changed some words in his essay. I would feel bad about it", a point also highlighted by Lee (2010). Consequently, to improve students' correction performance, peer editing could be attended to in class and immediate teacher feedback provided; this might help students with meaning-based activities.

Upon completion of task editing the students were requested to read their peers' feedback, which was generally thought to be helpful (Table 3, statement 2, mean = 3.87, SD = 0.90) since it prompted them to reflect on their errors and attempt to use grammatical accuracies in their subsequent tasks, thus improving their writing skills. Peer feedback, according to Rollinson (2005), "encourages a collaborative dialogue in which two-way feedback is established, and meaning is negotiated between the two parties" (p. 25). If taken seriously, feedback often leads to better understanding on the part of learners, as three of the students remarked. This concurs with Mackey's (2006) finding that his students acknowledged more noticing of language accuracy when feedback was provided, and that those who exhibited more noticing progressed faster than those who did not. Nevertheless, some of the students did not always perceive their peer feedback as effective. The comments written were sometimes vague and more explicit feedback would have been desirable. Here is an example of peer feedback:

We don't know how to correct Elena's mistakes. We think two are about grammar and one about vocabulary.

No information has been given regarding the specific mistakes, nor the decision made to solve the problem. The feedback seems to have been written in haste without being concerned about the errors to be attended to. In contrast to the above example, here is an example of more productive feedback:

Alberto, you have written a good essay. But there are some grammatical mistakes. Here are our corrections: In line 5, you should remove 'a' – We say 'research' and not 'a research' as the noun is uncountable. In line 4 it should be 'seemed' and not 'seems' because the context is past. In line 7 it should be 'easier than' and not 'easier that'. In line 15 'people considers …' should be 'people consider…' because 'people' is a plural noun. There is a spelling mistake in line 17- 'proffesion' is written with one 'f' and double 's'- 'profession'. I hope our corrections are useful.

This example illustrates the students' engagement in collaborative work to manage their problem-solving task, resulting in more specific feedback. The students, therefore, could improve their task performance after reflecting on their peer feedback. This finding supports Strijbos *et al.*'s (2010) view that elaborated feedback leads to better performance and outcomes. Despite this perceived benefit, peer feedback was limited to grammatical errors and no comments and suggestions were made on the content and organisation of the writing tasks. This corroborates similar results shown in previous research (Lin & Yang, 2011), which explains that students lack training in peer assessment and more effort and skills may be required in commenting on content and organisation.

Apart from their mutual engagement and collaboration in helping each other to improve their writing ability on the wiki, a student-centred tool, the students unanimously expressed their gratitude to their tutor for highlighting their errors prior to peer editing and the final revision of their corrections (Table 3, statement 6, mean = 4.61, SD = 0.66). They deemed teacher feedback more trustworthy and believed that without the tutor's assistance in pointing out the mistakes they would not have identified all the inaccuracies; moreover, the tutor's final revision of their editing built up their confidence. This is consistent with Lee's (2010) finding that the tutor should constantly monitor their editing process or provide them with some guidance. However, teacher feedback received opposing views from students in Lin and yang's (2011) study. Their results revealed that students felt more comfortable with their peers' comments due to their different levels of thinking.

CONCLUSION

The present study explored the effectiveness of using the smartphone as a means of reading articles with subsequent vocabulary acquisition together with a wiki for writing and collaborative editing and feedback. It has been perceived that the smartphone can empower learning anywhere and at any time, whilst allowing better access to knowledge. One significant benefit of the use of the smartphone in this particular study is that it fostered ubiquitous learning (Dashtestani, 2015; Kukulska-Hulme & Shield, 2008) since the students could perform their reading and vocabulary tasks while they were on the move, thereby adjusting to the information-savvy society in which we live. Another advantage of the smartphone is its portability (Chen & Desnoyelles, 2013; Kukulska-Hulme, 2013), which is closely linked to

Table 3. Peer editing and feedback

	Mean	Median	SD
1. I felt stimulated to edit my peers' essays.	3.90	4	0.90
2. I found my peers' feedback helpful.	3.87	4	0.90
3. I found it difficult to correct my peers' mistakes.	2.76	3	0.94
4. I learnt from correcting my peers' mistakes.	4.38	5	0.74
5. I used online tools (dictionaries, word references and spellcheckers) to correct the mistakes.	4.15	4	0.91
6. I found the tutor's final feedback helpful.	4.61	5	0.66

ubiquitous learning. This feature is perceived as a unique affordance of mobile learning. The fact that the participants reported that their phone was always on explains that students' learning style can be personalised to suit their needs (Sole, Calic & Neijmann, 2010). However, a restraint of the smartphone for reading purposes due to its small screen size, as the finding indicated, could be termed technological rather than pedagogical. The challenge may be for new technological advances to enhance the screen size so that learners can take full advantage of learning on the move.

Although the project lasted for only a semester, some progress in grammatical and lexical resources was notable. Focus on form is deemed vital for the balance of fluency and accuracy in computer-mediated instruction, a point made by Lee (2008) and Levy and Kennedy (2004). The current study has suggested that one of the main benefits of writing on a wiki is that students tend to pay more attention to form to improve language accuracy. Collaborative work on the wiki enabled the students to become more aware of linguistic inaccuracies, mainly those highlighted by the tutor, and strive hard to improve language accuracy; thereby helping them to become more proficient in linguistic accuracy, a point also made by Hsu and Lo (2018). Nonetheless, little correction was attended to in terms of meaning-making, content or organisation by those students who felt neither confident nor proficient enough to change their peers' work. Consequently, more time should be allocated to those students so that they can assimilate how errors can be edited as suggested by Sotoudehnamah & Pilehvari, (2016). More explicit explanations should be provided (Hyalnd & Hyland, 2006) to assist students to make necessary changes in their peers' work. Furthermore, as negotiating, problem-solving and decision-making (Aydin & Yildiz, 2014) play a critical role in improving language accuracy and writing ability, this resulted in confidence building (Khoii & Arabsarhangi, 2019). Increased motivation in writing was reported due to the students' familiarity with the subject of their essays through topical reading, unlike those found in their course books; the contextualised essays, therefore, led to their being more creative in writing. Peer feedback, however, was not always substantial, since some students were not equipped with the right skills for this task. Subsequently, as Lee (2010) suggests, the tutor's role is crucial in affording students guidance for effective feedback to be provided.

However, there are certain limitations in this study that should be addressed in future research. The small number of participants suggests that the results are not generalizable. Only one type of writing task, the essay, was assigned. It might be useful to explore diverse types of students' writing tasks to compare their approach to error correction and feedback. The participants worked individually when composing their essays and only collaborated for editing purposes. Exploring how students collaborate to produce their texts on wikis and attend to meaning construction might be beneficial. Moreover, there is no record of how the students discussed their views online in decision-making on error correction. This data would have been helpful. The fact that groups were reassigned for peer editing might have been disruptive for the students, making them occasionally uncomfortable. Therefore, it might be advisable to monitor how students work with the same partners. Additionally, the tutor's role was limited to only highlighting errors and revising peer editing. As such, it would be convenient to study tutor feedback and its impact on learning in future research.

Despite these limitations, this study has provided some valuable insights into how wikis and smartphones enabled students to collaborate, share knowledge and interact with each other in order to create learning contexts outside the traditional classroom. Peer editing and feedback can be deemed significant in the writing process and in fostering language accuracy. According to Brown and Adler (2008), collaborative work on wikis can benefit learners in their future professional lives. Similarly, in Blake's (2008) view, these technological tools can transform learners' learning environment by affording them the opportunity to adopt a self-learning approach and develop their ability to become critical not only of their own, but also their peers' writing (Hsu & Lo, 2018). Hence teachers should be encouraged to incorporate this novel approach into their teaching.

REFERENCES

Agca, R. K., & Özdemir, S. (2013). Foreign language vocabulary learning with mobile technologies. *Procedia: Social and Behavioral Sciences, 83*, 781–785. doi:10.1016/j.sbspro.2013.06.147

Ahmad, K. S., Armarego, J. & Sudweeks, F. (2017). The impact of utilising mobile assisted language learning (MALL) on vocabulary acquisition among migrant women English learners. *Interdisciplinary Journal of E-Skills and Lifelong learning*, 13, 38-57.

Ai, H. (2017). Graduated corrective feedback. *ReCALL, 29*(3), 313–334. doi:10.1017/S095834401700012X

Ally, M. (2013). Mobile learning: From research to practice to impact education. *Learning and Teaching in Higher Education: Gulf Perspectives, 10*(2), 1–10.

Arnold, N., Ducate, L., & Kost, C. (2009). Collaborative writing in wikis: Insights from culture projects in German classes. In L. Lomicka, & G. Lord (Eds.), *The next generation: Social networking and online collaboration in foreign language learning* (pp. 115–144). San Marcos, TX: CALICO.

Asraf, R. M., & Supian, N. (2017). Metacognition and mobile-assisted vocabulary learning. *Arab World English Journal, 8*(2), 16–35. doi:10.24093/awej/vol8no2.2

Aydin, Z., & Yildiz, S. (2014). Using wikis to promote collaborative EFL writing. *Language Learning & Technology, 18*(1), 160–180.

Barth, I., Spector-Cohen, E., Sitman, R., Jiang, G., Jiaotong, X., Liu, F., & Xu, Y. (2019). Beyond small chunks: Designing vocabulary OERs for mobile learning. *International Journal of Computer-Assisted Language Learning and Teaching, 9*(2), 79–97. doi:10.4018/IJCALLT.2019040105

Barton, M. D., & Heiman, J. R. (2012). Process, product, and potential: the archaeological assessment of collaborative, wiki-based student projects in the technical communication classroom. *Technical Communication Quarterly, 21*(1), 46–60. doi:10.1080/10572252.2012.626391

Bikowski, D., & Vithanage, R. (2016). Effects of web-based collaborative writing on individual L2 writing development. *Language Learning & Technology, 20*(1), 79–99.

Blake, R. J. (2008). *Brave new digital classroom: Technology and foreign language learning*. Washington, DC: Georgetown University Press.

Brophy, J. E. (2013). *Motivating students to learn*. New York: Routledge. doi:10.4324/9780203858318

Brown, S., & Adler, R. P. (2008). Minds on fire. Open education, the long trail, and learning 2.0. *EDUCAUSE Review, 43*(1), 16–32.

Çakmak, F., & Erçein, G. (2018). Effects of gloss type on text recall. *ReCALL, 30*(1), 24–43. doi:10.1017/S0958344017000155

Canham, N. (2017). Comparing Web 2.0 applications for peer feedback. *Conference paper: European Association of Computer Assisted language Learning*. Southampton, UK.

Chao, Y., & Lo, H. (2009). Students perceptions of Wiki-based collaborative writing for learners of English as a foreign language. *Interactive Learning Environments, 19*(4), 395–411. doi:10.1080/10494820903298662

Chen, B., & Denoyelles, A. (2013). Exploring students' mobile learning practices in higher education. *Educause Review Online*. Retrieved from http://er.educause.edu/articles/2013/10/exploring-students-practices-inhighereducationmobile-learning-

Chen, C.-M., Liu, H., & Huang, H.-B. (2019). Effects of a mobile game-based English vocabulary learning app on learners' perceptions learning performance: A case study of Taiwanese EFL learners. *ReCALL, 31*(2), 170–188. doi:10.1017/S0958344018000228

Chen, J. C., & Brown, K. L. (2012). The effects of authentic audience on English as a second language (ESL) writers: A task-based computer-mediated approach. *Computer Assisted Language Learning, 25*(5), 435–454. doi:10.1080/09588221.2011.606224

Chinnery, G. M. (2006). Emerging technologies: Going to the MALL (Mobile Assisted Language Learning). *Language Learning & Technology, 10*, 9–16.

Darmi, R., & Albion, P. (2014). A review of integrating mobile phones for language learning. In *Proceedings of the 10*th *International Conference Mobile learning IADIS'14*.

Dashtestani, R. (2015). Moving bravely towards mobile learning: Iranian students' use of mobile devices for learning English as a foreign language. *Computer Assisted Language Learning*. doi:10.1080/09588221.2015.1069360

Deborah, J. L., & Bodrova, E. (2001). Lev Vygotsky: Playing to learn. *Scholastic Early Childhood Today, 15*(4), 48.

Demirbilek, M. (2015). Social media and peer feedback: What do students really think about using wiki and Facebook as platforms for peer feedback? *Active Learning in Higher Education*, 1–14.

Ducate, L., Anderson, L., & Moreno, N. (2011). Wading through the world of wikis: An analysis of three wiki projects. *Foreign Language Annals, 44*(3), 495–524. doi:10.1111/j.1944-9720.2011.01144.x

Ducate, L. C. I, & Lomicka, L. L. (2008). Adventures in the blogosphere: From blog readers to blog writers. *Computer Assisted Language Learning, 21*(1), 9–28. doi:10.1080/09588220701865474

Ellis, R. (2009a). Corrective feedback and teacher development. *Journal of Linguistics and Language Teaching, 1*(1), 3–18.

Elola, I., & Oskoz, A. (2010). Collaborative writing: Fostering foreign language and writing conventions development. *Language Learning & Technology, 14*(3), 51–71.

Ferris, D. (2012). Written corrective feedback in second language acquisition and writing studies. *Language Teaching, 45*(04), 446–459. doi:10.1017/S0261444812000250

Ferris, D., & Roberts, B. (2001). Error feedback in L2 writing classes: How explicit does it need to be? *Journal of Second Language Writing, 10*(3), 161–184. doi:10.1016/S1060-3743(01)00039-X

Fitzgerald, J. (1987). Research on revision in writing. *Review of Educational Research*, *57*(4), 481–506. doi:10.3102/00346543057004481

Godwin-Jones, R. (2003). Blogs and wikis: Environments for on-line collaboration. *Language Learning & Technology*, *7*(2), 12–16.

Greene, R. L. (1989). Spacing effects in memory: evidence for a two-process account. *Experimental psychology: Learning, Memory, & Cognition*, *15*(3), 371–377. doi:10.1037/0278-7393.15.3.371

Gürkan, S. (2018). The effects of a mobile assisted vocabulary learning application on vocabulary learning. *Turkish Online Journal of Qualitative Inquiry*, *9*(3), 288–311. doi:10.17569/tojqi.407512

Hsu, H.-C., & Lo, Y.-F. (2018). Using wiki-mediated collaboration to foster L2 writing performance. *Language Learning & Technology*, *22*(3), 103–123.

Hsu, L. (2013). English as a foreign language learners perception of mobile assisted language learning: A crossnational study. *Computer Assisted Language Learning*, *26*(3), 197–213. doi:10.1080/09588221.2011.649485

Hudson, J. (2018). Using wikis for collaborative writing in the ELT classroom. *International Journal of Pedagogy and teacher. Education*, *2*(2), 413–426.

Hyland, K., & Hyland, F. (2006). Feedback on second language students writing. *Language Teaching*, *39*(02), 83–101. doi:10.1017/S0261444806003399

Karasavvidis, I. (2010). Wiki uses in higher education: Exploring barriers to successful implementation. *Interactive Learning Environments*, *18*(3), 219–231. doi:10.1080/10494820.2010.500514

Kassem, M. A. M. (2017). Developing business writing skills and reducing writing anxiety of EFL learners through wikis. *English Language Teaching*, *10*(3), 151–163. doi:10.5539/elt.v10n3p151

Kaufman, J. H., & Schunn, C. D. (2010). Students perceptions about peer assessment for writing: Their origin and impact on revision work. *Instructional Science*, *39*(3), 387–406. doi:10.100711251-010-9133-6

Kessler, G. (2009). Student-initiated attention to form in wiki-based collaborative writing. *Language Learning & Technology*, *13*(1), 79–95.

Kessler, G., & Bikowski, D. (2010). Developing collaborative autonomous learning abilities in computer mediated language learning: Attention to meaning among students in wiki space. *Computer Assisted Language Learning*, *23*(1), 41–58. doi:10.1080/09588220903467335

Kessler, G., Bikowski, D., & Boggs, J. (2012). Collaborative writing among second language learners in academic web-based projects. *Language Learning & Technology*, *16*(1), 91–109.

Khoii, R., & Arabsarhangi, Z. (2019). Developing young EFL learners' writing skill in wikis' collaborative environment. In M. Rahimi, & S. Rajaee (Eds.), Handbook of research on individual differences in computer-assisted language learning (pp. 345–374). Hershey, PA: IGI Global. doi:10.4018/978-1-5225-7663-1.ch067

Kost, C. R. (2011). Investigating writing strategies and revision behavior in collaborative wiki projects. *CALICO Journal*, *28*(3), 606–620. doi:10.11139/cj.28.3.606-620

Krashen, S. (1982). *Principles and practice in second language acquisition*. Oxford, UK: Pergamon.

Kukulska-Hulme, A. (2013). Mobile-assisted language learning. In C. Chapelle (Ed.), *The encyclopedia of applied linguistics* (pp. 3701–3709). New York: Wiley.

Kukulska-Hulme, A., & Shield, L. (2008). An overview of mobile assisted language learning: From content delivery to supported collaboration and interaction. *ReCALL, 20*(3), 271–289. doi:10.1017/S0958344008000335

Kurt, S. (2017). Wikis in education. How wikis are being used in the classroom. *Educational Technology, 2017*(March). Retrieved from https://educationaltechnology.net/educational-technology-articles/

Kuteeva, M. (2011). Wikis and academic writing: Changing the writer–reader relationship. *English for Specific Purposes, 30*(1), 44–57. doi:10.1016/j.esp.2010.04.007

Lamb, B. (2004). Wide open spaces wikis ready or not. *EDUCAUSE Review, 39*(5), 36–48.

Lee, L. (2008). Focus-on-form through collaborative scaffolding in expert-to-novice online interaction. *Language Learning & Technology, 12*(3), 53–72.

Lee, L. (2010). Exploring wiki-mediated collaborative writing: A case study in an elementary Spanish course. *CALICO Journal, 27*(2), 260–276. doi:10.11139/cj.27.2.260-276

Leong, D. J., & Bodrova, E. (2007). Vygotsky's zone of proximal development. *NAECS/SDE: Of Primary Interest*, 2(4).

Levy, M., & Kennedy, C. (2004). A task-cycling pedagogy using stimulated reflection and audio-conferencing in foreign language learning. *Language Learning & Technology, 8*(2), 50–69.

Li, M. (2012). Use of wikis in second/foreign language classes: A literature review. *CALL-EJ, 13*(1), 17–35.

Li, M., & Zhu, W. (2011). Patterns of computer-mediated interaction in small writing groups using wikis. *Computer Assisted Language Learning, 26*, 1–22.

Lin, W., & Yang, S. C. (2011). Exploring students' perceptions of integrating Wiki technology and peer feedback into writing courses. *English Teaching, 10*(2), 88–103.

Liou, H. C., & Lee, S. L. (2011). How wiki-based writing influences college students' collaborative and individual composing products, processes, and learners' perceptions. *International Journal of Computer-Assisted Language Learning and Teaching, 1*(1), 45–61. doi:10.4018/ijcallt.2011010104

Lu, M. (2008). Effectiveness of vocabulary learning via mobile phone. *Journal of Computer Assisted Learning, 24*(6), 515–525. doi:10.1111/j.1365-2729.2008.00289.x

Lund, A. (2008). Wikis: A collective approach to language production. *ReCALL, 20*(01), 35–54. doi:10.1017/S0958344008000414

Lundin, R. W. (2008). Teaching with Wikis: Toward a networked pedagogy. *Computers and Composition, 24*(5), 432–448. doi:10.1016/j.compcom.2008.06.001

Ma, Q. (2019). Examining the role of inter-group peer online feedback on wiki writing in an EAP context. *Computer Assisted Language Learning*, 1–20. doi:10.1080/09588221.2018.1556703

Mackey, A. (2006). Feedback, Noticing, and Instructed Second Language Learning. *Applied Linguistics*, *27*(3), 405–530. doi:10.1093/applin/ami051

Mak, B., & Coniam, D. (2008). Using wikis to enhance and develop writing skills among secondary school students in Hong Kong. *System*, *36*(3), 437–455. doi:10.1016/j.system.2008.02.004

Matthew, K. I., & Callaway, R. A. (2009). Wiki as a collaborative learning tool in a language arts methods class. *Journal of Research on Technology in Education*, *42*(1), 51–72. doi:10.1080/15391523.2009.10782541

McGrath, A. L., Taylor, A., & Pychyl, T. A. (2011). Writing helpful feedback: the influence of feedback type on students perceptions and writing performance. *The Canadian Journal for the Scholarship of Teaching and Learning*, *2*(2), 1–14. doi:10.5206/cjsotl-rcacea.2011.2.5

Miyazoe, T., & Anderson, T. (2010). Learning outcomes and students' perceptions of online writing: Simultaneous implementation of a forum, blog, and wiki in an EFL blended learning setting. *System*, *38*(2), 185–199. doi:10.1016/j.system.2010.03.006

Nami, F., & Marandi, S. S. (2013). Wikis as discussion forums: Exploring students' contribution and their attention to form. *Computer Assisted Language Learning*, *27*(6), 483–508. doi:10.1080/09588221.2013.770036

Ortega, L. (2009). *Understanding second language acquisition*. London, UK: Hodder Education.

Prensky, M. (2005). *What can you learn from a cell phone? Almost anything! The Innovate Gateway 1*. June/July.

Qian, K., & Tang, J. (2018). Researching mobile-assisted English language learning among adult distance learners in China: Emerging practices and learner perception of teacher role. *International Journal of Computer-Assisted Language Learning and Teaching*, *8*(3), 1–28. doi:10.4018/IJCALLT.2018070101

Reinders, H., & Hubbard, P. (2013). CALL and learner autonomy: Affordances and constraints. In M. Thomas, H. Reinders, & M. Warschauer (Eds.), *Contemporary Computer Assisted Language Learning* (pp. 359–375). London, UK: Continuum Books.

Reynolds, B. L., Wu, W. H., Liu, H. W., Kuo, S. Y., & Yeh, C. H. (2015). Towards a model of advanced learners' vocabulary acquisition: an investigation of12 vocabulary acquisition and retention by Taiwanese English majors. *Applied Linguistics Review*, *6*(1), 121–144. doi:10.1515/applirev-2015-0006

Richardson, W. (2006). *Blogs, wikis, podcasts, and other powerful web tools for classrooms*. Thousand Oaks, CA: Corwin Press.

Rollinson, P. (2005). Using peer feedback in the ESL writing class. *ELT Journal*, *59*(1), 23–30. doi:10.1093/elt/cci003

Sandberg, J., Maris, M., & de Geus, K. (2011). Mobile English learning: An evidence-based study with fifth graders. *Computers & Education*, *57*(1), 1334–1347. doi:10.1016/j.compedu.2011.01.015

Schmidt, R. (1995). Consciousness and foreign language learning: A tutorial on the role of attention and awareness in learning. In R. Schmidt (Ed.), *Attention and awareness in foreign language learning* (pp. 1–63). Honolulu, HI: University of Hawaii, Second Language Teaching & Curriculum Center.

Schmidt, R., & Frota, S. N. (1986). Developing basic conversational ability in a second language: A case study of an adult learner of Portuguese. In R. R. Day (Ed.), *Talking to learn: Conversation in second language acquisition* (pp. 237–326). Rowley, MA: Newbury House.

Sole, R. C., Calic, J., & Neijmann, D. (2010). A social and self-reflective approach to MALL. *ReCALL, 22*(1), 39–52. doi:10.1017/S0958344009990188

Sotoudehnamah, E., & Pilehvari, A. (2016). The impact of peer review on EFL learners' writing proficiency: Global and local aspects. *Porta Linguarum, 25*, 35–47.

Stockwell, G. (2007). Vocabulary on the move: Investigating an intelligent mobile phone-based vocabulary tutor. *Computer Assisted Language Learning, 20*(4), 365–383. doi:10.1080/09588220701745817

Stockwell, G. (2008). Investigating learner preparedness for and usage patterns of mobile learning. *ReCALL, 20*(3), 253–270. doi:10.1017/S0958344008000232

Stockwell, G., & Hubbard, P. (2013). *Some emerging principles for mobile-assisted language learning*. Monterey, CA: The International Research Foundation for English Language.

Storch, N. (2005). Collaborative writing: Product, process, and students' reflections. *Journal of Second Language Writing, 14*(3), 153–173. doi:10.1016/j.jslw.2005.05.002

Strijbos, J. W., Narciss, S., & Dünnebier, K. (2010). Peer feedback content and senders competence level in academic writing revision tasks: Are they critical for feedback perceptions and efficiency? *Learning and Instruction, 20*(4), 291–303. doi:10.1016/j.learninstruc.2009.08.008

Sung, Y. T., Chang, K. E., & Liu, T. C. (2016). The effects of integrating mobile devices with teaching and learning on students' learning performance. A meta-analysis and research synthesis. *Computers & Education, 94*, 252–275. doi:10.1016/j.compedu.2015.11.008

Swain, M. (2000). The output hypothesis and beyond. In J. Lantolf (Ed.), *Sociocultural theory and second language acquisition* (pp. 97–114). Oxford, UK: Oxford University Press.

Thornbury, S. (2004). *How to teach vocabulary*. Longman: Pearson Education Limited.

Thornton, P., & Houser, C. (2005). Using mobile phones in English education in Japan. *Journal of Computer Assisted Learning, 21*(3), 217–228. doi:10.1111/j.1365-2729.2005.00129.x

Topping, K. J. (1998). Peer assessment between students in colleges and universities. *Review of Educational Research, 68*(3), 249–276. doi:10.3102/00346543068003249

Truscott, J. (1998). Noticing in second language acquisition: a critical review. *Second Language Research, 14*(2), 103–135. doi:10.1191/026765898674803209

Umar, I., & Rathakrishnan, M. (2012). The effects of online teachers' social role and learning style on students' essay writing performance and critical thinking in a wiki environment. *Procedia: Social and Behavioral Sciences, 46*, 5730–5735. doi:10.1016/j.sbspro.2012.06.506

Van der Pol, J., Van den Berg, B. A. M., Admiraal, W. F., & Simons, P. R. J. (2008). The nature, reception, and use of online peer feedback in higher education. *Computers & Education*, *51*(4), 1804–1817. doi:10.1016/j.compedu.2008.06.001

Vygotsky, L. S. (1978). *Mind in society: The development of higher psychological processes*. Cambridge, MA: Harvard University Press.

Wang, Y.-C. (2015). Promoting collaborative writing through wikis: A new approach for advancing innovative and active learning in an ESP context. *Computer Assisted Language Learning*, *28*(6), 499–512. doi:10.1080/09588221.2014.881386

Warschauer, M. (2010). Invited commentary: new tools for teaching writing. *Language Learning & Technology*, *14*(1), 3–8.

Wenger, E. (1998). *Communities of practice: Learning, meaning, and identity*. New York, NY: Cambridge University Press. doi:10.1017/CBO9780511803932

West, J. A., & West, M. L. (2009). *Using wikis for online collaboration: The power of the read-write web*. San Francisco, CA: Jossey-Bass.

Wichadee, S. (2013). Improving students' writing ability through collaboration: A comparison between online wiki group and conventional face- to- face group. *TOJET: The Turkish Online Journal of Educational Technology*, *12*(3), 107–116.

Chapter 6
The Need to Engage With Smartphones and Social Network Sites (SNSs) at Korean Universities

Thomas E. Webster
Ewha Womans University, South Korea

ABSTRACT

The disparity between the pervasiveness of Smartphone and SNS use in Korean society, and the near absence of systematic engagement with educational approaches to their use could not be starker. This is even more perplexing in second language learning where contemporary communicative practices are underpinned by the assumption that they will enable students to apply lessons to real life circumstances outside the classroom. As found in an extensive study on teachers' perceptions and uses of technology, teachers often lack motivation to make changes owing to a lack of reliable resources, training, and professional development support. This chapter, therefore, provides the underpinning for a new theoretical approach to promoting a more culturally holistic engagement with technology, Smartphones, and SNS use at Korean universities and education in general.

INTRODUCTION

The inextricable links among language, literacy, and culture are well established in English as a second language (ESL) teaching and learning (Richards & Rogers, 2014). Drawing from this, communicative teaching practices, in particular, assume that through exposure to and practice with using authentic language in practical conditions, students will more likely be able to apply lessons learned to real life circumstances outside of the classroom (Ellis, 2012). This sociolinguistic approach to language teaching and learning finds its roots in many areas but none more so than in the pioneering work of the educational philosopher John Dewey. The collective work of scholars such as Dewey have provided the impetus for developing curriculum, syllabuses and lesson plans to reflect as closely as possible the demands of

DOI: 10.4018/978-1-7998-1282-1.ch006

reality for learners in their everyday lives. Further, given the future-orientation of the endeavor that is education, it is crucial that the future needs of students be taken equally into account. When considering the contemporary world, it is evident that computer technology has an impact on everyone's lives – even those who do not personally own a computer, smartphone, or mobile device. Governments, banks, retailers, publishers, farmers, and the food and entertainment industries as a whole are just a few examples of the overwhelming majority of areas in modern life that rely on computers to operate (Zhang & Aikman, 2007). However, the pervasiveness of technology in society has made slow progress into teaching and learning, and an understanding of proper pedagogy is still lacking (Schmid et al, 2014). There is evidence to suggest that this is primarily owing to a deficiency of reliable infrastructure and maintenance (Park & Son, 2009; Tondeur, van Keer, van Braak & Valcke, 2008; Webster & Son, 2012), an absence of teacher training and support (Kim, Kim, Lee, Spector & DeMeester, 2013), and a lack of teacher motivation for professional development (Schoepp, 2005). In Korean universities, teachers of English as a second language (ESL) and English as a foreign language (EFL) have increasingly become aware of the first two hindrances, though perhaps more reluctantly, the third. As Bates (2000) observed, these concerns can only become more pointed as society's use of technology increases: "More and more, learners will have developed extensive experience and skills in using information technologies in their nonacademic lives, and they will be increasingly unforgiving of institutions that seem out of touch with developments in the 'real' world" (p. 211).

Selwyn, in 2003, likewise pointed out, "[t]he ability to use information and communications technology (ICT) is now assumed by most commentators to be a prerequisite to living and working in the 'information society'" (pp. 99-100). And yet, in 2019, researchers continue to grapple with Larry Cuban's (2001) essential question posed nearly two decades ago: "Have teaching and learning changed as a consequence of...investment in computers and other technologies?" (p. 19).

In order to explore this issue, three of the most prevalent barriers to technology integration in Korea are first unpacked below. The importance of literacy and digital literacy are then discussed as the basis for a more holistic approach to the need to engage with technology, and in particular, smartphones at Korean universities and education in general.

BARRIERS TO TECHNOLOGY USE AT KOREAN UNIVERSITIES

The call to expand the view of the barriers to technology use beyond isolated variables to a more holistic consideration began nearly two decades ago (Becker, 2000; van den Berg, 2002). Even then, this may be seen as a natural reaction to the overabundance of specific barriers to integration that had been identified, with some implicitly suggesting that there are few factors in education which do not seem to play at least a minor role in technology integration. For instance, consider what Becker, in 2000, provided as an explanation of the necessary factors for successful integration:

However, under the right conditions – where teachers are personally comfortable and at least moderately skilled in using computers themselves, where the school's daily class schedule permits allocating time for students to use computers as part of class assignments, where enough equipment is available and convenient to permit computer activities to flow seamlessly alongside other learning tasks, and where teachers' personal philosophies support a student-centered, constructivist pedagogy that incorporates collaborative projects defined partly by student interest – computers are clearly becoming a valuable and well-functioning instructional tool. (p. 29)

Assuming that research into the barriers to integration is conducted to provide practical advice or guidelines on how to successfully integrate technology into the classroom, it is hard to imagine where interested teachers would begin to make adjustments based on the above suggestions. Therefore, a closer look at one of the most recent studies in a Korean context by Webster (2011) related to infrastructure, teacher development, and motivation for tertiary teachers of English in Korea is warranted.

Technology Infrastructure and Maintenance Issues at Korean Universities

Issues related to the barriers to technology integration are a central issue found in numerous research reports that are sometimes further investigated but just as often not (Lee, 2006). In one study by Park and Ertmer (2007), the authors correctly but misleadingly report that "First-order barriers [including lack of access to computers] are more easily recognized and easier to fix" (p. 247) than changing teachers' beliefs about technology use. While problems with access to technology may be easy to fix in theory, in practice, they can prove decidedly tenacious. As a result, most studies such as these do not explore the causes and effects of the issue even when problems with access to technology are reported by up to half of their participants, as was the case in a study by Tondeur, van Keer, van Braak and Valcke (2008). In contrast, one more recent study on teachers' perceptions and uses of technology in a Korean university English program did explore this issue (Webster, 2011). Findings indicate that the main external barrier to use stemmed from the prevalent maintenance policy referred to as "After Service" or simply "AS", which is employed by nearly all Korean businesses and institutions (Webster & Son, 2012). The AS policy, in fact, represents a reactive maintenance style often referred to as "fighting fires" since it is not preventive but instead focuses only on repairing breakdowns in the short-term (Starr et al, 2010). In Korean society, this practice is acceptable mostly owing to extremely punctual service providers who limit the duration of down time for consumers' products. However, as Webster and Son (2012) explained, the situation is more problematic at and has more significant repercussions for Korean universities:

The unfortunate result of AS maintenance policies at universities is that they inhibit reliable service that can ensure timely repairs of equipment for busy classrooms and guarantee a full and productive life for equipment that should be but as a result are not in high demand. (p. 112)

Moreover, participants in a study by Park and Son (2009) expressed the same concern, complaining that classroom computers were "very old and not in good condition" or "working slowly and need[ed] to be up-dated" (p. 93). A related issue involves the original design and setup of classroom technology. Again, teachers in the study by Webster (2011) reported irregular issues caused by poor design of the classroom technology, which proved frustrating for teachers or at times even inhibited use: "The system, the way they set it up is really awkward to use and it really, you know, it's not user-friendly for switching…ah, stuff around when you want to use different things (Rich, SSI#5)." (p. 163). Another aspect related to poor design encountered by teachers in the study by Park and Son (2009) was that "typical Korean classrooms designed for teacher-fronted lessons are not suitable for a CALL lesson" (p. 89). In other words, access to technology is an important first consideration that must be properly addressed concurrently or before other, higher-order barriers are considered.

Teacher Training and Support Issues at Korean Universities

The importance of teacher training and support is one of the most prevalent barriers addressed in the literature on technology use (Kim, Kim, Lee, Spector & DeMeester, 2013). In fact, providing consistent training and support for technology use "plays a crucial role in developing teachers' competency with computer applications" (Wozney, Vivek & Abrami, 2006, p. 175). However, Webster (2011) reported that most of the full-time teachers in his study (78.5%) did not feel that they were well-informed on how to use the resources available to them, and that only half (50.0%) had had some form of computer training in one or more of their workplaces, while the majority (82.3%) instead relied on fellow teachers for any informal training that they did receive. Moreover, despite expressed interest in technology training in the abstract, only a minority of teachers who had received some form of technology training in the past (35.7%) expressed a need for further training (Webster, 2011). However, owing to the lack of availability of training with specific or targeted goals and aims pertinent to teachers' needs, even interested teachers did not often pursue it:

Right, unless it's something short – like a 15 or 30...maximum 30-minute presentation – that (sic) I can bear with it, if it's a little slow. But if it's beyond that, it's just like, okay, I can use my time in a better way. (Stephen, SSI#8) (Webster, 2011, p. 141)

In another study conducted at secondary schools in Korea, teachers expressed a similar need for basic technology training that was best provided through in-service training courses (Park & Son, 2009). This was echoed and extended in a study by Ertmer and Park (n.d.), which found that teachers who engaged in "hands-on activities with a variety of examples, group work and PBL [problem-based learning] modeling activities" (p. 15) were able to gain practical insights into implementing student-centered activities using technology in classroom settings.

Teacher Motivation for Professional Development in Technology Use at Korean Universities

Teacher motivation for technology training as it relates to other professional development experiences and desires can be difficult to isolate and study (Schoepp, 2005). Kelchtermans (1996, as cited in van den Berg, 2002) put forward a comprehensive conception of "professional self-understanding" that stressed professional development as inextricably linked with teachers' professional lives such that technology decisions are made with the same fundamental considerations as any other classroom or professional decision. For instance, many teachers in Webster's (2011) study had begun their careers in other areas such as engineering or law but once inspired through experience in teaching English, sought to develop their credentials in language teaching owing chiefly to their sense of professionalism and self-efficacy:

I mean, I have a bachelor of commerce, and a JD law degree; a [Certification in English Language Teaching to Adults] CELTA, a [Degree in English Language Teaching to Adults] DELTA, and a MA-TESOL - Education is necessary to be competent (Sophie, SSI#13) (p. 178)

However, in the same study, teachers also acknowledged that they did not always see the practical use of technology, or value technology training enough to outweigh other more important needs:

Although I can't see just with the computer system what could...be done with a class of 35 with one computer and a screen. (Sophie, SSI#13) (Webster, 2011, p. 139)

I wish I had that knowledge, but I don't wish that strongly enough to be able to sacrifice something else in my life to make time to do that. (Russ, SSI#4) (Webster, 2011, p. 141)

The adverse repercussions of this lack of motivation to learn technology become more apparent when considering that the majority of teachers in the study (64.7%) stated that their students knew more about using computers than they did (Webster, 2011). As mentioned above, teachers can lack motivation for professional development when they have not had hands-on training that would otherwise enable them to realize the practical benefits and potential of technology use (Park & Son, 2009; Webster, 2011). Further, interestingly, Baek, Jung, and Kim (2008) in a study of 266 elementary and middle school teachers in Korea found that teachers who had had some experience using technology were more likely to employ it in their classrooms owing to external pressures. However, teachers in the study who had had little or no experience were more likely to use technology by choice. The researchers explain this apparent anomaly by pointing out teachers' adherence to governmental policies despite lack of conviction in its efficacy in use (Baek, Jung & Kim, 2008).

The effect of Korean faculty feeling pressure to use technology without having confidence in its benefits for classroom learning was also found to a lesser degree in Webster's (2011) study. Most Korean part-timers in the study (65%) felt that employing computers in the classroom was more work, while nearly half (45%) did not feel that computers performed any tasks better than more traditional means. However, almost all (80%) felt that computers and LCD projectors were an essential part of the classroom resources, while three quarters (75%) also agreed that all teachers will one day have to use computers for instructional purposes. Finally, as most part-time instructors (65%) and all full-time instructors (100%) agreed that computers are changing the skills that students need to be successful in life, it was telling that despite most of the full-timers (57.1%) saying that they did not regularly attend teacher development opportunities such as conferences which include technology training, a majority (71.4%) said that they were nevertheless satisfied with their knowledge and qualifications (Webster, 2011).

CULTURE, CRITICAL THINKING, AND DIGITAL LITERACY

Most of the barriers to and controversy surrounding the use of technology in the classroom can be reduced to a debate between two fundamental positions with various permutations: those who see technology as a useful tool that can make learning more efficient, interesting, and authentic; and, those who see it as an invasive or distracting dalliance without efficacy made worse by the high cost. Although there is some truth-value to both views, the underpinning assumption in the either/or dichotomy is a fallacious one. In fact, the commonly-held belief among supporters of technology use that "[a]fter all, technology is a tool, and as such it should be selected because it is the best tool for the job" (Murphy, DePasquale & McNamara, 2003, p. 2) is selling the real potential of technology short in such a way as to provide an unintended bulwark for opposition. Technology should not be seen merely as a tool – useful or otherwise – to perpetuating traditional learning approaches and techniques but more as integral to an educational experience that serves as a bridge between classroom learning and students' lives. As Klopfer, Osterweil, Groff and Haas (2009) express,

...there's a sharp disconnect between the way students are taught in school and the way the outside world approaches socialization, meaning-making, and accomplishment. It is critical that education not only seek to mitigate this disconnect in order to make these two 'worlds' more seamless, but of course also to leverage the power of these emerging technologies for instructional gain. (p. 3)

In fact, the impetus for attempting a unified connection between students' lives and their learning was best made by the American philosopher and educational reformer, John Dewey over a hundred years ago. He stressed that many well-intended curriculums, syllabuses and teachers inadvertently hinder the educational potential of their endeavors by not maintaining the crucial underpinning of relevance to students' lives. To make the case for why engagement with new technologies in education is warranted, we need to consider the educative value of the "outside world", and the necessary common threads of critical thinking and literacy relevant to both schooling and everyday living for students.

Cultural Complexity

Although largely based on anecdotal evidence, Johnson's (2005) thesis that participating in today's popular culture is becoming "more sophisticated, demanding more cognitive engagement with each passing year" (p. XV) seems nevertheless valid. However, more tentative is his belief that this process is making young people smarter. While this may also prove to be true, the question that remains to be demonstrated is whether this more complex engagement equates to smarter people or simply a society of individuals adapted to a more intricate culture (Robson, 2016). Similarly, Greenfeld (2014) worries that this internet-based complexity is implicitly conditioning us to form our opinions on skimmed through headlines, memes, and second-hand accounts of stories. Owing to the overwhelming amount of and complexity in information that we are exposed to every day, in this view, few end up taking the time to read any story beyond "mining the data" to be used for grist for subsequent conversations. By doing so, we have in essence, "outsourced our opinions to this loop of data" (Greenfeld, 2014, para. 13). Watching the ease and skill with which Korean university students these days use their "smartphones" to do short message service (SMS) chatting with friends or to navigate various forms of media via the Internet while on the way to classrooms is certainly testament to their skill at multitasking if not the mining that Greenfeld speaks of. However, as expressed by scholars such as Sherry Turkle (2011), the ubiquity of technology in everyday culture and life can have serious psychological and sociological implications that should be critically assessed by students, teachers, and society as a whole.

Critical Thinking and Digital Literacy

Critical thinking is an iterative process that involves the logical and open-minded assessment of information based on evidence. It is also often directly equated to success in the rapidly advancing demands of contemporary life (Marin & Halpern, 2011). Moreover, explicit teaching of critical thinking has shown to have direct benefits for students in their everyday decision-making. However, debate continues on how best to teach critical thinking skills effectively (Marin & Halpern, 2011). One framework for teaching critical thinking skills by van Gelder (2005) involves understanding of and approaches to six basic points: patience, practice, application, practical underpinning, creativity in problem-solving, and recognizing confirmation biases. Although there are numerous other critical thinking frameworks and assessment measures available online through sources such as the *Foundation for Critical Thinking*, and the *Reasoninglab*, the explicit and practical teaching of critical thinking skills in some form is crucial for transferring academic learning and student decision-making in to real life.

In terms of literacy, the United Nations Educational, Scientific and Cultural Organization (UNESCO, 2004) stressed that it is an evolving concept involving the ability to understand and communicate in written text for different purposes and situations. Explicit in this understanding is the notion that to be literate involves a practical, plural idea determined by people's communicative needs in the real world. They further emphasize the benefits of being literate as having: self-esteem; a sense of empowerment and participation; the ability to communicate; and, the recognition of cultural identity and diversity (UNESCO, 2004). This modern conception is based on the work of various literacy scholars such as Freire (1972, as cited in UNESCO, 2004) who emphasized the functional aspects of learning to read and write in order to encourage the learner to "question why things are the way they are and to undertake changing them for the better" (p. 9). Likewise, Gillmor (2008) developed a set of "Principles of a New Media Literacy" for consuming and creating information that are based on an application of critical thinking skills to new digital media sources and information. For consuming media, he suggests five "common sense principles": be skeptical of everything, recognizing different levels of credibility, avoiding confirmation biases (similar to van Gelder's [2005] sixth lesson of belief preservation above), asking many questions, and understanding how media works.

THE NEED TO ENGAGE WITH SMARTPHONES AND SOCIAL NETWORK SITES (SNSs) AT KOREAN UNIVERSITIES

Access to the Internet was considered so fundamental that "in 2016 the United Nations passed a nonbinding resolution to make disruption of Internet access a violation of human rights" (Pew, 2018). However, there is also a significant and persistent gap on Internet use between young and old, as well as educated and uneducated in all countries surveyed (Pew, 2018). As Palfrey and Gasser (2008) described in their book *Born digital: Understanding the first generation of digital natives*, anyone born after 1980 in developed countries can be referred to as "digital natives". They have had access to networked digital technologies for their entire lives, and unlike older "digital immigrants", live so much of their lives online that they do not innately separate their digital lives from their real lives. Moreover, digital natives share some fundamental lifestyle characteristics that can be thought of as representing a sea change in how social interactions take place:

They are joined by a set of common practices, including the amount of time they spend using digital technologies, their tendency to multitask, their tendency to express themselves and relate to one another in ways mediated by digital technologies, and their pattern of using the technologies to access and use information and create new knowledge and art forms. For these young people, new digital technologies – computers, cell phones, Sidekicks – are primary mediators of human-to-human connections. (Palfrey & Gasser, 2008, p. 4)

In the most recent report by the Pew Research Center (2019), by the end of 2018, global ownership of mobile devices continued to grow, with more than half of the five billion current users employing smartphones. In South Korea, the ownership rate of smartphones is an astounding 95% of the population with the remaining five percent also relying on some other form of mobile device (Pew, 2019). In terms of adult use of social networking sites (SNSs) such as Twitter, Instagram, and Facebook, both Israel and South Korea top the list of countries in the world, with 77% and 76%, respectively (Pew, 2019). However, surprisingly, emerging economies on the whole demonstrate an almost equal level of social media use with advanced economies despite having considerably lower rates of smartphone ownership (Pew, 2019). And although advanced economies such as South Korea continue to dominate emerging economies, the latter have seen smartphone adoption rates growing at a much greater pace, particularly among those 35 and under in age (Pew, 2019).

As a group, college students throughout the world have been rapid adopters of cell phone technology (Smith, Rainie, & Zickuhr, 2011), and make up 70 to 90 percent of Facebook users worldwide (Dahlstrom, de Boor, Grunwald, & Vockley, 2011; Lenhart, Purcell, Smith, & Zickuhr, 2010). Needless to say, smartphones and social media use are pervasive among university students throughout the world, but to what purpose they are put is an important consideration. To unpack how smartphones and social media are affecting students internationally and in Korea, an overview of this area is first presented below followed by a closer look at some of the benefits and drawbacks for use in education and their implications.

Background on and Attitudes Toward Smartphones and SNSs

As can be inferred above, the initial rush to integrate technology into education in the mid to late 1980s was judged by many scholars such as Larry Cuban (1986; 2000), and Henry Jay Becker (2000) to have been mostly a failure. Arguably, this was in large part owing to an over-emphasis on providing access to computers for as many students as possible, while neglecting proper pedagogical planning, training, and support for teachers and administrations. This culminated in an outcry to lessen the inequality of the "digital divide", which according to the Organization for Economic Co-operation and Development (OECD) unfairly denied individuals, households, businesses, and even geographic regions access and opportunities for using technology and the Internet (OECD, 2001). In Korea, trillions of Won were spent on information technology and communications (ICT)-related initiatives with the simple, but in hindsight profoundly wasteful approach of purchasing and provisioning as many schools as possible with the latest technologies without developing comprehensive plans for pedagogical use, necessary support, and required maintenance (Webster, 2011; Webster & Son, 2015).

Fast-forward to the invention of modern Smartphones, and subsequent widespread use of social networking sites (SNSs) from 2006-2008, and the debate over the effects of technology use in general and in education in particular shifted considerably though the sides remain essentially the same. That is, the ubiquitous, 24-hour availability of the Internet and SNSs afforded by Smartphones and other mobile devices can either be seen as a boon for learning and communication or a blight to essential educational foundations. Once again, South Korea is in the spotlight in this debate owing to the high demands placed on its adolescents students who on average devote "7 hours, 50 minutes per day [on study], which was much longer than that of other countries, which ranged from 3 to 6 hours" (Lee et al, 2018, p. 296).

The Benefits of Smartphones and SNSs in Education

For adolescents, the benefits of using mobile-, cell-, and smart- phones range from providing entertainment and the maintenance of interpersonal relationships to a fundamental means of maintaining self-identity and autonomy (Lee et al, 2018; Oksman & Turtianinen, 2004). Tertiary students likewise mostly use smartphones for texting friends and family, entertainment, or calling friends (Boumosleh &

Jaalouk, 2018), or educationally, to search for information on the Internet, access university portal sites, or exchange emails about school-related functions (Tossell, Kortum, Shepard, Rahmati & Zhong, 2015). In fact, mobile phones for these students "are an integral part of college life and culture. Even a casual observation of today's college students will reveal cell phones being used, both overtly and covertly, in every possible campus setting, including the classroom" (Leep, Barkley & Karpinski, 2015, p.1). Although, notably, it is also clear that a majority of students think of and use their phones for fun. A study by Feng, Wong, Y.K., Wong, L.Y., and Hossain (2019) indicated that 75% of students employed smartphones and the Internet mostly for entertainment purposes. Regarding SNSs, college students' opinions about and uses of various platforms have changed with time, but the most popular internationally usually include Facebook, Instagram, Twitter, WhatsApp and Snapchat, while local favorites find niche markets such as WeChat and Weibo in China, and Kakaostory and Band in South Korea (DeGennaro, T., 2019; Kim, H. J., Min, J.Y., Min, K. B., Lee, T. J., & Yoo, S. H., 2018; Lee, S. Y., Kim, M. W., McDonough, I., Mendoza, J. & Kim, M. S., 2017).

One study in Brazil characterized the multifarious benefits of using various SNS platforms in the following way:

WhatsApp is used to share quick information with close friends and family; Facebook is used to divulge content which they want to disseminate widely; Instagram is used to post careful and stylized constructed visual portraits of everyday life; Twitter is used to get news and comment about it; and Snapchat is for fun instantaneous communication with close friends (Boczkowski, Matassi, & Mitchelstein, 2018, p. 255).

Evident in the above study and internationally, is the fact that the popularity of SNSs "are primarily organized around people, not interests" (Boyd & Ellison, 2008, p. 219), and as such can be powerful forms of interpersonal social reform. In Korea, for instance, SNSs like Twitter can play a central role in mitigating the restraints of the overarching hierarchy imposed by traditional adherence to Confucian principles. As D.H. Lee (2013) expresses:

Traditionally, Koreans have emphasized personal connections based on school relationships, regionalism, and kinship. Personal connections, which are called 'Yeonjul', constitute an important condition for building up an individual's social status, sustaining a group's solidarity and fraternity, and affecting people's social lives [and therefore, significantly]...Twitter may provide individuals with a tool to widen personal networks beyond school relations, regionalism, and kinship and to share ideas and experiences through these networks (Yee, 2000; Kim 2003). (p. 277)

Beyond providing opportunities for negating issues related to social position, SNSs like Twitter can also promote connections that are "privately public" by allowing users to anonymously share intimate feelings about being "overwhelmed with burdensome social relations in Korean society" (Lee, D. H., 2013, p. 279). Moreover, a growing number of pedagogically-based smartphone applications and online tools are becoming available to help connect language teachers and learners through interactive feedback (Caruso, Fraschini, & Kuuse, 2019), curriculum and social communication applications (Zou, Li & Li, 2018), and even in creating virtual learning environments (Lawrence & Ahmed, 2018). In short, given the fact that Smartphones and SNSs are an essential part of college students' lives, and have demonstrable benefits for improving social connections and even the social structures that education is based upon, it seems confounding as to why there is a growing trend to restrict or ban their use in the classroom (Brooker, 2019).

The Drawbacks of Smartphones and SNSs in Education

Directly relevant to the knowledge that students are now "digital natives" (Palfrey & Gasser, 2008), the idea that Smartphone use should be considered addictive has continued to be pervasive, with one recent study by O'Donnell and Epstein (2019) even concluding that for the first time in research concerning college students, "smartphone use is more reinforcing than food" (p. 130). That is, incredibly, students in the study after "not having eaten for at least three hours, and not using a smartphone for two hours, individuals were still more motivated to work toward gaining portions of smartphone use than food" (O'Donnell & Epstein, 2019, p. 130). This presents a perplexing problem for education: students are born to use technology and Smartphones, but perhaps more for fun than study (Barkley & Lepp, 2013; Lepp, Barkley & Karpinski, 2015), while the benefits of use have not been agreed upon or confirmed. Coupled with the association of Smartphones with leisure – and even simply filling idle time (Matthews, Pierce & Tang, 2009; Tossell, 2012; Tossell, Kortum, Shepard, Rahmati & Zhong, 2015), the equally ubiquitous use of SNSs make identifying distinct effects of Smartphone use in education challenging. Many of the most recent studies on this topic have focused more on psychological factors of the students such as addictive risk factors and related lifestyle tendencies (Boumosleh & Jaalouk, 2018; Hawi & Samaha, 2016; Lee, D. H., 2013; Lee, J. W. et al, 2018; Lepp, Barkley & Karpinski, 2015).

Among the many factors studied, some of the most commonly identified negative effects of Smartphone and SNS use include distraction from study and overuse of multitasking, lower academic performance including fragmented learning styles and lower overall GPA, Cyberbullying, increased stress, lower exercise, sleep deprivation, and even associations with depression, smoking, increased family conflicts, and alcohol abuse. In terms of distraction, a study by Lepp, Barkley and Karpinski (2015) found that participants typically became distracted by media such as Facebook and texting "after less than six minutes of studying" (p. 2). This reinforced the findings of a study by etextbook seller CourseSmart and Wakefield Research that found that 38% of college students couldn't even go 10 minutes without using technology (Kessler, 2011). The flipside to Smartphone use for education is its seemingly boundless array of potential resources. However, as Tossell, Kortum, Shepard, Rahmati and Zhong (2015) found, "[w]hile the ubiquitous access to information and communication may prove valuable in specific situations, these situations may be so limited as to be inconsequential compared with the distractive power of the mobile platform" (p. 722).

Another interconnected mitigating factor for educational use of Smartphones and SNSs relates to what Sweller (1988; 1994) termed "cognitive load theory", and Salvucci and Taatgen (2008) described as the theory of "threaded cognition". Owing to the complexity of modern society, including the over-abundance of information available through technology, the processing power of humans is frequently exceeded, necessitating the use of multitasking as a feature of rather than as a fix for any shortcomings. In other words, we rely more and more on multitasking as a coping mechanism, and thereby sacrifice deep learning for more shallow, but wider understanding of an array of information. However, this necessary implicit skill for digital natives (Palfrey & Gasser, 2008) often leads to over-curated (see functional silo syndrome) lives and learning, lower scores on follow-up tests compared with non-multi-taskers (Lepp, Barkley, & Karpinski, 2015), and fragmented learning (Tossell, Kortum, Shepard, Rahmati & Zhong, 2015).

Further, Feng, Wong, Y.K., Wong, L.Y., and Hossain (2019)'s major finding was that having a high frequency of use, and larger number of Facebook friends had a negative influence on students' academic achievement. This was consistent with previous research showing educational issues related to overuse of Facebook and other SNSs (Boumosleh & Jaalouk, 2018; Junco, 2012; Karpinski, Kirschner, Ozer, Mellott, & Ochwo, 2013; Ravizza, Hambrick, & Fenn, 2014; Stollak, Vanderberg, Burklund, & Weiss, 2011). However, underpinning the influence of SNSs are important psychological factors such as perceived risk of Smartphone and SNS addiction. Although as of 2018, Smartphone and SNS were not listed on the Diagnostic and Statistical Manual of Mental Disorder (DSM-5), which is the standard for making psychiatric diagnoses, many adverse effects have been identified in various studies. For instance, Hawi and Samaha (2016) confirmed through binary logistic regression that students at high risk of Smartphone addiction were "less likely to achieve distinctive GPAs" (p. 87). This result confirmed the causal effects of high smartphone use and lessening learning commitments associated with lower GPAs found in two earlier studies (Junco and Cotton, 2012; Kim, Tak, & Lee, 2010), as well as two later studies (Boumosleh & Jaalouk, 2018; Lee et al, 2018). In South Korea in particular where Korean K-12 students have high demands on their time owing to heavy schoolwork and fierce competition for grades and jobs, an array of problems are common such as cyberbullying, increased stress, lower levels and frequency of exercise, irregular sleep patterns, and depression (Lee et al, 2018). Moreover, a new study of 4,512 Korean adolescents found that of the 338 who were identified as high risk on the Korean smart addiction scale (SAS), "more likely to have significant symptoms of depression, anxiety, ADHD, and to use tobacco and alcohol compared to those in the normal group" (Kim, S. G. et al, 2019, p. 5). Likewise, these issues were also found in a study of U.S. college students, including issues with smoking and excessive alcohol use (Lepp, Barkley, & Karpinski, 2015). On the whole, there seems to be a growing consensus that Smartphone and SNS use are detrimental to academic performance:

As such, the negative relationship between cell phone use and academic performance identified here could be attributed to students' decreased attention while studying or a diminished amount of time dedicated to uninterrupted studying. Indeed, a similar argument has been proffered to explain the negative relationship between general social-networking site use or Facebook use and academic performance (Karpinski et al., 2013; Kirschner & Karpinski, 2010). (Lepp, Barkley & Karpinski, 2015, p. 7)

Implications of Smartphone and SNS Use

In South Korea, where the existence of digital natives goes without saying, Korean officials and businesses have become aware of the real and potential for profit involved with Smartphone and SNS use, and are increasingly learning to efficiently mine the exchange of data. As Seo Kang-soo, President of the Korea Database Agency (KODB) expressed, "Data will become the world's newfound natural resource. If someone should ask me in the distant future what resources had driven the Korean economy in the 21st century…my answer would be 'data'" (Kim, 2014, p. 18). An equal (if somewhat hypocritical) concern and investment in data security and protection by banks, credit card companies and telecommunications operators have run parallel to these firms development of digital data mining tools for commercial purposes (Kang, 2014). The clear underpinning in all of these developments is that the use of and commercial investment in information and communication technologies (ICTs) primarily tethered to the Internet underpin nearly all aspects of contemporary life, and no more so than for students in South Korea.

It is perhaps not surprising then when, as alluded to above, many teachers of English at Korean universities believe that their students are more experienced at using new technologies than they are (Webster, 2011). However, this is not to say that students are consequently more adept at using them – especially for educational purposes. As a developer for Chrome at Google expressed, "Kids are very knowledgeable as consumers, but they don't necessarily know how the technologies work" (Murray, 2011, photo caption). This dovetails with the worry that the progress of modern society is making life more cognitively complex but not necessarily making citizens smarter (Robson, 2016). In fact, more and more researchers are finding that the pervasiveness of technology is having a decidedly negative effect not only on citizens' and students' intelligence, but also on their achievement, sociability, and sense of well-being (Yeboah & Ewur, 2014). This has led some teachers to sound alarms over the mounting problems in classrooms and to suggest or implement measures to limit or restrict access during lessons. One common response often found in South Korea is for teachers to politely ask their university students to turn off all devices upon entering the classroom (Webster, 2011). At some public schools in South Korea, teachers simply collect mobile devices from their students during school hours (Nam, 2013). In a more extreme measure, Korean officials in Seoul began installing an app called "iSmartKeeper" on students' smartphones in at least 11 public schools, which allows teachers to control or limit access during (and at times, after) classes (Souppouris & Jang, 2014). The app uses a "GPS geofencing" function that can locate students' positions in or out of class and automatically restrict functions or use when they enter school grounds or classrooms. The app additionally offers parents tools to control these utilities out of school if desired. However, apparently on at least one occasion, students learned how to circumvent the app, which led officials to lock down students' phones for hours even after they had left school (Souppouris & Jang, 2014).

Moreover, the Korean government likewise warned that 1 in 5 students were addicted to smartphones, as they had spent more than seven hours a day using them and had begun "experiencing symptoms such as anxiety, insomnia and depression when cut off from the device" (Nam, 2013, para. 4). As one possible solution, Government officials considered extending a current midnight curfew on computer use for children under16 years of age to include smartphone gaming software restrictions (Cain, 2014). Psychologist David Greenfield acknowledged the consensus, and further related that receiving email, in particular gives a form of "variable ratio reinforcement" (Doucleff & Aubrey, 2018, para. 11), whereby the receiver never knows when she or he will get a satisfying email and so checks over and over again like a compulsive gambler playing a slot machine.

Conversely, despite all of the portents about these "addictions", two other psychologists have taken more uniquely broader views of the issue. In 2008, John Grohol stated that SMS and texting addictions were no more of a problem than those predicted for but largely unrealized with radio or television addictions. He went on to mock use of the term "Internet addiction disorder" by suggesting that the researchers who coined it had merely appropriated the symptoms for pathological gambling and self-selected a sample of people to study who believed that they used the Internet excessively. In 2018, Grohol renewed his criticism through a large study of 1,319 Britons that revealed that, in fact, only 18 people had clinical "Internet addiction", though the study concluded that "over-engaging in websites…might be linked to psychological disorders like depression and addiction" (para. 3). Moreover, Turkle (2011) judged that the problem is indeed real and has serious repercussions but that it should not be considered as an "addiction" for a more instrumental reason:

It is, of course, tempting to talk about all of this in terms of addiction...But however apt the metaphor, we can ill afford the luxury of using it. Talking about addiction subverts our best thinking because it suggests that if there are problems, there is only one solution. To combat addiction, you have to discard the addicting substance. But we are not going to "get rid" of the Internet. We will not go "cold turkey" or forbid cell phones to our children. We are not going to stop the music or go back to television as the family hearth. (pp. 293-294)

The key, she believes to addressing this pressing issue lies in reestablishing basic interpersonal skills such as restoring good manners by talking with colleagues, friends and family while concurrently turning off the devices while in the company of others. She believes that it is "time to look again toward the virtues of solitude, deliberateness, and living fully in the moment" (Turkle, 2011, p. 296). Turkle (2011) ends her book by positing that by not addressing what new technologies mean in our lives, we have essentially become the human guinea pigs in our own experiments, which has resulted in a denigrating need for the devices, which keep us busy rather than satisfied.

In terms of education, it is here where the crux of this paper lies. By not properly engaging with technology including Smartphones and SNSs in education, we have not only allowed a festering social problem to propagate, but have most poignantly failed our essential mission as educators. That is, our primary mission is not to transmit cloistered postulates of learning to a new generation but to kindle students' curiosity, critical thinking skills, and sense of wonder at the increasingly digital world in which we all live in and will increasingly inhabit in the future. Consider the fact that an overwhelming majority of people in modern societies owns and relies on smartphones and yet an equally overwhelming majority has never been taught about the benefits and dangers of their use (imagine if smartphones were powerful sports cars!). Further, it is a considerable paradox that universities as esteemed as Harvard College continue to express the long-held desire for "the advancement and education of youth...[as a] foundation upon which self-reliance and habits of lifelong learning are built" (Lewis, 1997, para. 3), and yet in 2018 continue to sequester technology and digital issues into specialized vocationally-oriented courses ranging from science to art. Parents have additionally come to assume the desire for use of new technologies in learning, but this has not been realized in classrooms owing to various institutional logistics and restrictions (Hudson, 2014). As Attwell and Hughes (2010) express, this has led to a growing concern that formal education is quickly becoming obsolete.

This viability concern at universities has also been stated in purely economic terms in a UNESCO publication, which warns that, "[a]t the political level, the ideology of detachment of university degrees and their academic curricula from the labour markets can be regarded as a negative trend in university development" (Maclean & Pavlova, 2013, p. 70). By downplaying or ignoring the need to engage with Smartphones and SNSs effectively in their classrooms, teachers are in danger of having what former United States Secretary of Education, Lamar Alexander envisioned for education come to fruition: "designing schools that shift from a teachers/community base to central administrators, and employ technology with low-cost, non-professional classroom assistants" (Spillane & Shapiro, 1992, p. 279). Therefore, it is imperative that educators seriously attend to and become active participants in new literacy practices based on the integration of technology. This requires substantial time and openness to the kinds of frustrations, challenges, and life-enhancing experiences that students experience in and out of the classroom – in essence, it requires teachers to become students again. As Ramsey and Fitzgibbons (2005) remind teachers: "If we are not learners, we cannot help others to learn" (p. 345). Tertiary teachers are first and foremost models of higher learning for students and so should be conversant in modern methods of learning that are underpinned by the use of technology, and Smartphones and social networking sites (SNSs) in particular.

Further, there is considerable evidence that students not only want and expect to learn about and use the latest technology in their classrooms, but view banning use by teachers and administrators as creating a "generational conflict" (Mavhunga, Kibirige, Chigonga, & Ramaboka, 2016). Perhaps most tellingly, students themselves have recognized and expressed desire for a regulatory framework to become educated in the proper way to employ Smartphones and SNSs (Mavhunga, Kibirige, Chigonga, & Ramaboka, 2016). For example, undergraduate students at Rice University who had not previously owned a Smartphone were given iPhones to assist in their education and asked to evaluate their experiences before and after using them for study (Tossell, Kortum, Shepard, Rahmati, & Zhong, 2015). Contrary to the researchers' expectations, students became highly critical of the devices despite having favorable opinions prior to use:

[S]tudents felt that their preparation was impaired with access to the Internet and other resources through their smartphones. This attenuation could have been driven by usability issues such as small screen space, awkward text entry and long page loading delays. Users may have wanted to use their devices to support educational activities (as indicated by the high volume of usage early in the study), but technology limitations could have hindered this desire to manifest consistently over time. (p. 722)

The researchers concluded that providing students with access to Smartphones without specific training and directed learning activities was detrimental, not because use of such devices was incompatible, but "might rather be due to the fact the current model of education does not require this type of informal learning. Smartphones support ubiquitous informal learning opportunities, but the educational model being used currently provides limited need for this beneficial activity" (Tossell, Kortum, Shepard, Rahmati, & Zhong, 2015, p. 722). In short, Smarphones and SNSs are not designed for education and vice versa, and so without addressing this disparity, these technologies represent both a lost opportunity, and an impediment to traditional ways of learning.

CONCLUSION

All practical methods of teaching English to non-native speakers require teachers to include various degrees of cultural information as the basis for situating learning. Moreover, numerous philosophers and scholars of general education through the years have likewise stressed the central importance of continuation and consistency between students' lives and their educational experiences (Rudd & Tyldesley, 2006). However, the contrast between the pervasiveness of Smartphone and SNS use in Korean society and the failure to engage with related educational issues could not be starker. Tertiary English educators in Korea, it would seem, have largely been accepting of this disparity by implicitly – or explicitly – ignoring the need to educate themselves and students in new literacies that are underpinned by new technology use employed throughout society. As illustrated, the repercussions of this oversight have far-reaching implications not only for teachers of English at Korean universities and education on the whole, but also for the future of socialization in Korean society and throughout the world. As John Dewey (1938) would remind us,

The educator more than the member of any other profession is concerned to have a long look ahead... The educator by the very nature of his work is obliged to see his present work in terms of what it accomplishes, or fails to accomplish, for a future whose objects are linked with those of the present (pp. 75-76).

We must develop a rigorous regulatory and pedagogical approach to guiding students (and ourselves!) in the proper use of Smartphones and SNSs, or we risk forever being the punch line of the joke about the ancient Greek traveler who upon encountering all the modern innovations to life in our world, is in amazement and disbelief at the "magic" until he enters a classroom and exclaims: "Ah, I am home!".

REFERENCES

Attwell, G., & Hughes, J. (2010). Pedagogic approaches to using technology for learning: Literature review. *Lifelong Learning UK*. Retrieved from http://webarchive.nationalarchives.gov.uk/20110414152025/http:/www.lluk.org/wp-content/uploads/2011/01/Pedagogical-appraches-for-using-technology-literature-review-january-11-FINAL.pdf

Baek, Y. K., Jung, J. Y., & Kim, B. K. (2008). What makes teachers use technology in the classroom? Exploring the factors affecting facilitation of technology with a Korean sample. *Computers & Education*, *50*(1), 224–234. doi:10.1016/j.compedu.2006.05.002

Barkley, J., & Lepp, A. (2013). Cellular telephone use is associated with greater sedentary behavior independent of leisure-time physical activity. *Applied Physiology, Nutrition, and Metabolism*, *38*(S1), 1023. Retrieved from https://www.ncbi.nlm.nih.gov/pmc/articles/PMC4815203/

Bates, A. (2000). *Managing technological change: Strategies for college and university leaders*. San Francisco, CA: Jossey-Bass.

Becker, H. (2000). Findings from the teaching, learning, and computing survey: Is Larry Cuban right? *Education Policy Analysis Archives*, *51*(8), 1–32. Retrieved from http://www.crito.uci.edu/tlc/findings/ccsso.pdf

Boczkowski, P., Matassi, M., & Mitchelstein, E. (2018). How young users deal with multiple platforms: The role of meaning-making in social media repertoires. *Journal of Computer-Mediated Communication*, *23*(5), 245–259. doi:10.1093/jcmc/zmy012

Boumosleh, J., & Jaalouk, D. (2018). Smartphone addiction among university students and its relationship with academic performance. *Global Journal of Health Science*, *10*(1), 48–59. doi:10.5539/gjhs.v10n1p48

Boyd, D., & Ellison, N. (2008). Social network sites: Definition, history, and scholarship. *Journal of Computer-Mediated Communication*, *13*(1), 210–230. doi:10.1111/j.1083-6101.2007.00393.x

Brooker, J. (2019). Why banning phones from schools is a backward step for education: Instead, let's treat this as an opportunity to help young people today become productive members of society. *Podium Online*. Retrieved from https://thenextweb.com/podium/2019/03/23/why-banning-phones-from-schools-is-a-backward-step-for-education/

Cain, G. (2014). The South Korean government wants to impose a curfew on smartphone use. *Global-Post Online*. Retrieved from https://www.pri.org/stories/2014-04-14/south-korean-government-wants-impose-curfew-smartphone-use

Caruso, M., Fraschini, N., & Kuuse, S. (2019). Online tools for feedback engagement in second language learning. *International Journal of Computer-Assisted Language Learning and Teaching*, *9*(1), 58–78. doi:10.4018/IJCALLT.2019010104

Cuban, L. (2001). *Oversold and underused: Computers in the classroom*. Cambridge, MA: Harvard University Press.

Dahlstrom, E., de Boor, T., Grunwald, P., & Vockley, M. (2011). ECAR National study of students and information technology in higer education, 2011. *EDUCAUSE Center for Applied Research*. Retrieved from http://grunwald.com/pdfs/EDUCAUSE_Grunwald_College_Student_Tech_Study.pdf

Degennaro, T. (2019). Ten most popular social media sites in China (2019 updated). Retrieved from https://www.dragonsocial.net/blog/social-media-in-china/

DELNI. (1998). Lifelong learning: A new learning culture for all, Retrieved from http://www.delni.gov.uk/acfbb7f.pdf

Dewey, J. (1938). *Experience and education*. New York: Collier Books, Macmillan.

Doucleff, M., & Aubrey, A. (2018). Smartphone detox: How to power down in a wired world. NPR Morning Edition. Retrieved from https://www.npr.org/sections/health-shots/2018/02/12/584389201/smartphone-detox-how-to-power-down-in-a-wired-world

Ellis, R. (2012). *Language teaching research & language pedagogy*. West Sussex, UK: Wiley-Blackwell. doi:10.1002/9781118271643

Ertmer, P., & Park, S. H. (n.d.). Changing teachers' beliefs toward classroom technology use: The potential of problem-based learning. Retrieved from http://www.edci.purdue.edu/ertmer/docs/earli09_ertmer_park.pdf

Feng, S., Wong, Y. K., Wong, L. Y., & Hossain, L. (2019). The Internet and Facebook usage on academic distraction of college students. *Computers & Education*, *134*, 41–49. doi:10.1016/j.compedu.2019.02.005

Gillmor, D. (2008). *Principles for a new media literacy*. Harvard, MA: Berkman Center for Internet & Society at Harvard University. Retrieved from https://cyber.law.harvard.edu/sites/cyber.law.harvard.edu/files/Principles%20for%20a%20New%20Media%20Literacy_MR.pdf

Gray, R. (2011, Jan. 2). Facebook generation suffer information withdrawal syndrome. *The telegraph*. Retrieved from http://www.telegraph.co.uk/technology/news/8235302/Facebook-generation-suffer-information-withdrawal-syndrome.html

Greenfeld, K. (2014). Faking cultural literacy. *New York Times Online*. Retrieved from https://www.nytimes.com/2014/05/25/opinion/sunday/faking-cultural-literacy.html

Grohol, J. (2008). SMS addiction and texting addiction. *Psych Central*. Retrieved from http://psychcentral.com/blog/archives/2008/03/01/sms-addiction-and-texting-addiction/

Grohol, J. (2018). Internet addiction and depression. *Psych Central*. Retrieved from https://psychcentral.com/blog/internet-addiction-and-depression/

Hawi, N., & Samaha, M. (2016). To excel or not to excel: Strong evidence on the adverse effect of smartphone addiction on academic performance. *Computers & Education, 98*, 81–89. doi:10.1016/j.compedu.2016.03.007

Hudson, H. (2014). *Do your students know more about technology than you do?* Retrieved from http://www.scholastic.com/teachers/article/do-your-students-know-more-about-technology-you-do

International Center for Media & the Public Agenda (ICMPA). (2014). *The world unplugged*. Retrieved from http://theworldunplugged.wordpress.com/about/international-center-for-media-the-public-agenda/

Johnson, S. (2005). *Everything bad is good for you: How today's popular culture is actually making us smarter*. New York: Penguin Group.

Junco, R. (2012). In-class multitasking and academic performance. *Computers in Human Behavior, 28*(6), 2236–2243. doi:10.1016/j.chb.2012.06.031

Junco, R., & Cotton, S. (2012). No A 4 U: The relationship between multitasking and academic performance. *Computers & Education, 59*(2), 505–514. doi:10.1016/j.compedu.2011.12.023

Kang, S. J. (2014). The leadership on a safe and secure cyberspace. *Korea IT Times Global New Network* (pp. 26-27). Retrieved from http://www.koreaittimes.com/pdf/2014_04.pdf

Karpinski, A., Kirschner, P., Ozer, I., Mellott, J., & Ochwo, P. (2013). An exploration of social networking site use, multitasking, and academic performance among United States and European university students. *Computers in Human Behavior, 29*(3), 1182–1192. doi:10.1016/j.chb.2012.10.011

Kessler, S. (2011, May 31). 38% of college students can't go 10 minutes without tech (STATS). *Mashable Asia*. Retrieved from https://mashable.com/video/digital-art-tablet-review/

Kim, A., Tak, H., & Lee, C. (2010). The development and validation of a learning flow scale for adults. *The Korean Journal of Educational Psychology, 24*, 39–59. Retrieved from http://www.newnonmun.com/article=193913

Kim, A., Tak, H., & Lee, C. (2010). The development and validation of a learning flow scale for adults. *The Korean Journal of Educational Psychology, 24*, 39–59. Retrieved from http://www.newnonmun.com/article=193913

Kim, C. M., Kim, M. K., Lee, C. J., Spector, M., & DeMeester, K. (2013). Teacher beliefs and technology integration. *Teaching and Teacher Education, 29*, 76–85. doi:10.1016/j.tate.2012.08.005

Kim, H. J., Min, J. Y., Min, K. B., Lee, T. J., & Yoo, S. H. (2018). Relationship among family environment, self-control, friendship quality, and adolescents' smartphone addiction in South Korea: Findings from nationwide data. *PLoS One, 13*(2), 1–13. doi:10.1371/journal.pone.0190896 PMID:29401496

Kim, S. G., Park, J., Kim, H. T., Pan, Z., Lee, Y., & McIntyre, R. (2019). The relationship between smartphone addiction and symptoms of depression, anxiety, and attention-deficit/hyperactivity in South Korean adolescents. *Annals of General Psychiatry, 18*(1), 1–8. doi:10.118612991-019-0224-8 PMID:30899316

Kim, Y. N. (2014, April 1). The power of big data, the power of Korea: Who would dare to come forward to try estimating big data technology's growth potential? Korea IT Times Global New Network (pp. 18-19). Retrieved from http://www.koreaittimes.com/pdf/2014_04.pdf

Kirschner, P., & Karpinski, A. (2010). Facebook and academic performance. *Computers in Human Behavior*, *26*(6), 1237–1245. doi:10.1016/j.chb.2010.03.024

Klopfer, E., Osterweil, S., Groff, J., & Haas, J. (2009). The instructional power of digital games social networking simulations and how teachers can leverage them. *Using the technology of today, in the classroom today*. Cambridge, MA: The Education Arcade, MIT, Creative Commons. Retrieved from http://education.mit.edu/papers/GamesSimsSocNets_EdArcade.pdf

Lawrence, G., & Ahmed, F. (2018). Pedagogical insights into hyper-immersive virtual world language learning environments. *International Journal of Computer-Assisted Language Learning and Teaching*, *8*(1), 1–14. doi:10.4018/IJCALLT.2018010101

Lee, D. H. (2013). Smartphones, mobile social space, and new sociality in Korea. *Mobile Media & Communication*, *1*(3), 269–284. doi:10.1177/2050157913486790

Lee, J. W., Sung, M. J., Song, S. H., Lee, Y. M., Lee, J. J., Cho, S. M., ... Shin, Y. M. (2018). Psychological factors associated with smartphone addiction in South Korean adolescents. *The Journal of Early Adolescence*, *38*(3), 288–302. doi:10.1177/0272431616670751

Lee, S. H. (2006). *Korean higher education: Its emergence, development & future challenges*. Seoul, South Korea: Hakjisa Publisher.

Lee, S. Y., Kim, M. S., Mendoza, J., & McDonough, I. (2018). Addicted to cellphones: Exploring the psychometric properties between the nomophobia questionnaire and obsessiveness in college students. *Heliyon (London)*, *4*(11), 1–21. doi:10.1016/j.heliyon.2018.e00895 PMID:30426100

Lee, S. Y., Kim, M. W., McDonough, I., Mendoza, J., & Kim, M. S. (2017). The effects of mobile phone use and emotion-regulation style on college students' learning. *Applied Cognitive Psychology*, *31*(3), 360–366. doi:10.1002/acp.3323

Lee, Y. K., Chang, C. T., Lin, Y., & Cheng, Z. H. (2014). The dark side of smartphone usage: Psychological traits, compulsive behavior, and technostress. *Computers in Human Behavior*, *31*, 373–383. doi:10.1016/j.chb.2013.10.047

Lenhart, A., Purcell, K., Smith, A., & Zickuhr, K. (2010). Social media & mobile Internet use among teens and young adults. *Pew Internet & American Life Project*. Retrieved from https://files.eric.ed.gov/fulltext/ED525056.pdf

Lepp, A., Barkley, J., & Karpinski, A. (2015). The relationship between cell phone use and academic performance in a sample of U.S. college students. *SAGE Open*, 1–9.

Lewis, H. (1997). The mission of Harvard College. *Harvard University*. Retrieved from http://www.harvard.edu/faqs/mission-statement

Maclean, R., & Pavlova, M. (2013). Vocationalization of secondary and higher education: Pathways to the world of work. In UNESCO-UNEVOC, *Revisiting global trend in TVET* (pp. 42-85). Retrieved from http://www.unevoc.unesco.org/fileadmin/up/2013_epub_revisiting_global_trends_in_tvet_chapter2.pdf

Marin, L., & Halpern, D. (2011). Pedagogy for developing critical thinking in adolescents: Explicit instruction produces greatest gains. *Thinking Skills and Creativity*, *6*(1), 1–13. doi:10.1016/j.tsc.2010.08.002

Matthews, T., Pierce, J., & Tang, J. (2009). No smartphone is an island: The impact of places, situations, and other devices on smartphone use. IBM Technical Report #RJ10452. Retrieved from https://domino.research.ibm.com/library/cyberdig.nsf/papers/F5FD878B5B062ACA85257635004EC3F5/$File/rj10452.pdf

Mavhunga, F., Kibirige, I., Chigonga, B., & Ramaboka, M. (2016). Smartphones in public secondary schools: Views of matric graduates. *Perspectives in Education*, *34*(3), 72–85. doi:10.18820/2519593X/pie.v34i3.6

Murphy, K., DePasquale, R., & McNamara, E. (2003). Meaningful connections: Using technology in primary classrooms. *The National Association for the Education of Young Children (NAEYC)*. Retrieved from http://www.naeyc.org/files/yc/file/200311/TechInPrimaryClassrooms.pdf

Murray, J. (2011, Nov. 11). Do students know more about technology than their teachers? *The Guardian* (online edition). Retrieved from http://www.theguardian.com/education/2011/nov/21/multiple-choice-students-teachers-technology

Nam, I. S. (2013, July 23). A rising addiction among youths: Smartphones. *The Wall Street Journal* (online edition). Retrieved from http://online.wsj.com/news/articles/SB100014241278873242634045786l5162292157222

O'Donnell, S., & Epstein, L. (2019). Smartphones are more reinforcing than food for students. *Addictive Behaviors*, *90*, 124–133. doi:10.1016/j.addbeh.2018.10.018 PMID:30390436

Oksman, V., & Turtianinen, J. (2004). Mobile communication as a social stage: Meanings of mobile communication in everyday life among teenagers in Finland. *New Media & Society*, *6*(3), 319–339. doi:10.1177/1461444804042518

Palfrey, J., & Gasser, U. (2008). *Born digital: Understanding the first generation of digital natives*. New York: Basic Books.

Park, C. N., & Son, J.-B. (2009). Implementing computer-assisted language learning in the EFL classroom: Teachers' perceptions and perspectives. *International Journal of Pedagogies and Learning*, *5*(2), 80–101. doi:10.5172/ijpl.5.2.80

Park, S. H., & Ertmer, P. (2007). Impact of problem-based learning (PBL) on teachers' beliefs regarding technology use. *Journal of Research on Technology in Education*, *40*(2), 247–267. doi:10.1080/15391523.2007.10782507

Pew Research. (2018). *Social media use continues to rise in developing countries but plateaus across developed ones*. Retrieved from http://www.pewglobal.org/2018/06/19/social-media-use-continues-to-rise-in-developing-countries-but-plateaus-across-developed-ones/#table

Poushter, J., Bishop, C., & Chwe, H. (2019). Social media use continues to rise in developing countries but plateaus across developed ones: Digital divides remain, both within and across countries. Pew Research Center: Global Attitudes & Trends. Retrieved from https://www.pewglobal.org/2018/06/19/social-media-use-continues-to-rise-in-developing-countries-but-plateaus-across-developed-ones/#table

Ramsey, V., & Fitzgibbons, D. (2005). Being in the classroom. *Journal of Management Education, 29*(2), 333–356. doi:10.1177/1052562904271144

Ravizza, S., Hambrick, D., & Fenn, K. (2014). Non-academic Internet use in the classroom is negatively related to classroom learning regardless of intellectual ability. *Computers & Education, 78*, 109–114. doi:10.1016/j.compedu.2014.05.007

Richards, J., & Rogers, T. (2014). *Approaches and methods in language teaching* (3rd ed.). Cambridge, UK: Cambridge University Press.

Robson, D. (2016). Our IQs have never been higher – but it hasn't made us smarter. *BBC Online*. Retrieved from http://www.bbc.com/future/story/20160929-our-iqs-have-never-been-higher-but-it-hasnt-made-us-smart

Rudd, A., & Tyldesley, A. (2006). *Literacy and ICT in the primary school*. London, UK: David Fulton Publishers.

Salvucci, D., & Taatgen, N. (2008). Threaded cognition: An integrated theory of concurrent multitasking. *Psychological Review, 115*(1), 101–130. doi:10.1037/0033-295X.115.1.101 PMID:18211187

Schmid, R., Bernard, R., Borokhovski, E., Tamim, R., Abrami, P., Surkes, M., ... Woods, J. (2014). The effects of technology use in postsecondary education: A meta-analysis of classroom applications. *Computers & Education, 72*, 271–291. doi:10.1016/j.compedu.2013.11.002

Schoepp, K. (2005). Barriers to technology integration in a technology-rich environment. *Learning and Teaching in Higher Education: Gulf Perspectives, 2*(1), 1–24.

Selwyn, N. (2003). Apart from technology: Understanding people's non-use of information and communication technologies in everyday life. *Technology in Society, 25*(1), 99–116. doi:10.1016/S0160-791X(02)00062-3

Smith, A., Rainie, L., & Zickuhr, K. (2011). College students and technology. Pew Research Center. Retrieved from https://www.pewinternet.org/2011/07/19/college-students-and-technology/

Souppouris, A., & Jang, H. J. (2014, March 20). South Korean schools are remotely disabling students' smartphones. *The Verge*. Retrieved from http://www.theverge.com/2014/3/20/5528842/korean-schools-block-smartphones-in-class-ismartkeeper

Spillane, M., & Shapiro, B. (1992). A small circle of friends. *Nation (New York, N.Y.), 25*(8), 279–281.

Starr, A., Al-Najjar, B., Holmberg, K., Jantunen, E., Bellew, J., & Albarbar, A. (2010). Maintenance today and future trends. In K. Holmberg, A. Adgar, A. Arnaiz, E. Jantunen, J. Mascolo, & S. Mekid (Eds.), *E-maintenance* (pp. 5–37). London, UK: Springer-Verlag. doi:10.1007/978-1-84996-205-6_2

Stollak, M., Vanderberg, A., Burklund, A., & Weiss, S. (2011). Getting social: The impact of social networking usage on grades among college students. In *Proceedings from ASBBS Annual Conference* (pp. 859-865). Retrieved from http://asbs.org/files/2011/ASBBS2011v1/PDF/S/StollakM.pdf

Sung, W. J. (2016). A study of the digital divide in the current phrase of the information age: The moderating effect of smartphones. *Information Policy*, *21*(3), 291–306. doi:10.3233/IP-160398

Sweller, J. (1988). Cognitive load during problem solving: Effects on learning. *Cognitive Science*, *12*(2), 257–285. doi:10.120715516709cog1202_4

Sweller, J. (1994). Cognitive load theory, learning difficulty, and instructional design. *Learning and Instruction*, *4*(4), 295–312. doi:10.1016/0959-4752(94)90003-5

Taylor, K., & Silver, L. (2019). Smartphone ownership is growing rapidly around the world, but not always equally: In emerging economies, technology use still much more common among young people and the well-educated. Pew Research Center. Retrieved from https://www.pewglobal.org/2019/02/05/smartphone-ownership-is-growing-rapidly-around-the-world-but-not-always-equally/

The United Nations Educational, Scientific and Cultural Organization (UNESCO). (2004). The plurality of literacy and its implications for policies and programmes. UNESCO Education Sector Position Paper. Retrieved from http://unesdoc.unesco.org/images/0013/001362/136246e.pdf

Tondeur, J., van Keer, H., van Braak, J., & Valcke, M. (2008). ICT integration in the classroom: Challenging the potential of a school policy. *Computers & Education*, *51*(1), 212–223. doi:10.1016/j.compedu.2007.05.003

Tossell, C. (2012). An empirical analysis of internet use on smartphones: Characterizing visit patterns and user differences. (Unpublished Doctoral Dissertation, Rice University). Retrieved from https://scholarship.rice.edu/bitstream/handle/1911/64626/TOSSELL-THESIS.pdf?sequence=1&isAllowed=y

Tossell, C., Kortum, P., Shepard, C., Rahmati, A., & Zhong, L. (2015). You can lead a horse to water but you can't make him learn: Smartphone use in higher education. *British Journal of Educational Technology*, *46*(4), 713–724. doi:10.1111/bjet.12176

Turkle, S. (2011). *Alone together: Why we expect more from technology and less from each other*. New York: Basic Books.

van den Berg, R. (2002). Teacher's meanings regarding educational practice. *Review of Educational Research*, *72*(4), 577–625. doi:10.3102/00346543072004577

van Gelder, T. (2005). Teaching critical thinking: Some lessons from cognitive science. *College Teaching*, *53*(1), 41–46. doi:10.3200/CTCH.53.1.41-48

Webster, T. (2011). *Doing what works: A substantive grounded theory of teachers' perceptions and uses of technology in a Korean university general English department.* (Unpublished doctoral dissertation). Toowoomba, Australia: The University of Southern Queensland. Retrieved from http://eprints.usq.edu.au/19651/2/Webster_2011_whole.pdf

Webster, T., & Son, J.-B. (2012). Implementing proactive maintenance policies to address problems with access to technology at Korean universities. *International Journal of Pedagogies and Learning*, *7*(2), 109–121. doi:10.5172/ijpl.2012.7.2.109

Webster, T. E., & Son, J.-B. (2015). Doing what works: A grounded theory case study of technology use by teachers of English at a Korean university. *Computers & Education*, *80*, 84–94. doi:10.1016/j.compedu.2014.08.012

Wozney, L., Vivek, V., & Abrami, P. (2006). Implementing computer technologies: Teachers' perceptions and practices. *Journal of Technology and Teacher Education*, *14*(1), 173–207. Retrieved from https://www.learntechlib.org/primary/p/5437/

Yeboah, J., & Ewur, G. (2014). The impact of Whatsapp Messenger usage on students' performance in tertiary institutions in Ghana. *Journal of Education and Practice*, *5*(6), 157–164.

Zhang, P., & Aikman, S. (2007, July 22-27). *Attitudes in ICT acceptance and use.* Paper presented at the International Conference on Human Computer Interaction, Beijing, China.

Zou, B., Li, H., & Li, J. (2018). Exploring a curriculum app and a social communication app for EFL learning. *Computer Assisted Language Learning*, *31*(7), 694–713. doi:10.1080/09588221.2018.1438474

Section 3
Online-Integrated Learning

Chapter 7
An Exploratory Study of Using Personal Blogs for L2 Writing in Fully Online Language Courses

Lina Lee
University of New Hampshire, USA

ABSTRACT

The chapter reports the results of an exploratory study examining the use of personal blogs for the development of L2 writing skills in fully online language courses. The chapter outlines the methodology of the blog project including pedagogical objectives, task design, selection of digital tools, and implementation. The study involved 48 beginning students who used blogs for their writing assignments over the course of two consecutive summers. Both quantitative and qualitative data collected from post surveys, blog entries, and comments, and final interviews were analyzed. The results indicated that students perceived blogging as an effective tool for building their writing skills. Moreover, the chapter revealed that feedback scaffolding affected students' efforts to make improvement on both content and form. The study concludes that while writing performance can be assessed by the implementation of a well-designed blog project, sufficient time for feedback interaction and strategies for effective use of feedback are vital to foster reflective thinking and collaborative learning.

INTRODUCTION

In recent years, the process-oriented approach to L2 writing has been well received in the field of language teaching because it encourages students to actively participate in the writing process of planning, drafting, revising and editing. Upon receiving feedback from the instructor, students reflect on the comments and incorporate them into revisions to improve the quality of writing (Lam, 2013). Nevertheless, writing through a cyclical approach is a time-consuming task in the traditional classroom setting. Given the rapid growth of emerging technologies, computer-mediated communication (CMC) technology has been integrated into today's language classroom to support L2 writing (Çiftçi & Aslan, 2019; Godwin-Jones, 2018). Among other CMC tools, blogs have received substantial attention from L2 practitioners.

DOI: 10.4018/978-1-7998-1282-1.ch007

The use of blogs affords the opportunity for students to work independently (e.g., content creation), and collaboratively (e.g., peer feedback) during the writing process (Armstrong & Retterer, 2008; Lee, 2010; Richardson, 2011). In the process of blogging, students assume multiple roles, as they post their own entries, and read and respond to each other's postings. According to Lee (2014), blogging is not simply a process of practicing writing skills. Rather, it is a socially mediated activity through which ideas are circulated, shared and exchanged with a global audience. To this view, network-based writing encourages students to pay attention to the writer-reader interaction, and to think critically about how their writing might be reflected by their readers. As a result, students tend to produce more thoughtful responses. Also archived posts in reverse chronological order empower students to use metacognitive skills to monitor and assess their own writing performance (Sun & Chang, 2012).

As to feedback on CMC, L2 researchers have underscored that scaffolding feedback through asynchronous interaction draws students' attention to focus on linguistic problems and make necessary adjustments to improve their communicative competence (Lee, 2008; Vinagre & Muñoz, 2011; Ware & Kessler, 2013). Peer feedback through blogging strengthens learners' writing skills by expanding their lexicon and improving their grammatical accuracy and further develops their interlanguage (Alsubaie & Madine, 2018; Çiftçi & Kocoglu, 2012; Lee, 2010; Lin, 2015). In addition, network-based publishing also fosters learner autonomy, as students to take charge of decision-making on what, how much and when to publish their work (Lee & Markey, 2014). Given that blogs are asynchronous CMC, students write at their own pace without time pressure so reducing writing anxiety (Cequena & Gustilo, 2014). Finally, the instantaneous nature of content publishing for a broad audience rather than for a sole instructor increases students' motivation to produce quality work (Lee, 2016).

To date, L2 researchers have found that blogging has a positive impact on the development of writing skills and intercultural competence (e.g., Elola & Oskoz, 2008; Hegelheimer & Lee, 2013; Lee, 2017; Shao & Crook, 2015). For example, personal blogs foster self-expression and self-reflection (Stickler & Hampel, 2010). The use of blogs also promotes learners' interaction and collaboration through computer-mediated feedback in the process of L2 writing (Lee, 2016; Sun, 2010). Although the existing research is valuable to understanding blog technology in L2 instruction, most studies focus on advanced learners in blended learning settings. Studies on using asynchronous CMC for L2 writing within a fully online context at the beginning level is clearly needed to bring new insights into the impact of blogging on the development of writing performance. Thus, the current study aims to explore the use of personal blogs for L2 writing in two fully online elementary language courses. In particular, it examines the role of task, peer feedback and other factors that influence students' engagement in the writing process and their writing performance.

LITERATURE REVIEW

Personal Blogs for L2 Writing

Blogs haven been increasingly implemented in L2 instruction (e.g., Aydin, 2014; de Andrés Martínez, 2012; Lee, 2011a; Murray & Hourigan, 2008;; Pinkman, 2005; Vurdien, 2013). According to Hegelheimer and Lee (2013), blogging promotes the process approach to writing and focuses on the writing itself rather than the final product, as it involves a cycle of writing, reading and commenting on each other's entries, and making revisions. Among many benefits of using blogs for L2 writing, researchers have highlighted the development of personal writing styles and critical thinking skills (Hourigan & Murray, 2010; Lee, 2017; Sattar, 2015). Sun and Chang (2012) in their recent study explored how students' collaborative dialogues via blogging encouraged them to actively and reflectively engage in the writing process. Another study by Stickler and Hampel (2010) reported that the use of blogs enabled the intermediate German students to reflect on both language and form through social engagement. In addition, L2 studies have shown that blogging keeps students motivated and builds their confidence in writing because of the awareness of authorship and the existence of a real audience (e.g., Chen & Brown, 2012; Lee, 2012a). For example, several researchers found that the integration of learner-centered blogs into EFL writing instruction enhanced students' writing performance and increased their motivation to write (Lin, 2015; Trajtemberg & Yiakoumetti, 2011).

Other studies have reported challenges of using blogs for L2 instruction. For example, Blackmore-Squires (2010) argues that students may not feel comfortable having others read their writing due to the nature of blogs as an open platform. In her blog study, Vurdien (2013) found that not all students expressed a strong interest in the topics assigned by the instructor, and some were less motivated to participate because they viewed writing tasks as extra assignments. Another concern is that blogs as asynchronous CMC may not encourage social presence and community building due to lack of a timestamp and insufficient interpersonal communication (Rourke & Kanuka, 2009). For example, Lee (2016), in her recent CMC study found that students tended to forget to log into the site to read and respond to their peers' comments. Previous studies have reported that poor linguistic and cognitive skills affect L2 writing performance in blogging. The instructor should guide and monitor students through purposeful interaction and collaboration to ensure quality of writing (Lin, 2014; Wu 2015). To help students develop reflective learning strategies, teachers should provide them with a structured guidance framework (Hourigan & Murray, 2010).

Peer Feedback on Asynchronous CMC

Given the emergence of process-based writing, effective feedback is essential for the development of L2 writing, especially in online learning environments. In addition to teacher feedback, peer feedback is often incorporated into the writing process and can result in better writing performance (Hyland & Hyland, 2006). Peer feedback involves commenting on each other's work and providing suggests for the improvement of the original work. From a socio-cognitive perspective, peer feedback is embedded within a social context through which learners work collaboratively to exchange ideas, and solve linguistic problems (Lee, 2012b). CMC researchers have reported that peer feedback through blogging is beneficial for language development; especially writing skills (e.g., Chen, 2012; Nguyen, 2012; Ware & O'Dowd, 2008). Furthermore, peer scaffolding has a positive impact on learners' cognitive and social interaction skills. For example, peer feedback helped ESL students reflect on their learning process, and improve their self-editing and reflective skills (Gedera, 2012). Xu and Yu (2018) in their blog study demonstrated how peer feedback training enhanced students' engagement with feedback tasks during the collaborative activities in EFL writing classrooms. Similarly, Yang and Meng (2013) found that less-proficient students made more error correction during text revision than the more-proficient students did after they received online feedback training. Other blog studies reported that EFL students commented on their peers' blogs using various types of feedback, such as clarification, explanation and suggestion. As a result, they improved their writing in revised drafts (Çiftçi & Kocoglu, 2012; Pham & Usaha, 2015). Lee (2012b) found that peer feedback allowed students to reflect not only on their peers' postings but also on their own work. Significantly, peer feedback draws learners' attention to focus on form, make the connection between meaning and form that leads to error correction (Lee, 2008; Vinagre & Lera, 2008).

The ability to give meaningful feedback and sufficient time for reflection on language plays a crucial role in the feedback process. For example, Lee and Markey (2014) in their study of Spanish-American telecollaboration found that advanced language learners who were trained to become language teachers were well equipped with metalinguistic knowledge to fully explain certain grammar rules. Given asynchronous computer-mediated feedback is delayed, the lack of a timestamp in blogs may not facilitate the offering of peer comments and responses in a timely manner. To increase feedback responses, communication in real time using synchronous tools, such as *Skype* and *Zoom* should be considered as an alternative to delayed feedback via blogging. Another potential drawback of peer feedback is that students may not have sufficient metalinguistic knowledge to fully explain grammar rules to provide accurate comments and make effective corrections (Ware & O'Dowd, 2008). Other findings show that students are reluctant to offer candid comments in an open virtual environment because they do not feel adequately connected to their peers or are not confident in their own L2 knowledge (Lee & Markey, 2014). Consequently, they fail to offer meaningful and constructive comments in an online blogging environment. As suggested by Lee (2012b), specific instructions on how to effectively provide and use feedback in conjunction with appropriate training needs to be made available to learners in order to ensure the quality of feedback.

RESEARCH QUESTIONS

The three central questions addressed in this study are as follows:

1. How do beginning language students view the use of personal blogs in support of the development of L2 writing?
2. Do topics and tasks affect the way students participate in the process of blog writing?
3. What impact does computer-mediated peer feedback have on the blog writing process?

METHODOLOGY

Context of the Study

The study was set up using two fully online sections of a second semester beginning Spanish course (Elementary II) over two consecutive summers. The aim of the course was to expose students to the target language (input), and to using the target language to express meaning (output) through real-world tasks. In addition to input-based practices via the electronic platform *MySpanishLab* provided by the textbook publisher, course materials that focused on output-based activities which were created and housed in a private class wiki via *Wikispaces*[1]. The class wiki was embedded in *Blackboard*[2] to ensure the security and privacy of the students. Only the students and instructor had access to course materials. The class wiki contained a collection of wiki pages, which listed all course information, including course description, course components, weekly calendar, tools, grading and resources. A teacher-made video using the *Tegrity*, a lecture capture software, was used to provide students with step-by step instructions on how to use the wiki site and digital tools (e.g., *VoiceThread*[3], in conjunction with video tutorials from

YouTube. In addition to other online assignments (e.g., voice recordings), personal blogs were used for writing assignments, and were worth 20% of the final course grade. The blog-based writing set three main objectives: (1) to develop students' written communication skills; (2) to create an online community where the students could share and exchange ideas with each other through social interaction; and (3) to foster linguistic awareness through peer feedback as part of the blog revision process. It was hoped that blogging would motivate students to actively engage in writing and peer interaction through the provision of feedback.

Participants

The participants were 48 students who enrolled in Elementary Spanish II courses. Based on the pre-survey questionnaire, the participants were native speakers of English and had a basic knowledge of Spanish vocabulary and structures. More than 90% of the students had successfully completed the first semester of introductory Spanish (Elementary I), before enrolling in Elementary Spanish II. The participants were 67% female, 33% male, and between the ages of 19 and 32. Fewer than 10% of the students were sophomores (n = 4), 10% were juniors (n = 5), more than 70% were seniors (n = 35) and fewer than 10% were non-degree students (n = 4). None of them were Spanish majors or minors. Since more than 90% of the students (n = 46) enrolled in the course in order to fulfill the institutional foreign language graduation requirement and were not particularly interested in taking Spanish for personal enjoyment, they were not considered to be highly motivated language learners. Only two non-traditional students who had worked in Mexico and Costa Rica for a short period of time enrolled in the course due to personal interest in learning Spanish. In terms of computer knowledge and skills, the majority of students were competent users of Web 2.0 technology, as they grew up in the digital age. In addition, most students had taken an online course offered by the university prior to the study, thus they were familiar with *Blackboard* used by the researcher's institution.

Task Design

The project was designed based on task-based activities supported by Chapelle's (2001), six criteria for CALL task appropriateness (e.g., learner fit, meaning focus, authenticity). Task-based writing was employed to promote the use of the target language rather than to acquire new language knowledge. Based on major themes of chapters, various types of blog tasks were created to develop student language skills and cultural knowledge (Table 1).

Meaning-focused tasks with an emphasis on certain grammar structures or vocabulary were created to enable students to use the target language to express ideas (content) and practice linguistic form (grammar). For example, blog assignment #1 shown in Table 1 required students to use the imperfect to describe their childhood activities, whereas they used the food and vocation vocabulary to describe their favorite holiday (assignment #2). While some blog tasks required students to demonstrate their knowledge and understanding of the target culture by reading or searching online resources (assignment 4), others allowed them to write creatively. For example, one of the assignments was to use the two distinct aspects of the past tense (preterit vs. imperfect) to create a photo story to share it in their blogs.

Table 1. Sample topics and tasks for blog assignments

Topic	Description of Task
#1 "Mi niñez" (My childhood)	For this assignment, you will use a list of guided questions to write a short paragraph about your childhood. Read my childhood and use it as a model to write your own. Be sure to post your favorite childhood pictures. Read your peers' postings and use "Comment" to write your comments and/or ask questions about your peers' childhood.
#2 "*Mi día festivo favorito*" (My favorite holiday)	In your blog, write an entry to describe your favorite holiday. Describe how you celebrate the holiday, with whom you usually spend the day and what activities you do to spend the day. Feel free to use photos to support your writing. Be sure to read and make comments on your peers' blogs.
#3 "Mi viaje ideal" (My ideal trip)	Using this Google Map site (www.google.com/maps), search for one of the Spanish-speaking countries you would like to visit after you graduate from the university. In your blog, describe the country you would like to visit and why. Also tell us places you would like to see, food you would like to try, etc. Be sure to post pictures/videos to share with your peers. Read and make comments on your peers' blogs.
#4 "Frida Kahlo y sus pinturas" (Frida Kahlo and her paintings)	Using the links posted in our wiki, read the biography of the famous Mexican painter, Frida Kahlo, her artwork and style. Visit Frida Kahlo's Museum "La Casa Azul" (Blue House) (http://www.museofridakahlo.org.mx/en/) to learn more about her paintings. Write a blog entry to share and exchange ideas with peers. Be sure to make comments on your peers' blogs.
#5 "Una carta a Tomás" (A letter to Thomas)	For this blog assignment, you need to read the email message from Thomas (p. 114/e-book), and write a letter in which you give him some advice to help solve his problems. Be sure to use the present subjunctive to give advice, and make comments on your peers' postings.

Procedure

As part of the course requirement, each student kept a personal blog throughout the course. *Blogger*, one of the free blog publishing tools from *Google* was used to create personal blogs. Each week students were responsible for posting two entries using various types of tasks (see Table 1). Upon completion of the first blog assignment, the instructor collected the blog addresses and posted them to the *Blogger* page in the class wiki. The instructor divided the class into small groups of 6 students who were asked to read, comment on, and respond to each other's entries. The small group size enabled team members to become quickly acquainted with each other so that they felt comfortable making contributions. To facilitate scaffolding through peer feedback, and increase interaction and collaboration among students, the instructor assigned one linguistically strong student to each group. The instructor acted as a facilitator to guide students through the revision process. Individual contributions and collaborative effort are less likely to occur without proper guidance. Hence the instructor provided guidelines to the students explaining how to contribute to blogging and provide content and language use focused feedback to each other. Since the students were still developing their writing skills and did not have sufficient knowledge to offer linguistic feedback beyond the basics, the instructor provided them with a list of common errors that beginning students make along with examples to facilitate the revision process and error correction (see Table 2).

Students used the comment feature of the blog to interact and respond to each other. To maintain a high level of interaction, the instructor sent emails to remind students to participate in the feedback process. Using comments received from their peers, students revised their blog entries accordingly. Students were given one week to draft and comment on each blog assignment. As to criteria for writing

Table 2. Sample basic Spanish errors with examples

Verbs to express "to be"	Examples with *errors
Tener años = to describe age	*¿Cuántos años eres? (How old are you?)
Tener calor = to feel hot	*Soy calor. (I'm hot.)
Estar = to describe physical and emotional conditions	*Soy nervioso. (I'm nervous.)
False cognates	**Examples with *errors**
Asistir = to attend vs. ayudar = to help Embarazada = pregnant vs. avergonzada = embarrassed	Voy a *asistir mi amigo. (I'm going to attend my friend). Me siento *embarazada. (I feel pregnant).
Noun-adjective agreement	**Example with *errors**
perros pequeños = masculine; plural	Tengo dos perros *pequeño. (I have two small dogs).
Escritora favorita = feminine, singular	Mi escritora *favorito es JK Rowling. (My favorite writer is JK Rowling.)
Informal vs. informal "you"	**Example with *errors**
Usted = formal you; with older people, boss at work or strangers. Tú = informal you; with people that you know, such as family or friends.	¿Cómo *estás? (How are you?) – But you are talking to the president Trump. Recomiendo que no *salga esta noche. (I recommend that you don't go out tonight.) – But you are talking to your sister.
Spelling & accent marks	Example with *errors
imposible = impossible Habló = He talked.	Es *impossible para mí. (It is impossible for me.). *Hablo con mi hermana anoche. (He talked to my sister last night.)

evaluation, the instructor used a holistic rubric to give an overall rating for each blog performance (For alternative rubrics, see Ishikawa, 2018).

DATA COLLECTION AND ANALYSIS

Multiple sources of data collection were used to understand students' views about the effectiveness of blogging, task design and peer feedback on the development of their writing skills: (1) online post-surveys, (2) student-generated blogs, and (3) end-of-course interviews.

Online Post-Surveys

The online survey consisted of 12 statements and used a 5-point Likert scale ranging from *Strongly Disagree* to *Strongly Agree* to gauge different viewpoints. Students indicated their level of satisfaction by ranking the questions from 1 to 5 (5 being the highest score). The survey elicited responses in three areas: (1) the effectiveness of blogs for online writing, (2) the affordance of task type, and (3) the role of feedback and scaffolding. 79% of the students (n = 38) voluntarily completed the survey via *SurveyMonkey*.

Student-Generated Blogs

Qualitative data analysis was used to allow the researcher to trace the development of beginning students' writing, and provide additional evidence to illustrate and support the findings. Student-generated blog posts added another dimension to the data collection. Blog posts archived in reverse chronological order provide greater insight into how individuals construct and negotiate meaning through the provision of feedback, and make progress in their writing through the revising and editing process. Blog comments were used to illustrate how students co-constructed L2 knowledge through negotiation of meaning (content), whereas blog posts were employed to exhibit how individual students made improvement in their writing through feedback scaffolding (form).

End-of-Course Interviews

At the end of the semester, the instructor conducted small group interviews with students to secure in-depth understanding of how their experiences with blogs affected the way they view online writing and the impact of peer feedback on their writing performance. Each group consisted of 5-6 students. Each interview lasted approximately 40 minutes and was recorded digitally for data analysis. Responses on similar topics were grouped together and incorporated into the survey results for discussion.

FINDINGS AND DISCUSSION

Effectiveness of Using Personal Blogs for Online Writing

The mean score displayed in Table 3 records student reactions to the effectiveness of using blogs for online writing.

Overall, students found blogging effective for the development of their L2 writing skills (statement 1), and agreed that they benefitted from creating and reading blog entries (statement 2). During the interviews, the majority of the students expressed satisfaction with the use of blogs for writing assignments. They repeatedly commented on how much they enjoyed connecting socially with their peers via blogging. The following comment exemplifies the sentiment:

To be honest, I felt somewhat isolated and disconnected in this online course. Blogging helped me connect with my peers and it created a small community where we helped each other through the revision cycle. I learned a great deal from reading my peers' blogs. I found them interesting. I enjoyed working with my classmates.

Another student expressed her positive attitude towards blogging:

Table 3. Student reactions to the use of blogs for online writing

Statements of the Survey	Mean	SD
1. Blogging is an effective way for me to develop my writing skills.	4.38	0.52
2. I benefited from writing blog entries and reading my peers' posts.	4.29	0.55
3. I found blogging to be time-consuming.	4.56	0.44
4. Blog tasks were interesting and meaningful to me.	4.15	0.51
5. I preferred to choose my own topics for blog assignments.	2.43	0.62
6. Participating in the revision process of blogging helped me improve my writing.	3.68	0.29

To be honest, I really don't like to write. I often feel unmotivated to write because it takes a huge effort for me to produce an essay. Blogging is different from writing essays. I liked how we wrote for a real purpose and a real audience; not just for the teacher. I enjoyed writing blog entries and shared them with my peers. We all worked together to help each other improve Spanish. I think blogging is a great way to practice your language skills. I highly recommend it to any language students.

The above findings demonstrated that personal blogs not only facilitated collaborative learning but also encouraged self-expression through a social learning environment (de Andrés Martínez, 2012; Gunduz, 2016; Lee, 2010).

The high rate of statement 3 (Mean =4.56) indicated that many students experienced difficulties keeping up with their blog assignments. According to participant survey data, more than 60% of the students worked full-time during the summer while taking this online course. Online learning invariably requires students to have a degree of autonomy. This finding suggests that a lack of time commitment contributes to student performance. As mentioned previously, the majority of the students enrolled in the online course to satisfy the foreign language requirement for graduation. It is possible that they were not aware of how much time they needed to devote to completing the blog assignments. For example, one student said that he'd had no idea how much time it would take him to complete entries, and read and comment on his peers' blogs. Although online learning affords students greater flexibility and convenience than traditional learning, it requires adequate self-regulation and self-determination to engage in the learning process as suggested by other researchers (e.g., Lee, 2016; Schunk & Zimmerman, 2008).

With respect to the effectiveness of blog tasks, the results showed that both assigned and self-selected topics afforded novice learners the opportunity to develop L2 writing skills. More than 80% of the students found the blog topics stimulating because they allowed them to use the target language in a meaningful manner (statement 4). They especially liked how topics were related to their personal interests and experiences. For example, one student used Spanish properly to describe her favorite TV show, whereas another student wrote about one of his fondest childhood memories. Moreover, blog posts regarding daily routines, hobbies and future plans helped students get to know each other on a more personal level. One student, for example, explained the following during the final interview:

Due to the lack of face-to-face interaction, I felt isolated and disconnected in this online course. Also I'm kind of a shy and quite person. I often find it difficult to express myself in front of people. I didn't know anyone in this class. But reading my peers' personal stories with photos helped me get to know them better. After using blog writing for a couple of weeks, I felt more connected and more comfortable interacting with my peers.

The finding revealed that photos added a personal touch to their blogs and helped them craft their stories in a dynamic way. The data seems to suggest that personal topics aroused students' motivation, reduced their anxiety and promoted social interaction, which have been repeatedly addressed in the previous studies (e.g., Lee, 2016).

When asked about their preference for teacher-assigned versus free topics (statement 5), students slightly favored using teacher-assigned topics (51%) over choosing their own topics (49%). This suggests that students preferred having a mix of teacher assigned topics and individually chosen topics. The following excerpts from the final interviews demonstrate how students enjoyed both teacher-made and student-chosen blog topics:

- I really liked the tasks assigned by the instructor because they were related to real-life situations and cultural topics. Teacher prompts gave clear directions for how to build the content that connected to the vocabulary and the grammar that we learned from previous chapters.
- I was glad that we were allowed to choose our own topics for some of writing assignments. I really wanted to write about something that interests me most. I love music. My favorite Latin singer is Carlos Vives. I wrote about his song "la bicicleta" with Shakira. I also embedded his YouTube video in my blog so my classmates could listen to the song. To my surprise, I received many comments on my posting. We had a good discussion about Latin pop songs and our favorite singers. That was really cool!

Despite the fact that students found blog assignments fun and engaging, it appears that beginning students feel less confident expressing their ideas when using self-selected topics, as they are not fully capable of expressing complex ideas in L2. One student, for example, explained the following during the final interview:

To be honest, I had a hard time deciding what to write when we were given free topics due to my limited language ability. I would love to write something about Picasso's work but I wouldn't know how to describe my feelings on Picasso's paintings and the reasons for his fame in Spanish. I'd prefer to use teacher-assigned topics.

While it is important to integrate topics of student choice and interest in L2 writing, free topics may not be suitable for novice learners, not due to their content knowledge, but because of their limited linguistic ability, meaning their ability to describe the topic in the target language. Nevertheless, the results revealed that nearly 50% of the students were in favor of using their own writing topics and many of them chose familiar topics, such as a memorable place, my favorite TV show or an ideal summer vacation. As suggested by Lee (2010), topic choice affected the amount of writing that students produced and the degree to which they interacted with each other. A closer look at the data shows that students tended to write longer entries using topics of their choice, whereas they produced shorter but more accurate writing using teacher-assigned topics. This finding corroborates the results of previous studies (Bonzo, 2008; Dickinson, 2014) showing that students produced a greater variety of lexical items and wrote with a greater fluency when they selected their own topics than when the topics were assigned to them. It is possible that students are more motivated to write when they are given the freedom to choose topics that they are familiar with, while teacher-guided tasks gave them more control over the vocabulary and grammatical structures used. The study suggests that a balanced approach to topic selection should be adopted to keep students motivated and engaged in the writing process.

As shown in Table 3, more than 80% of the students affirmed that blogging had a positive impact on the development of their writing (statement 6). There appeared to be a clear consensus among the students that interactive blog comments afforded them the opportunity to participate actively in the learning process. They indicated that using blogs not only gave them a personal space to write but also opened up a social place for them to interact with each other. The following blog comments exhibit that beginning students engaged actively in sharing their thoughts as illustrated in the following exchange on healthy eating (translated to English):

Student A: *Maybe you can add bad cholesterol from eating junk food. Do you think some people eat too much fast food? When I'm hungry, I eat yogurt with fruit. It has a lot of fiber and less sugar. I also drink a lot of water.*

Student B: *Interesting! But I like to eat a good burger with homemade fries ☺! I don't buy hamburgers in fast food restaurants like Burger King or McDonalds. My mom makes the best burgers. I do exercise and I run everyday.*

Student C: *I think it's important to mention 'red meat' in your blog. We shouldn't eat red meat like beef. Red meat is bad for you.*

Student A: *I agree with you. I'm a vegetarian. I don't like meat.*

Student B: *Thanks for your comments. I'll add those points.*

To build communicative language competence, students need to have the opportunity to engage in real-world tasks that require them to go beyond their traditional role as responder to the instructor's questions. The above example demonstrated that beginning students were able to express ideas and negotiate meaning through interactive exchange, which enhanced their interpersonal skills, one of the ACTFL three modes of communication (interpersonal, interpretive, presentational).

Computer-Medicated Peer Feedback in Blog Writing

Regarding peer feedback, students were asked to rate six statements to find out the role of peer feedback in blog writing (Table 4).

80% of the students enjoyed interacting with their peers through writing comments on each other's blogs (statement 7), and more than 60% of the students found peer feedback valuable and helpful for revising and improving their writing (statement 8). Peer feedback mediated through blogging was useful to students in terms of correcting their own errors, as this student commented during the final interview:

I have a lot of problems with my writing. My classmates in my group were able to help me with my grammar mistakes. I made careless mistakes, such as wrong articles or incorrect verb conjugations. I found their comments helpful. Once I received the feedback, I knew how to go by fixing them in my blog.

Table 4. Student views of peer feedback via blogging

Statements of the Survey	Mean	SD
7. I enjoyed making comments on my peers' blog entries.	4.01	0.47
8. The feedback I received from my peers was helpful.	3.23	0.57
9. Peer feedback motivated me to make revisions and improve my writing.	3.62	0.51
10. Peer comments allowed me to reflect upon my own writing.	4.05	0.41
11. I felt comfortable discussing linguistic errors with my peers.	2.67	0.38
12. Peer feedback along with instructor comments were useful for me.	3.84	0.26

A closer look at blog interactive comments revealed that students tended to provide local comments on language use. For example, one linguistically strong student explained to his peer about the difference between 'ser' vs. 'estar' (to be) with examples to illustrate her points:

You need to use 'ser' to describe occupation. Ella 'es' profesora not 'está' profesora in the third sentence. Also you need to change mi perro 'es' to 'está' en el patio because you are talking about the location. You can also find more information on pp. 78-79. I hope this helps.

To respond to his peer's feedback, the student wrote:

Thanks for your help. I still have a lot of trouble with these two verbs. I should review my notes and do a few online Quizlet exercises. I'll make changes on my blog.

A similar finding was reported in the study by Ware (2011). Students tended to make error corrections when clear explanations were given during the peer review process.

While there is no guarantee that peer feedback and error correction have long term impact on the development of L2 writing, the results affirmed that beginning students benefited from peer scaffolding (statement 9), as shown in the following unedited blog posts during the second week and the fifth week of class. (* = linguistic error):

*En el futuro viajaré a Barcelona, España porque me gusta Europa. Barcelona es *un ciudad muy *bonito. En Barcelona, visitaré La Rambla, el Parque Cuell y el Museo Picasso. Mis amigos y yo *comeramos *mucho tapas y paella de mariscos. Tomaré *mucho cervezas ... (Week 2)*

[In the future I will travel to Barcelona, Spain because I like Europe. Barcelona

is a beautiful country. In Barcelona, I will visit La Rambla and Guell Park and Picasso Museum. My friends and I will eat a lot of snacks and seafood paella. I will drink a lot of beer ...]

As the above example illustrates, the student had difficulty in the noun-adjective agreement, such as un (masculine), vs. una (feminine), ciudad ''bonito'' (masculine), versus ''bonita'' (feminine), and ''mucho'' (masculine-singular), tapas vs. muchas (feminine-plural), tapas. By the fifth week, her writing did show her understanding of the agreement between nouns and adjectives by using 'muchas,' 'bonitos,' and 'deliciosa' correctly illustrated in the following example:

*"En la noche dejábamos muchas galletas y leche en la mesa *por Santa. Mis padres daban *nos regalos bonitos. Comíamos una cena deliciosa con mis tíos y primos ..." (Week 5)*

[At night we used to leave many cookies and milk on the table for Santa. My parents gave us pretty gifts. We ate a delicious dinner with my aunts, uncles and cousins ...]

As CMC researchers pointed out, blog writing tends to promote fluency over accuracy (Lee 2010b) and linguistics problems tend to go by the wayside because learners primarily focus on conveying ideas. The finding proved that the inclusion of peer feedback on form as part of the blog exchange enabled students to pay attention to linguistic forms, help them make error corrections on their original entries, and further improve language accuracy.

The findings revealed that most students (81%) agreed that using peer feedback encouraged them to reflect on their own writing (statement 10). The following example exhibited how one student responded to his peer's comment about the magical world created in the Harry Potter series:

Interesting point. I never thought about the bad influence that Harry's witchcraft has on teen fantasy. I hope children understand that Harry Potter is a fictional character. I should add something about parental guidance and good virtues in Potter books. What do you think?

The above comment suggests that peer feedback strengthens learners' reflective thinking and content quality, as reported in previous studies (e.g., Lee, 2011b).

In line with the findings reported in other CMC studies (e.g., Ware & O'Dowd, 2008), students used affective comments, such as compliments to diminish anxiety or intimidation during CMC feedback interaction. Words of appraisal like 'very good,' 'excellent' and 'awesome' appeared repeatedly, as shown in the following quotation:

Your blog looks awesome with a lot of pictures. You also write very well. I hardly can find any mistakes.

Students also expressed empathy towards their peers' writing. For example, one student wrote:

I understand how you feel. I have trouble with my writing as well. I had only two years of Spanish in high school. It's been four years. I forgot most of it. I've been struggling with this class.

This result coincides with the findings in the study conducted by Lee and Markey (2014), who found that students expressed themselves appropriately in a social context by using effective pragmatic strategies to interact with each other. It is likely that due to the missing paralinguistic cues in CMC, students were conscious of the need to be polite and show empathy before giving negative feedback.

When asking students to rate their comfort level with leaving comments, the results showed that more than 50% of the students did not feel comfortable providing linguistic feedback to their peers (statement 11). Students pointed out that they read mostly for content rather than looked at grammar mistakes. They expressed reluctance to comment on their peers' blogs because they lacked confidence in their own writing and were not able to give meaningful feedback. According to Wu (2015), students may not know how to give and use feedback, and thus should be trained on how to use online feedback effectively. The results indicated that peer commentary feedback in conjunction with teacher feedback proved beneficial to the majority of beginning students (statement 12). One student made the following comment during the final interview:

I found the instructor's error codes very helpful. I was able to identify some of my peers' grammar errors. However, I must say that some of the suggestions made by my classmates are somewhat confusing. For me, I'd prefer not to make comments on language use and have the teacher make error correction.

Although peer feedback fosters attention to linguistic form at the basic level, novice students with low language proficiency are not equipped to make error correction. Instead, teacher linguistic feedback plays a vital role in the revision process of L2 writing. The following excerpt demonstrated how much a beginning student valued the instructor's corrective feedback:

I appreciate the constructive feedback that the instructor gave me. In most cases, I was able to make error correction in my blog. I found the explanations precise and easily understandable. Making error correction helped me improve my writing. At the end of the semester, I gained confidence in my writing abilities.

The finding is consistent with the one found in Lee's CMC study (2016) showing that effective expert scaffolding on focus on form brings students' attention to linguistic problems and help them build form-meaning connections through blogging.

LIMITATIONS AND SUGGESTIONS FOR FUTURE RESEARCH

Although the findings of this study have shed light on our understanding of the impact of using personal blogs on L2 writing, much more research is still needed. Clearly, the course content and design of one single instructor cannot be representative of the multitude of online learning settings available. Additionally, the study recognizes the short duration of a five-week summer session. Future research would need to look at increasing course length to determine the impact of blog writing regarding how L2 learners individually and collaboratively work in the virtual environment over a greater period of time. Due to the lack of a control group performing the same tasks, it is not feasible to document whether students were more productive in terms of the quantity or quality of their output with blog writing as opposed to more traditional writing methods. Another limitation of this study is that the data collection only included a post-survey. A future study focusing on the comparison of the results of pre- and post-surveys will contribute to a better understanding of task design, personal reflection and peer feedback through blogging. Finally, more detailed investigation into the quality of feedback, including learning effect on language accuracy will further our knowledge about using computer-mediated feedback to support online writing.

PEDAGOGICAL IMPLICATIONS AND CONCLUSION

Despite some challenges reported, the blog project showed how beginning students used personal blogs for L2 writing in ways that are pedagogically effective. The findings are noteworthy and point to important implications for L2 writing instruction. Firstly, the application of blogs itself does not guarantee the success of learning outcomes. Tasks that are linguistically and cognitively suitable for students to engage in different stages of online writing are pivotal for implementing successful blog projects. Secondly, linguistic feedback is essential for the development of language accuracy, and should be integrated into L2 writing instruction to bring students' attention to focus on form without the sacrifice of the focus on meaning. Learners with limited linguistic knowledge are not equipped to give grammar explanations with a high degree of accuracy. To this end, scaffolding provided by the instructor is indispensible in order to ensure language accuracy and avoid fossilization. Thirdly, to promote deeper reflection, the instructor needs to guide students through the peer commenting process, and offer them strategies for critical thinking to prompt in-depth and thoughtful responses. Finally, blog writing offers students an open and social place where they get acquainted with each other, establish interpersonal relationships and build up self-confidence in order to surmount linguistic and sociolinguistic barriers in a fully online learning environment.

As stated by Lee (2016), in our globalized world, there is an ever-increasing demand for language learners to attain the ability to communicate effectively with others. Effective communication involves not only speaking but also writing skills. The study showed that computer-mediated writing using personal blogs provided learners with a superb venue for them to develop written communication skills through social engagement. The application of blogs supports cognitive, social and affective dimensions of online writing by allowing students to learn independently and collaboratively with their peers. The findings revealed that both teacher-made and self-selected topics were suitable for students to engage in the blog writing process. Significantly, peer feedback and instructor scaffolding afforded beginning students the opportunity to notice and reflect on language use and make error correction. Despite the fact that time and place independence offers students the flexibility and convenience of online learning, the results demonstrated that some students failed to self-regulate their own learning due to a busy work schedule or a lack of commitment to online coursework. Consequently, they did not fully participate in blog discussions, nor did they provide timely feedback. To ensure engaged learning in a fully online language course, the instructor should find ways to create social presence and foster a sense of community among students. The study concludes that allocating sufficient time to complete each blog writing assignment and making personal commitment to online contributions are indispensable for maximum online communication and collaboration.

REFERENCES

Alsubaie, A., & Madine, A. (2018). The effect of using blogs to enhance the writing skill of English language learners at a Saudi University. *Global Journal of Educational Studies*, *4*(1), 13–30. doi:10.5296/gjes.v4i1.12224

Armstrong, K., & Retterer, O. (2008). Blogging as L2 writing: A case study. *AACE Journal*, *16*(3), 233–251.

Aydin, S. (2014). The use of blogs in learning English as a foreign language. [MIJE]. *Mevlana International Journal of Education*, *4*(1), 244–259. doi:10.13054/mije.13.79.4.1

Blackmore-Squires, S. (2010). *An investigation into the use of s blog as a tool to improve writing in the second language classroom.* (Unpublished MA dissertation, University of Manchester, UK).

Bonzo, D. (2008). To assign topics or not: Observing fluency and complexity in intermediate foreign language writing. *Foreign Language Annals*, *41*(4), 722–735. doi:10.1111/j.1944-9720.2008.tb03327.x

Cequena, M. B., & Gustilo, L. (2014). Can Weblogs reduce writing anxiety and facilitate improvement in writing skills? *Asian Journal of English Language Studies*, *2*, 1–23.

Chapelle, C. A. (2001). *Computer applications in second language acquisition: Foundations for teaching, testing and research.* Cambridge, UK: Cambridge University Press. doi:10.1017/CBO9781139524681

Chen, J. C., & Brown, K. L. (2012). The effects of authentic audience on English as a second language (ESL) writers: A task-based, computer-mediated approach. *Computer Assisted Language Learning, 25*(5), 435–454. doi:10.1080/09588221.2011.606224

Chen, K. T. (2012). Blog-based peer reviewing in EFL writing classrooms for Chinese speakers. *Computers and Composition, 29*(4), 280–291. doi:10.1016/j.compcom.2012.09.004

Çiftçi, H., & Aslan, E. (2019). Computer-mediated communication in the L2 writing process: A review of studies between 2000 and 2017. [IJCALLT]. *International Journal of Computer-Assisted Language Learning and Teaching, 9*(2), 19–36. doi:10.4018/IJCALLT.2019040102

Çiftçi, H., & Kocoglu, Z. (2012). Effects of peer e-feedback on Turkish EFL students' writing performance. *Journal of Educational Computing Research, 46*(1), 61–84. doi:10.2190/EC.46.1.c

de Andrés Martínez, C. (2012). Developing metacognition at a distance: Sharing students' learning strategies on a reflective blog. *Computer Assisted Language Learning, 25*(2), 199–212. doi:10.1080/09588221.2011.636056

Dickinson, P. (2014). The effect of topic-selection control on EFL writing fluency. *Journal of Niigata University of International and Information Studies, 17*, 15–25.

Elola, I., & Oskoz, A. (2008). Blogging: Fostering intercultural competence development in foreign language and study abroad contexts. *Foreign Language Annals, 41*(3), 454–477. doi:10.1111/j.1944-9720.2008.tb03307.x

Gedera, D. (2012). The dynamics of blog peer feedback in ESL classroom. *Teaching English with Technology, 12*(4), 16–30.

Godwin-Jones, R. (2018). Second language writing online: An update. *Language Learning & Technology, 22*(1), 1–15.

Gunduz, M. (2016). Promoting interaction through blogging in language classrooms. [IJRES]. *International Journal of Research in Education and Science, 2*(2), 438–443. doi:10.21890/ijres.82857

Hegelheimer, V., & Lee, J. (2013). The role of technology in teaching and researching writing. In M. Thomas, H. Reinders, & M. Warschauer (Eds.), *Contemporary computer-assisted language learning* (pp. 287–302). London, UK: Bloomsbury.

Hourigan, T., & Murray, L. (2010). Using blogs to help language students to develop reflective learning strategies: Towards a pedagogical framework. *Australasian Journal of Educational Technology, 26*(2), 209–225. doi:10.14742/ajet.1091

Hyland, K., & Hyland, F. (2006). Feedback on second language student's writing. *Language Teaching, 39*(2), 83–101. doi:10.1017/S0261444806003399

Ishikawa, S. (2018). Composition of three kinds of alternative essay-rating methods to the ESL composition profile. [IJCALLT]. *International Journal of Computer-Assisted Language Learning and Teaching, 8*(4), 32–44. doi:10.4018/IJCALLT.2018100103

Lam, R. (2013). The relationship between assessment types and text revision. *ELT Journal*, *67*(4), 446–458. doi:10.1093/elt/cct034

Lee, L. (2008). Focus on form through collaborative scaffolding in expert-to-novice online interaction. *Language Learning & Technology*, *12*(3), 53–72.

Lee, L. (2010). Fostering reflective writing and interactive exchange through blogging in an advanced language course. *ReCALL*, *22*(2), 212–227. doi:10.1017/S095834401000008X

Lee, L. (2011a). Blogging: Promoting learner autonomy and intercultural competence through study abroad. *Language Learning & Technology*, *15*(3), 87–109.

Lee, L. (2011b). Focus on form through peer feedback in a Spanish-American telecollaborative exchange. *Language Awareness*, *20*(4), 343–357. doi:10.1080/09658416.2011.592589

Lee, L. (2012a). Engaging study abroad students in intercultural learning through blogging and ethnographic interviews. *Foreign Language Annals*, *45*(1), 7–21.

Lee, L. (2012b). Linguistic feedback and focus on form through expert scaffolding in L2 blog writing. In G. Kessler, A. Oskoz, & I. Elola (Eds.), *Technology use across writing contexts* (pp. 57–80). CALICO Book Series.

Lee, L. (2016). Autonomous learning through task-based instruction in fully online language courses. *Language Learning & Technology*, *20*(2), 81–97.

Lee, L. (2017). Extending the intercultural learning after study abroad through a telecollaborative exchange. In J. Jackson, & S. Oguro (Eds.), *Intercultural Interventions in Study Abroad* (pp. 137–154). London, UK: Routledge Publishing. doi:10.4324/9781315276595-9

Lee, L., & Markey, A. (2014). A study of learners' perceptions of online intercultural exchange through Web 2.0 technologies. *ReCALL*, *26*(3), 1–20. doi:10.1017/S0958344014000111

Lin, M. H. (2014). Effects of classroom blogging on ESL student writers: An empirical reassessment. *The Asia-Pacific Education Researcher*, *23*(3), 577–590. doi:10.100740299-013-0131-8

Lin, M. H. (2015). Learner-centered blogging: A preliminary investigation of EFL student writers' experience. *Journal of Educational Technology & Society*, *18*(4), 446–458.

Murray, L., & Hourigan, T. (2008). Blogs for specific purposes: Expressivist or socio-cognitivist approach? *ReCALL*, *20*(1), 82–97. doi:10.1017/S0958344008000719

Nguyen, P. T. (2012). Peer feedback on second language writing through blogs: The case of a Vietnamese EFL classroom. [IJCALLT]. *International Journal of Computer-Assisted Language Learning and Teaching*, *2*(1), 13–23. doi:10.4018/ijcallt.2012010102

Pham, V. P. H., & Usaha, S. (2016). Blog-based peer response for L2 writing revision. *Computer Assisted Language Learning*, *29*(4), 724–748. doi:10.1080/09588221.2015.1026355

Pinkman, K. (2005). Using blogs in the foreign classroom: Encouraging learner independence. *JALT CALL Journal*, *1*(1), 12–24.

Richardson, W. (2011). *Blogs, wikis, podcasts, and other powerful Web tools for classrooms* (3rd ed.). Thousand Oaks, CA: Corwin Press.

Rourke, L., & Kanuka, H. (2009). Learning in communities of inquiry: A review of the literature. *Journal of Distance Education*, *23*(1), 19–48.

Sattar, S. (2015). Learning via blogging: The ESL/EFL perspective. [JEd]. *GSTF Journal on Education*, *3*(1), 7–12.

Schunk, D. H., & Zimmerman, B. J. (Eds.). (2008). *Motivation and self-regulated Learning: Theory, research, and applications*. New York, NY: Lawrence Erlbaum.

Shao, Y., & Crook, C. (2015). The potential of a mobile group blog to support cultural learning among overseas students. *Journal of Studies in International Education*, *19*(5), 1–14. doi:10.1177/1028315315574101

Stickler, U., & Hampel, R. (2010). Cyber Deutsch: Language production and user preferences in a Moodle VLE. *CALICO Journal*, *28*(1), 49–73. doi:10.11139/cj.28.1.49-73

Sun, Y. C. (2010). Extensive writing in foreign-language classrooms: A blogging approach. *Innovations in Education and Teaching International*, *47*(3), 327–339. doi:10.1080/14703297.2010.498184

Sun, Y. C., & Chang, Y. J. (2012). Blogging to learn: Becoming EFL academic writers through collaborative dialogues. *Language Learning & Technology*, *16*(1), 43–61.

Trajtemberg, C., & Yiakoumetti, A. (2011). Weblogs: A tool for EFL interaction, expression, and self-evaluation. *ELT Journal*, *65*(4), 437–445. doi:10.1093/elt/ccr015

Vinagre, M., & Lera, M. (2008). The role of error correction in online exchanges. In F. Zhang, & B. Barber (Eds.), *Handbook of research on computer-enhanced language acquisition and learning* (pp. 326–341). Hershey, PA: IGI Global. doi:10.4018/978-1-59904-895-6.ch019

Vinagre, M., & Munoz, B. (2011). Computer-mediated corrective feedback and language accuracy in telecollaborative exchanges. *Language Learning & Technology*, *15*(1), 72–103.

Vurdien, R. (2013). Enhancing writing skills through blogging in an advanced English as a foreign Language class in Spain. *Computer Assisted Language Learning*, *26*(2), 126–143. doi:10.1080/09588221.2011.639784

Ware, P. (2011). Computer-generated feedback on student writing. *TESOL Quarterly*, *45*(4), 769–775. doi:10.5054/tq.2011.272525

Ware, P., & Kessler, G. (2013). CALL and digital feedback. In M. Thomas, H. Reinders, & M. Warschauer (Eds.), *Contemporary Computer-Assisted Language Learning* (pp. 323–339). London, UK: Continuum.

Ware, P., & O'Dowd, R. (2008). Peer feedback on language form in telecollaboration. *Language Learning & Technology*, *12*(1), 43–63.

Wu, H. (2015). *The effects of blog-supported collaborative writing on writing performance, writing anxiety and perceptions of EFL college students in Taiwan*. (Doctoral Dissertation, University of South Florida).

Xu, Q., & Yu, S. (2018). An action research on computer-mediated communication (CMC) peer feedback in EFL writing context. *The Asia-Pacific Education Researcher*, *27*(3), 207–216. doi:10.100740299-018-0379-0

Yang, Y. F., & Meng, W. T. (2013). The effects of online feedback training on students' text revision. *Language Learning & Technology*, *17*(2), 220–238.

ENDNOTES

1 It should be noted that *Wikispaces* is no longer available. Due to cost issues, the private *Wikispaces* site closed down on January 31, 2019.

2 *Canvas* replaced *Blackboard* at the researcher's institution. Current students are enrolled into *Canvas* courses.

3 *VoiceThread* is a multimodal communication platform that allows users to create multimedia slideshows and share them with others through interactive comments. The author's university owns a departmental license for students to use *VoiceThread*.

Chapter 8
Chinese English Teachers' Perspectives on "hMOOC Flipped Blends":
Project BMELTE (Blending MOOCs Into ELT Education)

Marina Orsini-Jones
https://orcid.org/0000-0001-5250-5682
Coventry University, UK

Bin Zou
https://orcid.org/0000-0002-4863-0998
Xi'an Jiaotong-Liverpool University, China

ABSTRACT

This chapter reports two related studies involving experienced university teachers of English language and literature from China, who engaged in reflection on how to blend FutureLearn MOOCs (Massive Open Online Courses) into their existing English Language Teaching (ELT) curricula while attending courses at Coventry University (UK). The first study relates to 12 lecturers who enrolled on an 'upskilling' English for Academic Purposes (EAP) summer course in academic year 2016-2017. The second one relates to the experience of 5 visiting scholars who attended classes on module Theories, Methods, and Approaches to Language Learning and Teaching on a postgraduate course (Master's of Art) in English Language Teaching and Applied Linguistics in academic years 2017-2018 and 2018-2019. The MA integrates 'off-the-shelf' MOOCs into its curriculum. The chapter investigates the Chinese teachers' perspectives on the adoption of 'hMOOC' distributed flip blends in a Chinese ELT context.

DOI: 10.4018/978-1-7998-1282-1.ch008

INTRODUCTION: A METAREFLECTIVE APPROACH TO MOOC INTEGRATION

This chapter discusses the reflections on the adoption and implementation of a flipped-MOOC curricular integration approach by two groups of experienced teachers of English language and literature from different universities in mainland China. The first group of lecturers (twelve in total) came from Nanjing Agricultural University (NAU) and were attending a teacher education 'upskilling' English for Academic Purposes (EAP) summer course at Coventry University (CU) in the UK in the summer of academic year 2016-2017. The second group consisted of five English and College English[1] tutors attending classes on the MA in English Language Teaching and Applied Linguistics, also at Coventry University, in academic years 2017-2018 and 2018-2019. These tutors were from, respectively: Guangdong University of Foreign Studies, Dalian Maritime University, Guangzhou University, Fuzhou University and Xiamen University and participated in the classes for module *Theories and Methods of Language Learning and Teaching*, where a MOOC had been integrated.

The two studies are mainly qualitative – even if they include some quantitative data. They both stemmed from a British Council ELTRA (English Language Teaching Research Award) project: B-MELTT (Blending MOOCs for English Language Teacher Training) (Orsini-Jones, Conde, Bothwick, Zou & Ma, 2018).

The choice of renaming the project 'BMELTE' (Blending MOOCs for English Language Teacher Education) was deliberate (also refer to the video by Orsini-Jones 2018 on this). The replacement of "teacher training" with "teacher education" aims to stress the value put on the development of an autonomous and reflective approach to teaching practice, in line with Dewey's educational philosophy (1933) and its more recent applications to ELT (Mann & Walsh, 2017).

Borg argues that English language teachers' individual perceptions and beliefs can be strengthened and extended through their education (2011) and, as reported by Mann and Walsh (2017, p.7) reflection is "fundamental to individual education and personal growth". Schön introduced the concepts of "reflection-in-action" (while carrying out the educational experience) and "on- action" after the educational event has taken place (1983) which can support teachers' active learning. Killion and Todnem coined "reflection-for-action" (1991 in Mann & Walsh 2017, p. 8), a future-oriented action which implies a certain level of prediction. For the two studies discussed here a reflective approach underpinned by action research "in-action" - while experiencing a MOOC -, "on action" - after having carried out tasks on the MOOC -, and "for action" - thinking how a MOOC could be integrated into future curricula - was adopted. Participants actively engaged in metareflective practice (Flavell, 1979; Efkledis, 2006), recording their thoughts on their teaching perceptions, beliefs and practice while engaging with MOOCs and reflecting on how they could integrate them into their curricula in the future.

There is evidence that the utilisation of digital learning platforms like MOOCs can foster learner autonomy (Cappellini, Lewis & Mompean, 2017) and, as a consequence to this, in the context of the BMELTE project, teachers' agency. As discussed in Orsini-Jones et al. (2018, p.6), the blended MOOC BMELTE approach aims to address the marginalisation of technology in the professional development of English teachers. Most key texts on ELT used in teacher education (e.g. Richards & Rodgers, 2014) do not appear to fully address the online dimension, its affordances and how transformative effective engagement with technology can prove to be for teachers' agency. Active learning supported by a distributed MOOC blend, can be empowering for ELT practitioners, can help them develop critical digital literacy and encourage them to approach the integration of technology into teaching in a holistic way though experiential learning.

At the same time, engaging with a MOOC on language learning, and teaching and being fully immersed in it, can support Chinese teachers' English language acquisition and enhance their awareness of the variety of communication modes available through a MOOC, while enabling them to also practise English. As argued by Dixon and Thomas (2015), digitally mediated environments can enable sophisticated linguistic exchanges.

THE 'DISTRIBUTED FLIP MOOC BLEND'

According to Li, Zhang, Bonk and Guo (2015, p.4), "a Massive Open Online Course (MOOC) is an 'online course aimed at unlimited participation and open access via the Web'", and 'the term MOOC was first introduced by George Siemens and Stephen Dowes in 2008 when they described an experimental online course named "Connectivism and Connective Knowledge" that had 25 paid enrollments (for credit) with around 2,200 non-credit, non fee paying students (ibid.) '. Lee and Rofe (2016) argue that the acronym was only popularised in November 2012 when *The New York Times* published 'The Year of the MOOC' (Pappano, 2012). Lee and Rofe (2016) also discuss the proliferation of MOOC types and denominations. Their list includes the definition coined by Sandeen (2013) and further explored by Joseph-Israel (2013) and Kim (2015): the 'hMOOCs' (hybrid MOOCs), MOOCs that are used and integrated into existing degree courses. In the studies reported here the hMOOC model has been implemented. At CU various action research studies have been carried out to investigate English teachers' and MA in English Language Teaching students' reflections on the integration of MOOCs into existing curricula (Orsini-Jones, 2015; Orsini-Jones et al. 2015; Orsini-Jones, Altamimi & Conde 2017; Orsini-Jones, Zou, Borthwick & Conde, 2017; Orsini-Jones et al. 2018; Orsini-Jones & Cerveró, 2019). In BMELTE the content of a FutureLearn MOOC becomes an integral part of an existing curriculum in an institution that is not involved in the development of the MOOC itself. Sandeen also refers to the 'h-MOOC 3.0' as a 'distributed flip' model (2013).

The hMOOC blended flip model can be 'distributed' in various ways. For example, in the September 2017 BMELLT implementation cycle, students from CU, from the University of Applied Sciences in Utrecht (HU) and from three universities in China - Xi'an Jiaotong-Liverpool University (XJTLU), Sichuan International Studies University (SISU) and East China University of Science and Technology (ECUST) – were first of all accessing materials online on Task-Based Language Learning (TBLL) on the FutureLearn MOOC *Understanding Language: Learning and Teaching* (created by the British Council in collaboration with the University of Southampton, Borthwick, 2017), secondly they were reflecting on these materials online amongst themselves on a dedicated Moodle platforms and then, in the case of CU and SISU, they were also having face-to-face discussions in their respective classes on said materials and they furthermore engaged in synchronous Collaborative Online International Learning (COIL) discussions via Skype.

Another feature that distinguishes BMELTT/BMELTE from other related studies on MOOC blends, consists in the fact that it does not directly relate to the integration into the curriculum of an 'L-MOOC' (Language Learning MOOC, such as 'Italian for beginners', see Motzo & Proudfoot, 2017), but of MOOCs aimed at stimulating reflections on blended and online learning and other teacher education themes for language teachers, such as *Understanding Language, Learning and Teaching* and *Teaching for Success: the Classroom and the World,* or of MOOCs for other subjects, such as *Business Fundamentals: Effec-*

tive Communication or *Basic Science: Understanding Experiments*, to support the reflection on how to teach English for Specific Purposes.

The blended MOOC flip curricular integration has proven to be quite successful to date (Orsini-Jones et al., 2017; Orsini-Jones et al., 2018; Orsini-Jones & Cerveró 2019), but some issues have arisen due to changes to the way FutureLearn MOOCs are distributed that occurred in 2017. Up to 2016, the MOOCs offered by the UK-based FutureLearn platform (linked to the Open University, https://www.futurelearn.com/courses) were characterised by open access and learning at a distance that allowed their users to self-regulate their own learning, determining when, how and with what content and activities they would engage with (Hood, Littlejohn & Milligan, 2015). MOOCs used to share the "anytime, anywhere principle of m-learning[2]", as defined by Kukulska-Hulme & Shield (2008, p. 281), by allowing students to complete their studies at their own pace. In 2017 however, FutureLearn MOOCs, like the ones used for this study, started limiting time access. Participants have to pay for a subscription if they want continuous access to the MOOC they have been engaged with after the course – which normally lasts between three and six weeks - terminates. This major change put under discussion the initial conceptualisation of FutureLearn MOOCs as 'disruptive' open access technologies, as they used to be Open Educational Resources (OERs) on a massive scale.

The acronym 'MOOC' was already being debated before 2017 (Orsini-Jones et al. 2015) because MOOCs can only be fully accessed in certain parts of the world and not others; the concept of 'course' in an environment in which a tutor cannot moderate effectively due to the number of participants has also been debated *(ibid.)*. Since 2017 FutureLearn MOOCs have become less 'open' and probably, as a consequence to this, less 'massive' due to the subscription fee required after a number of weeks from initial enrolment. The evolution of MOOC accessibility calls for a re-definition of terms of reference and also has implications for those who, like the authors of this piece, used to regularly integrate them into their curricula because they were OERs.

However, MOOCs still provide sufficient value added and 'flipped mode' potential to be an interesting way of enhancing an existing curriculum, as reiterated by Zhang (2017), who used a MOOC blend at Shenzen University in China to support the teaching of College English. Quoting Abeysekera and Dawson (2014), Zhang lists the key features of a flipped approach facilitated by the integration of a MOOC (2017, p. 17):

- most information-transmission teaching happens out of class;
- classroom time can be utilised for active learning and social-collaborative tasks; and
- students are required to complete pre- and/or post-class activities to fully benefit from in-class work.

Up to 2015, most publications on MOOCs by Chinese scholars (e.g. Chen, 2014; Chen, 2015; Ma & Hu, 2015; Zhang, 2015), appeared to focus on MOOC platforms and studies in the USA. Many articles did not appear to provide information on how to use MOOCs or discuss effective approaches to MOOC integration into existing classes, particularly with reference to TESOL/ELT courses. It was also reported that Chinese students were reluctant to engage with discussion forums online, and for this reason Chinese scholars suggested integrating blended learning strategies and flipped classroom approaches when using MOOCs for English teaching and learning (e.g. Chen, 2015). Luo (2017) argues that Chinese students feel more confident interacting in class after having studied MOOCs outside classroom time in flipped mode, unlike their U.S.A. counterparts, who enjoy online interaction on MOOC forums. Similar findings emerged from a previous BMELTET study (Orsini-Jones et al., 2018), where participants from China studying in the UK had expressed a certain reluctance to engage online on the MOOC and declared to be more comfortable with post-MOOC classroom engagement in flipped mode.

Suo & Chi (2018) explored blended learning using MOOCs in an intercultural foreign language teaching and learning context. They used an intercultural course on FutureLearn and participants were 49 sophomore (second year) students. Participating students worked on the MOOC for self-study after class and then discussed and shared their understanding in class. The study found that self-study on the MOOC enhanced students' autonomous learning and flip blend collaboration and the teacher's support in class reinforced their critical thinking. Students and staff alike valued the interactions with learners from other countries on the MOOC, which provided a real intercultural context. Jiang, & Hu (2018) also found that flip blend learning in MOOC contexts can enhance effective EFL learning and teaching and achieve innovation in college EFL teaching. In their study, Juiang and Hu (2018), reported that the teachers utilized the video materials on the MOOC, which students watched out of class. The teachers organized collaborative activities and group discussions based on such videos, which appeared to raise students' motivation and learning efficiency.

Luo (2018) investigated further flipped learning with an EFL MOOC she had designed. The 11 participating teachers provided positive comments on flipped classrooms with the MOOC after its implementation. They asserted that a flipped approach can improve students' autonomous learning and effectiveness in the classroom. The majority of the 342 participating students also expressed positive views about the distributed flip blend used in conjunction with their teachers' support in class. The blend enabled them to dynamically interact with others in group discussions because they had watched the relevant videos before each class.

In view of the experience of teaching teachers (or would be teachers) about MOOCs, despite the limitation to access caused by the introduction of subscription fees, which echoes the evolution of other popular OERs (Open Educational Resources), MOOCs can still be utilised to stimulate reflection on learning and teaching in general and language learning and teaching in particular. Also, there is a growing interest for MOOCs in China. A number of online systems have provided platforms for teachers to deliver MOOC courses (Klobus, Macintosh & Murphy, 2015). Many Chinese universities are keen to use MOOC platforms to deliver their courses which are free to their own students as well as students from other universities. For example, Xuetang Zaixian (https://www.xuetangx.com/), - with involvement, amongst others, of Tsinghua University, Fudan University, Taiwan Tsinghua University and Taiwan Chiao Tung University - and Chinese University MOOC (http://www.icourse163.org/) - with support from Beijing University, Nanjing University and Zhejing University - are two popular online platforms for many universities to deliver their MOOC courses.

Although there are studies in Chinese exploring the opportunity for EFL (English as Foreign Language) teachers to integrate MOOCs into their curricula (e.g. Ma & Hu, 2014; Chen, 2015), many teachers are still not aware of the scope of MOOCs and how to use them effectively even if there is a strong drive from the Chinese government to support MOOC developments. The low completion rates on MOOCs, the lack of good quality materials and valid assessment tasks have also been identified as problematic issues for MOOCs in China (Chen, 2014).

Despite the issues above, another benefit of utilising MOOCs for teacher education is the exposure to massive social-collaborative opportunities they provide and the participation in a global 'community of practice' (Wenger Trayner & Wenger Trayner, 2015) they afford. As illustrated by Ferguson, Coughlan and Heredotou (2016), quoted in Motzo and Proudfoot (2017, pp. 89-90), "the MOOCs hosted by FutureLearn are underpinned by the pedagogy of conversational learning with a learning environment that aims to foster social interaction and collaboration between learners mainly through the use of embedded tools such as discussions".

The Chinese English teachers involved in BMELTE engaged in active reflection on their MOOC experience and provided constructive feedback on it, highlighting the added value of the flipped blend, its social-collaborative aspects and the added value of enriching their English, while actively reflecting on how to teach English, while at the same time expressing their reservations towards this hMOOC flip.

METHODOLOGY

The research methodology approach was based on related studies (Orsini-Jones et al., 2015; Orsini-Jones, 2015; Orsini-Jones et al., 2017) that had preceded the implementation of this 'spin off' of the BMELTT project. A grounded mixed-method approach was adopted: both qualitative and quantitative data were collected, with a stronger focus on qualitative data. The teachers were actively involved in the study and there were some autoethnographic elements to it too (Mackey & Gass, 2005, p.77). With both groups of teachers involved, the main data sources used were:

1. A pre-MOOC and a post-MOOC online survey administered through the JISC Online Surveys tool (formerly Bristol Online Survey, BOS: a survey provider that complies with the General Data Protection Regulation introduced in Europe in May 2018) to involve participants in individual meta-reflections before and after they engaged with the MOOC modelled on previous cycles of the project.
2. The analysis of the discussion postings relating to the MOOC integration and blended-MOOC task design posted by the participants in Moodle (which is also GDPR compliant).
3. The analysis of the reflective report by two of the participants who collated both their views on MOOC blends and those of the other participants in individual interviews carried out with the summer school participants at NAU on their return to China.
4. The analysis of the reflections by the five teachers in the second group (2017-2018 and 2018-2019);
5. The reflections that stemmed from a post-MOOC focus group with the participants from NAU four months after the summer school had finished, when the initial survey results were analysed and triangulated. The focus group took place in China.
6. The reflections that stemmed from the creation of a video (Orsini-Jones, 2018) based on this paper by the teachers in the second group
7. Semi-structured interviews carried out with the tutors attending classes on the MA at Coventry University.

The research questions of this study focused on the participating teachers' beliefs regarding an autonomous approach to language learning and teaching facilitated by a MOOC, their views on online learning and whether or not they perceived a non-language specific MOOC as a useful platform to use to teach General English:

The overall questions set by the researchers where:

1. Can a 'flipped MOOC' integration approach support the teaching of English in China?

2. What is the teachers' perception of online and blended learning?
3. What recommendations could be made for the purpose of English teacher education in China following this project?

Informed consent was sought and obtained from all participants, in compliance with the Coventry University ethics governance requirements.

THE PRE-MOOC BRISTOL ONLINE SURVEY

The Pre-MOOC survey consisted of two sections. The first one, adapted from a related study by Orsini-Jones et al. (2015), included two types of questions:

1. Specific open questions that were used to gather sufficient 'biodata information' from the participants such as nationality, university affiliation, mode of study, L1 (language 1), age, gender, English language proficiency, and previous teaching experience (Mackey & Gass, 2016, p.177).
2. Short-answer questions that allowed participants to express their opinions, attitudes, and expectations towards MOOC integration into existing curricula.

The second section covered attitudinal statements in Likert-scale format, which were based on the work on autonomy in language education by Palfreyman (2003) and Benson (2007). This part of the survey aimed to identify participants' beliefs on learner autonomy in English language teaching and learning, with particular reference to the development of autonomy in online settings. It also aimed to investigate their attitudes towards online and blended learning.

FEEDBACK FROM THE FIRST GROUP OF TEACHERS FROM NANJING AGRICULTURAL UNIVERSITY (NAU)

The twelve teachers involved were all female and aged 31-50. Their proficiency in English was high, ranging between IELTS 6 (CEFR B2) to IELTS 7 and above (CEFR C2). The length of their teaching experience varied between six and 23 years. Eleven out of 12 stated that they knew what a MOOC was and three of them stated that they had taken part in a MOOC before. However, they all declared that they had never taken part in a course involving reflecting on a MOOC for the purpose of integrating it into their curricula. In reply to the question 'What are your beliefs regarding online learning', four participating teachers stated that "convenience" was a positive factor when considering online solutions, but two expressed concerns relating to both ITS problematic issues that might occur and the possible negative impact of a loss of face-to-face contact.

It was also interesting to see the replies to beliefs regarding language learning online, where most teachers from NAU agreed it was useful, but more for teacher education than for language learners.

THE MOOC SELECTED FOR THE NAU TEACHERS: FUTURELEARN BUSINESS FUNDAMENTALS: EFFECTIVE COMMUNICATION

Although most of the teachers involved in the study were teaching General English, the MOOC used was *Business Fundamentals: Effective Communication* (FutureLearn) by the Open University, to explore how it could be used to teach either ESP (English for Specific Purposes) or General English. The choice was dictated by convenience and suitability, that is to say what MOOC was available at the time the group of teachers was in England and that could be useful to them for the purpose of discussing how to blend MOOCs in ELT.

The teachers used the selected MOOC in conjunction with Moodle. A dedicated Moodle website had been created for the summer school. They were asked to do some preparatory work before engaging with the MOOC. This consisted of:

1. Filling in the Pre-MOOC survey;
2. Reading background information on MOOC integration (e.g. Orsini-Jones, 2015);
3. Watching the presentation on MOOCs by Stephen Bax given at the BMELTT symposium held at Coventry University in July 2017 (Bax, 2018).

In class, during a three-hour lecture/workshop session that followed the pre-MOOC work, the teachers were asked to register for the FutureLearn MOOC selected, and engage in an initial navigational workshop on the learning environment. The workshop included trying out the social-collaborative functions within the MOOC, by either posting their thoughts in the 'comments' section or 'lurk' in that environment to evaluate it.

The teachers were then asked to carry on with the MOOC outside classroom time, select an activity in the MOOC and design a blended learning task based on it. Most teachers had to teach communication skills for their General English courses in China, so the MOOC appeared to be appropriate for their needs. The out-of-class task design work was followed by a 'flipped' seminar/workshop on both the English contained in the MOOC and a reflection on how the MOOC could be blended into their ELT.

At the end of the week, the teachers were asked to post their blended-MOOC-inspired tasks online in the relevant asynchronous forum in Moodle to share and discuss them. The tasks created were interesting and imaginative and were shared and analysed in class face-to-face. Two sample tasks posted in the discussion forum in Moodle are reproduced below, one for General English and one for translation:

Box 1. Sample task 1 for B1 level students – general English

Class activities: step 1 Watch the video: What is LinkedIn (on the MOOC)? (1 minute) step 2 Ask Ss questions about LinkedIn, e.g. What they can do with LinkedIn? (2 minutes) step 3 Ask Ss to work in groups of 3-4, share their experience of using social media (8 minutes) What social media do you use most often? Why? What do you usually do on them? What are the benefits? How long do you spend on them? Discuss the advantages and disadvantages of using social media step 4 One spokesman of each group present their conclusion in 1 minute

Box 2. Sample task two for English major students studying interpreting B2/C1 level (20 min task)

Pre-class: **purpose:** to know about the course (on the MOOC) and the video clip **Task one (pre-class)**: reading (3m.) read what is networking. **Task two (pre-class)**: shadow reading aloud (3.25m. X 3) and have one of the readings recorded **In-class** **purpose:** to know more about the video **Task three (in-class):** listening comprehension (3.25m.+3m.) Students are asked to listen to the video three times and answer a few questions. What are the advantages of social networking according to three speakers? **Task four (in-class):** blank-filling (3.25+2m.) Take away the key words about the advantages and do blank-filling. **purpose: interpreting practice** **Task five (in-class)**: sight interpreting (4m.) Give students the printed transcript and do sight interpreting **Task six (in-class)**: simulated consecutive interpreting (4m.) One student reads James's words and the other interprets. There are 7 pairs. **Task seven (in-class)**: simulated consecutive interpreting (4m.) Exchange recorded readings, listen to the partner's reading and do consecutive interpreting. There are 8 pairs of students.

On the whole the teachers from NAU appeared to have found the creation of the tasks based on the MOOC content stimulating and were very positive about this 'new to them' reflective experience.

THE FOCUS GROUP TRIANGULATION WITH THE POST-MOOC SURVEY RESULTS: NAU SUMMER SCHOOL GROUP

Eleven out of the twelve lecturers who had taken part in the summer school in July-August 2017 took part in a focus group in Nanjing coordinated by the Principal Investigator in November 2017. They were shown the results of their pre-and post-MOOC surveys and asked to discuss the three questions posed earlier:

- Did they think that a 'flipped MOOC' integration approach could support the teaching of English in China, with particular reference to NAU?
- What were their views on online and blended learning?
- What recommendations could be made for the purpose of English teacher education in China following their experience on this project?

In line with the definition of action research by McNiff, this paper describes "research with" (1988:4):

It is research WITH rather than research ON. (…) (It) encourages teachers to become adventurous and critical in their thinking, to develop theories and rationales for their practice, and to give reasoned justification for their public claims to professional knowledge. It is this systematic ENQUIRY MADE PUBLIC which distinguishes the activity as research.

The post-MOOC survey consisted of three sections. The first section, which was similar to the first section of the pre-MOOC survey, included a multiple-choice item that asked for the degree of participation with the MOOC. This question aimed to reveal the possible correlation between the degree of participation and the degree of change in participants' beliefs after they engaged with the MOOC. The second section of the survey consisted of Likert-scale type statements relating to participant's perceptions and attitudes regarding their MOOC experience.

In reply to question 6: "Are you considering blending an existing MOOC into your curriculum', all twelve tutors replied that they were. However, when the focus group was carried out in November, it transpired that only the same four tutors who were using MOOCs before they had attended the summer school were blending MOOCs into their curricula. The reasons provided in the focus group by the 'non-adopters' were:

1. Curricular constraints;
2. Slow server/ITS issues on campus;
3. Unsuitability of existing MOOCs for their teaching/learning needs;
4. Fear of increased workload;
5. Lack of value attached to MOOC developments by management (as opposed to publishing research papers);
6. Lack of personalized feedback provided on the activities on the MOOC;
7. Concerns about 'losing face' (existing 'off the shelf' MOOCs as a threat to the teacher's authority, as the teachers felt they might not be able to answer specific questions on the material covered).

Point seven above was further discussed during the focus group and appeared to have an intercultural dimension linked to the Chinese expectations about teacher knowledge and the Confucius tradition that a teacher is perceived to be 'omniscient', one of the participants stated:

Many teachers believe that, since the task of teaching has traditionally been defined as transmitting wisdom, imparting knowledge and solving doubts, the teachers are expected to provide feedback and answers to students whenever students have got any doubts. If teachers fail to provide accurate and clear keys to the answers, the students will often feel depressed and the teachers themselves will also feel embarrassed. This traditional expectation makes teachers feel under great pressure when they are facing the amount of information on a MOOC. Thus, a lot of teachers are reluctant to give students the freedom to choose from a number of MOOC sources in order to achieve some controlling effects.

The fear of 'losing face' and/or control was mentioned by most participants who stated that they would prefer to design their own MOOCs, rather than adopt existing ones, to be in control of the content and the activities and be able to provide appropriate feedback in a confident way. It also emerged that the definition of what a MOOC is was quite 'fuzzy', according to another participant:

When it comes to how to define "online and blended learning", opinions vary. In the context English teaching in Chinese universities, online and blended learning have many other names like MOOC blend, MOOC flip, MOOC integration, blended classroom, and flipped classroom. They are similar concepts with different meanings but without clear boundaries. Among them, MOOC, MOOC blend and flipped classroom are new emerging concepts that are frequently mentioned by English teachers in Chinese universities. However, misunderstanding and confusion of concepts may occur.

What emerged was a rather broad definition of what MOOCs are. The MOOC acronym would appear to be associated with any online course, whether open or closed, whether free or carrying a subscription fee, including textbook-based online materials, as demonstrated by the teacher's feedback on MOOCs below, where the 'MOOC video clips' would probably be defined as 'additional courseware material' in other ELT teaching contexts, e.g. in the UK:

A textbook I once used called New Target English published by Shanghai Foreign Language Education Press provides ready-to-use courseware for teachers. The well-planned courseware is comprised of PPTs, audios and videos. A significant portion of those multi-media files are MOOC video clips.

In both the post-MOOC survey and in the focus group, all participating teachers agreed that using the MOOC to reflect on their practice and to develop an autonomous approach to language learning and teaching had supported their personal development as ELT specialists. They all valued the experience for their Continuous Professional Development (CPD). So, although some expressed doubts about blending MOOCs into their curricula, all agreed that they had found the reflective teacher education MOOC blend on the summer school very beneficial for their personal development.

THE SECOND GROUP OF TEACHERS: VISITING SCHOLARS IN ACADEMIC YEARS 2017-2018 AND 2018-2019

The five teachers involved in the BMELTE project were three female and two male, aged 29-60. Like with the teachers from NAU, their proficiency in English was high, ranging between IELTS 6 (CEFR B2) to IELTS 7 and above (CEFR C2). The length of their teaching experience varied between seven and over thirty years. Four out of five stated that they knew what a MOOC was and two of them stated that they had taken part in a MOOC before. However, like the teachers from NAU, they all stated that they had never taken part in a course involving reflecting on a MOOC for the purpose of integrating it into their curricula to enhance reflection on English language teaching.

As with the NAU teachers, the following broad questions were posed after the Pre-MOOC and Post MOOC surveys were administered, but a semi-structured interview format was used instead of a focus group:

- Did they think that a 'flipped MOOC' integration approach could support the teaching of English in China?
- What were their views on online and blended learning?
- What recommendations could be made for the purpose of English teacher education in China following their experience on this project?

All five teachers attended the classes for module *Theories, methods and approaches of language learning and teaching* where the MOOC Understanding Language: Learning and Teaching - by the University of Southampton and the British Council - had been integrated to implement BMELTE. As already reported in Orsini-Jones et al. (2018, p. 10), this MOOC was designed to act primarily as a marketing tool to increase student recruitment on a jointly run online Master's in English Language Teaching delivered by the University of Southampton with the British Council. It offers a 'taste' of key concepts in the study of applied linguistics and runs over five weeks, featuring a different topic each week: language learning, language teaching, technology in teaching, Global English and a research week. Course content reflects some activities and topics covered on the Masters in ELT both at the University of Southampton and at Coventry University and is delivered by a range of staff from the Applied Linguistics Department at the University of Southampton and the British Council, via short videos and linked discussion questions. It aims to be academic but approachable in tone. There are also texts to read, tasks to engage in and interactive elements, such as polls. Learners discuss and respond to questions or tasks in comment areas attached to each activity and the notion of 'learning as a conversation' is at the core of the learning design (Laurillard 2002). All FutureLearn MOOCs include sections that enable participants to engage in an online dialogue with other participants and/or the moderators in the forums for each unit, as well as with the materials available.

Unlike the teachers from NAU, the scholars did not have dedicated sessions. They carried out the same BMELTE activities as the other students in the class. BMELTE for these scholars involved the addition of telecollaboration or Collaborative Online International Learning (COIL, see Orsini-Jones & Lee, 2018) with partners in Spain to discuss the themes of the MOOC. They:

- Participated in face-to-face classroom interactions discussing the topics that were common to the MOOC and the syllabus (e.g. Task-Based Learning; Content and Language Integrated Learning; Online Language Learning and Teaching);
- Participated in the relevant discussion on the Moodle website that related to the topics covered;
- Took part in the Moodle website discussions that had been created specifically to share knowledge with the Coventry Spanish partners from La Florida Universitària in València, who were also taking part in the MOOC blend through telecollaboration;
- Shared knowledge on the MOOC via the 'comments' (forums) section and engaged in the live webinars offered on the MOOC;
- Filled in the pre- and post- MOOC surveys; and
- Took part in semi-structured interviews about their experience once the course was completed.

The feedback from this group of Chinese scholars was mixed. One of them stated that she did not believe in online learning (semi-structured interviews, 2017, participant A):

When we learn something online, we don't take it seriously. For me, when I learn something online, it's entertainment and I don't take it very seriously. And, it's my problem because I am a little bit behind the time. On the computer, online, I just want to send messages, get information...I can't think, I can't analyse through the computer. So, I can watch movies on computer or just listening to speech on computer, but I don't think I will...I can learn something, but I will not take it seriously. I just kind of get extra material to relax myself.

The above participant did not appear to see to the connection between the online environment (the MOOC) and its blended integration into the face-to-face classroom, possibly because of her beliefs on online learning, but it was quite interesting to see how she answered the question: 'Did the engagement with the MOOC give you new ideas on how to teach?', see below (semi-structured interviews, 2017, participant A):

It didn't give me new ideas on how to teach, but it made me think a lot. Why... I just think why the lecturer want to tell me this? What's the purpose? How can I apply it into my teaching? And it made me very puzzled sometimes. And I tried to find an answer, and perhaps at least it made me think that's good.

Participant A appeared therefore to admit that engaging with the MOOC had triggered some level of reflection and critical thinking on her practice, which was exactly what the investigators were hoping for.

Another participant (B) felt that the blend was useful for the purpose of stimulating reflection on learning and teaching, but he thought that the stress on the MOOC was too commercial (promoting the MA at Southampton University) and the coverage of the course material too superficial. For these reasons he suggested that students in China should be given a selection of MOOCs to choose from, preferably MOOCs designed in China and incorporating authentic materials in English, like TED talks. He felt that MOOCs designed in China catered better for the intercultural and linguistic needs of Chinese students and teachers.

The third participant (C) highlighted the advantages of utilising a MOOC, namely the 'any time/anywhere' opportunities offered to learners and the ability that learners have to make the most of the accessibility features of the FutureLearn MOOCs, such as subtitles and transcripts available for all video clips that can be used to create further language learning activities. He however pointed out that in some parts of China it can be a challenge to stream and watch videos due to server issues.

The fourth participant (D) stated that she had made extensive use of MOOCs when teaching in China, recommending MOOCs related to the topics discussed in class. She suggested the use of the Chinese MOOC *Introducing China in English* (http://moocs.unipus.cn/course/70) that she had embedded into her course *Chinese Culture in English* for non –English majors. She felt it was a good platform for students to share their opinions with their peers from the different parts of the country. The scholar had had access to the results from the first study with the NAU teachers before her interview and stated that she, unlike some of the NAU lecturers, was not worried about 'losing face' by integrating 'off the shelf' MOOCs in her curriculum. She stated (semi-structured interview, participant D, 2019):

I do not think we are afraid of using MOOCs just because teachers should be "sages on stages". In the first class of the course, teachers can explain to the students that in the Information Age, it is impossible for teachers to know everything. University students are smart enough to accept this belief. Sometimes the teacher's role is to work together with students to get problems solved.

Participant E agreed with the above statement and added that she had made extensive use of the h-MOOC model, flipping classroom delivery with the mediation of MOOC videos. She also stated that she had found BMELTE so useful that she had decided to do a little autoethnographical study based on the use of another FutureLearn MOOC that she had selected herself while in Coventry: *TESOL Strategies: Enriching Classroom (TSEC),* designed by staff at the School of Education at the University of Glasgow, and that she had also paid for an upgrade to have continuous access to it. She did however stress that hMOOC flip blends can be time-consuming to implement in ELT practice and that, therefore, she would probably not be able to implement the blend herself on her return to China.

With reference to the research questions set, four out of five scholars were in favour of h-MOOC blends and the integration of blended and online learning both in their teaching practice and in their continuous professional development. However, one of them continued to harbour very strong skepticism towards any type of e-learning, despite the fact that they had stated that the BMELTE experience had given them 'teaching practice food for thought'.

All of the visiting scholars has some reservations about autonomous learning and the role that technology can play in supporting it. One stated in fact that autonomy is a Western concept that has been adopted in China, but that it is not fully understood there and therefore is challenging to implement.

It also appeared, like with the teachers from NAU, that the concept of MOOC embraced a wider connotation than in the UK. When asked to provide an example of a MOOC in China, the teachers provided materials that appeared to be uploaded in Virtual Learning Environments like Moodle, initially for institutional use, but then opened for free access. These would probably be considered 'courseware', rather than courses, in other educational contexts, as normally in the UK and the USA a MOOC is supported by a MOOC platform, such as FutureLearn in the UK.

CONCLUSION

The research questions posed for this study were:

1. Can a 'flipped MOOC' integration approach support the teaching of English in China?
2. What is the teachers' perception of online and blended learning?
3. What recommendations could be made for the purpose of English teacher education in China following this project?

With reference to question 1, it appeared that all the teachers consulted used flipped models for ELT, but that some of them were reluctant to utilise 'off-the-shelf' MOOCs for their blends for the reasons highlighted above. All participating tutors were acquainted with online and blended learning and most made use of these in their learning and teaching practice. Most teachers appeared to have become 'converted' to the use of MOOCs for their own Continuous Professional Development, but also highlighted the constraints in their local teaching contexts that might prevent them from implementing an hMOOC flipped blend.

Most stated that they could see MOOCs like the ready-made FutureLearn ones as an 'add-on' for students to do in their own time, as an extra resource to use, as opposed to being a core aspect blended into their own curriculum. Some were developing their own online courses or using Chinese courses created for ELT.

With reference to question 2, while some of the replies provided were in line with those given by tutors in other countries too (in Britain for example, see Orsini-Jones, et al., 2015), such as the difficulty in integrating a MOOC into an existing curriculum and the extra workload in redesigning the syllabus to accommodate the blend, one aspect stood out as 'context specific', that is to say the way the MOOC acronym has been understood in China, where a MOOC could be an institutional online course supported by a VLE, or even a section of an online course, possibly attached to and/or supporting an existing textbook (e.g. support courseware).

Having said that, the definition of what a MOOC stands for is becoming blurred in Western contexts too, as demonstrated by the website by Gimeno, based in Spain, and titled 'Ana Gimeno MOOC and Free Online Courses' (https://www.mooc-list.com/instructor/ana-gimeno, 2019). It would appear that the conceptualisation of what a MOOC is, is becoming fuzzy in all teaching contexts, not only in China.

Borthwick (personal communication, July 2017), who has authored FutureLearn MOOCs, reports that FutureLearn have introduced business models which broaden the interpretation of 'MOOC.' Borthwick now frequently uses the term 'online courses which reach a mass audience' rather than 'MOOC,' in relation to most courses run through the FutureLearn platform. This is because the course material is open and freely available during the course run, but if learners wish to retain access to course content, they are now required to pay a fee, an 'upgrade'. So according to Borthwick, even in the UK the picture is becoming more nuanced and so many of the definitions do not reflect current reality anymore (or at least the range of current realities).

As for question 3, the authors of this paper have greatly benefitted from this exchange of ideas on MOOC research and practice for the purpose of ELT teacher education. The joint cross-continental discussion has helped all participants and the principal investigators to uncover aspects of online learning and blended learning they had not considered before and see their language learning and teaching practice from different intercultural perspectives. So, even if doubts were expressed regarding the adoption of a flipped MOOC blend by some of the participants, all agreed that they had gained new insights into ELT theory and practice.

With reference to Stephen Bax's work on the normalisation of technology (2003; 2011 & 2018) this might suggest that the original version of the pioneering Open Educational Resource (OER) MOOCs might not become 'normalised' and rather be renamed as 'online courses'. However, as the 'MOOC' acronym has been adopted and promoted by the Ministry of Education in China (Ma et al., 2018; also see http://www.icourses.cn/home), it might also be possible that the definition/understanding of MOOCs specific to the Chinese context is already normalised in China as 'online courses', not necessarily massive, not necessarily open. Or it could also be that courses similar to MOOCs in format, but on a smaller scale, will be more normalised than MOOCs. SPOCs (Small Private Online Courses) are for example becoming popular (see Zhang, Zhang & Jin, 2018). Other hMOOC examples include institutions and teachers in China asking FutureLearn to use their videos from relevant MOOCs and flip the classroom by using these videos only, rather than the whole MOOC (Borthwick, personal communication, 28 June 2019).

The two studies reported here were small-scale projects, so we need to exert caution before we can generalise their results. It is hoped that they can be scaled up to more Chinese teachers and to other universities in China to verify the validity of the findings and further explore how distributed flip hMOOC blends are perceived.

ACKNOWLEDGEMENT

We would like to thank all the staff and students who have participated in our study on the distributed flip MOOC blend curricular integration since 2014 and in particular the lecturers from Nanjing Agricultural University in China and the visiting scholars auditing classes at Coventry University who gave us consent to use the data reported here. We would also like to thank Kate Borthwick, from the University of Southampton, who provided useful insights on MOOCs.

REFERENCES

Abeysekera, L., & Dawson, P. (2014). Motivation and cognition load in the flipped classroom: Definition, rational and a call for research. *Higher Education Research & Development, 34*(1), 1–14. doi:10.1080/07294360.2014.934336

Bax, S. (2003). CALL – Past, present and future. *System, 31*(11), 13–28. doi:10.1016/S0346-251X(02)00071-4

Bax, S. (2011). Normalisation revisited: the effective use of technology in language education. *International Journal of Computer-Assisted Language Learning and Teaching, 1*(2), 1–15. doi:10.4018/ijcallt.2011040101

Bax, S. (2018). MOOCs as a new technology: approaches to normalising the MOOC experience for our learners; paper posthumously transcribed by Marina Orsini-Jones. In M. Orsini-Jones, & S. Smith (Eds.), Flipping the blend through MOOCs, MALL, and OIL – new directions in CALL (pp. 9-16). Research-publishing.net. doi:10.14705/rpnet.2018.23.785

Benson, P. (2007). Autonomy in language teaching and learning. *Language Teaching, 40*(1), 21–40. doi:10.1017/S0261444806003958

Borg, S. (2011). The impact of in-service teacher education on language teachers' beliefs. *System, 39*(3), 370–380. doi:10.1016/j.system.2011.07.009

Borthwick, K. (2018). What our MOOC did next: embedding, exploiting, and extending an existing MOOC to fit strategic purposes and priorities. In M. Orsini-Jones, & S. Smith (Eds.), Flipping the blend through MOOCs, MALL and OIL – new directions in CALL (pp. 17-23). Dublin, Ireland: Research-publishing.net. doi:10.14705/rpnet.2018.23.786

Cappellini, M., Lewis, T., & Rivens Mompean, A. (2017). *Learner Autonomy and Web 2.0.* Sheffield, UK: Equinox.

Chen, B. (2014). MOOCs: Contributions and dilemmas. *TEFLE, 157*, 38–43.

Chen, J. (2015). MOOCs and foreign language teaching studies in the big data era: challenges and opportunities. *TEFLE, 1*, 3–8.

Chinnery, G. M. (2006). Going to the MALL: Mobile assisted language learning. *Language Learning & Technology, 10*(1), 9–16. Retrieved from https://www.learntechlib.org/p/74432/

Dewey, J. (1933). *How we think: A restatement of the relation pf reflective thinking to the educative process* (Revised ed.). Boston, MA: D.C. Heath.

Ding, Y., & Jiang, X. (2016). *Exploring hot topics of MOOC research in China and abroad: a co-word analysis*. Paper presented at the International Symposium on CALL, Qingdao, China.

Dixon, E., & Thomas, M. (2015). *Researching language learner interactions online: from social media to MOOCs. CALICO*. Monograph Series.

Donaghue, H. (2003). An instrument to elicit teachers' beliefs and assumptions. *ELT Journal, 57*(4), 344–351. doi:10.1093/elt/57.4.344

Efkledis, A. (2006). Metacognition, affect, and conceptual difficulty. In J. H. F. Meyer, & R. Land (Eds.), *Overcoming barriers to student understanding: Threshold concepts and troublesome knowledge. London, UK.* (pp. 48–69). Falmer, UK: Routledge.

Ferguson, R., Coughlan, T., & Heredotou, C. (2016). *MOOCs: what the open university research tells us. The Open University*. Milton Keynes: Institute of Educational Technology.

Flavell, J. (1979). Metacognition and cognitive monitoring: A new era cognitive-developmental inquiry. *The American Psychologist*, *34*(10), 906–911. doi:10.1037/0003-066X.34.10.906

FutureLearn. (n.d.). Retrieved from https://www.futurelearn.com

Gimeno, A. (2019) Ana Gimeno MOOC and free online courses. Retrieved from https://www.mooc-list.com/instructor/ana-gimeno

Gimeno-Sanz, A. (2017). Designing a MOOC for learners of Spanish: exploring learner usage and satisfaction. In K. Borthwick, L. Bradley & S. Thouësny (Eds), CALL in a climate of change: adapting to turbulent global conditions – short papers from EUROCALL 2017 (pp. 122-127). Research-publishing.net. https://doi.org/. eurocall2017.700 doi:10.14705/rpnet.2017

Hood, N., Littlejohn, A., & Milligan, C. (2015). Context counts: How learners' contexts influence learning in a MOOC. *Computers & Education*, *91*, 83–91. doi:10.1016/j.compedu.2015.10.019

Jiang, Y., & Hu, J. S. (2018). A study on the large-scale instruction mechanism of SPOC-based college English flipped classroom. *TEFLE*, *4*, 9–15.

Joseph-Israel, M. (2013). Effectiveness of integrating MOOCs in traditional classrooms for undergraduate students. *IRRODL. The International Review of Open and Distributed Learning*, *16*(5). doi:10.19173/irrodl.v16i5.2222

Killion, J. P., & Todnem, G. R. (1991). A process for personal theory building. *Educational Leadership*, *48*(6), 14–16.

Kim, P. (Ed.). (2015). *Massive open online courses: the MOOC revolution*. New York: Routledge.

Klobus, J., Mackintosh, B., & Murphy, J. (2015). The anatomy of MOOCs. In P. Kim (Ed.), *Massive open online courses: the MOOC revolution*. New York: Routledge.

Kukulska-Hulme, A., & Shield, L. (2008). An overview of mobile assisted language learning: From content delivery to supported collaboration and interaction. *ReCALL: The Journal of EUROCALL*, *20*(3), 271–289. doi:10.1017/S0958344008000335

Laurillard (2002). Rethinking University Teaching: A Framework for the Effective. Use of Learning Technologies, 2nd ed. London: Routledge Falmer.

Lee, Y., & Rofe, J. S. (2016). Pedagogy and flipped assessment: experience of designing and running a MOOC on research methods. *Open Learning: The Journal of Open, Distance and e-Learning, 31*(2), 116-129, doi:10.1080/02680513.2016.1188690

Li, Y., Zhang, M., Bonk, C. J., & Guo, N. (2015). Integrating MOOC and flipped classroom practice in a traditional undergraduate course: students' experience and perceptions. [iJET]. *International Journal of Emerging Technologies in Learning*, *10*(6), 4–10. doi:10.3991/ijet.v10i6.4708

Luo, R. (2017). A study of autonomous foreign language learning in the Internet environment- An investigation on MOOCs in the USA and China. *Foreign Language World*, *6*, 29–36.

Luo, S. (2018). Evaluating the learning environment of MOOC-based college English flipped classrooms. *TEFLE*, *4*, 16–22.

Ma, W., & Hu, J. (2015). On the impact of international MOOCs and redesign of college English curriculum. *CAFLT*, *157*, 48–54.

Ma, W., Kuang, S., Su, X., & Liu, S. (2018). A study on college English instruction in a MOOC-based flipped classroom in China. In J. Colpaert (Ed.), pp. 260-270. *Proceedings of the 19th International CALL Research Conference CALL Your Data*, Brugge (Belgium) University of Antwerp.

Mackey, A., & Gass, S. M. (2005). *Second language research: methods and design*. London, UK: Routledge.

Mann, S., & Walsh, S. (2017). *Reflective practice in English language teaching: research-based principles and practices*. Abingdon, UK: Routledge. doi:10.4324/9781315733395

McNiff, J. (1988). *Action research: Principles and practices*. London, UK: Routledge. doi:10.4324/9780203305676

Motzo, A., & Proudfoot, A. (2017). MOOCs for language learning – opportunities and challenges: the case of the Open University Italian Beginners' MOOCs. In Q. Kan, & S. Bax (Eds.), Beyond the language classroom: Researching MOOCs and other innovations. (pp. 85-98). Dublin, Ireland: Research Publishing.net.

Orsini-Jones, M. (2015). Integrating a MOOC into the MA in English Language Teaching at Coventry University. York, UK: Higher Education Academy. Retrieved from https://www.heacademy.ac.uk/sites/default/files/marina_orsini_jones_final.pdf

Orsini-Jones, M. (2018) Chinese English teachers' perspectives on "distributed flip MOOC blends": From BMELTT to BMELTE'. Coventry, UK: Coventry University. Retrieved from https://vilte.warwick.ac.uk/items/show/49?

Orsini-Jones, M., Altamimi, S., & Conde, B. (2017). Integrating a MOOC into the postgraduate ELT curriculum: Reflecting on students' beliefs with a MOOC blend. In Q. Kan, & S. Bax (Eds.), *Beyond the language classroom: researching MOOCS and other innovations* (pp. 71-83). Dublin, Ireland: Researchpublishing.net. doi:10.14705/rpnet.2017.mooc2016.672

Orsini-Jones, M., & Cerveró Carrascosa, A. (2019). BMELTET – Blending MOOCs into English language teacher education with telecollaboration. In A. Plutino, K. Borthwick, & E. Corradini (Eds.), *New educational landscapes: innovative perspectives in language learning and technology* (pp. 1-7). Research-publishing.net.

Orsini-Jones, M., & Lee, F. (2018). *Intercultural communicative competence for global citizenship: identifying rules of engagement in telecollaboration*. Basingstoke, UK: Palgrave MacMillan. doi:10.1057/978-1-137-58103-7

Orsini-Jones, M., Pibworth-Dolinski, L., Cribb, M., Brick, B., Gazeley-Eke, Z., Leinster, H., & Lloyd, E. (2015). Learning about language learning on a MOOC: how massive, open, online and "course"? In F. Helm, L. Bradley, M. Guarda, & S. Thouësny (Eds.), *Critical CALL – Proceedings of the 2015 EUROCALL Conference,* Padova, Italy (pp. 450-457). Dublin, Ireland: Research-publishing.net. doi:10.14705/rpnet.2015.000374

Orsini-Jones, M., Zou, B., Borthwick, K., & Conde, B. (2017). BMELTT (Blending MOOCs for English language teacher training): a 'distributed MOOC flip' to explore local and global ELT contexts and beliefs (pp. 608-625). In R. Kern, J. Colpaert, A. Aerts, & M. Kaiser, *Proceedings of the XVIIIth International CALL Conference: CALL in Context*, UC Berkeley. Retrieved from http://call2017.language.berkeley.edu/wpcontent/uploads/2017/07/CALL2017_proceedings.pdf

Orsini-Jones, M., Zou, B., Hu, Y., & Li, W. (2017). Chinese English teachers' perspectives on "distributed flip MOOC blends": From BMELTT to BMELTE, special issue of IJCALLT, 7(4), pp. 1-14.

Palfreyman, D. (2003). The representation of learner autonomy and learner independence in organizational culture. In D. Palfreyman, & R. C. Smith (Eds.), *Learner autonomy across cultures: Language education perspectives* (pp. 183–200). Basingstoke, UK: Palgrave Macmillan. doi:10.1057/9780230504684_11

Pappano, L. (2014, Nov. 12). The year of the MOOC. *The New York Times*. Retrieved from https://www.nytimes.com/2012/11/04/education/edlife/massive-open-online-courses-are-multiplying-at-a-rapid-pace.html

Richards, J. C., & Rodgers, T. S. (2014). *Approaches and methods in language teaching* (3rd ed.). New York: CUP.

Sandeen, C. (2013). Integrating MOOCs into traditional higher education: the emerging "MOOC 3.0" Era. *Change*, *45*(6), 34–39. doi:10.1080/00091383.2013.842103

Schön, D. (1983). *The reflective practitioner: how professionals think in action*. New York: Basic Books.

Suo, G. F., & Chi, R. B. (2018). Blended learning in intercultural foreign language teaching based on MOOCs. *Foreign Language World*, *3*, 89–96.

Wenger-Trayner, E., & Wenger-Trayner, B. (2015). Introduction to communities of practice: a brief overview of the concept and its uses. Retrieved from https://wenger-trayner.com/introduction-to-communities-of-practice/

Zhang, E., Zhang, W., & Jin, C. (2018). SPOC-based flipped classroom of college English: Construction of an effective learning model. [iJET]. *International Journal of Emerging Technology*, *13*(01), 37–45. doi:10.3991/ijet.v13i01.7513

Zhang, X. (2017). Researching into a MOOC embedded flipped classroom model for college English reading and writing course. In Q. Kan, & S. Bax (Eds.), Beyond the language classroom: researching MOOCs and other innovations (pp. 15-27). Dublin, Ireland: Research-publishing.net. doi:10.14705/rpnet.2017.mooc2016.668

Zheng, Y., & Cheng, L. (2008). Test review: college English test (CET) in China. *Language Testing*, *25*(3), 408–417. doi:10.1177/0265532208092433

ENDNOTES

1 'College English' refers to the preparation for the main English test taken by Chinese students – the College English Test (CET) – that is also required by many employers as proof of English proficiency in China. According to Zheng and Cheng (2008, p. 408): 'The purpose of the CET is to examine the English proficiency of undergraduate students in China and ensure that Chinese undergraduates reach the required English levels specified in the National College English Teaching Syllabuses (NCETS)'.

2 *Mobile Assisted Language Learning*, which refers to the use of mobile devices as a tool for language learning instruction (Chinnery, 2006, p. 9).

Chapter 9
English Language Learner Motivation in the Digital Technology Classroom:
A Case Study of a Vocational University in Indonesia

Baetty Baetty
https://orcid.org/0000-0002-7473-3050
Politeknik Negeri Padang, Indonesia

Michael Thomas
University of Central Lancashire, UK

ABSTRACT

This chapter investigates learner motivation in an English as a foreign language writing classroom in an Indonesian university. Its originality arises from the fact that no substantive studies have explored learner motivation in the digital classroom in Indonesian higher education. A mixed methods data collection process was conducted involving 144 students from three-year groups who responded to an online questionnaire. Two classes from Year 1 (47 students) were taken as a sample to observe the learning process between an existing group that was introduced to the learning of English writing through Edmodo. The other group used traditional materials for their writing tasks. The findings are significant in that the high levels of motivation reported by the students were not reflected in the way they completed their writing tasks as the use of technology affected their motivation in complex ways. In conclusion, the study encourages future research in Indonesia that measures English students' motivation and technology-mediated writing task performance through longitudinal studies.

DOI: 10.4018/978-1-7998-1282-1.ch009

INTRODUCTION

Previous research has suggested that the Indonesian education curriculum is heavily dependent on teacher-centred and deductive approaches to learning English as a Foreign Language (EFL) and this has led to lower levels of learner motivation (Mattarima & Hamdan, 2011, 2016). Most reseach studies have focused on receptive skills (Araminta & Halimi, 2015; Pammu, Amir & Maasum, 2014) and this is because Indonesian students typically prioritise reading and listening over productive skills such as writing and speaking (Sukandi & Syafar, 2018). Although in the global context of EFL and computer-assisted language learning (CALL) there have been numerous studies of learner motivation (Hannibal Jensen, 2019; Ushioda, 2013), they have not explored the issue in Indonesian higher education in any substantive way. Nevertheless, several preliminary studies (Aulia, Yulastri & Sari, 2014; Aulia, Yulastri & Handayani, 2016; Yulastri, 2015a, 2015b; Yulastri, Aulia & Saptopramono, 2016) have indicated that combining the use of online platforms such as Edmondo alongside more learner-centred approaches may significantly improve students' motivation in classroom contexts. This claim warrants further investigation in this paper.

In order to address these gaps in the research on learner motivation and learning technologies in Indonesia, this chapter investigates language learner motivation in two technology-mediated classes with students at a vocational higher education institution in western Indonesia in which task-based language teaching (TBLT) was used as the main instructional approach. Following a review of the research literature on learner motivation and TBLT usage in the Asian context, the methodology describes the research framework of the study. Findings are then discussed in relation to Gardner's model of motivation. Finally, the limitations and implications of the study are explored, prior to identifying areas for future research in this area.

BACKGROUND

Language Learner Motivation

The reason behind a student choosing to learn a new language is a key motivational factor influencing the language learning process and many second language acquisition (SLA) studies over the past 40 years have examined motivation in and outside the language classroom (Dörnyei, 2001a, 2001b; Ellis, 2015; Gardner & Lambert, 1959). Gardener (1985) identified three key components in studies on motivation: motivational effort, the desire to learn the language, and learners' attitude towards learning the language. Dörnyei and Ushioda (2013) stressed the importance of persistence in this respect, i.e. the continuance of an action in spite of difficulty and opposition. Nevertheless, while extensive research literature exists on motivation, it remains an abstract concept that is difficult to measure (Barba, Kennedy & Ainley, 2016; Crookes & Schmidt, 1989; Dörnyei & Ottó, 1998; Gardner, 1985).

Motivation has been defined from a psychological perspective as (a) having purposes, intents, aims, goals and decisions (Young, 1961), (b) the process whereby goal-directed activity is instigated and sustained (Schunk, Meece & Pintrich, 2008), and (c) the drive that pushes people to do activities with purpose (Deci & Ryan, 1985). Motivation can also be defined as a process (Schunk et al., 2008) that grows and changes over time. It is complex and non-deterministic because it is an abstract construct that deals with intentions rather than results.

Types of Motivation

In an effort to define motivation several key types have been identified (Clément, Gardner & Smythe, 1980; Dörnyei, 2001a; Gardner & Lambert, 1972; Gardner & Smythe, 1981). In a seminal early study that still warrants attention, Young (1961) defined intrinsic motivation as the willingness to do or to learn something without expecting incentives for doing so. Extrinsic motivation was perceived as incentive-driven, whereas intrinsic motivation was more self-sustaining in orientation.

The categories of extrinsic and intrinsic motivation are in many ways equivalent to the instrumental and integrative types of motivation used by Gardner and Lambert (1972) who defined integrated motivation as the 'willingness' to be liked and valued members of a language community. Instrumental motivation is a desire to learn a language to fulfil utilitarian goals such as the need to obtain a job or pass an examination.

Young's definition of motivation as "purpose, intent, aim, goal, and decision" is a good starting point to understand what is going in the mind of a language learner (Young, 1961, p. 6), though the five keywords that emerge from his research lack consideration of the 'in-between states' which may take place during the learning process. Young also drew a distinction between motives and habits. By developing good habits, students can reach their goals guided by teachers during the initial stages of language learning. This may gradually lead to independent learning as they establish greater motivation. If this is the case, any distinction between habits and motives is of little importance. Young's definition ignores the dynamic and process-oriented element of motivation. Likewise, the instrumental/extrinsic or integrative/intrinsic oppositions tend to ignore the fact that learning a new language might not solely be either instrumental or integrated but a combination of both in ways that are uniquely dependent on the learner and the learning context.

There have been a limited number of studies on EFL motivation in Indonesian among junior high school students. Lamb (2004a, 2004b, 2007), for example, found that over 20 months students' instrumental motivation increased slightly although their integrative motivation did not. Classroom-related variables emerged as the most important aspects of learning and monotonous classroom procedures, incomprehensible lessons, and the fear of reprimand were highly demotivating to students.

For the purposes of this paper, motivation is defined in terms of the instrumental and integrative types used by Gardner and Lambert (1972), while it also recognises that the static interpretation advanced initially by Young (1961) needs to be seen as a complex and dynamic process that is based on multiple internal and contextual factors that are subject to change.

TBLT and Writing

Authentic task-based approaches to education started to be used in schools in the 1970s (Richards & Rodgers, 2001) and in language teaching in the early 1980s (Prabhu, 1987). Consequently, TBLT flourished in the 1980s and 1990s (Skehan, 1998) arising from dissatisfaction with communicative language teaching (CLT) which still relied on grammar-based instruction. TBLT promoted an authentic way of learning languages aimed at meaning-focused activities in which the linguistic focus emerged incidentally at the end of the learning sequence. Numerous researchers have defined task as a consequence (see Ellis, 2003; Van den Branden, 2016) and while there is no common agreement, several key principles reoccur in the research. Firstly, tasks are classroom activities that enable students to use words and phrases to convey meaning or intentions. Tasks mainly focus on meaning and process, and they require an outcome.

The characteristics of *tasks*: 1) involve a primary focus on semantic and pragmatic meaning, 2) have some kind of 'gap' (i.e. a need to convey information, to express an opinion or to infer the meaning), 3) provide freedom for choosing the linguistic or non-linguistic resources that learners need to complete their task, and 4) have a clearly defined, non-linguistic outcome, i.e. the language serves as the means for achieving the outcome, not as an end in its own right (Ellis, 2003, 2009).

Arising from this, Ellis (2003), Nunan (2004), Samuda (2013), and Willis (1996) categorised classroom task frameworks into three main types that can be summarised as pre-task, task and post-task, although they used different terms in their research. The frameworks from Willis (1996), Samuda (2001) and Ellis (2003) are applicable to the research in this study as they involve a series of task stages, the last of which involves a review of the language element. The emphasis is first placed on meaning. The teacher introduces focus-on-form ('FonF') when improved grammar is taught at the end of the learning process through recap activities. 'FonF' refers to an approach to language education in which learners are only made aware of the grammatical form of language features when they are already able to use it communicatively. This two-step method (focus on meaning followed by FoF) has been shown to relax students, enabling them to learn in a more effective and enjoyable way as students focus on delivering their message instead of correct utterances (Bao & Du, 2015; Chen, 2016).

After careful review of the four TBLT frameworks suggested above, Willis's framework was chosen for this study as the final stage includes a clear emphasis on language focus. It differentiates this cycle from the stages of teaching language skills that is also divided into three stages: pre-, during, and post- activities. In the *pre-task* teachers introduce the topic and the task, highlighting useful words and phrases, helping students to understand task instructions and preparing them to attempt the tasks. Students may hear a recording of others doing a similar task for example. The second phase that Willis introduced involves the *task cycle*: task, planning and reporting. Students work in pairs or a small group. The teacher monitors the activities and maintains distance to allow students to do their work. Students then prepare to report to the class orally or in writing. This report explains how they completed the work and what they decided or learnt in the process. Following that, students present their report to the class. They may also exchange written reports and compare the results with other students. The final stage in Willis' framework is the *language focus* which is divided into analysis and practice at the end of the class. In this phase students are expected to be able to analyse and discuss specific features of the text or transcript of the recording.

Few previous research studies have investigated the success of the TBLT approach in improving English writing skills, and even fewer have examined the specific Indonesian context. In this chapter, writing refers to the production of reports and scripts used in broadcast media, as the students were studying on a Broadcasting English course to teach them the skills and language use required in the industry. In the broader context of research on TBLT and writing insights can be obtained from Abrams and Byrd (2017), for example, who recorded how collaborative, meaning-focused writing tasks improved grammatical accuracy, lexical richness, and the overall quality of students' writing. Yasuda (2017) also noted that TBLT combined with Systemic Functional Linguistics (SFL) and genre-based tasks were effective in improving English writing skills, particularly in writing for college students. Moreover, Talebi, Aidinlou and Farhadi (2015) reported that writing task development was confirmed in their study, but that improvements in grammatical accuracy were less pronounced. While the study was conducted in Iran and generalisability of the research is problematic, the main weakness of the research was the failure to address how information gaps could enhance writing ability. Addressing the specific Indonesian context, Sundari, Febriyanti and Saragih (2018) argue that writing is a complex matter for students, as it is not "a single entity; rather, it involves other aspects, such as mastery of grammar and vocabulary, the social context, and the targeted audience" (p. 275). Above all, it "requires a lot of effort, especially in foreign languages" and learners typically need higher levels of motivation". The authors found that students were more highly motivated by rewriting stories and by doing homework assignments in place of group work; that the content of the writing tasks should "adaptive and relevant to global and national issues" (p. 279); and above all, that the writing tasks appeared authentic.

Task-Based Language Teaching in Asia

Returning to the Indonesian context, several research studies have indicated that the application of TBLT in similar Asian contexts has been problematic (Carless, 2003; Ellis, 2003; Littlewood, 2014; Mustafa, 2010; Ortega, 2012). Carless (2009) noted that EFL teaching in Asia was characterised by 1) large class sizes, 2) an examination-oriented system, 3) lack of teaching expertise in task-based approaches, 4) a preference for Presentation-Practice-Production (PPP) teaching, 5) direct grammar instruction, 6) teacher-centred, and 7) non-interactive forms of teaching. Carless also pointed out that TBLT conflicted with the Confucian-heritage culture in Hong Kong.

Other researchers suggest that learning strategies and study time (Helmke & Tuyet, 1999) and achievement-oriented attitudes and motivation (Le Ha, 2014) also inhibit English language learning in Asia. Thirdly, Littlewood (2007) reported that non-student-oriented activities, grammar translation methods and audio-lingual methods led to passive learning. In particular, Littlewood noted five concerns relating to the implementation of CLT and TBLT in East Asian classrooms: 1) classroom management, 2) avoidance of English, 3) minimal demands on language competence, 4) incompatibility with public assessment demands, and 5) conflict with established educational values and tradition.

In discussing the implementation of TBLT in teaching EFL curricula in Japan, Iran and Indonesia, Ortega (2012) argued that students' passive learning style, low motivation to learn, high dependency on teachers, and large class sizes could be overcome by a "glocalized" approach to TBLT in which teachers would be required to combine traditions by "thinking globally" and "acting locally". Similarly, Ellis (2015) agreed with the suggestion of Littlewood (2007) that in South East Asia, TBLT could be combined effectively with traditional language teaching approaches rather than supplant them (e.g., PPP and grammar-based teaching). Despite being a possible solution to motivation issues, as suggested by Carless (2009) in a broader context, Mufida, Mukhyaiyar, and Radjab (2013) observed that the implementation of TBLT in Indonesia was challenging as a result of local institutional and social factors.

Arising from the above review, the following research question was identified: How do Indonesian EFL students' perceptions about motivation to learn English writing skills predict their experience in the digital TBLT writing classroom? Related to this, two hypotheses were confirmed:

H1: There is a significant correlation between motivation and performance in writing classes as indicated by the Final Score in the Writing 1 module.

H2: There is a significant difference in motivation between the technology group that learned to write through the use of PCs and the non-PC group.

METHODOLOGY

Participants

In addressing the gap identified in the literature review about the lack of studies on the Indonesian context, data for this study were collected from students at a vocational university located in West Sumatra. The university offered a three-year study programme that focussed on applied sciences and aimed to equip graduates with the technical skills needed by local industries. The participants included students aged 17–25 in the English Department and a total of 144 (m=37, f=107) were observed in three different modules: Writing 1 (Classes 1A and 1B), Technical Writing 1 (Classes 2A and 2B), and a Workshop for TV Broadcasting (Classes 3A and 3B), focusing mainly on writing skills. The students had been studying English as a compulsory subject for eight years from primary to high school. English was taught as a foreign language to these students and they were generally proficient in at least two languages (at least one local language and a national language) and they averaged 302 points (range 115–565) in their TOEIC scores.

Materials

In Writing 1 the first-year students learned basic writing skills such as combining sentences and paragraph writing in a general English context. Students in Year 2 studied English for Specific Purposes (ESP) such as writing English correspondence and essays. In their final year of taught classes, the students in Year 3 learned writing for the specific genre of broadcasting, including news scripts, radio talk shows scripts, and a short TV production show in English.

The TBLT framework was implemented alongside relevant digital technology usage during the writing tasks. For example, students sat in a multimedia laboratory for Writing 1 and Technical Writing 1 and in a separate studio for TV and Radio Broadcasting. For Years 1 and 2 the dominant technology used was Internet-enabled computers. However, authentic broadcasting equipment, audio systems, and professional cameras were used in the Year 3 workshops. The students' activities were structured according to the three stages of TBLT identified by Willis (1996) involving pre-task, task, and language focus activities.

Procedures

First, the participants completed an online questionnaire and asked to rate their learning experience on a five-point Likert scale, where 1 was "Strongly Disagree" and 5 was ''Strongly Agree''. The questionnaire was divided into six parts but only the first two parts are discussed in this paper as they relate specifically to the research question; a copy of the questionnaire showing the parts used is provided in Appendix I. Part 1 (Items 1–3) explored the students' motivation to learn English in the vocational institution, the reasons for choosing to study in the English Department, and a statement relating to their choice of the English Department in their entry test. Part 2 (Items 4-6) focused on motivation, writing and task performance and explored the students' perception of the relation between the themes in the study.

Data were also taken from the learning process and the post-learning process to generate results for correlative studies. Document analysis was used in relation to the process of learning using tasks and digital technology, particularly in the second and last cycle in the framework of tasks based on Willis (1996): the task and the post-task. In relation to outcomes, scores from Assignment, Mid Semester-Test, and Semester-Test variables were grouped in relation to help understand the task-in-process and the task-as-outcome, which was based on Final Scores, namely, the overall score achieved at the end of the entire semester. Documents that contained learning outcomes (i.e. the scores achieved from writing modules) were analysed to identify variables related to the learning process. This standard was then correlated with other statistical results from the questionnaires.

Observations were conducted in several different classes that implemented the TBLT approach. Direct observation was made on three occasions for classes A and B in Year 1 and Year 2, while classes in Year 3 classes A and were observed once. The procedure followed the guidelines developed by Dörnyei's "Motivation Orientation in Language Teaching" (MOLT) scheme and the variables included attention, participation and volunteering initiative as shown in Table 1.

Table 1. Motivation variables observed (Guilloteaux & Dörnyei, 2008)

The Year 1 groups received different treatments: one class was taught using Internet technology, such as Edmodo and computer applications, and the other used conventional tools such as pens, pencils, paper and printed dictionaries.

Data Analysis

Correlation studies on motivation, the use of digital technologies and writing proficiency were carried out using the Spearman correlation (Furlong, Lovelace & Lovelace, 2000) to analyse the relationship between motivation and attitude towards English learning, and motivation and attitude towards the English writing modules. Both data and methodological triangulation were used to maintain construct validity (Silverman, 2014). Interrater agreement on NVivo was used to ensure the reliability of the qualitative coding and reliability achieved 78% in agreement (Mackey & Gass, 2005). The validity and reliability of the questionnaire were tested at the pilot stage using Cronbach's Alpha (Tavakol & Dennick, 2011). Potential threats to validity, and the strategies employed to minimise these when merging data in concurrent convergent, embedded, transformative, and multiphase designs are listed by Creswell and Plano Clark (2011). These were taken into account and the study ensured its internal validity by using a logical model to draw an accurate conclusion (Yin, 2014). The variables described in Table 1 were used to record the classroom motivational behaviour.

Variables	Description
Attention	Students look like they are paying attention; they are looking at the teacher and following her movement, looking at other students contributing to the task, or making physical responses.
Participation	Learners are actively interacting with the task and working on the assignment
Volunteering for teacher-fronted activity	At least one-third of the students are willingly volunteering without being coaxed by the teacher.

FINDINGS

English Learning Motivation (ELM)

The research examined the numbers of students by year of entry that chose the English Department as their first, second, or third option. The results are shown in Table 2.

Table 2. Rank of entry year

Overall, 44% of students opted to study English as their first choice and a further 44% as their second choice. However, there were small differences between years of entry. The figures were 87.5% in Year 1, 82.6% in Year 2, and 96.8% in Year 3. Nevertheless, far fewer students in Years 1 (41.7%) and 2 (34.8%) chose English as their first option compared with Year 3 (61.3%) due to changes in entry standards.

Students from each year group indicated that they had a high level of motivation to learn English (see Figure 1) with 52% very willing to learn the language and a further 32% who had a high willingness. A similar picture was given by students for choosing to study in the English Department (see Figure 2)

The majority of students responded that they wanted to be able to communicate well in English (58%), while 28% chose to study in order to obtain a good job (see Figure 2).

A summary of the twelve classroom observations that took place is shown in Table 3 and indicates a contrasting finding between the questionnaire results and the classroom observations.

Table 3. Classroom observation summary

Students responded differently according to the way the lecturers conducted the classes and it was evident that attention, participation and volunteering varied. Both classes paid attention to the lecturers' instructions. However, students' attention in Class 1A was rather unfocused; some were busy with their

			Classes by Year of Entry			Total
			Year 1	Year 2	Year 3	
Rank of Entry Option	First	Number of Students	20	16	19	55
		Percentage of Students	41.7%	34.8%	61.30%	44%
	Second	Number of Students	22	22	11	55
		Percentage of Students	45.8%	47.8%	35.50%	44%
	Third	Number of Students	6	7	1	14
		Percentage of Students	12.5%	15.2%	3.20%	11.20%
	Missing	Number of Students	0	1	0	1
		Percentage of Students	0%	2.2%	0%	0.80%
Total		Number of Students	48	46	31	125
		Percentage of Students	100%	100%	100%	100%

Figure 1. Item 1, willingness to learn English

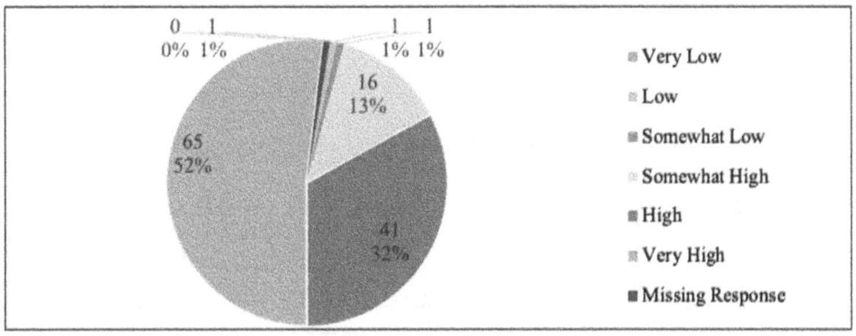

Figure 2. Item 2. My main reason for choosing the English department

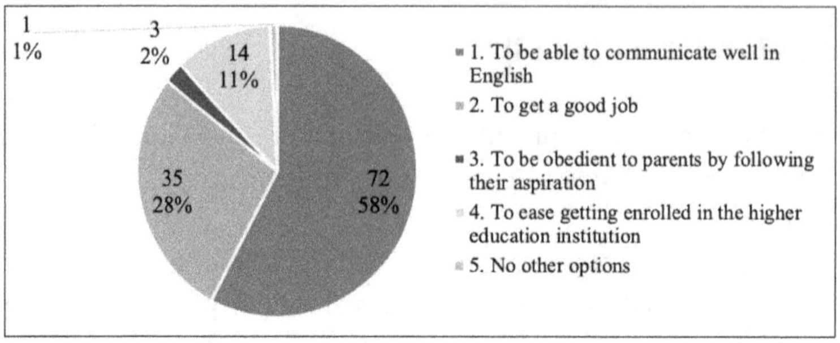

monitors, while others paid attention to the lecturers. In comparison, attention during the pre-task session in Class 1B was focused; students listened to and read from the same resources when the lecturer guided them to read a writing sample together from the screen projector.

Even though both classes in Year 2 used PCs in their learning, there were differences in their motivational behaviour. Class 2B paid more attention in the three task-based cycles compared with those in Class 2A. Observation strongly suggested that the varying competences and personalities of the four lecturers teaching the course heavily influenced student behaviour.

Observation recorded that students in Class 1B were more active in using different tools and were not limited to Google Translate and other online and offline dictionaries. They also used specific Indonesian dictionary applications, YouTube and websites to complete their writing tasks. Students' participation and volunteering were broadly similar in each class with the more extrovert students dominating participation and volunteering. However, the more experienced lecturers were able to ensure a more equal form of participation.

The first session of the task cycle was not engaging for students, but feedback sessions were reported as stimulating. Students in the non-Edmodo-based class became active and walked around approaching their peers and lecturers to obtain feedback and to question the feedback they received. Students from the

Class	Learners' Motivated Behaviour		
	Attention	Participation	Volunteering
1A	• Divided attention	• Dominated by the same students	• Dominated by the same student but the lecturer took control to enable other students to participate
1B	• Attentive activities	• Dominated by the same students • Active in getting access to different resources and the lecturers	• Dominated by the same student but the lecturer took control to enable other students to participate
2A	• Divided attention	• Dominated by the same students	• Lack of volunteering
2B	• Divided Attention	• Dominated by the same students	• Lecturer regulated the volunteering but students indicated a willingness to volunteer

Edmodo-based classes demonstrated curiosity and made sure that their peers responded to their writing. They talked to each other and reminded each other of their roles as feedback providers.

The students in Class 1B were greatly handicapped as their only resource was their handwriting books which had to be taken in person to the feedback providers although they too walked and talked freely to each other and to lecturers to obtain this. As the students' wish to learn English was driven by non-language and cultural-related factors, their motivation was often weak and their main writing tasks were frequently not completed within the time limit. However, their willingness, as indicated by their effort to approach the lecturers to obtain feedback at the end of the task cycles, was high.

The Relationship Between ELM and Writing Task Completion

The correlation between the students' reported levels of motivation, technology and their performance in task completion is presented according to the following hypotheses and findings from inferential statistics. These results were then compared with the qualitative findings to draw conclusions. Two hypotheses were posed for the research question.

Hypothesis 1: There is a significant correlation between motivation and performance in writing classes as indicated by the Final Score in the Writing 1 module.

Hypothesis 2: There is a significant difference between the technology group that learned to write through the use of PCs and the non-PC group.

Correlations were made between motivation levels as reported in the questionnaire and variables from the Assignments, Mid-Test, Semester-Test (the final semester examination) and Final Scores (the scores that students achieved for the entire semester). Because the data were not normally distributed (except for the Final Score variable), Kendal's Tau and Spearman's Rho tests were run. The significant value was set at 0.5. In instances where the two tests differed, the Kendal's Tau result was accepted as likely to be the more accurate. To check the answer for Hypothesis 1 the variables were correlated separately. A Pearson product-moment correlation was run to determine the relationship between motivation and the final score in the writing modules (see Table 4).

Table 4. Correlation between motivation and final scores in the writing modules

Although there was a positive correlation between the motivation level and the Final scores, the correlation was not statistically significant ($r = - 0.74$, $n = 125$, $p = .410$) and it was concluded that there was no relationship between the final scores in Writing 1 and the motivation levels (see Table 5).

Table 5. Correlation between motivation level and task-in process scores

		Motivation Level	Final Score
Motivation Level	Pearson Correlation	1	.062
	Sig. (2-tailed)		.491
	N	124	124
Final Score	Pearson Correlation	.062	1
	Sig. (2-tailed)	.491	
	N	124	124

None of the three scores were statistically significant although the Assignment Score had the strongest correlation coefficient (r = .108, p = .236) and the Mid-Test scores the lowest (r = .026, p = .771).

The results from Year 1 were examined in more detail as it was hypothesised that the utilisation of technology might affect changes of motivation and writing proficiency (Hypothesis 2). Students in Class 1A (M = 74.59, SD = 3.850, n = 22) used technology when learning Writing 1 through task-based activities. Students of Class 1B (M = 77.42, SD = 3.384, n = 26) did not. A t-test was conducted to analyse the data and the results are shown in Table 6.

Table 6. Independent sample test

The t-test assumed that the standard deviations were the same (less than 4.0). F = .394 and the score of .534 was above the significant level. Therefore, the Equal Variance Assumed was used to check for the t-value (-2.712) and the significant level was .009, which was ≥ .05. Therefore, the null hypothesis was accepted and the difference between the use of technology and non-technology in these two classes was significant. There was a significant relationship between having been exposed to technology and students' writing skills (t (46) = - 2.712, p < .05).

A Kruskal-Wallis test was run to investigate whether exposure to the use of technology was associated with the student's performance in writing classes (see Table 7).

			Motivation Level	Assignment Score	Mid-Test Score	Semester-Test Score
Spearman's rho	Motivation Level	Correlation Coefficient	1.000	.108	.026	.069
		Sig. (2-tailed)		.236	.771	.449
		N	124	123	124	124
	Assignment Score	Correlation Coefficient	.108	1.000	.334**	.544**
		Sig. (2-tailed)	.236		.000	.000
		N	123	124	124	124
	Mid-Test Score	Correlation Coefficient	.026	.334**	1.000	.464**
		Sig. (2-tailed)	.771	.000		.000
		N	124	124	125	125
	Semester-Test Score	Correlation Coefficient	.069	.544**	.464**	1.000
		Sig. (2-tailed)	.449	.000	.000	
		N	124	124	125	125

**. Correlation is significant at the 0.01 level (2-tailed).

		Levine's Test for Equality of Variances		t-test for Equality of Means						
									95% Confidence Interval of the Difference	
		F	Sig.	t	df	Sig. (2-tailed)	Mean Difference	Std. Error Difference	Lower	Upper
Final Score	Equal variances assumed	.394	.534	-2.712	46	.009	-2.832	1.044	-4.934	-.730
	Equal variances not assumed			-2.683	42.261	.010	-2.832	1.056	-4.962	-.702

Table 7. Kruskal-Wallis results on Motivation and the Task-in Process variables.

There were no significant differences in the Assignment, Mid-Term Test, and Semester-Test Scores between 'somewhat high', 'high', and 'very highly' motivated students.

The Assignment Score was not significantly different for students of these three groups in terms of motivation levels $\chi2(2) = 1.426$, $p = .490$, with a mean rank of the Assignment Score 17.00 for 'somewhat high', 25.85 for 'high' and 24.76 for 'very highly' motivated students. There was also no significant difference in the Mid-Test score $\chi2(2) = .511$, $p = .775$, with a mean rank Assignment Score of 19.75 for 'somewhat high', 25.03 for 'high' and 24.87 for 'very highly motivated' students. Similarly, there was no significant difference between the Semester-Test Score $\chi2(2) = .957$, $p = .620$, with a mean rank Assignment Score of 19.25 for 'somewhat high', 23.44 for 'high', and 25.94 for 'very highly' motivated students.

The Mann-Whitney U Test was used to investigate the differences between two independent groups i.e. Classes 1A and 1B (see Table 8).

Table 8. Mann-Whitney U test results

The Assignment and semester-Test Scores show significant differences compared to the Mid-Test score between Classes 1A and 1B. The Assignment Score in Class 1B were statistically significant and higher than the Class 1A ($U = 118$, $p = .000$) with a mean rank of the Assignment Score 30.96 for 1B and 16.86 for 1A. Similar findings were noted for the Semester-Test Score. Class 1B had a significant difference compared to 1A ($U = 130$, $p = .001$) with a mean rank Semester-Test score of 30.50 for 1B and 17.41 for Class 1A.

However, there were no significant differences between these two classes in the Mid-Test Scores ($U = 243$, $p = .370$). This variable also appeared to differ in mean rank. While Class 1B had higher scores for Assignment and Semester-Test, Class 1A had higher scores in a mean rank of 26.45 for 1A and 22.85 for Class 1B. Arising from these results, the findings for research question 1 are summarised in Table 9.

Table 9. The quantitative findings

As is evident in Table 9, there was no association between motivation and the task-in-process and task-as-outcomes. And the use of PC or non-PC (in Classes 1A and 1B) did not influence the performance in writing classes.

To conclude, the correlation between the students' reported level of motivation, the use of technology, and the students' actual performance in task completion was also evaluated qualitatively by generating answers from coded transcripts. It is not possible to correlate quantitative datasets with qualitative datasets, thus the term 'correlation' was replaced with the synonymous word 'relationship'. The results of the correlation analysis were disappointing, and no significant correlations were identified.

The correlation was analysed between motivation and task-as-outcome which was measured by the students' Final Scores. Although there was a strong, positive correlation between the Motivation Levels

	Assignment Score	Mid-Test Score	Semester-Test Score	Final Score
Chi-Square	1.426	.511	.800	.957
df	2	2	2	2
Asymp. Sig.	.490	.775	.670	.620
a. Kruskal Wallis Test				
b. Grouping Variable: Motivation Level				

	Assignment Score	Mid-Test Score	Semester-Test Score
Mann-Whitney U	118.000	243.000	130.000
Wilcoxon W	371.000	594.000	383.000
Z	-3.619	-.896	-3.253
Asymp. Sig. (2-tailed)	.000	.370	.001
a. Grouping Variable: Class			

	Hypotheses	Variables		Findings	Conclusion
1	H_0: there is a significant correlation between motivation and performances in writing classes. H_1: there is no significant correlation between motivation and performances in writing classes.	1.1 Motivation and Task-in Process	1.1.1 Motivation and Assignment Score	Not significant (r = .108, p = .236)	Ho = Rejected
			1.1.2 Motivation and Mid-Test Score	Not significant (r = .026, p = .771)	Ho = Rejected
			1.1.3 Motivation and Semester Test Score	Not significant (r =.069, p = .449)	Ho = Rejected
		1.2 Task-as Outcomes	1.2.4 Motivation and Final Score	Not significant (r = - 0.74, n = 125, p = .410)	Ho = Rejected
2	H_0: there is a significant difference between the PC-based group and the non-PC-group. H_1: there is no significant difference between the PC-based group and the non-PC-group	2.1 There was an association between the use of technology and performance in Writing 1 module (t (46) = - 2.712, $p < .05$			Ho = Accepted
		2.2 There were no statistical differences between motivation level and task-in process (assignment, mid-test, and semester-test scores variables) and motivation level and the task-in process and task-as outcome (Final Score variable)			Ho = Accepted

and the Final Score it was not statistically significant (r = - 0.74, n = 125, p = .410). Four variables were analysed to examine the relationship between motivation and writing skills (task-in-process). None of the results were statistically significant.

For the task-in process, the first variable examined was the students' actual performance when carrying out task-based activities as measured by the results of their weekly writing task or Assignment Score. Spearman's Rho correlation coefficient was used to analyse the results and there was a weak positive correlation between the Motivation Levels and Assignment Score (r= .108, n= 123, p = .236).

The second variable examined was the relationship between Motivation Levels and writing skills as measured by the Mid-Test Score was also investigated using Spearman's product-moment correlation coefficient (r= .026, n= 124, p = .771). It was weaker than the Assignment Score's correlation.

The third variable studied was the relationship between Motivation Levels and writing skills as measured by Semester-Test Score - also using Spearman's Rho correlation coefficient. There was a weak correlation between Motivation Levels and Semester-Test Score, but it was stronger than the Mid-Test Score variables (r = 069, n = 124, p =.449).

The fourth variable examined was the relationship between Motivation and task-based activities as measured by Assignment Score, again using Spearman's Rho correlation coefficient. There was a weak positive correlation between the Motivation Level and Assignment Score (r= .108, n= 123, p = .236).

An initial objective of the research was to identify the role of motivation in the learning of English writing through technology-mediated TBLT in an Indonesian HEI. It was found that using technology affected students' motivation in completing their writing tasks both positively and negatively. In particular it was the software, applications or websites that were important in keeping the students motivated to complete their required tasks.

The study found that access to digital tools was the dominant factor in facilitating the learning of English writing skills and that it was access to digital tools that facilitated learning regardless of the stated reason to learn or the professed degree of motivation. This conclusion was made on the basis of Gardner's model (2007). It is also evident that learner motivation fluctuated based on the classroom situation. The motivation that was reported on item 1 of the students' questionnaire was compared with the observed language learning motivation (Guilloteaux & Dörnyei, 2008) derived from the classroom observation notes. Classroom behaviour, persistence in following the sequence of tasks, and language retention were all recorded, as these four elements combined to help explain motivation to study a foreign language within a challenging classroom environment. Accordingly, the data suggested that the task cycles followed by the learners successfully built up their individual levels of persistence and this, in turn, influenced their classmates in a snowball effect which by the end of the cycle had generated motivation to learn across the group.

DISCUSSION

Reflections on Language Learning Motivation

Dörnyei (1990) and Oxford and Shearin (1994) suggested that instrumental motivation and the need for achievement are associated with foreign language learning. And, more specifically, Lauder (2010) claimed that instrumental motivation was a significant factor among Indonesian students in learning English as they saw it as a means to gain access to international markets, further academic studies, and professional life. However, this study observed that a high level of motivation did not influence students' classroom behaviour and that only two Year 3 and five Year 2 students achieved scores of 95 points. However, five Year 1 students achieved only 85 for their highest Semester Test score.

It was evident that the students had a higher level of instrumental as opposed to integrative motivation as they had no real need to use English in direct daily communication. It is therefore possible to conclude that the majority of students did not have a genuine interest in English learning as the language was only understood as a stepping-stone for their future career and was not seen as a significant part of an identity that they wanted or needed to develop further.

Although 57.6% of the questionnaire respondents indicated that they wanted to be able to communicate well in English, no 'drive' was observable during classroom activities and students did not display the attitude of those who wanted to be successful. This finding is in agreement with that of Kenny (2017) who found that students with poor proficiency in English still wished to attend university to study English as a major subject. More specifically, Lauder (2010) claimed instrumental motivation was a significant factor among Indonesian students in learning English as they saw it as a means to gain access to international markets, further academic studies, and professional life. Lauder's observation helps us to understand the findings from the current study. Although the students claimed to be highly motivated, their actual level was not sufficient to make them engage voluntarily in their learning activities, especially in writing modules, which they considered to be a boring activity.

It is clear, however, language learning motivation is subject to change and while instrumental motivation was dominant in the observed students, integrated motivation was identified in the responses to item

2 on the questionnaire, although not confirmed during classroom observation. Regardless of the findings on the motivation types, we do not consider classification important. This conclusion is in agreement with Gardner (2007) who found that the intensity of the motivation is more crucial in L2 learning than classifying motivation as integrative, instrumental, or as extrinsic and intrinsic. In our study students said that they chose to study English so that they could communicate in English, and it was this ability that motivated them. The students did not specify the communication channel they wished to use, probably because in Indonesia EFL learning, oral communication is commonly referred to communication and the students wished to improve their ability in this regard. Nevertheless, at all levels of teaching, a grammar-focused and reading-based learning system dominates the English learning context in Indonesia (Sulistiyo, 2016). The national foreign language teaching curriculum is outcomes-based at the higher education level and aims to develop the four language skills equally (Solikhah, 2015). However, this does not happen in practice. Musthafa (2015) found that teaching in Indonesia was heavily biased towards the improvement of speaking English rather than the other skills. Therefore, this study found that in responding to the online questionnaire, students automatically understood the successful learning of English in terms of being competent in speaking and ignored English writing competence. Students therefore rated their motivation to learn English in terms of becoming a fluent English speaker rather than writer.

These findings are also in agreement with Gardner's (2007) claim on classroom learning. To pass the module with good scores became the dominant reason for students based on classroom observation. The students who did not have integrative learning motivation were influenced by the learning atmosphere in the technology-mediated TBL writing classes. According to the qualitative data, students displayed shifting motivational drives as both integrated and instrumental motivation was evident. As Gardner divided motivation into language learning and classroom learning motivation, it was evident that the classroom environment may have played an important role in strengthening language learner motivation. In the case of low levels of motivation, which were identified with the instrumental type, the classroom environment that utilised the technology-mediated TBLT approach enabled the students to stay motivated throughout their writing skills development.

A similar concept was identified by Bower (2017) who claimed that learners' motivation, the learning context and the environment influence and shape each other. These three factors co-exist in classroom contexts where changes in the level and types of motivation can happen. Similarly, this study did not find it necessary to classify motivation into particular types because of the sociocultural context of learning of English as a first foreign language in Indonesia. Motivation emerges as a result as more developmental in orientation (Lauder, 2010). Thus, looking at the intensity of the motivation was more significant in this respect. This was because the openness to cultural identification was included in integrative motive. It also included openness to cultural identification as an element that is likely associated with attaining the ultimate level of achievement. We argue that in vocational higher education, learning English is expected to be more externally oriented because of the expectations of the system, the quality of the programme, the interest, enthusiasm, and skills of the teacher, the adequacy of the materials, the curriculum, and the class atmosphere. All of these factors play a role in the motivation of the students.

The results of the study suggest a connection between the use of technology, with its ease of access to content, to improve the learning of English writing skills. The students' difficulties in bringing and using printed dictionaries were found to have contributed to their unwillingness to perform well in the writing task completion exercises. In contrast the ease and lack of effort needed to find useful digital tools to complete the writing tasks improved the students' motivation and their willingness to complete the writing task. The quantitative data were only collected once, and it was therefore not possible to measure changes in motivation adequately over time. However, it was evident from observation of the students from Years 2 and 3, that they had experienced changes in motivation at different stages of the learning process. This finding was derived from different students who recalled how their motivation developed over time and followed classroom learning motivation as proposed by Gardner (2007).

For the Year 3 it was evident from observation that they demonstrated change in their motivation depending on the learning context. For example, as they progressed to the next level of study they found different tools to assist them in their learning and they became more confident in their English skills. This increase in confidence also affected their motivational intensity and their motivation types. Consequently, students also became more motivated in their English writing skills and in completing their writing tasks. This finding was in line with those of Busse and Walter (2013) who suggested that students' continued motivation at university level was affected by their perceived progress. When students felt that they had made progress in mastering English, they became more motivated to learn. The improved motivation was also associated with increasing enjoyment in the learning process.

In terms of answering the research question which guided the study our analysis has compared the results from the questionnaire with those from classroom observation. No significant positive relationship was found between motivation and 1) Assignment Score, 2) the Mid-Test Score, 3) the Semester-Test Score, or 4) the Final Score. There were no statistical differences between Motivation Levels and task-in process (Assignment, Mid Semester-Test, and Semester Test variables) and task-as-outcome (Final Score). However, the association between the use of technology and the performance in Writing 1 module was confirmed. The learning of writing skills using technology-mediated TBLT approaches did not significantly influence the students' motivation in terms of quantitative findings. This outcome was expected as the literature records that the success of learning is not only measured by the scores (Gardner, 2010).

It is evident that motivation changes over time; it is influenced by numerous, unfixed and uncontrollable factors and is hard to measure (Dörnyei, 2001a). We thus recognise that our measure of motivation, extracted from the qualitative data, may have been related to a specific trait. Similar findings were recorded by Lo and Hyland (2007) in their study in Hong Kong who found that a new writing programme improved students' writing engagement and motivation but also resulted in lower writing scores for accuracy and organisation, especially among the more able students. Encouraging students to write about topics of interest and relevance to them, and providing them with a genuine audience for their may be liberating and confidence-building. In the case of our data, the use of smartphones which can access vocabulary-searching tools, and the use of PCs to access a wide range of internet-based tools, did not improve students' motivation to complete their writing tasks.

The Effects of Culture on Motivation

Gardner's model (2007) can help to explain why the findings in the study were not statistically significant. Even though the results of the study were not significant, students who went through this learning cycle found that learning through technology-mediated TBLT approaches was preferred. The students were familiar with the general writing culture and educational context of their study, but they were not accustomed to task-based learning cycles. They initially found the cycles of pre-task (planning), task (writing, giving feedback, and rewriting), and language focus (analysis and practice) challenging. However, as the students became used to the new cultural and educational context and more familiar with using English, their attitude to learning the language improved, as did their motivation. Students who had completed their three-year programme reported that they gained an advantage by using the TBLT approach through the use of technological applications.

CONCLUSION

This study has identified three main outcomes relating to learner motivation: 1) the factors that affect the motivation to improve English writing skills, 2) the use of computer technology, and 3) the way students accomplished their English writing tasks. According to much of the research literature on language learner motivation, it is regarded as either instrumental/extrinsic or integrative/intrinsic. However, it is evident from this study that this model is overly static and simplistic in the Indonesian HE context; motivation to learn a new language might not solely be either instrumental or integrated but a combination of both at different times that is dependent on the unique context of the learner. Utilising quantitative and qualitative findings in order to answer the research question (How do Indonesian EFL students' perceptions about their motivation to learn English predict their experience in the technology-mediated TBLT classroom?), the findings suggest that the Indonesian EFL learners were highly motivated to study English for economic development, such as personal development or employability. The use of digital technology, such as e-portfolios, classroom management systems, digital online and offline dictionaries, and other internet-facilitated equipment in the learning of English writing skills, motivated the students. The questionnaire results indicated that the students had very high levels of motivation in learning English in Indonesia, however, they were not enthusiastic about working on the first draft of their writing tasks. This session seemed to be very time-consuming. Students were not motivated to complete their writing on time. Even though the students reported wanting to learn the English language, they were not motivated to take an active role in the learning process. Moreover, the students mentioned that they lacked the confidence to write because of limited vocabulary. Similar to other Asian cultures, Indonesian students were dominated by dependency on their teacher and they relied on instructions and guidelines from the lecturers.

Implications and Limitations

Firstly, in relation to pedagogical implications, when discussing English learning motivation levels, findings suggest that language learning motivation was affected by classroom learning motivation. Even though a student had a high level of motivation or had integrative or intrinsic motivation for learning English, it was not necessarily reflected in their attitude to writing classes. It is recommended that lecturers identify their students' English learning motivation at the beginning of the semester. By doing so, adjustments to the teaching design and materials can then be made in order to fulfil the students' needs, and to improve motivational strategies that are needed in the learning process.

The second implication relates to future research. While the study has attempted to investigate motivational issues based on Gardner's (2007) model, more research is required to investigate the effectiveness of the model to embrace all of its elements.

The most significant limitation of this study refers to the nature of the data. The study was designed for a specific, local context in Indonesia. Since every classroom is unique, the results of the study are not generalisable. Nevertheless, they do provide insights into the specific local context that will be of value to practitioners, curriculum designers and researchers and further encourage future experimental and longitudinal studies of English writing in digital classrooms in Indonesia.

REFERENCES

Abrams, Z., & Byrd, D. R. (2017). The effects of meaning-focused pre-tasks on beginning-level L2 writing in German: An exploratory study. *Language Teaching Research*, *21*(4), 434–453. doi:10.1177/1362168815627383

Almutairi, S. (2014). *Managing and analysing task-based interaction in digital tabletop environments*. Newcastle Upon Tyne, UK: Unpublished University of Newcastle Upon Tyne.

Araminta, L. D., & Halimi, S. S. (2015). ASEAN economic community 2015: Needs analysis of Universitas Indonesia's engineering students. *Indonesian Journal of Applied Linguistics*, *5*(1), 11–18. doi:10.17509/ijal.v5i1.841

Aulia, D., Yulastri, D., & Handayani, W. (2016). The use of e-portfolio for improving students' English skills: A pilot study in English department, the State Polytechnic of Padang. *Journal Polingua*, *5*(2), 52–59.

Aulia, D., Yulastri, D., & Sari, I. (2014). The use of portfolio to improve translation ability of English department students in State Polytechnic of Padang. *Proceedings of ISELT FBS Universitas Negeri Padang*, *2*, 100–106.

Bao, R., & Du, X. (2015). Implementation of task-based language teaching in Chinese as a foreign language: Benefits and challenges. *Language, Culture, and Curriculum*, *28*(3), 291–310. doi:10.1080/07908318.2015.1058392

Barba, P., Kennedy, G., & Ainley, M. (2016). The role of students' motivation and participation in predicting performance in a MOOC motivation and participation in MOOCs. *Journal of Computer Assisted Learning*, *32*(3), 218–231. doi:10.1111/jcal.12130

Bower, K. (2017). Explaining motivation in language learning: A framework for evaluation and research. *Language Learning Journal*, 1–17. doi:10.1080/09571736.2017.1321035

Busse, V., & Walter, C. (2013). Foreign language learning motivation in higher education: A longitudinal study of motivational changes and their causes. *Modern Language Journal*, *97*(2), 435–456. doi:10.1111/j.1540-4781.2013.12004.x

Carless, D. R. (2003). Factors in the implementation of task-based teaching in primary schools. *System*, *31*(4), 485–500. doi:10.1016/j.system.2003.03.002

Carless, D. R. (2009). Revisiting the TBLT versus PPP debate: Voices from Hong Kong. *Asian Journal of English Language Teaching*, *19*(1), 49–66.

Chen, J. C. (2016). The crossroads of English language learners, task-based instruction, and 3D multi-user virtual learning in *Second Life*. *Computers & Education*, *102*, 152–171. doi:10.1016/j.compedu.2016.08.004

Clément, R., Gardner, R. C., & Smythe, P. C. (1980). Social and individual factors in second language acquisition. *Canadian Journal of Behavioural Science, 12*(4), 293–302. doi:10.1037/h0081081

Creswell, J. W., & Plano Clark, V. L. (2011). *Designing and conducting mixed methods research* (2nd ed.). London, UK: Sage.

Crookes, G., & Schmidt, R. (1989). Motivation: Reopening the research agenda. *University of Hawai'i working papers in English as a second language, 8*(1), 217-256.

Deci, E. L., & Ryan, R. M. (1985). *Intrinsic motivation and self-determination in human behavior.* London, UK: Plenum Press. doi:10.1007/978-1-4899-2271-7

Dörnyei, Z. (1990). Conceptualizing motivation in foreign-language learning. *Language Learning, 40*(1), 45–78. doi:10.1111/j.1467-1770.1990.tb00954.x

Dörnyei, Z. (2001a). *Motivational strategies in the language classroom.* Cambridge, UK: Cambridge University Press. doi:10.1017/CBO9780511667343

Dörnyei, Z. (2001b). *Teaching and researching motivation.* Harlow, UK: Longman.

Dörnyei, Z., & Ottó, I. (1998). Motivation in action: A process model of L2 motivation. *Working papers in applied linguistics (Thames Valley University, London), 4*, 43-69.

Dörnyei, Z., & Ushioda, E. (2013). *Teaching and researching motivation* (2nd ed.). London, UK: Taylor and Francis.

Ellis, R. (2003). *Task-based language learning and teaching.* Oxford, UK: Oxford University Press.

Ellis, R. (2009). Task-based language teaching: Sorting out the misunderstandings. *International Journal of Applied Linguistics, 19*(3), 221–246. doi:10.1111/j.1473-4192.2009.00231.x

Ellis, R. (2015). The study of second language acquisition (2nd ed.). Oxford, UK: Oxford University Press.

Furlong, N. E., Lovelace, K. L., & Lovelace, E. A. (2000). *Research methods and statistics: An integrated approach.* Belmont: Wadsworth/Thomson Learning.

Gardner, R. C. (1985). *Social psychology and second language learning: The role of attitudes and motivation.* London, UK: Arnold.

Gardner, R. C. (2007). Motivation and second language acquisition. *Porta Linguarum, 8*, 9–20.

Gardner, R. C. (2010). *Motivation and second language acquisition: The socio-educational model.* Oxford, UK: Peter Lang.

Gardner, R. C., & Lambert, W. E. (1959). Motivational variables in second-language acquisition. *Canadian Journal of Psychology/Revue. Canadian Psychology, 13*(4), 266–272. doi:10.1037/h0083787

Gardner, R. C., & Lambert, W. E. (1972). *Attitudes and motivation in second language learning.* Massachusetts: Newbury House.

Gardner, R. C., & Smythe, P. C. (1981). On the development of the attitude/motivation test battery. *Canadian Modern Language Review, 37*(3), 510–525. doi:10.3138/cmlr.37.3.510

Guilloteaux, M. J., & Dörnyei, Z. (2008). Motivating language learners: A classroom-oriented investigation of the effects of motivational strategies on student motivation. *TESOL Quarterly*, *42*(1), 55–77. doi:10.1002/j.1545-7249.2008.tb00207.x

Hannibal Jensen, S. (2019). Language learning in the wild: A young user perspective. *Language Learning & Technology*, *23*(1), 72–86.

Helmke, A., & Tuyet, V. T. A. (1999). Do Asian and western students learn in different way? An empirical study on motivation, study time, and learning strategies of German and Vietnamese university students. *Asia Pacific Journal of Education*, *19*(2), 30–44. doi:10.1080/0218879990190204

Huizingh, E. (2007). *Applied statistics with SPSS*. London, UK: Sage. doi:10.4135/9781446249390

Kenny, N. (2017). Developing communicative competence through task based approach. In N. Stojković, M. Tošić, & V. Nejković (Eds.), *Synergies of English for specific purposes and language learning technologies* (pp. 78–88). Cambridge Scholars Publishing.

Lamb, M. (2004a). Integrative motivation in a globalizing world. *System*, *32*(1), 3–19. doi:10.1016/j.system.2003.04.002

Lamb, M. (2004b). 'It depends on the students themselves': Independent language learning at an Indonesian state school.

Lamb, M. (2007). The impact of school on EFL learning motivation: An Indonesian case study. *TESOL Quarterly*, *41*(4), 757–780. doi:10.1002/j.1545-7249.2007.tb00102.x

Lauder, A. (2010). The status and function of English in Indonesia: A review of key factors. *MAKARA of Social Sciences and Humanities Series, 12*(1).

Le Ha, P. (2014). The politics of naming: Critiquing "learner-centred" and "teacher as facilitator" in English language and humanities classrooms. *Asia-Pacific Journal of Teacher Education*, *42*(4), 392–405. doi:10.1080/1359866X.2014.956048

Littlewood, W. (2007). Communicative and task-based language teaching in East Asian classrooms. *Language Teaching*, *40*(03), 243–249. doi:10.1017/S0261444807004363

Littlewood, W. (2014). Communication-oriented language teaching: Where are we now? where do we go from here? *Language Teaching*, *47*(3), 349–362. doi:10.1017/S0261444812000134

Lo, J., & Hyland, F. (2007). Enhancing students' engagement and motivation in writing: The case of primary students in Hong Kong. *Journal of Second Language Writing*, *16*(4), 219–237. doi:10.1016/j.jslw.2007.06.002

MacIntyre, P. D., & Blackie, R. A. (2012). Action control, motivated strategies, and integrative motivation as predictors of language learning affect and the intention to continue learning French. *System*, *40*(4), 533–543. doi:10.1016/j.system.2012.10.014

Mackey, A., & Gass, S. (2005). *Second language research: Methodology and design*. Mahwah, NJ: Erlbaum.

Mattarima, K., & Hamdan, A. R. (2011). Learners' motivation and learning strategies in English foreign language (EFI) in Indonesian context. *Journal of Edupres, 1*, 100–108.

Mattarima, K., & Hamdan, A. R. (2016). The teaching constraints of English as a foreign language in Indonesia: The context of school-based curriculum. *Sosiohumanika, 4*(2), 287–300.

Mufida, A. R., Mukhyaiyar, M., & Radjab, D. (2013). The effect of content-based instruction and task-based language teaching on the second semester students' speaking skill and students' speaking motivation of English Department Islamic University Indragiri. [ELT]. *English Language Teaching, 1*(3).

Mustafa, Z. (2010). Teachers' levels of use in the adoption of task-based language teaching in Malaysian classrooms. *The International Journal of Interdisciplinary Social Sciences: Annual Review, 5*(3), 127–138. doi:10.18848/1833-1882/CGP/v05i03/51621

Musthafa, B. (2015). Communicative language teaching in Indonesia: Issues of theoretical assumptions and challenges in the classroom practice. *TEFLIN Journal, 12*(2), 184–193.

Nunan, D. (2004). *Task-based language teaching* (Rev. ed.). Cambridge, UK: Cambridge University Press. doi:10.1017/CBO9780511667336

Ortega, L. (2012). Task-based language teaching in foreign language contexts: One pragmatist's view. Paper presented at the *Plenary delivered at JASELE Conference*, Nagoya, Japan.

Oxford, R., & Shearin, J. (1994). Language learning motivation: Expanding the theoretical framework. *Modern Language Journal, 78*(1), 12–28. doi:10.1111/j.1540-4781.1994.tb02011.x

Pammu, A., Amir, Z., & Maasum, T. N. R. T. M. (2014). Metacognitive reading strategies of less proficient tertiary learners: A case study of EFL learners at a public university in Makassar, Indonesia. *Procedia: Social and Behavioral Sciences, 118*, 357–364. doi:10.1016/j.sbspro.2014.02.049

Prabhu, N. S. (1987). *Second language pedagogy*. Oxford University Press Oxford.

Richards, J. C., & Rodgers, T. S. (2001). Approaches and methods in language teaching (2nd ed.). Cambridge, UK: Cambridge University Press. doi:10.1017/CBO9780511667305

Samuda, V. (2001). Guiding relationships between form and meaning during task performance: The role of the teacher. In M. Bygate, P. Skehan, & M. Swain (Eds.), *Researching pedagogic tasks: Second language learning, teaching and testing* (pp. 119–140). Harlow, UK: Longman.

Samuda, V. (2013). Guiding relationships between form and meaning during task performance: The role of the teacher. In M. Bygate, P. Skehan, & M. Swain (Eds.), *Researching pedagogic tasks: Second language learning, teaching and testing* (pp. 119–162). London, UK: Routledge.

Schunk, D. H., Meece, J. R., & Pintrich, P. R. (2008). *Motivation in education: Theory, research, and applications* (3rd ed.). Harlow, UK: Pearson Education Ltd.

Seedhouse, P., & Almutairi, S. (2009). A holistic approach to task-based interaction. *International Journal of Applied Linguistics, 19*(3), 311–338. doi:10.1111/j.1473-4192.2009.00243.x

Silverman, D. (2014). *Interpreting qualitative data* (5th ed.). London, UK: Sage.

Skehan, P. (1998). *A cognitive approach to language learning*. Oxford University Press.

Solikhah, I. (2015). KKNI dalam kurikulum berbasis learning outcomes. (Indonesian National Framework in learning outcome Curriculum) *LINGUA: Journal of Language. Literature and Teaching*, *12*(1), 1–22. doi:10.30957/lingua.v12i1.68

Sukandi, S. S., & Syafar, D. N. (2018). EFL students' responses to learning basic reading and writing skills. *Studies in English Language and Education*, *5*(1), 40–53. doi:10.24815iele.v5i1.8419

Sulistiyo, U. (2016). Learning English as a foreign language in an Indonesian university: A study of non-English department students' preferred activities inside and outside the classroom. [Indonesian Journal of English Teaching]. *IJET*, *5*(1), 1–26. doi:10.15642/ijet2.2016.5.1.1-26

Sundari, H., Febriyanti, R., & Saragih, G. (2018). Using task-based materials in teaching writing for EFL classes in Indonesia. *International Journal of Applied Linguistics and English Literature*, *7*(3), 119–124. doi:10.7575/aiac.ijalel.v.7n.3p.119

Talebi, Z., Aidinlou, N. A., & Farhadi, S. (2015). Form-based approaches vs. task-based approaches. *International Journal of Applied Linguistics and English Literature*, *4*(4), 137–143.

Tavakol, M., & Dennick, R. (2011). Making sense of Cronbach's alpha. *International Journal of Medical Education*, *2*, 53–55. doi:10.5116/ijme.4dfb.8dfd PMID:28029643

Ushioda, E. (2013). Motivation matters in mobile language learning: A brief commentary. *Language Learning & Technology*, *17*(3), 1–5.

Van den Branden, K. (2016). Task-based language teaching. In G. Hall (Ed.), *The Routledge handbook of English language teaching* (pp. 238–252). Routledge.

Willis, J. (1996). *A framework for task-based learning*. Harlow, UK: Longman.

Yasuda, S. (2017). Toward a framework for linking linguistic knowledge and writing expertise: Interplay between SFL-based genre pedagogy and task-based language teaching. *TESOL Quarterly*, *51*(3), 576–606. doi:10.1002/tesq.383

Yin, R. K. (2014). *Case study research: Design and methods* (5th ed.). London, UK: Sage.

Young, P. T. (1961). Motivation and emotion: A survey of the determinants of human and animal activity.

Yulastri, D. (2015a). Building students' writing skill by using Edmodo. *Journal Polingua*, *4*(2), 47–51.

Yulastri, D. (2015b). Enriching students' vocabulary by using charade game. Proceeding Research Interchange between Politeknik Negeri Padang, Indonesia and Leyte Normal University, Philippines, 1, 57-62.

Yulastri, D., Aulia, D., & Saptopramono, H. (2016). The use of Edmodo to improve the writing ability of English department students of State Polytechnic of Padang. *Journal Polingua*, *5*(2), 67–72.

APPENDIX I

Extract From the Online questionnaire for Students (Part I and II)

Instructions

This questionnaire is aimed at investigating your responses on language learning motivation, attitude and opinion about the use of technology in learning English writing skills through task-based learning.

You are required to answer the following questions related to the use of technology in learning English writing in [name removed]. It is not an examination, there is no "right" or "wrong" answer. Your own opinion is highly appreciated. Thank you.

Part I: Motivation to Learn English in Vocational Institution

1. My willingness to learn English is:

□ 1 □ 2 □ 3 □ 4 □ 5 □ 6
Very Low Very High

2. My main reason for choosing the English Department in this vocational institution is (Choose one that match your reason):
   To be able to communicate well in English □
   To get a good job □
   To be obedient to parents by following their aspiration □
   To ease getting enrolled in the higher education institution □
   No other options □
3. On the national vocational institution entry examination, this English Department at [name removed] was my choice on (Choose one that matches your choice):

   The first option □ The second option □ The third/last option □

Part II: Motivation and Writing Task Performance

4. My motivation has positive effect on my willingness to do the writing tasks.

□ 1 □ 2 □ 3 □ 4 □ 5 □ 6
Completely Disagree Completely Agree

5. Working on the English writing tasks motivates me to improve my English writing skills.

   □ 1 □ 2 □ 3 □ 4 □ 5 □ 6
   Completely Disagree Completely Agree

6. The use of technology in completing the writing tasks makes the learning of English writing more interesting

   □ 1 □ 2 □ 3 □ 4 □ 5 □ 6
   Completely Disagree Completely Agree

Chapter 10
Toward the Future of Computer-Assisted Language Testing:
Assessing Spoken Performance Through Semi-Direct Tests

Ethan Douglas Quaid
https://orcid.org/0000-0003-2682-2347
Xi'an Jiaotong-Liverpool University, China

Alex Barrett
https://orcid.org/0000-0003-1229-9743
Xi'an Jiaotong-Liverpool University, China

ABSTRACT

Semi-direct speaking tests have become an increasingly favored method of assessing spoken performance in recent years. Underpinning evidence for their continued development and use has been largely contingent on language testing and assessment researchers' claim of their interchangeability with more traditional, direct face-to-face oral proficiency interviews through theoretical and empirical investigations from multiple perspectives. This chapter initially provides background and research synopses of four significant test facets that have formed the bases for semi-direct and direct speaking test comparison studies. These are followed by the inclusion of a recent case study comparing test taker output from a computer-based Aptis speaking test and a purposively developed identical face-to-face oral proficiency interview that found a slight register shift which may be viewed as advantageous for semi-direct speaking tests. Finally, future research directions are proposed in light of the recent developments in the semi-direct speaking testing research presented throughout this chapter.

DOI: 10.4018/978-1-7998-1282-1.ch010

INTRODUCTION

Computer-based (CB) and computer-mediated (CM) testing is today, more than ever, being seen as the future of language assessment, primarily through the former's increasing role in testing contexts. The broadening use of computer-based oral proficiency interviews (CB-OPI) by test developers has necessitated that myriad studies be conducted by language testing and assessment researchers in order that this delivery mode is underpinned by sound empirical knowledge. This research has provided a growing body of evidence suggesting a degree of interchangeability between CB and face-to-face oral proficiency interviews (OPI). This chapter firstly reviews CB speaking tests' comparability with OPIs by providing synopses of background and current research findings pertaining to four of the most significant test facets supporting arguments for the use of semi-direct speaking tests over their direct counterparts.

Practicality is the first of these test facets and arguably the most important from a test developers and administering institution's perspective. Representing the second test factor is face validity which has proven to be instrumental in the decision-making process when considering the development and use of semi-direct speaking tests. Test reliability and concurrent validity are essential test measurement factors, and hence have been chosen as the latter two facets to be included within this chapter examining direct and semi-direct speaking test interchangeability. Research studies encapsulating these four test facets have often promoted the development and use of semi-direct speaking tests, and this has led to concerns that the important factor of test taker spoken output from performances has often been overlooked (Shohamy, 1994; Weir, 2005; Zhou, 2015).

The second half of this chapter examines and contrasts test taker spoken output in direct and semi-direct speaking test delivery modes by the use of a recent case study investigating the equivalence of spoken language register in test event performances. This exemplified case study provides additional empirical evidence supporting the interchangeability of test taker output register in direct and semi-direct speaking tests, by comparing spoken output elicited from four Chinese first language users of intermediate level spoken English in a British Council *Aptis General* CB-OPI and a purposively designed identical face-to-face direct OPI version. The results from this differentiation provide additional empirical evidence contributing toward establishing the equivalence of CB and face-to-face test delivery modes in a foreign language speaking test context. In particular, the validation of CB input as an elicitation instrument through interpretation of performance.

DIRECT AND SEMI-DIRECT SPEAKING TESTS

Clark (1979) labels direct speaking tests as consisting of "procedures in which the examinee is asked to engage in a face-to-face communicative exchange with one or more human interlocutors" (p.36). However, a truly direct test measures proficiency inside the identified target language use (TLU) domain, and therefore it is preferable to identify test directness on a cline between the indirect structural model and live performance in the TLU domain as the most direct. Mirroring Clark's (1979) communicative exchange, Luoma (1997) states "the main characteristic of the live test mode is that interaction in it is two-directional", and asserts that "the construct assessed is clearly related to spoken interaction" (p. 44). Although these suppositions were likely to be a given, when early theoretical models underpinned language testing, today the relatively scripted nature of many speaking tests, especially those termed as being high stakes, may well have rendered them problematic. Thus, Fulcher's (2014) view that direct testing only implies that *direct* involves live physical interaction with a human interlocutor and nothing more will be applied, and henceforth a direct test will be represented by a face-to-face OPI throughout the remainder of this chapter.

Semi-direct speaking tests are defined for the purpose of this chapter as tests that elicit spoken performance by means of non-human or technology-assisted elicitation procedures. This description encompasses both the early audio tape-based simulated oral proficiency interviews (SOPI) and today's CB mode of testing, as well as CM test input found in the mode of video-conferencing. Much criticism has been leveled at semi-direct testing from language test developers, researchers and users alike, and thus merely establishing some form of parity between delivery modes has been a primary concern for the field of language assessment and testing. Nonetheless, CB and CM speaking tests' increased practicality is a test quality that most literature argues is supportive of these delivery modes.

PRACTICALITY

Practicality is the extent to which resources support the design and development of the test as well as its ongoing use. A semi-direct test certainly provides a more superior practical alternative, because of the "flexibility with which it can be administered" (Dooey, 2008, p. 30). Semi-direct speaking tests can be conducted with large groups of candidates completing the test simultaneously meaning a shorter period of time is generally needed for administration of the test (Yonezaki, 2016); whereas face-to-face OPIs often necessitate additional procedural tasks, that require supplemental human, material, and time resources. Semi-direct testing can also be "especially pertinent in foreign language testing situations in which it is difficult to establish a reliable pool of qualified interviewers" (Choi, 2014, p. 546).

In an increasingly automated world, issues in video and audio quality are less of a concern for developers and administrators of CM language tests, due to any breakdown of communication being the exception rather than the norm. For example, studies (Kim & Craig, 2012; Loranc-Paszylk, 2015) investigating videoconferencing as a semi-direct delivery mode for language testing have found that in terms of delivery this mode is stable enough to be considered an alternative to more traditional face-to-face direct input. Additionally, Nakatsuhara, Inoue, Berry, and Galaczi (2017a) have asserted that while reducing many of the practical challenges for speaking test delivery, the CM videoconferencing delivery mode does not subvert the construct of interaction of a face-to-face OPI. However, this is not a universally agreed position for all semi-direct modes of delivery as Brooks and Swain (2014) state that CB-OPIs can limit interaction, and this could then affect the predictive validity of performance during tests to performance in TLU domains.

The practicality of CB and CM testing also benefits test takers by allowing them to complete a spoken language proficiency test, needing only access to a computer connected to the internet. This provides a wider constituency of test takers whom may be located in remote geographical areas, where it is impossible to conduct OPIs, with accessibility to a test (Nakatsuhara et al., 2017a). This inclusiveness encourages equal opportunity and fairness to be realized for all potential test takers which are important factors not to be overlooked in the social dimension of language testing.

Practicality advantages of CB speaking tests have been reported by Chinese *Aptis* CB-OPI test takers with the test being found to be "easy and convenient to operate" (Zheng & Zhang, 2017). Moreover, an interesting recent study exploring the use of the CM video-conferencing delivery mode for the International English Language Testing System (IELTS) also reported participants finding the test easier than the long-standing traditional OPI equivalent (Berry, Nakatsuhara, Inoue, & Galaczi, 2018).

Institutional test score users are important stakeholders for whom CB and CM speaking tests can also provide distinct practicality advantages. Perhaps the most significant of these is that test results can be made available to them faster, enabling program entry decisions to be made in a timelier manner, which is increasingly important in the now internationalized education sector. Likewise, decision-making for migration and work purposes is able to be completed in a timelier manner, allowing government bodies and employers to streamline administrative processes.

Evidently, there are numerous practicality benefits for the continued implementation and use of semi-direct speaking tests; however, possible risks to their feasibility cannot be discounted. These include test takers' lack of computer familiarity leading to construct-irrelevant variance and possible test security issues. Furthermore, the procedural tasks, which require additional administration to complete, and the use of human, material and time resources in conducting face-to-face OPIs may well be insignificant when considering the alternative of developing or purchasing a CB speaking test, which could be especially prohibitive in terms of monetary cost for smaller institutional test score users.

These issues notwithstanding, a practicality advantage has led to ever-increasing support for the continued introduction of new semi-direct speaking tests, and encourages established tests of both high and low stakes denomination to replace their direct OPI with the CB or CM delivery mode. However, Weir's (2005) heretical view that "practicality is simply not a necessary condition for validity" (p. 49) leads us to examine three further test factors, which could demonstrate semi-direct tests' parity with their direct OPI counterparts, beginning with face validity.

FACE VALIDITY

Face validity refers to how test developers, institutional test score users and associated stakeholders, in addition to the test takers themselves, perceive the test to be an accurate and fair measure of spoken performance, as well as their affective variables toward a test delivery mode more generally. Interchanging a live interlocutor with a computer may seem counterintuitive for a proficiency assessment measuring speaking ability, and hence the face validity of CB-OPIs is often seen as being key to their success. In contrast to a recent study conducted by Alutumi (2018) that suggests positive attitudes were indicated towards integrating computer-assisted language learning for TOEFL iBT exam preparation training, research findings have shown mixed results as to how test takers feel about actually using computers during oral assessment procedures.

An early study by Kenyon and Malabanga (2001) compared test taker attitude toward both a SOPI and CB-OPI and compared them with their affective variables in direct OPIs. Participants who took both the SOPI and the CB-OPI found the CB exam to be less difficult due to its adaptive nature, but otherwise both tests scored similarly. The two semi-direct tests were then compared to an OPI and results indicated that participants felt the differently mediated exams to be similar. Despite this likeness, participants in this study felt the face-to-face OPI was more personal and consequently inspired language that was more conversational and thereupon more closely aligned with *real-life* speaking scenarios.

A later study by Surface, Poncheri, and Bhavsar (2008) included a comparative question of preference between direct and semi-direct oral proficiency tests and their results indicated a predilection for the OPI, although it was speculated that this was due primarily to respondents' dislike of an avatar used in the CB-OPI and less to do with skepticism concerning the validity of the test. Test takers' predilection for OPIs was corroborated by Qian (2009) who measured test-taker preference between the IELTS OPI and an in-house semi-direct OPI at the Hong Kong Polytechnic University. Furthermore, a more recent study by Yonezaki (2016) demonstrated a definitive preference for the direct test. Test taker comments elicited centered on the preference for a speaking test that was similar to natural daily life interaction, although a few respondents mentioned a preference for the semi-direct test as they felt more nervous when confronted with a live interlocutor.

Zhan and Wan (2016) measured test taker opinions of a semi-direct OPI used in China which showed that participants felt "their pragmatic and strategic competencies in communication were not measured" (p. 373), because the CB test seemed inauthentic. It should be noted though that Zhan and Wan (2016) were not comparing their CB-OPI to an OPI, and thus participants did not have the benefit of an explicit contrast. Lastly, Dunlea et al. (2018) measured test-taker preference in Vietnam between face-to-face and CB tests in their examination of concurrent validity between the *Aptis* and a similar non-computerized OPI, finding a strong preference for the face-to-face test as well, with 74% of respondents agreeing or strongly agreeing to a preference for it.

The evidence seems to indicate a preference by test takers for OPIs due to reasons of authenticity and natural speech production which it is perceived can only arise from human-human interaction. This seems to be incongruent with seminal research in human-computer interaction which testifies that people tend to interact with computers similarly to how they would with people (Reeves & Nass, 1996). Despite this, examining test taker affective variables through general preference toward direct and semi-direct tests is just one aspect of face validity.

A second important characteristic of face validity is the determination of whether a test taker feels an assessment fairly and accurately measures the constructs it purports to measure. For example, Amengual-Pizarro and Garcia-Laborda (2017) discovered that test takers who took both direct and semi-direct OPIs found that the CB-OPI was a perfectly valid measure of oral competence. This perception of the CB-OPIs validity was due to the study participants noting that the CB-OPI was "convenient, intuitive, and user-friendly" (p. 32).

Zheng and Zhang (2017) measured test taker attitudes to both a CB test and a paper based test that measured the four major skills and revealed that test takers found advantages and disadvantages to both formats without a clear preference for one over the other, although it was discovered that the speaking portion of the CB test was the most difficult for participants. On the other end of the spectrum, a study conducted by Stricker and Attali (2010) which measured attitudes toward the *TOEFL iBT* found the speaking section of the exam garnered many more unfavorable opinions compared to the sections of the test assessing the other three language use skills.

Overall, test takers tend to feel that face-to-face OPIs are preferable. Therefore, continued development and adoption of semi-direct speaking tests may encounter some resistance with test takers who feel that a more accurate assessment of their speaking can only be achieved in direct OPIs. As artificial intelligence continues to develop, a CB-OPI which can adapt and perhaps personalize the experience of CB-OPIs, without compromising test reliability, could well be a valid solution.

RELIABILITY

Test reliability is the consistency of test performance measurement. It is typically examined in two ways: test-retest reliability (consistency in test performance when a test taker takes the same test twice) and rater agreement (consistency in intra- and inter-rating). Thompson, Cox, and Knapp's (2016) study found a high degree of reliability in both test-retest and rater agreement for an OPI and CB-OPI, which confirmed results from previous studies (Abadin, Fried, Good, & Surface, 2012; Surface, Harman, Watson, & Thompson, 2009; Surface, Poncheri, & Bhavsar, 2008).

More recent studies examining the scoring reliability of high profile CB-OPIs have underscored this delivery mode's consistency in the rating of test taker performance. For instance, Schmidgall's (2017) study analyzed the reliability of the Test Of English for International Communication (TOEIC) speaking scores across different levels of the scoring procedure using the G-theory framework and found the dependability of the TOEIC Speaking scale scores was relatively high.

Despite the potential test-retest reliability of both OPIs and CB-OPIs, detractors have put forth valid points, regarding construct irrevelant variance. Lazarton's (1996) study examining the types of linguistic and interactional support that an interlocutor provides to the test taker in an OPI found that the "potential for uneven interview performance in a face-to-face interview is one reason that [semi-direct tests] are so appealing i.e. they remove the variability that a live interlocutor introduces" (p.154).

An example of interlocutor corruption of test taker output in OPIs was found by Reemann, Alas, and Liiv (2013), who discovered that deviations from the OPI script by interlocutors correlated with their gender in Estonia. In their study, female interlocutors tended to be more accommodative and generous with time, which resulted in lower test reliability. This perhaps demonstrates that despite present-day procedures of standardization and other strict interlocutor procedural guidelines in fixing input frames, a human element in test delivery will always include the possibility of error or aberration. And conversely, test takers in OPIs, through the presence of a human interlocutor, are afforded the opportunity to interrupt the relatively formatted test input discourse, which is an additional nuance to test reliability.

Arguments supporting the continued use of OPIs are partly based upon the notion that they can provide opportunities to elicit a wider range of discourse moves from test takers and therefore it is claimed that they could more accurately reflect spoken interaction. Seedhouse and Morales (2017) have proposed a fourth part to be included into the IELTS OPI, enabling interlocutor question followed by test taker response discourse exchanges to be reversed. Results from their study suggest that these atypical sequence of exchanges were successfully elicited, along with a variety of other speech acts. Furthermore, additional rating data were retrieved from the performances throughout this proposed new section that provided a clear distinction between stronger and weaker test takers. Nonetheless, introducing candidate-led interaction into OPIs may affect opportunities for test takers of varying ability to demonstrate their competence and thus affect the reliability of the test.

Questions as to the reliability of SOPIs have been put forth by Young-Ju (2007) which also affect CB-OPIs. Namely, Young-Ju (2007) discovered that SOPI raters tended to listen to recordings selectively. For instance, raters would begin listening to task three first, and if the test taker performed well there, would then move to task four or five. However, they would skip these subsequent tasks and focus on tasks one or two if the performance in task three was not successful. Selective listening deprives the examinee of a holistic appraisal of their interview and is important due to the frequently given expectation that test taker performance is rated throughout all parts of a test. This example of selective listening to test taker performance by raters cannot be as easily amended in OPIs. Young-Ju's (2007) findings were based on a sample size that was too small to determine if this selective listening behavior affected reliability; nevertheless, this does warrant further investigation. It is worth noting, however, that the irregularity identified by Young-Ju (2007) is not associated with the delivery of the test and hence could be rectified during the rating process.

During the documented recent revision of the *Aptis* CB-OPI speaking rating scales, Fairburn and Dunlea (2017) noted that although inter-rater agreement was high using the new scales, minor inconsistencies in the rating of performances were primarily attributable to the rater effects of leniency or severity and a tendency to mark centrally within the scale producing a restricted range of scores. Considering these findings that well-developed rating scales and rater training and standardization can improve the accuracy and consistency of test scores, much is still unknown of the cognitive processes employed by raters when making scoring decisions and further research investigating this construct irrelevant facet would be beneficial.

One way of increasing the reliability of test scores is to utilize double-marking of test event performances by raters. Through the use of pre-marked control items regularly interspersed within the performances to be rated, both inter- and intra-rating can be monitored. Whilst the benefits of incorporating second-marking are numerous, questions remain as to its accuracy for OPIs, because a live test event performance cannot be replicated. The use of audio and audio-visual recordings of OPIs for double-marking has recently been brought into focus with Beltran (2016) reporting no significant differences between the rating of audio and audio-visual speaking test performances, because despite there being variability between scores, these remained within a comparable range. However, the raters participating in this study expressed a preference for the audio-visual input mode, due to it "allowing for a more complete and straightforward scoring experience" (Beltran, 2016, p.15).

Nevertheless, a smaller study investigating the rating of live, audio-visual and audio only input modes of the IELTS speaking test conducted by Nakatsuhara, Inoue and Taylor (2017b) reported significant differences in the scores awarded for audio recorded spoken performances and live test events. It was proposed that this finding demonstrates narrower constructs are being assessed in the audio input mode. Consistency between scores of performances in the audio-visual and live modes was reported as being much closer as raters were able to notice paralinguistic features that contribute toward discourse expected in *real-life* interaction.

Semi-direct speaking test score consistency has been shown to possess the reliability which is required to facilitate high-quality decisions. This is important as interpretations must be meaningful, impartial, generalizable and relevant. Furthermore, the stability of interlocutor input throughout successive administrations of a test along with the degree of rater agreement achievable when a test event performance is scored by audio only suggests that reliability is a test quality wherein semi-direct tests can claim interchangeability with their direct counterparts. However, concurrent validity evidence of test scores between these two delivery modes that demonstrate the predictive ability of CB-OPIs to accurately reference performance, and thus scores, in OPIs is also essential.

CONCURRENT VALIDITY

As it is proposed that semi-direct speaking tests be substituted for OPIs, concurrent validity is of high importance to all test stakeholders. Much of the research investigating direct and semi-direct speaking test interchangeability has focused on concurrent validation that involves equating test scores between direct and semi-direct tests. This research has often used the OPI as the criterion behavior, with the presumption that it is always the semi-direct tests' validity that needs to be established. Clark (1979) initially argued that a correlation figure of 0.9 or higher would be an appropriate level of agreement to suggest interchangeability; yet a subsequent study by Clark and Swinton (1980) found that scores on the TSE and OPI correlated at $r = 0.80$ and they concluded that the TSE was a reasonable alternative.

With the Center for Applied Linguistics' introduction of the first SOPIs designed to test less commonly taught languages in the late 1980s, subsequent research from Stansfield (1991) reported Pearson correlations of 0.89 – 0.95 in the OPI and SOPI variants leading to the proposal that the SOPI correlates so highly with the OPI that it seems safe to say that both measures test the same abilities. Moreover, on the basis of Stansfield and Kenyon's (1992a, 1992b) research, it was concluded that the OPI and SOPI are highly comparable measures of oral language proficiency and can be viewed as parallel tests in two different formats.

More recent studies investigating the concurrent validity of CB-OPIs include those by Rosenfeld, Bernstein, and Balogh (2005) and Mousavi (2009) and have found that comparisons of test taker scores between the delivery modes correlate highly, signaling the possibility that no adverse effects are to be found. Additionally, Surface, Poncheri, and Bhavsar (2008) conducted an OPI to CB-OPI concurrent validity study with 99 Korean learners of English and found that absolute agreement on final scores between the two tests was 63%, but increased to 98% when considering adjacent agreement alongside the absolute rating. Moreover, Thompson, Cox, and Knapp (2016) found that 55% of test-takers who took both an OPI and CB-OPI had the same score on both exams with this percentage increasing to 97% for scores with adjacent category agreement.

The most recent published study, Dunlea et al. (2018), had very similar results to both the Surface et al. (2008) and Thompson et al. (2016) studies, but used a test that measured all four skills. Comparing 384 Vietnamese students who took both a paper based English proficiency test and the *Aptis* CB-OPI, Dunlea el al. (2018) found 66% exact agreement, and 99% agreement when including adjacent placement. From the results of the above-mentioned studies, it can be seen that exact agreement typically falls below acceptable standards, yet is impressively high when accounting for adjacent agreement. Adjacent agreement could be a fair concession in justifying the overall validity between direct and semi-direct OPIs; however, serious repercussions within the allowance could exist. For instance, if adjacent scores straddled threshold levels, such as intermediate-high and advanced-low, a test taker may be affected by one test format over the other if entry requirements sought only advanced placements.

Yonezaki (2016) conducted a comparison study between direct and semi-direct speaking assessments with Japanese participants and found no statistically significant differences between scores. This study also compared the speaking criteria separately to determine if specific skills may differ between test formats. Although fluency and accuracy were slightly better in the direct test, and the other two criteria of volume and content showed marginally superior numbers for the semi-direct test, Yonezaki (2016) concluded no significant differences among these scoring criteria between test formats.

Kim and Craig's (2012) interesting experimental study validating a CM video conferenced speaking test compared this delivery mode with a face-to-face OPI and found "no significant difference in performance between test modes, neither overall nor across analytic scoring features" (p.257). In addition, Ockey, Koyama, Setoguchi, and Sun (2015) compared the *TOEFL iBT* speaking scores of 222 Japanese university students to their performances on face-to-face or group oral assessments in their university English classes and also found a strong relationship between their performances.

Kim and Craig's (2012) validation study results were later found to be representative as Nakatsuhara et al.'s (2017b) comparison between video conferenced OPIs and face-to-face OPIs also found no significant differences in overall test scores or in performance in rating scale criteria (fluency, lexis, grammar, and pronunciation). Nakatsuhara et al. (2017b) also analyzed language functions elicited from each test format and from 30 language functions examined, only clarification, comparison, and suggestion showed significant differences in use between test modes. The differences were explained by questionnaire feedback which showed that the sound quality of the video conferencing tests was moderately unreliable in part one of the test, where the differences were found.

As evidenced from the research presented, there is some degree of concurrent validity between direct and semi-direct speaking tests, but Shohamy (1994), Weir (2005) and Zhou (2015) agree that high correlations between delivery modes of a test provide necessary but insufficient evidence of their interchangeability, because of the need to investigate the equivalence of direct and semi-direct speaking tests from multiple perspectives. Concerns generated include lower test validity because of the possibility of obscuring or introducing mode-specific features indicating potential disparities that may prove detrimental to the way in which assessment scores are interpreted and include test taker spoken output.

TEST TAKER OUTPUT

Early Speaking test theorem argued that direct tests are the better measures of speaking ability due to their close relationship between test context and *real-life*, yet acknowledged that the language elicited is unrepresentative of *real-life* conversational discourse, because test takers are aware that they are talking to a language assessor (Clark, 1979).

A relatively small number of studies have investigated the equivalence of test taker output in direct and semi-direct speaking tests, and those which have (Choi, 2014; O'Loughlin, 2001; Shohamy 1994; Zhou, 2008) have used closely matched tasks, serving to complicate potential output divisions due to the difficulties experienced in separating task effect from mode effect. The following abridged version of a recent published study entitled *Output register parallelism in an identical direct and semi-direct speaking test: A case study* (Quaid, 2018) represents an example of research investigating this facet of test mode comparability. For brevity, the introduction and conclusion sections have been excluded from presentation, whereupon the study can be joined at the following literature review stage that details previous research findings of salient language register features to be investigated in the study.

LITERATURE REVIEW

Rhetorical Functions and Structure

Shohamy (1994) defined rhetorical functions as the nature of the input or prompt used to elicit test taker output, while rhetorical structure referred to the underlying discourse organization of the speech event in its entirety. Shohamy (1994) found both were different in her study, because the OPI mainly consisted of direct interrogatives and the SOPI of declarative instructional prompts. Two possible explanations for these differences could be task effect or the now relatively dated speaking test used in the comparison, which predominantly used a *task-response-new task* rhetorical structure. The latter is a more likely explanation as differing types of interaction have been included in more recent CB-OPIs that allow inferences to be made about performance in a myriad of contexts (Laborda, 2010), and thus later studies (O'Loughlin, 2001; Choi, 2014) have shown that the rhetorical functions and structure are highly comparable in monologic tasks of direct and semi-direct speaking tests.

Agreement of research findings relating to the similarities between the rhetorical functions and structure in test taker output in direct and semi-direct versions of monologic test tasks appears to be within sight. However, less agreement has been reached with regard to the similarity of prosodic features and contextualization in test taker output between delivery modes.

Prosodic Features and Contextualization

Shohamy (1994) and O'Loughlin (2001) agreed that the prosodic features of test taker output differed, with the semi-direct tests monologic tasks encouraging less variation in intonation and voice range: Kiddle and Kormos (2011) concurred with Shohamy (1994) and O'Loughlin's (2001) earlier research findings in their study, which compared test taker output from an OPI with a CB-OPI using a purpose developed speaking test. Results showed that there was a statistically significant difference in pronunciation performance in monologic speaking tasks, when the test taker response was delivered via a microphone on a computer, yet in a more recent study, Choi (2014) noted that the OPI and SOPI performance samples did not show any distinctive patterns or characteristics in terms of average tone and pitch shifts, and thus concluded that prosodic features were very similar.

Shohamy (1994) reported on the differing test taker spoken discourses elicited by the two versions of the test and contextualization was proposed as a major contributing factor. This was signaled by test taker laughter, addressing of the interlocutor directly, sharing personal information and referring to physical objects located within the testing environment to explain or demonstrate a point being made. Shohamy (1994) remarked that "context alone seems to be more powerful than the elicitation tasks themselves" (p.118). Nonetheless, Shohamy, Donitsa-Schmidt and Waizer (1993) did concede that it was unclear if these facets of contextualization were a result of not controlling for task effect. However, O'Loughlin (2001) found no evidence of similar contextualization in either version of the *access* speaking test. Furthermore, Choi (2014) labelled contextualization as being very similar in both delivery modes.

To examine contextualization is one method of determining interpersonal differences in elicited test taker discourse; however, lexical density analyses have provided an alternative tool with which to investigate possible output register variation.

Lexical Density

Shohamy (1994) found that the OPI output contained 40 per cent lexical items and 60 per cent functional items approximately whilst these figures were reversed for the semi-direct test. On this basis, it was argued that the language output possessed greater literateness in the semi-direct test. Similarly, O'Loughlin (2001) reported a smaller but statistically significant difference between modes, and suggested that the lack of interlocutor verbal feedback during the semi-direct test could explain this difference, because even in monologic tasks during the direct test, interlocutors provided reactive tokens to the test takers.

Zhou (2008) found her lexical density results conflicted with those of Shohamy (1994) and O'Loughlin (2001), because there were no significant differences between the OPI and CB-OPI. Zhou (2008) proposed the disparity of this finding "may be attributable to that the tasks used... were more parallel in various aspects across modes" (p. 203). It is likely that Shohamy (1994) and O'Loughlin's (2001) inclusion of open tasks was a key contributor to the task effect noted in their studies, as ultimately the range and frequency of lexical items within test taker output are subject to the demands of the task.

Choi (2014) documented that output from the semi-direct test had a slightly higher lexical density than the OPI throughout all task types in his study. Whilst agreeing that task type contributed to output lexical density, Choi put forward an alternate proposition to O'Loughlin (2001) in that his closed narration tasks elicited more lexically dense output than the open description tasks. This discrepancy may well be due to the two studies not being comparable, because the majority of Choi's (2014) tasks allowed for test taker planning time, which could be a source of lexical density variation.

Syntactic Complexity

Shohamy (1994) reported a possible difference between connecters used in the OPI and SOPI. A subsequent study conducted by Luoma (1997) agreed and showed that there was a possible difference in a tendency towards more coordination on the tape-mediated test. Luoma (1997) showed that there were almost twice as many coordinating conjunctions during the performances in the tape-based test, but a ratio of only 4:3 respectively in test taker output from the face-to-face test. The sets' range of coordinating and subordinating conjunctions were almost identical between modes, although some less frequently used were perhaps more mode specific, and may have implied slight register variation. During the face-to-face test, informal vague list completers such as *and_stuff* and *and_everything* were found, yet none were discovered in output from the tape-mediated test.

Luoma (1997) also noted unexpected de-contextualization of the direct test event, which was found within subordinating conjunction use in addressing the interlocutor, whereby test takers used *as_it_says* during the face-to-face test, whilst deciding to acknowledge the speaker in the tape-mediated equivalent with *as_you_have_said*. Shohamy (1994) found that the OPI test taker output contained a variety of discourse connectives, whereas these were restricted during the SOPI. In direct contrast, O'Loughlin (2001) reported that output from both versions of the *access* test's monologic tasks showed an equally broad range of discourse linkers, but that they were used less frequently during the semi-direct test.

Choi (2014) found that the types and numbers of discourse connectives and markers in test taker output were identical in both the direct and semi-direct versions of the test tasks used in his study. These findings are interesting because we may expect a number of specific cohesive devices to be found in test taker output from semi-direct speaking tests, illustrating what many researchers (O'Loughlin, 2001; Shohamy 1994; Zhou 2008) have described as a more formal register or style, with a higher degree of literateness and cohesion.

From syntactic complexity analyses of test taker output between delivery modes at AS-unit and clausal level, while using monologic tasks, Zhou (2008) reported no significant difference in the syntactic complexity of the output examined, although the means of syntactic complexity measures were slightly higher in the CB-OPI. Furthermore, Choi's (2014) study, also using monologic tasks, similarly showed that the semi-direct test was prone to elicit longer and more complex utterances.

RESEARCH QUESTIONS

1. Can test taker output register equivalence be shown in an identical semi-direct and direct version of the *Aptis General* speaking test?
2. What output features are primary contributors toward any register shift found?

METHODS

The present study used an alternate methodological approach to determining test taker output equivalence in direct and semi-direct speaking tests. In contrast to all previous studies referenced in this paper, identical test task type and content were used and interlocutor effect was successfully minimized. Figure 1 provides an overview of the counter-balanced study design.

MATERIAL

Aptis General CB-OPI

The *Aptis General* Speaking test (British Council, 2018) was used to form the basis of this study. The test is delivered as a CB-OPI and consists of four parts using monologic tasks, whose full specifications are available in O'Sullivan and Dunlea (2015). A number of these specifications are identical throughout all four tasks, such as the CB delivery mode and the pre-recorded and scripted features of the tasks, but task feature specifications that do differ by task type and/or number are summarized below.

The online practice version of the *Aptis General* speaking test (2016) was chosen in preference to current live versions to minimize test security risks, enable immediate access to data for stimulated recall

Figure 1. Study design

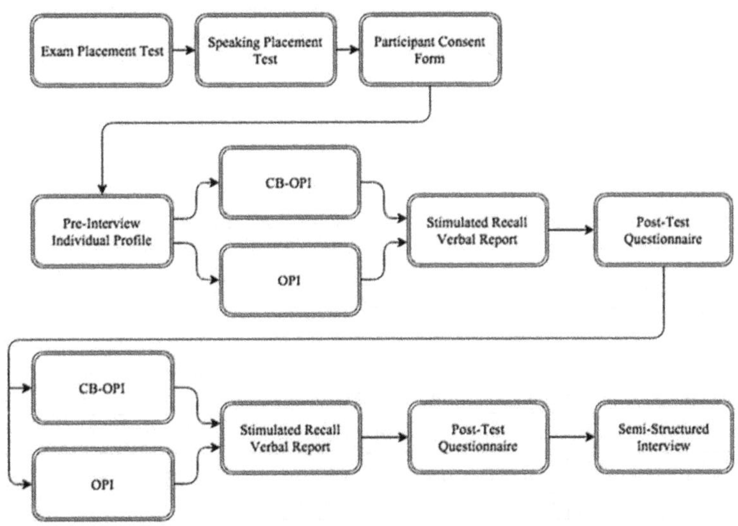

Table 1. Task feature differences

Specification	*Task 1*	*Task 2*	*Task 3*	*Task 4*
Task level (CEFR)	A1, A2	B1	B1	B2
Rubric presentation	Aural, written	Aural, written, visual	Aural, written, visual	Aural, written, visual
Response format	Q&A	Q&A	Q&A	Long turn
Interaction	Interlocutor - candidate	Interlocutor - candidate	Interlocutor - candidate	Candidate only

verbal report interviews and allow for unedited publication of this study. No changes were made to this standard version of the *Aptis* General speaking test for delivery. The CB *Aptis General* speaking test was fully transcribed, interlocutor input modified and visual prompts printed for face-to-face delivery.

Participants

A pool of 30 participants was invited to complete Cambridge English Language Assessment's (2016) Adult Learners' General English exam placement test (EPT). Four respondents were identified from their EPT scores as minimally lower-intermediate English language users and completed a face-to-face speaking placement test (SPT) in order to establish the validity of the scores attained from the EPT with regard to their speaking ability. Pseudonyms were assigned to all participants for the reporting of this study to protect identities and maintain confidentiality agreements.

The participants were female and of Chinese nationality with a corresponding L1, who were 18-35 years old and had excellent familiarity with computing and technology. Emily and Katrina were studying English in company-organized classes at the time of the data collection sessions, but only one lesson was completed during the five-day span of the data collection phases, and this related to salutations and closings in business emails and therefore was not deemed to be of consequence for this study's results. All four participants reported some familiarity with the *Aptis General* Speaking test format, although none had completed the online practice version of the test used in this study.

Table 2. Participants' EPT score, recommended exam and SPT Level

Participant	*EPT score*	*Recommended Cambridge English exam*	*SPT level*
Elena	22	Cambridge English Advanced (CAE) / Cambridge English Proficiency (CPE)	Upper-intermediate
Chloe	25	Cambridge English Proficiency (CPE)	Intermediate
Emily	24	Cambridge English Proficiency (CPE)	Intermediate
Katrina	21	Cambridge English First (FCE) / Cambridge English Advanced (CAE)	Lower-intermediate

Procedure

The participants were divided into two groups that were assigned to complete alternate test delivery formats during each of the two data collection sessions. The CB practice version of the *Aptis General* Speaking test was administered in standard format in a computer laboratory, and participants' spoken performances were captured by an audio DRD recorder. The face-to-face OPI delivery was conducted in a quiet room adjoining the computer laboratory.

Situational practicality demanded that the two data collection sessions were conducted within a five-day period. No unreasonable practice or recency effect were noted during the second data collection session. Participants were not informed of task nature or content before either of the sessions. The instructions to participants and researcher protocol for the stimulated recall interviews were adapted from Mackay and Gass (2000). The self-report interviews were conducted immediately after each administration of the speaking test. The DRD recorder containing the participants spoken output from the OPIs was placed between the participant and the researcher, and both parties were able to pause the recording on listening to the tests to comment or ask questions. A limitation of selecting the online practice version was that the test was unable to be paused after each task for the verbal report to be conducted using the audio recordings as stimuli, and therefore the full tests needed to be administered before initiation of the stimulated recall phases.

The second data collection session differed by inclusion of a semi-structured interview conducted at the end of the session that allowed participants to expand on and contrast their responses in the two post-test questionnaires. This interview was co-constructed in that both the participant and the interviewer could select salient responses from the post-test questionnaires to form part of the interview.

Analyses and Results

Spoken output data from the four participants were transcribed following conversation analysis transcription notation conventions that were recommended by Atkinson and Heritage (1984), and subsequently adopted by Lazaraton (2002), to investigate test taker output in OPIs. Transcription of the spoken performances was primarily carried out by the lead investigator; however, twenty-five per cent of the raw data was double-coded by a trained research assistant to validate the accuracy of the coded transcripts. The spoken data from the stimulated recall and semi-structured post-test interviews were not transcribed, save for excerpts presented in this study.

Foster, Tonkyn, and Wigglesworth (2000) define AS-units as being "a single speaker's utterance consisting of an independent clause, or sub-clausal unit, together with any subordinate clause(s) associated with either" (p. 365). Foster et al.'s AS-unit was chosen as the basic syntactic speech element best suited to the syntactic complexity analyses in this study, as it was considered a better measure than others, such as T- and C-units which are inadequate to deal with a full analysis of spoken discourse, because multiple unit definitions inhibit studies being replicated with any real accuracy.

Rhetorical Functions and Structure

The rhetorical functions and structure of the performance samples elicited from the OPI and the CB-OPI were comparable. The variance of item input in the test, containing both task instructions and direct questions, ensured maximum flexibility of the discourse event. Non-conformation to standard *question–*

answer–question traditional OPI form, or _task-performance–new task_ discourse units, typical of some early semi-direct speaking tests, encouraged a wider range of discourse exchanges: _task–performance-question–answer_. Deviation from this myriad of exchange forms was rare, and was only found in the OPI when test takers made requests for instruction clarification:

[Katrina: OPI, Task 4 Instructions]

116 IN you now have two minutes? to talk?

117 PD for each question or all the three? (.2) the three ok. .hhh! (.)

((looks at interlocutor who nods))

Test taker output was similar between modes at a macro-structure level, sharing many common features. The following excerpts clearly illustrate the similar discourse organization of the texts elicited:

[Elena: CB-OPI, Task 1, Item 2]

17 EL well basically? there is no pattern or theme for me t(hhh)o do in

18 my free time, .hhh! (.2) um i just simply like (.) reading books.

19 (.) (*er watching*) some films (.2) or listen to some music, .hhh

20 (.5) and it really all depends on my (*moods,*) (.2) <not

21 some> kind of thing i have to do. .hhh (.5) so basically free

22 time (*for me*) is, do >whatever i want?!< (*and*) do it

23 <whenever (*i want?*)> (.5) ok,

[Elena: OPI, Task 1, Item 2]

19 EL (%ah?%) well what i like to do in my free time is to. (.) do.

20 almost (.) nothing, or just lying down? .hhh ah reading some

21 books? or watching some tvs, .hhh (.) so? basically free time is

22 for me is to do >whatever i want,< there's no such thing

23 as, .hhh (.) (*um*) tch like i'll go? (.) jogging or something

*24 like >that it?< all depends on my (*mood,*) (1.5)*

25 (%ok?%) (.) ah (%i'm ready.%) tch

The discourse functions in test taker output at the level of act were also highly comparable throughout the tests.

Contextualization and Prosodic Features

A higher degree of contextualization was found in the output from the direct OPI. Discourse markers indicative of more interactive exchanges were found throughout test taker output in the direct versions of the test, and their relative absence within the elicited discourse of the semi-direct CB-OPI was marked. A salient example was Elena's frequent use of *you know*, when attempting to seek interlocutor agreement:

[Elena: OPI, Part 3, Item 1, Response]

82 playing basketball you can see a lot of people,.hhh (.) you know?

*83 chasing the balls? (.) (*and*) you know fighting er with*

During Elena's output in the CB-OPI, no seemingly direct attempts were made to address the interlocutor. The second person pronoun *you* was instead used in isolation to achieve personal reference to a lesser degree. To exemplify this, the following excerpt from CB-OPI output sought to advise personally and generically of entry to a museum:

[Elena: CB-OPI, Part 2, Item 2, Response]

*52 (*er*) it is free admission so you can go >whenever< you want*

This both generic and personal use of *you* by participants was frequently observed in both test delivery modes, and individual test task items were almost certainly an important factor in its use.

Discourse particles were used frequently by all participants in the OPI at the end of turns, to seek agreement from the interlocutor of the quality or length of their response. The most frequent of these was *OK?* used with rising intonation:

[Chloe: OPI, Part 3, Item 3, Response]

92 so (.2) um: basketball is more difficult. it's (.8) ok?%

This directly contrasted with their use in the CB-OPI as a hesitation filler at the beginning of turns or as a signal of turn completion, which were equally identifiable by the use of flat continuing intonation:

[Katrina, CB-OPI, Part 1, Item 1, Response]

*10 PD ok. (.) (*there a:re four*) members in my family. (.) .hhh! my*

Additional evidence of test taker contextualization during the OPIs was found in laughter, requests for clarification of task instructions and in more interpersonal turn completion signals used with rising intonation.

Lexical Density

To give an overall impression of the performances in each mode, word counts were taken per task and item for each participant. A word count calculation resulted in overall test means per delivery mode of CB-OPI *782.75:797.75* OPI. This result, coupled with the individual task/item word counts in Table 3, suggested that both versions elicited a very similar amount of ratable language.

To investigate claims of spoken output register variation between delivery modes, lexical density analyses of the test takers' performances were conducted. The taxonomy framework originally proposed by Halliday (1989), and subsequently revised and used by O'Loughlin (2001) and Choi (2014), was adopted as the item classification system used in these analyses. It was decided that no distinction be made between high and low frequency lexical items, so as to be able to effectively compare results with the most similar and recent studies (Choi 2014, Zhou 2008), as well as those which were broadly relevant to this current investigation (O'Loughlin, 2001; Shohamy, 1994).

An analysis of all collected spoken data produced very similar overall lexical density mode percentage medians of CB-OPI *40.614:40.329* OPI. Figure 2 shows these overall mean values distributed into percentage figures per test task item.

The CB-OPI elicited minimally greater lexically dense output in two task items, although more noticeable is a strikingly similar overall pattern in the lexical density of output per individual test task item between delivery modes.

Syntactic Complexity

An analysis of the total occurrence of all conjunctions was found to be CB-OPI *231:277* OPI. Therefore, a relatively even distribution was found between modes. A similar ratio of coordination and subordination was also present: CB-OPI coordination *65.4:34.6* subordination, and OPI coordination *67.1:32.9* subordination. Table 4 presents occurrence by conjunction type, identifier, number used, and their frequency of use among all conjunctions found in the tests.

To determine complexity at the level of AS-unit, three additional analyses were conducted and the first of these was the number of words per AS-unit.

Table 3. Mean output word count per task item

Delivery mode	*Task 1*			*Task 2*			*Task 3*			*Task 4*
	Item 1	*Item 2*	*Item 3*	*Item 1*	*Item 2*	*Item 3*	*Item 1*	*Item 2*	*Item 3*	*Item*
CB-OPI	50.5	49	48.25	72.5	78	80.75	70.75	65.5	74.25	193.25
OPI	53.75	56	46.75	74.75	76	72.75	69	65.25	89.25	195

Figure 2. Mean lexical density percentage values per test task item

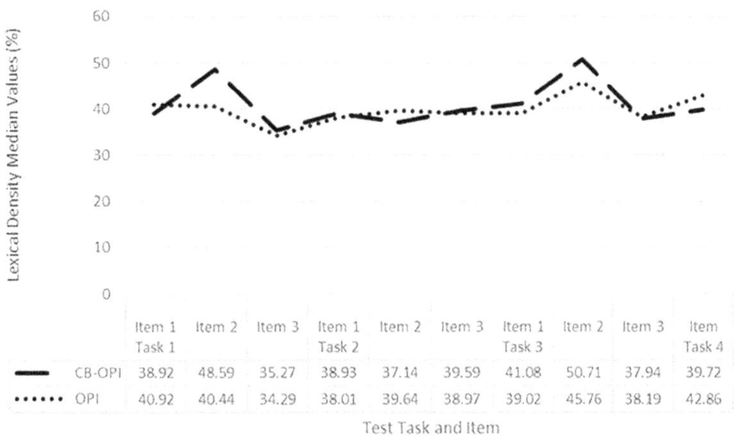

Table 4. Phrasal and clausal conjunction type and frequency

CB-OPI coordinators			*OPI coordinators*		
Conjunction	*No.*	*%**	*Conjunction*	*No.*	*%**
and	100	43.2	and	109	39.3
so	19	8.2	so	35	12.6
but	18	7.7	but	21	7.5
or	14	6	or	21	7.5
not only… also	1	0.4			
CB-OPI subordinators			*OPI subordinators*		
Conjunction	*No.*	*%**	*Conjunction*	*No.*	*%**
because	30	12.9	that	24	8.6
that	19	8.2	because	21	7.5
when	8	3.4	when	16	5.7
which	4	1.7	if (whether)	9	3.2
as	3	1.2	what	6	2.1
if, how, what, whatever, while	2 each	0.8	whatever	3	1
			even though, how	2	0.7
			however, who, as, which, after whenever, while, as long as	1 each	0.3
since, whenever who, where, without,	1 each	0.4			

* Percentage of conjunction in test mode for ease of comparison

Three participants used more words per AS-unit during the CB-OPI; however, Elena's output did not conform to this overall trend, because she used more words per AS-unit in the OPI. The second analysis investigated the number of clauses per AS-unit, and within these results a pattern for all participants emerged. Table 6 shows a greater percentage of clauses per AS-unit in output from the CB-OPI, albeit marginally for Emily and Katrina.

Finally, an analysis of the number of subordinate clauses per AS-unit revealed that three of the four participants used moderately more subordinating clauses in the CB-OPI, whilst Elena used subordination equally in both versions of the test.

The results of the syntactic complexity analyses were comparable between modes. The OPI elicited minimally more linking of phrases in the output retrieved, but at clausal and AS-unit level the CB-OPI output possessed only minimally levels of higher syntactic complexity and subordination.

Discussion

The rhetorical functions and structure of the discourse during the test events were very similar and this was perhaps most relevant to the test itself, because findings between studies have differed according to the nature of the task item input. Atypical from the early version of a semi-direct test that formed the basis of Shohamy's (1994) study, a combination of questions and task prompts are used to form input in the newer *Aptis General* CB-OPI. This results in a relatively more varied speaking test discourse in both direct and semi-direct delivery formats.

Prosodic feature differences were not immediately apparent when analyzing the transcribed and fully-coded test performances. However, on re-listening to the complete audio-recorded tests to gain an overall impression, it was difficult not to agree with previous research findings (Kiddle and Kormos,

Table 5. Words per AS-unit

Participant	*Elena*	*Chloe*	*Emily*	*Katrina*
CB-OPI	10.46	11.22	10.69	10.88
OPI	11.02	10.08	10.55	10.13

Table 6. Clauses per AS-unit

Participant	*Elena*	*Chloe*	*Emily*	*Katrina*
CB-OPI	1.64	1.64	1.52	1.51
OPI	1.54	1.55	1.48	1.49

Table 7. Subordinate clauses per AS-unit

Participant	*Elena*	*Chloe*	*Emily*	*Katrina*
CB-OPI	0.47	0.57	0.4	0.3
OPI	0.47	0.43	0.36	0.2

2011; O'Loughlin, 2001; Shohamy, 1994) that monologic-tasked semi-direct tests encourage marginally less variation in intonation and voice range and sound more monotonous.

A more concrete difference was that in the OPIs paralinguistic and prosodic features were often responsible for contextualization by way of test takers attempting to build a relationship with the interlocutor. For example, and exemplifying the non-verbalized contextualization frequently found in the OPIs, Elena reported that she glanced at the interlocutor, who was checking the timer, when she suspected her response was too short in part three. From this non-verbal exchange, she interpreted the need to continue her turn. Furthermore, a verbalized example found more frequently was Elena's use of *you know* when attempting to seek interlocutor agreement. It was unclear from the spoken data from the OPI whether this was expressed consciously or unconsciously and if it was rhetorical in nature or if some means of non-verbal response was desired.

The use and pronunciation of discourse markers for contextualization was prevalent throughout the OPI performances and were normally marked by rising intonation. A possible explanation for the test takers interpersonal behavior was revealed in the post-test interviews, when Katrina explained that it "felt like she was actually talking to someone", and Elena said that "it really felt like an interaction between two people". This insinuates that the mere presence of an unresponsive human interlocutor can affect the tenor and register of test taker output and that contextualization and interactiveness may well have been the most sensitive measure of difference in this study, although this degree of interactiveness had a relatively minor effect on the quantity or lexical density of the elicited spoken output.

Along with the findings of previous studies (Luoma, 1997; Shohamy, 1994; Zhou, 2008), overall output word counts were similar between modes. In general, the CB-OPI elicited minimally higher lexically dense output, supporting previous related research (Choi, 2014; O'Loughlin, 2001; Zhou, 2008), which partly controlled for interlocutor effect and used closely matched or identical monologic test tasks. These results imply that Shohamy's (1994) findings of significantly greater lexical density in the semi-direct test may not be robust and may have resulted from task and interlocutor effect.

Lexical density variance was found between individual test task items. Conforming to lexical density theory, less literateness was generally demonstrated during test takers' response to the everyday conversational and contextualized input; whereas more was found in output elicited from decontextualized situational items.

Phrase level syntactic complexity was relatively similar in test taker output from the direct and semi-direct test in this study, although slightly more conjunctions overall were found in the output from the OPI than the corresponding CB-OPI. This disagreed with Luoma's (1997) earlier finding that the overall difference in frequency of conjunction use between modes was much larger. A possible explanation for this greater difference may be that the test tasks used by Luoma were not identical in structure.

Luoma (1997) showed that there were almost twice as many coordinating conjunctions during the performances on the tape-based test, but a ratio of only 4:3 respectively in test taker output from the face-to-face test. This finding was also not replicated in this present study, because although performances in both delivery modes contained a higher frequency of coordinating conjunction use, the ratios between coordination and subordination conjunctions were relatively stable between modes. However, the supposition of minimally more complex grammatical structure being representative of test takers' output in CB-OPIs was confirmed, when examining the participants' performances at AS-unit and clausal level.

Overall, more words per AS-unit were used in the CB-OPI, and differences were also found in the number of clauses and subordinating clauses per AS-unit, with the CB-OPI output containing minimally higher syntactic complexity means. These findings corroborated those of Choi (2014) and Zhou (2008), although any difference in syntactic complexity between modes was unlikely to be significant should larger test taker output data samples have been analyzed. Nonetheless, Brooks and Swain (2014) have shown a significant decrease in syntactic complexity in output from the speaking section of the CB *TOEFL iBT™* to conversation in university contexts. Syntactic complexity is therefore likely to increase as spoken discourse becomes of a less interactive and formal nature.

Nevertheless, the importance of the syntactic complexity results for this present study should not be underestimated, because the performance samples elicited in the CB-OPI were "more likely to contain longer and more complex sentences" (Choi, 2014, p.563). Responsibility for this can only be reasonably assigned to mode effect, inside which interlocutor effect and the resulting increased test discourse interactiveness are intricately and unavoidably interwoven.

Summary

Test taker output register equivalence is perhaps unachievable in identical semi- direct and direct versions of speaking tests, as there may be the tendency for CB-OPIs to elicit test taker output leaning toward the minimally more formal, written and literate. This register variance is primarily attributable to interlocutor effect, a facet of mode effect, which leads to a higher degree of interactiveness in direct test events.

However, the tendency for semi-direct tests to elicit minimally higher lexical density and syntactic complexity in spoken output should be seen as advantageous for both test taker and delivery mode. Lexical and grammatical range and complexity are frequently found in band descriptors of criterion-referenced speaking tests, and in encouraging the use of more lexically dense and syntactically complex output, semi-direct tests more accurately reflect true ability.

Case Study Limitations

Several limitations should be remembered when interpreting the results of this case study. Firstly, the study was necessarily sample dependent, which prevent the generalizability of findings because the participants were from a narrowly defined population that is unlikely to be fully representative of a broader second language English user population. Secondly, the use of identical task type and content could have encouraged recency effect in the participants' performances during the second administration of the test. And the possibility of increasing familiarity with the interlocutor was also present, as the researcher acted as both interviewer and interlocutor throughout the sampling and data collection phases of the study. It is also feasible that if a female had acted as the interlocutor, performance results may have differed (O'Sullivan, 2000).

FUTURE RESEARCH DIRECTIONS

It is clear from the four selected test facets synopsized in the first part of this chapter that evidence through progressive studies has provided a foundation on which to continue to develop and implement semi-direct speaking tests. The use of CM video-conferencing in second language speaking assessment is currently an under researched delivery mode and has been less widely used than CB testing. Further research on the CM video-conferencing test delivery mode's practicality could focus on test takers' untrue perception that sound quality affected their performance when, in fact, the connection remained stable

(Nakatsuhara et al., 2017a). Similarly, further investigations into the online stability of CB tests input and written and/or visual prompts are essential if inclusiveness, via equal opportunity and fairness, for test takers is a primary aim of semi-direct speaking test delivery.

Much research has been conducted on test taker affective variables toward direct and semi-direct speaking tests. Reduced nervousness during completion of a semi-direct speaking test has been experienced by many, due to a human interlocutor not being present. This is an area of investigation that could support the face validity of CB speaking tests with further generalizable research. Additional studies are also needed to examine if test takers feel that CB speaking tests accurately measure the constructs they purport to.

CB-OPI test-retest reliability studies have been generally positive, although additional themed research as new tests are developed would further support findings to date. In terms of rater reliability more research is needed to explore the cognitive processes employed when completing the marking of audio and audio-visual speaking tests, including the rater effects of leniency or severity and a tendency to mark centrally within rating scales producing a restricted range of scores. In addition, studies addressing how the gender of interlocutors affects test taker performance and the test event more generally would be beneficial.

The concurrent validity of test scores between delivery modes has been found to be highly accordant when accounting for adjacent agreement, yet when this is excluded, exact agreement can fall below acceptable tolerances. Although adjacent agreement of scores may be acceptable for low stakes tests, it is less so for those of high stakes denomination. It is thus important for these tests to regularly commit to improving absolute agreement through ongoing research.

The exampled case study in the latter part of this chapter suggests that future research could include a larger generalizable comparative replication study or an investigation of interlocutor effect's relationship with output register, by administering OPIs to test takers with unfamiliar and moderately familiar interlocutors and examine the contextualization and interactiveness in the spoken output retrieved. An awareness of how familiarity in the interlocutor–test taker relationship can affect output in OPIs could influence speaking test delivery practices.

CONCLUSION

The purpose of this chapter was to examine the equivalence of semi-direct CB and CM speaking tests and their more traditional face-to-face direct counterparts through four essential test facets, indicative of their interchangeability, and highlight the comparability of test taker output elicited through direct and semi-direct input delivery modes.

The practicality advantages of CB and CM speaking tests are marked for test takers, test score users and large-scale test developers, yet for smaller would be institutional level developers, costs can be prohibitive. Through a number of studies investigating the face validity of direct and semi-direct speaking test delivery modes, it has been found that test takers' affective behavior toward direct OPIs often acknowledges that a perceived, but untrue, fundamental change takes place in that they are engaged in a *real-life* conversation during the face-to-face test. It is therefore likely that direct speaking tests' current higher face validity is a primary justification for their continued use.

Numerous benefits are apparent for the development and use of CB-OPIs with regard to the reliability of input achievable and test scores. The absence of a human interlocutor ensures that task input is stable within and between test events and thus the factor of deviation in the resulting spoken discourse is a non-entity. Perhaps the most significant challenge for CB and CM delivery modes is the effective rating of test takers' audio-visual and audio only output, given paralinguistic features indicative of spoken discourse are absent.

To date, concurrent validity has been one of the most highly researched areas of semi-direct and direct speaking test interchangeability and results have consistently shown that test scores are often highly comparable. This apparent degree of equivalence is a primary contributor to the ongoing development and continued use of CB speaking tests, albeit the issue of absolute versus adjacent currently remains problematic and requires further clarification.

The results from the exemplified case study showed that spoken output throughout test takers' performances was highly comparable between delivery modes. Evidence revealed that differences in the elicited spoken discourse from the test performances is a result of the two different contexts in which the language is elicited. This discourse differentiation manifested itself through the participants' increased output interactiveness via contextualization of the test event in the direct OPI that led to a slight shift in output register akin to the spoken and less literate.

Today, computer-based speaking tests appear to be a feasible alternative to traditional face-to-face oral proficiency interviews. Evidence testifying to this semi-direct delivery mode's reliability and concurrent validity with OPIs, along with the relatively high degree of similarity in test taker elicited discourse provides a stable base from which to encourage the development and use of semi-direct speaking tests. Just as the higher degree of practicality achievable in semi-direct speaking tests cannot be a singular justification for their continued development and implementation, a somewhat higher degree of face validity for direct OPIs should perhaps not be the primary rationale for their ongoing use.

REFERENCES

Abadin, H., Fried, D., Good, G., & Surface, E. (2012). *Reliability study of the ACTFL OPI in Chinese, Portuguese, Russian, Spanish, German, and English for the ACE review*. Raleigh, NC: SWA Consulting.

Alotumi, M. (2018). The effect of CALL-based instruction on students' score attainment on the TOEFL iBT in a Yemeni context. *International Journal of Computer-Assisted Language Learning and Teaching*, *8*(1), 50–64. doi:10.4018/IJCALLT.2018010104

Amengual-Pizarro, M., & Garcia-Laborda, J. (2017). Analysing test-takers' views on a computer-based speaking test. *Profile: Issues in Teachers' Professional Development*, *19*(1), 23–38.

Atkinson, J. M., & Heritage, J. (Eds.). (1984). *Structures of social action: Studies in conversational analysis*. Cambridge, UK: Cambridge University Press.

Beltran, J. (2016). The effects of visual input on scoring a speaking achievement test. *Working papers in TESOL & Applied Linguistics, 16*(2), 1-23. doi:10.7916/D8543VDT

Berry, V., Nakatsuhara, F., Inoue, C., & Galaczi, E. (2018). *Exploring the use of video-conferencing technology to deliver the IELTS speaking test: Phase 3 technical trial*. Retrieved from https://www.ielts.org/-/media/research-reports/ielts-research-partner-paper-4.ashx

British Council. (2018). *What is Aptis*. Retrieved from https://www.britishcouncil.my/exam/aptis/what

British Council. (2016). *Aptis general speaking test: Practice version.* Retrieved from https://www.britishcouncil.org/aptis-practice-tests/AptisSpeakingPractice/

Brooks, L., & Swain, M. (2014). Contextualizing performances: Comparing performances during TOEFL iBT™ and real-life academic speaking activities. *Language Assessment Quarterly, 11*(4), 353–373. doi:10.1080/15434303.2014.947532

Cambridge English Language Assessment. (2018). *Test your English - adult learners.* Retrieved from http://www.cambridgeenglish.org/in/test-your-english/adult-learners/

Choi, I. (2014). The comparability of direct and semi-direct oral proficiency interviews in a foreign language context: A case study with advanced Korean learners of English. *Language Research, 50*(2), 545-568. doi:10371/93290/1/12

Clark, J. L. D. (1979). Direct versus semi-direct tests of speaking proficiency. In E. J. Briere & F. B. Hinofotis (Eds.), *Concepts in language testing: Some recent studies* (pp. 35–49). Washington, DC: TESOL.

Clark, J. L. D., & Swinton, S. S. (1980). The test of spoken English as a measure of communicative ability in English-medium instructional settings. *TOEFL Research Report, 7*, 1–68. doi:10.1002/j.2333-8504.1980.tb01230.x

Dooey, P. (2008). Language testing and technology: Problems of transition to a new era. *ReCALL, 20*(1), 21–34. doi:10.1017/S0958344008000311

Dunlea, J., Spiby, R., Nguyen, Q., Nguyen, H., Nguyen, Y., Nguyen, T., . . . Bui, S. (2018). *Aptis-VSTEP comparability study: Investigating the usage of two EFL tests in the context of higher education in Vietnam* (VS/2018/001). Retrieved from https://www.britishcouncil.org/sites/default/files/aptis-vstep_study.pdf

Fairbairn, J., & Dunlea, J. (2017). *Speaking and writing rating scales revision technical report* (TR/2017/001). Retrieved from https://www.britishcouncil.org/exam/aptis/research/publications/scale-revision

Foster, P., Tonkyn, A., & Wigglesworth, G. (2000). Measuring spoken language: A unit for all reasons. *Applied Linguistics, 21*(3), 354–375. doi:10.1093/applin/21.3.354

Fulcher, G. (2014). *Testing second language speaking.* Oxon, UK: Routledge. doi:10.4324/9781315837376

Halliday, M. A. K. (1989). *Spoken and written language* (2nd ed.). Oxford, UK: Oxford University Press.

Kenyon, D. M., & Malabonga, V. (2001). Comparing examinee attitudes toward computer-assisted and other oral proficiency assessments. *Language Learning & Technology, 5*(2), 60.

Kiddle, T., & Kormos, J. (2011). The effect of mode of response on a semi-direct test of oral proficiency. *Language Assessment Quarterly, 8*(4), 342–360. doi:10.1080/15434303.2011.613503

Kim, J., & Craig, D. A. (2012). Validation of a video-conferenced speaking test. *Computer Assisted Language Learning, 25*(3), 257–275. doi:10.1080/09588221.2011.649482

Laborda, J. G. (2010). Contextual clues in semi-direct interviews for computer-assisted language testing. *Procedia - Social and Behavioral Sciences 2.* 3591-3595. doi:10.1016/j.sbspro.2010.03.557

Lazaraton, A. (1996). Interlocutor support in oral proficiency interviews: The case of CASE. *Language Testing*, *13*(2), 151–172. doi:10.1177/026553229601300202

Lazaraton, A. (2002). *A qualitative approach to the validation of oral language tests. Studies in Language Testing, 14*. Cambridge, UK: Cambridge University Press.

Loranc-Paszylk, B. (2015). Videoconferencing as a tool for developing speaking skills. In M. Pawlak, & E. Waniek-Klimczak (Eds.), *Issues in teaching, learning, and testing speaking in a second language* (pp. 189–203). London, UK: Springer. doi:10.1007/978-3-642-38339-7_12

Luoma, S. (1997). *Comparability of a tape-mediated and face-to-face test of speaking: A triangulation study* (Licentiate thesis). Retrieved from http://urn.fi/URN:NBN:fi:jyu-1997698892

Mackay, A., & Gass, S. M. (2000). *Stimulated recall methodology in second language Research*. Mahwah, NJ: Lawrence Erlbaum Associates.

Mousavi, S. A. (2009). Multimedia as a test method facet in oral proficiency tests. *International Journal of Pedagogies & Learning*, *5*(1), 37–48. doi:10.5172/ijpl.5.1.37

Nakatsuhara, F., Inoue, C., Berry, V., & Galaczi, E. (2017a). Exploring the use of video-conferencing technology in the assessment of spoken language: A mixed-methods study. *Language Assessment Quarterly*, *14*(1), 1–18. doi:10.1080/15434303.2016.1263637

Nakatsuhara, F., Inoue, C., & Taylor, L. (2017b). *An investigation into double-marking methods: comparing live, audio and video rating of performance on the IELTS speaking test*. Retrieved from https://www.ielts.org/teaching-and-research/research-reports/ielts_online_rr_2017-1

Ockey, G., Koyama, D., Setoguchi, E., & Sun, A. (2015). The extent to which TOEFL iBT speaking scores are associated with performance on oral language tasks and oral ability components for Japanese university students. *Language Testing*, *32*(1), 39–62. doi:10.1177/0265532214538014

O'Loughlin. (2001). *The equivalence of direct and semi-direct speaking tests. Studies in Language Testing, 13*. Cambridge, UK: Cambridge University Press.

O'Sullivan, B. (2000). Exploring gender and oral proficiency interview performance. *System*, *28*(3), 373–386. doi:10.1016/S0346-251X(00)00018-X

O'Sullivan, B., & Dunlea, J. (2015). *Aptis general technical manual: Version 1* (TR/2015/005). Retrieved from https://www.britishcouncil.org/aptis-general-technical-manual-version-10

Qian, D. (2009). Comparing direct and semi-direct modes for speaking assessment: Affective effects on test takers. *Language Assessment Quarterly*, *6*(2), 113–125. doi:10.1080/15434300902800059

Quaid, E. D. (2018). Output register parallelism in an identical direct and semi-direct speaking test: A case study. *International Journal of Computer-Assisted Language Learning and Teaching*, *8*(2), 75–91. doi:10.4018/IJCALLT.2018040105

Reemann, E., Alas, E., & Liiv, S. (2013). Interviewer behaviour during oral proficiency interviews: A gender perspective. *Eesti Rakenduslingvistika Uhingu Aastaraamat*, (9), 209-226. doi:10.5128/ERYa9.14

Reeves, B., & Nass, C. (1996). *The media equation: How people treat computers, television, and new media like real people and places*. Cambridge, UK: Cambridge University Press.

Rosenfeld, E., Bernstein, J., & Balogh, J. (2005). Validation of an automatic measurement of Spanish speaking proficiency. *The Journal of the Acoustical Society of America, 117*(4), 2428–2428. doi:10.1121/1.4786630

Schmidgall, J. E. (2017). *The consistency of TOEIC speaking scores across ratings and tasks* (Research Report No. RR-17-46). Princeton, NJ: Educational Testing Service. doi:10.1002/ets2.12178

Seedhouse, P., & Morales, S. (2017). *Candidates questioning examiners in the IELTS speaking test: An intervention study*. Retrieved from https://www.ielts.org/-/media/research-reports/ielts_online_rr_2017-5.ashx

Shohamy, E. (1994). The validity of direct versus semi-direct oral tests. *Language Testing, 11*(2), 99–123. doi:10.1177/026553229401100202

Shohamy, E., Donitsa-Schmidt, S., & Waizer, R. (1993). *The effect of the elicitation mode on the language samples obtained in oral tests*. Paper presented at the 15th Language Testing Research Colloquium, Cambridge, UK.

Stansfield, C. W. (1991). A comparative analysis of simulated and direct oral interviews. Anivan, S. (Ed.), Current developments in language testing (pp. 199–209). Singapore: SEAMEO RELC.

Stansfield, C. W., & Kenyon, D. (1992a). The development and validation of a simulated oral proficiency interview. *Modern Language Journal, 72*(2), 129–141. doi:10.1111/j.1540-4781.1992.tb01093.x

Stansfield, C. W., & Kenyon, D. (1992b). Research on the comparability of the oral proficiency interview and the simulated oral proficiency interview. *System, 20*(3), 347–364. doi:10.1016/0346-251X(92)90045-5

Stricker, L. J., & Attali, Y. (2010). *Test takers' attitudes about the TOEFL iBT™*. ETS TOEFL iBT Report No. iBT-13. Retrieved from https://onlinelibrary.wiley.com/doi/pdf/10.1002/j.2333-8504.2010.tb02209.x

Surface, E. A., Poncheri, R. M., & Bhavsar, K. S. (2008). *Two studies investigating the reliability and validity of the English ACTFL OPIc with Korean test takers*. Retrieved from https://www.languagetesting.com/research

Surface, E. A., Harman, R. P., Watson, A. M., & Thompson, L. F. (2009). *Are human and computer-administered interviews comparable?* Paper presented at the 24th annual meeting of the Society for Industrial and Organizational Psychology, New Orleans, LA.

Thompson, G. L., Cox, T. L., & Knapp, N. (2016). Comparing the OPI and OPIc: The effect of test method on oral proficiency scores and student preference. *Foreign Language Annals, 49*(1), 75–92. doi:10.1111/flan.12178

Weir, C. J. (2005). *Language testing and validation: An evidenced-based approach*. London, UK: Palgrave Macmillan. doi:10.1057/9780230514577

Yonezaki, M. (2016). A comparative analysis of semi-direct speaking testing and direct speaking testing for Japanese EFL learners. *International Journal of Curriculum Development and Practice*, *18*(1), 27–38. doi:10.18993/jcrdaen.18.1_27

Lee, Y.-J. (2007). The multimedia assisted test of English speaking: The SOPI Approach. *Language Assessment Quarterly*, *4*(4), 352–366. doi:10.1080/15434300701533661

Zhan, Y., & Wan, Z. H. (2016). Test takers' beliefs and experiences of a high-stakes computer-based English listening and speaking test. *RELC Journal*, *47*(3), 363–376. doi:10.1177/0033688216631174

Zheng, Y., & Zhang, Y. (2017). *Aptis in China: Exploring test-taker perceptions of its test validity and practicality* (AR-G/2017/6). Retrieved from https://www.britishcouncil.org/sites/default/files/ying_layout.pdf

Zhou, Y. J. (2008). A comparison of speech samples of monologic tasks in speaking tests between computer-delivered and face-to-face modes. *Japan Language Testing Association Journal*, *11*, 189–208. doi:10.20622/jltaj.11.0_189

Zhou, Y. J. (2015). Computer-delivered or face-to-face: Effects of delivery mode on the testing of second language speaking. *Language Testing in Asia*, *5*(2), 1–16. doi:10.118640468-014-0012-y

ADDITIONAL READING

Chapelle, C. A., & Douglas, D. (2006). *Assessing language through computer technology*. Cambridge, UK: Cambridge University Press. doi:10.1017/CBO9780511733116

Cheung, Y.-R. (2017). Validation of technology-assisted language tests. In C, A. Chapelle, & S. Sauro (Eds.), The handbook of technology and second language teaching and learning (pp. 332-347). Hoboken, NJ: Wiley Blackwell. doi:10.1002/9781118914069.ch22

Choi, I. (2014). The comparability of direct and semi-direct oral proficiency interviews in a foreign language context: A case study with advanced Korean learners of English. *Language Research*, 50(2), 545-568. doi: 10371/93290/1/12

Guoxing, Yu., & Zhang, J. (2017). Computer-Based English Language Testing in China: Present and Future. *Language Assessment Quarterly*, *14*(2), 177–188. doi:10.1080/15434303.2017.1303704

O'Loughlin, K. (2001). *The equivalence of direct and semi-direct speaking tests. Studies in Language Testing, 13*. Cambridge, UK: Cambridge University Press.

Qian, D. (2009). Comparing direct and semi-direct modes for speaking assessment: Affective effects on test takers. *Language Assessment Quarterly*, *6*(2), 113–125. doi:10.1080/15434300902800059

Schmidgall, J. E., & Powers, D. E. (2017). Technology and high-stakes language testing. In C, A. Chapelle, & S. Sauro (Eds.), The handbook of technology and second language teaching and learning (pp. 317-331). Hoboken, NJ: Wiley Blackwell. doi:10.1002/9781118914069.ch21

Valencia Robles, J. (2017). Anxiety in language testing: The APTIS case. *Profile: Issues in Teachers'. Professional Development, 19*(Suppl. 1), 39–50. doi:10.15446/profile.v19n_sup1.68575

Zhou, Y. J. (2015). Computer-delivered or face-to-face: Effects of delivery mode on the testing of second language speaking. *Language Testing in Asia, 5*(2), 1–16. doi:10.118640468-014-0012-y

KEY TERMS AND DEFINITIONS

Adjacent Agreement: A rating within one sub-level such as advanced-low and advanced- mid.

Concurrent Validity: The degree of test taker score equivalence between two tests, with one test acting as the criterion behavior.

Construct Irrelevant Variance: The introduction of extraneous, uncontrolled variables not reflected in the constructs tested that affect assessment outcomes.

Face Validity: The degree to which a test appears to measure the identified constructs (knowledge and/or abilities) it purports to measure based on the subjective judgment of test stakeholders.

Lexical Density: A quantitative measure of the relationship between lexical and grammatical items in spoken and written discourse.

Output: In the context of this chapter, output refers to test takers' spoken language elicited from a speaking test.

Prosodic Features: Suprasegmental units and forms that occur when sounds are placed together in connected speech. For example, intonation, pitch, stress and rhythm.

Simulated Oral Proficiency Interview (SOPI): First generation semi-direct speaking test that often used tape-mediated delivery in lieu of computers.

Target Language Use (TLU) Domain: The context or situation(s) where the test taker will be using the language on completion of the test.

Chapter 11
What Constitutes an Effective Instructional Video?
Perspectives From Chinese EFL Learners

Yan Ding
https://orcid.org/0000-0002-4579-8250
Beijing Jiaotong University, China

ABSTRACT

Online English courses have been developing rapidly in the past few years. As instructional videos play a central role in such courses, what constitutes an effective instruction video becomes a critical question for online English course developers. This chapter offers perspectives of EFL learners on this issue via content analysis of their feedback on existing instructional videos used in online English courses. The data consisted of 51 learners' comments on three micro-courses and 3,510 learner reviews on 41 English MOOCs. Analysis of the data revealed the most favorable features of an instructional video, the means to actualize these features, and learners' perceptions of different aspects of the physical design of an instructional video. The findings provided video producers with suggestions on the design and production of instructional videos used in online English courses.

INTRODUCTION

English micro-courses and MOOCs are gaining in popularity rapidly during the past few years. [1] Central to these online English courses are the instructional videos produced by course instructors. [2] First, instructional videos constitute an essential component of these courses which are organized either as a single instructional video or a sequence of instructional videos interspersed with other resources and learning activities (Educourse, 2012; Guo, Kim, & Rubin, 2014). Second, they serve as a predominant way of transmitting information and instructions to students (Khalil, Brunner, & Ebner, 2015). Third, online learners often paid most or even all of their attention to instructional videos (Breslow et al., 2013; Kizilcec, Piech, & Schneider, 2013). Finally, these instructional videos are also a source of authentic language input and an opportunity for learners to be engaged in language and culture (Sokolik, 2014).

DOI: 10.4018/978-1-7998-1282-1.ch011

Due to the critical role of instructional videos, it is very important for developers of online English courses to design videos that cater for the needs and interests of EFL learners. However, direct feedback of EFL learners on these instructional videos has been rarely considered. To address the gap, the present study provided an explorative investigation of the perspectives of EFL learners on instructional videos. The findings are expected to provide video producers with suggestions on the design and production of instructional videos used in online English courses.

LITERATURE REVIEW

A number of studies have examined the design and production of instructional videos used in online courses on subjects other than English. They presented a range of findings and suggestions concerning the physical design, content design, and structure of an instruction video.

Studies that investigated the physical design of a video mainly dealt with the presentation style, speaking rate, caption, length, navigation support and visual transition of a video.[3] With respect to presentation style, the results indicated that talking-head style videos were slightly more popular and resulted in better learning performance than drawing-board style videos (Ilioudi, Giannakos, & Chorianopoulos, 2013); drawing-board style videos and PowerPoint-slide style videos enjoyed similar popularity (Cross, Bayyapunedi, Cutrell, Agarwal, & Thies, 2013); lecturing videos interspersing PowerPoint slides with an instructor's talking head were more engaging than slides alone (Guo et al., 2014); and drawing-board style tutorial videos were more engaging than PowerPoint-slide ones (Guo et al., 2014).[4] As for speaking rate, caption and length, it was shown that videos where instructors spoke fairly fast with high enthusiasm were more engaging (Guo et al., 2014); videos with captions resulted in better learning performance than those without captions (Wang, Hao, & Lu, 2014); and shorter videos, ideally less than six minutes, were much more engaging (Guo et al., 2014). Regarding navigation support and visual transition, it was suggested that navigation support all through the content should be provided (Chorianopoulos & Giannakos, 2013; Kim et al., 2014), while abrupt visual transitions should be avoided (Kim et al., 2014).

Several studies presented findings that were useful for designing the content of a video. Coccoli, Iacono, and Vercelli (2015) and Zhu, Pei, and Shang (2017) revealed that narrative-style videos with gamification design were more engaging than lecture-style videos. Swarts (2012) discovered that highly-rated tutorial videos spent more time doing and explaining steps than either doing or explaining alone and their instructional messages were easily identified, understood and applied.

A few studies offered suggestions concerning the structure of a video. Zheng, Wang, Wang, and Bai (2012) suggested that a MOOC video should typically include an opening, a question that captures the essence of the video, explanation of the question, revision, in-video quizzes and answers, announcement of the main content of the next video, and an ending. Kovacs (2016) concluded that in-video quizzes could be added to a video to improve learners' engagement with the video. Swarts (2012) advised presenting an outline of the lesson to be learned at the beginning of a video.

In addition to the studies mentioned above, there have been a few studies that investigated or touched upon instructional videos used in online language courses. They offered suggestions concerning the physical design, content design, and language use of the videos.

The physical features that were mentioned in these studies included presentation style, speaking rate, caption, and length. As for presentation style, Ma and He (2017) found out that highly-rated instructional videos for English micro-courses were able to integrate different presentation styles. Fontana and Leffa

(2018), by contrast, advocated a single presentation style—the one where a teacher is present in the video and interacts with the people on the other side. As to speaking rate, Li and Zhao (2015) suggested that instructors should set their speaking rate above a threshold (200 wpm for advanced learners and 150 wpm for intermediate learners), as speaking rate below the threshold could not facilitate listening comprehension nor provide helpful language input.[5] They also suggested that instructors should add more over-2-second speech pauses while retaining the threshold speaking rate, so that audience could understand the video better and have more time for visual aids. Regarding caption, Fontana and Leffa (2018) held that course instructors needed to offer subtitles in different languages. As for length, Carlos, Verónica, and Guerrero (2017), Fontana and Leffa (2018), and Teixeira and Mota (2014) suggested that instructional videos in online language courses should be short, ideally no more than ten minutes.

With respect to content design, Perifanou (2016) and Sokolik (2014) proposed that language MOOC producers should avoid lecture-style videos and adopt a story/situation-based model instead in order to immerse learners in a rich environment, an example of the model being the French language course "French in Action" where romantic comedy segments were interspersed among grammar and vocabulary lessons. Ma and He (2017) observed that effective instructional videos featured rich, interesting, complete, and well-organized content on attractive and practical topics, delivered using diverse teaching methods and complete and logical teaching procedure.

Finally, with regard to the use of language, Ma and He (2017) found that instructors in effective English-course videos all spoke native-like, fluent, and powerful English with standard pronunciation and intonation. Li and Zhao (2015) suggested that instructors should use elaborated language (mean length around 15 words per sentence) to provide meaningful input.

Though they offered useful findings and suggestions, previous studies do not suffice for guiding the design and production of instructional videos for online English courses. To begin with, suggestions concerning instructional videos on other subjects may not apply to instructional videos for language courses. As pointed out by Sokolik (2014), unlike those in other courses, instructional videos in language courses are not only a way of delivering lectures, but also a source of authentic language input and an opportunity for students to be engaged in the culture and language. This may bring about different requirements for instructional videos used in language courses, which could only be discovered by studies dealing specifically with instructional videos for language courses. Unfortunately, there have been only a few such studies. Further research is needed to provide a more comprehensive understanding of the topic.

More importantly, previous studies, including those on language courses and those on non-language courses, have generally neglected direct feedback from learners which are essential for the design and production of instructional videos that cater for learners' needs and interests. A portion of these studies based their conclusions on researchers' own experiences (Chorianopoulos & Giannakos, 2013; Coccoli et al., 2015; Zheng et al., 2012; Zhu et al., 2017), analysis of high-rated videos (Swarts, 2012), review of the literature (Carlos et al., 2017; Fontana & Leffa, 2018; Li & Zhao, 2015; Perifanou 2016; Sokolik, 2014; Teixeira & Mota, 2014), or analysis of experts' and teachers' feedback (Ma & He, 2017), where learners' opinions were not considered at all.

Another portion of the studies did take learners' response into consideration, but they mainly looked at implicit user data, namely, interaction logs (Guo et al., 2014; Kim et al., 2014; Kovacs, 2016) and learning performances (Ilioudi et al., 2013; Wang et al., 2014). Though they can indicate students' preferences, these behavioral data cannot reveal students' feelings and views. Cross et al. (2013) was the only study that examined direct feedback from learners, but it only examined the presentation style of the videos. In fact, all the studies that analyzed learners' implicit or explicit responses were only concerned with the physical features, i.e. presentation style, speaking rate, caption, and length of the videos. Learner data on other aspects of instructional videos have not been collected and analyzed.

To sum up, previous research has not been adequate for guiding the design and production of instructional videos for online English courses due to the neglect of direct feedback from EFL learners.

RESEARCH QUESTIONS

The present study was conducted to address the gap. It provided an explorative investigation of the perspectives of EFL learners on instructional videos used in online English courses so as to offer suggestions on the design and production of such instructional videos. The specific research questions it intended to answer include the following.

RQ1: What features of instructional videos are most praised and desired by EFL learners?
RQ2: What means can be used to actualize these favorable features of instructional videos?
RQ3: How do EFL learners respond to the physical design of an instructional video?

METHODOLOGY

The present study adopted the method of content analysis. The procedure of content analysis mainly includes collecting and preparing the data, coding the data, counting and weighting, and drawing conclusions (List, 2002). The details will be presented below.

Data Collection and Preparation

Two sets of data were collected. The first set was learners' feedback on three instructional videos used in online English micro-courses, which was elicited specially for the present study. The participants were 51 second-year, non-English-major undergraduates in a Chinese university. They were asked to watch three instructional videos successively in class, and then write down whatever comments they had on the videos either in Chinese or English. The participants were not asked any questions about specific features of the videos in order not to introduce preconceived categories to the data (Hsieh & Shannon, 2006).

The details of the three videos are shown in Table 1. All the videos were produced for the 2016 national contest of micro-courses for foreign language learning. They were chosen for their different physical features and experts' ratings—V1 and V2 won respectively the first prize and the second prize in the national final, whereas V3 won the second prize in the provincial contest but failed to advance to the final. Videos with different features were supposed to be able to elicit more responses than those with similar features.

As a few students only commented on one or two of the videos, a total number of 141 comments were collected from the 51 participants. 86 of them were written primarily in Chinese, and the remaining 55 were written primarily in English, with code-switching and language mix appearing frequently in comments of both languages. Taken together, the comments amounted to 16,601 words. Each comment was assigned a source code in the form of "SnumberVnumber", where "Snumber" indicates the participant

Table 1. Physical features of the instructional videos for online English micro-courses

Code	Title	Length	Speaking Rate	Presentation Style	Caption	Music
V1	Hello, metaphor	8'02''	114 wpm	Talking-head & PowerPoint-slide	Yes	No
V2	How to avoid plagiarism	6'57''	135 wpm	PowerPoint-slide	No	Yes
V3	British Gentleman & Chinese *Junzi*	9'55''	163 wpm	Drawing-board & animation	No	Yes

and "Vnumber" indicates the video. For example, a comment with the source code S11V2 indicates that it is a comment made by participant 11 on video 2.

The second set of data consisted of learner reviews on 41 English MOOCs offered in iCourse, the biggest MOOC provider in China. The 41 MOOCs included 24 MOOCs on English for General Purpose (EGP), 13 MOOCs on English for Specific Purposes (ESP) or English for Academic Purposes (EAP), and four on cultural basics of English-speaking countries. All of the MOOCs were organized around instructional videos, assessments, and assignments. The instructional videos in the MOOCs were diverse in length, speaking rate, presentation style, use of instructional language, accessibility of caption and background music, etc. By the time of data collection (i.e. September 24, 2018), these MOOCs had received 3,510 reviews. The learner reviews covered a variety of aspects of the courses, but only those concerned with instructional videos were analyzed in the present study. The learner reviews on MOOCs were not assigned a source code, as it was unclear who posted a review or which specific video a review referred to. The second set of data was much larger in size, but less specified and detailed than the first set.

Data Coding

Data coding was conducted with the aid of QDA Miner 5. It consisted of three rounds. The first round of data coding, which aimed to answer RQ1, focused on the strengths and weaknesses of each video mentioned by the learners. Keywords that learners uttered to describe the videos were identified and grouped into meaningful categories. The categories were then given a code label, each of which represented a feature of the videos. Note that analysis of weaknesses mentioned by the students could reveal favorable features as much as analysis of strengths, as weaknesses could be interpreted as absence of favorable features. For instance, when a student stated "the video was boring", it could be assumed that the student regarded being interesting as a desired feature of a video. For this reason, expressions like "the video was boring" were put in the same coding category with expressions like "the video was interesting".

The second round of data coding, which was intended to answer RQ2, focused on the parts of comments where students explained explicitly why they thought a video possessed or lacked a favorable feature. To code comments of this type, the keywords that explained the reason were noted down and categorized. The categories of keywords were then given a code label. Comments where the participants only noticed a feature of a video without noting its cause or consequence were not analyzed in this stage. For instance, comments like "the examples make the video easier to understand" and "it is too fast; I can't understand it" were included, but comments that simply stated "the examples are wonderful" or "the video is too fast" were excluded.

To answer RQ3, a third round of data coding was conducted, where the focus was shifted to the parts of comments that made an evaluation of the physical design of a video. In this stage, comments were first categorized according to the aspects of physical design they mentioned, such as presentation style, background music, etc. They were further divided into positive and negative ones to reveal learners' response to different physical features of an instructional video.

Counting, Weighting, and Drawing Conclusions

Subsequent to data coding, the frequencies and percentages of each code were generated automatically by QDA Miner 5. Conclusions were drawn on the basis of the codes identified as well as frequencies and relative importance (i.e. percentages) of the codes.

RESULTS

The Most Favorable Features of a Video

Table 2 lists 10 favorable features whose percentages were more than 1% in the first set of data (i.e. the micro-course data). It can be seen from Table 2 that the most favorable features (% Codes > 10%) were "easily understood", "interesting and attractive", and "clear and logical".

Table 3 lists 12 favorable features whose percentages were more than 1% in the second set of data (i.e. the MOOC data). As can be seen from Table 3, the most favorable (% Codes > 10%) in this set of data were "useful and practical", "rich in content", "interesting and attractive", "detailed", "easily understood", and "clear and logical".

A comparison between Table 2 and Table 3 shows that in the MOOC data, three more features—"useful and practical", "rich in content", "detailed"—manifested themselves as the most favorable features. The difference might be attributed to the following two facts. First, the MOOC learners were larger in size and more heterogeneous than the micro-course subjects. Second, whereas the micro-course videos were

Table 2. Favorable features of an instructional video (micro-courses)

Code	Count	%Codes
easily understood	103	29.5%
interesting and attractive	101	28.9%
clear and logical	54	15.5%
rich in content	23	6.6%
memorable	15	4.3%
convincing	13	3.7%
specialized	11	3.2%
interactive	9	2.6%
creative	8	2.3%
inspiring and thought-provoking	6	1.7%

Table 3. Favorable features of an instructional video (MOOCs)

Code	Count	% Codes
useful and practical	292	19.4%
rich in content	238	15.8%
interesting and attractive	221	14.7%
detailed	205	13.7%
easily understood	193	12.8%
clear and logical	184	12.3%
concise	42	2.8%
inspiring and thought-provoking	35	2.3%
concrete	30	2.0%
systematic	26	1.7%
creative	19	1.3%
specialized	17	1.1%

evaluated in a classroom experiment context, the MOOC videos were reviewed in real learning contexts that were much more complex. Considering that instructional videos for online English courses are mostly produced to be learnt by heterogeneous learners in a real learning context, it is reasonable to give the MOOC data more credibility in the first round of analysis and conclude that "useful and practical", "rich in content", "interesting and attractive", "detailed", "easily understood", and "clear and logical" are the most favorable features of an instructional video used in online English courses.

Means to Actualize the Most Favorable Features of a Video

Table 4 presents reasons the participants provided to explain why a micro-course video possessed a favorable feature, from which means to actualize "easily understood", "interesting and attractive", and "clear and logical" can be derived. Reasons that were mentioned only once were categorized into "others". "Count" indicates how many times an item in the "reason" column was said to be the reason why a video possessed a desired feature.

It can be seen from Table 4 that some of the means were frequently mentioned. Those that were mentioned at least five times include various visual aids (picture, color, text, and caption), animation, example/exemplification, rate, background music, inserted movie clip, dialogical design, and outline and summary. How these means help to actualize a favorable feature will be illustrated below by citing excerpts of participants' comments.

Visual aids: Pictures were said to be able to make a video easier to understand, as illustrated in (1), and more interesting and attractive, as illustrated in (2).[6]

(1) *The pictures are clear. For example, the picture that goes with the metaphor "snake of traffic" shows lines of vehicles that are just like snakes, which makes it very easy for people to understand the metaphor.(S9V1, translated)*

Table 4. Means to actualize the most favorable features of an instructional video (micro-courses)

Feature	Reason		Count	% Code
easily understood	visual aids	picture	13	13.1%
		text	11	11.1%
		caption	10	10.1%
	example/exemplification		30	30.3%
	rate		8	8.1%
	animation		6	6.1%
	outline		4	4.0%
	classification		3	3.0%
	definition		3	3.0%
	comparison and contrast		3	3.0%
	in-video quiz		2	2.0%
	quotation		2	2.0%
	language		2	2.0%
	others		2	2.0%
	Total		99	100%
interesting and attractive	visual aids	picture	13	14.9%
		color	5	5.7%
	animation		15	17.2%
	inserted movie clip		11	12.6%
	example/exemplification		11	12.6%
	background music		11	12.6%
	dialogic design		7	8.0%
	overall design		4	4.6%
	instructor		3	3.4%
	topic		2	2.3%
	others		4	4.6%
	Total		87	100%
clear and logical	outline		4	66.7%
	summary		2	33.3%
	Total		6	100%

(2) *The video uses pictures to draw people's attention. It makes people want to learn more.(S31V2, translated)*

Text and caption were only related to understanding. Caption was shown to be a much desired feature, as illustrated in (3).

(3) *It is a shame that the video does not have captions. Sometimes I cannot understand what the speaker says.(S14V3, translated)*

Text, however, received more negative comments. A few participants deemed it to be helpful, as illustrated in (4), but more participants complained about the inappropriate use of text, chiefly textual overload in V2, as illustrated in (5).

(4) *And there appear some words, the key points are also underlined to make it easy to understand. (S25V3)*
(5) *Besides, there are so many words on the PPT, so we cannot read it and think it twice in the short time.(S33V2)*

Color was able to make a video more attractive, as illustrated in (6).

(6) *The PowerPoint slides use brilliant and vibrant colors, which make them attractive.(S25V1)*

Animation: Animation in V3 was frequently mentioned as a means to make the video more attractive and interesting. It was also said to be able to make the video easier to understand. These positive effects of animation are illustrated in (7) and (8).

(7) *What impressed me is that the lecture used animated characters. The animated characters are very interesting. I think we should use animated characters to attract students' interest in class.(S51V3)*
(8) *And this video just makes almost everything into cartoon. So it is easier for us to understand the content of the video, this is good. (S24V3)*

Example/exemplification: It was the most frequently mentioned way to help the audience understand a video and also a frequently mentioned way to make a video more attractive and interesting. The positive effects of examples, especially those that the audience were familiar with, are illustrated in (9) and (10).

(9) *When she talked about the metaphor is implicit, she made an example of snow white. We are all familiar with snow white. Thus, it's very easy to understand.(S16V1)*
(10) *When the Harry Potter appears, students get interested in the lesson. It is a good way to attract students' attention by using their favorite things as example.(S11V2)*

Dull examples were not able to fulfill the function, though, as shown in (11).

(11) *Some examples are dull and unable to arouse students' enthusiasm for learning the topic.(S39V1, translated)*

Rate: Rate was said to be a factor that influenced understanding. Two participants praised the rate of V1 and V3, as illustrated in (12), while six participants complained about the rate of V2, as illustrated in (13).

(12) *In addition, the teacher is at a moderate speed and we can easily understand what she said.(S51V1)*

(13) *It is too fast; I can't understand it.(S17V2, translated)*

It should be noted that the term "rate" here does not mean the speaking rate of the instructor. Instead, it refers to the overall rate of a video, which is determined by the total amount of information—including that presented in the audio mode and that presented in the visual mode—and the length of the video. In the present study, the visual aids in V1 and V3 mainly repeated or reinforced audio information, whereas the visual aids in V2 encoded a large amount of new information. In other words, the overall rate of V2 was in fact even higher than that of V3. This explains why V2 was widely criticized for being too fast, though the speaking rate of V2 is not the highest.

Inserted movie clip: It could make a video more interesting and attractive. Participants thought highly of the beginning of V2 where the instructor used a clip taken from the TV sitcom "Friends" to introduce metaphor, as illustrated in (14).

(14) *The most impressive part is the movie part, the shoes or hat metaphor is very interesting.(S3V1)*

Background music: It could also give the videos greater appeal. Though one participant noted that background music of V2 was distracting, seven participants mentioned in ten comments that background music was helpful in keeping their attention to the videos, as illustrated in (15).

(15) *The background music is soft and comfortable. It helps us to listen to the teacher carefully. (S16V2)*

Dialogic design: The dialogic design of V3, where two animated characters talked about and demonstrated the similarities and differences between British Gentleman and Chinese *Junzi*, was thought to be a reason why V3 was attractive, as illustrated in (16).

(16) *We can learn a lot of things that we want to know from their conversation. This form is novel and able to arouse my interest. (S22V3, translated)*

Outline and summary: They could make the audience feel that a video was clearly structured, as illustrated in (17) and (18).[7]

(17) *The structure is very clear, with the outline in the beginning of video giving the audience a general idea of the main content. (S9V1, translated)*
(18) *There is also a summary at the end of the video, which allows us to get the train of thought of the video more clearly. (S1V3, translated)*

They were also said to be able to facilitate understanding and recalling, as shown in (19) and (20).

(19) *The teacher put the contents in advance to make students know what they will learn today, making them understand the contents easily.(S11V2)*
(20) *The final summary offered by the instructor can help students to review the main content of the lecture and remember the key points better. (S19V3, translated)*

Analysis of the MOOC data confirmed that role of the above-mentioned means in actualizing a favorable feature.[8] For example, quotation (21) shows that examples can make a video "easy to understand"; quotation (22) shows that summary can make a video "clear and logical"; and quotation (23) shows that dialogic design can make a video "interesting and attractive". [9]

(21) *The instruction is clear, and the analysis is thorough. Each point is followed by examples to make us understand the point better (translated).*
(22) *Every lesson is logically organized, and the best part is the mind map summarizing the lesson, which cannot be more thoughtful (translated).*
(23) *I like the section called "seven mouths and eight tongues", where the three instructors teach English by having a conversation. This method of teaching is very lively and impressive (translated).*

Analysis of the MOOC data also revealed means to actualize the other three most favorable features—"useful and practical", "rich in content" and "detailed", which are illustrated below via excerpts of learner reviews.

The videos of a course were said to be "useful and practical" when the contents could solve the problem of the learners or satisfy their needs, as illustrated in (24) and (25).[10]

(24) *I just started learning the course today, and I already felt that it was very useful to me. Before I learned the course, I really did not know that my method of reading the literature was problematic. I became aware of my problem after a few lessons. I hope that everyone can watch the videos carefully. They are really practical and useful.*
(25) *This is the first MOOC I have taken. I chose the MOOC as I wanted to learn some skills of translation. I have completed the course this week. It has indeed taught me a lot of skills, very practical.*

The "richness" of course videos lies in the range and diversity of topics included in the course, as shown in (26) and (27).

(26) *The contents of the course are quite comprehensive, including topics such as meeting, introduction, giving gifts, things to avoid in conversation, etc. I know more about these topics after learning the course, and I gain a knowledge of English for international communication from the course.*
(27) *I have been attracted by the course from the first lesson. The contents of the course are rich. It examines the topic from multiples angles such as geography, history, and culture.*

Finally, the feature of "detailed" can be achieved through all-round exposition of a topic, illustrated in (28), emphasis on the subtleties, illustrated in (29), or close analysis of the English language, illustrated in (30). It sometimes intertwines with richness, as shown in (28).

(28) *The contents of the course are rich and detailed. In order to help learners fully understand what English for academic communication is, the teacher explains its background, principles, and features in great detail.*
(29) *The lesson taught by Professor X is very detailed. Professor X pays attention to the subtleties, which demonstrates his high level of disciplinary knowledge.*

(30) *I have just started the first unit, and I think I can understand it. That is all because of the detailed and thorough explanation provided by the teacher. I particularly like the morphological analysis of the new words.*

Responses to the Physical Design of a Video

As shown in Table 5, the micro-course participants commented on a range of physical features of the course videos. As some of the features has been discussed in the previous section, this section will focus on what has not been discussed, namely, negative comments on visual aids, and comments on the instructor, PowerPoint-slide style, quality of sound and picture, and length of a video.

Visual aids: Negative comments on the use of picture, caption, and color were very few. The only negative comment on picture stated that too many pictures in V3 made the video less systematic. The only negative comment on caption stated that the caption of V1 may distract audience' attention from other content of the video. The few negative remarks on color stated that the color design in some parts of the videos was ugly. The use of text was deemed to be more problematic, however. In addition to the problem of textual overload mentioned in the previous section, participants were also critical of the inappropriate use of keywords, as shown in (31) and (32).

(31) Some slides are not good enough. For example, the keyword on one of the slides should be "your idea", but I didn't find it immediately on the slide. Then I found it at the bottom of the slide. The words are small and not bold. (S9V2, translated)

Table 5. Responses to the physical design of a video (micro-courses)

Physical design		Count			%Code
		Positive	Negative	Total	
visual aids	picture	24	1	25	13.6%
	text	4	17	21	11.4%
	color	17	4	21	11.4%
	caption	10	1	11	6.0%
instructor	appearance and manner	9	6	15	8.2%
	pronunciation and intonation	12	0	12	6.5%
rate		5	21	26	14.1%
animation		24	0	24	13.0%
background music		16	1	17	9.2%
the PowerPoint-slide style		5	0	5	2.7%
quality of sound and picture		1	4	5	2.7%
length		0	2	2	1.1%
Total		119	65	184	100%

(32)But this video has too few words on the screen. The important information is given only orally, and we will forget it soon. Thus, I suggest that more words should be shown on the screen. (S39V3, translated)

Instructor: The appearance and manner of the instructor in V1, who was the only instructor that showed herself in the video, was controversial, with nine participants thinking highly of her appearance, smile, clothes, and gestures while another six participants being critical of her body language and facial expression. The pronunciation and intonation of all the three instructors were paid complements.

The PowerPoint-slide style: Five participants showed their appreciation of the PowerPoint-slide style of V2 for its "cleanness" and practicality, as illustrated in (33) and (34).

(33) Across this video, there is no real people and just a human sound exists. And l think the voice make the video clean.(S25V2)

(34) Her micro course uses a popular style of web course where teacher doesn't show and the video is like a ppt. I prefer this kind of idea, because teacher doesn't need to show on the small scene and we can have a bigger place to get the ideas of the video.(S33V2)

Quality of sound and picture: One participant wrote that the pictures in V1 were of high quality, while another two participants stated in four comments that sounds of the videos were not clear enough.

Length: Two participants said that V1 (8'02'') and V3 (9'55'') were too long, and no one showed dissatisfaction with the length of V2 (6'57'').

MOOC learners' responses to the physical design of MOOC videos are presented in Table 6, from which it can be seen that the physical features that MOOC learners and micro-course participants paid attention to were almost the same. Their overall responses to the features were different in terms of counts, percentages, or the ratios of positive to negative comments, though. However, what matters here is not the counts and percentages of positive and negative comments that a feature received or the overall polarity of the comments, but the reasons why a feature received positive and negative comments. The details of the reasons will be presented below.

Instructor: The pronunciation and intonation of most MOOC instructors were praised as clear, accurate, or standard. However, a few course instructors and student actors (i.e. those who participated in role-plays recorded in course videos) were said to have an accent, as illustrated in (35).

(35) The teacher has a strange accent. She pronounced /ei/ as something like /a/ in words like "basic" and "patient".

The appearance and manner of the MOOC instructors also received predominantly positive reviews, with 109 of the 111 commenters stating that they were attracted by the instructors' good looks and/or pleasant voice, as illustrated in (36). Of the only two negative reviews, one said that a course instructor "always gets a long face as if somebody owed him money", and the other one showed dissatisfaction with another course instructor's "clumsy and old-fashioned" clothing.

(36) The instructor has a beautiful appearance and a sweet voice. At first, I just wanted to have a try, but now I am so fascinated that I cannot stop.

Table 6. Responses to the physical design of a video (MOOCs)

Physical design		Count			% Code
		Positive	Negative	Total	
instructor	pronunciation and intonation	180	20	200	33.3%
	appearance and manner	109	2	111	18.5%
visual aids	caption	69	2	71	11.8%
	text	0	1	1	0.2%
rate		59	31	90	15.0%
English-only instruction		50	10	60	10.0%
quality of sound and picture		30	6	36	6.0%
length		19	5	24	4.0%
background music		0	5	5	0.8%
animation		1	2	3	0.5%
Total		518	83	601	100%

Visual aids: Caption was the most frequently commented type of visual aid. Most MOOC commenters believed caption helped them to understand a course better, whereas lack of caption posed problems for understanding. However, two MOOC learners, commenting on two different courses, asked whether the course instructors could remove the Chinese caption to create an immersive English-learning environment. The other three types of visual aid, namely, color, picture, and text, received very little attention in the MOOC dataset. No MOOC learners commented on the use of color and picture, and only 1 of the 3,510 learner reviews mentioned the use of text, saying that the typeface used in the videos of a course was ugly. One possible reason for the lack of attention on these features (and some other features that will be mentioned below) might be that their effects on learning outcomes were so trivial that MOOC learners, who were primarily concerned with their achievements rather than evaluation of the course videos, did not notice them or did not bother to mention them in their reviews. Future research is needed to verify the speculation.

Rate: A total of 59 commenters showed satisfaction with the speaking rate of the course videos they watched, whereas 31 regarded the speaking rate as too fast or too slow. Note that learners' comments on the speaking rate of the same course videos might vary. For example, there were four learners commenting on the speaking rate of the videos of *College English Writing I*. Three of them deemed it appropriate, whereas the other one thought that it was too fast. The difference might be due to individual factors such as language proficiency or learning styles, which need to be verified by evidence from a separate study.

English-only instruction: The feature was mentioned only in the MOOC data, probably because some MOOC videos used English-only instruction, whereas others used a combination of English and Chinese, the fact of which made comparison between English-instruction and bilingual instruction possible and natural. A majority of the commenters preferred English-only instruction, considering it an opportunity for them to be immersed in an English environment. By contrast, ten commenters preferred bilingual instruction which was easier for them to follow.

Quality of sound and picture: Whereas 30 commenters said the videos they watched were slick productions and well made, six commenters complained that the sound in the videos they watched was not clear enough and the resolution was not high enough.

Length: A total of 19 MOOC learners listed short videos as a strength of a course, as short videos could retain learner attention and reduce boredom. However, five MOOC learners, commenting on four different courses, said that videos less than five minutes were too short to be substantial.

Background music: Five MOOC learners mentioned that the background music of videos of two MOOCs was too loud.

Animation: One commenter thought highly of the use of animation in videos of one MOOC. Two other commenters said that the animation in the videos of another MOOC was so much that it caused a headache.

DISCUSSION

Based on the results presented above, the present section offers the following suggestions concerning the overall features, structure, content design, presentation style, rate, language, caption, on-screen text, background music, and length of an instructional video used in online English courses.

Overall features: The most favorable features of an instructional video used in online English courses include "useful and practical", "rich in content", "interesting and attractive", "detailed", "easily understood", and "clear and logical". How to actualize these features in a video should be video producers' primary concern.

Structure: The present study supports the suggestions of Swarts (2012) and Zheng et al. (2012) that outline and summary should be added to a video, as the results showed that they could facilitate audience's understanding of the structure and ideas of a video. Kovacs' (2016) suggestion of adding in-video quizzes can be partly supported by the present study which revealed that the in-video quizzes of micro-course videos V1 and V2 might help the audience to understand the lesson better. The function of in-video quizzes was not prominent, though, judging from the fact that only two participants mentioned this. Nor were the in-video quizzes reported to help draw the participants' attention, which appears to be contrary to Kovacs' (2016) expectation that in-video quizzes would improve learners' engagement with a video. One possible reason for this contradiction is the difference between the in-video quizzes: the in-video quizzes in Kovacs' (2016) study were short, automatically-graded questions that appeared in the middle of a video, whereas those in the present study were more complicated tasks appearing at the end of a video.

Content design: Video producers should include abundant examples that are close to the life of the target audience, as they were said by many participants to be very helpful for making a video more easily understood and more attractive. In addition, video producers may insert movie clips and adopt a dialogic design to make a video more interesting and attractive. Considering that movie clips and dialogic design are story and situation based, these findings can be related to the conclusions of previous studies that story/situation-based style and narrative style in general were more engaging than lecturing-style (Coccoli et al. 2015; Sokolik, 2014; Zhu et al. 2017). Therefore, video producers may try different story/situation-based designs or intersperse a lecturing style video with story/situation-based style parts.

Presentation style: Animation was shown to be a popular presentation style, though the overuse of animation may be disturbing. In addition, in contrary to previous research which revealed or suggested that the PowerPoint-slide style was less popular than the talking-head style or the drawing-board style (Guo et al., 2014; Fontana & Leffa, 2018), the results of the present study suggest that the PowerPoint-slide style is not an inferior option. The data in the present study showed no sign of audience's dissatisfaction with this presentation style. Instead, five micro-course participants expressed explicitly their appreciation for the style.

Rate: The overall rate, rather than the speaking rate, of a video was found to be a major factor that influenced learners' understanding. Unfortunately, extant studies have only examined the speaking rate of a video (Guo et al., 2014; Li & Zhao, 2015), and to determine the best overall rate of a video is a very complicated question that may take a number of empirical studies to answer. At present, however, video producers may draw on extant research by: (1) taking Li and Zhao's (2015) advice concerning the speaking rate of a video for EFL learners, namely, retaining the threshold speaking rate (200 w/min for advanced learners and 150 w/min for intermediate learners) while adding more over-2-second speech pauses, and (2) making sure that visual aids only repeat or reinforce the information delivered in the audio mode, the practice of which not only complies with multimedia learning principles (Mayer & Moreno, 2003; Salmond & Smith, 2011), but also ensures that the overall rate will not be much higher than the speaking rate and will thus be acceptable.

Language: The pronunciation and intonation of the instructor attracted the attention of a fairly large portion of audience and was possibly a key criterion that they use to evaluate a video. Therefore, in line with the finding of Ma and He (2017), the present study suggests that the audio message in a video should be delivered in native-like English with standard pronunciation and intonation. In addition, as most learners preferred English-only instruction to bilingual instruction, video producers are advised to use English as the medium of instruction.

Caption: Caption was shown to be a desired feature in the present study, and was associated with better performance in previous research (Wang et al., 2014). However, considering the opposing views that captions may distract one's attention from other content of a video and that subtitles in one's native language may ruin an English-immersive environment, captions and subtitles in multiple languages are best offered as an option. Such setting is readily provided in most platforms for online courses.

On-screen text: The results of the present study revealed three main problems with respect to the use of on-screen text, i.e., textual overload, illustrated in excerpt (5); indiscriminate keywords, illustrated in (31); and lack of keywords, illustrated in (32). To avoid the problems, video producers, especially those who want to produce PowerPoint-slide style videos, are advised to adopt a PowerPoint design that was proved to be effective and popular, i.e. to put on a slide a few key terms or phrases as short as possible, coupled with high-quality supporting images (Mayer & Moreno, 2003; Mollerup, 2014; Pate et al. 2016; Reynolds, 2008; Salmond & Smith, 2011). Video producers are also advised to use large fonts (Blokzijl & Naeff, 2004).

Background music: Background music was commented on by a number of participants. Their remarks on the role of background music in attention-keeping are in line with findings of previous research on arousal which showed that music could augment arousal levels and in turn lead to more concentrated attention (Levasseur & Sawyer, 2006). With respect to the type of music to be used, the present study can only provide a general advice, namely, to use soft music, on the basis of a few participants' comments. More concrete suggestions could, however, be derived from research on the effects of background music on listeners' performance on cognitive tasks, which indicated that slow-tempo (80-110 bpm), soft (lower than 60dB), rhythmically simple, and repetitive instrumental music was optimally arousing and able to improve performance on cognitive tasks (de Groot, 2006; Felix, 1993; Hallam, Price, & Katsarou, 2002;

Kiger, 1989), whereas vocal pop music with lyrics, and fast-tempo (140-150bpm), loud (over 72 dB), rhythmically complex, non-repetitive instrumental music had negative effects on listeners' performance (Cassidy & MacDonald, 2007; de Groot & Smedinga, 2014; Furnham & Strbac, 2002; Thompson, Schellenberg, & Letnic, 2011). Nevertheless, further research is still needed to examine the use of background music in instructional videos, as this involves more complicated issues such as sound mixing.

Length: The fact that only two participants complained about the length of V1 (8'02'') and V3 (9'55'') and no one showed dissatisfaction with the length of V2 (6'57'') seems to suggest that, in contrast to the six-minute limit proposed by Guo et al. (2014), videos shorter than ten minutes are generally acceptable and those shorter than seven minutes are even more satisfactory. The suggestion is tentative, however, given that the videos analyzed in the present study were all prize winners and that factors such as the attractiveness of a video might influence learners' perception of the length of the video. For instance, a learner may find a six-minute boring video to be long, but an eight-minute attractive video to be perfect in length. In addition, the results also show that videos that are shorter than five minutes might be considered as over-short and criticized for lack of substance. Thus, the best range of the length of a video seems to be between five to seven minutes.

CONCLUSION

To sum up, the present study provided an explorative investigation of the perspectives of EFL learners on instructional videos used in online English courses. Through content analysis of students' comments on three micro-course videos and learner reviews on 41 MOOCs, it revealed the most favorable features of an instructional video used in online English courses, the means to actualize these features, and students' perceptions of different aspects of the physical design of an instructional video. Based on the results, it raised a number of suggestions concerning the overall features, structure, content design, presentation style, rate, language, caption, on-screen text, background music, and length of an instructional video used in online English courses. These suggestions are expected to help make a video more popular with EFL learners.

ACKNOWLEDGMENT

This research was supported by the Social Science Foundation of Beijing [grant number 16YJC018]. The author would like to thank Professor Xueqing Jiang at Beijing Jiaotong University and Associate Professor Huizhong Shen at the University of Sydney for their insight and expertise that greatly assisted the research.

REFERENCES

Blokzijl, W., & Naeff, R. (2004). The instructor as stagehand: Dutch student responses to PowerPoint. *Business Communication Quarterly*, *67*(1), 70–77. doi:10.1177/1080569903262046

Breslow, L., Pritchard, D. E., de Boer, J., Stump, G. S., Ho, A. D., & Seaton, D. T. (2013). Studying learning in the worldwide classroom: Research into edX's first MOOC. *Research and Practice in Assessment*, *8*(1), 13–25.

Carlos, A. M. F., Verónica, E. C. R., & Guerrero, J. S. (2017). BLMOOCs, a proposal for the design of Language MOOCs in a Blended context. *International Conference on Edemocracy & Egovernment* (pp.265-268). IEEE.

Cassidy, G., & MacDonald, R. (2007). The effect of background music and background noise on the task performance of introverts and extraverts. *Psychology of Music*, *35*(3), 517–537. doi:10.1177/0305735607076444

Chorianopoulos, K., & Giannakos, M. N. (2013). Usability design for video lectures. In *Proceedings of the 11th European Conference on Interactive TV and Video* (pp. 163-164). New York, NY: ACM. 10.1145/2465958.2465982

Coccoli, M., Iacono, S., & Vercelli, G. (2015). Applying gamification techniques to enhance the effectiveness of video-lessons. *Journal of E-Learning and Knowledge Society*, *11*(3), 73–84.

Cross, A., Bayyapunedi, M., Cutrell, E., Agarwal, A., & Thies, W. (2013). TypeRighting: combining the benefits of handwriting and typeface in online educational videos. In *Proceedings of the SIGCHI Conference on Human Factors in Computing Systems* (pp. 793-796). New York, NY: ACM. 10.1145/2470654.2470766

de Groot, A. M. B. (2006). Effects of stimulus characteristics and background music on foreign language vocabulary learning and forgetting. *Language Learning*, *56*(3), 463–506. doi:10.1111/j.1467-9922.2006.00374.x

Educause. (2012). 7 things you should know about microlectures. Retrieved from https://library.educause.edu/resources/2012/11/7-things-you-should-know-about-microlectures

Felix, U. (1993). The contribution of background music to the enhancement of learning in Suggestopedia: A critical review of the literature. *Journal of the Society for Accelerative Learning and Teaching*, *18*, 277–303.

Fontana, M. V. L., & Leffa, V. L. (2018). MOOCs for language teaching: A study on CALL from the connectivist perspective. *Alfa: Revista de Linguistica*, *62*(1), 73–86.

Furnham, A., & Strbac, L. (2002). Music is as distracting as noises: The differential distraction of background music and noise on the cognitive test performance of introverts and extraverts. *Ergonomics*, *45*(3), 203–217. doi:10.1080/00140130210121932 PMID:11964204

Guo, P. J., Kim, J., & Rubin, R. (2014). How video production affects student engagement: an empirical study of MOOC videos. In *Proceedings of the First ACM Conference on Learning @ Scale Conference* (pp. 41-50). New York, NY: ACM. 10.1145/2556325.2566239

Hallam, S., Price, J., & Katsarou, G. (2002). The effects of background music on primary school pupils' task performance'. *Educational Studies*, *28*(2), 112–122. doi:10.1080/03055690220124551

Hsieh, H. F., & Shannon, S. E. (2005). Three approaches to qualitative content analysis. *Qualitative Health Research*, *15*(9), 1277–1288. doi:10.1177/1049732305276687 PMID:16204405

Ilioudi, C., Giannakos, M. N., & Chorianopoulos, K. (2013). Investigating differences among the commonly used video lecture styles. In *Proceedings of the 2013 Workshop on Analytics on Video-based Learning* (pp. 21–26). Retrieved from http://ceur-ws.org/Vol-983/

Khalil, M., Brunner, H., & Ebner, M. (2015). Evaluation grid for xMOOCs. *International Journal of Emerging Technologies in Learning, 10*(4), 40–45. doi:10.3991/ijet.v10i4.4653

Kiger, D. M. (1989). Effects of music information load on a reading comprehension task. *Perceptual and Motor Skills, 69*(2), 531–534. doi:10.2466/pms.1989.69.2.531 PMID:2717361

Kim, J., Guo, P. J., Seaton, D. T., Mitros, P., Gajos, K. Z., & Miller, R. C. (2014). Understanding in-video dropouts and interaction peaks in online lecture videos. In *Proceedings of the First ACM Conference on Learning @ Scale Conference* (pp. 31-40). New York, NY: ACM. 10.1145/2556325.2566237

Kizilcec, R. F., Piech, C., & Schneider, E. (2013). Deconstructing disengagement: Analyzing learner subpopulations in massive open online courses. In *Proceedings of the Third International Conference on Learning Analytics and Knowledge* (pp. 170-179). New York, NY: ACM. 10.1145/2460296.2460330

Kovacs, G. (2016). Effects of in-video quizzes on MOOC lecture viewing. In *Proceedings of the Third ACM Conference on Learning* (pp. 31-40). New York, NY: ACM. 10.1145/2876034.2876041

Levasseur, D. G., & Sawyer, J. K. (2006). Pedagogy meets PowerPoint: A research review of the effects of computer-generated slides in the classroom. *Review of Communication, 6*(1-2), 101–123. doi:10.1080/15358590600763383

Li, H., & Zhao, D. M. (2015). Teacher talk and its effects in the micro-course of College English. *Technology Enhanced Foreign Language Education, 165*, 15–20.

List, D. (2002). *Know your audience: A practical guide to media research.* Retrieved from http://www.audiencedialogue.net/kya.html

Ma, W. L., & He, J. J. (2017). A study on characteristics of excellent micro-lectures of foreign languages. *Technology Enhanced Foreign Language Education, 174*, 22–26.

Mollerup, P. (2014). Slide presentations, seriously. *Visible Language, 48*(1), 4–21.

Perifanou, M. (2016). Designing strategies for an efficient language MOOC. In S. Papadima-Sophocleous, L. Bradley, & S. Thouësny (Eds.), CALL communities and culture – short papers from EUROCALL 2016 (pp. 380-385). Research-publishing.net. doi:10.14705/rpnet.2016.eurocall2016.592

Reynolds, G. (2008). *Presentation Zen: Simple ideas on presentation design and delivery.* Upper Saddle River, NJ: New Riders Press.

Salmond, R., & Smith, D. T. (2011). Cheating death-by-PowerPoint: Effective use of visual aids at professional conferences. *PS, Political Science & Politics, 44*(3), 589–596. doi:10.1017/S1049096511000813

Sokolik, M. (2014). What constitutes an effective language MOOC? In E. Martin-Monje, & E. Bárcena (Eds.), *Language MOOCs: Providing learning, transcending boundaries* (pp. 16–32). Berlin, Germany: Walter de Gruyter.

Swarts, J. (2012). New modes of help: Best practices for instructional video. *Technical Communication (Washington)*, *59*(3), 195–206.

Teixeira, A. M., & Mota, J. (2014). A proposal for the methodological design of collaborative language MOOCs. In E. Martin-Monje, & E. Bárcena (Eds.), *Language MOOCs: Providing learning, transcending boundaries* (pp. 33–47). Berlin, Germany: Walter de Gruyter. doi:10.2478/9783110420067.3

Thompson, W. F., Schellenberg, E. G., & Letnic, A. K. (2012). Fast and loud background music disrupts reading comprehension. *Psychology of Music*, *40*(6), 700–708. doi:10.1177/0305735611400173

Wang, J., Hao, Y. H., & Lu, J. L. (2014). The effect of the presentation styles of videos on the effectiveness of autonomous learning. *Curriculum and Teaching*, (03): 93–99.

Zheng, J., Wang, Y. N., Wang, K. L., & Bai, Y. (2012). A study into the design of micro-lecturing videos. *China Educational Technology,* (04), 21-24.

Zhu, Y., Pei, L., & Shang, J. (2017). Improving video engagement by gamification: A proposed design of MOOC videos. In *Proceedings of the International Conference on Blended Learning* (pp. 433-444). New York, NY: Springer. 10.1007/978-3-319-59360-9_38

ENDNOTES

1 Micro-courses are also known as micro-lectures. They usually consist of a short recorded video presentation on a single, tightly defined topic and learning activities that reinforce lecture topics (Educause, 2012). MOOCs refer to Massive Open Online Courses. Most MOOCs of the current generation are organized around instructional videos, assignments, and assessments provided by course instructors, and are seen to mimic the structure of university courses (Khalil et al., 2015).

2 In this paper, "online English courses", "English micro-courses", and "English MOOCs" were defined as online courses, micro-courses, and MOOCs related particularly to the learning of English as a foreign language. They are on topics that are usually covered in the curriculum for EFL students in formal education, such as English vocabulary and grammar, English listening, speaking, reading, writing and translation skills, English for specific or academic purposes, and the cultural basics of English-speaking countries.

3 The presentation styles mentioned in the paper include (1) talking-head, i.e. shot of an instructor talking at a desk; (2) drawing-board, i.e. screencasting of digital tablets with voice-over; (3) PowerPoint-slide, i.e. screencasting of PowerPoint slide presentation with voice-over; and (4) animation, i.e. animated images with voice-over.

4 Guo et al. (2014) distinguished between lecturing videos and tutorial videos. The former gave mini-lectures, whereas the latter showed step-by-step problem solving walkthroughs.

5 Speaking rate was calculated as average number of words per minute (wpm), obtained by dividing the number of words in a speech by the duration of the speech (regular speech pauses included).

6 The comments that were written in English were cited in their original form without any editing, whereas the Chinese comments were translated by the author.

7 Most participants did not state explicitly the reasons why they thought a video was clearly and logically. Instead, they usually provided positive comments on the structure of a video prior to

or after their summary of the video where they depicted what the instructor did part by part. In other words, participants gave positive comments on the structure of the videos once they found themselves capable of dividing the videos into distinct parts.

8 As they were all very low and thus meaningless in statistical sense, the frequencies of the codes revealed in the second round of analysis of the MOOC data were not presented in the text.

9 Reviews that talked about "the contents of the course" or "the instruction" were assumed to be concerned with "the contents of course videos", as the contents of these MOOCs were predominately transmitted through videos.

10 It is worth noting that, as illustrated by the examples, the features "useful and practical" and "rich in content" were usually mentioned when a reviewer evaluated all the videos of a MOOC as a whole instead of focusing on an individual video. This might also be one of the reasons why the two features were prominent in the MOOC data but not the micro-course data.

Chapter 12
Using Blogs to Motivate English as a Foreign Language Writers

Selami Aydin
Istanbul Medeniyet University, Turkey

Emrah Özdemir
Balikesir University, Turkey

ABSTRACT

Not many studies have been present on the effects of blogging, particularly with respect to English as a Foreign Language (EFL) writing motivation. Those studies did not focus on the effect of the use of blogs on Turkish EFL learners' writing motivation. Thus, this chapter examines how the use of blogs affects EFL writing motivation among EFL learners in a Turkish EFL learning context. A questionnaire interrogating demographic information, a pre-test and a post-test measuring writing achievement were administered to a group of participants including 48 language learners. According to results, blogging on its own does not increase motivation; however, the process-based writing instruction mainly has positive influences on EFL learners' motivation in both traditional pen-paper and blog environments. Thus, EFL teachers need to know that the use of blogs does not increase motivation among Turkish EFL learners. To increase their motivation level, it is also recommended that teachers should use a writing environment where their students are encouraged to write in the target language.

INTRODUCTION

Writing as a productive skill in the foreign language learning process is a process and a product in which tangible and intellectual factors have an important role (Sokolik, 2003). Since the 1950s, writing instructions including process and project-based activities have become more common due to the change in paradigm from teacher-oriented instructions to learner-oriented instructions (Brown, 1987). Thus, in EFL classes, writing is used for controlling the learning process, minimizing errors, teaching punctuation, determining the English level of students, consolidating vocabulary, boosting memory and developing creative thinking skills (Nightingale, 1988). However, as Boscolo and Hidi (2007) under-

DOI: 10.4018/978-1-7998-1282-1.ch012

line, the lack of motivation in writing instruction is as one of the considerable problems to overcome. In addition, the environment in which the learner is expected to write is also one of the key factors for cultivating motivation.

The lack of motivation among learners causes certain problems regarding writing. First, learners consider writing difficult and have a common belief that they do not possess the intellectual capacity required to express themselves in written English (Erkan & Saban, 2011). Students have trouble with writing not just linguistically, but in a communicative manner as well (Ismail, 2011). Second, learners have negative attitudes towards writing; thus, they tend to see writing and its processes as time-consuming and tedious (Owston & Wideman, 1997). Third, because of the testing system, which does not include adequate writing sections, learners are likely to regard writing as unnecessary. In other words, learners focus more on reading comprehension and grammatical correctness owing to the demand of exams and curriculum (Huang, 2005). Last, while research shows the superiority of computer integrated writing instruction over traditional pen-paper writing in terms of motivation and achievement (Chuo, 2007; Owston & Wideman, 1997; Sullivan, & Pratt, 1996; Zhu et al., 2015), computer-based writing instruction has been neglected in EFL classes. In conclusion, by considering the studies that are in favor of positive settings for writing motivation, more attention is necessary for the environment in which learners are expected to write.

With the rapid technological developments in the field of ICT, the course of English learning and teaching has drastically changed. Educators and scholars have been seeking alternative ways to integrate ICTs into language learning classrooms as an alternative and a complementary to traditional learning environments. In addition, the generation after 90s has grown up in a technology-oriented world where they were exposed to computers. Thus, the term digital natives is used for individuals who have been familiar with the technology since birth (Kirschner & Karpinski, 2010; Prensky, 2001; Sánchez, Cortijo, & Javed, 2014; Tapscott & Williams, 2010). Due to the technological developments and increasing familiarity of the students with the ICT, educators and researchers have been urged to explore alternative ways to incorporate the recent technologies into language learning environments and create new instructional settings utilizing recent technological developments.

The latest technological developments have paved the way for the integration of writing and computers. This approach is reinforced by technology by providing both collaborative writing opportunities and skill development using computer-based programs. Teachers and students may benefit from all these innovations. As one of these tools, Weblog or its short form blog is an asynchronous means of communication and usually ascribed to John Barger who was one of the foremost bloggers in 1997 (Ducate & Lomicka, 2005). Considering the growing trend, blogs have become a very important tool and environment for communication among web users, which help the development of creative thinking, reading, writing, autonomy and collaboration. According to Ducate and Lomicka (2008), blogs contribute literacy in a number of ways, especially reading and writing skills, as they create a learning environment in which language learners can share and discuss their ideas. In addition to creating an interactive environment, blogs are helpful in terms of announcing assignments, keeping records, giving feedback and taking part in discussions, which enables teachers and students to access the information through virtual world whenever or wherever it is needed.

In terms of EFL learning, using blogs is useful due to several reasons. First, blogs are practical tools for learning, as they are easily accessible and most of them are free of charge (Murray & Hourigan, 2008). Learners can start to utilize them as soon as they find a computer with an internet connection. Second, blogs contribute to collaboration among learners. The students' feelings about group identity increase by commenting on their writing (Ducate & Lomicka, 2008; Murray & Hourigan, 2008). Third, they contribute to the feedback process (Dippold, 2009). Fourth, the use of blogs develops learners' thinking skills in an organized way and develops their research skills (Aydin, 2014; Richardson, 2010). Next, writing on a blog is not an activity that is done for one time. It is a gradual process similar to writing a diary entry. Finally, while writing on a blog, learners consider the target audiences' needs. They adjust the level of their writing without feeling the pressure of face-to-face communication (Richardson, 2010). However, few empirical studies have investigated the effect of blogging on EFL writing motivation. Thus, there is a need to provide empirical and theoretical foundations to use blogs to increase writing motivation in language classes. Below, before a brief review of the literature on the process-based approach, writing motivation and blogging effect on writing motivation is presented, a theoretical background and related terms and concepts used throughout the study are mentioned.

THEORETICAL FRAMEWORK

As a productive skill, writing means to express one's feelings, ideas, knowledge, plans, and comments in a written form. It is widely accepted as one of the most challenging skills for foreign language learners to develop (Allen & Corder, 1974), as it requires complex mental processes in which learners are expected to not only have y thoughts and ideas but also express these ideas and thoughts on paper.

For Raimes (1991), there are four different approaches to second and foreign language writing, which emerge at different times and still have an impact on teaching writing as *Form-focused Approach*, *Genre-based Approach*, *Reader-dominated Approach*, and *Process-based Approach.* The focus of this study was on the *Process-based Approach.* According to the Process-based Approach, writing consists of various stages such as brainstorming, planning, drafting, revising, editing and publishing. In this approach, concepts such as audience, interaction with classmates and teacher are especially emphasized (Arslan & Şahin-Kızıl, 2010). It can be stated that the *Process-based Approach* in writing is similar to writing a blog in terms of their processes, as they both emphasize the importance of collaboration. In addition, as blogs help students write in coordination, blogging increases learners' writing motivation (Lacina & Griffith, 2012).

Motivations can be defined as a need, desire that activates or stimulates behavior and gives it direction (Kleinginna & Kleinginna, 1981). In terms of foreign language learning, motivation includes attitudes and emotional conditions that affect the amount of effort and the desire to learn (Ellis, 1997). In the *Socio-educational Model*, two types of motivation are mentioned as instrumental and integrative (Brown, 1987). In the scope of *Self-determination Theory*, motivation can be categorized as intrinsic and extrinsic (Deci &Ryan, 1985). It can be pointed out that writing requires instrumental motivation as using writing knowledge can be a way of gaining prestige or economic profits, whereas learners have integrative motivation to be integrated into the target culture. In addition, writing both requires intrinsic and extrinsic motivation, as writing performance and achievement relate to innate pleasures and emotional or pragmatic reasons (Zimmerman & Kitsantas, 2007).

Several theories and approaches are associated with teaching through blogs. First, *Constructivism*, defined as a theory in which learners develop meaning, based on the relationship between what they already know and what they have just come across (Resnick, 1989). *Constructivism* might have an effect on online writing with regard to the cognitive processes that learners face. Benson (2013) underlines that learners study collaboratively with others during social interaction. By this way, they can develop high-order cognitive processes through observation, analysis and evaluation. While writing online, students have to think more carefully about what to write and whether their writing is appropriate and effective in a particular context. Second, *Critical theory,* originated at the beginning of 1920s in the Frankfurt school was another theory that is related to the use of blogs for writing. Herbert Marcuse, Max Horkheimer Leo Lowenthal, T. W. Adorno, and Erich Fromm were the pioneers of this school of thought. In critical theory, social institutions and associations are not accepted as sole data. Instead, it emphasizes intellectual and societal roots regarding how the phenomena occur and change over time. Additionally, it investigates the relationship between social structure, ideology and language. Critical theory involves critical literacy research, critical pedagogy, and critical discourse analysis (Pennycook, 2001). In terms of language learning, critical theory asserts that knowledge is constructed through societal relations, which is similar to constructivism. This approach suggests that individuals learn new information through various forms of social interaction which involves social change and political stance. According to this approach, learning is seen as a process of interaction with social context, including the possibility of political action and social change (Thanasoulas, 2000). Third, *Humanism* is the other approach which were developed as a reaction to behaviorism by Abraham Maslow and Carl Rogers. This theory mainly focuses on learners. Proponents of this theory claim that learning occur in a relaxing and learner-centered atmosphere. The fundamental notion of humanism is that everybody has a potential to learn under certain circumstances. In a humanistic learning environment, learners have the autonomy and are responsible for their own learning, which is necessary for teaching through blogs. Fourth, *Collaborative Learning,* which is defined as a status in which at least two learners try to learn new things together (Dillenburg, 1999), is closely related to Piaget and Vygotsky's views which assert that a great many of cognitive processes occur during collaboration (Brandon & Hollingshead, 1999). In computer-based learning environments, collaboration is significant, as students learn new information thanks to the interaction among group members by making comments, reviewing and criticizing. Fifth, according to *Situated Cognition,* knowledge can be affected by the culture, activities, and context in which it is used and situated because of these factors (Brown et al., 1989).Learning is an expected result of the social interaction among learners during online exchanges. Sixth, according to *Autonomous Learning,* the learner has the responsibility of his or her own learning process. For blogging, autonomy means writing on a personalized website, free of time constraints of traditional classes. Lastly, *Self-determination* relates to humans' basic psychological needs, namely, the reason for human behaviors is the need to control and choose freely what and how they behave. The learning situations backing self-determination and autonomy are favorable with regard to learners' motivation, concentration, creativity and intellectual development in a blog environment. Blogs are also an ideal environment for writing by providing opportunities to learners such as writing for different audiences, on different topics, working without pressure from teachers, free from constraints of time and place (Sun, 2010), which might have an effect on motivation.

LITERATURE REVIEW

Now an agreement among scholars with regard to the advantages of the Process-based Approach has been reached. To begin with, to discover how process writing contributes to writing skills, Ho (2006) investigated 200 primary school students. Interviews, questionnaires and observations were used to gather the data. Ho (2006) found that writing instruction with a process-based approach was advantageous for students with not only higher but also lower levels. In another study, Muncie (2002) found that a positive correlation existed between process-based writing and vocabulary development. On the other hand, not all studies were in favor of the positive effects of writing as a process approach. For instance, in a review of several quasi-experimental and experimental studies, Graham and Sandmel (2011) found no any significant effect of writing instruction with a Process-based Approach to students' writing skills and motivation and writing skills. Additionally, in a study carried out on freshmen, Barnhisel et al. (2012) identified that the Process-based approach did not have a positive effect on writing. To conclude, research indicated that process-based writing approach is beneficial for vocabulary development at lower and upper levels, while the use of the approach has no impact on motivation and writing performance.

Early motivational studies on writing mostly emphasized apprehension (Daly, 1978; Daly & Wilson, 1983; Faigley et al., 1981). However, after the introduction of Social Cognitive Theory, research focused on writing motivation in terms of self-efficacy. For instance, Pajares (2003) asserted that the students' self-confidence about their writing skills had an effect on their motivation. In addition, Zhang and Guo (2012) examined 66 Chinese EFL learners to examine the relationship between EFL writing motivation and self-efficacy. They found that EFL writing motivation, self-efficacy and writing competence had a positive and considerable correlation for freshmen but not for sophomores. Interest is another variable that has a positive effect on writing (Albin et al., 1996). Lo and Hyland (2007) conducted a study on young ESL writers as a part of an action research project that aimed to improve learners' motivation and engagement based on their own socio-cultural context. They found that interest and relevant topics had a confidence-building effect on young learners. Lam and Law (2007) carried out a survey to find whether instructional practices were connected to students' motivation and performance. They discovered that the more motivating strategies the teachers used, the more the students were motivated. In conclusion, research demonstrates that self-confidence, self-efficacy and interest have positive effects on writing motivation.

Along with the developments of computer technologies and the Internet, research appeared on blogs that provide many different opportunities to both teachers and language learners (Aydın, 2014). To begin with, in a study conducted to examine the utilization of blogs, Noytim (2010) found that the students thought blogs as a useful tool to develop reading, vocabulary and writing skills as well as thinking, self-expression and social interaction skills. Moreover, Kocoglu (2009) investigated whether the use of blogs had a role in improving writing among EFL learners. Results showed that blogs were useful for learners to improve writing skills. In an action research conducted with 30 tertiary level EFL learners, Sulistyo, Mukminatien, Cahyono, and Saukah (2019) investigated how Blog-Assisted Language Learning (BALL) improve writing performance in terms of complexity, accuracy, and fluency. In the study they found positive improvements in writing achievement and collaboration. Sulistyo, Mukminatien, Cahyono, and Saukah (2019) conducted a study with 50 secondary school students in Thailand to investigate the effect of the use of blogs for writing. A mixed method was employed in the study. The results demonstrated that blog writing group outperformed the traditional writing group in writing ability test. Al-Qallaf and Al-Mutairi (2016) examined the effect of blogs on teaching writing. In the study that was conducted with 23 fifth grade students in Kuwait and used mixed methods, they found that learners had significant gains in terms of writing lengthy and more accurate sentences. Vurdien (2013) aimed to explore possible influences of blogs on feedback. in the five-month study, the students created personal blogs in which activities were mainly about the writing tasks such as writing letters, reports, proposals and articles. She concluded that blogs helped comprehend the influence of the learners' feedback better, to develop writing skills in special tasks and to increase collaboration. In addition, Arslan and Şahin-Kızıl (2010) carried out a study to investigate the influence of blog-oriented writing instruction on the overall writing performance. In this quasi-experimental study, the results showed that writing in the Process-based Approach has a significant effect on the development of students' writing. Last, in a study carried out by Sun (2010), blogs were found to be useful in terms of stimulating learner autonomy, boosting students' motivation and the development of students' writing skills. In brief, research indicated that blogs could be seen as useful tools for improving writing skills, collaborative writing, writing performance and autonomous writing.

The number of studies on the use of blogs on motivation in EFL context is limited. Among those studies, Nair et al. (2013) carried out a quasi-experimental research, including 154 undergraduate students to explore the effects of blogs on learners' attitudes during two semesters. In the study, two types of blogs, individual and interactive, were compared. They found that interactive blogs had positive effects on academic achievement and peer interaction. In terms of motivation, both groups displayed positive attitudes towards writing. In their research, Deng and Yuen (2012) investigated student teachers' perceptions towards academic blogging and motivational factors. Questionnaires, interviews and content analysis were used to collect data. Findings demonstrated that students' perceptions of blogs played an important role in motivation. Nair et al. (2013) compared traditional writing and online blogs. The participants, 224 students and four teachers were assigned to produce two paper-based and two blog-oriented products. Although there were problems with the students' submission rates and teachers' negative perceptions about the burden of online tasks, blogs might have a positive influence on writing performance. Lee (2017) investigated to what extent assignments submitted through blogs can facilitate writing and how students feel after blog based instruction. The results demonstrated that learners had positive attitudes towards the blog use as it facilitate collaboration and cooperation. In addition, the results showed significant gains in terms of learners' attention levels. Liu (2016) conducted an exploratory study with 42 freshman students in a Taiwanese university to examine the effect of blended instruction including the use of blogs on actual learning performance of students. The results showed that the blogging group were more willing to communicate and had more positive attitudes. Mabuan (2018) examined a corpus of blogs written by 58 freshman university students studying tourism in the Philippines. The results showed that students viewed blogs as a feasible platform since the learners had freedom to express their views as well as developing writing skills. Hindley, Clughen, and Rawden (2018) investigated the implementation of blog writing in a final year undergraduate module. In the study using a mixed method approach for data collection and analysis, they found that the use of blogs greatly enhanced student engagement.

Although most of the studies on the use of blogs in writing classes have generally yielded positive results, there are some studies emphasizing the negative points need to be considered. Hamuddin, Syahdan, and Kurniawan (2018) conducted a qualitative study which investigates 10 highly recognized papers. The results showed that cyberbullying is a serious problem for EFL bloggers. Liu (2016) highlighted that lack of simultaneous peer interaction, and willingness, and heavy workload and timing issues were among the major problems which were encountered. Yao (2019) reported that a small number of students expressed negative attitudes towards peer reviewing by preferring their writing to be evaluated by more experienced writers not their peers.

In conclusion, this study aims to explore the differences between traditional writing environments and blog-oriented environments in terms of EFL writing motivation. For this purpose, the study addresses the following research questions:

- Does blogging have an effect on EFL learners' writing motivation levels?

- Is there a difference between traditional writing environments and blog-oriented writing environments in terms of EFL writing motivation?

METHODOLOGY

Design

To investigate the effect of blogging on EFL learners' writing motivation, the study was designed to be experimental. Data were collected from a background questionnaire and Payne's (2012) Academic Writing Motivation Questionnaire (AWMQ) (See Appendix 1). In the study, the positivistic paradigm is preferred, as it investigates observable behaviors that can be measured through experimental methods (Lincoln & Guba, 1994). One of the most common features of the positivistic paradigm is the use of scientific method including a generalization of findings, control and experimental groups, pre and posttest design, and statistical analysis procedures. The effect of blogging on writing motivation was examined through quantitative methods so that the researcher could keep the distance and act independently of the thing being investigated to deal with bias and objectivity issues (Craswell, 1994).

Before the research, all of the participants were informed about the purposes, significance and methodology of the study. Then, the approval of ethical review board was obtained through the administration of Education Faculty. Finally, the participants signed the consent form assuring that their participation was voluntary.

Participants

Forty-eight students at the English Language Teaching (ELT) Department of Balikesir University participated in the research. All of the participants were freshmen, as their writing class was taught during the first two semesters of the program. The participants were at the advanced level of English as a foreign language. The participants were 18 (37.5%) male and 30 (62.5%) female students. The gender distribution of the participants was a reflection of the overall population in the ELT department. The mean age of the students was 18.9 in the range of 18 and 26. They all studied EFL during their high school education where they enrolled in English departments that involved 10 to 12 hours of English classes in a week when they were in 10th grade at high school. They also intensively studied English in the 10^{th,} 11th and 12th grades. The mean score as an indication of their academic achievement was 2.85. The mean scores were their official test results in the range of 0 and 4 obtained from the formal examination results from their classes they attended during the semester. The classes they took during the first semester of the academic year were Contextual Grammar, Listening and Pronunciation, Advanced Reading and Writing and Oral Communication Skills. For the indication of their language proficiency, the scores they got from Foreign Language Examination (FLE) were examined. FLE, as a determinant while attending a university by Student Selection and Placement Center in Turkey, consisted of 80 questions including 15 grammar questions, five cloze items, eight sentence completion, 12 translation sentences from Turkish into English and English into Turkish, 15 reading items, five restatements of sentences, five paragraph completion exercises, five situational items, five dialog completion items and five irrelevant sentence questions. As an indication of participants' writing achievement and the homogeneity of the groups

TOEFL writing items were used to assign the participants to two groups as control and experimental. The inter-rater reliability coefficient was found to be 0.90 for pre-test results of the writing the writing test.

Procedure

A three-step procedure was used in the study: (1) administration of background questionnaire and the AWMQ, (2) instruction, (3) re-administration of the AWMQ. In the third week of the Fall semester of 2014, the background questionnaire and the AWMQ were conducted. Then, participants were placed in accordance with the results obtained from the AWMQ in control (x=3.30; SD=3.6) and experimental groups (x=3.31; SD=3.39) as mean scores and standard deviations showed a balance in accordance with the control and experimental group. Then, four-week writing instruction within the scope of the Process-based Approach was given to the participants in the control and experimental groups in the practice process. During the process, the tasks of the control group were completed in traditional pen-paper writing, whereas the ones in the experimental group were completed on blogs. As a note, all of the participants in two groups had the same process during their writing instruction as detailed in Table 1. Finally, for the comparison of the two groups at the end of the semester, the AWMQ were re-administered.

Instruction

The study lasted for four weeks, as this period was considered as adequate to comprehend the basic steps of process-based writing. Participants in both groups took the same process-based instruction However, the writing tasks in the control group were completed through the traditional pen-paper writing in classrooms, whereas the ones in the experimental group were completed through weblogs as seen in Appendix 2. The students in the experimental group completed the tasks and feedback processes apart from the regular class hours. The students followed the necessary steps of the Process-based Approach in the scope of Flower and Hayes' (1981) process writing including the steps such as planning, drafting and revising.

Week 1

In the first week, the necessary steps for writing a descriptive essay were introduced. The participants were informed about how to use the descriptive language and organize an essay, which includes an introduction, a thesis statement, body paragraphs and a conclusion. After descriptive and non-descriptive essay samples were introduced, they read an example descriptive essay and did several exercises. Then, they were asked to write a descriptive essay about restaurants. Before they started to write, they followed some steps to gather ideas for their essay. Next, they used these ideas while making an outline. At the beginning of the outline, they wrote some introductory ideas and a thesis statement before they wrote two body paragraphs including descriptive language about the features of the topic the chose. At the end, they wrote a conclusion paragraph involving final opinions. With the help of the outline they made, they wrote a four-paragraph essay that involved a descriptive language. Finally, before editing, they read their partners' essays and discussed with them. The students revised and rewrote their essays according to the feedback given by their peers. Then, after the essays were read by the teacher and given feedback, they wrote their final draft and edited their writing.

Week 2

The second week covered the organization of narrative essays. The subjects were informed about how to organize an essay including previous personal experience or a memorable event and to express the order of events by using time words and time clauses. Then, they read an example of the narrative essay and answered the questions that aimed to focus on the features of the narrative essay. Before writing, the students had a brainstorming session to plan their essays and started to write an outline by listing some introductory ideas. Next, they wrote three body paragraphs including narrative language about the event they were influenced. At the end, they wrote a conclusion paragraph involving final opinions. With the help of the outline they made, they were expected to write a narrative essay including the correct ordering of the events and use of time words and clauses. They completed the tasks and made comments on their partners' writing pieces. After they revised and rewrote their essays according to the feedback given by their peers, the essays were read by the teacher and given feedback. Finally, they wrote their final draft and edited their writing.

Week 3

The third week involved writing a compare and contrast essay. The participants were explained how to describe two subjects being compared and contrasted and organize body paragraphs by using techniques such as point-by-point essay in which students choose three or more key points to compare and contrast. Then, they read an example of compare and contrast essay. After practicing the structures they learned, they prepared to plan their own five-paragraph essays. Before starting, they brainstormed to gather new ideas about their essays, chose two topics to compare and contrast and decided the technique they were going to use. They wrote their ideas in a chart and started to make an outline. They wrote some introductory ideas and a thesis statement, three body paragraphs including the comparing and contrasting language about the selected two topics. At the end, they wrote a conclusion paragraph involving final opinions. With the help of the outline they made, they wrote a five-paragraph essay which involved a compare and contrast language. Finally, before editing, they read their partners' papers, revised and rewrote their essays according to the feedback given by their peers. Then, after they received teacher feedback, they wrote their final draft and edited their writing.

Week 4

In the last week, cause and effect essay that includes the reasons and the results of an event, situation or action was introduced in details. Before they started to write, they followed some steps to gather ideas for their essay. After they wrote their ideas on a chart, they used these ideas to make an outline. At the beginning of the outline, they wrote some introductory ideas and a thesis statement. Then, they wrote three body paragraphs supporting their arguments and a conclusion involving final opinions. By means of the outline they made, they wrote a five-paragraph essay that involved causes and effect technique. Finally, before editing, they read their partners' pieces, revised and rewrote their essays according to the feedback given by their peers and teachers. Finally, they wrote their final draft and edited their writing.

Instruments

The study used two instruments to collect data: A background questionnaire and writing motivation scale. First, a background questionnaire was used to interrogate gender, age, academic achievement and FLE scores. The second tool administered in the study to see participants' motivation levels was Payne's (2012) Academic Writing Motivation Questionnaire (AWMQ), including 37 items. The questionnaire was Likert-type that was assessed on a scale one to five (never = 1, rarely = 2, sometimes = 3, usually = 4, always = 5).

The questionnaire was aimed to measure to what extent the students are motivated regarding writing.

Data Analysis

Statistical Package for Social Sciences (SPSS) was used with the aim of analyzing the data. For this purpose, the mean scores, maximum and minimum values for the participants' ages were computed. Then, the number and percentage of participants' gender were calculated, before mean scores, minimum and maximum values and standard deviations for participants' academic achievement scores were found. Then, a similar process was gone through for participants' FLE and writing achievement scores by calculating mean scores and standard deviations. Then, the reliability coefficients of the AWMQ in Cronbach's Alpha Model and percentages of variance were computed for pre-and post-tests. For the pretest, the reliability coefficient was 0.91 whereas the percentage of variance was 77.36. Moreover,

Table 1. Instruction process for control and experimental groups

<table>
<tr><th>Weeks</th><th>Tasks</th><th>Grammar</th><th>Vocabulary</th><th>Process</th></tr>
<tr><td>Week 1</td><td>Writing a descriptive essay
a. Organizing a descriptive essay
b. Using descriptive language by giving clear mental picture of the subject of the essay</td><td>1. Using definite and indefinite articles
a. Using correct articles with nouns and noun phrases</td><td>Using descriptive adjectives and adverbs</td><td rowspan="4">Brainstorming
Planning
First draft
Peer feedback
Second draft
Teacher feedback
Final draft
•
•
•</td></tr>
<tr><td>Week 2</td><td>Writing a narrative essay
a. Organizing a narrative essay
b. Expressing the order of events</td><td>1. Using Past Perfect Tense
a. Ordering the events in the past
b. Using the Past Perfect Tense with time clauses</td><td>Using past time clauses and subordinators</td></tr>
<tr><td>Week 3</td><td>Writing a compare and contrast essay
a. Organizing a compare and contrast essay
a. Organizing body paragraphs of a compare and contrast essay in accordance with point by point and blocks</td><td>Using subordinators and transitions to compare and contrast</td><td>Using the dictionary to distinguish between homonyms</td></tr>
<tr><td>Week 4</td><td>Writing a cause and effect essay
a. Organizing a compare and contrast essay
b. Structuring a cause and effect essay in accordance with reasons (causes) and results (effects)</td><td>1. Using agents with the passive voice</td><td>Using cause and effect collocations</td></tr>
</table>

for the post-test, the reliability coefficient was 0.75 and percentage of variance was 76.94. The results presented in Table 2 indicated that reliability and validity of the data were obtained.

RESULTS

Instruction Effect on Writing Motivation in a Traditional Writing Environment

As shown in Table 3, the paired sample test results that were aimed at exploring whether there was a considerable difference between pre-test and post-test results of the control group indicated that only five items significantly differed in terms of the pre- and post-tests scores. First, the values indicated that the participants who enjoyed writing significantly increased (p=.02). Namely, there was a noticeable improvement in emotions regarding writing. Second, the participants' statements about their positive feelings to write down their thoughts significantly differed (p=.03). This showed that they liked writing down their ideas more at the end of the experiment. Moreover, there existed to be a significant difference (p=.04) between values, which showed that they enjoyed creative writing assignments. That is to say, the participants' beliefs about creative writing increased considerably. Finally, the values demonstrated that spelling was easy for them (p=.05), which showed an obvious improvement.

As shown in Table 4, the paired sample test results were used to see whether there was a significant difference between the pre-test and post-test results of the experimental group. The results demonstrated that only six items statistically differed. Initially, the values demonstrated a statistically significant increase in terms of enjoying writing (p=.01), doing creative writing assignments (p=.05), classes that require a lot of writing (p=.04) and writing literary analysis papers (.04). In other words, there were substantial improvements in feelings in relation to writing. Moreover, there was a significant difference (p=.04)

Table 2. Reliability coefficients and percentage of variance for the AWMQ

	Reliability coefficients (Cronbach's Alpha)	% of the Variance
Pre-test	0.91	77.36
Post-test	0.75	76.94

Table 3. Pre- and post-test comparison of the items in the AWMQ for the control group

	Paired Differences					T	Df	Sig. (2-tailed)
	Mean	Std. Deviation	Std. Error Mean	95% Confidence Interval of the Difference				
				Lower	Upper			
I enjoy writing.	.56	.89	.22	.08	1.03	2.52	15	.02
I like to write down my thoughts.	.56	.96	.24	.04	1.07	2.33	15	.03
I enjoy creative writing assignments.	.56	1.03	.25	.01	1.11	2.18	15	.04
Spelling is easy for me.	.37	.71	.17	-.00	.75	2.08	15	.05

between values showing that they would rather have written an essay than answer multiple-choice questions. Finally, the values showing that they wanted others to recognize them as a good writer differed (p=.01), as there existed to be a clear improvement.

Instruction Effect on Writing Motivation in a Blogging Environment

In order to see whether there was a difference between the control group and experimental group, both the pre-test and post-test scores for both groups were compared. As shown in Table 5, there was no statistically significant difference between the scores obtained from control and experimental groups in terms of writing motivation except for their statement on having more opportunities to write in classes. The significance level of the item was found to be.02 that showed a significant difference.

To see whether there was any difference between the control group and experimental group after the treatment, both pre-test and post-test scores for both groups were compared. As given in Table 6, there was no statistically significant difference between groups in terms of writing motivation, except for the statement that the participants made about their pleasure from creative writing assignments, the significance level of which was .05, and their comment on practicing writing in order to improve their skills, which had a significance level of .01.

Table 4. Pre- and post-test comparison of the items in the AWMQ for the experimental group

	Paired Differences					T	Df	Sig. (2-tailed)
	Mean	Std. Deviation	Std. Error Mean	95% Confidence Interval of the Difference				
				Lower	Upper			
I enjoy writing.	.43	.62	.15	.10	.77	2.78	15	.01
I enjoy creative writing assignments.	.50	.96	.24	-.01	1.01	2.07	15	.05
I like classes that require a lot of writing.	.43	.81	.20	.00	.87	2.15	15	.04
I enjoy writing literary analysis papers.	-.75	1.34	.33	-1.46	-.03	-2.23	15	.04
I would rather write an essay than answer multiple-choice questions.	-.50	.89	.22	-.97	-.02	-2.23	15	.04
I want others to recognize me as a good writer.	-.56	.81	.20	-.99	-.12	-2.76	15	.01

Table 5. Comparison of the pre-test items in the AWMQ for control and experimental groups

	Group	Mean	Std. Deviation	Std. Error Mean	F	Sig.
I would like to have more opportunities to write in classes.	Control Group	2.90	.68	.14	5.40	.02
	Experimental Group	3.15	1.21	.27		

CONCLUSION

Three conclusions were reached in the study. The first conclusion is that the use of Process-based Approach has mainly no significant effects on writing motivation. Namely, learners have nearly the same level of motivation related to emotions about writing, self-assessment for the mastery of writing, assessment from others and future expectations after the instruction. This demonstrates that process-based learning does not affect the level of motivation levels among learners who write in a traditional writing environment. Yet, process-based writing in a traditional environment increases motivation the enjoyment of writing, writing down thoughts, creative writing assignments and easiness of spelling. The second conclusion is that the level of motivation does not increase considerably for blog writers. On the other hand, EFL writers feel motivated in terms of enjoyment of writing, writing down their thoughts, participating classes that require a lot of writing, pleasure taken from writing literary analysis papers, preference of writing essays to answer multiple questions and wishes about being recognized as a good writer. The final conclusion is that apart from enjoyment from creative writing assignments and writing practice to improve skills, there is no considerable difference between traditional and blog writing in terms of writing motivation.

DISCUSSION

As Yakut and Aydın (2015) stated, the reason why there is not a significant difference between a language learning setting with a traditional and blog environment is in relation to several factors. First, students who used blogs to carry out their activities perceive problems with regard to blogs because of technical concerns. Second, research shows that EFL learners lack experience in navigating the use of blogs in their educational activities. Third, throughout their education, they were in traditional pen–paper classroom environment and completed traditional pen–paper tasks (Yakut & Aydin, 20015).

A brief comparison of the conclusions to the ones in previous research is provided below. The conclusion reached in the research contradicts with the results of previous studies. For example, Kocoglu (2009) found that the utilization of blogs had a role in developing writing skills and increasing interest. Lee (2017) demonstrated positive attitudes towards the use of blogs and increasing collaboration and cooperation. Liu (2016) found the blogging group were more willing to communicate and had more positive attitudes. Additionally, Lin et al. (2014) stated that when compared to the traditional pen-and-paper writing, blogging helps learners to improve their writing. Mabuan (2018) showed that students viewed blogs as a feasible platform since the learners had freedom to express their views as well as developing

Table 6. Comparison of the post-test items in the AWMQ for control and experimental groups

	Group	Mean	Std. Deviation	Std. Error Mean	F	Sig.
I enjoy creative writing assignments.	Control Group	3.79	.84	.19	4.01	.05
	Experimental Group	4.05	1.23	.27		
I practice writing in order to improve my skills.	Control Group	3.57	1.42	.32	6.71	.01
	Experimental Group	2.95	.99	.22		

writing skills. Hindley et al (2018) found that the use of blogs greatly enhanced student engagement. With regard to motivation, this study found that the use of the Process-based Approach does not directly affect writing motivation. Furthermore, the blog writing environment does not foster the level of motivation for writing, which is similar to the findings that demonstrate blog writing instruction does not have an effect on motivation (Nair et al., 2013). Results are also in contradiction with the results showing the positive effect of blog writing on motivation (Aydin, 2014; Vurdien, 2013). Finally, in terms of writing motivation, no considerable difference is observed in this study between traditional and blog writing, which is in contrast with the findings of the study claiming that blogs may have a relative contribution to writing motivation (Arslan & Şahin-Kızıl, 2010).

By considering the results, some practical recommendations can be made. First, target groups should know that compared to traditional learning environments, the use of blogs does not have any extra advantages. The use of blogs does not improve writing more improvement than traditional learning environments with regard to writing motivation. Second, EFL teachers should seek ways to improve motivation, as motivation is considered as one of the fundamental constituents of EFL learning. Additionally, material and curriculum developers and policy makers should develop and design new approaches, methods, techniques and procedures to meet learners' needs in terms of motivation. In addition, authentic materials stimulating learners' desires significantly must be developed. Teachers also need to know that using blog-oriented instruction may not improve EFL learners' writing motivation. That is because they should integrate blogs into their classes as a complementary environment to traditional pen-paper writing. As a final note, teachers, material developers, curriculum developers and policy-makers should cooperate to create an encouraging and motivating language-learning environment that helps improve students' writing motivation.

The first limitation of the research is that 48 EFL learners. The second limitation is the experimental research design that involves control and experimental group assignment of the participants in accordance with writing achievement pre-test results. The third limitation is that the instruction process lasted for four weeks. Finally, the data collected regarding EFL writing motivation is limited to the AWMQ developed by Payne (2012).

As well as Process-based Approach, further research should focus on other writing approaches such as Reader/audience-dominated, Genre-based, and Form-focused approaches. Research should also focus on the variables that can have an effect on writing and motivation such as affective states, self-efficacy beliefs, attitudes and perceptions. Additionally, social media and other Web 2.0 tools such as podcasts and wikis should be researched. As well as experimental studies, there is a need for qualitative and descriptive studies. Moreover, in terms of EFL writing motivation, demographic variables and proficiency levels should be investigated. Research in the Turkish EFL context should also focus on more generic issues such as perceptions, attitudes and factors that may have an influence on educational technology use in Turkey, as there is a considerable gap between the amount of research and the number teachers and students and technology investments.

REFERENCES

Abazaoğlu, I., Yıldırım, O., & Yıldızhan, Y. (2014). Teacher profile in Turkey]. *Turkish Studies: International Periodical for the Languages, Literature, and History of Turkish or Turkic*, *9*(2), 1–20.

Al-Qallaf, C. L., & Al-Mutairi, A. S. (2016). Digital literacy and digital content supports learning: The impact of blogs on teaching English as a foreign language. *The Electronic Library*, *34*(3), 522–547. doi:10.1108/EL-05-2015-0076

Albin, M. L., Benton, S. L., & Khramtsova, I. (1996). Individual differences in interest and narrative writing. *Contemporary Educational Psychology*, *21*(4), 305–324. doi:10.1006/ceps.1996.0024 PMID:8979867

Allen, J. P., & Corder, S. Pit. (1974). Techniques in applied linguistics. London, UK: Oxford University Press.

Arslan, R. Ş., & Şahin-Kızıl, A. (2010). How can the use of blog software facilitate the writing process of English language learners? *Computer Assisted Language Learning*, *23*(3), 183–197. doi:10.1080/09588221.2010.486575

Aydin, S. (2014). The use of blogs in learning English as a foreign language. *Mevlana International Journal of Education*, *4*(1), 244–259. doi:10.13054/mije.13.79.4.1

Barnhisel, G., Stoddard, E., & Gorman, J. (2012). Incorporating process-based writing pedagogy into first-year learning communities. *The Journal of General Education*, *61*(4), 461–487. doi:10.1353/jge.2012.0041

Benson, P. (2013). *Teaching and researching: Autonomy in language learning*. New York: Routledge.

Boscolo, P., & Hidi, S. (2007). The multiple meanings of motivation to write. In P. Boscolo, & S. Hidi (Eds.), *Writing and Motivation* (pp. 1–14). Bingley, UK: Emerald.

Brandon, D. P., & Hollingshead, A. B. (1999). Collaborative learning and computer-supported groups. *Communication Education*, *48*(2), 109–126. doi:10.1080/03634529909379159

Brown, D. H. (1987). *Principles of language learning and teaching*. New Jersey: Prentice-Hall.

Brown, J. S., Collins, A., & Duguid, P. (1989). Situated cognition and the culture of learning. *Educational Researcher*, *18*(1), 32–42. doi:10.3102/0013189X018001032

Chuo, T. W. I. (2007). The effects of the WebQuest writing instruction program on EFL learners' writing performance, writing apprehension, and perception. *TESL-EJ*, *11*(3), 1–27.

Cook, V. (2013). *Second language learning and language teaching, 4th Ed.* New York: Routledge.

Daly, J. A. (1978). Writing apprehension and writing competency. *The Journal of Educational Research*, *72*(1), 10–14. doi:10.1080/00220671.1978.10885110

Daly, J. A., & Wilson, D. A. (1983). Writing apprehension, self-esteem, and personality. *Research in the Teaching of English*, *17*(4), 327–341.

Deci, E. L., & Ryan, R. M. (1985). The general causality orientations scale: Self-determination in personality. *Journal of Research in Personality*, *19*(2), 109–134. doi:10.1016/0092-6566(85)90023-6

Deng, L., & Yuen, H. K. (2012). Understanding student perceptions and motivation towards academic blogs: An exploratory study. *Australasian Journal of Educational Technology*, *28*(1), 48–66. doi:10.14742/ajet.883

Dillenbourg, P. (1999). Collaborative learning: Cognitive and computational approaches. Advances in learning and instruction series. Elsevier Science, Inc., Madison Square Station, New York.

Dippold, D. (2009). Peer feedback through blogs: Student and teacher perceptions in an advanced German class. *ReCALL, 21*(1), 18–36. doi:10.1017/S095834400900010X

Ducate, L. C., & Lomicka, L. L. (2005). Exploring the blogosphere: Use of weblogs in the foreign language classroom. *Foreign Language Annals, 38*(3), 410–421. doi:10.1111/j.1944-9720.2005.tb02227.x

Ducate, L. C. 1, & Lomicka, L. L. (2008). Adventures in the blogosphere: From blog readers to blog writers. *Computer Assisted Language Learning, 21*(1), 9–28. doi:10.1080/09588220701865474

Ellis, R. (1997). *The study of second language acquisition*. New York: Oxford University Press.

Erkan, D. Y., & Saban, A. I. (2011). Writing performance relative to writing apprehension, self-efficacy in writing, and attitudes towards writing: A correlational study in Turkish tertiary-level EFL. *The Asian EFL Journal Quarterly, 13*(1), 163–191.

Faigley, L., Daly, J. A., & Witte, S. P. (1981). The role of writing apprehension in writing performance and competence. *The Journal of Educational Research, 75*(1), 16–21. doi:10.1080/00220671.1981.10885348

Flower, L., & Hayes, J. R. (1981). A cognitive process theory of writing. *College Composition and Communication, 32*(4), 365–387. doi:10.2307/356600

Gardner, R. C., & Lambert, W. E. (1972). Attitudes and motivation in second-language Learning. Rowley, MA: Newbury.

Graham, S., & Sandmel, K. (2011). The process writing approach: A meta-analysis. *The Journal of Educational Research, 104*(6), 396–407. doi:10.1080/00220671.2010.488703

Guba, E. G., & Lincoln, Y. S. (1994). Competing paradigms in qualitative research. Handbook of qualitative research, 2(163-194), 105.

Hamuddin, B., Syahdan, S., & Kurniawan, K. (2018). Cyberbullying on students' blog: Exploring bully in digital era. *ELT-Lectura, 5*(2), 189–197. doi:10.31849/elt-lectura.v5i2.1700

Hindley, D., Clughen, L., & Rawden, B. (2018). Implementing blog writing as a tool for promoting student engagement and literacy development. *RAISE: Student Engagement in Higher Education Journal, 2*(2), 133–140.

Ho, B. (2006). Using the process approach to teach writing in 6 Hong Kong primary classrooms. *New Horizons in Education*. Retrieved from ERIC Database (EJ847597) from http://eric.ed.gov/?id=EJ847597

Huang, J. (2005). A diary study of difficulties and constraints in EFL learning. *System, 33*(4), 609–621. doi:10.1016/j.system.2005.04.001

Ismail, S. A. A. (2011). Exploring students' perceptions of ESL writing. *English Language Teaching, 4*(2), 73–84. doi:10.5539/elt.v4n2p73

Kirschner, P. A., & Karpinski, A. C. (2010). Facebook® and academic performance. *Computers in Human Behavior*, *26*(6), 1237–1245. doi:10.1016/j.chb.2010.03.024

Kleinginna, P. R. Jr, & Kleinginna, A. M. (1981). A categorized list of emotion definitions, with suggestions for a consensual definition. *Motivation and Emotion*, *5*(4), 263–291. doi:10.1007/BF00993889

Kocoglu, Z. (2009). Weblog use in EFL writing class. *Ankara University Journal of Faculty of Educational Sciences*, *42*(1), 311–327.

Kohsamut, T., & Sucaromana, U. (2017). Using blog to enhance English writing skill among high school students in Thailand. *PEOPLE: International Journal of Social Sciences*, *3*(2), 1337–1348.

Lacina, J., & Griffith, R. (2012). Blogging as a means of crafting writing. *The Reading Teacher*, *66*(4), 316–320. doi:10.1002/TRTR.01128

Lam, S. F., & Law, Y. K. (2007). The roles of instructional practices and motivation in writing performance. *Journal of Experimental Education*, *75*(2), 145–164. doi:10.3200/JEXE.75.2.145-164

Lee, L. (2017). Learners' perceptions of the effectiveness of blogging for L2 writing in fully online language courses. [IJCALLT]. *International Journal of Computer-Assisted Language Learning and Teaching*, *7*(1), 19–33. doi:10.4018/IJCALLT.2017010102

Lin, M. H., Li, J. J., Hung, P. Y., & Huang, H. W. (2014). Blogging a journal: Changing students' writing skills and perceptions. *ELT Journal*, *68*(4), 422–431. doi:10.1093/elt/ccu032

Liu, M. H. (2016). Blending a class video blog to optimize student learning outcomes in higher education. *The Internet and Higher Education*, *30*, 44–53. doi:10.1016/j.iheduc.2016.03.001

Lo, J., & Hyland, F. (2007). Enhancing students' engagement and motivation in writing: The case of primary students in Hong Kong. *Journal of Second Language Writing*, *16*(4), 219–237. doi:10.1016/j.jslw.2007.06.002

Mabuan, R. A. (2018). Using blogs in teaching tertiary ESL writing. *English Review: Journal of English Education*, *6*(2), 1–10.

Muncie, J. (2002). Process writing and vocabulary development: Comparing lexical frequency profiles across drafts. *System*, *30*(2), 225–235. doi:10.1016/S0346-251X(02)00006-4

Murray, L., & Hourigan, T. (2008). Blogs for specific purposes: Expressivist or socio-cognitivist approach? *ReCALL*, *20*(01), 82–97. doi:10.1017/S0958344008000719

Nair, S. S., Tay, L. Y., & Koh, J. H. L. (2013). Students' motivation and teachers' teaching practices towards the use of blogs for writing of online journals. *Educational Media International*, *50*(2), 108–119. doi:10.1080/09523987.2013.795351

Nation, I. S. P., & Newton, J. (2008). *Teaching ESL/EFL listening and speaking*. New York: Routledge. doi:10.4324/9780203891704

Nightingale, P. (1988). Understanding processes and problems in student writing. *Studies in Higher Education*, *13*(3), 263–283. doi:10.1080/03075078812331377720

Noytim, U. (2010). Weblogs enhancing EFL students' English language learning. *Procedia: Social and Behavioral Sciences*, *2*(2), 1127–1132. doi:10.1016/j.sbspro.2010.03.159

Okan, Z. (2008). Computing laboratory classes as language learning environments. *Learning Environments Research*, *11*(1), 31–48. doi:10.100710984-007-9035-y

Owston, R. D., & Wideman, H. H. (1997). Word processors and children's writing in a high-computer-access setting. *Journal of Research on Computing in Education*, *30*(2), 202–220. doi:10.1080/08886504.1997.10782223

Pajares, F. (2003). Self-efficacy beliefs, motivation, and achievement in writing: A review of the literature. *Reading & Writing Quarterly*, *19*(2), 139–158. doi:10.1080/10573560308222

Payne, A. R. (2012). *Development of the academic writing motivation questionnaire.* (Doctoral Dissertation, University of Georgia).

Pennycook, A. (2001). *Critical applied linguistics: A critical introduction.* Routledge. doi:10.4324/9781410600790

Prensky, M. (2001). Digital natives, digital immigrants part 1. *On the Horizon*, *9*(5), 1–6. doi:10.1108/10748120110424816

Raimes, A. (1991). Out of the woods: Emerging traditions in the teaching of writing. *TESOL Quarterly*, *25*(3), 407–429. doi:10.2307/3586978

Resnick, L. B. (1989). *Knowing, learning, and instruction: Essays in honor of Robert Glaser.* New Jersey: Lawrence Erlbaum Associates.

Richardson, W. (2010). *Blogs, wikis, podcasts, and other powerful web tools for classrooms*. London, UK: Sage.

Sánchez, R. A., Cortijo, V., & Javed, U. (2014). Students' perceptions of Facebook for academic purposes. *Computers & Education*, *70*, 138–149. doi:10.1016/j.compedu.2013.08.012

Sokolik, M. (2003). Writing. In D. Nunan (Ed.), *Practical English language teaching* (pp. 87–88). New York: McGraw-Hill.

Sulistyo, T., Mukminatien, N., Cahyono, B. Y., & Saukah, A. (2019). Enhancing learners' writing performance through blog-assisted language Learning. *International Journal of Emerging Technologies in Learning*, *14*(9), 61–73. doi:10.3991/ijet.v14i09.9535

Sullivan, N., & Pratt, E. (1996). A comparative study of two ESL writing environments: A computer-assisted classroom and a traditional oral classroom. *System*, *24*(4), 491–501. doi:10.1016/S0346-251X(96)00044-9

Sun, Y. C. (2010). Extensive writing in foreign-language classrooms: A blogging approach. *Innovations in Education and Teaching International*, *47*(3), 327–339. doi:10.1080/14703297.2010.498184

Tapscott, D., & Williams, A. D. (2010). Innovating the 21st-century university: It's time. *EDUCAUSE Review*, *45*(1), 16–29.

Thanasoulas, D. (2000). What is learner autonomy and how can it be fostered. *The Internet TESL Journal, 6*(11), 37–48.

Turkish Ministry of Development. (2015). *Public investments of information and communication technologies*. Department of Information Society. Retrieved from http://www.bilgitoplumu.gov.tr/wp-content/uploads/2015/04/2015_Kamu_BIT_Yatirimlari_Raporu.pdf

Vurdien, R. (2013). Enhancing writing skills through blogging in an advanced English as a foreign language class in Spain. *Computer Assisted Language Learning, 26*(2), 126–143. doi:10.1080/09588221.2011.639784

Yakut, A. D., & Aydın, S. (2015). An experimental study on the effects of the use of blogs on EFL reading comprehension. *Innovation in Language Learning and Teaching, 11*(1), 1–16. doi:10.1080/17501229.2015.1006634

Yaman, H. (2009). Teachers' views on the applicability of the Turkish course curriculum in crowded primary classrooms. *Educational Sciences: Theory and Practice, 9*(1), 349–359.

Yao, C. (2019, March). How peer review affects Chinese adult college students' English writing acquisition in a computer assisted online learning environment? [IOP Publishing]. *Journal of Physics: Conference Series, 1176*(2), 022044. doi:10.1088/1742-6596/1176/2/022044

Zhang, Y., & Guo, H. (2012). A study of English writing and domain-specific motivation and self-efficacy of Chinese EFL learners. *Journal of Pan-Pacific Association of Applied Linguistics, 16*(2), 101–121.

Zhu, Y., Mark Shum, S. K., Brian Tse, S. K., & Liu, J. J. (2015). Word-processor or pencil-and-paper? A comparison of students' writing in Chinese as a foreign language. *Computer Assisted Language Learning*, (ahead-of-print), 1-22.

Zimmerman, B. J., & Kitsantas, A. (2007). A writer's discipline: The development of self-regulatory skill. In P. Boscolo, & S. Hidi (Eds.), *Writing and motivation* (pp. 51–69). Oxford, UK: Elsevier.

APPENDIX 1: BACKGROUND QUESTIONNAIRE AND THE AWMQ

Dear participant,
A questionnaire was presented below to examine the relationship between motivation and EFL writing. Please read the questions and mark the most appropriate choice. I would like to thank for your kind participation.

Table 7. Emrah Özdemir

Part 1: Background Questionnaire					
Your age ______	Your gender Female (1) Male (2)				
Group Pen-paper (1) Blog (2)	Your academic achievement score ________				
Part 2. Attitudes and perceptions towards EFL writing					
Statements	Never	Rarely	Sometimes	Usually	Always
01. I enjoy writing.	(1)	(2)	(3)	(4)	(5)
02. I like to write down my thoughts.	(1)	(2)	(3)	(4)	(5)
03. I use correct grammar in my writing.	(1)	(2)	(3)	(4)	(5)
04. I complete a writing assignment even when it is difficult.	(1)	(2)	(3)	(4)	(5)
05. Being a good writer will help me do well academically.	(1)	(2)	(3)	(4)	(5)
06. I write as well as other students.	(1)	(2)	(3)	(4)	(5)
07. I write more than the minimum on writing assignments.	(1)	(2)	(3)	(4)	(5)
08. I put a lot of effort into my writing.	(1)	(2)	(3)	(4)	(5)
09. I like to participate in written online discussions.	(1)	(2)	(3)	(4)	(5)
10. I like to get feedback from an instructor on my writing.	(1)	(2)	(3)	(4)	(5)
11. I am able to clearly express my ideas in writing.	(1)	(2)	(3)	(4)	(5)
12. I easily focus on what I am writing.	(1)	(2)	(3)	(4)	(5)
13. I like my writing to be graded.	(1)	(2)	(3)	(4)	(5)
14. I am more likely to succeed if I can write well.	(1)	(2)	(3)	(4)	(5)
15. It is easy for me to write good essays.	(1)	(2)	(3)	(4)	(5)
16. I enjoy creative writing assignments.	(1)	(2)	(3)	(4)	(5)
17. I like classes that require a lot of writing.	(1)	(2)	(3)	(4)	(5)
18. I plan how I am going to write something before I write it.	(1)	(2)	(3)	(4)	(5)
19. Becoming a better writer is important to me.	(1)	(2)	(3)	(4)	(5)
20. Being a better writer will help me in my career.	(1)	(2)	(3)	(4)	(5)
21. It is important to me that I make an A on a writing assignment.	(1)	(2)	(3)	(4)	(5)

continued on following page

Table 7. Continued

Part 1: Background Questionnaire					
22. I enjoy writing assignments that challenge me.	(1)	(2)	(3)	(4)	(5)
23. I revise my writing before submitting an assignment.	(1)	(2)	(3)	(4)	(5)
24. Punctuation is easy for me.	(1)	(2)	(3)	(4)	(5)
25. I enjoy writing literary analysis papers.	(1)	(2)	(3)	(4)	(5)
26. I like to write even if my writing will not be graded.	(1)	(2)	(3)	(4)	(5)
27. I like others to read what I have written.	(1)	(2)	(3)	(4)	(5)
28. I enjoy writing research papers.	(1)	(2)	(3)	(4)	(5)
29. I would like to have more opportunities to write in classes.	(1)	(2)	(3)	(4)	(5)
30. Being a good writer is important in getting a good job.	(1)	(2)	(3)	(4)	(5)
31. I practice writing in order to improve my skills.	(1)	(2)	(3)	(4)	(5)
32. I want the highest grade in the class on a writing assignment.	(1)	(2)	(3)	(4)	(5)
33. I would rather write an essay than answer multiple-choice questions.	(1)	(2)	(3)	(4)	(5)
34. I want others to recognize me as a good writer.	(1)	(2)	(3)	(4)	(5)
35. Spelling is easy for me.	(1)	(2)	(3)	(4)	(5)
36. Choosing the right word is easy for me.	(1)	(2)	(3)	(4)	(5)
37. I am motivated to write in my classes.	(1)	(2)	(3)	(4)	(5)

Figure 1.

tension type headache attacks.

Conclusion: Foods can have good or bad effects. But we should take them how much we need. If we eat so much, we will have so many illnesses. So; we take care well ourselves.

c) Write

PROS AND CONS OF FOOD

I want to tell about that effects of science on food, good effects and bad effects. People are impressed by these effects.
Food has good effects. For example; Food increases your energy levels.They provide better mental function.Cruciferous vegetables support the body in fighting cancer.Berries contain flavonoids that slow aging and avocados lower your bad cholesterol.You have less chance of getting sick.A healthy diet can keep your weight in check and help build an attractive physique.
Food has also bad effects. For example; Any food can cause an allergy.Specific food may cause bad breath. Red meat and processed foods have a negative impact on body odor attractiveness.Most foods contain carbohydrates can cause gas.Many foods high in vitamin C have natural diuretic properties and can lead to frequent bathroom visits.Foods may cause high blood pressure. Food may trigger not only migraine but also tension type headache attacks.
Food can have good or bad effects. But we should take them how much we need. If we eat so much, we will have so many illnesses. So; we take care well ourselves.

d) Rewrite

PROS AND CONS OF FOOD

Figure 2.

REVISE AND EDIT

a) *Peer Review*

1) Is there a clear opinion expressed about the effect science has had on the food we eat)
2) Does the introduction contain a thesis statement that clearly states the opinion?
3) Is it clear how each of the effects supports the thesis statement? Are there any ideas that don't support it?
4) Are the effects supported by fact, examples, and descriptions?
5) Are the paragraphs connected logically using transitions?

SELF-ASSESSMENT

Does the essay clearly describe three effects of science on the food we eat? *Yes*
Does the essay contain an introduction, three body paragraphs, and a conclusion? *Yes*
Does the essay use cause and effect collocations appropriately? *Yes*
Are passive verbs used correctly? Are agents included and omitted appropriately? *No*
Does the essay include vocabulary from the unit? *Yes*
Did you check the essay for punctuation, spelling, and grammar? *Yes*

B) VOCABULARY

Training in Brainstorming and Developing Writing Skills

Chapter 13
Mobilisation and Enactment of Malaysian ESL Teachers' Technological Pedagogical Content Knowledge:
From Professional Learning to Professional Practice

Cynthia C. James
University of Cambridge, UK

Kean Wah Lee
https://orcid.org/0000-0003-3644-0086
University of Nottingham Malaysia, Malaysia

ABSTRACT

This chapter is a review of a three-year journey into exploring the development, mobilisation, and enactment of Malaysian ESL teachers' technological pedagogical content knowledge through a professional learning community known as 'Going Digital'. The first part of the chapter summarises the investigation on the effectiveness of the TPACK-IDDIRR + PLC as a transformative model of professional development to engender technology integration practices in the classroom. The findings reveal that the model is effective in enhancing technology integration practices of ESL teachers. In the second part, individual experiences of four members of the 'Going Digital' are narratively explored to understand the mobilisation and enactment of TPACK from professional development to practice in the classroom. The affordances and constraints of technology integration is explored in the third part. The chapter concludes with discussions on the interconnectedness of knowledge, context, and identity; and how it has led to the proposition of the model for TPACK mobilisation, appropriation, and enactment.

DOI: 10.4018/978-1-7998-1282-1.ch013

INTRODUCTION

Research and scholarship on technology integration in the language classrooms are increasing in number since the last decade (Kessler, 2018; Warschauer, 2000; Warschauer & Healey, 1998; Wu, 2014). This is mainly attributable to the prominence and ubiquity of technology in modern daily lives which have stirred the interests among researchers in the field to examine the use and impacts of technology on language education (Chapelle, 2009; Keengwe & Kang, 2011; Kessler, 2018). Despite all the enthusiasms, the levels of penetration and success of technology integration (Mishra & Koehler, 2006) are still shown to be discouraging, as reported by a number of studies on the challenges and barriers faced by teachers in integrating technology at classroom levels (e.g. Christ, Arya, & Liu, 2019; Herro, Quigley, & Cian, 2019; Regan et al., 2019; Vasinda, Ryter, Hathcock, & Wang, 2017). Substantial bodies of research identified teacher knowledge and perception of technology as among the reasons that contribute towards the low level of penetration and success of technology integration in the classrooms (e.g. Aljaloud, Billingsley, & Kwan, 2019; Muhaimin et al., 2019; Regan et al., 2019).

At the same time, researchers in the field of in-service teacher development have consistently worked on exploring approaches and strategies for effective and sustainable teacher professional development, as shown in a number of research and scholarships (Mak & Pun, 2015; Mohammadi & Moradi, 2017; Onguko, 2014; Zhukova, 2018). Literatures in the field of continuous professional development (CPD) for teachers have explored and offer comparisons of the various models of CPD for teachers to provide some insights to what an 'ideal' model of CPD, particularly the ones that promote both continuous and sustainable development, should look like. Kennedy (2005) for example identified a number of key models of CPD and classified them in relation to their capacity for supporting professional autonomy and transformative practice. The transmission category refers to models of CPD which are conceived as fulfilling the function of preparing teachers to implement reforms. The transitional category includes models of CPD which can be placed in between the transmission and transformative categories. These CPD models are considered 'transitional' in the sense that they have the capacity to support underlying agendas compatible with either of the other two categories. The transformative category includes models of CPD which are conceived as supporting teachers in contributing to and shaping education policy and practices (Kennedy, 2005, p. 248). Various literatures have established how the needs of 21st century learners' have changed tremendously compared to yesteryears, and how teachers should adapt and tailor their pedagogical approaches to accommodate these needs better (Greenlaw, 2015; Herman, 2012; Maretich, 2017; Prensky, 2009). As the need for transforming methodology and instructions in the classroom is becoming one of the most prominent topic when discussing 21st century education, it can be argued that teacher professional development should also undergo transformation.

In an attempt to answer this call for transformation, this chapter aims to examine the experiences of Malaysian ESL teachers participating in a transformative TPACK-based professional development which adopted the IDDIRR instructional design (Introduce, Demonstrate, Develop, Implement, Reflect, Revise). In the first part of this chapter, the teachers' perceptions of the effectiveness of the professional development model in engendering technology integration practices in their ESL classroom will be analysed. The second part will discuss the teachers' mobilisation and enactment of TPACK from the professional development setting to their professional practice in the classroom. The affordances and constraints of technology integration in the ESL classroom will be explored in the third part.

BACKGROUND

This chapter aims to explore this phenomenon in the educational context of Malaysia. The choice of Malaysia as the focus of study is justified by the initiatives for education reform in the country which started since more than a decade ago, which include technology integration in education as one of the main agendas. A considerable amount of time has passed between the launch of policy on education reform and the latest implementations based on the policy. It seems pertinent to start analysing to what extent the implementations are impactful, and to explore the potential course of action for the future based on the information gathered.

"Malaysia: The Way Forward (Vision 2020)" is a book written by the Prime Minister of Malaysia, Tun Dr. Mahathir Mohamad which outlined the nation's desire to become a "fully-developed nation" by the year 2020 (Mohamad (Tun), 1991, p. 1). To achieve this, one of the things Malaysia aims to establish is "a scientific and progressive society, a society that is innovative and forward looking, one that is not only a consumer of technology but also a contributor to the scientific and technological civilisation of the future" (p. 2). The Malaysia Ministry of Education responded to this vision by drawing up a Policy on ICT in Education (2010) and outlining eleven shifts to transform the education system in its Education Blueprint (2013-2025). The Policy stated that "more and more integration of ICT into the mainstream education" is necessary in order "to transform and revamp the Malaysian education system" (*Policy on ICT in Education*, 2010, p. 14). In the same vein, the Blueprint listed "leveraging ICT to scale up quality learning across Malaysia" as one of the eleven shifts for education reform (Ministry of Education Malaysia, 2013, p. E20).

More than two decades have passed since the inception of Vision 2020. The Policy is in its penultimate year towards a decade, and the Blueprint is now entering its sixth year of implementation. Throughout the years, the aims and goals outlined in both the Policy as well as the Blueprint have instigated a substantial amount of initiatives at multiple levels to consolidate the use of ICT in schools and education institutions across Malaysia. A number of studies have been conducted by local researchers to examine the impacts of some of these initiatives. Findings from these research echoed the conclusion drawn by several studies which pointed to teacher knowledge and perception of technology as the main factors that contribute towards the low levels of penetration and success of technology integration in the classrooms (e.g. Nikian, Nor, & Aziz, 2013; Simin & Sani, 2015; Thang, Lin, Mahmud, Ismail, & Zabidi, 2014; Umar & Hassan, 2015).

To provide an example, Umar & Hassan (2015) conducted a survey on 2,661 primary and secondary school teachers in Malaysia and found out that despite ICT being perceived as bringing positive impacts on the teachers' teaching and students' learning, the integration was reported to be at the low level. Umar & Hassan claimed that this low level of integration "impede the success of all ICT initiatives introduced by the ministry [of Education]" (p. 2015). They also drew attention to the need for teachers to undergo training to make technology integration in the classroom more impactful. Another example is Thang et al's (2014) study on the concerns of ESL instructors in a Malaysian public university. The findings revealed that some instructors' resistance to technology "could lead to failure in technology integration" (p. 311). Nikian, Nor and Aziz's (2013) study on Malaysian ESL teachers' perception of applying technology in the classroom contributed another insight to this phenomenon. The participants in this research were reported to be users of technology in the classroom and had positive perceptions of technology. However, all of them believed that it is crucial for them to undergo training to enhance their technological knowledge. The study also listed a few constraints to effective technology integration. This included the lack of technology equipment, minimal technical support, absence of access to certain facilities and time constraint.

Teacher Knowledge and Technological Pedagogical Content Knowledge (TPACK)

Teacher cognition is an overarching area of research that seeks to understand teachers thinking, knowledge and beliefs, and their relationships to practices in the classroom (Borg, 2003, 2015). The notion that teachers are active and thinking decision makers who play an important role in determining what is going on in the classroom is the impetus for research on teacher cognition (Borg, 2015). One of the research areas under the field of teacher cognition is teacher knowledge. Mishra & Koehler's (2006) technological pedagogical content knowledge framework, commonly known as TPCK or TPACK, is one of the most recent contribution in the field of teacher knowledge. The TPACK framework incorporates a technological knowledge domain into Shulman's (1986) concept of pedagogical content knowledge (PCK). The framework demonstrates an interplay among knowledge of technology, pedagogy and content. It describes how this interplay is crucial for meaningful technology integration in the classroom.

Mishra & Koehler introduced TPACK as a framework to help teachers develop "nuanced understandings" of the dynamic equilibrium among the three components (p. 1030). They argued that the traditional methods of training for technology integration such as workshops and courses are no longer relevant in helping teachers integrate technology effectively in the classroom (p. 1032). They advocated the 'learning-technology-by-design' approach that enables teachers to be engaged in educational technology design which encourages them to understand the complexity of the relationships between the three domains (p. 1038). To provide an overview of the TPACK framework, Mishra & Koehler (2006) described seven knowledge domains: pedagogical knowledge (PK), content knowledge (CK), technological knowledge (TK), pedagogical content knowledge (PCK), technological content knowledge (TCK), technological pedagogical knowledge (TPK) and technological pedagogical content knowledge (TPACK).

Pedagogical knowledge (PK) refers to the knowledge of the nature of teaching and learning which includes teaching methods, classroom management, instructional planning, assessment of student learning, etc. Content knowledge (CK) refers to the knowledge of the subject matter to be taught. Technological knowledge (TK) is a continually changing and evolving knowledge base that includes knowledge of technology for information processing, communications and problem solving. TK focuses on the productive application of technology in both work and daily life.

Pedagogical content knowledge (PCK) describes the knowledge of pedagogies, teaching practices and planning processes applicable and appropriate to teaching a given subject matter. Technological content knowledge (TCK) is defined as the relationship between subject matter and technology, including knowledge of technology that has influenced and is used in exploring a given content discipline. Technological pedagogical knowledge (TPK), on the other hand, is knowledge of the technological influence on teaching and learning, as well as the affordances and constraints of technology in regard to educational designs and strategies. Technological pedagogical content knowledge (TPACK) is the domain that characterises the knowledge of complex interactions among principle domains (content, pedagogy and technology).

According to Judi Harris, Koehler, & Mishra (2009), the TPACK framework "seeks to assist the development of better techniques for discovering and describing how technology-related professional knowledge is implemented and instantiated in practice" (p. 67). This allows teachers or educators to better understand the varied levels of technological integration. Moreover, it enables teachers and educators to go beyond the simplified approaches of treating technology as an "add on". Instead, they can focus on the connections between technology, content and pedagogy in the classroom context. Figure 1 summarises the TPACK model as described by Mishra & Koehler (2006).

Recently, there is also a growing number of studies investigating the development of TPACK and its complex relationship with its different knowledge components (Beriswill, Bracey, Sherman-Morris, Huang, & Lee, 2016; Celik, Sahin, & Akturk, 2014; Chaemchoy, 2017). However, there is a dearth of literature investigating teacher experiences of professional development and self-ownership in creating teaching and learning tools for local usage; with the exception of Lee, Ng, & Tan (2014). Lee et al. examined technological pedagogical content knowledge (TPACK) development with a group of Malaysian teachers. They found that the process of designing and implementing digital materials was helpful for integrating technology into the curriculum. The processes of material development allowed teachers to mobilise their multiple knowledge on curricular contents, education and technology. The adoption of this framework for teacher professional development particularly that of in-service ESL teachers, is timely and relevant. This is if the knowledge of teachers can be advanced as a result of the learning environment and experiences provided by professional development sessions. These exposures include new perspectives on teaching and learning that hold promises of more effective pedagogical practice in classrooms which will enhance student learning; such as the school of thought of constructivism, sociocultural theory and ideas like communities of practices, technological mediated learning, mental models, modelling, conceptual change and mediations.

Figure 1. Graphic presentation of technological pedagogical content knowledge framework

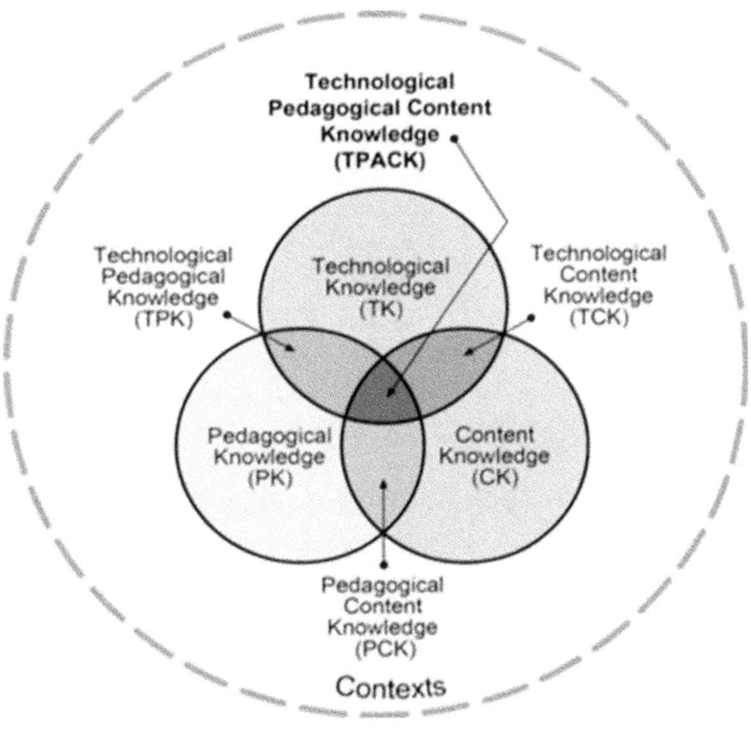

The TPACK-IDDIRR Model

The conceptual model that underpins the approach adopted in this study is the IDDIRR (Introduce, Demonstrate, Develop, Implement, Reflect, Revise) model (Lee & Kim, 2014). The TPACK-IDDIR model is shown in Figure 2 below.

In order to facilitate teachers' TPACK development, the technology integration sessions should include explicit and systematic procedures. Based on the TPACK-IDDIRR model, the role of the trainer or facilitator is to introduce and demonstrate. The training should include a discussion of definitions and teaching examples relevant to TPACK. The purpose is to enhance the understanding of TPACK domains among teachers. The development stage is undertaken by teachers; they should be involved in the development of several lesson plans that integrate various technological tools to enhance the connection of technology to specific content and pedagogy. The development of lesson plans should be followed by the implementation of a technology-integrated lesson in the classroom to help transfer that knowledge to practice.

For learning to occur, the implementation stage must be followed by a reflection on the TPACK-based lesson, along with a revision of that lesson. The TPACK-IDDIRR model, when adopted in professional development programmes for teachers, provides opportunities for sustainable development as it fulfils most of the criteria for effective professional development; i.e. it takes into account the appropriateness of the needs of individual classrooms, it provides opportunities for teachers to collaborate and it is grounded on the main objective of enhancing student learning and achievements.

Figure 2. The TPACK-IDDIRR Model (Lee & Kim, 2014)

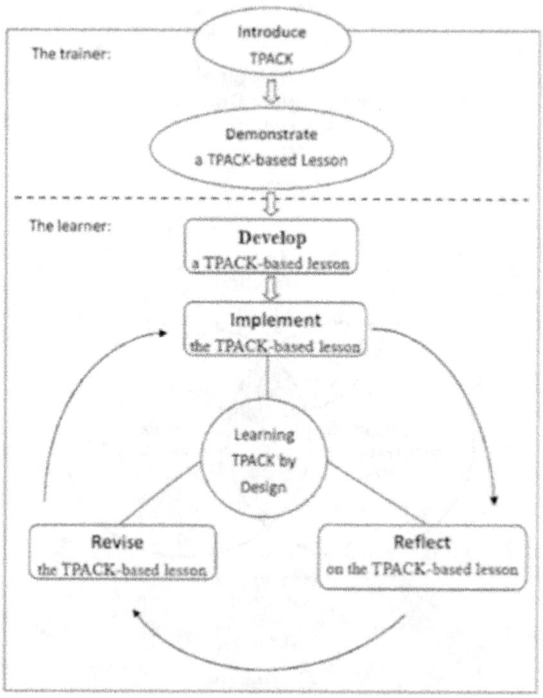

TPACK, Second Language Education, and Teacher Professional Development

Despite the large bodies of research on technology integration in language education, there is a dearth of literature discussing the TPACK framework in the context of second or foreign language education (Judi Harris, Koehler, & Mishra, 2009). For instance, Belo, Belo, McKenney, Voogt, & Bradley (2016) reviewed studies on TPACK and language teaching from 2002 to 2012 and discovered only 46 studies on language teaching and learning that incorporated the TPACK framework as part of their research designs. Narrowing the search to the specific context of English as a second language (ESL) would reveal greater paucity (Koçoğlu, 2009).

Current research in the field are heavily focusing on the different ways TPACK can be measured using different types of instruments. For example, Abbitt (2011) reported to have reviewed more than 300 unique publications which included journal articles and conference proceedings focusing on measuring the TPACK of both pre-service and in-service teachers through various instruments such as self-assessment surveys, classroom observations, teachers' reflective journals and assessment of classroom artifacts. TPACK research on actual classroom practices are also quite substantial in number, but many are focusing on the application of TPACK in Science and Mathematics pedagogy (J. B. Harris & Hofer, 2017; Jang & Tsai, 2012; Koh, Chai, & Lee, 2015).

The intention of the TPACK framework as proposed by Mishra & Koehler (2006) was to "transform the conceptualisation and the practice of teacher education, teacher training, and teachers' professional development" (p. 1019). Brantley-Dias & Ertmer (2013) echoed this by pointing out that TPACK was originally "intended for teacher educators" and that it should provide a way for teachers to discuss technology and the knowledge needed to make its application in the classroom successful (p. 107). There are quite extensive amount of research focusing on the impacts of particular teacher training models on the TPACK acquisition of teachers (Brantley-Dias & Ertmer, 2013; Cavanagh & Koehler, 2013). However, many of these studies focused on pre-service teachers and conducted in teacher preparation programme settings (Dong, Chai, Sang, Koh, & Tsai, 2015; Koh, Chai, & Lim, 2017). Hofer & Harris (2012) pointed that experienced teachers' greater familiarity with teaching and curriculum caused them to have distinctive knowledge of technology. Spires, Hervey, & Watson (2013) stated that different groups of teachers with different levels of expertise bring different strengths to TPACK-based professional development for teachers. More TPACK research focusing on in-service teachers should contribute to more knowledge and insights on technology integration in education.

Professional Learning Community as a Platform of Teacher Professional Development to Enhance Technology Integration in the Classroom

The concept of professional learning community (PLC) is based on an idea developed by the business sector. The concept is based on the utilisation of organisation members' capacity to learn and acquire skills through collaborative professional learning (Vescio, Ross, & Adams, 2008). The idea has been modified to suit the education context, where the concept of a learning organisation was turned into a learning community that works together to build collaborative cultures among teachers (M. Park & So, 2014; Spencer, 2016; Thompson, Gregg, & Niska, 2004).

The implementation of professional learning communities in education context is grounded on two assumptions. The first assumption is that knowledge is situated in the day-to-day and first-hand experiences of teachers. Therefore, it is best understood through critical reflection with others who share the same experiences. The second assumption is that when teachers are actively engaged in professional development activities through PLC, their professional knowledge will increase, and students' learning will enhance as a result (Buysse, Sparkman, & Wesley, 2003). In addition to the two assumptions, DuFour & DuFour (2010) introduced Three Big Ideas to be incorporated in the implementation of PLC, i.e. the commitment to high levels of learning for all students, the imperative of a collaborative and collective effort to fulfil that commitment and the intense focus on results that enables a school to respond to the needs of each student, inform teacher practices and fuel continuous improvement (p. 77). Also fundamental in the PLC framework are the five dimensions conceptualised by Hord (1997) and later modified by Hipp & Huffman (2003). The five dimensions are supportive and shared leadership; shared values, norms, vision and mission; collective learning and application of learning; supportive conditions; and shared personal practice. These dimensions are widely accepted as valid constructs to measure the effectiveness of PLC in schools and institutions (Abbot, Lee, & Rossiter, 2018; Blitz & Schulman, 2016; Guskey, 2014; Song & Choi, 2017). In line with the principles underpinned by the two assumptions, the Three Big Ideas, and the five dimensions, various research on the impacts of PLC on the enhancement of student learning have consistently pointed towards its valuable role in supporting the professional development of teachers (Brissenden-Smith, Moreno, Peloquin, Radiloff, & Wachtel, 2018; Brown, Horn, & King, 2018; Easton, 2015).

Due to its ability to link professional development and classroom practices, PLC is rapidly gaining acceptance as an effective model of professional development to enhance teachers' technology integration practices in the classroom (Cheah, Chai, & Toh, 2019; Thoma, Hutchison, Johnson, Johnson, & Stromer, 2017). For example, Thoma et al. (2017) found that PLC is effective in improving teachers' use of technology in literacy instructions because it provides opportunities for teachers to develop common formative assessment as well as gives them ample time to learn from one another and from a facilitator (knowledgeable peer). Ertmer & Ottenbreit-Leftwich (2010) in discussing the importance of teacher self-efficacy in ensuring effective technology integration practices argued that "time and effort should be devoted to increasing teachers' confidence for using technology…to achieve student learning objectives" (p. 261). To increase teachers' confidence and personal mastery, teachers should be given the opportunities to work with knowledgeable peers within a PLC setting where professional development can be situated within the context of teachers' ongoing works (Ertmer & Ottenbreit-Leftwich, 2010). In Malaysia, PLC is increasingly gaining popularity, as indicated by a number of studies conducted in local contexts. Besides shown to be effective as a strategy to improve schools' performances, the findings from these studies also pointed towards the merit of PLC as a conduit to enhance teachers' professional and instructional practices (Abdullah & A. Ghani, 2014; Hassan, Ahmad, & Boon, 2018; Saad, Walsh, Mallaburn, & Brundrett, 2017; Tahir et al., 2013).

Cheah et al. (2019) highlighted the need for "creating cohesive TPACK development spaces across communities" through effective management of the contradictions between teachers' personal and contextual factors (p. 161). They referred to the term "TPACK in-design" and TPACK in-action" which described the mobilisation of knowledge from the design context (professional development in a PLC outside the school) to the context where TPACK is put in action (within-school PLC). This aptly describes the main interest of this chapter.

PART 1: EXPLORING ESL TEACHERS' TPACK DEVELOPMENT THROUGH PROFESSIONAL LEARNING COMMUNITY

Context

'Going Digital' is the name given to a professional learning community formed by a group of ESL practitioners in Malaysia in 2016. A total of 18 participants volunteered to take part in this year-long study. The participants are between the ages of 31 to 49, with teaching experiences ranging from 8 to 26 years. Out of 18 participants, 5 of them taught in primary schools, 8 taught in secondary schools and 2 taught at pre-university level. 3 participants were attached to the district education office as teacher coaches and facilitators for English literacy. 38.8% (7) of participants taught in urban schools, 27.8% (5) taught in suburban schools, 16.7% (3) taught in villages and rural areas, while 16.7% (3) were attached to the district education office as teacher coaches and facilitators. 16.7% (3) of participants were male, while 83.3% (15) were female.

The community was formed with the main purpose of providing a professional yet friendly and conducive platforms for its members to share knowledge about technology integration in the classroom, to collaborate on technology-based projects and to inspire one another. The members of the community got together once or twice every month to engage in interactive workshops and teacher-sharing sessions. The members also communicated regularly through a WhatsApp group chat. Records of the community's activities as well as samples of technology-based projects and artifacts can be accessed through the 'Going Digital' website (www.goingdigitalkotakinabalu.weebly.com).

A Transformative Model of Teacher Professional Development

A series of technology-integrated sessions were conducted to provide teachers with the opportunity and platform to exchange ideas, learn from each other and collaborate (see Table 1). The sessions were accomplished based on the PLC model of teacher sharing sessions (TSS); whereby, no trainer or instructor was present – everyone in the room was an expert in his/her own right. There was a group leader who played the role of the main facilitator during the sessions. However, her role was more as a coordinator to ensure that everything ran smoothly rather than as an expert or 'source of knowledge'. This was in line with the first dimension of PLC, which is supportive and shared leadership. In this learning community, everyone was a leader, and everyone supported each other. In addition to providing a conducive and safe environment (as outlined in the third dimension of PLC), some 'digital natives' (i.e., pre-service teachers) were recruited as facilitators (knowledgeable peers) since they are more adept at using various technological tools. Their role was to offer support in the technical aspect as 'digital immigrants' embarked on the journey of exploring various technological tools to develop their digital language learning materials and technology-based lessons.

These sessions via TSS adopted the TPACK-IDDIRR model where teachers were first introduced to the TPACK framework and technology-based lessons through samples and demonstrations. They were then given the opportunity to design their own technology-based lessons and to develop tools that can support lesson delivery. This was either done individually or in groups. Teachers were given time in between sessions to implement these lessons in their own classrooms. After implementation, the teachers reflected on the strengths and weaknesses, along with what went well and what needed to be changed or improved. Based on these reflections, the teachers worked on improving or revising their lesson plans

Table 1. The project phases and activities involved

Phase	Mode (Support)	Activities
Introduce (I) Demonstrate (D)	Face-to-face (TSS 1)	Introduction to TPACK Demonstration of TPACK-based lessons
Develop (D)	Face-to-face (TSS 2)	Participants develop TPACK-based lessons.
Implement (I)	Not face-to-face (Online)	Participants implement TPACK- based lessons in the classroom.
Reflect (R)	Face-to-face (TSS 3)	Participants showcase TPACK- based lessons and share their reflections. Participants obtain feedback from other participants.

and digital language learning materials. This process provided teachers with the avenue for collective learning and application in accordance with PLC's third dimension.

The IRR stage (Implement, Reflect, Revise) of the model was cyclical and repetitively conducted to provide teachers with an opportunity to experience the design process more than once (Lee & Kim, 2014). The iterative characteristic of the model, as pointed out by Lee & Kim (2014), is important as it will enhance teachers' learning of TPACK (p. 443). To further cater to the fifth dimension of PLC, which is "shared personal practice", the TSS was extended beyond face-to-face sessions to include an online platform where all classroom practices, digital materials, lesson plans and reflections of teachers were shared through a website specifically designed for this purpose. Teachers contributed to the content of the website by sending their revised lesson plans, materials and reflections as many times as they liked while undergoing the iterative process of implementing, reflecting and revising. This online extension to PLC provided teachers with additional support to ensure that their TPACK development is sustainable beyond face-to-face sessions.

This model of professional development is part of the second dimension of PLC, which is shared missions or objectives. The members of this learning community work on the same mission to enhance the quality of learning for their students. They engage in collaborative and collective efforts to improve student outcomes, thereby consummating the Three Big Ideas of PLC (Dufour & DuFour, 2010). Figure 3 displays the design of this model which combines the TPACK framework, the TPACK-IDDIRR model and professional learning community (PLC).

Capturing ESL Teachers' Experiences with the TPACK-IDDIRR + PLC Model

To capture the teachers' experiences of adopting the IDDIRR instructional design model to develop technology-based lessons for their ESL classrooms, data were collected through three main instruments. i.e. surveys, interviews and written reflections.

- **Reflective Log**

The teachers were requested to keep a reflective log. They were told to record what was significant to them as they underwent the IDDIRR instructional design stages. They shared their reflections on a website (http://goingdigitalkotakinabalu.weebly.com) specifically designed for this purpose.

Figure 3. TPACK-IDDIRR + PLC Framework

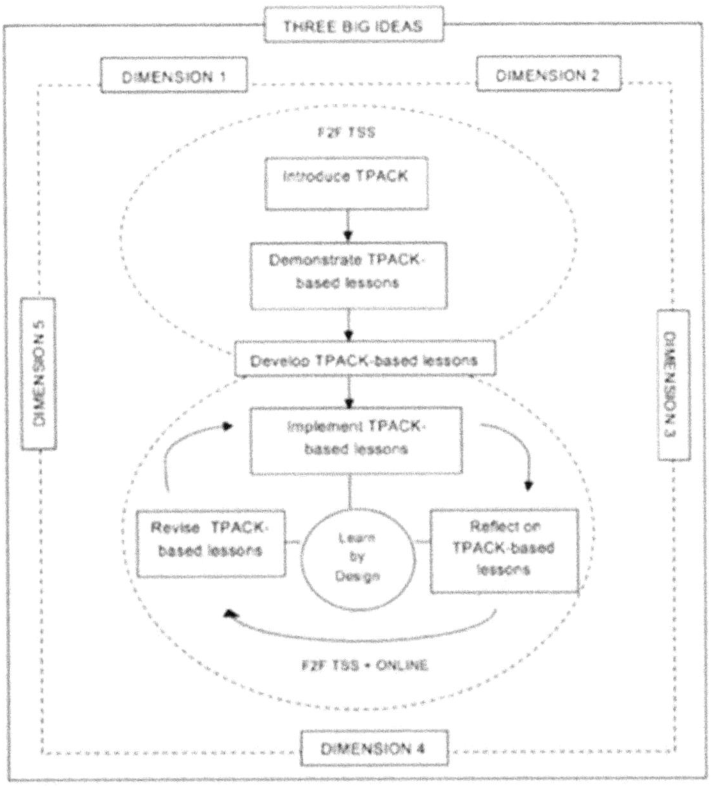

- **Questionnaire**

Besides reflection, a self-constructed questionnaire consisting of seven items with a four-point Likert scale was handed out to the teachers so as to gather their insights on professional development activities of the project. The Likert scale ranged from 1- Strongly Disagree, 2 – Disagree, 3 – Agree to 4 – Strongly Agree. The seven items focused on how professional development activities provided teachers with:

- The knowledge of how to effectively integrate educational technologies to increase student opportunities of interacting with ideas;
- The knowledge and skills necessary to flexibly incorporate new tools and resources into content and teaching methods to enhance learning;
- Teaching methods that use technology to teach content and provide learners with the opportunity to interact with ideas;
- An understanding of what makes certain concepts difficult to learn for students and how technology can be used to improve student learning;
- An understanding of how to integrate technology to build upon students' prior knowledge of subject matters;

- An understanding of how to operate classroom technologies as well as incorporating them into particular content area or grade level to enhance student learning;
- Providing strong technological pedagogical content knowledge.
    - **Interview**

Interviews were conducted in small groups of 3-4 teachers based on availability through informal meetings and WhatsApp discussions. The interview questions were designed to elicit teacher experiences in planning, designing and implementing technology-based lessons hinged on the IDDIRR framework. The interviews were audio-recorded and selectively documented for analysis. See Appendix A for the interview protocol.

Summary of Findings

The findings suggest that teachers perceive the professional development sessions which adopted the TPACK - IDDIRR + PLC model as effective in inspiring them to integrate more technology in their English language classrooms. It appears that the TPACK-IDDIRR instructional design framework (Lee & Kim, 2014) provided teachers with a 'structured' approach to integrate technology that is both explicit and systematic to work with. The positive endorsement was reflected in all seven items of the survey, demonstrating that teachers have acquired the necessary knowledge and skills needed to integrate technology into their practice. The feedback obtained via reflections and interviews affirm that the TPACK - IDDIRR + PLC model helped teachers see how technology integration can increase their teaching effectiveness in numerous ways. This was supported by Lee & Kim's (2014) study, leading to the conclusion that this form of professional development has the potential to be adopted as a model to enhance teachers' TPACK. The model appears to be helpful in providing teachers with a platform to learn how technology can affect student education and improve their teaching in several ways.

The findings further suggest that PLC has provided teachers with a safe and conducive environment to learn and be inspired. The presence of more knowledgeable peers in PLC gave the much-needed support for teachers, particularly in the technical aspects of technology. The teachers appreciated the friendly learning atmosphere and felt less vulnerable since no one was seen as an expert. The findings of this study are similar to previous research investigating the impacts of PLC in regard to the advancement of teacher knowledge (Brissenden-Smith, Moreno, Peloquin, Radiloff, & Wachtel, 2018; Brown, Horn, & King, 2018; Easton, 2015).

The results also pointed towards the need for teacher professional development to be extended beyond the conventional face-to-face sessions. They should include additional and continuous support in the form of online platforms such as websites or other interactive social media platforms. The websites and social media platforms act like an e-portfolio for teachers to share their reflections. The TPACK-IDDIRR framework seemed to have helped teachers focus their reflections on the domains of TK, CK, PK, TCK, PCK, TPK and TPACK. These findings are similar to Ching et al.'s (2016) results on enhancing graduate students' reflections in e-portfolios using the TPACK framework.

The findings highlight the importance of teachers' pedagogical, subject and technological knowledge, as well as the presence of a supportive PLC for teachers' TPACK acquisition. In most previous studies, TPACK was taught as integrated knowledge (Mishra & Koehler, 2006). This study's findings echo Lee & Kim's (2014) research which suggest that isolated domains of TPACK should be introduced in a structured manner within a supportive environment for change to occur. The use of dedicated websites and social media sharing are needed to provide teachers with an avenue for sharing their best practices and reflections. In other words, an online site will function as a huge e-portfolio to track updates and development among PLC members (Ching, Yang, Baek, & Baldwin, 2016).

PART 2: FROM PROFESSIONAL LEARNING TO PROFESSIONAL PRACTICE

TPACK includes discussions on the inferential and application aspects of the framework. The inferential aspect refers to how teacher trainers can use the framework to predict the contexts for effective teaching with technology which enables them to design and implement training programmes that are relevant and helpful for teachers. Application refers to how TPACK can help teachers and students explore learning contexts that can employ technology as an enhancing tool for better understanding of the subject matter (J. Harris et al., 2009; Mishra & Koehler, 2006).

These inferential and application aspects of TPACK point towards the contexts in which the framework operates. The inferential aspect discusses the framework's application in a professional development setting, while the application aspect adopts the framework in classroom setting. In this chapter, these two aspects are contextualised within the scope of ESL teachers' professional development and classroom practices. Figure 4 demonstrates how the two contexts interconnect.

Figure 4 demonstrates the TPACK framework in two different contexts, i.e. the professional development context and the professional practice context. The professional development context refers to TPACK-based teacher trainings while the professional practice context refers to classrooms and schools where teachers practice what they learn from their trainings. The intersection between the contexts represents the transition phase when teachers move from training to practice.

Judi Harris, Grandgenett, & Hofer (2010) developed a TPACK-based technology integration instrument where the components of technology, pedagogy and content are contextualised within the classroom setting. This chapter will further specify this contextualisation by focusing on the specific area of English as a Second Language (ESL). In this chapter, 'technology' refers specifically to the technology selections for teaching and learning which include hardware, software, tools and resources appropriate and

Figure 4. Mobilisation of TPACK between two ESL contexts

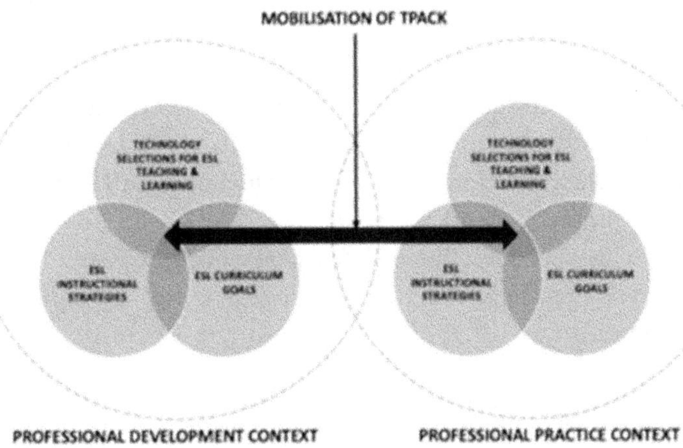

relevant for ESL classroom context. 'Pedagogy' is described as the instructional strategies and classroom approaches for the teaching of English as a second language. 'Content' is defined as the learning goals and standards as specified by the ESL curriculum.

Mobilisation and Enactment of Teacher Knowledge

Research in the field of teacher knowledge mobilisation mainly concerns with the transfer of knowledge from research to practice (La Velle & Flores, 2018; Levin, 2013; Naidorf, 2014; Younie et al., 2018). In this chapter, however, the mobilisation of teacher knowledge refers to the movement of knowledge from professional development context to classroom practice. It describes a post-training / pre-enactment phase where teachers usually do some reflections and self-evaluations, consider the affordances and constraints of technology integration, evaluate their strengths and weaknesses, as well as think deeply about students' needs and the most effective pedagogical strategies before adopting what they have learned into practice.

La Velle & Flores (2018) defined knowledge mobilisation as the "transfer of available knowledge into active use" (p. 28). To describe the movements of knowledge from learning to practice, La Velle & Flores used terms such as "knowledge acquisition" (where teachers acquire knowledge from research, or in the context of this chapter, professional development), "knowledge mobilisation" (the transition between knowledge acquisition to classroom practice) and "knowledge utilisation" (referring to how the knowledge is utilised in classroom teaching). Longhurst, Jones, & Campbell (2017) used the term "knowledge appropriation" to describe the enactment of knowledge acquired from a professional development in the classroom. Braun, Maguire, & Ball (2010) pointed out that understanding of the factors that influence the reasons and ways teachers enact the knowledge from professional development is essential for the design, implementation and funding of future teacher professional learning.

'Zooming In': Making Sense of Individual Experiences of Teachers

The successful execution of the TPACK-IDDIRR + PLC model had inspired the authors to 'zoom-in' on individual experiences of the members of the 'Going Digital' community, as a follow-up to the study by K. W. Lee & James (2018). A follow-up is important for a number of reasons. First, it can address the matters that were absent from the previous study, such as the personal experiences of ESL teachers as individual learners, and how these teachers mobilise the knowledge acquired through the professional learning community into technology integration practices in the ESL classrooms. This is in line with Creswell & Poth's (2017) view on the importance of follow-up, which listed furthering an end in a particular study and reviewing new developments as among the reasons for follow-up research. Secondly, follow-ups could also "be conducted subsequent to the original research to ascertain if an intervention has changed the lives of the study participants" (Salkind, 2010, p. 2). It is worth exploring whether a teacher learning community which was formed two years ago and is still active to this very day is still able to impact its members' professional practices.

To provide multiplicity of perspectives, four ESL teachers who represented different types of schools, years of experiences and levels of technological skills were selected as participants. Table 2 summarises the profiles of each participant.

Strategy of Inquiry

For this follow-up study, narrative inquiry was adopted as a strategy of inquiry. Narrative accounts of each participant's experiences were constructed by adopting the "three-dimensional narrative inquiry space" framework, where the commonplaces of temporality, sociality and place were taken into account (D. J. Clandinin & Connelly, 1994, 2004; J. D. Clandinin, 2013). Temporality refers to the participants' reflections of their past (participation in 'Going Digital'), present (their current practice) and future (plans and insights). Sociality describes the participants' interactions with their environment, with the 'Going Digital' and their schools' communities, and with the milieus. Sociality also refers to inward interactions and personal reflections, aesthetics, feelings and moral dispositions (Clandinin, 2013). In this study, place can refer to both physical places (e.g. school, classroom, outside school) and metaphorical places (e.g. "the digital oceans", the "real world").

To construct the narrative accounts, the participants' individual experiences were captured through teachers' project reports and interviews.

- **Teachers' Project Reports**

The participants were requested to write up a report of the technology-based projects that they conducted in their classrooms following their participation in the 'Going Digital.' To guide the teachers, a report outline was provided (See Appendix B).

- **Interview**

The purpose of the interview was to capture stories and information that were not recorded in the project report. The interview provided the participants with the chance to reflect on their experiences of transitioning between the 'Going Digital' professional development to their professional practice in the classroom.

Teachers' Narrative Accounts

Data from the teachers' project reports and the interviews were used to construct narrative accounts of the participants' experiences of participating in the 'Going Digital' community and practicing what they learned in the classroom. To ensure accurate representations of the teachers' personal experiences, each narrative went through what was referred to as the first level of analysis by Clandinin (2013). This

Table 2. Profiles of participants

Participant	Age	Teaching Experience	Context
Arsyad	Early 30	7 years	Sports school, sub-urban area
Erica	Early 40	14 years	Primary school, rural area
Adele	Early 40	17 years	Convent (all-girls) secondary school, urban area
Lim	Early 40	17 years	Chinese secondary school, urban area

Table 3. Summary of the participants' narrative accounts

Arsyad: 'The Young Teacher'
Arsyad taught in a sports boarding school located in the suburban area. The school catered to young athletes who represented the country in various sports and games. Arsyad described himself as a young teacher who knew a lot about technology and the importance of integrating technology in his ESL lessons. As the youngest participant, Arsyad was very impressed to see teachers who were way more experienced taking part in 'Going Digital.' He recalled saying to himself: "What excuse do you have? You're still young, there's so much you can do." Arsyad did not find much difficulty in adopting what he had learned from 'Going Digital' to his practice in the classroom. Instead of technological competence, he defined challenges in terms of identifying the most pertinent approaches to technology integration that could make learning meaningful for his students. Before coming up with his technology-based project, Arsyad reflected on his 'failed' 'A Word A Day' and 'Book Review' projects. Arsyad recalled his frustrations over the dwindling interests in the two activities among the students. For 'A Word A Day,' the same word would stay on the board for weeks. As for the 'Book Review,' most students relied heavily on the teachers to provide them with the texts, rather than working on them independently. Despite this, Arsyad realised that his students were not completely apathetic when it came to the use of English language in daily conversations. The students actually did use English voluntarily when interacting with one another on social media like Facebook and Instagram. Arsyad noticed his students' aptitudes towards vlogging and video-making, so he decided "to manipulate this inclination" by coming up with what he called the 60-Second Project. The 60-Second Project required students to record a 60-second video of themselves talking about a topic of their choice. A topic could be chosen based on a pre-determined list of themes. The project started with students conducting research on their chosen topic at the school's language lab. It was quite an impressive language lab – well-equipped with 25 computers, LCD projectors, headphones, audio speakers and good Internet connection. Once the research was done, students went out to shoot their videos. After the recordings were completed, students worked on the editing which were mostly done using free mobile phones video-editing apps. Arsyad held a video-watching session in the classroom on the 6th week, and he found the responses from the students to be inspiring. Arsyad was elated to witness how the videos were able to spark interesting and meaningful conversations among his students. The final products were uploaded on the project's official Instagram account, the InstaStoryTellers19 (https://www.instagram.com/instastorytellers19/). Arsyad's challenges came in the form of negotiating the tensions between the students' many responsibilities – as learners, as athletes and as examination candidates. For Arsyad, this was the biggest challenge he had to face in executing technology-based projects because according to him, "we want them to engage in lessons, definitely. But at the same time, it's always at the back of our mind that we want them to perform well in their examinations as well." Another challenge was the school rule which forbid the use of mobile phones by students. This made the decision to conduct a project using mobile phones a challenging endeavour. Although Arsyad was able to seek permission from the school warden, he still thought that the lack of freedom restricted the students to a certain degree, because only "phones with basic functions" were allowed. Another thing Arsyad wished he could have done differently was the way the selection of topics and themes for the videos were done. For future projects, he hoped to give the students more independence and autonomy to explore options and alternatives, and to discover their vast potentials in the process. He planned to expand a project that he was currently doing with his pre-university students which integrated the literature circle approach with technology through the use of TED-talk videos.
Erica: 'The Simple Teacher'
The rural primary school was located about 100 kilometres from the state capital. Erica had worked in the school for nine years as an ESL teacher. She was in her early 40's and had 14 years of experience under her belt. As far as technology is concerned, Erica admitted that she was "probably not very good at it" but she loved it very much. She enjoyed exchanging ideas and learning about tools and apps to integrate technology in her ESL lessons with other members of the 'Going Digital' community. Although she confessed that not all of the tools and apps shared were directly applicable to her rural classroom, she appreciated the new knowledge that she gained. The idea of getting students to be "the doer" sat well with Erica's teaching philosophy. Erica described herself as a "simple person" who liked "direct and transparent things." As a language teacher, this meant getting her students to "learn by doing." In Erica's words: "If they want to learn speaking, they need to speak. It's all about doing it." This is evident through the technology-based project that Erica chose to conduct with her Year 4 (age 10) students. She wanted to improve her students narrative writing skills, so she decided to do the digital storytelling project. The inspiration came after learning about an app called Voki, which exploited the combination of images, voices and texts to tell a story. Erica thought it was a fun app to use in her classroom, but due to the poor Internet connection in her school she was not able to share it with her students. She realised that basic Microsoft Office applications such as the PowerPoint was provided for free in all the school's computers and netbooks – and that they required no Internet connection. Erica decided to use PowerPoint as a tool to help her students blend images, voices and texts to create their own digital stories. Erica's students enjoyed creating digital stories very much, but they were frustrated by the poor Internet connection and "low-performing hardware" provided by the school. Erica was concerned that this might cause some of the students to lose interest. To keep the momentum going, Erica resolved these issues by allowing the students to use her own mobile Internet hotspot. Although she realised that the outdated equipment and poor Internet connection provided extra challenges to her effort of integrating technology in her ESL lessons, Erica was determined to do it because "the students enjoyed learning using computers" and that "the school is the only place where they can get access to computers." Erica also admitted to using technology as a "bait" to "attract students to learn English in a different way, in a high-tech way." Knowing that they would have the opportunity to use the computer to convert their stories into digital format made the students excited about writing, "in a way that they had never done before." The success of the digital storytelling project inspired Erica to conduct similar projects in the future, perhaps in a larger scale. For future projects, she hoped to explore the use of digital storytelling in improving her students' listening and speaking skills.
Adele: 'The Digital Immigrant Teacher'
Adele had been teaching English in the all-girls convent school for almost her entire career. As far as technology is concerned, the self-professed "digital immigrant" described herself as someone "whose bragging rights are only limited to Microsoft Word and maybe PowerPoint." Adele described her participation in the 'Going Digital' community as an experience that had opened up her eyes "to the endless possibilities of exploiting the programmes and applications available for classroom use." Despite being greatly inspired, she also believed that it was something that was totally out of her comfort zone. She described it as a "plunge into the deep end of the digital ocean from the highest cliff." However, the peer support that she received from other members of the community enabled her to derive the optimal benefits from the learning experience. Despite her lack of confidence in her technological skills, Adele was motivated to explore ways she could use technology "to enrich the classroom experience." She decided to explore the potentials of PowToon, a free online software for creating animated presentations, which she was introduced to at 'Going Digital.' Adele decided to take this 'plunge' with 28 students in her Form 4 (age 16) class. Working in groups, the students would need to come up with animated presentations to describe themselves and their group members using metaphors, riddles and imagery. Through this project, the students were able to learn how to use metaphors, riddles and imagery to describe someone or something. But more than that, Adele was also happy that the students were able "to exploit a digital tool to make their presentation more interesting, which would be valuable for their future, especially in college or university." Just like any other technology-based project, Adele's PowToon project was not immune to challenges. Internet connection seemed to be the main problem, despite the school's urban location. As an animation creator software, PowToon required high-speed Internet connection for it to function effectively. Adele tried to solve the problem by seeking permission from the school administrators to allow the students to bring their mobile hotspot or portable wi-fi to school. Another big challenge was the lack of computers. The school did not have a computer lab, and the laptops available for use were very limited. Again, Adele managed to resolve this issue by getting the school administrators to grant the permission for students to bring their laptops to school. Since not every student was in a possession of a laptop, Adele needed to make slight rearrangements to the students' groupings. This was to ensure that every group had at least one laptop to work with. At the inception of the project, Adele did not have a lot of confidence in using and teaching her students how to use PowToon. As the project progressed, Adele gradually discovered that these initial worries did not actually matter. To make up for her "lack of technological competence," the students "took the lead" as they "explored the programme together." Adele believed that in order to make her digital 'migration' successful, she needed to keep "an open mind and an open heart." She needed "to pick up the courage to conduct trials and errors and be better." For her future projects, she hoped to explore "other programmes that are less demanding on Internet speed" to ensure a more seamless experience for all the students.
Lim: 'The Practical Teacher'

continued on following page

Table 3. Continued

Arsyad: 'The Young Teacher'
Lim recounted that the use of technology in education had been "a long-time fascination" for him. He had always been intrigued by the potentials of technology, how it "changes the dynamics of the classroom" and how "it allows materials to be presented in a myriad of ways." However, he also admitted that his use of technology in the classroom had "mostly been borne out of practicality," i.e. technology offered him the affordance to "reuse materials repeatedly with only slight modifications." To provide an example, Lim explained that he used a lot of "recyclable" PowerPoint slides, videos and music in his language lessons. Occasionally, he would use Microsoft Word for the students to type in "some sort of input, such as an answer to a question." When it came to assessments, however, Lim still adhered to "more traditional means – copied exercises, or through the exercises found in a workbook." Lim was well-aware of the possibility of using technology to conduct assessments. At various points in his teaching career, he had had the opportunity to use digital assessment tools like Authorware and Hot Potatoes. While being "very capable" assessment tools, Lim believed the drawbacks for both were "the steep learning curve, as well as the time needed to prepare an assessment." Lim was introduced to Kahoot! during a sharing session in 'Going Digital.' He "quickly saw how it could be used as a means to evaluate what has been learned." Lim realised how much he enjoyed taking part in the Kahoot! quiz carried out during the session, and how well it reinforced his understanding of the content being shared earlier. For him, "Kahoot! seemed to tick all the right boxes in an assessment tool – it was fun and engaging, and most importantly, it seemed easy enough to set up." As he did further explorations, Lim discovered a function on Kahoot! that makes it possible to obtain more detailed analysis of the students' responses. With this new discovery, Lim was enthusiastic to carry out a Kahoot! session with his students. He decided to focus on assessing his students' mastery of Simple Past and Past Continuous. To prepare his students, Lim conducted a series of four lessons. The Kahoot! session was carried out in the school library over two 40-minute sessions. Lim used the schools' Chromebooks and Internet connection. The school had enough Chromebooks for each and every 35 students. However, from past experiences of using the school's Internet connection, too many users would normally cause laggings and delays. In order to overcome this problem, Lim decided to reduce the number of users by putting the students in groups of five. The students were supposed to take turns answering the questions individually. Lim was delighted to discover that by "downloading the game results data from the Kahoot! website in Microsoft Excel format", he was able to find out the number of players who joined the quiz, the number of questions played, the overall performance, individual or group scores and number of correct answers obtained, overview of all answers given by every player/group to each question as well as individual question analysis. In Lim's words, "just by the click of a button, Kahoot! takes away all the pain out of data gathering and data analysis." After analysing the Kahoot! data, Lim also realised that his students "still faced some fundamental problems in their understanding of the whole aspect of both tenses as evidenced by their scores." Lim attributed this to his teaching approach. He admitted to have fallen back to his "conventional approach to teaching the Simple Past and Past Continuous" through mere explanations and drillings. In future lessons, Lim considered using enquiry-based learning approaches to enhance his teaching and the students' understanding. He believed that this approach might be able to help his students "to understand the reasons for learning what they need to learn." In terms of using technology as a tool for assessment, Lim hoped to use Kahoot! as "an integral part" of his classroom assessment. He also saw the possibilities of integrating Kahoot! into reading and writing lessons in the future.

involved the composing of the narrative accounts of the participants' unique experiences and negotiating the compositions until each participant feels that the account "represent something of who they are and are becoming" (Clandinin, 2013, p. 132). Table 3 presents the summaries of the narrative accounts of each participant.

Mobilisation: The 'Transition Phase'

The narrative accounts consisted of three main parts, i.e. the participants' experiences of participating in the 'Going Digital' professional development, their experiences of putting into practice what they had learned from the professional development, and the phase in between these two, which will be referred to in this chapter as the 'transition phase.' This is the phase where the mobilisation of knowledge from

Table 4. Mobilisation of teacher knowledge

Participant	'Going Digital' (Professional Development)	Transition Phase (Mobilisation)	Classroom (Professional Practice)
Arsyad	Young teacher, motivated by more experienced teachers	Identifying pertinent teaching approaches	Video project to enhance speaking skills among students
Erica	Gained lots of knowledge that could not be directly applied to her rural classroom	Adopting and tailoring	Digital Storytelling project using PowerPoint to teach narrative writing
Adele	Saw the community as a "safe place" with plenty of peer support	"Taking the plunge", letting students to "take the lead" and explore	PowToon project to teach metaphors, riddles and imagery
Lim	Learned new tools that infuse "fun element" to practicality	Exploring, experimenting and discovering new knowledge	Using Kahoot! as a tool for classroom assessments

Table 5. Interplay among the knowledge of technology, pedagogy and content

Participant	Technology Selection (Technological Knowledge)	Instructions & Teaching Approaches (Pedagogical Knowledge)	Curriculum Goals (Content Knowledge)
Arsyad	Mobile phones, video-editing apps, Instagram	Project-based Learning (PBL)	Speaking skills
Erica	PowerPoint, netbooks	Scaffolded writing, digital storytelling	Narrative writing / creative writing
Adele	Laptops, PowToon, portable Internet connection (hotspot)	Collaborative learning, constructivist approach	Metaphors, imagery and riddles
Lim	Chromebooks, Kahoot!	Classroom assessment	Grammar: simple past, past continuous

professional development to professional practice occurred. Table 4 presents a summary of the participants' experiences as they transitioned from the professional development context in the 'Going Digital' community to their professional practice context in the classroom.

Although all of the four teachers participated in the same professional development, we could observe four different responses to the experience and four different ways the teachers decided to translate learning to practice. The responses of the participants in the transition phase can be summarised as follows:

- **Focusing on Pedagogical Approaches**

Arsyad, after being inspired by the veteran teachers in the 'Going Digital' community, decided to reflect upon his past teaching experiences and to use the reflection to identify pertinent teaching approaches.

- **Focusing on Context**

Erica described how most of the skills that she acquired from the professional development were not directly applicable due to the unique context of her rural primary classroom. She responded by adopting and tailoring her technology-based project based on the availability of facilities in her school.

- **Focusing on Learning Experiences (of Both Teacher and Learners)**

Adele, a self-professed 'digital immigrant,' referred to the 'Going Digital' community as a safe place where plenty of peer support were available. Her transitionary experience was described as a "plunge," where she decided to embark on a collaborative discovery and exploration with her 'digital native' students.

- **Focusing on Teacher Knowledge**

As someone who was highly-skilled in technology, Lim used the transition phase to learn more about the features and functions of Kahoot! and how the online quiz generator could potentially be used to enhance the effectiveness of his classroom assessment, while increasing learners' engagement in the process.

Enactment: Putting Knowledge Into Practice

Enactment of knowledge refers to how teachers put into practice the knowledge that they have acquired from a training. In this study, enactment of knowledge will be analysed through the interplay of the knowledge of technology, pedagogy and content. To focus specifically on the context of the teaching of English as a Second Language (ESL), 'technological knowledge' represents the technology selection for use in the ESL classroom, 'pedagogical knowledge' refers to ESL instructions and teaching approaches, while 'content knowledge' describes the curriculum goals of an ESL lesson (Judi Harris, Grandgenett, & Hofer, 2010). Table 5 summarises the interplay among the knowledge of technology, pedagogy and content as presented in each participant's narrative account.

PART 3: AFFORDANCES AND CONSTRAINTS OF TECHNOLOGY INTEGRATION IN THE ESL CLASSROOM

Mishra & Koehler (2006) posited that understanding of the affordances and constraints of technology integration is important as it helps teachers to represent content and identify pertinent teaching approaches. In addition to the understanding of affordances and constraints, the participants' narrative accounts also reveal every teacher's future plans for technology integration. Table 6 summarises the affordances and constraints as well as the future plans of each participant as described in their narratives.

In sum, the participants identified the following as among the affordances of technology integration in the ESL classroom:

- Teaching and learning with technology enhance learners' engagement
- Teaching and learning with technology increase learners' motivation to learn
- Learning with technology provides students with the opportunities to learn 'soft skills' like collaboration (e.g. group work in PowToon project and Kahoot! quiz), creativity (e.g. creating videos and digital stories) and skills that can be used in 'real-life' settings (e.g. skills to create "captivating presentations" using PowToon, speaking skills).
- Technology improves efficiency in the classroom (e.g. materials are "recyclable", data analysis can be done with "just the click of a button")

The following are the challenges, constraints and tensions faced by the participants in integrating technology in the classroom:

- **Issues With Lack of Equipment and Facilities**

With the exception of the sports school with its impressive language lab and good Internet connection, all the other schools were dealing with issues of lack of equipment and facilities. The convent secondary school had no computer lab at all. The rural primary school had some netbooks, but they were all reported to be "outdated" and "low-performing." It also had very poor Internet connection. The Chinese secondary school had a library with enough Chromebooks for 35 students, but Internet connection was a bit unstable.

Table 6. Affordances, constraints, and future plans

Participant	Affordances of technology integration	Constraints, challenges and tensions	Future plans
Arsyad	Enhances students' engagement; can be utilised to "manipulate students' inclination" towards any interests.	Juggling roles: students, athletes, examination candidates. Tension between meaningful learning and preparing for examination. Issues with freedom – students were not allowed to use mobile phones in school.	To allow more independence and autonomy for students. To integrate the literature circle approach with TED-talk videos.
Erica	Increases students' motivation to learn – technology used as a "bait." As a result, students were writing "in a way they have never done before."	Poor Internet connection; outdated equipment.	To extend the use of digital storytelling in the teaching of listening and speaking skills.
Adele	Provides the soft skills necessary for life after secondary school, i.e. tools to conduct "captivating presentations." Makes learning more engaging.	Poor Internet connection. Lack of equipment. The teacher's lack of confidence to use technology as a "digital immigrant."	To explore other tools that are "less demanding on Internet speed." To continue to be "open-minded" about what technology can offer.
Lim	Practicality: digital materials are easily "recyclable"; in the case of Kahoot! – data analysis is a useful and time-saving feature. Infuses the "fun element" in learning and classroom assessment.	Poor Internet connection. The tension between the use of technology with pedagogy approaches and knowledge of good assessment instrument.	To adopt enquiry-based approach to enhance students' understanding of the topic. To continue to use Kahoot! as an "integral tool for classroom assessment" and also for teaching reading and writing.

- **Tensions With School Policy on Technology Use**

Some of the participants had to deal with issues with the school's policy of not allowing students to bring technology tools like mobile phones and laptops to school. Arsyad had to seek permission from the hostel warden before his students could use their mobile phones to create their 60-second videos. Adele had to carry out repeated visits to the school administrator's office so her students could bring their laptops and portable Internet to school to work on their PowToon project.

- **Issues of Teacher's Confidence in Using and Teaching With Technology**

This is an issue specifically for Adele, who identified herself as a "digital immigrant." However, it is worth noting that despite this low self-efficacy, Adele was able to carry out her PowToon project quite successfully.

- **Issues With Interplay Between Technology and Teaching Approaches, i.e. Technological Pedagogical Knowledge (TPK)**

This is clearly demonstrated through Lim's experience of using Kahoot! as a classroom assessment tool. Despite his learners' positive classroom experience with Kahoot!, Lim realised that his students were still not able to master the fundamentals of Simple Past and Past Continuous, as reflected by their scores in the quiz. Lim attributed this to his ineffective teaching strategy, i.e. his pedagogical knowledge.

DISCUSSION

Clandinin (2013) described the second level of analysis in narrative inquiry as the process of looking across the individual narrative accounts to identify resonant threads or patterns (p. 132). Creswell (2014) referred to the practice of identifying common meaning from lived experiences as the essentials of experience. These resonances or common meanings do not necessarily represent similarities, but more importantly delineate unifying themes that help us make sense of the participants' experiences in a more holistic manner. Resonances in this chapter will be discussed in terms of how TPACK intersects with many different variables that contribute towards the construction of the participants' experiences of transitioning from learning in the 'Going Digital' community to practice in the ESL classroom.

- **TPACK and Teacher's Self-Efficacy**

Studies have shown that teacher knowledge and self-efficacy influence how teachers respond to their training in technology integration and how they adopt the knowledge in classroom practice (Abbott, 2016; Ertmer & Ottenbreit-Leftwich, 2010; Joo, Park, & Lim, 2018). The connection between knowledge and self-efficacy is evident in the way each of the participant chose to respond to their learning experiences in the 'Going Digital' community. Young and tech-savvy Arsyad decided to focus on the best pedagogical strategy because he was confident in his ability to use technology in his classroom. Lim, who was also very competent in technology, chose to employ his knowledge of technology by exploring the extra functions and features of Kahoot! which was not shared during the 'Going Digital' sharing session. Erica, on the other hand, saw herself as a moderately competent technology user. Her focus was on context, i.e. on what was most convenient in terms of availability and ease of use. Perhaps the participant with the lowest level of self-efficacy was Adele, who identified herself as the 'digital immigrant.' She took the 'plunge' by deciding to let her students take the lead because she was not confident in her ability to teach with technology.

- **TPACK and Teacher's Identity**

Besides knowledge and self-efficacy, teacher identity also plays a role in how a teacher chooses to integrate (or not to integrate) technology in his or her classroom (Abbott, 2016; Curwood, 2014; Ertmer & Ottenbreit-Leftwich, 2010; Hew & Brush, 2007; Shelton, 2018). According to Bukor (2015), teacher identity is developed through the articulation of personal and professional beliefs about being a teacher. It is rooted in various sources such as experiences, personality, professional practice and emotions. Abbot (2016) posited that "barriers were created if the use of technology did not fit comfortably into [teachers'] personal and professional identities" (p. 20). The narrative accounts reveal how each participant projected their identity and beliefs about being a teacher. For example, Arsyad, the Young Teacher, strongly believed in the importance of technology integration. Observing the veteran teachers participating in the 'Going Digital' community prompted him to self-question: "What excuse do you have? You're so young, there's so much you can do." He refused to be "complacent," and expressed that resorting to "chalk-and-talk" teaching is his biggest fear as a teacher.

Erica, the Simple Teacher, preferred to keep things as simple as possible. Her projected identity as a teacher was evident through her way of handling the issues with tools and facilities in her school. To deal with the almost non-existent Internet connection, Erica decided to scrap Internet out of the picture. She used PowerPoint because the software is available for free in all computers in the school.

Adele, the Digital Immigrant Teacher, dealt with real anxieties associated with an immigrant. She recounted issues of unfamiliarity, emphasising on learning journey and exploration into the unknown. She also shared a lot about the importance of being "open-minded." In describing her experience of integrating technology in her ESL lesson, Adele used the 'ocean' metaphor a lot, e.g. "taking the plunge," "will I sink or swim?", "diving from the highest cliff to the deepest ocean." Not surprisingly, she also decided to choose 'metaphors' as one of the learning contents for her technology-based classroom project. She referred to her whole experience of conducting the project as a "migration", i.e. from the safe place of the 'Going Digital' community where peer support was available to the alien 'digital native' world of her Generation Z students.

For Lim, the Practical Teacher, practicality is obviously of utmost importance. He chose Kahoot! as his technology tool because it "ticks all the boxes" for practicality and usability. Lim's top criteria for technology selection include user-friendliness, recyclability and time-saving feature (e.g. "just by the click of a button," data can be generated). Lim compared Kahoot! with Authorware and Hot Potatoes which he believed scored lower in terms of practicality as both software require a large amount of time to set up and involve a "steep learning curve."

- **TPACK and Context**

As for context, Somekh (2008) contended that: "Teachers are not 'free agents' and their use of ICT for teaching and learning depends on the interlocking cultural, social and organisational contexts in which they live and work" (p. 450). This view is echoed by many studies on the role of contexts in technology integration in the classroom (e.g. Cheah et al., 2019; Ertmer & Ottenbreit-Leftwich, 2010; Liu, Ritzhaupt, Dawson, & Barron, 2017; Swallow & Olofson, 2017). It is obvious from the narrative accounts of the participants how the distinctive context of every school determines the choices of technology tools, pedagogical approaches and curricular content. For example, the unique context of the sports boarding school required Arsyad to negotiate the tensions created by the juggling of the students' responsibilities as athletes, learners and examination candidates. His decision to limit the length of videos to 60 seconds was influenced by the need to accommodate the student-athletes' busy schedules. Another example of how context come into play in determining the direction of technology integration is Erica's school in the rural area. Due to the unavailability of good Internet connection, the project had to be conducted using tools that require no Internet connection, i.e. the PowerPoint.

The role of context is also evident in Adele's experience. Dealing with students who were highly proficient not just in technology use, but also in the English language informed Adele's decision of choosing a more complex subject matter (metaphors, riddles and imageries) as her curriculum focus. Despite her own lack of confidence in using technology, Adele had a lot faith in her students' abilities to learn PowToon through collaborative exploration and discovery. The context of her learners clearly influenced Adele's management of the interplay among the domains of technology, pedagogy and content in her teaching.

- **TPACK and Teachers' Understanding of the Affordances and Constraints of Technology Integration**

From the participants' narrative accounts, mobilisation of knowledge is not just visible through the teachers' descriptions of their experiences being in the transition phase, where the professional development had just ended, and classroom practice was about to start. A glimpse of how new knowledge, or to put it in Shulman's (1986) term, new comprehension after undergoing the first cycle of technology-based project can be seen through the participants' depiction of their future plans. As pointed out by Mishra & Koehler (2006), the understanding of affordances and constraints of technology integration assisted teachers in representing content and identifying pertinent teaching approaches. The participants gained more nuanced understanding of the affordances and constraints after executing the first technology-based project following their participations in the 'Going Digital.'

Many studies have pointed towards the importance of developing the awareness of the affordances and constraints of technology in enhancing teachers' technology integration practices. For example, Tseng, Lien, & Chen (2016) conducted a study on the development of teacher knowledge via web conferencing technology and found that the teachers' TPACK grew due to increased awareness of the affordances and constraints of web conferencing technology in foreign language teaching environment. Another example is a study by Evans, Nino, Deater-Deckard, & Chang (2015) which found that using the TPACK framework to evaluate the affordances and constraints of a learning game useful in enhancing technology integration in the classroom. The increasing awareness of the importance of understanding the affordances and constraints of technology to ensure successful mobilisation and enactment of TPACK is evident through the growing number of studies dedicated to the subject (e.g. Antonenko, Dawson, & Sahay, 2017; Bakir, Devers, & Hug, 2016; Burke & Hughes, 2018).

A MODEL OF TPACK MOBILISATION, APPROPRIATION AND ENACTMENT

The mobilisation of knowledge from professional development to practice in the classroom has often been a concern (Van Duzor, 2011). Dimmock (2016) posited that "instead of the traditional dissemination through one-off workshops, seminars or discussions, knowledge mediation and knowledge application should be in line with the new accounts of professional learning mobilisation" (pp. 40-41). Despite this, there is a dearth of study outlining how the mobilisation of knowledge from professional development to the classroom can be assisted in systematic and helpful ways.

According to O' Dwyer (2018), "the likelihood of new learning being implemented in practice is increased when the gap between the professional development and classroom practice is reduced" (p. 354). Also, in order for a professional development to be successful, it needs to be consistent with classroom practice (Hill, Blazar, & Lynch, 2015). The 'gap' that O' Dwyer referred to can be decreased by ensuring that professional development is linked to and consistent with classroom practices.

This section aims to explore ways of reducing the gap between professional development and professional practice by paying specific attention to the 'link in between', i.e. what occurs in the transition phase. It is what we referred to earlier as the post-training / pre-enactment stage – where professional development ends and classroom practice starts. It is a phase that links these two contexts together. According to Shulman (1986), new comprehension does not automatically occur even after evaluation and reflection. Specific strategies are needed to assist the transition from learning to enactment. The authors believe that the proposition of a model that can potentially guide teachers in linking their learning to practice is timely and relevant, particularly in the field of TPACK and technology integration in the ESL classroom.

The authors would like to propose a model of TPACK mobilisation and enactment that aims to offer a guide for teacher self-evaluation and reflections following a TPACK-based professional development. The model aims to capture the interconnectedness among knowledge, context and identity as well as the considerations of the affordances and constraints of technology integration. The model allows teachers to ponder on the selection of technology tools, instructional strategies and curriculum goals for their ESL classrooms by tapping into the knowledge that they acquire from professional development and linking it with their professional practices. The model is shown in Figure 5 below.

- Post-Training Evaluation

The authors proposed that every TPACK-based professional development should end with a post-training evaluation, to mark the beginning of the pre-enactment phase which should link the professional development with classroom practice. Post-training evaluation can be carried out by getting teachers to evaluate the professional development effectiveness, and by reflecting upon their experiences of participating in the professional development.

- Self-Evaluation

Self-evaluation is the stage where teachers reflect on their identity and knowledge by analysing their pedagogical beliefs and self-efficacy.

- Context Evaluation

Figure 5. Model of TPACK mobilisation, appropriation and enactment

Context evaluation involves thinking about their school and classroom's unique circumstances, their learners' needs, aptitudes, competency or dispositions, as well as other contextual factors such as organisational routines, policy, the milieus and etc.

• Evaluation of Affordances and Constraints

Considering the affordances and constraints at the outset of every technology integration practice is pertinent as it gears teachers towards proper appropriation of knowledge (Antonenko, Dawson, & Sahay, 2017; Bakir, Devers, & Hug, 2016; Burke & Hughes, 2018).

• Knowledge Appropriation

Longhurst, Jones & Campbell (2017) define appropriation as "a process where an individual adopts, uses and modifies pedagogical tools within and influenced by specific social or cultural contexts" (p. 366). They also stated that the "implementation of conceptual and practical pedagogies from professional development with acceptable adaptation" is the epitome of the concept of appropriation (p. 366). Appropriation is an important stage in the pre-enactment stage, as it helps teachers to adopt and tailor their pedagogical strategies, curriculum content and technological resources according to the practical and contextual needs of the classroom and learners (Shulman, 1986).

• Knowledge Enactment

Knowledge enactment is the stage where TPACK is fully mobilised from professional development to professional practice in the classroom.

FUTURE RESEARCH DIRECTIONS

This chapter is a small step towards understanding how teachers respond to TPACK-based professional development and how they mobilise as well as enact the knowledge they acquire from the professional development to practice in the classroom. However, more research into recognising the diverse factors that influence teachers' professional development experiences and the social contexts that mediate individual implementation are needed in order to better understand teachers' contextual appropriation from professional learning experiences (Bourke, Mentis, & O'Neill, 2013).

The authors would be very interested in exploring the potentials of the proposed model of TPACK mobilisation, appropriation and enactment as a tool to support and assist teachers in linking their professional development experiences to classroom practices. Further investigations into the concept, the continuum as well as the varying degrees of knowledge appropriation as described by Longhurst, Jones & Campbell (2017) with a specific focus on TPACK and language teaching and learning is a worthy research pursuit.

CONCLUSION

This chapter recapitulates a three-year journey into the study of Malaysian ESL teachers' TPACK development and practice. It started with the formation of the 'Going Digital' which incorporated the principles of professional learning community into the TPACK framework and Lee & Kim's (2014) ID-DIRR instructional design. The TPACK - IDDIRR + PLC model was adopted to explore its effectiveness in inspiring in-service teachers to integrate technology in their English language classrooms. The results indicate that this model has the potential to be adopted to enhance teachers' TPACK. The findings further imply that this model provides in-service teachers with a platform to improve their practices in integrating technology within their classrooms. The supporting context (PLC) provided a safe and conducive environment for in-service teachers to learn and be inspired. The presence of more knowledgeable individuals (peers and student teachers) in PLC yielded the much-needed support for teachers to learn the technical aspects of integrating technology with their content and pedagogical knowledge. Beyond the favourable evidence accrued, the findings also suggest that teacher professional development should be extended beyond the conventional face-to-face sessions. They should include additional and continuous support in the form of online platforms such as websites or interactive social media platforms to continuously motivate and change teachers' mindsets and practices for 21st century teaching.

Progressing from the first part of the study, the authors embarked on another journey to make sense of the individual experiences of the teachers in mobilising their TPACK from the 'Going Digital' professional development to their practices in the classroom through narrative inquiry. The findings revealed interesting interconnectedness among knowledge, context and identity; teachers' understanding of the affordances and constraints of technology integration; and how they impacted teachers' practices. These findings inspired the proposition of the model for TPACK mobilisation, appropriation and enactment, which the authors hope to explore further in subsequent research.

Despite strongly advocating for the broadening of the conception of good teaching to include the idea that "teaching is effective only when combined with relevant ICT tools and resources" (Ertmer & Ottenbreit-Leftwich, 2010, p. 259), Ertmer & Ottenbreit-Leftwich acknowledged that technology is "always in a state of flux" and that "learning about technology is equivalent to asking teachers to hit a moving target" (p. 260). Through the inquiry into teachers' narrative experiences of integrating technology in their ESL classrooms, this study hopes to pave the way towards exploring the possibility of an emphasised focus on teachers' contexts, the shaping of teachers' identities and the development of self-efficacy through teacher professional development, mobilisation of knowledge, and enactment of knowledge in the classroom. The main intent is not to 'hit the moving target,' but rather to help teachers gain a more nuanced understanding of TPACK so that technology can be employed to benefit learners in more practical and contextualised manners.

ACKNOWLEDGMENT

This research received no specific grant from any funding agency in the public, commercial, or not-for-profit sectors.

REFERENCES

Abbitt, J. T. (2011). Measuring technological pedagogical content knowledge in preservice teacher education: a review of current methods and instruments. *Journal of Research on Technology in Education, 43*(4), 281–300. doi:10.1080/15391523.2011.10782573

Abbot, M. L., Lee, K. K., & Rossiter, M. J. (2018). Evaluating the effectiveness and functionality of professional learning communities in adult ESL programs. *TESL Canada Journal, 35*(2), 1–25. doi:10.18806/tesl.v35i2.1288

Abbott, R. (2016). *Embracing digital technologies in classroom practice: the impact of teacher identity*. 26.

Abdullah, Z., & Ghani, A., M. F. (2014). Professional learning community in secondary schools community in Malaysia. [EduLearn]. *Journal of Education and Learning, 8*(3), 227. doi:10.11591/edulearn.v8i3.265

Aljaloud, A., Billingsley, W., & Kwan, P. (2019). Factors that influence teachers' decisions to use smartphone clicker apps to enhance teacher-student interactions in university classrooms in Saudi Arabia. *Learning: Research and Practice, 5*(1), 67–86. doi:10.1080/23735082.2018.1459802

Antonenko, P. D., Dawson, K., & Sahay, S. (2017). A framework for aligning needs, abilities, and affordances to inform design and practice of educational technologies. *British Journal of Educational Technology, 48*(4), 916–927. doi:10.1111/bjet.12466

Bakir, N., Devers, C., & Hug, B. (2016). Affordances and constraints of a blended course in a teacher professional development program. *Journal of Educational Multimedia and Hypermedia, 25*(4), 323–341.

Belo, N., Belo, N., McKenney, S., Voogt, J., & Bradley, B. (2016). Teacher knowledge for using technology to foster early literacy: A literature review. *Computers in Human Behavior, 60*, 372–383. doi:10.1016/j.chb.2016.02.053

Beriswill, J. E., Bracey, P. S., Sherman-Morris, K., Huang, K., & Lee, S. J. (2016). Professional development for promoting 21st century skills and common core state standards in foreign language and social studies classrooms. *TechTrends, 60*(1), 77–84. doi:10.100711528-015-0004-5

Blitz, C. L., & Schulman, R. (2016). *Measurement instruments for assessing the performance of professional learning communities. REL 2016-144*. Retrieved from https://eric.ed.gov/?q=measuring+the+effectiveness+of+professional+learning+community+in+schools+&pr=on&id=ED568594

Borg, S. (2003). Teacher cognition in language teaching: A review of research on what language teachers think, know, believe, and do. *Language Teaching, 36*(2), 81–109. doi:10.1017/S0261444803001903

Borg, S. (2015). *Teacher cognition and language education*. London, UK: Bloomsbury Academic.

Bourke, R., Mentis, M., & O'Neill, J. (2013). Using activity theory to evaluate a professional learning and development initiative in the use of narrative assessment. *Cambridge Journal of Education, 43*(1), 35–50. doi:10.1080/0305764X.2012.749214

Brantley-Dias, L., & Ertmer, P. A. (2013). Goldilocks and TPACK: Is the construct 'Just Right?'. *Journal of Research on Technology in Education, 46*(2), 103–128. doi:10.1080/15391523.2013.10782615

Braun, A., Maguire, M., & Ball, S. J. (2010). Policy enactments in the UK secondary school: examining policy, practice and school positioning. *Journal of Education Policy*, *25*(4), 547–560. doi:10.1080/02680931003698544

Brissenden-Smith, K., Moreno, A., Peloquin, L., Radiloff, J., & Wachtel, J. (2018). Growing opportunities: collaboration nurtures and supports early learning educators. *Learning Professional*, *39*(3), 42–46.

Brown, B. D., Horn, R. S., & King, G. (2018). The effective implementation of professional learning communities. *Alabama Journal of Educational Leadership*, *5*, 53–59.

Bugueño, W. (2013). Using TPACK to promote effective language teaching in an ESL/EFL classroom. *Graduate Research Papers*. Retrieved from https://scholarworks.uni.edu/grp/150

Bukor, E. (2015). Exploring teacher identity from a holistic perspective: Reconstructing and reconnecting personal and professional selves. *Teachers and Teaching*, *21*(3), 305–327. doi:10.1080/13540602.2014.953818

Burke, A., & Hughes, J. (2018). A shifting landscape: using tablets to support learning in students with diverse abilities. *Technology, Pedagogy, and Education*, *27*(2), 183–198. doi:10.1080/1475939X.2017.1396492

Buysse, V., Sparkman, K. L., & Wesley, P. W. (2003). Communities of practice: connecting what we know with what we do. *Exceptional Children*, *69*(3), 263–277. doi:10.1177/001440290306900301

Cavanagh, R. F., & Koehler, M. J. (2013). A turn toward specifying validity criteria in the measurement of technological pedagogical content knowledge (TPACK). *Journal of Research on Technology in Education*, *46*(2), 129–148. doi:10.1080/15391523.2013.10782616

Celik, I., Sahin, I., & Akturk, A. O. (2014). Analysis of the relations among the components of technological pedagogical and content knowledge (TPACK): A structural equation model. *Journal of Educational Computing Research*, *51*(1), 1–22. doi:10.2190/EC.51.1.a

Chaemchoy, S. (2017, February). An investigation of Thai Principals' Technology Leadership and Understanding of Mobile Technology in Education: Apply the TPACK Framework. *Advanced Science Letters*, *23*(2), 1134–1139.

Chapelle, C. A. (2009). The relationship between second language acquisition theory and computer-assisted language learning. *Modern Language Journal*, *93*(s1), 741–753. doi:10.1111/j.1540-4781.2009.00970.x

Cheah, Y. H., Chai, C. S., & Toh, Y. (2019). Traversing the context of professional learning communities: Development and implementation of technological pedagogical content knowledge of a primary science teacher. *Research in Science & Technological Education*, *37*(2), 147–167. doi:10.1080/02635143.2018.1504765

Cheng, K.-H. (2017). A survey of native language teachers' technological pedagogical and content knowledge (TPACK) in Taiwan. *Computer Assisted Language Learning*, *30*(7), 692–708. doi:10.1080/09588221.2017.1349805

Ching, Y.-H., Yang, D., Baek, Y., & Baldwin, S. (2016). Enhancing graduate students' reflection in e-portfolios using the TPACK framework. *Australasian Journal of Educational Technology, 32*(5), 108–122. doi:10.14742/ajet.2830

Christ, T., Arya, P., & Liu, Y. (2019). Technology integration in literacy lessons: challenges and successes. *Literacy Research and Instruction, 58*(1), 49–66. doi:10.1080/19388071.2018.1554732

Clandinin, D. J., & Connelly, F. M. (1994). Personal experience methods. In *Handbook of qualitative research* (pp. 413–427). Thousand Oaks, CA: Sage.

Clandinin, D. J., & Connelly, F. M. (2004). *Narrative inquiry: Experience and story in qualitative research.* San Francisco, CA: Jossey Bass.

Clandinin, J. D. (2013). *Engaging in narrative inquiry.* New York: Routledge.

Creswell, J. W. (2014). Educational research: Pearson New International Edition: Planning, conducting, and evaluating quantitative and qualitative research (4th ed.). Harlow, UK: Pearson.

Curwood, J. S. (2014). Between continuity and change: Identities and narratives within teacher professional development. *Teaching Education, 25*(2), 156–183. doi:10.1080/10476210.2012.755159

Dimmock, C. (2016). Conceptualising the research–practice–professional development nexus: Mobilising schools as 'research-engaged' professional learning communities. *Professional Development in Education, 42*(1), 36–53. doi:10.1080/19415257.2014.963884

Dong, Y., Chai, C. S., Sang, G.-Y., Koh, J. H. L., & Tsai, C.-C. (2015). Exploring the profiles and interplays of pre-service and in-service teachers' technological pedagogical content knowledge (TPACK) in China. *Journal of Educational Technology & Society, 18*(1), 158–169.

DuFour, R., & DuFour, R. (2010). The role of professional learning communities in advancing 21st century skills. In J. A. Bellanca (Ed.), 21st century skills: rethinking how students learn (pp. 77–95). Bloomington, IN: Solution Tree Press.

Easton, L. B. (2015). The 5 habits of effective PLCs. *Journal of Staff Development, 36*(6), 24.

Ertmer, P. A., & Ottenbreit-Leftwich, A. T. (2010). Teacher technology change: how knowledge, confidence, beliefs, and culture intersect. *Journal of Research on Technology in Education, 42*(3), 255–284. doi:10.1080/15391523.2010.10782551

Evans, M. A., Nino, M., Deater-Deckard, K., & Chang, M. (2015). School-wide adoption of a mathematics learning game in a middle school setting: Using the TPACK framework to analyze effects on practice. *The Asia-Pacific Education Researcher, 24*(3), 495–504. doi:10.100740299-014-0225-y

Greenlaw, J. (2015). Deconstructing the metanarrative of the 21st century skills movement. *Educational Philosophy and Theory, 47*(9), 894–903. doi:10.1080/00131857.2015.1035156

Guskey, T. R. (2014). Planning professional learning. *Educational Leadership, 71*(8), 10–16.

Harris, J., Grandgenett, N., & Hofer, M. (2010, March 29). *Testing a TPACK-based technology integration assessment rubric.* 3833–3840. Retrieved from https://www.learntechlib.org/primary/p/33978/

Harris, J., Koehler, M., & Mishra, P. (2009). What is technological pedagogical content knowledge? *Contemporary Issues in Technology & Teacher Education*, 9.

Harris, J. B., & Hofer, M. J. (2017). "TPACK stories": Schools and school districts repurposing a theoretical construct for technology-related professional development. *Journal of Research on Technology in Education, 49*(1–2), 1–15. doi:10.1080/15391523.2017.1295408

Hassan, R., Ahmad, J., & Boon, Y. (2018). Professional learning community in Malaysia. *International Journal of Engineering*, 12.

Herman, J. M. (2012). Creating balance in the new age of technology. *Montessori Life: A Publication of the American Montessori Society, 24*(3), 36–43.

Herro, D., Quigley, C., & Cian, H. (2019). The challenges of STEAM instruction: Lessons from the field. *Action in Teacher Education, 41*(2), 172–190. doi:10.1080/01626620.2018.1551159

Hew, K. F., & Brush, T. (2007). Integrating technology into K-12 teaching and learning: current knowledge gaps and recommendations for future research. *Educational Technology Research and Development, 55*(3), 223–252. doi:10.100711423-006-9022-5

Hill, H. C., Blazar, D., & Lynch, K. (2015). Resources for teaching: examining personal and institutional predictors of high-quality instruction. *AERA Open, 1*(4). Retrieved from https://eric.ed.gov/?q=hill%2c+blazar+%26+lynch+2015&pr=on&id=EJ1194657

Hipp, K. K., & Huffman, J. B. (2003). *Professional learning communities: Assessment--Development--Effects*. Retrieved from https://eric.ed.gov/?id=ED482255

Hofer, M., & Harris, J. (2012, March 5). *TPACK research with inservice teachers: Where's the TCK?* 4704–4709. Retrieved from https://www.learntechlib.org/primary/p/40352/

Hord, S. M. (1997). *Professional learning communities: communities of continuous inquiry and improvement*. Retrieved from https://eric.ed.gov/?id=ED410659

Jang, S.-J., & Tsai, M.-F. (2012). Exploring the TPACK of Taiwanese elementary mathematics and science teachers with respect to use of interactive whiteboards. *Computers & Education, 59*(2), 327–338. doi:10.1016/j.compedu.2012.02.003

Joo, Y. J., Park, S., & Lim, E. (2018). Factors influencing preservice teachers' intention to use technology: TPACK, teacher self-efficacy, and technology acceptance model. *Journal of Educational Technology & Society, 21*(3), 48–59.

Keengwe, J., & Kang, J.-J. (2011). A review of empirical research on blended learning in teacher education programs. *Education and Information Technologies, 18*(3), 479–493. doi:10.100710639-011-9182-8

Kennedy, A. (2005). Models of continuing professional development: A framework for analysis. *Journal of In-service Education, 31*(2), 235–250. doi:10.1080/13674580500200277

Kessler, G. (2018). Technology and the future of language teaching. *Foreign Language Annals, 51*(1), 205–218. doi:10.1111/flan.12318

Koçoğlu, Z. (2009). Exploring the technological pedagogical content knowledge of pre-service teachers in language education. *Procedia: Social and Behavioral Sciences*, *1*(1), 2734–2737. doi:10.1016/j.sbspro.2009.01.485

Koh, J. H. L., Chai, C. S., & Lee, M.-H. (2015). Technological pedagogical content knowledge (TPACK) for pedagogical improvement: editorial for special issue on TPACK. *The Asia-Pacific Education Researcher*, *24*(3), 459–462. doi:10.100740299-015-0241-6

Koh, J. H. L., Chai, C. S., & Lim, W. Y. (2017). Teacher professional development for TPACK-21CL: Effects on teacher ICT integration and student outcomes. *Journal of Educational Computing Research*, *55*(2), 172–196. doi:10.1177/0735633116656848

La Velle, L., & Flores, M. A. (2018). Perspectives on evidence-based knowledge for teachers: Acquisition, mobilisation and utilisation. *Journal of Education for Teaching*, *44*(5), 524–538. doi:10.1080/02607476.2018.1516345

Lee, C.-J., & Kim, C. (2014). An implementation study of a TPACK-based instructional design model in a technology integration course. *Educational Technology Research and Development*, *62*(4), 437–460. doi:10.100711423-014-9335-8

Lee, K. W., & James, C. C. (2018). Exploring a transformative teacher professional development model to engender technology integration in the 21st century ESL language classrooms. [IJCALLT]. *International Journal of Computer-Assisted Language Learning and Teaching*, *8*(4), 13–31. doi:10.4018/IJCALLT.2018100102

Lee, K. W., Ng, S. I., & Tan, C. K. (2014). Developing Malaysian ESL teachers technological pedagogical content knowledge with digital materials. In S. In (Ed.), *Computer-Assisted Language Learning: Learners, Teachers & Tools* (pp. 97–121). Newcastle upon Tyne, UK: Cambridge Publishing Press.

Levin, B. (2013). To know is not enough: Research knowledge and its use. *Review of Education*, *1*(1), 2–31. doi:10.1002/rev3.3001

Liu, F., Ritzhaupt, A. D., Dawson, K., & Barron, A. E. (2017). Explaining technology integration in K-12 classrooms: a multilevel path analysis model. *Educational Technology Research and Development*, *65*(4), 795–813. doi:10.100711423-016-9487-9

Longhurst, M. L., Jones, S. H., & Campbell, T. (2017). Factors influencing teacher appropriation of professional learning focused on the use of technology in science classrooms. *Teacher Development*, *21*(3), 365–387. doi:10.1080/13664530.2016.1273848

Mahathir, M. (1991). Malaysia: the way forward (Vision 2020). Malaysian Business Council.

Mak, B., & Pun, S.-H. (2015). Cultivating a teacher community of practice for sustainable professional development: beyond planned efforts. *Teachers and Teaching*, *21*(1), 4–21. doi:10.1080/13540602.2014.928120

Maretich, K. (2017). Data in the digital age: charting the way for multimedia learning. *Australian Primary Mathematics Classroom*, *22*(4), 22–26.

Ministry of Education Malaysia. (2013). *Malaysia education blueprint 2013-2025 (Preschool to post-secondary education)*. Ministry of Education Malaysia.

Mishra, P., & Koehler, M. J. (2006). Technological pedagogical content knowledge: a framework for teacher knowledge. *Teachers College Record, 108*(6), 1017–1054. doi:10.1111/j.1467-9620.2006.00684.x

Mohammadi, M., & Moradi, K. (2017). Exploring change in EFL teachers' perceptions of professional development. *Journal of Teacher Education for Sustainability, 19*(1), 22–42. doi:10.1515/jtes-2017-0002

Muhaimin, M., Habibi, A., Mukminin, A., Saudagar, F., Pratama, R., Wahyuni, S., ... Indrayana, B. (2019). A sequential explanatory investigation of TPACK: Indonesian science teachers' survey and perspective. *Journal of Technology and Science Education, 9*(3), 269–281. doi:10.3926/jotse.662

Naidorf, J. (2014). Knowledge utility: from social relevance to knowledge mobilization. *Education Policy Analysis Archives, 22*(89). Retrieved from https://eric.ed.gov/?q=Naidorf%2c+J.+2014.+%e2%80%9cKnowledge+Utility%3a+From+Social+Relevance+to+Knowledge+Mobilization.%e2%80%9d+Education+Policy+Analysis+Archives+22+(89)%3a+1%e2%80%9331.&pr=on&id=EJ1050049

Nikian, S., Nor, F. M., & Aziz, M. A. (2013). Malaysian teachers' perception of applying technology in the classroom. *Procedia: Social and Behavioral Sciences, 103*, 621–627. doi:10.1016/j.sbspro.2013.10.380

O' Dwyer, A. (2018). An insight into how a constructivist professional development program can influence practice in six high school chemistry classrooms. *Journal of Science Teacher Education, 29*(5), 353–377. doi:10.1080/1046560X.2018.1457348

Onguko, B. B. (2014). JiFUNzeni: A blended learning approach for sustainable teachers' professional development. *Electronic Journal of E-Learning, 12*(1), 77–88.

Park, M., & So, K. (2014). Opportunities and challenges for teacher professional development: a case of collaborative learning community in South Korea. *International Education Studies, 7*(7), 96–108. doi:10.5539/ies.v7n7p96

Policy on ICT in education. (2010). (p. 104).

Prensky, M. (2009). H. sapiens digital: from digital immigrants and digital natives to digital wisdom. *Innovate: Journal of Online Education, 5*(3).

Regan, K., Evmenova, A. S., Sacco, D., Schwartzer, J., Chirinos, D. S., & Hughes, M. D. (2019). Teacher perceptions of integrating technology in writing. *Technology, Pedagogy, and Education, 28*(1), 1–19. doi:10.1080/1475939X.2018.1561507

Saad, K. A., Walsh, B., Mallaburn, A., & Brundrett, M. (2017). Exploring the implementation of professional learning communities in Malaysian schools. *International Journal of Education. Psychology and Counselling, 2*(5), 1–18.

Salkind, N. (2010). *Encyclopedia of Research Design*. doi:10.4135/9781412961288

Shelton, C. (2018). "You have to teach to your personality": Caring, sharing, and teaching with technology. *Australasian Journal of Educational Technology, 34*(4). doi:10.14742/ajet.3557

Shulman, L. S. (1986). Those who understand: knowledge growth in teaching. *Educational Researcher*, *15*(2), 4–14. doi:10.3102/0013189X015002004

Simin, G., & Sani, I. M. (2015). *Effectiveness of ICT integration in Malaysian schools: a quantitative analysis. 2*, 12.

Somekh, B. (2008). Factors affecting teachers' pedagogical adoption of ICT. In J. Voogt, & G. Knezek (Eds.), *International handbook of information technology in primary and secondary education* (pp. 449–460). doi:10.1007/978-0-387-73315-9_27

Song, K.-O., & Choi, J. (2017). Structural analysis of factors that influence professional learning communities in Korean elementary schools. *International Electronic Journal of Elementary Education*, *10*(1), 1–9.

Spencer, E. J. (2016). Professional learning communities: keeping the focus on instructional practice. *Kappa Delta Pi Record*, *52*(2), 83–85. doi:10.1080/00228958.2016.1156544

Spires, H., Hervey, L., & Watson, T. (2013). Scaffolding the TPACK framework in reading and language arts: new literacies, new minds. In *Research on Technology in English Education*. Information Age Publishing.

Swallow, M. J. C., & Olofson, M. W. (2017). Contextual understandings in the TPACK framework. *Journal of Research on Technology in Education*, *49*(3-4), 228–244. doi:10.1080/15391523.2017.1347537

Tahir, L. M., Said, M. N. H. M., Ali, M. F., Samah, N. A., Daud, K., & Mohtar, T. H. (2013). Examining the professional learning community practices: an empirical comparison from Malaysian universities clusters. *Procedia: Social and Behavioral Sciences*, *97*, 105–113. doi:10.1016/j.sbspro.2013.10.210

Thang, S. M., Lin, L. K., Mahmud, N., Ismail, K., & Zabidi, N. A. (2014). Technology integration in the form of digital storytelling: Mapping the concerns of four Malaysian ESL instructors. *Computer Assisted Language Learning*, *27*(4), 311–329. doi:10.1080/09588221.2014.903979

Thoma, J., Hutchison, A., Johnson, D., Johnson, K., & Stromer, E. (2017). Planning for technology integration in a professional learning community. *The Reading Teacher*, *71*(2), 167–175. doi:10.1002/trtr.1604

Thompson, S. C., Gregg, L., & Niska, J. M. (2004). Professional learning communities, leadership, and student learning. *RMLE Online: Research in Middle Level Education*, *28*(1), 1–15. doi:10.1080/19404476.2004.11658173

Tseng, J.-J., Lien, Y.-J., & Chen, H.-J. (2016). Using a teacher support group to develop teacher knowledge of mandarin teaching via web conferencing technology. *Computer Assisted Language Learning*, *29*(1), 127–147. doi:10.1080/09588221.2014.903978

Umar, I. N., & Hassan, A. S. A. (2015). Malaysian teachers' levels of ICT integration and its perceived impact on teaching and learning. *Procedia: Social and Behavioral Sciences*, *197*, 2015–2021. doi:10.1016/j.sbspro.2015.07.586

Van Duzor, A. (2011). Capitalizing on teacher expertise: motivations for contemplating transfer from professional development to the classroom. *Journal of Science Education and Technology*, *20*(4), 363–374. doi:10.100710956-010-9258-z

Vasinda, S., Ryter, D. A., Hathcock, S., & Wang, Q. (2017). Access is not enough: a collaborative auto-ethnographic study of affordances and challenges of teacher educators' iPad integration in elementary education methods courses. [CITE Journal]. *Contemporary Issues in Technology & Teacher Education, 17*(3).

Vescio, V., Ross, D., & Adams, A. (2008). A review of research on the impact of professional learning communities on teaching practice and student learning. *Teaching and Teacher Education, 24*(1), 80–91. doi:10.1016/j.tate.2007.01.004

Warschauer, M. (2000). The changing global economy and the future of English teaching. *TESOL Quarterly, 34*(3), 511–535. doi:10.2307/3587741

Warschauer, M., & Healey, D. (1998). Computers and language learning: An overview. *Language Teaching, 31*(2), 57–71. doi:10.1017/S0261444800012970

Wu, Y.-L. (2014). The impact of technology on language learning. In J. H. Park, Y. Pan, C.-S. Kim, & Y. Yang (Eds.), Future Information Technology (pp. 727–731). Springer Berlin. doi:10.1007/978-3-642-55038-6_112

Younie, S., Audain, J., Eloff, I., Leask, M., Procter, R., & Shelton, C. (2018). Mobilising knowledge through global partnerships to support research-informed teaching: Five models for translational research. *Journal of Education for Teaching, 44*(5), 574–589. doi:10.1080/02607476.2018.1516348

Zhukova, O. (2018). Novice teachers' concerns, early professional experiences and development: implications for theory and practice. *Discourse and Communication for Sustainable Education, 9*(1), 100–114. doi:10.2478/dcse-2018-0008

ADDITIONAL READING

Chai, C. S., Koh, J. H. L., & Tsai, C.-C. (2013). A review of technological pedagogical content knowledge. [Retrieved from Scopus.]. *Journal of Educational Technology & Society, 16*(2), 31–51.

Ertmer, P. A. (2005). Teacher pedagogical beliefs: The final frontier in our quest for technology integration? *Educational Technology Research and Development, 53*(4), 25–39. doi:10.1007/BF02504683

Harris, J., Koehler, M., & Mishra, P. (2009). What Is Technological Pedagogical Content Knowledge? *Contemporary Issues in Technology & Teacher Education*, ▪▪▪, 9.

Koh, J. H. L., Chai, C. S., & Lee, M.-H. (2015). Technological Pedagogical Content Knowledge (TPACK) for Pedagogical Improvement: Editorial for Special Issue on TPACK. *The Asia-Pacific Education Researcher, 24*(3), 459–462. doi:10.100740299-015-0241-6

Porras-Hernández, L. H., & Salinas-Amescua, B. (2013). Strengthening TPACK: A broader notion of context and the use of teacher's narratives to reveal knowledge construction. *Journal of Educational Computing Research, 48*(2), 223–244. doi:10.2190/EC.48.2.f

Role of Educational Technologies Utilizing the TPACK Framework and 21st Century Pedagogies: Academics' Perspectives. (n.d.). Retrieved 16 June 2019, from The International Academic Forum (IAFOR) website: https://iafor.org/journal/iafor-journal-of-education/volume-6-issue-3/article-3/

Voogt, J., Fisser, P., Pareja Roblin, N., Tondeur, J., & van Braak, J. (2013). Technological pedagogical content knowledge - A review of the literature. *Journal of Computer Assisted Learning*, *29*(2), 109–121. doi:10.1111/j.1365-2729.2012.00487.x

Willermark, S. (2018). Technological Pedagogical and Content Knowledge: A Review of Empirical Studies Published From 2011 to 2016. *Journal of Educational Computing Research*, *56*(3), 315–343. doi:10.1177/0735633117713114

KEY TERMS AND DEFINITIONS

Knowledge Appropriation: Adaptation, adoption and tailoring of pedagogical strategies, curriculum contents and technological resources to suit the practical and contextual needs of classrooms and learners.

Knowledge Enactment: The act of putting into practice in the classroom the knowledge or skills acquired from learning or training.

Knowledge Mobilisation: Movement of knowledge from professional development context to classroom practices.

Professional Development: Engagement with activities or events to acquire or enhance knowledge and skills in certain pedagogical, curricular or instructional areas with the objective of improving classroom practices.

Professional Practice: Classroom approaches, pedagogical techniques and management of resources, contents and learners during the curriculum delivery process.

Technology-Based Projects: Teaching and learning activities that utilise technology, conducted either in the classroom or outside the classroom.

Technology Integration Practice: The utilisation of technology tools, facilities and resources in the classroom.

APPENDIX 1

Interview Protocol

1. In what ways the skills you presented in your product be applied into real life setting or workplace? (TPCK)
2. Was/were the selected skill(s) important? Why do you think so? (PK)
3. How did educational technology (e.g. Web 2.0 Tools – Teaching and learning softwares/online learning activities) help in teaching and learning? (TPCK)
4. Do you think it was important to integrate educational technology into curriculum-based learning? Why do you think so? (TPCK)
5. What were the changes you wish you could have made during the planning, designing, and implementation stage and how could the changes affect teaching and learning ? (TPCK)
6. How could you further improve your classroom management/teaching method? (PCK)
7. Did your product benefit your learners in terms of their knowledge and soft skills? (TPCK) Why do you think so?
8. Do you think about your teaching approaches work well with the application of educational technology? If so, in what way? If not, why? (TPCK)
9. How did your instructions and product impact the learners? If so, in what way? If not, why? (TPCK)

APPENDIX 2

Writing Guideline for Technology-Based Project Report

Phase 1: Introduction – The Planning Stage

This section of the article captures the author's experiences in the 'Introduce' and 'Demonstrate' phases of the TPACK-IDDIRR model. It answers the following questions:

- What were the aims/objectives of the project?
- What were the expected outcomes of the project?
- What were the challenges faced throughout the planning stage and how did the author solve the issues?

Phase 2: Design and Development

This section describes the experiences of the author throughout the 'Development' phase. It provides the answers to the following questions:

- How did the author adapt the suitable syllabus/topics to integrate technology in the classroom?
- How did the author analyse the suitability of the digital tools used in the project?
- What were the teaching or learning issues/concerns/skills that the project wanted to focus on?
- What were the reasons for addressing the issues/concerns/skills?
- What digital tools were selected for the project and what were the reasons for the selection?

· What were the challenges/limitations faced during the development phase and how did the author solve them?

Phase 3: Implementation

This section describes what the author went through during the 'Implementation' phase. It provides the answers to the following questions:

· Where was the project conducted?
· Who were the participants?
· How many participants were involved in the project?
· How long did it take for the project to be completed?
· How was the project conducted? Ð the methods, the timeline, whether it was a group or individual work etc.
· What form of assessment did the author use to measure the impacts/effectiveness of the project?
· In what ways can the outputs from the project be applied into real-life setting/workplace?
· What were the challenges/limitations faced during the implementation stage and how did the author solve the issues?

Phase 4: Reflection

In this section, the author shares his/her reflection on the experience of conducting the project. The author may also share thoughts and feedbacks about the project from the learners' perspectives.

· What was the biggest challenge/limitation that the author faced when conducting the project?
· How did the author overcome the challenge/limitation?
· What was the author's overall thoughts about the impact of the project on his/her teaching?
· How did the project impact learners?
· Was there any feedback from learners? What did the learners say about how the project had impacted their learning?

Phase 5: Revision – What's next?

This section describes the changes/improvements that the author had done, or planned to do, in order to make the project better. It also answers the following questions:

· What area/s of the project can be further improved?
· Does the author's teaching approach work well with educational technology? If so, in what way? If not, why?
· What's next? How would the author bring the project further to the next level? Is there any future plan?

Chapter 14
Exploring Pre-Service Teachers' Developmental Trajectories of Digital Literacies

Le Wang
Qingdao University, China

Yi Luo
Tianjin Foreign Studies University, China

Pengpeng Feng
Sun Yat-sen University, China

ABSTRACT

Digital literacies are gaining popularity in teacher education over the past decade, but little research has been conducted on the developmental trajectories of pre-service teachers' digital literacies. Adopting a case study, four L2 Chinese pre-service teachers were examined during the spring semester of 2016 when they assisted teaching in a wiki writing classroom. Data was collected through semi-structured interviews and observation diaries. Drawing upon the framework of digital literacies, this chapter identifies the core components of digital literacies in a wiki-based collaborative writing context: attitudes towards technology and application (Thinking), task organization and feedback provision (Doing), modes and genres (Meaning), teacher-student relations (Relating), and roles and responsibilities (Being), and further explores pre-service teachers' developmental trajectories of digital literacies before concluding with a discussion of implications for instruction and teacher education.

INTRODUCTION

Literacy, known as the skills and abilities to read and write, has long been considered an indispensable component in language education. Under the trend of the digital technology revolution, digital literacies emerged in response to digital tools that facilitate interaction between people and the world through the

DOI: 10.4018/978-1-7998-1282-1.ch014

practices of reading, writing and communication (Hafner, Chik, & Jones, 2015). In Australia, Britain and the United States, the national education offices have incorporated digital literacies into their curricula and emphasized the importance of digital technology in school education practice (Pullen & Cole, 2010). They have noted that literacy focusing solely on reading and writing has been no longer able to meet social and pedagogical needs, and that digital technology should be incorporated in schooling as a form of mediation.

From the 1990s onwards, digital technology has been gaining widespread popularity in higher education because of the growing digitalization (Kirkwook & Price, 2013). Pre-service teachers, growing up in a digital era, have more access to digital technology and are more comfortable with its use, and their own digital literacies are becoming a vital issue in determining what and how they will do in their future teaching practice. According to Raith & Hegelheimer (2010), the application of digital technology has been identified as a basic skill for teacher education, and teachers are expected to embrace relevant technologies and apply them to their literacy teaching practices. However, there are different requirements of digital literacies in and out of educational contexts. Pre-service teachers' digital practices in informal context cannot necessarily be transformed into digital literacies in the educational setting. It is suggested that pedagogical use of digital technology should be embedded in education programs to improve current teaching and develop new approaches (Kirschner et al, 2008). In the global context, UNESCO's *ICT Competency Standards for Teachers* (2008) called on educational faculties to combine literacy education and digital technology in teacher education and preparation. Although wiki-based collaborative writing (WCW) has been gaining increasing popularity in literacy education, the use of wikis in Chinese writing in Mainland China is only at an early stage (Li et al., 2014).

Previous literatures examine pre-service teachers' beliefs about digital literacies development (e.g., Güneş & Bahçivan, 2018; List, 2019), while no research has ever focused on the development process in the WCW context. Therefore, there is a need to trace the developmental trajectories of pre-service teachers' digital literacies by comparing their past learning experiences with current teaching reflections within the digital literacies framework proposed by Jones & Hafner (2012), which serves as the analytic lens to show the complex nature of literacy development. Adopting a case study approach, this study explores how pre-service teachers develop their digital literacies through a wiki-based writing class and attempts to answer the following research questions:

1. What are the core components of pre-service teachers' digital literacies in the WCW context?
2. What developmental trajectories of pre-service teachers' digital literacies can be traced in a WCW context?

THEROTICAL FRAMEWORK

Digital Literacies

Gilster (1997) was among the first to define digital literacies, which means "the ability to understand and use information in multiple formats from a wide variety of sources when it is presented via computers." According to Dudency et al. (2013), it refers to "the individual and social skills needed to effectively interpret, manage, share and create meaning in the growing range of digital communication channels." From the definitions, it is evident that digital literacies are meaning-making skills that can be identified and categorized in digital settings (Eshet, 2004; Calvani et al., 2009; Pegrum, 2011). Similarly, Calvani et al. (2009) notes that 'the competence we are dealing with entails a critical understanding of technologies, a cognitive and cultural appreciation, and in particular the ability to select and manage information, along with relational and ethical awareness'. Taking notice of the differences of pre-service teachers' digital literacies in and out of educational contexts, Krumsvik (2014) proposes and develops a digital competence model for teachers and teacher educators in a Norwegian context. This model consists of four core components: basic digital skills, didactic ICT (Information Communications Technology)-competence, learning strategies and digital awareness. In sum, the dimensions above enable us to reflect on different kinds of actions, social relationships and ways of thinking, but they fail to take different kinds of meanings and social identities into account.

Although a set of frameworks are put forward to study digital literacy development, only a few are based on language learning and technology. In order to reveal the development of digital literacies in WCW context, this study adopts the framework of Hafner *et al.* (2015) with is located in the language and educational technology scope as the analytical lens. According to Hafner *et al.* (2015), digital literacies are the practices of reading, writing and communication through digital tools that facilitate interaction between people and the world. Adopting a sociocultural perspective, the authors view digital tools as mediations. Although the ability to use mediations (blogs, chats, wikis, etc.) reflects learners' digital literacies, knowing how to use those tools does not necessarily make one digitally literate, because the development of digital literacies involves many other dimensions as well.

Jones & Hafner (2012) points out that digital tools enable us to 'do new things, think in new ways, express new kinds of meaning, establish new kinds of relationships and be new kinds of people', and digital literacies are concerned with "what we can do, what we can mean, how we can relate to others, how or what we can think and who we can be", i.e. doing, meaning, relating, thinking and being (see Fig. 1). This division involves all the aforementioned important dimensions (e.g. Calvani et al., 2009; Dudency et al., 2013; Krumsvik, 2014; Hafner et al., 2015), and it is a comprehensive model to investigate pre-service teachers' development of digital literacies. Informed by the framework, this study adopted this model as the analytical lens for investigating how pre-service teachers develop their digital literacies during the transition from being a student to being a teacher through reflection and classroom observation.

Specifically, *Doing* means what digital tools allow us to do in the physical worlds. For instance, blogs enable us to write online, and search engines allow people to seek information online, which has dramatically changed our societies and cultures by offering us new abilities to handle daily routines. *Meaning* refers to what and how people express in digital situations, such as commenting on a blog written by peers. Web pages and hypertexts are carriers commonly used to express multimodal meaning, including characters, visual images, audios, videos, etc. *Relating* means relationships that people can have in particular situations, and different tools make us form different relations with others. When commenting on blog essays, individuals may ask questions for confirmation and contribute their own feelings and reflections. *Thinking* represents what people think about reality. For instance, people hold different views on participating digital communication. In terms of sharing information on social media, it is perceived that people may violate others' privacy by uploading a group photograph, which shows that privacy is no longer an individual matter as previously assumed. *Being* is social identity that people assume to fulfill their roles and claim their rights in a specific situation. In online affinity spaces, for instance, one may adopt a leading role as he or she creates a group to share information, and others are members or beneficiaries who receive it.

Figure 1. Dimensions of digital literacies (based on Jones & Hafner, 2012)

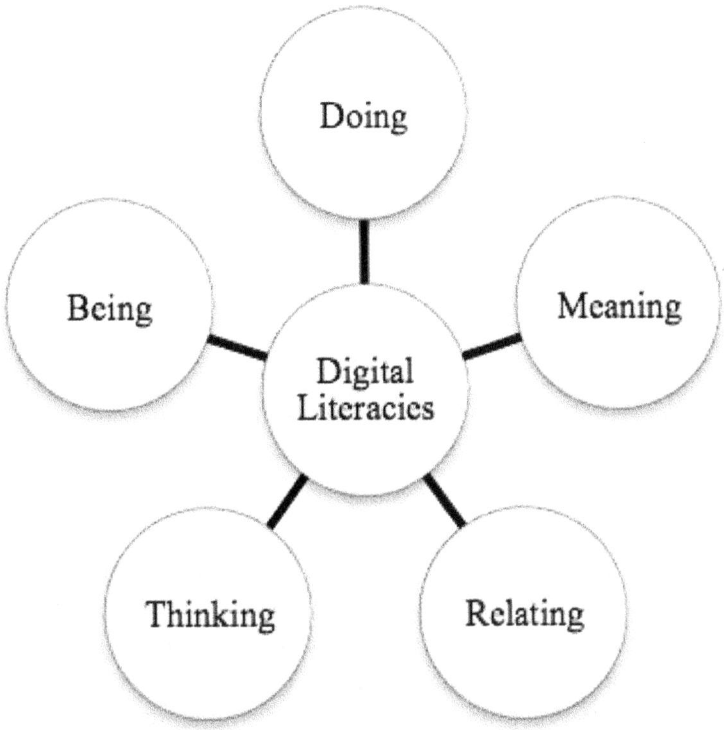

LITERATURE REVIEW

The Development of Digital Literacies

Previous literature has identified three conceptions of digital literacies development: digital literacy as an automatic process, digital literacy as a set of skills, and sociocultural perspective on digital literacy (List, 2019). As an automatic process, digital literacy is acquired automatically through exposure to and use of digital tools by pre-service teachers who grow up as digital natives (Margaryan *et al.*, 2011). Digital literacies can also be understood as an inter-related set of skills. Sefton *et al.* (2009) defines digital literacies as basic ICT skills and more advanced skills regarding the critical and creative affordances of digital tools. One of the latest researches, van Laar (2017), constructed a model including 21st century skills, information literacy, and new media literacy. But, according to Thorne (2013:193), digital literacies are not only a set of technical skills. With a sociocultural perspective, digital literacies are viewed as meaningful participation in online communities (Limberg et al., 2012).

WCW and Digital Literacies

With the advancement of writing tools, traditional paper-and-pencil writing is extended to digital media writing. Thus, two forms of writing task design attract our attention, i.e. paper-based individual writing and wiki-based collaborative writing. In terms of writing instruction, there is a controversy over the two in L1 and L2 writing teaching (Nunan, 2015). With the former approach, teachers are expected to select and explain various samples for learners to imitate and provide feedback on accuracy after learners hand in their work, which may result in learners' lack of critical thinking and writing styles as they have few opportunities to share ideas with their peers and are confined in the model essay (Pozzi, 2008). The latter approach, however, emphasizes cooperation, interaction and re-writing activities that foster teamwork spirit, improve writing skills and enhance target language learning (Woo et al., 2010; Liou et al., 2011; Wang et al., 2012).

Wiki technology pushes collaborative writing forward and provides a platform for writing practice. In recent years, WCW pedagogy has been acclaimed effective in improving writing instruction. Previous studies also investigate learners' perceptions of and attitudes towards WCW (e.g., Arnold et al., 2009; Aydin & Yildiz, 2014), proving that WCW pedagogy is recognized as a way to enhance learners' motivation (Warschauer, 2000), improve their writing skills (Mak & Coniam, 2008), strengthen reader-friendly awareness (Lin et al., 2010) and foster L2 writing performance (Hsu & Lo, 2018).

In terms of teacher education, WCW pedagogy is practical in expanding teachers' pedagogical knowledge (Li et al., 2012). Given the benefits, teacher educators are encouraged to embed technology-assisted writing instruction and the collaborative process approach in pre-service teachers' training programs (Drent & Meelissen, 2008).

WCW pedagogy, as an important approach to developing digital literacies, enables learners to make joint efforts to write online and provide mutual feedback. The central affordance of wikis is to set up an online platform for collaboration, co-construction and peer production where learners express their understanding of and viewpoints on a certain topic and establish a learning community where they exchange knowledge and information (Tan, 2011). In such a community, learners can be either a team leader in charge of the whole writing task or a team member assigned to complete the task. If WCW is to be adopted by L2 learners, they need to be able to write collaboratively and play their respective roles in the writing process on top of knowing how to operate a wiki.

Digital Literacies and Pre-Service Teacher Education

Although digital literacies, especially digital competence, are duly stressed in teacher education, previous studies paid special attention to a) perceptions of digital literacies in pre-service teacher education, especially digital tools affordances ('Thinking') and b) approaches to developing pre-service teachers' digital literacies.

In terms of digital literacies, two themes are highlighted in pre-service teacher education: a) digital literacies as linked to out-of-school practice; b) digital literacies as proving collaborative learning (Nascimento & Knobel, 2017). Previous research show that the didactic use of the tools provides both challenges and opportunities for learning and future teaching. On one hand, some pre-service teachers hold a positive attitude towards digital tools and are willing to use these technologies for the benefits they can bring (Kumar & Vigil, 2010). For example, digital technology can support and extend classroom discussion, create a professional learning community, provide greater opportunities for reflection, enhance critical thinking and learner autonomy, and foster appreciations (Sardegna & Dugartsyrenova, 2014). On the other hand, some pre-service teachers express their fears of using digital tools in their future teaching as these tools are not promoted in the teacher education program (Sang et al., 2010), so they do not develop a good digital awareness.

As for approaches to developing pre-service teachers' digital literacies, previous literature identifies that modeling digital technology for teaching, scaffolding their learning experience, and reflecting with pedagogical use of digital technology are proved to be feasible in facilitating digital literacies development (Enochsson & Rizza, 2009; Tondeur et al., 2012). As experiencing digital technology through teaching practice has proved to be feasible in facilitating the development of digital literacies (Røkenes & Krumsvik, 2014), there is a need to trace pre-service teachers' developmental trajectories. To fill the void identified above, the present study draws on a case study to explore how pre-service teachers develop their digital literacies through a WCW context.

METHODS

Study Context and Participants

The pre-service teacher education program in this study was part of a TCSOL (Teaching Chinese to Speakers of Other Languages) M.A. program for the spring semester of 2016 in a key university in Southern China. Twenty pre-service teachers took part in "language teaching resources: theory and practice" that focused on two of the most important and indispensable sections – classroom observation and teaching practice as an elective course. When illustrating online writing platform, the teacher educator in this course distinguished two approaches: paper-based individual writing and WCW. The former represents mere literacies, while the latter stands for digital literacies. According to the curriculum, the pre-service teachers were asked to observe at least two classes in a week and provide students with advice on their homework during the semester.

In order to explore the factors affecting the task design of WCW, the first author randomly selected four pre-service teachers enrolling in the course of "language teaching resources: theory and practice" as participants in this study and invited them to observe an 18-week intermediate Chinese writing classroom. Tony, Sara, John and Kate (all pseudonyms, see Table 1 for participants' information) were observers in a writing classroom among whom John and Kate were overseas pre-service teachers who majored in Chinese, while Tony and Sara were Chinese majoring in English and TCSOL, respectively, during their B.A. studies. This study involved both Chinese and oversea participants, with the aim of seeking opinions from pre-service teachers of different backgrounds. Before entering the classroom, all of them were trained to operate a wiki in order to have a good understanding of collaborative writing.

In this study, we focused on an 18-week intermediate Chinese writing. Except for the mid-term and final exams, there was a total of 16 weeks' writing practice time. Pansy, the teacher of this writing course, was a female teacher with a master's degree, and has taught Chinese for 3 years. Before the study, the first author introduced the concept of WCW and technical operation to Pansy. She believed that WCW was a new type of writing teaching model and was willing to participate in the experiment. According

Table 1.Pre-service teachers personal information

Name	Gender	Nationality	Second Languages
Tony	Male	China	English, French
Sara	Female	China	English, German
John	Male	Vietnam	Chinese, English
Kate	Female	Poland	Chinese, English

to the students' actual level and teaching plan, Pansy selected 4 cooperative writing tasks (see Table 2) in *The New Chinese Writing Course Book* (Luo Qingsong, Chinese Language Teaching Press, 2012).

As the learners did not have the experience of writing on a wiki platform, Pansy introduced the wiki platform to her students at the very beginning of the writing course during which she talked about the operation system of wikis and advised the students to create multimodal compositions if need be. Then, the four participants helped learners to operate wikis in practice. When the wiki platform was used for the first time, Pansy directed to group the learners. There were 16 students in the class that could be divided into four groups (ABCD), and group members took turns to be the team leader. To facilitate the learners, each of the four participants was responsible for the direction of a group.

As for the task process, learners immediately joined the group discussion once they had received writing tasks, reporting each person's point of view and ideas. The team leader was responsible for coordinating the division of labor, controlling the progress and handing in the final draft, while team members wrote a paragraph by each person in the wiki writing. After the drafting period, the team members evaluated mutually and uploaded the final version to the platform to get the whole class involved in the modification where the content, diction, punctuation, logic and ideas were the major concerns.

Data Collection and Analysis

The study employed a case study methodology (Stake, 1988) in which pre-service teachers' developmental trajectories of digital literacies were revealed. According to Stake (1988), a case study is defined as "a study of a bounded system, emphasizing the unity and wholeness of that system, but confining the attention to those aspects that are relevant to the research problem at the time". In the study, the methods of semi-structured interviews (Boling et al., 2014), participant observation (Merriam & Tisdell, 2016) and diaries (Numrich, 1996) were used to collect data.

Data from the interviews were gathered twice – one at the very beginning and the other at the end of the semester. Four 20-minute semi-structured interviews were conducted in the first round to invite the participants to talk about their past writing and learning experiences and views on teaching writing with digital technology. Before the interviews, all participants had taken the course 'TCSOL Theory and Practice' whereby they were learning how to teach writing. They were then asked to observe writing classes to learn how to combine what they had learned about the theories regarding teaching. The purpose of the participant observation was to help pre-service teachers accumulate teaching experience with digital technology and collect the data used to understand how four pre-service teachers developed their digital literacies in an educational context. The second four 20-minute interviews and diaries were conducted at the end of the semester to reflect what they had observed and learned. The interviews were

Table 2. Topics and writing tasks within the semester

No.	Topics	Tasks
1	Narrate small things in everyday life	A memorable gift
2	Introduce a place, describe the environment	My school
3	Lyrical narrative	Stories of learning Chinese
4	Explain the steps and methods	Introduce a sport

audio-recorded and the teaching reflection diaries were written in Chinese. Data were transcribed and translated into English, followed by member checking to ensure accuracy.

To analyze the data, we followed the procedures suggested by Boling et al. (2014) and the framework of digital literacies (Jones & Hafner, 2012) for data coding. By identifying, categorizing and describing the data, we coded the transcripts of the interviews and diaries and further divided the dimensions of digital literacies (Doing, Meaning, Relating, Thinking and Being) into several sub-categories. In coding 'Doing', for instance, when reading the interview transcripts and dairies, we identified that pre-service teachers in the current study mainly mentioned two major activities in a WCW context, i.e. task design and feedback provision, which echoes the definition 'Doing' termed by Jones and Hafner (2012). Thus, we combined them into the category of 'Doing'.

FINDINGS

Drawing upon the framework of digital literacies, the data analysis indicates that the core components of pre-service teachers' digital literacies in the WCW context are: attitudes towards technology and application (Thinking), task design and feedback provision (Doing), modes and genres (Meaning), teacher-student relations (Relating), roles and responsibilities (Being).

Attitudes Towards Technology and Application (Thinking)

The use of digital tools is a basic skill ensuring pre-service teachers' development of digital literacies. The findings show that four pre-service teachers' attitudes towards technology and application have gone through a complex process. To be specific, they underwent changes in attitudes towards teaching writing with wikis. For instance, Sara and Kate admitted that at the very beginning they were worried about technical problems because they were not adept at operating digital tools, nor were they confident that students were able to handle wiki-related problems in a short time. However, after their classroom observation and exposure to wikis, they realized that wiki technology was not as difficult as they had expected. For example,

I thought wiki technology was difficult to grasp before I understood it better. What happens if students do not know how to operate wikis? I myself do not want to spend time teaching them how to use wikis because that is far beyond my teaching objective. But later, I found that wiki, like blogs and other social tools, is not that difficult to operate. (Kate, E1)

The excerpt above shows that the female pre-service teacher, Kate, did not seem confident in the application of wikis to writing instruction until she grasped the core technology, while male teachers, Tony and John, reported that they preferred teaching writing with a wiki as it could motivate learners to write on a platform that provides an encouraging environment, indicating that they held a positive attitude towards wiki-based writing instruction.

More noticeably, one of the pre-service teachers, Sara, thought that wiki technology still had some room to improve in that some of the functions were not user-friendly. For example, the comparison function was not that direct and concrete, and students still needed time to distinguish the difference between the original and final versions. She suggested that wiki technology learn from Microsoft Word's Comment function and allow for detailed annotations.

When asked whether pre-service teachers would like to apply the wiki platform to their future Chinese language teaching, Chinese and international pre-service teachers demonstrated different views. Chinese pre-service teachers, Tony and Sara, held that they would like to try WCW as the main approach because wikis provided a platform that helps students learn and make progress. They expressed positive attitudes towards using wikis in their teaching.

According to my observation, wikis are a good tool for facilitating writing instruction for the following reasons. First, group discussions lay the foundation for brainstorming ideas and gathering opinions. Second, positive feedback strengthens students' confidence in writing and motivated them to be more creative. Third, I found most of the students expanded their vocabulary and constructed longer sentences. Therefore, I prefer this approach to teaching writing. (Tony, E2)

Previously as a student, I tended to read and learn essays written by my classmates and peers for accumulation and imitation. I did not prefer the samples provided by my teacher, and I do not think I can write that well. Therefore, wiki-based writing is a good choice. (Sara, E3)

However, international pre-service teachers expressed opposition against the use of wikis. John and Kate expressed their concerns about the application of wikis, and pointed out that students might not support wiki-based Chinese writing because they were afraid that online writing might prevent them from writing Chinese characters. John said,

The Chinese writing system is unique to students like me because they have to spend a lot of time understanding the system. When writing online, we do not write, but type instead. The typing software provides choices of the same sound, and we do not have to write characters. (John, E4)

This indicates that although WCW has been gaining popularity and developed rapidly in L2 English writing, the efforts to promote the use of L2 Chinese WCW may face resistance by Chinese learners. Chinese characters, unlike English ones, are harder to acquire. Chinese learners need more practice till they are able to read and write the Chinese characters smoothly. Evidently, it is essential to find a solution to this issue. Given this, Kate suggested that we combine online and offline writing in Chinese WCW, and those teachers construct a clear plan when organizing WCW, especially a plan for group control and monitoring. The following excerpt details Kate's suggestions on how to carry out Chinese WCW.

I am not sure if I will adopt wiki-based writing for the whole semester; maybe I will use wikis for half of the tasks. On one hand, I have to train students' Chinese character writing skills. On the other hand, I am afraid that I have to balance the relations of students and take charge of operating the wiki platform, which will take a lot of time. In my future teaching, I'd like to adopt both writing approaches. At the very beginning of the semester, I will ask them to write with wikis to check whether they prefer it and will adjust accordingly until they feel and perform best in a group setting. (Kate, E5)

Task Design and Feedback Provision (Doing)

Task design was found in the study to be a key 'doing' activity in which wikis were used to help teachers adopt new teaching models in a writing classroom, which usually involves a series of tasks. By examining pre-service teachers' past learning experiences, the current study found the following three kinds: textbook-oriented, instruction-oriented and interaction-oriented task design.

Under textbook-oriented task design, textbooks provide various sources of writing exercises and dictate teachers' teaching practices. After students complete such exercises, teachers provide answers and a few comments. This approach is echoed in Tony's story, as he recalled that his teacher asked him to complete various writing exercises on textbooks. He explained,

During my undergraduate study, my teacher relied on a textbook to teach a writing class, and organized classroom tasks according to the arrangement of the textbook. A writing class, as I understand it, is designed to cover a variety of exercises, such as error correction, punctuation and title writing, and paragraph development. (Tony, E6)

In instruction-oriented task design, teachers are responsible for giving instructions to learners by providing samples, explanations and analyses. John and Kate pointed out that their Chinese teaching class was in fact organized in this way. As John reported,

At the very beginning of each lesson, the teacher told us the topic and provided us with model essays. After that, she analyzed the introduction, the main body and the conclusion one after another, from which we could learn diction and sentence structures, and form an outline for writing our own essays. (John, E7)

Interaction-oriented task design means learning takes place in an interactive way among teachers and learners, as reflected in German writing lessons. As Sara put it,

My German teacher used to conduct his class by posing questions and organizing group discussions during which we shared our opinions. (Sara, E8)

Compared with task designs mentioned above, the participants reported that WCW helped develop their digital literacies through new platforms that facilitated collaborative learning. As John put it,

Wiki-based writing introduces to the class new ideas. Through in-class group discussion and collaborative writing, learners become more interested in writing and feel more motivated. In this process, we may have the opportunity to read essays written by other people and learn new language points. (John, D1)

Designing a coherent WCW task is a necessary part in completing a writing task. One of the participants, Kate, expressed her concern that the current WCW task design in Pansy's class might not help students develop good writing skills because limited writing practice expected of each student in such a task – often one paragraph or so – is not enough to bring about any substantial benefits for students.

I just wonder whether this type of collaboration will benefit students' writing. According to my experience, students tend to write a paragraph each time; will this method enable them to write an entire es-

say? Focusing on one paragraph does not guarantee that they will develop the skills necessary to write an essay. (Kate, E9)

It is obvious that teachers offer learners advice on division of labor, and that a one-student-one-paragraph policy is only one way of such division. Therefore, more approaches must be taken into account, such as individual writing followed by collaborative comments, as well as 'sequential writing', the process by which a student works on an essay before passing it on to the next student to improve the work.

In terms of process writing, four pre-service teachers showed varied views with respect to what impacts it might exert to students and how it was put into practice. Tony and Sara recognized that process writing was a plus for both teachers and students.

In the writing process, teachers are able to grasp learners' language development, and learners can deepen their understanding of language forms by constant revisions. (Tony, E10)

John and Kate, however, were concerned about learners' increasing fatigue resulting from the constant revisions expected of them.

I am not quite in favor of the idea of process writing. Correcting one version several times may lead to more trouble for learners, as they have to confront mistakes, which, of course, erases the sense of freshness. Moreover, they do not have enough opportunities to have access to other topics and vocabulary due to time constraints. (John, E11)

This indicates that teachers should take into account the revision times and task types in process writing. Since learners do not enjoy tedious revisions, teachers are advised to control revision times required and subject learners to different tasks. More importantly, each stage of a writing task should be directed to a specific focus, such as diction, grammar, structuring and views.

Feedback provision, especially in a digital form, is another part of digital literacies that all participants developed in educational contexts. Moreover, participants stated that although written notes and emails were commonly used communication tools, they often increased the time needed for teachers to offer feedback. With the wiki platform, learners are able to receive comments and inspiration quickly and effectively, whether from their teachers or peers. Tony and Kate stated,

Most of the time, my teacher adopted paper-and-pencil feedback. We seldom used digital feedback, say, emails, which was perhaps once in a semester. Both methods of feedback provision took a week or so. By the time we received feedback, we nearly forgot what we have written. But wikis may be more efficient as we can get others' comments once we pose our essay on the platform. (Tony, E12)

Adopting a wiki-based writing approach is seen as a positive way to enhance learners' individuality. Previously, an individual process writing approach depended on teachers' feedback and treated teachers as the only source of learning. As a result, students failed to develop their writing style and exchange ideas through interactions and cooperation in groups. (Kate, D2)

This indicates that the participants have noticed that digital feedback provision differs from traditional teacher-centered and paper-mediated feedback in how long it takes and how many people offer comments.

Although wikis had their merits, the current study found that there were still issues that teachers need to pay attention to. For instance, the standard of evaluation should be taken in account as individual and collaborative work each follow different rules. As Sara argued,

Teachers can easily judge an individual's writing based on certain criteria, but when it comes to collaborative writing, teachers should be more mindful of the division of labor and members' contributions in a group setting when providing feedback. (Sara, D3)

They suggest that the criteria for evaluating collaborative process writing need to be reconsidered to ensure feedback validity. Teachers, therefore, should be encouraged to find new criteria to judge the performances of learners and groups separately.

Modes and Genres (Meaning)

By participating in this study, four pre-service teachers realized that modes and genres are two important parts in 'meaning' making process. Previously, learners used monomodal resources (i.e. Chinese characters) to express their meaning. With the implementation of digital technology, they noticed that learners tended to adopt new modes in WCW practices, such as visual images, diagrams, charts and figures, tapping into multimodal resources to make their writing stand out. Sara mentioned,

Online writing enables us to use language in a creative way. During my field practice in an international school, students would like to present their collaborative work with pictures, hypertext and charts, making their work attractive and presentable. In this way, they adopted different ways to design their work and expressed meaningful ideas. (Sara, E13)

According to Sara, multimodal resources should be used effectively to facilitate meaningful expressions. In WCW, teachers are advised to encourage students to present their collaborative work in a multimodal way where the resources are integrated to convey meaning.

In addition to modes, pre-service teachers also consider the genre as another factor in 'meaning' making as different meanings vary in different genres. However, not all of the genres are suitable for adopting into a WCW task. Therefore, it is advised that appropriate genres and interesting topics be selected for collaborative writing. Kate mentioned,

Students may not work well with each other if the genre of a writing task is not preferable for collaborative purposes, such as resumes and notices. Topics about which they have nothing to say or which may cause conflicts may not be chosen for collaborative writing. (Kate, D4)

Teacher-Student Relations (Relating)

Pre-service teachers' digital literacies on 'relating' are reflected by their comparison and contrast on how individual product writing and WCW alter the relations between teachers and students. Previously in individual product writing, teachers interacted with learners through classroom instruction and organizing group activities, but seldom interacted with students outside of class. The interaction was often focused on grammar, vocabulary and writing skills, making the learning process a knowledge-based one. In the study, pre-service teachers reported that relations between teachers and students were relatively stable in individual product writing and that students viewed teachers as the authority of language and the only source of feedback. But they also emphasized that WCW exposed teachers to more opportunities to interact with students online and provided personalized instructions. The following excerpt shows that by organizing WCW, teachers become closer to students as the writing process increases interaction and forms interpersonal relations.

Teachers may provide advice on how to improve students' writing and constantly encourage them to move on by pointing out the progress students have made in the writing process. In turn, students may find joy in committing to the writing process, and I believe that students would like to talk to their teachers about issues other than errors and mistakes. (John, E14)

The findings further show that teachers have an important role to play in maintaining harmonious relations with students. Tony, in particular, stressed the importance of the roles teachers played in WCW.

Teachers are responsible for designing writing tasks, monitoring the writing process and giving advice on group structuring, writing skills and emotional support, and mutual feedback among learners could never replace the teachers' role, regardless of how well wiki-based collaborative process writing is organized. (Tony, E15)

Leaners' interactions are confined in a classroom setting in individual product writing. WCW, however, promotes co-relations between students by constructing a community bestowed with interaction, communication and cooperation. In such cases, it is possible that students rely on each other to complete writing tasks or projects, breaking the restrictions of time and space and allowing them to communicate anywhere at any time. In the study, Sara and John demonstrated that WCW improved relations among students in three important aspects. First, wiki serves as an instant feedback tool that provides technical support in connecting students in a group or in a class. Second, collaborative writing gives learners a fresh experience of writing, heightening their awareness of cooperation and a sense of collectivism. Third, commenting on the work of other groups makes mutual learning possible, and students' interactions promote mutual understanding and cognitive development.

In addition, all of the pre-service teachers believed that the relations among students could be strengthened with the help of teachers. Kate suggested that teachers create a collaborative environment in and out of the classroom where the individual's style, age, gender and characters are considered in grouping for collaborative writing. As she explained,

Group work may run smoothly if different levels of students are arranged in one group and group leaders are carefully chosen to ensure useful peer feedback, which is very important in the writing process. (Kate, E16)

Roles and Responsibilities (Being)

Pre-service teachers reported that both teachers and students experienced more diversified identities in collaborative process writing than individual product writing can ever afford, which is conducive to performing and enjoying different roles and responsibilities. In this study, Sara and Kate explained the changes from the teachers' perspective. Sara reported,

I think how teachers view their roles is very important. Previously in individual product writing, teachers dominated classroom teaching and feedback provision. With the incorporation of collaborative process writing, teachers are no longer the only reader and feedback provider; they are organizers, participants, supervisors and tutors in the discussion period. (Sara, E17)

This indicates that teachers are not placed in the center of writing teaching any more, and it is students who take charge of the writing process. Meanwhile, teachers have more roles and therefore, should perform more duties in the writing process. That is to say, mere classroom instruction is far from sufficient. The interaction between teachers and students in discussions and the exchange of ideas and thoughts are the key benefits of WCW.

According to John, students played different roles in a series of WCW activities, such as discussion, reading and writing, peer revision and feedback provision. More importantly, they had to switch their roles for different writing tasks because each activity constituted a way of learning. For example, group discussion required learners to think and talk actively to ensure the stream of interactions, while writing called for using language skills and cultural knowledge to communicate ideas and thoughts. The following excerpt shows that different roles were in action in different activities where students were pleased to face such development of identities.

Through my observation, I saw students actively performing their duties and readying themselves to face the challenges. A boy in Class B told me that he was glad to read and comment on his peer's work. In such a case, he believed that being a reader and a judge was a fresh experience. Another boy was happy to become a team leader in the writing, although it was only once. He said, 'I've dreamed for a long time to become a commander, and this time, in wiki-based writing, my dream came true.' (John, D5)

This shows that in WCW, different roles, such as readers, judges, team leaders and members, brought learners different experiences, resulting in increased enjoyment of the writing process. In order to facilitate WCW, John further suggested that it be a good idea for teachers to encourage students to perform different duties and play different roles, and that the roles of team leaders and members shift over time to expose students to different learning experiences. Moreover, John planned to encourage his students to share their stories of collaborative writing and leadership experience in the future.

DISCUSSION

Adopting WCW as a case, this study explores the developmental trajectories of four pre-service teachers' digital literacies within an educational environment.

The findings reveal that the participants experienced changed attitudes towards digital technology and its application. At the beginning of the semester, they expressed their doubts about teaching writing with wikis before they were exposed to wiki technology as they lacked basic trainings. After one semester, however, they overcame the fear of failing to rise up to the challenge posed by wiki technology. As Tan (2011) points out, if one is able to write an email or edit a Microsoft Word document, he or she should have no problem creating and editing wikis. Despite this, not all pre-service teachers are willing to embrace or try those new writing techniques. Therefore, this study finds it necessary to take how pre-service teachers really think about digital tools into account in their development of digital literacies, in an attempt to answer the call of Instefjord & Munthe (2015) to focus more empirical research on what is behind a teacher's willingness or reluctance to use wiki technology.

With an in-depth analysis of the perceptions of pre-service teachers in question, this study unequivocally reveals that their attitudes towards wiki technology and its applications ('Thinking') vary by gender and cultural background. The gender difference underlined in the current study is reflected in the fact that male teachers are more willing to accept and learn digital technology than female teachers. As List (2019) argued, some pre-service teachers acquired digital literacies automatically through their exploration of digital tools. Since male teachers tend to get access to digital tools, the autonomy-focused and technology-based conceptions may explain why male teachers developed their digital literacies more smoothly than female teachers in this dimension. According to Li et al. (2014), most of the students in their study developed a more positive attitude towards writing after adopting a WCW approach, but our study exhibits marked impacts of cultural backgrounds on swaying the pre-service teachers' attitudes towards WCW, demonstrating that Chinese teachers are more inclined to use wiki technology than their international counterparts. The reason why there exists this difference is that unlike Chinese teachers, international teachers know — whether from their own learning experience or their more frequent talks with students — most of their students' concern over how the use of wikis may lead to fewer opportunities to write Chinese characters. Although one of the pre-service teachers, Kate, believed that the concern was well-founded, she still recognized the benefits of wikis and developed her digital literacies by proposing a new approach that combines WCW and traditional paper-and-pencil writing, so that teachers can promote learners' Chinese character writing abilities as well as digital literacies.

The findings in relation to 'task design' echo those previous studies on collaborative writing strategies. Sharples et al. (1993) identifies sequential writing (one student works on the essay before passing it on to the next student), parallel writing (each student takes charge of a certain part of the essay), and reciprocal writing (students discuss, draft and respond to each other simultaneously). As it was the first time that WCW has been conducted, teachers and students in this study were relatively inexperienced in 'task design' to the extent that teachers only guided learners to follow a parallel writing strategy in the whole semester. At last, pre-service teachers in the current study noticed that different strategies should be well embedded in 'task design'. For example, reciprocal writing could be used at the pre-writing stage and sequential writing at the feedback stage. In terms of parallel writing, this study argues that a one-student-one-paragraph policy in WCW is not suitable because students cannot receive basic trainings on writing a coherent and integrated essay, but team members may have different roles to play based on their interests and competence, which indicates that four pre-service teachers acquire the core strategies in 'task design'.

A WCW approach goes through the stages of planning, drafting, providing feedback, revising and publishing (Li et al., 2012; Oskaz & Elola, 2014), of which feedback provision and revising caused the biggest concern among pre-service teachers. The current study reflects the development of pre-service teachers' digital literacies by arguing that tedious revising work may annoy and discourage learners, revealing a new source of criticism for process writing other than those identified in previous studies, such as its failure to foster factual writing (Nunan, 2015). More importantly, our study demonstrates that digital feedback provision, according to pre-service teachers in the study, is more complex than that on papers, as students are expected to work with teachers to comment on others' essays. This complexity calls for an evaluation of not only individual performance and the language of writing products, as highlighted by previous studies on feedback (Elola & Oskoz, 2016), but also students' teamwork and critical thinking.

In the study, although four pre-service teachers did not know the term 'multimodality', one of them did notice that students tended to use different ways to make 'meaning' on the wiki platform, whether by the use of tables, images or characters, which reflects that pre-services teachers' development in the perception of meaning-making resources and process. Tagg (2015) points out that language is by no means the only resource to make meaning, and that other resources, such as orthography, typography, font and images, are also available for writers. The use of multiple resources can have the benefit of making writing products more effective, as demonstrated by Aukerman & Schuldt (2016) through their experiment that clearly shows "pictures can say more things", especially when students are working on an expository writing task to introduce, for instance, a particular aspect of their country or culture. In light of this well-tested advantage, Gitsaki et al. (2010) suggests that various multimodal resources be used appropriately and purposefully in teaching. Other than the use of meaning-making multimodal resources, this study also adopts a genre-based teaching approach developed by Badger & White (2000), who argue that since writing is always bound by social context, a good writer should be able to choose and command a genre that best reflects a given social context. This makes it necessary for learners to not only gain a deep understanding of various genres, but also know how to put them into effective uses in a particular social context that they may encounter in their daily lives. This study extends the use of the genre-based teaching approach to WCW, and identified modes and genres as two key factors to be considered in the development of pre-service teachers digital literacies.

Unlike most of the previous studies on 'Relating' that are either concerned with teacher-student relations or relations among students (e.g. Jones & Hafner, 2012; Hung, 2016), the findings reveal that teachers, as authorities, may have constructive roles in helping students handle conflicts when a student is discontent with peer contributions. Thus, as teachers become mediators to maintain students' relations in WCW, they experience various identities, roles and responsibilities. This indicates that like students, teachers are also subject to development in terms of 'Being'. By involving teachers in a wiki task, this study puts equal emphasis on the roles of teachers and students, as opposed to previous studies that only stressed students' roles (e.g. Yu & Lee, 2016). The findings of this study illustrate 'Relating' and 'Being' from both the students and teachers' perspectives, which enables teacher educators to cultivate pre-service teachers' digital literacies with a new and equal approach.

Finally, it is clear from the study that although pre-service teachers in this study would like to try and adopt digital technology in future writing instruction, their digital literacies still had room to improve. "Doing" is not the only dimension that pre-service teachers need to focus on. They ought to develop their digital literacies in other four dimensions as no milestones have been found in the current study. Therefore, this study suggests that courses regarding digital literacies be embedded in the teacher education program. In fact, there are some improvements, such as the introduction of relevant courses in teacher education. According to Lo & Clarke (2010), a 12-hour course 'New Literacies' will be required of English language pre-service teachers in Hong Kong. They proposed that teacher educators implement digital technologies in the curriculum to make the current teacher education more multimodal, participative and collaborative, and that teacher educators need to infuse new literacies in training programs and daily practices. Since it is widely acknowledged that digital literacy is one of the most significant and essential competence in 21st century (Vavik & Salomon, 2015), there is a reason to believe that pre-service teachers who are digitally literate will provide high-quality and up-to-date education for the students.

IMPLICATIONS

Drawing upon the digital literacies framework (Jones & Hafner, 2012) and WCW pedagogy, this study focuses on four pre-service teachers' development of digital literacies. The findings have theoretical, empirical and practical implications for language teaching as well as teacher education.

A theoretical implication of this study is the application of a digital literacies framework to analyze qualitative data. Based on the transcription of interviews and dairies, the current study has further formed an extended framework to provide a panorama of WCW by detailing five dimensions (e.g. Doing, Meaning, Relating, Thinking and Being) as shown in Fig. 2. In this framework, 'modes and genre' (Meaning) is placed at the center surrounded by other dimensions because WCW aims to make meanings through the means of other dimensions. Moreover, leveraging the activity theory arguing that community and division of labor are two important factors in the activity system (Engeström, 2001; Lantolf & Thorne, 2013), the current framework develops to benefit both teachers and learners as a writing task can never be successful without the joint efforts of teachers and students. Consequently, applying this extended framework as an analytical model can help teacher educators and policy-makers understand what digital tasks are and should be in the educational context. Moreover, this framework may be used to examine other collaborative activities, such as collaborative oral presentations, blog writing and computer-assisted translation projects.

Empirically, this study contributes illuminating insights into wiki-based collaborative process L2 Chinese writing, which is scarcely studied in China. Instead of studying pre-service teachers' digital literacies in their teaching and daily lives (Burnett, 2011), this study attempts to examine how classroom observations changed their perceptions of WCW and the necessary measures for improving the current standard of instruction, which may serve as a guidance to implement an action research in the further studies.

Finally, the findings suggest that digital literacies be included in teaching and teacher education, which is of practical importance in a pedagogical setting. With the rapid advancement of digital technology, literacy education is undergoing significant changes to the extent that the image-and-screen replace print-

Figure 2. Dimensions of pre-service teachers' digital literacies (based on Jones & Hafner, 2012)

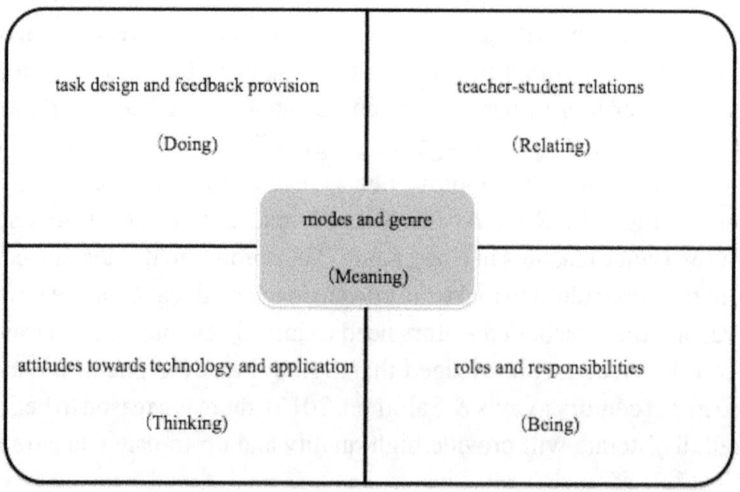

and-page as modes and media in communication (Kress, 2003). As today's young pre-service teachers and students grow up in a digital world, multiliteracies, which involve multiple identities and multiple modes in intercultural communications, are becoming the objective of literacy education (Kerin, 2009). For teaching, the concept of 'digital literacies' offers opportunities and challenges to both teachers and teacher educators. With such a background, the instructor of the intermediate L2 Chinese writing class in our study is responsive to the emergence of the new needs for developing students' digital literacies. From this perspective, this study suggests that teachers put WCW in the right place and adopt such an approach in their teaching if technology permits. For teacher education, a digitally literate teacher is supposed to grasp a set of skills and competencies regarding educational technology. To this end, this study proposes that pre-service teacher' digital literacies be developed through various ways. For instance, apart from WCW observation, courses regarding digital literacies should be embedded and digital activities be designed in teacher education program, as apparent in Hong Kong EFL teacher education (Lo & Clarke, 2010).

LIMITATIONS AND FURTHER RESEARCH

With a small scale, this study nevertheless sheds light on the core components and developmental trajectories of four pre-service teachers' digital literacies in a wiki-based collaborative writing context. To the benefit of further studies, this study suggests that mixed methods of research design be incorporated to study the development of teachers' digital literacies in other contexts. A general recommendation is that a larger number of pre-service and in-service teachers should be evolved to investigate how they develop digital literacies in educational contexts by adopting quantitative and qualitative methods. Moreover, an action research should be conducted as it can help teachers and teacher educators adopt theories to better understand and illustrate their WCW teaching practice to reflect and improve the wiki writing classroom (Burns, 2011). As this study is among the initial efforts to explore the development trajectories of pre-service teachers' digital literacies in a WCW context, we suggest that more empirical studies should investigate pre-service teachers' developmental stages and features of digital literacies, and explore how WCW affects learners' attitudes and competencies in writing. As we believe our digital literacies framework is built on a sociocultural perspective, WCW can also be applied to other collaborative activities, and more of such research is encouraged to find strategies, identities and meaning-making processes.

REFERENCES

Arnold, N., Ducate, L., & Kost, C. (2009). Collaborative writing in wikis: Insights from culture projects in German class. In L. Lomicka, & G. Lord (Eds.), *The next generation: Social networking and online collaboration in foreign language learning* (pp. 115–144). San Marcos, TX: CALICO.

Aukerman, M., & Schuldt, L. C. (2016). "The pictures can say more things": Change across time in young children's references to images and words during text discussion. *Reading Research Quarterly*, *51*(3), 267–287. doi:10.1002/rrq.138

Aydin, Z., & Yildiz, S. (2014). Using wikis to promote collaborative EFL writing. *Language Learning & Technology*, *18*(1), 160–180.

Badger, R., & Write, G. (2000). A process genre approach to teaching writing. *ELT Journal, 54*(2), 153–160. doi:10.1093/elt/54.2.153

Boling, E. C., Holan, E., Horbatt, B., Hough, M., Jean-Louis, J., Khurana, C., ... Spiezio, C. (2014). Using online tools for communication and collaboration: Understanding educators' experiences in an online course. *Internet & Higher Education, 23*, 48–55. doi:10.1016/j.iheduc.2014.07.002

Burnett, C. (2011). Pre-service teachers' digital literacy practices: Exploring contingency in identity and digital literacy in and out of educational contexts. *Language and Education, 25*(5), 433–449. doi :10.1080/09500782.2011.584347

Burns, A. (2011). *Doing action research in English language teaching: A guide for practitioners*. Beijing, China: Foreign Language Teaching and Research Press.

Calvani, A., Fini, A., & Ranieri, M. (2009). Assessing digital competence in secondary education. Issues, models and instruments. In M. Learning (Ed.), *Issues in information and media literacy: education, practice, and pedagogy* (pp. 153–172). Santa Rosa, CA: Information Science Press.

Dingli, A., & Seychell, D. (2015). *The new digital natives*. Berlin, Germany: Springer. doi:10.1007/978-3-662-46590-5

Drent, M., & Meelissen, M. (2008). Which factors obstruct or stimulate teacher educators to use ICT innovatively? *Computers & Education, 51*(1), 187–199. doi:10.1016/j.compedu.2007.05.001

Dudeney, G., Hockly, N., & Pegrum, M. (2013). *Digital literacies: Research and Resources in language teaching*. London, UK: Routledge.

Egbert, J. L., Shahrokni, S. A., Zhang, X., Yahia, I. A., Borysenko, N., Mohamed, A. F. S., ... Aljarih, F. (2018). Planning for future inquiry: Gaps in the call research. [IJCALLT]. *International Journal of Computer-Assisted Language Learning and Teaching, 8*(2), 39–59. doi:10.4018/IJCALLT.2018040103

Elola, I., & Oskoz, A. (2016). Supporting second language writing using multimodal feedback. *Foreign Language Annals, 49*(1), 58–74. doi:10.1111/flan.12183

Engeström, Y. (2001). Expansive learning at work: toward an activity theoretical reconceptualization. *Journal of Education and Work, 14*(1), 133–156. doi:10.1080/13639080020028747

Enochsson, A. B., & Rizza, C. (2009). ICT in initial teacher training: Research review (38). *OECD Education Working Paper*: OECD Publishing.

Eshet-Alkalai, Y. (2004). Digital literacy: A conceptual framework for survival skills in the digital era. *Journal of Educational Multimedia and Hypermedia, 13*(1), 93–106.

Gilster, P. (1997). *Digital Literacy*. New York: John Wiley & Sons.

Gitsaki, C., Ya'akub, A., & Honan, E. (2010). ICT integration in second language writing: a Malay language case study. In D. L. Pullen, & D. R. Cole (Eds.), Multiliteracies and technology enhanced education: social practices and the global classroom. Hershey, PA: IGI Global. doi:10.4018/978-1-60566-673-0.ch011

Güneş, E., & Bahçivan, E. (2018). A mixed research-based model for pre-service science teachers' digital literacy: Responses to "which beliefs" and "how and why they interact" questions. *Computers & Education, 118*, 96–106. doi:10.1016/j.compedu.2017.11.012

Hafner, C. A., Chik, A., & Jones, R. H. (2015). Digital literacies and language learning. *Language Learning & Technology, 19*(3), 1–7.

Hsu, H.-C., & Lo, Y.-F. (2018). Using wiki-mediated collaboration to foster L2 writing performance. *Language Learning & Technology, 22*(3), 103–123.

Hung, S. T. A. (2016). Enhancing feedback provision through multimodal video technology. *Computers & Education, 98*, 90–101. doi:10.1016/j.compedu.2016.03.009

Instefjord, E., & Munthe, E. (2015). Preparing pre-service teachers to integrate technology: An analysis of the emphasis on digital competence in teacher education curricula. *European Journal of Teacher Education, 39*, 1–17.

Jones, R. H., & Hafner, C. A. (2012). *Understanding digital literacies: a practical introduction*. London, UK: Routledge. doi:10.4324/9780203095317

Kerin, R. (2009). Digital portraits: teacher education and multiliteracies pedagogy. In V. Carrington, & M. Robinson (Eds.), *Digital literacies: social learning and classroom practice*. London, UK: Sage. doi:10.4135/9781446288238.n9

Kirkwood, A., & Price, L. (2013). Technology-enhanced learning and teaching in higher education: What is 'enhanced' and how do we know? A critical literature review. *Learning, Media, and Technology, 39*(1), 6–36. doi:10.1080/17439884.2013.770404

Kirschner, P., Wubbels, T., & Brekelmans, M. (2008). *Benchmarks for teacher education programs in the pedagogical use of ict.international handbook of information technology in primary and secondary education*. US: Springer.

Kress, G. (2003). *Literacy in the new media age*. London, UK: Routledge.

Krumsvik, R. J. (2014). Teacher educators' digital competence. *Scandinavian Journal of Educational Research, 58*(3), 269–280. doi:10.1080/00313831.2012.726273

Kumar, S., & Vigil, K. (2010). Pre-service teachers' perspectives on web 2.0 integration in teacher education courses. In J. Sanchez, & K. Zhang (Eds.), *Proceedings of e-learn: world conference on e-learning in corporate, government, healthcare, and higher education, 1908-1913*.

Lantolf, J. P., & Thorne, S. L. (2013). *Sociocultural theory and the genesis of second language development*. Shanghai, China: Shanghai Foreign Language Education Press.

Li, X., Chu, S. K. W., & Ki, W. W. (2014). The effects of a wiki-based collaborative process writing pedagogy on writing ability and attitudes among upper primary school students in mainland China. *Computers & Education, 77*, 151–169. doi:10.1016/j.compedu.2014.04.019

Li, X., Chu, S. K. W., Ki, W. W., & Woo, M. (2012). Using a wiki-based collaborative process writing pedagogy to facilitate collaborative writing among Chinese primary school students. *Australasian Journal of Educational Technology, 28*(1), 159–181. doi:10.14742/ajet.889

Limberg, L., Sundin, O., & Talja, S. (2012). Three theoretical perspectives on information literacy. *Hum. IT: J. Inf. Technol. Stud. Hum. Sci., 11*(2).

Lin, L., Cranton, P., & Bridglall, B. (2010). Psychological type and asynchronous written dialogue in adult learning. *Teachers College Record, 107*(8), 1788–1813. doi:10.1111/j.1467-9620.2005.00542.x

Liou, H. C., & Lee, S. L. (2011). How wiki-based writing influences college students' collaborative and individual composing products, processes, and learners' perceptions. [IJCALLT]. *International Journal of Computer-Assisted Language Learning and Teaching, 1*(1), 45–61. doi:10.4018/ijcallt.2011010104

List, A. (2019). Defining digital literacy development: An examination of pre- service teachers' beliefs. *Computers & Education, 138*, 146–158. doi:10.1016/j.compedu.2019.03.009

Lo, M., & Clarke, M. (2010). Practicing or preaching? Teacher educators and student teachers appropriating new literacies. In D. L. Pullen, & D. R. Cole (Eds.), *Multiliteracies and technology enhanced education: social practice and the global classroom*. New York: Information Science Reference. doi:10.4018/978-1-60566-673-0.ch010

Mak, B., & Coniam, D. (2008). Using wikis to enhance and develop writing skills among secondary school students in Hong Kong. *System, 36*(3), 437–455. doi:10.1016/j.system.2008.02.004

Margaryan, A., Littlejohn, A., & Vojt, G. (2011). Are digital natives a myth or reality? University students' use of digital technologies. *Computers & Education, 56*(2), 429–440. doi:10.1016/j.compedu.2010.09.004

Merriam, S. B., & Tisdell, E. J. (2016). *Qualitative research: a guide to design and implementation* (4th ed.). Jossey Bass.

Nascimento, A. K., & Knobel, M. (2017). What's to be learned? A review of sociocultural digital literacies research within pre-service teacher education. *Nordic Journal of Digital Literacy, 12*(3), 67–88. doi:10.18261/issn.1891-943x-2017-03-03

Numrich, C. (1996). On becoming a language teacher: Insights from diary studies. *TESOL Quarterly, 30*(1), 131–153. doi:10.2307/3587610

Nunan, D. (2015). *Teaching English to speakers of other languages: an introduction*. London, UK: Routledge. doi:10.4324/9781315740553

Oskaz, A., & Elola, I. (2014). Promoting foreign language collaborative writing through the use of Web 2.0 tools and tasks. In M. González-Lloret, & L. Ortega (Eds.), *Technology-mediated TBLT: Researching technology and tasks*. Amsterdam, The Netherlands: John Benjamins Publishing. doi:10.1075/tblt.6.05osk

Pegrum, M. (2011). Modified, multiplied, and (re-) mixed: Social media and digital literacies. In M. Thomas (Ed.), *Digital Education: opportunities for social collaboration* (pp. 9–35). Basingstoke, UK: Palgrave Macmillan. doi:10.1057/9780230118003_2

Peled, Y., Shalom, O., & Sharon, R. (2014). Characterization of pre-service teachers' attitude to feedback in a wiki-environment framework. *Interactive Learning Environments*, *22*(5), 578–593. doi:10.1080/10494820.2012.731002

Pozzi, F. (2008). Teaching dimension in web-based learning communities. *International Journal of Web-Based Learning and Teaching Technologies*, *3*(3), 34–43. doi:10.4018/jwltt.2008070103

Pullen, D. L., & Cole, D. R. (2010). *Multiliteracies and technology enhanced education: social practice and the global classroom*. New York: Information Science Reference. doi:10.4018/978-1-60566-673-0

Raith, T., & Hegelheimer, V. (2010). Teacher development, TBLT and technology. In M. Thomas, & H. Reinders (Eds.), *Task-based language learning and teaching with technology*. London, UK: Continuum International Publishing Group.

Røkenes, F. M., & Krumsvik, R. J. (2014). Development of student teachers' digital competence in teacher education: A literature review. *Nordic Journal of Digital Literacy*, *9*(4), 250–280.

Sang, G., Valcke, M., Braak, J. V., & Tondeur, J. (2010). Student teachers' thinking processes and ict integration: Predictors of prospective teaching behaviors with educational technology. *Computers & Education*, *54*(1), 103–112. doi:10.1016/j.compedu.2009.07.010

Sardegna, V. G., & Dugartsyrenova, V. A. (2014). Pre-service foreign language teachers' perspectives on learning with technology. *Foreign Language Annals*, *47*(1), 147–167. doi:10.1111/flan.12078

Sharples, M., Goodlet, J. S., Beck, E. E., Wood, C. C., Easterbrook, S. M., & Plowman, L. (1993). *Research issues in the study of computer supported collaborative writing*. London, UK: Springer. doi:10.1007/978-1-4471-2007-0

Stake, R. (1988). Case study methods in educational research: Seeking sweet water. In R. M. Jaeger (Ed.), *Complementary methods for research in education*. Washington, DC: American Educational Research Association.

Tagg, C. (2015). *Exploring digital communication: Language in action*. London, UK: Routledge. doi:10.4324/9781315727165

Tan, A. (2011). Why write with wikis? In C. M. L. Ho, K. T. Anderson, & A. P. Leong (Eds.), *Transforming literacies and language: multimodality and literacy in the new media age*. London, UK: Continuum.

Thorne, S. (2013). Digital literacies. In M. Hawkins (Ed.), *Framing languages and literacies: socially situated views and perspectives* (pp. 192–218). New York: Routledge.

Tondeur, J., van Braak, J., Sang, G., Voogt, J., Fisser, P., & Ottenbreit-Leftwich, A. (2012). Preparing pre-service teachers to integrate technology in education: A synthesis of qualitative evidence. *Computers & Education*, *59*(1), 134–144. doi:10.1016/j.compedu.2011.10.009

United Nations Educational, Scientific and Cultural Organization (UNESCO). (2008). *ICT competency standards for teachers – competency standard modules*. Retrieved from http://unesdoc.unesco.org/images/0015/001562/156207e.pdf

van Laar, E., van Deursen, A. J., van Dijk, J. A., & de Haan, J. (2017). The relation between 21st-century skills and digital skills: A systematic literature review. *Computers in Human Behavior*, *72*, 577–588. doi:10.1016/j.chb.2017.03.010

Vavik, L., & Salomon, G. (2015). Twenty First Century skills vs. disciplinary studies. In Handbook of research on technology tools for real-world skill development (pp. 1-12). Hershey, PA: IGI Global.

Wang, D., Zou, B., & Xing, M. (2012). Interactive learning between Chinese students learning English and English students leaning Chinese on the platform of wiki. [IJCALLT]. *International Journal of Computer-Assisted Language Learning and Teaching*, *1*(3), 70–85. doi:10.4018/ijcallt.2011070105

Warschauer, M. (2000). The death of cyberspace and the rebirth of CALL. *English Teachers Journal*, *1*, 61–67.

Woo, M., Chu, S., Ho, A., & Li, X. (2010). Collaborative writing with a wiki in a primary five English classroom. *Managing knowledge for global and collaborative innovations*. 193-206.

Yu, S., & Lee, I. (2016). Exploring Chinese students' strategy use in a cooperative peer feedback writing group. *System*, *58*, 1–11. doi:10.1016/j.system.2016.02.005

Section 4

Virtual Reality

Chapter 15
Avatar Teaching and Learning:
Examining Language Teaching and Learning Practices in Virtual Reality Environments

Geoff Lawrence
https://orcid.org/0000-0002-5759-815X
York University, Canada

Farhana Ahmed
https://orcid.org/0000-0001-6163-7468
York University, Canada

ABSTRACT

This chapter examines the pedagogical potential of immersive social virtual worlds (SVWs) in language teaching and learning. Recognizing the language learning affordances of immersive virtual environments, this research examines a study analyzing the beliefs and practices of 'Karelia Kondor', an avatar-learner and teacher of languages with a decade of diverse experiences in Second Life (SL), one of the first widely used SVWs. Findings highlight the relevance of a hyper-immersive and emotionally engaging conceptual model informing language teaching approaches within these rapidly evolving environments. When supported pedagogically, the activities illustrated demonstrate the potential of these immersive approaches to create communities of practice and affinity spaces by fostering investment and autonomy in the language learning process through shared target language experiences. The chapter concludes with a summary of pedagogical insights to inform the use of these hyper-immersive environments in language teaching and learning.

DOI: 10.4018/978-1-7998-1282-1.ch015

INTRODUCTION

Three-dimensional (3-D) virtual and augmented reality media are increasingly being recognized as ideal environments for second/additional language teaching and learning. Virtual world[1] (VW) learning platforms that began with Active Worlds, Second Life (SL) and Open Wonderland have evolved into mobile-friendly augmented reality[2] and virtual world environments including Oculus Rift, Pokemon Go and Project Sansar[3] that have the potential to add an interactive, simulative and immersive dimension into language teaching practices (Buckley & Perez, 2019; Deutschmann & Panichi, 2009; Lin & Lan, 2015; Loke, 2015; Panichi, 2015; Scrivner, Madewell; Wang, 2017). These emerging environments offer the potential of hyper-immersive, multimodal target language simulations that cognitively, kinesthetically and emotionally engage learners, activating a range of linguistic, cultural and collaborative resources that can facilitate linguistic, intercultural and 21st century skills (Deutschmann & Panichi, 2009; Hanewald, 2013; Lin & Lan, 2015; Shrestha & Harrison, 2019).

Second Life (SL) was launched in 2003 and quickly became one of the most prominent and accessible 3-D multi-user social virtual world (SVW) environments used in education (Wang, 2017). Research on SL focused on suggesting ways to use this platform in education (Hismanoglu, 2012), analyzing the environment and its language learning potential (Panichi, 2015). However, many teachers remain unclear how to integrate these dynamic platforms into their language learning environments.

The field of language instruction has been slow to embrace immersive technologies in teaching practices as "there is still not a clear vision of how to integrate these technologies in a stable way into an educational process" (Martin-Gutierrez et al., 2017, as cited in Scrivner et al., 2019, p. 56). Although the use of these environments tend to be increasingly seen as promising for language learning, there remains a dearth of research examining teacher perspectives on the potential, relevance and approaches needed in 3-D VW language education (Lin & Lan, 2015). There is minimal research documenting task design and pedagogical approaches relevant for language teaching/learning in SVWs. In addition, little if any research has examined VW teaching practices through the eyes of an experienced avatar language learner and teacher.

The purpose of this chapter is to provide pedagogical insights into the potential uses of SVWs in language teaching and learning. This chapter will revisit and update an article reporting on a unique study examining the beliefs and practices of an avatar learner and teacher with extensive plurilingual experiences in SL (Lawrence & Ahmed, 2018), a teacher who immersed herself within these environments in varied teaching and learning roles using a range of languages over a 10-year period. Findings will be shared from this study that examined interviews with 'Karelia Kondor', who learned Italian as an adult, taught French to secondary students and designed a range of virtual world curricula. She designed and facilitated telecollaborative German language game-based exchanges and participated extensively in educational communities of practice, all within SL. The study examined the following question: What experiences and pedagogical insights inform language teaching and learning practices within these online immersive environments?

This chapter offers perspectives on hyper-immersive SVWs, their benefits, limitations and the pedagogical potential to inform language teaching within these platforms. The chapter will begin with a definition of SVWs, outlining the affordances and limitations of these environments. The relevance of sociocultural theories to inform SVW use and this study will then be examined, followed by the study's methodology and a profile of this key informant. An analysis of findings, organized by key themes identified in the data will then be discussed. Links between these themes and language teaching practices and theories will follow. Pedagogical insights to guide teaching practices within these unique environments and the need for future research will conclude the chapter.

DEFINING SOCIAL VIRTUAL WORLDS

3-D VWs have been defined by Kozlova & Priven (2015, p. 83) as the most complex modern technologies for their synchronous, multimodal communication, their simulation of real-life experiences and learning spaces that are conceptually different from face-to-face classroom and other online learning environments. Loke (2015, p. 112) defines VWs as "computer-based, multi-user virtual environments that simulate real or fictional life and that users experience using their graphical representations or avatars." According to Panichi (2015, p. 465), the most significant characteristics of 3-D VWs is the immersive nature of the platform, impacting language learning activities and learner engagement. Hanewald (2013) categorizes virtual worlds as either gaming virtual worlds, SVWs or educational virtual worlds. Educational VWs are characterized by experiential learning, having active in-world experiences based on learning particular content or through simulations (Hanewald, 2013, p. 238). Although the gaming and socializing aspects of VWs initially attracted many users, the educational possibilities are now drawing more institutions to explore classroom applications within these environments.

In spite of their original intentions, educators and researchers are now working with a range of SVWs to understand the pedagogical principles, theories and practices that can inform the use of these tools in language teaching and learning. The emerging potential of these environments that fray the boundaries between study and play (Sykes, Oskoz, & Thorne, 2016, p. 176) has captured an increasing range of educators, researchers and prompted the study outlined below. This research embraces Mayrath, Traphagan, Heikes and Trivedi's (2011) definition that SVWs like SL are not a game, but a social virtual world that "provides a platform for users to create and/or explore places and spaces…enhancing student engagement, facilitating collaboration and providing situated learning opportunities that are unavailable in traditional learning environments" (p.126). This definition resonates with the varied experiences of Karelia Kondor, as a language learner and then as a teacher in SL.

AFFORDANCES OF SVWs

SVWs are an evolution of Web 2.0 tools that are designed to be social and collaborative environments (Sadler & Dooly, 2014), offering simulated interactions within immersive spaces. Hismanoglu (2012) concludes that virtual worlds like SL are particularly appropriate for teaching and learning foreign languages due to their immersive environments. They provide learners with life-like situations to interact socially, exchange cultural information, construct meaning collaboratively in authentic-like contexts which might be costly or impossible to replicate in real life (Hismanoglu, 2012, p. 105). Some of the distinguishing features of SL in relation to language learning can be listed as follows:

- *The multimodal nature of SL, provides multiple communication channels and a variety of feedback;*
- *The accessible nature of these open environments provide opportunities for learner-centered interactions involving target language speakers and a diverse group of interlocutors;*

- *The anonymity of avatars can reduce affective filters where learners take more risks and engage in language play;*
- *Personalized avatars provide enhanced feelings of co-presence leading to high degree of engagement;*
- *Tasks designed to facilitate interaction enhance participation and provide opportunities for using the target language;*
- *The supportive atmosphere engendered by interaction strengthens group cohesion and develops collaborative social relationships.*

(Peterson, 2011, pp. 69-70)

Providing a sense of community, belonging and collaborative learning opportunities through resources for learners and teachers makes SVWs unique platforms, worthy of consideration in language education (Duncan, Miller, & Jiang, 2012; Hanewald, 2013; Peterson, 2012; Wang, Lefaiver, Wang, & Hunt, 2011). For example, the interactive nature of SL facilitates teaching online by not just speaking into a microphone, but by acting, performing and collaborating with students, affording learners dynamic learning to complement the traditional language classroom (Wang, et al., 2011, p. 33). Peterson's (2012, p. 20) study on EFL learner collaborations suggests that SL provides an arena for learner-centered social interaction offering opportunities for target language practice and the development of autonomy. Virtual environments have also been reported to provide a positive affective dimension to the language learning experience and have made students more engaged and autonomous learners (Sama & Wu, 2019, p. 73). Furthermore, the technology-enhanced interaction within these environments facilitates the consistent production of target language output and learner centered rather than teacher led interaction (Peterson, 2010, p. 289).

In addition, the mediated experiences of simulated SVW environments encourage learners to experiment with varied communicative norms, developing pragmatic competence (Sykes et al., 2016). Such environments reduce learners' affective filters, enabling risk-taking in the learning process and a willingness to shift perspectives and play while learning (Lin & Lan, 2015). Interactions in these environments can thereby facilitate intercultural awareness and competence (Diehl & Prins, 2008). For example, learners adopting a gender or ethnic background different than their own can interact through a different perspective and expand their worldviews through such simulations (Diehl & Prins, 2008). This fluid identity affordance allows learners to play with identity and work with imagined communities (Norton, 2013) actualizing visions in the target language that can foster investment and learning (Dörnyei, 2009).

As a result, SVW platforms offer educators a range of affective dimensions to learning that can deepen motivation and learning. For example, principles of gamification can be used in task design to enhance learner engagement, interaction and cognition. By integrating elements of gamification such as mechanics and game-thinking (i.e., offering options, challenges, competition and rewards) in esthetically engaging environments, engagement and risk-taking can be sustained and notions of failure and mistakes can be reframed as a necessary part of task completion, skill development and learning (Dominguez et al., 2013). Leveraging elements of gamification in task design and teaching practices can contribute to affinity spaces where learners share expertise in common activities with similar goals, developing practices, knowledge and/or skills (Gee & Hayes, 2012).

LIMITATIONS OF SVWs

The most widely cited limitations of SVWs include the digital literacies required to effectively interact within these emerging environments (Sykes et al., 2016; Wang, 2017). These include a steep learning curve and technical difficulties to use these platforms, making it time-consuming for educators to integrate into classroom learning (Wang, 2017). Other constraining factors include hardware issues, digital access and expenses involved in purchasing, enhancing or maintaining one's learning environment, as in SL, one can purchase 'land' and accessories to enhance interactions, avatars and environments (Hismanoglu, 2012). There are concerns around security working with young learners in some of these open environments (Lee & Warren, 2007). Issues like identity masking, theft and cyberbullying can pose a serious concern for teachers wanting to use these environments with learners of any age (Lee & Warren, 2007).

In addition, maneuvering avatars to their full potential can require practice and time. Sykes et al. (2016) identify pragmatic control of the communicative norms used within a specific online community as time-consuming but necessary for full participation in these environments. Examining EFL teaching in SL, Wang et al. (2011, p. 35) identified technical problems like frozen screens, delayed audio and pedagogical problems, along with challenging classroom management as impediments to successful language learning. Teachers in this study reported issues like students walking or flying away from instructional sites, straying off topic or not speaking at all, avatars lacking facial expressions and body language leading to the teacher's inability to anticipate comprehension (Wang et al., 2011, p. 35). The study stresses the need for SVW-specific classroom management guidelines. "Too much functionality" and the diverse simulated environments can distract students, while teachers complained that when observing students' performance, the avatars' body language and expressions were not as intuitive as those in a traditional classroom (Duncan et al., 2012, p. 12).

The flexible, expansive nature of SVW platforms necessitates dramatic shifts in teacher and learner roles. Unless activities within these environments are acutely structured, learners in these environments can change identities, locations and move around freely. Learners have intense autonomy and numerous distractions that can prevent them from focusing on a language learning task. In addition, teachers need to adopt new roles as a learning 'observer', a guide/facilitator, a task 'director' and someone often responsible for tech guidance and support. Such changes can be daunting for instructors and learners to adopt, necessitating a supportive approach to fully orient learners and instructors to these new educational roles.

SOCIOCULTURALLY-INFORMED PEDAGOGY

Several interrelated language teaching and learning theories inform the use of SVWs in language education and help shed perspectives on the pedagogical findings discussed below. Sociocultural theory (SCT) highlights the interconnected roles of the social context, the teacher as facilitator and the mediational tools used for language learning and teaching (Lantolf, 2011). The rapidly changing influence of technology on language use and the need for language work to be within a learner's reach, the zone of proximal development, continue to inform language teaching practices with technology. "SCT is very much concerned with concrete classroom activities and its impact on learning" (Lantolf, 2011, p. 43) and this is very much being explored in SL through task-based learning. The ability to combine multimodal verbal, visual and kinesthetic activities in an SVW task can lead towards a deep, multi-level understanding of language use (Sykes et al., 2016). Such multisensory learning in these environments can be enhanced by emotional engagement (Swain, 2013), contributing to situated learning where learning is embedded within experiential activities within these immersive environments (Lave & Wenger, 1990).

Embedded within this SCT framework is the mediational role of identities and particularly imagined identities (Norton, 2013) and one's idealized L2 self, as discussed in Dörnyei's (2009) L2 self-motivation system that help mediate learning. Immersive interactions with extensive imagery enhancement in these environments help learners visualize their ideal L2 self that can enhance target language-and-culture curiosity, investment and learning (Dörnyei, 2009, p. 34). This experimentation with identity and work with emotion can reduce inhibitions and foster a reflective mindfulness that can deepen motivation, metacognitive and strategic skills, social connections and learning beyond the classroom (Sykes et al., 2016). As a result, SVW simulations can facilitate affinity spaces as noted above where value is placed on shared experiences, prompting reflection, meaning-making and informal learning within these shared situated learning experiences (Gee, 2005). This multi-faceted SCT perspective sheds a valuable perspective on L2 learning in SVWs that will be discussed in the research below.

EXAMINING DIMENSIONS OF AVATAR LANGUAGE TEACHING AND LEARNING: A STUDY

The study below examines the experiences, beliefs and reflections from a unique key informant, an educator who has spent over a decade teaching and learning a range of languages using varied approaches in SL (Lawrence & Ahmed, 2018). As noted above, this exploratory study examined and documented the teaching and learning practices of Karelia Kondor, a language teacher and learner who ventured into SL when virtual reality (VR) was first emerging and used it in varied capacities to teach and learn languages. The study's methodology is outlined below, followed by details on this educator's background and beliefs. This is followed by a discussion and analysis of findings related to these practices.

METHODOLOGY

This study adopted a qualitative research approach combining semi-structured interviews with document analysis to elicit and analyze Karelia Kondor's experiences and perceptions as a key informant within SL. Given this study's focus examining the lived experiences of Karelia, documenting her beliefs, reflections and perceptions as a highly experienced teacher-learner within SL, a qualitative analysis was used to contextualize these stories, to identify patterns of benefits, limitations within SVWs and to develop pedagogical insights from this key informant's lived experiences and voice.

Two 60-minute audio-recorded interviews were conducted using Google+ Hangouts. The researchers shared the interview questions (see Appendix 1) with the participant one week prior to the interview to provide preparation time to revisit past classroom experiences and to allow the participant to share relevant documents. The interview data was fully transcribed and then thematically coded by the researchers over the period of eight weeks using NVIVO 10 to identify and refine recurring themes within her responses. Transcribed data was shared with the participant to ensure member checks, so "data [and findings were] mutually constructed by the researcher and the researched" (Wertz, Charmaz, McMullen, Josselson, Anderson & McSpadden, 2011, p. 169). Other data sources like participant reflections on email exchanges, videos on her use of SL in teaching and learning, her personal blogs were used to interpret, analyse and triangulate selected themes and findings. An autobiographical Youtube video detailing her Italian learning experiences was also reviewed to establish a close encounter with the participant's 'language learner self'. All these documents were reviewed, seeking recurring patterns, corroborating and disconfirming instances to ensure reliability (Stake, 1995).

KARELIA KONDOR: BACKGROUND AND BELIEFS

Karelia has a background teaching French, German, music, and beginner Italian to secondary school students and English pronunciation to adults in England. She has worked as a language teacher and has always been involved with online language teaching approaches. She was an early adopter of online approaches in the late 1990s, working for a school that received funding to demonstrate how information technology can improve learner experience. Since then she's "never looked back" and has been extremely active in online learning, being an innovator using SVWs in her teaching and learning. She has networked with other educators interested in online approaches through her work in professional associations and online teacher communities. She admitted loving "the fact that you could get so much information from other teachers being online".

She "stumbled across" SL through a professional development opportunity. In response to a colleague's invitation to attend a conference, she created her avatar and began her journey on SL. "I thought this is fantastic, you can go along and get professional development from the comfort of your chair, and enjoy it." A comment in a conference document she attended got Karelia very motivated and thinking, "to convince teachers of really how good something is, very often if they've experienced it as a learner, that's the best sort of insight you can give them" (Allen, 2010, 1:20). She noted the power of communities of practice, the friends she has made who have helped with her teaching and learning journey in SL. "Even when I talk about it [now], I can't help but be excited about it." She has continued to share a range of SL teaching strategies through her blogs and videos. Karelia was seen as an ideal participant for this type of study as she had the experience of being both a student and a teacher on the SL platform as Coles believes that "a good instructor learns only when he becomes a willing student, eager to be taught" (as cited in Connelly & Clandinin, 1990, p.22).

FINDINGS AND ANALYSIS

The findings below are organized under themes identified through the analysis of this avatar-learner-teacher's experiences in SL. The findings are presented and analyzed noting links to the theoretical perspectives outlined above.

Hyper-Immersive and Emotionally Engaging Action-Oriented Learning

A consistent language learning benefit that emerged when speaking to Karelia was the potential of these environments to offer hyper-immersive, situated multimodal learning that engages learners in fun, emotionally engaging, purposeful action-oriented tasks. "You've got to give them a reason to talk" she stressed, citing the power of immersive, purposeful interactions in language learning, noting that these media are a practical alternative to target language immersion for the language classroom (Peterson,

2011). Karelia notes, "the real benefit is this feeling of being immersed, because people will say for any learning [to take place], if you feel immersed, you feel engaged, especially if there's some sort of emotion involved."

Karelia cited the example of a multi-lesson activity she experienced as an Italian language learner in an informal class held weekly in SL with adult learners who worked collaboratively to create a machinima, a film recorded by the learners in SL that they would develop, star in and eventually watch together. Because this film was being prepared in an open environment in SL, an Italian-speaking colleague of the teacher dropped in and offered to play a part in this film. As a result, the learners gained the benefit of interactions and feedback from this Italian-speaking individual. Karelia commented that these experiences can be "more memorable if you're with a French or Italian speaker."

The instructor divided the activity into subtasks. Initially learners created the characters, the storyline and assigned parts around the film's title "A Hairdresser's Husband". In their roles, the learners then began creating their dialogues, working in separate sound parcels in SL where the teacher flew in, listened and provided guidance. Karelia noted that while listening to students, the teacher would transcribe the dialogue so it was all captured. "If we said something incorrect, she'd correct us and every now and then a note card would pop up saying here's the latest of what you've said". Karelia praised this scaffolded, multimodal approach that provided instant corrective feedback fostering noticing and a focus on linguistic form and meaning (Hismanoglu, 2012; Schmidt, 1990). The learners eventually performed the film in a set prepared by this teacher who also filmed the movie within SL using Fraps[4]. The teacher's recording of the film within SL allowed the students to watch the movie and their performances in Italian through a celebratory event where the learners dressed up and attended a mock Academy Award screening in a cinema, got 'Oscars' and then went out partying in SL.

This multi-staged task demonstrates a situated action-oriented task-based approach to learning where learners engage in goal-oriented tasks, strategically activating specific competencies in a set of purposeful actions that exercise a range of language skills (Ellis, 2006; Piccardo, 2014). Such an approach "makes learning tangible, palpable, and meaningful" (Piccardo, 2014, p. 27). It also leverages the benefits of task-based learning where teaching aims to create meaningful authentic contexts in which language learning capacity can be nurtured rather than learning language through a structural approach (Ellis, 2006). In addition, the use of a machinima as an action-oriented reflective teaching tool has been reported to deepen the engagement of language learners (Shrestha & Harrison, 2019, p. 37).

Karelia noted a strong degree of emotional investment in this task, a concept that has informed her own SVW pedagogy. She noted, "It didn't feel like learning…instead a real feeling of being immersed in Italian and connected with each other". This feeling is reiterated in one of her blogs commenting about her French teaching experiences in SL, "There is no doubt in my mind that language sticks better when you have been fully immersed in a situation where you came across it for the first time, whether physically or emotionally." (Kondor, 2016, para 1). Such emotional engagement describes the possibility for these hyper-immersive environments to create affinity spaces where individuals are drawn together in an absorbing activity where informal language learning happens (Gee, 2005) but where the power of language play and emotional involvement takes precedence (Swain, 2013). Such tasks in SVW environments leverage the often unrecognized power of emotion to spark and fuel cognition (Swain, 2013), creating opportunities for learners to gain embodied experience with concepts and language which can lead to situated understanding and long-term retention (Gee & Hayes, 2011).

Gamifying Language Learning

In discussions with Karelia, she reinforced the relevance of gamification in SVW learning. She stated that the experiential learning opportunities in life-like game-based situations make learning memorable and meaningful, "playing games in 3-dimensional consequences" (Kondor, 2013, 2:31). As a student learning Italian in SL, she gave an example of a vocabulary game where students are seated on chairs and lifted up with every correct word they provide. Once at the top, students had to solve a word search embedded in a wall. When solved, the wall fell apart and allowed the student avatars to move onto the next level of the game. She recalled getting gifts like scooters as recognition of their successful feat in this vocabulary competition. She remarked that these fun games and activities made students relax in each other's company and that "the gifts encouraged them to have a go" (Kondor, 2013, 3:15). This example illustrates the power of integrating game-based approaches that are creative while being language-focused to facilitate language acquisition through a heightened motivational state (Flores, 2015).

Karelia later shared another successful game-based telecollaborative activity that she developed in collaboration with a Dutch secondary school teacher. She met this teacher in SL and then offline at a conference and decided to collaborate on a game-based project in SL where his Dutch learners of German had to interact with Karelia's English learners of German. With the help of a game developer they designed a game using principles of game-based learning, attending to the mechanics (i.e., objectives, rules, processes), the dynamics (i.e., player behaviour) and the emotions (i.e., the players' state of mind throughout the game) of the desired game-based activity (Pitarch, 2018). In this game, paired students had to go through a scenario of six doors representing different levels. Students had to solve a series of problems, exchange information, like passwords in German, to open a sequence of doors to move through levels of the game. The telecollaborative nature of this game where the participants did not share the same first language encouraged learners to communicate using the target language of German throughout the game. Karelia described this game as a great success as it engaged learners through competitive interaction and successful task completion that involved language tasks. Karelia stressed the importance of designing "games that required [students] to communicate, because so often with these games, communication is not needed."

Facilitative Stress and Tech-Talk Learning

Another type of emotionally charged interaction that Karelia identified as endemic to SL is the need for learners in these SVWs to use 'tech-talk' to troubleshoot navigation and communication problems, common in these immersive environments. She remarked that this type of authentic target language communication seems to recur in SL given its unfamiliarity to many learners (Wang, 2017). She highlighted this type of interaction as often emotionally charged and therefore a prime opportunity for language learning.

SL is where things often go wrong...so you find that you get in an emotional state about how you do something. It may sound really odd, but it's things like: can you hear me? My microphone's not working.

She noted having had many of these experiences as a learner. "It makes it more memorable because you're there and you really need to communicate". Her initial mistakes, like, sitting on people, actually led to asking for help and learning, as "doing things wrong provokes laughter which supposes a real human thing, breaking down barriers" (Kondor, 2013, 1:32). Reinforcing a teaching approach that actively works with emotion, she added that the facilitative stress and emotion around these interactions "make the memory of this interaction and language stick".

Authentic Interactions Emphasizing Listening and Speaking

Karelia noted that teachers using SL can create what sometimes is lacking in the language classroom, "genuine interactions, not made-up ones". She highlighted the ability of activities in these virtual environments to provide extensive opportunities for practicing speaking and listening skills, areas that are often lacking in traditional classroom contexts. "At the productive stage, that's the bit where SL absolutely beats anything that you can do in your own classroom", she noted. Karelia commented that as she is walking around the streets of Paris in SL projecting SL-mediated interactions in front of her students (discussed below), they may see a notice and because it is in context and meaningful, "it's more likely to stick than any amount of repetition and drilling I might do in the classroom".

Admitting that some people do not see interactions in SL as authentic, Karelia responded, "it's a real person sitting behind that avatar...you want to talk to them, get to know them...this is real life and these are real people". Karelia remarked that interactions in SL can be more engaging and authentic than a role play rehearsed by the lockers or from following lessons in a text. She adds, "it is comfortably over and above what you can offer in a normal teaching situation" (Allen, 2010, 4:52). Scrivner, et al. (2019) also found that the immersive aspect of VW technologies provide "students with active control and more authentic experiences; thus, helping them learn more effectively and increase their retention" (p. 55). The result of this collaborative research at Indiana University which investigated the impact of mobile immersive technologies (i.e., Aurasma, ThingLink, and Google Cardboard) for foreign language teaching and learning found that augmented reality successfully supported the learning of vocabulary and listening skills, whereas virtual reality enhanced cultural learning with spatial immersion (p. 69). Usage-based linguistics also 'claims that language is ultimately learned through exposure to authentic language exemplars and through the meaningful use of language as means of actual communication (Lech & Harris, 2019, p. 43).

In her second interview, Karelia emphasized that the presence of an actual person behind an avatar makes the interactions "genuine", "not made up ones" and provides a reason for learners to interact, "a motivation for having interaction because you get to know the people, you want to talk to them". Highlighting the link between these types of interactions and language acquisition, Sama and Wu (2019) found in a study examining an online "Talk Abroad" (TA) video-synchronous communication tool, that Italian language learners made significant increases in oral proficiency (especially in accuracy and fluency), and in autonomy in linguistic development and self-regulated learning strategies (p. 73). Students reported being more engaged and motivated to use Italian in their everyday life (p. 90). Students expressed excitement and engagement in being able to participate in the online conversation partner sessions. All students reported having had a positive affective experience, as they became more engaged and autonomous learners as the course progressed (p. 90). They also mentioned that it was especially good practice as it was "similar to real life" (p. 86).

Identity Manipulation and Engagement

A key aspect to engaging learners in meaningful and fun interactions in SVWs appears to be the fact that everyone adopts an avatar, a unique and alternate identity in the SL environment. Karelia stressed the affective benefit of this: "People are more anxious about speaking [in another language] but behind the avatar, people will speak more openly". She also noted that "people say you can hide behind your mask...I feel sometimes that a mask lets you be yourself". These thoughts reflect research on the notion that avatars can reduce inhibitions, affective filters and encourage risk-taking, which can be useful in extending one's language proficiency (Gee & Hayes, 2011; Peterson, 2011).

Karelia noted the potential engagement when interacting through an avatar that became an idealized vision of herself (Dörnyei, 2009). This feeling is further echoed in her autobiographical video (Kondor, 2013, 6:50).

The 3D environment sets it apart, your avatar becomes you, you cannot help but be kinesthetically involved in learning as you move about the world, manipulate objects, type for chat...And there are plenty of studies which indicate that this sort of learning has great results.

She contrasted her learner identity of her Italian character in the machinima discussed above, with her offline 'self'.

[The teacher] had this fantastic [film] set...we were in a hairdressing salon...having our hair done and speaking and listening in Italian all the time...Later I had a lovely black dress. We all got our Oscars... and like, see, I'm quite an ordinary person, really.

Such identity manipulation affords learners the ability to embody different communicative roles in a simulated space, developing pragmatic functions in varied contexts (Sykes et al., 2016). When describing her French SL identity that she uses to teach French secondary students, she notes sarcastically, "They [my students] saw my avatar, which already made them laugh, because of course, I said, I make her look just like me, mid 20's, pink hair" (see Figure 1 below).

Language-and-Culture Learning

In her Italian SL classes, Karelia's Italian language teacher invited Karelia and her classmates into an environment in SL that recreated the island of Sardinia. "You had a group of people so proud of their heritage and of their history, that they'd recreated elements of Sardinia, and we all walked around, and they would introduce us to these ancient monuments and aspects of their lives/cultures which they'd recreated." Karelia added that this integrated a focus on culture-and-language learning, elements that can be forgotten in a classroom context. In this lesson students were given an emic understanding of these cultural elements, shared by insiders with investment in this culture, facilitating an intercultural learning environment where languages and cultures can be recreated and explored (Sykes et al., 2016).

VR technology allows for the incorporation of cultural and communicative aspects of language learning. In contrast to traditional images and videos used in language classes, VR offers a 360 degree view of an environment that enables participants to experience an immersive spatial environment that is effective for language learning (Scrivner, et al., 2019, p. 59). Telecollaborative experiences in foreign language learning have also been reported to have supported enhanced intercultural exchanges and competences (Gomez, 2019, pp. 151, 161). For example, the ability to easily adopt a new identity, to experience interactions and the behaviour of others through this new identity in SVWs can expand worldviews and perspectives on one's cultural self and the complexity of other cultures and experiences (Hasler, 2011).

Figure 1. An image of Karelia Kondor © 2009, Helen Myers. (Used with permission)

Karelia described their visit to Sardinia in SL as a valuable intercultural language learning experience where these Sardinian hosts facilitated intercultural learning while enhancing language skills. For example, throughout these exchanges, students and these Sardinian hosts were speaking and writing while Karelia's teacher would mediate difficult phrases when the group did not understand. In fact, the experience was so memorable that Karelia made connections with some of these Sardinian individuals and pursued offline learning with several of them after.

Fostering Communities of Practice

As noted, a recurring theme in discussions with Karelia was the potential of SL to provide networks that extended learning through different contexts. Her experiences as a language learner were storied with anecdotes about dynamic language learning communities of practice that she would leverage as a learner and teacher. According to Karelia, these interactions fueled ongoing language learning, teacher education and friendships. She noted initially making friends with English teachers who were happy to speak with her as a first language English speaker. "...that's how I made friends, and then they helped my language learning as some of them were German, some French, some Italian. They would involve me in their lessons, and I made friends with them." For example, some of her Italian speaking classmates asked if she could help them with their English pronunciation. This prompted her to offer weekly English pronunciation classes with some of these classmates. These quickly evolved into a form of tandem learning as these collaborators shared their linguistic and cultural knowledge with each other.

Karelia reported using these teacher communities to help with questions around French language and culture.

...if I had a query about language, I could just pop into [this French speaking community] and find someone, and they'd loved to know that people were interested in learning about their culture and language.

These examples of socially mediated learning illustrate the power of these hyper-immersive environments to facilitate online communities of practice where a group of individuals (teachers in this case) engage in ongoing collective learning in a shared practice (Wenger, 1998). Karelia and these teachers interact and leverage collective knowledge, resources and experiences to refine individual language learning and teaching practices through shared experiences that build investment in the community. These interactions consequently transform the communities, the interactive networks and build competence through these sustainable, dynamic connections (Siemens, 2005).

A Web-Enhanced Teacher-Mediated Approach for Younger Learners

In discussing SL limitations, Karelia noted that SL is ideally for a "self-motivated IT savvy adult" (Allen, 2010, 4:06). Recognizing the inherent security challenges in SVW environments inhibiting use with younger learners, Karelia adopted a web-enhanced interactive approach that she used with her secondary school French learners. Karelia considered these activities her most successful SL teaching experiences. She invited guest French speakers from her SL communities and would project herself interacting with these individuals in SL using a laptop and projector in front of her students in her classroom. This provided her students with authentic language-and-culture input that they would actively use in class. She began this with her French language sixth form students[5] and developed a series of lessons that reflected curricular goals of the course; each lesson involved at least one pre-planned simulation with a French speaking colleague that Karelia would then project in front of her class.

She would design each episode ahead of time with her guest speaker(s) so each person knew her/his role, their interactions and the learning outcomes of the class. She would introduce her students to the forthcoming interactions in class and assign them tasks to perform before, during and after the interactions. For example, one of her most memorable lessons was inviting a retired French language teacher who interacted as a chic, French avatar to join Karelia in finding a holiday home in Arcachon, France. She assigned her students homework, using the vocabulary they heard, to write a description of their own homes to promote as a holiday rental. In the projected interaction, the two avatars visited a number of holiday homes in the SL town of Arcachon, touring around each home and discussing each home's pros and cons. Students were tasked with transcribing new vocabulary, asking questions to clarify vocabulary and preparing to argue for their preferred holiday home. As they explored these homes, Karelia and her friend introduced idiomatic language and wrote down any new expression so students could see it on the screen as well as hear it.

Karelia declared that the homework she got from her students after this activity was far better in terms of lexical and rhetorical outcomes than their usual work responding to a text-based assignment. She noted that students had used a larger breadth of vocabulary and expressions, many that were used in the activity. "I've never had such fantastic results...I know I can't put it down to that one lesson but… it did seem to capture their imagination." She added, "I had a parent's evening the next week and I think nearly every parent talked about that lesson…they had a teacher crazy enough to do this." Nevertheless, Karelia admitted this took substantial time and preparation to work with her SL colleagues to prepare this SL simulation to project in front of her students. Although Karelia admitted that student learning tended to be heightened with this type of simulated language input, there were some students who expressed frustration that they could not directly participate in these simulations and were limited to the role of observers.

PEDAGOGICAL GUIDELINES

Karelia's insights from this study and the literature discussed above inform the following pedagogical guidelines that can be used to guide SVW use in language teaching and learning. These pedagogical guidelines are listed in four categories. The first three are ones that Karelia highlighted as essential when integrating these platforms into one's language teaching practice (Lawrence & Ahmed, 2018, p. 10). The fourth has been added to help guide teaching practices in SVW environments.

1. Task design and preparation
    - Connect with a mentor or community who has teaching experience in these environments to help guide you.
    - Choose action-oriented, project-based tasks that are goal-oriented, require collaboration and transactional language that involve relevant situated learning (i.e., role plays, describing an environment, visiting a tourist office).
    - Integrate gaming principles and emotion into task design (i.e., considering gaming mechanics, design, emotion) (Pitarch, 2018).
    - Integrate skills in situations where learners have to speak/listen, read and write, exercising both fluency and accuracy to find and convey information.
    - Methodically prepare the task embedding short and focused sub-tasks with time limits to maintain attention and limit distractions.
    - Prepare tasks and follow guidelines to effectively foster autonomy, putting learners in control of their language learning (Benson, 2011, pp. 121- 197).
2. Defining communicative norms and developing autonomous learning strategies
    - SVWs create unique interactive environments so teachers must explicitly discuss and practice turn-taking strategies, communicative practices, and feedback strategies like tapping avatars, as non-verbal cues will be lacking.
    - Conduct a pre-task in-class activity to orient learners to specific language use, terminology, the necessary skills and communication strategies needed.
    - Orient learners to autonomous learning strategies that can be used in a task and transferred to language learning beyond the program.
    - Hold a tech-talk practice session using the target language within the SVW environment, negotiating troubleshooting norms; this can develop transferable target language strategies to navigate tech issues that are likely to occur.
    - Consider supporting learner autonomy by consulting the six approaches associated with the development of learner autonomy in language learning and teaching practices (Benson, 2011, pp. 125-196).
    - If intercultural learning is desired, build in explicit learning about one's cultural self, culture-general learning (i.e., general categories of cultural behaviour), intercultural communication and reflection strategies and processes to examine miscommunication (Lawrence, 2013).
3. SVW and tech design
    - Choose an SVW environment with a simple design: flat surfaces, no rivers or trees; have your avatars readily clothed when students log in and create a no-fly zone to prevent students from flying off during lessons. Ensure everyone is equipped with working headphones and speakers.

  - Ensure all safeguarding is in place. Password protect educational spaces, restricting access to anyone without the link or password, particularly if teaching young learners. As noted above, younger learners can also be spectator-participants, actively using interactions they observe.
  - Start with less demanding tech-activities, simple games or tasks that do not make the tech requirements more demanding than the language requirements.
  - Orient yourself fully to the technology and learning environment and plan to remove any student whose tech is interfering with the rest of the class (prepare students with a backup lesson should technology fail and a student must withdraw).
  - If possible have a readily available tech-support (or tech savvy mentor) during the activity.
4. In-world teaching
  - Ensure learners are well oriented to task responsibilities before task initiation (preparing/distributing a task responsibility checklist if needed).
  - Establish pre-task peer mentoring teams for in-world tech support so learners know who to ask if tech support is needed.
  - Adopt a facilitative role during the task, supporting learners when/as needed.
  - Actively observe interactions, providing language and learning feedback.
  - Note areas of language use, misuse and topics to debrief with learners to guide classroom teaching.
  - Engage in active reflection to improve task design, SVW pedagogy and areas for further self-development.
  - Record newly planned sessions as they are taking place in-world, for reflection and improvement of task design.

CONCLUDING THOUGHTS

This research suggests that SVWs offer language learning programs a range of affordances. These emerging environments offer the potential of multimodal target language immersive experiences that emotionally engage learners in situated, task-based learning, activating language use, noticing, play and emotional responses that can result in learning that sticks (Hanewald, 2013; Swain, 2013). Tech-talk interactions can build transferable linguistic, sociolinguistic and strategic competences that are relevant for today's digital age (Hanewald, 2013; Wang, 2017). Avatar identities can encourage linguistic risk-taking, target language output and error awareness within the language learning process (de Jong Derrington, 2013). Avatar-mediated interactions can provide a "cloak of anonymity" and the "adoption of a new persona" (de Jong Derrington, 2013, p. 147) that can forge imagined identities that can build intercultural competence, intrinsic motivation, fueling language-and-culture learning efforts (Norton, 2013). When well designed, SVW activities can leverage elements of play and gamification to deepen learner investment and learning communities (Gee & Hayes, 2011). As illustrated by Karelia's experiences, the social connections possible in these virtual worlds can connect learners to communities of practice that can spark affinity spaces (Gee, 2005) and ongoing language-and-culture learning. For teachers, such communities can provide professional resources to help refine language-and-culture knowledge and practices.

However, SVWs have serious educational limitations. As Karelia noted, the communicative interactions within these environments currently omit naturalistic visual and non-verbal cues that influence conveyed meaning (Duncan, et al., 2012, p. 12). If not supported by sound, complementary pedagogy, sociolinguistic and intercultural learning within these environments can be seriously constrained. This is where learner-centred, task-based pedagogy offered in a blended learning environment where activities are conducted in SVWs and in a face-to-face or synchronous classroom environment can engage learners in complementary experiences. Recognizing these limitations, Karelia uses these environments as an enhancement to learning, to primarily foster language production. As Karelia affirmed, interactions are most successful when mediated by the instructor. This raises questions about the role of teacher presence and its impact on pedagogy. Does the learning experience become more teacher-centred or are there ways to scaffold learner-centred interactions as a teacher would in a classroom context? Thomas and Schneider's (2018) study investigating language learning in 3D VWs "reinforces the argument that creating opportunities for pedagogical purposes in virtual worlds implies that teachers need to change their perspectives to take advantages of the affordances offered" (p. 20). This is where more action-research on SVW pedagogy would be useful.

While these limitations outlined may be resolved with adaptations, a prohibitive barrier to SVW use is the need for time. As emphasized above, lesson preparation for these activities, even with guest interactors/interlocutors, requires a substantial investment of time and preparation. And unfortunately, time acts as a great inhibitor of many technology-mediated language teaching approaches (Lawrence, 2014). This may be where professional communities of practice can help offer templates and tools to scaffold the teaching process.

Nevertheless, the potential of these 3-D virtual worlds for language education is promising. Emerging forms of virtual reality continue to expand and in the future will likely offer a more naturalistic resemblance of communicative interaction. Karelia and other early adopters have forged a path into the use of these mediums for language learning and teaching. Karelia's use of SL interactions as a web-enhanced language learning tool is an encouraging example of a differentiated practice serving a specific group of learners to complement face-to-face learning. As Karelia commented, "SL is something they will not forget. It's the pleasure that you see in your learners, that's the promise of learning."

REFERENCES

Allen, C. [Karelia Kondor- Teachmeet Second Life]. (2010, May 9). *Karelia Kondor (Helen Myres) presentation at the first Teachmeet Second Life talking about learning languages using Second Life* [Video file]. Retrieved from https://www.youtube.com/watch?v=LhTAmHM34gE

Benson, P. (2011). *Teaching and researching: Autonomy in language learning*. London, UK: Pearson Education Limited.

Connelly, F. M., & Clandinin, J. D. (1990). Stories of experience and narrative inquiry. *Educational Researcher, 19*(5), 2–14. doi:10.3102/0013189X019005002

de Jong Derrington, M. (2013). Second language acquisition by immersive and collaborative task-based learning in a virtual world. In M. Childs, & A. Peachey (Eds.), *Understanding learning in virtual worlds* (pp. 135–163). London, UK: Springer. doi:10.1007/978-1-4471-5370-2_8

Deutschmann, M., & Panichi, L. (2009). Talking into empty space? Signalling involvement in a virtual language classroom in Second Life. *Language Awareness, 18*(3-4), 310–328. doi:10.1080/09658410903197306

Diehl, W. C., & Prins, E. (2008). Unintended outcomes in Second Life: Intercultural literacy and cultural identity in a virtual world. *Language and Intercultural Communication*, *8*(2), 101–118. doi:10.1080/14708470802139619

Dominguez, A., Saenz-de-Navarrete, J., de Marcos, L., Fernandez-Sanz, L., Pages, C., & Martinez-Herraiz, J.-J. (2013). Gamifying learning experiences: Practical implications and outcomes. *Computers & Education*, *63*, 380–392. doi:10.1016/j.compedu.2012.12.020

Dörnyei, Z. (2009). The L2 motivational self system. In Z. Dörnyei, & E. Ushioda (Eds.), *Motivation, language identity and the L2 self* (pp. 9–42). Bristol: Multilingual Matters. doi:10.21832/9781847691293-003

Duncan, I., Miller, A., & Jiang, S. (2012). A taxonomy of virtual worlds usage in education. *British Journal of Educational Technology*, *43*(6), 949–964. doi:10.1111/j.1467-8535.2011.01263.x

Flores, J. F. F. (2015). Using gamification to enhance second language learning. *Digital Education Review, (27)*, 32-54.

Gee, J. P., & Hayes, E. (2012). Nurturing affinity spaces and game-based learning. In *Games, learning, and society: Learning and meaning in the digital age* (pp. 129–153). Cambridge University Press; doi:10.1017/CBO9781139031127.015

Gee, J. P., & Hayes, E. R. (2011). *Language and learning in the digital age*. New York, NY: Routledge. doi:10.4324/9780203830918

Gomez, M. V. G. (2019). Developing soft skills in higher education foreign language programs. Initial insights into telecollaboration. In M. L. Carrio-Pastor (Ed.), *Teaching language and teaching literature in virtual environments* (pp. 151–161). Singapore: Springer Nature Singapore Pte Ltd. doi:10.1007/978-981-13-1358-5_8

Hanewald, R. (2013). Learners and collaborative learning in virtual worlds: A review of the literature. *Turkish Online Journal of Distance Education*, *14*(2), 233–247.

Hasler, B. S. (2011). Intercultural collaborative learning in virtual worlds. In R. Hindrichs, & C. Wankel (Eds.), *Transforming virtual world learning* (pp. 265–304). Bingley, UK: Emerald Group Publishing. doi:10.1108/S2044-9968(2011)0000004015

Hismanoglu, M. (2012). Integrating second life into an EFL classroom: A new dimension in foreign language learning and teaching. *International Journal on New Trends in Education and Their Implications*, *3*(4), 100–111.

Kondor, K. [Karelia Kondor: Language learning in second life - An introduction]. (2013, Nov. 21). *Karelia Kondor: Language learning in second life - an introduction* [Video file]. Retrieved from https://www.youtube.com/watch?v=D9ks7jOdJ88&t=2s

Kondor, K. (2016, March 5). Le Louvre in second life [Blog post]. Retrieved from https://kareliakondor.wordpress.com/2016/03/

Kozlova, I., & Priven, D. (2015). ESL teacher training in 3D virtual worlds. *Language Learning & Technology*, *19*(1), 83–101.

Lantolf, J. P. (2011). The sociocultural approach to second language acquisition: Sociocultural theory, second language acquisition, and artificial L2 development. In D. Atkinson (Ed.), *Alternative approaches to second language acquisition* (pp. 24–47). New York, NY: Taylor & Francis.

Lave, J., & Wenger, E. (1990). *Situated learning: Legitimate peripheral participation*. Cambridge, UK: Cambridge University Press.

Lawrence, G. (2013). A working model for intercultural learning and engagement in collaborative online language learning environments. *Intercultural Education*, *24*(4), 303–314. doi:10.1080/14675986.2013.809247

Lawrence, G. (2014). The role of teachers and their beliefs in implementing technology-mediated language learning: Implications for teacher development and research. *IJCALLT, 4*(4), 59-75.

Lawrence, G., & Ahmed, F. (2018). Pedagogical insights into hyper-immersive virtual world language learning environments. *International Journal of Computer-Assisted Language Learning and Teaching*, *8*(1), 1–14. doi:10.4018/IJCALLT.2018010101

Lech, I. B., & Harris, L. N. (2019). Language learning in the virtual wild. In M. L. Carrio-Pastor (Ed.), Teaching language and teaching literature in virtual environments (pp. 39 -53). Springer, Singapore: Springer Nature Singapore Pte Ltd. doi:10.1007/978-981-13-1358-5_3

Lee, C. Y., & Warren, M. (2007). Security issues within virtual worlds such as second life. *Proceedings of 5th Australian Information Security Management Conference* (pp. 151-161). Perth, Australia: Edith Cowan University.

Lin, T. J., & Lan, Y. J. (2015). Language learning in virtual reality environments: Past, present, and future. *Journal of Educational Technology & Society*, *18*(4), 486–497.

Loke, S. K. (2015). How do virtual world experiences bring about learning? A critical review of theories. *Australasian Journal of Educational Technology*, *31*(1), 112–122. doi:10.14742/ajet.2532

Mayrath, M. C., Traphagan, T., Heikes, E. J., & Trivedi, A. (2011). Instructional design best practices for Second Life: A case study from a college-level English course. *Interactive Learning Environments*, *19*(2), 125–142. doi:10.1080/10494820802602568

Norton, B. (2013). *Identity and language learning: Extending the conversation* (2nd ed.). Bristol, UK: Multilingual Matters. doi:10.21832/9781783090563

Panichi, L. (2015). A critical analysis of learner participation in virtual worlds: How can virtual worlds inform our pedagogy? In F. Helm, L. Bradley, M. Guarda, & S. Thouesny (Eds.), *Critical CALL–Proceedings of the 2015 EUROCALL Conference,* Padova, Italy (pp. 464-469). Dublin, Ireland: Research-publishing.net.

Peterson, M. (2010). Learner participation patterns and strategy use in Second Life: An exploratory case study. *ReCALL*, *22*(3), 273–292. doi:10.1017/S0958344010000169

Peterson, M. (2011). Towards a research agenda for the use of three-dimensional virtual worlds in language learning. *CALICO Journal*, *29*(1), 67–80. doi:10.11139/cj.29.1.67-80

Peterson, M. (2012). EFL learner collaborative interaction in Second Life. *ReCALL, 24*(1), 20–39. doi:10.1017/S0958344011000279

Piccardo, E. (2014). *From communicative to action-oriented: A research pathway*. Retrieved from https://www.coe.int/t/dg4/linguistic/Source/CSC605_Research_Guide_English.pdf

Pitarch, R. C. (2018). An approach to digital game-based learning: Video-games principles and applications in foreign language teaching. *Journal of Language Teaching Research, 9*(6), 1147–1159. doi:10.17507/jltr.0906.04

Sadler, R., & Dooly, M. (2014). Language learning in virtual worlds: Research and practice. In M. Thomas, H. Reinders, & M. Warschauer (Eds.), *Contemporary computer-assisted language learning* (pp. 159–182). New York, NY: Bloomsbury.

Sama, C. M., & Wu, Y. (2019). Integrating "Talk Abroad" into the intermediate foreign language course: Building learner autonomy and engagement through video conversations with native speakers. In M. L. Carrio-Pastor (Ed.), *Teaching language and teaching literature in virtual environments* (pp. 73–94). Singapore: Springer Nature Singapore Pte Ltd. doi:10.1007/978-981-13-1358-5_5

Schmidt, R. (1990). The role of consciousness in second language learning. *Applied Linguistics, 11*(2), 129–158. doi:10.1093/applin/11.2.129

Scrivner, O., Madewell, J., Buckley, C., & Perez, N. (2019). Best practices in the use of augmented and virtual reality technologies for SLA: Design, implementation and feedback. In M. L. Carrio-Pastor (Ed.), Teaching language and teaching literature in virtual environments (pp. 55-70). Springer, Singapore: Springer Nature Singapore Pte Ltd.

Shrestha, S., & Harrison, T. (2019). Using machinima as teaching and learning materials: A Nepalese case study. *International Journal of Computer-Assisted Language Learning and Teaching, 9*(2), 37–52. doi:10.4018/IJCALLT.2019040103

Siemens, G. (2005). Connectivism: A learning theory for the digital age. *International Journal of Instructional Technology & Distance Learning, 2*(1). Retrieved from http://itdl.org/Journal/Jan_05/article01.htm

Swain, M. (2013). The inseparability of cognition and emotion in second language learning. *Language Teaching, 46*(2), 195–207. doi:10.1017/S0261444811000486

Sykes, J. M., Oskoz, A., & Thorne, S. L. (2016). Web 2.0, synthetic immersive environments, and mobile resources for language education. In G. Kessler (Ed.), *Landmarks in CALL research* (pp. 160–183). Bristol, CT: Equinox.

Thomas, M., & Schneider, C. (2018). Language teaching in 3D virtual worlds with machinima: Reflecting on an online machinima teacher training course. *International Journal of Computer-Assisted Language Learning and Teaching, 8*(2), 20–38. doi:10.4018/IJCALLT.2018040102

Wang, A. (2017). Using Second Life in an English course: How does the technology affect participation? *International Journal of Computer-Assisted Language Learning and Teaching, 7*(1), 66–85. doi:10.4018/IJCALLT.2017010105

Wang, C. X., Lefaiver, M. L. M., Wang, Q., & Hunt, C. (2011). Teaching in an EFL program in second life: Student teachers' perspectives and implications. *Journal of Educational Technology Development and Exchange*, *4*(1), 27–40. doi:10.18785/jetde.0401.03

Wenger, E. (1998). *Communities of practice: Learning, meaning and identity*. Cambridge, UK: Cambridge University Press. doi:10.1017/CBO9780511803932

Wertz, F. J., Charmaz, K., McMullen, L. M., Josselson, R., Anderson, R., & McSpadden, E. (2011). *Five ways of doing qualitative analysis*. New York, NY: Guilford.

ENDNOTES

1. Virtual worlds are computer-simulated environments where avatars (graphical representations of the users) interact.
2. Augmented reality provides a view of reality where specific elements are enhanced or augmented by computer-generated input.
3. Project Sansar will be the updated version of Second Life. For details, see: https://www.engadget.com/2016/08/31/second-life-sansar-creators-open/
4. See http://www.fraps.com/ for more information.
5. Sixth form in UK schools tends to be students between 16 and 18 years of age in senior years of secondary school.

APPENDIX

Interview questions

Interview 1: Questions

1. From your perspectives as a learner and a teacher in social virtual worlds (VWs), what are the *benefits* of language learning in VWs? What are the *limitations* of these environments?
2. What are your perspectives of language learning pedagogy/methods needed in VWs vs. methods needed in traditional classroom-based language teaching environments?
3. Can you describe any specific AHA moments or exemplary virtual world tasks/interactions you experienced as a learner or teacher? Any reflections from these?
4. Reflecting on your VW learning and/or teaching, how do these experiences inform your thinking about task design and/or educational practices in general?
5. To guide teachers and researchers interested in VW language teaching/learning, what are your takeaways from your avatar/learner experiences on virtual world design and interactions/learning in these environments?

Interview 2: Questions

1. Please elaborate on specific examples of teaching/learning you have experienced in Second Life that may illustrate benefits/limitations of VWs.
2. Have you formally integrated Second Life into your course syllabi or assignments when teaching with this? Or as a learner using Second Life, did you receive any assignments/documents outlining how Second Life was going to be (or should be) used? If so, would you consider sharing examples of this documentation with us?
3. What pedagogical insights and strategies would you say these interactions taught you? How have you used them in your teaching practices? How would you recommend they be dealt with in teaching practices?
4. You had said previously, 'learning which is done in an interactive context with some sort of emotional attachment tends to stick more'. Can you please give concrete examples of such interactions on Second Life?

Chapter 16
Using a Complex Technology in a Language Course:
Examining Second Life in Terms of Participation

Airong Wang
Xi'an Jiaotong-Liverpool University, China

ABSTRACT

In this chapter, how the complex technology of Second Life affects participation in an English course is investigated. With the aim of exploring gender issues, the special affordance of Second Life, i.e. voice-morphing together with sound-isolated parcels, was used. The data set consists of about 33 hours of audio recordings and chat logs of 8,315 words. The results show that in audio10.8% of the course time deals with technological challenges, while in chat 69.2% of the words contribute to technology. Three challenges interfering with participation were identified: software complexity, unreliable functionality of Second Life, and hardware and connectivity issues. To deal with these problems, pedagogical facilitators, technological facilitators, and Second Life -experienced peers made a significant contribution. Based on the results, this chapter analyzes whether Second Life can be widely used in language education, how affordances of it can be learned and taught, and scenarios where Second Life can and cannot be used.

INTRODUCTION

Three-dimensional (3D) virtual worlds have made a special contribution to language education, among various research interests and applications of technologies in/to language education, such as mobile learning, VR (Virtual reality), and blended learning. Although there are different 3D virtual worlds (e.g., World of Warcraft, Quest Atlantis, OpenSim), Second Life (SL) is still the dominant one applied (Gamage, Tretiakov, & Crump, 2011, p. 2407) and heavily-researched (e.g. Chen, 2018; Palomeque & Pujolà, 2018; Melchor-Couto, 2017; Wang, 2017a; Wang, 2017b). For example, Melchor-Couto (2017) investigates the reduced anxiety provided by the anonymity of SL in foreign language oral-interactions.

DOI: 10.4018/978-1-7998-1282-1.ch016

Zheng (2012) studies negotiation among Chinese language learners who use resources in SL and Chinese signs to participate in problem-solving activities. Peterson (2012) examines EFL learners' engagement in SL interactions, their attitudes towards using SL, and how SL facilitates their language output. It has been reported that learning a foreign language in SL is engaging, which, in turn, motivates student participation (e.g., Peterson & Swier, 2018; Wehner, Gump, & Downey, 2011; Peterson, 2012; Hsu, 2015). *Participation* in this type of environment means that 'students not only listen and observe, but also contribute (in speech, in writing or through actions) to the interaction' (Wang, Deutschmann, & Steinvall, 2013, p. 4). When mapping and analysing factors affecting participation in 3D virtual worlds, Wang et al. (2013) emphasize the SL technology often constitutes a key factor affecting student participation.

Although active participation, regarded as a 'prerequisite' (p. 4) for learning a foreign language in social collaborations in SL (Wang et al., 2013), is highly dependent on the technology working as it should, previous research has not dealt with this question sufficiently (e.g., Inman, Wright, & Hartman, 2010; Liou, 2011; Barr, 2013; Wang et al., 2013; Wang, 2015). For instance, Wang (2015) mentions the technical issues that hindered participation in an English course in SL, her focus lies on the strategies and roles the teacher used and played to solve these problems. Only in her recent work, Wang (2017a) highlights and analyzes situations, for a language course, where SL can be used and cannot be adopted, based on the English courses she has observed and studied in SL.

BACKGROUND

It has been suggested that technology adoption depends on the complexity of a technology set against the perceived advantages the technology may bring (Rogers, 2003; Venkatesh, Morris, Davis, & Davis, 2003). A technology that is easy to understand and to use is adopted more rapidly than a technology that requires 'new skills and understandings' (Rogers, 2003, p. 16). Nonetheless, a complex technology may be acceptable when its use is associated with many perceived advantages. According to Nielsen's (1993) model of system acceptability, some attributes concerning the practical acceptability of a system are important, namely: usefulness, cost, compatibility, and reliability. Usefulness refers to whether the system can do what it is needed and whether it has a high usability: easy to learn, efficient to use, easy to remember its functions for users, few errors made by users when they use it, and users feel subjectively pleased. Compatibility mainly addresses whether a system is compatible with other existing systems, and reliability concerns whether a system is reliable. As these three attributes constitute the basic criteria for evaluating a technology, they will be used to analyze participation in SL in the course under investigation.

In the following sections, the attributes of SL to language education, and the technical complexity and requirements of SL are presented.

The Learning Environment SL

SL is an Internet-based 3D virtual world launched by Linden Lab in 2003 with audio integrated in 2007. SL offers avatars that can be modified by users. Avatars in SL can perform some actions, such as running, walking, sitting, or flying; they can also teleport to different in-world geographical regions (called islands) by a simple click on the teleport button. Furthermore, SL avatars can share digital artifacts, such as notecards (digital documents used to save detailed information), and manipulate in-world objects by, for instance, building a virtual classroom or uploading a PowerPoint to a virtual screen.

SL affords multiple communication modes. The synchronous audio communication mode includes public audio, group audio, and private audio. The proximity requirement for using the public audio is 60 virtual in-world meters, while no proximity requirements exist for the group and private audio (Wigham & Chanier, 2013, p. 76). Apart from these free audio tools, SL also offers a purchasable voice-morphing tool by which a feminine voice can be morphed into a masculine voice, and vice versa. Therefore, there is potential for exploring gender in SL to raise language learners' awareness of gender issues, especially in the sociolinguistics context. The text chat communication mode consists of multidirectional synchronous local and group chat, as well as asynchronous and synchronous instant messaging. The public audio and the local chat are open to avatars within a certain in-world distance (usually within 20 meters for the local chat), whereas the group audio and chat are only available to the members of that group. Private audio and chat can only be used between two avatars. SL also provides limited non-verbal communication. This is either generated by users choosing an action deliberately, such as 'orienting their avatar and positioning their avatar with respect to others' (Wigham & Chanier, 2013, p. 67), or it may be predefined by the program, for example, an avatar is set automatically to the posture of falling asleep after remaining inactive in the audio or chat communication for several minutes. There are also a number of pre-programmed gestures, such as laughing and crying, which users can activate by clicking options on a list. The synchronous audio and chat are the primary communication modes in SL (Henderson, Huang, Grant, & Henderson, 2009, p. 464).

Using SL in Language Teaching and Learning

SL is a potentially rich environment for authentic and collaborative language teaching and learning. Using SL, language instructors can use innovative designs for course activities, partly as a result of SL being user-defined (Wehner et al., 2011). In an English and French course studied by Wigham and Chanier (2013), the course team used the building affordance of SL to design a collaborative building activity for architecture students. The design introduced the students to building techniques, and more importantly, to an authentic language learning context, where the students collaboratively practiced oral skills and developed communication skills with regard to referencing of objects (Wigham & Chanier, 2013). Building tasks have also been implemented in EFL course to study the learners' negotiation of meaning during that process when they were using voice chat (Chen, 2018). Apart from the building affordance, course instructors can also exploit the various open virtual communities that exist in SL to immerse students in authentic foreign language learning. For example, course designs may involve exploring 'environments that may represent cultural expressions of a target language community' (Deutschmann & Panichi, 2013, p. 69), or map a city in real life (Chen, 2018).

The presence of avatars in SL has been shown to be conducive to enhancing language awareness and participation. As avatars in SL can perform some non-verbal communication, such as laughing or crying, language learners get a feeling that they communicate in the target language as they would in real life (Blasing, 2010; Thomas, 2013). This visual nature of SL, in turn, draws language learners' attention to 'linguistic accuracy' when they collaborate with native speakers in SL, according to Blasing (2010, p. 104). However, Chen (2016) criticizes, "The lack of these paralinguistic features (e.g., eye contact) can also result in the removal of nonverbal support" (p. 161). However, some researchers agree that the presence of personalized avatars could enhance English learners' sense of engagement and improve their communication (Peterson & Swier, 2018; Chen, 2016; Peterson, 2012; Thomas, 2013). MacIntyre (1995) emphasizes, 'anxiety may cause deficits in cognitive processing and impair task performance'

(p. 92). The anonymity provided by user-controlled avatars in SL may thus help reduce the anxiety of foreign language learners, which is beneficial for enhancing participation (e.g., Melchor-Couto, 2017; Gamage et al., 2011; Wang et al., 2013).

In addition, the 3D nature of SL has the potential for demonstrating linguistic concepts in ways that may be unachievable using other online tools (Deutschmann & Panichi, 2013). For example, in an Italian course for beginners examined by Deutschmann and Panichi (2013), Italian learners were instructed to perform actions such as sitting down and standing up. These movements '[do] not only teach the basic vocabulary associated with movement, but also [illustrate] the grammatical form of giving instructions' (Deutschmann & Panichi, 2013, p. 78).

However, these above affordances of SL, i.e. 'what is available to the person to do something with' (van Lier, 2004, p. 91), are highly dependent on the technology working and the users' technical proficiency in using SL. As Stockwell (2012) explains, '[w]hile technologies possess inherent affordances, the manifestation of these affordances will differ depending on the user' (p. 7). From an ecological perspective, learners are active agents in perceiving and using resources, and only those who can perceive 'the affordances from the large array of resources' (p. 556) in SL have the potential of using these (Zheng, 2012). Liu and Chen (2017) emphasizes how teachers perceive the affordances of a technology and implement them in an English course could largely decide how well the students can take control of the technology in learning. Therefore, it can be argued, "teachers could pinpoint affordances so that learners will be aware of the various possibilities the technology provides and choose what they need" (Liu & Chen, 2017, p. 83).

Nonetheless, learning through playing games can be 'pleasantly frustrating' (Gee, 2007). Playing the games is 'doable' but 'challenging' as it requires players to have adequate technical competence.

Technical Demands of SL and Previous Studies

SL has specific demands on technology. For example, SL requires a cable or a DSL Internet connection, computers with a minimum of 1 GB or more memory (4 GB or more recommended), and latest drivers for graphics cards. SL also has critical requirements for the operation system, computer processors, computer memory, and screen resolution (for more details, see http://secondlife.com/support/system-requirements/). If these requirements are not met, it is difficult to run SL or run it smoothly.

Although not focusing on technology in particular, previous research has discussed some types of technical problems with SL. Such technical problems include the long downloading time of SL and software crashes (Chen, 2016; Inman et al., 2010, p. 53), and the need for a fast Internet connection, without which, voice problems occur (Chen, 2016) and could lead to more than half of student feeling frustrated (Liou, 2011). Users need a broadband Internet connection when logging into SL from home computers, and users may face software crashes when using 'sophisticated university computing labs' (p. 552) due to busy Internet traffic caused by many users logging into SL at the same time (Cooke-Plagwitz, 2008).

Another problem concerns audio quality. The volume in SL may be experienced as too high or too low, echoes and background noises are frequently reported, learners fail to use headsets, there is audio break up, or learners are unable to activate the audio (Wang et al., 2013; Wang, 2014; Wang, 2015). SL maintenance also causes problems (Wang et al., 2013). SL only informs users a few minutes before a certain region is shut down for maintenance. If this happens at the middle of a language course, a class has to move to another region in SL or wait for the maintenance to be completed.

Other reported technical problems include PowerPoint slides not uploading and that it takes time for language learners to acquaint themselves with the software (Baker, Wentz, & Woods, 2009, p. 62). Furthermore, the unintuitive interface of SL is complicated for users to master (Cooke-Plagwitz, 2008). Wang et al. (2013) report that undesirable amount of course time in their study was spent dealing with technical problems.

Previous research has given some suggestions for dealing with SL technology. From the perspective of language learners, technical readiness, i.e. training language learners to use SL before a language course starts, is necessary (e.g., Peterson, 2012; Cooke-Plagwitz, 2008). Such training deserves 'at least one class period' (p. 553) under the guidance of a SL-experienced user (Cooke-Plagwitz, 2008). Users have to acquire 'basic gestures, movements and camera skills' in using SL (Salmon, 2009, p. 527). From the perspective of course organizers, language teachers should master SL technology first, and motivate students to be patient (Liu & Chen, 2017; Baker et al., 2009). It is suggested that technical support during a course is important (Wang, 2017a; Wang, 2017b; Wang, Song, Stone, & Yan, 2009). These all point out that SL is a technically demanding environment. Below shows the cases where SL is suitable and is not suitable for a language course (Wang, 2017a).

Building on previous studies, the present study examines technical challenges in relation to participation, especially when voice-morphing and sound isolated parcels are used. There are three research questions:

- Research question 1: What proportion of the course time was spent dealing with technical challenges?
- Research question 2: What types of technical challenges hindered participation in this course?
- Research question 3: How were technical challenges avoided or solved in this course?

MATERIAL AND METHOD

The Course Under Study

The topic of the English course under study was gender, sociolinguistics and second language education. It was offered to student teachers of English (hereafter students) by Umeå University, Sweden. The course was organized around two problem-based tasks where the students were given an opportunity to discuss issues in small groups together with invited professionals, who were experienced users of SL and active in language research. An added course aim was thus to provide the students with an opportunity to practice their English skills in an authentic context. Another course aim was to 'introduce the students to the use of Web 2.0 tools in language education' (Wang, Steinvall, & Deutschmann, 2014). Finally, the course design contained a hidden agenda of which the students were not aware, namely to expose students to male and female simulations of the same person in order to investigate whether or not they judged the person differently depending on the gender. For this purpose, a male pedagogical facilitator used the voice-morphing option available in SL to swap between the roles of male and female facilitators.

The course participants were as follows. There was one male pedagogical facilitator, who used three avatars, two of which were voice-morphed into feminine and masculine voices respectively (cf. Deutschmann, Steinvall, & Lagerström, 2011). There were two technical facilitators and one course teacher. Furthermore, there were 32 third-term students of English and 11 invited professionals, who collaborated in the course activities. It is assumed that the students had general computer skills; however,

Figure 1a. Scenarios in which Second Life is suitable, figure 1b. Scenarios in which Second Life is not suitable

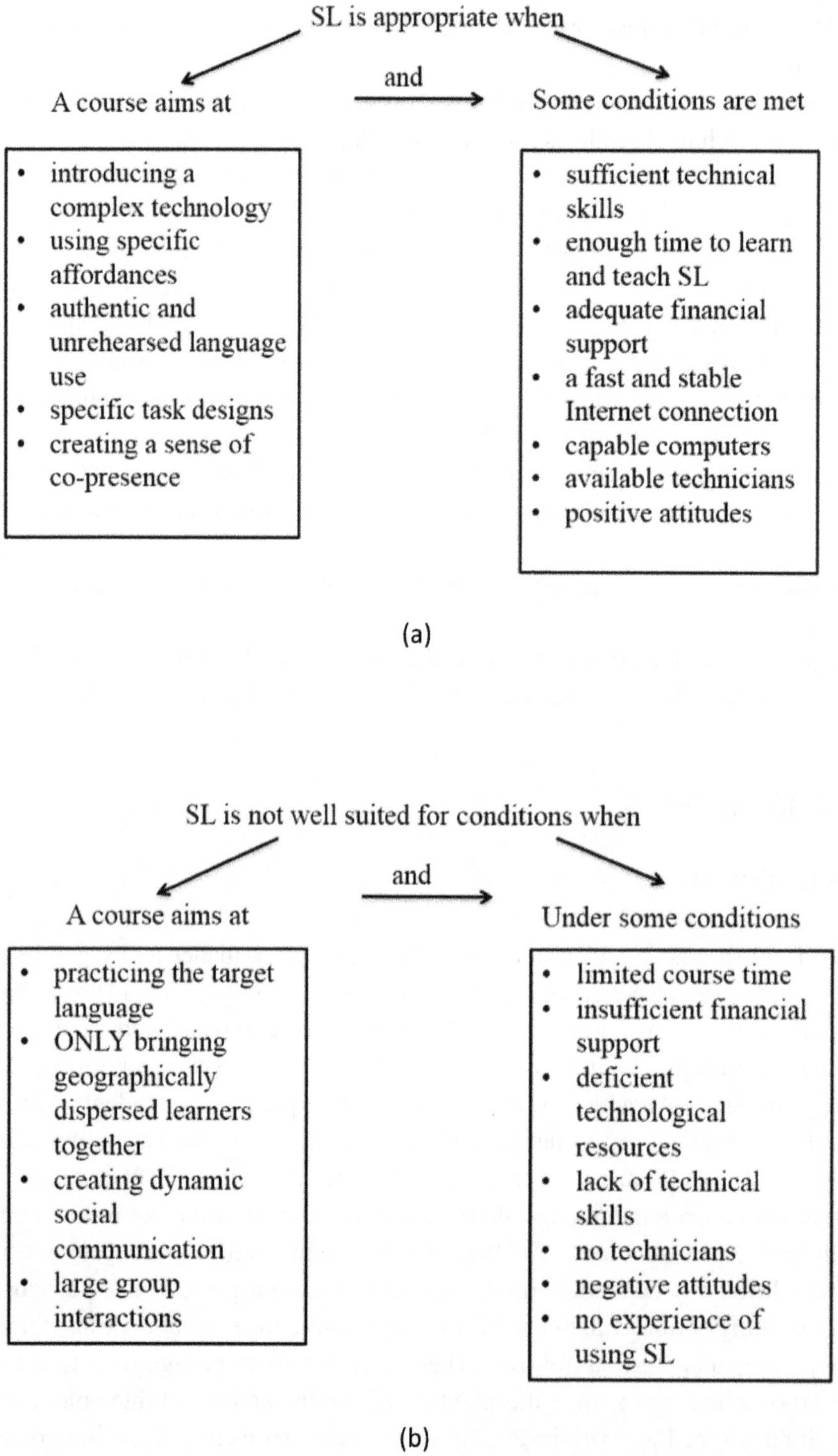

none of them had had prior experience of using SL. The invited professionals were enrolled from different European countries using social networks in SL. Of the 11 invited professionals, two were native English speakers and the rest were highly fluent in English (cf. Wang et al., 2014). The university laboratory offered computers that matched the required software and hardware requirements for running SL and a fast Internet connection to students, while no such facilities were available for the invited professionals who were not based at Umeå University, Sweden.

The course consisted of four sessions. The first session was a technical and social initiation. In this session, the male pedagogical facilitator and the two technical facilitators taught all the participants how to use SL functions, especially the local chat, the public audio, and the notecards. The two technical facilitators also provided technical guidance in real life to students present at the laboratory. Students were taught how to teleport to another island and to find their way back to the course island, and were guided on how to modify their avatars. Moreover, the participants were given the contact details of their peers so that they could learn more about SL from each other, and they were encouraged to explore SL in their spare time. Note that the students had unrestricted access to the university laboratory.

Following this initiation session, there were two workshop sessions. During the two workshops, the students and the invited professionals worked in groups of three or four within sound isolated parcels in SL. Using the affordance of manipulating in-world objects, the sound isolated parcels were set up so that the group members could conduct their group discussions without disturbance from other ongoing conversations (cf. Wang et al., 2014). Moreover, all the groups could use the local chat to signal for technical assistance easily. The technical and pedagogical facilitators could survey the groups efficiently and move between the groups quickly. Figure 1 represents the sound parcels in the course under study, i.e. the six rectangular spaces, outlined in red.

Outside the sound parcels, the area with 'red chairs' (bottom left in Figure 1) was a public place for all the participants. Workshop 1 included group discussions where the participants were asked to discuss statements from the course literature by referring to data collected from a fictitious language classroom (cf. Wang et al., 2014). In Workshop 2, the participants were asked to use their own experience, combined with the expertise of the invited professionals to create an online lesson for secondary school pupils (cf.

Figure 2. Sound isolated parcels (adapted from Deutschmann et al., 2011)

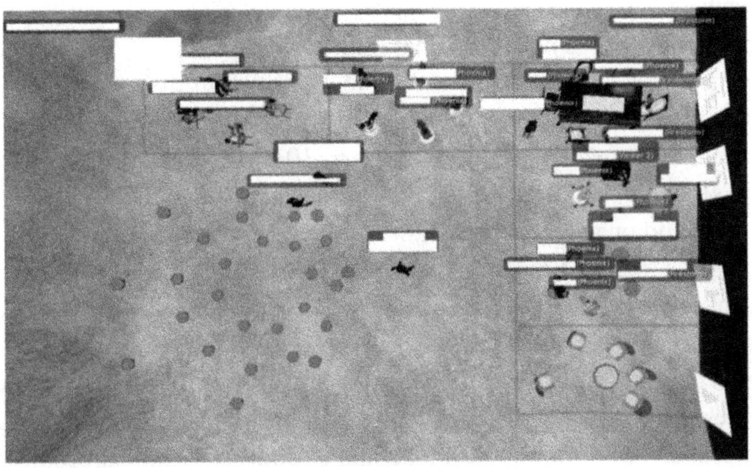

Wang et al., 2014). In both workshops, special attention was paid to gender issues. The last session was a debriefing that included the students' evaluation of the course and the voice morphed avatars.

Data Collection and Analysis

All the four course sessions were recorded using the video recording software Camtasia, and all local chat logs (there was no access to the private chats and the group chats) during the four course sessions were saved. Due to technical problems, approximately three hours of group discussions were not recorded successfully. The total length of the recordings is 33 hours, two minutes and 38 seconds, and the total number of words in the chat logs is 8315. The length of the recordings for each course session varies: three hours, two minutes and 50 seconds of the initiation session, 28 hours, two minutes and 47 seconds of the two workshops (note here that each sound parcel generated its own recordings), and one hour, 57 minutes and one second of the debriefing session. The number of words in the chat logs of the four course sessions also differs: 2549 words in the initiation session, 5428 words in the two workshops, and 338 words in the debriefing session.

To answer the three research questions, the audio and chat data were analyzed in the following ways. Firstly, all parts in the recordings dedicated to technical challenges were noted, i.e. time started and ended, and then the time spent dealing with technology was calculated. Secondly, words related to technical challenges in the chat logs were identified and counted. The chat logs were not counted on the basis of time because the time that the participants spent on typing was unknown. Finally, all technical challenges were grouped into different categories that emerged from the recordings and the chat logs. These categories include (a) software complexity, (b) unreliable functionality of the software, and (c) hardware and connectivity.

RESULTS

Proportions of Technical Challenges

To answer research question 1, '[w]hat proportion of the course time was spent dealing with technical challenges?', the proportions of exchanges dealing with technical challenges were calculated in the audio and chat data respectively.

In the audio data, a total of three hours and 35 minutes (out of 33 hours, two minutes and 38 seconds) was devoted to technical challenges, corresponding to 10.8% of all the course sessions. One hour, 15 minutes and 10 seconds (out of three hours, two minutes and 50 seconds), i.e. 41.1%, of the initiation session concerned technology, whereas only two hours, 10 minutes and 43 seconds (out of 28 hours, two minutes, and 50 seconds), i.e. 7.8%, of the two workshops, and eight minutes and 58 seconds (out of one hour, 57 minutes and one second), i.e. 7.7%, of the debriefing session was spent on technology.

In the local chat data, a total of 5754 words out of 8315 (69.2%) concerned technology. The number of words dealing with technology in the four course sessions also varies: 1453 words out of 2549 words, i.e. 57%, in the initiation session; as many as 4137 words out of 5428 words, i.e. 76%, in the two workshops; and 164 words out of 338 words, i.e. 48%, in the debriefing session. The reason for these high proportions of the technology-related words is that all the participants in this course were encouraged to use audio as the primary communication mode and to confine technical problems to chat to avoid disrupting ongoing discussions (cf. Wang et al., 2014). The rest of the chat, i.e. 30.8%, was used for socializing (cf. Wang et al., 2014), such as greetings, farewells, and compliments.

Types of Technical Challenges

This subsection answers research question 2, '[w]hat types of technical challenges hindered participation in this course?'.

Software Complexity

The participants' unfamiliarity with the communication modes available in SL. For example, some students could not hear other participants whose volume was low, and those students did not know how to turn up individual volume using the in-world settings, as shown in example (1)[1].

(1) (from audio)

S1: I'm just having some trouble with the sound I can hear you very well but not the girls erm

[…]

S1: faintly but yes er how did you turn the=

Some participants forgot to unlock their 'talk' buttons, resulting in that they failed to be heard by other participants. In contrast, some participants forgot to lock their 'talk' buttons when they were not speaking, leading to echoes when their peers were talking, as example (2) shows. Typos in the chat output have not been corrected in the examples.

(2) (from chat)

TF1: Echo is coing from S1

S2: I turned my sound off?

Certain students were outside sound parcels, and they could not be heard or hear when other participants were inside the sound parcels, and vice versa. In example (3), MP pointed this out to some students who were standing within a sound parcel while others were talking outside in the public area (see Figure 1).

(3) (from chat)

MP: you should be aware of the fact tha if you stand by tables and chairs

MP: you will not be able to hear me

Apart from these issues, two groups tried without success to use the group chat, which was due to unknown problems as they explained in the audio. This issue with chat was neither noticed by the pedagogical facilitators and the TFs nor did the participants seek help from them. Other groups did not use this affordance of SL. Wigham and Chanier (2013) and Wang (2015) also find that the group chat is infrequently used in SL.

In addition, some basic functions in SL seem complex for beginners. Some students had problems teleporting, finding it difficult to find the location using the in-world search function. Others had problems adjusting sunlight in SL (SL offers the 'sun' option to imitate four different positions: sunrise, midday, sunset, and midnight), or changing display names above avatars' heads. Example (4) shows that S3 was frustrated about not being able to edit her avatar's name.

(4) (from chat)

S3: How the heck do I change my name? Like S17 has

S3: Or sort of edit it

There was one student who did not know how to find the course program that was saved in a notecard.

Orienting avatars also puzzled SL beginners. For example, it was noted that some avatars would sit with their backs towards other participants. Others had problems working out how to seat themselves on appropriate places, as shown in example (5).

(5) (from audio)

IP1: would you like to sit on the chair?

S4: yeah sure ((stood up and sat on the chair))

The co-presence of in-world avatars gave the impression that some participants were active in SL when they were in fact away from their computers. For instance, MP kept speaking to IP2, whose avatar was in an active status. When IP2 did not respond in audio, MP tried to use chat. Until then it was unknown that IP2 had wandered off from the computer in real-life, as illustrated in example (6).

(6) (from chat)

MP: IP2

IP2: yeah sorry I wasn't there

In SL, an avatar is automatically set to show one's status as 'falling to sleep' after remaining inactive for several minutes, but in this example the period of inactivity was not long enough for an inactive status to be indicted by the avatar.

In summary, some participants especially the 'newbies' (novices) in SL did not master the affordances of this complex environment, which is reflected by the conversation in example (7) between MP and TF2.

(7) (from chat)

TF2: lots of confusion this time

TF2: taking a bit of time

MP: often confusing when there're many newbies

The participants' comments highlight that SL is not easy to master, the participants thus struggle to achieve a high level of efficiency in using it and they make errors (see Nielsen, 1993). Based on these results, it can be argued that the usability of SL may be low in terms of motivating participation.

Unreliable Functionality of the Software

One unreliable function of SL relates to the sound parcels, especially in the case of the voice-morphed avatars whose volume became too high almost every time they entered a sound parcel. See example (8).

(8) (from audio)

FV: hi, hi sorry to interrupt you ((high volume)), umm, no ok sorry this is about group erm it was group 5's got some problems with their peer so

IP3: oh that was very loud in my my ((coughing)) sorry [in my headphone]. did- did you really understand what the person said? did you recognize?

S5: [yeah very loud]

S3: no idea

((FV left))

As illustrated in this example, the participants could not recognize who was talking due to the high volume although they previously had met FV in SL. To further complicate the matters, the audio in one of the sound parcels was malfunctioning.

Another problem concerned the audio and chat communication modes. Firstly, there was distorted sound. The distorted sound applied particularly to the voice-morphed avatars and one IP in the two workshops. When the voice-morphed avatars entered a sound parcel, their sound was sometimes distorted and caused a great deal of noise. Interestingly, when the pedagogical facilitators and one TF pointed out that the IP's sound was distorted, their group members thought that the IP's sound was acceptable. In other words, not all the participants experienced the same sound conditions. Additionally, for one IP and several students there was a serious sound problem: i.e. they could neither hear others nor be heard. Examples (9) and (10) show that the 'talk' button in SL did not work in these instances.

(9) (from chat)

S6: I can't even press my talk button

(10) (from chat)

S7: I disconnected and connected again and now my talk button is gone..

Finally, with regard to audio issues, for one student and an IP, instant messaging did not function.

SL crashing was also a problem. This issue was experienced by some students, by some IPs, and even by MF. See example (11).

(11) (from audio)

S8: I am sorry about that are we still on the sa::me same statement? my program shut down.

Another way in which the functions in SL can be unreliable concerns the avatars. There were some trivial problems, such as the hair of one student's avatar disappearing, and the hair color of another student's avatar could not be changed, which distracted the students from participation, because they did not know how to solve them.

The different viewers of SL also contributed to some technical malfunctions. When the course was conducted, Linden Lab launched three different viewers: Phoenix, Firestorm, and Viewer 2. The software responded very differently depending on which viewer was used. Some participants complained that it took a long time to log into SL, especially with the Phoenix viewer. One typical example is that one student could not log into the Phoenix viewer at all, as shown in example (12).

(12) (from audio)

S9: erm well, what can I say about myself I () I'm er well () just the ()

IP4: oh it's breaking up and up

S10: yeah

[…]

S11: dodgy mike

[…]

S9: yeah I know I was try- () I wa- () -ng to connect to the big computer upstairs and they didn't let me in on the Phoenix viewer so I don't know what () happening so now I have my little tiny thing here […]

Another example is that for the invited professional IP4, the Phoenix viewer kept crashing. For some participants, Viewer 2 did not work: IP4 could not use Viewer 2 either, commenting in the chat, 'deaf and mute with viewer two'.

Hardware and Connectivity

One type of hardware problem included computers with low capacity. Some participants' computers, including two IPs' computers, crashed. For instance, the low capacity of S9's computer led to sound breaking up (see example (12)). Moreover, IP4 typed in chat that she had to uninstall some programs to make space for SL to run (although it remained unknown what programs she uninstalled).

Problems relating to headsets constitute another hardware issue. Several students and one IP did not have headsets, leading to echoes that were caused by sound feedback from their audio channels. Some students' headsets did not work, some students forgot to turn off headsets when they were not speaking, leading to echoes when others were speaking, and several students and IP3 forgot to turn on headsets, resulting in their being unheard, as shown in example (13).

(13) (from audio)

S5: ok so shall we begin or what [()]

IP3: [((laughter))] the funny thing cos I was saying the same thing with my microphone off

One student hardly participated for about 20 minutes in one two-hour workshop as the student's audio volume kept going down. In the end, TF1 worked out that the student had two operative microphones, which caused the problem, as shown in example (14).

(14) (from audio)

TF1: she had two mikes on earlier so that was the problem earlier [...] one is off and then turned both of them off […]

Slow Internet connections caused the following problems. PowerPoint slides did not upload in the virtual screen. The sound of many participants, including some students, IPs, and the pedagogical facilitators, occasionally broke up. Moreover, slow Internet connections led to avatar problems. Some avatars were stuck, for example, in mid-air, on a chair, or on a table, or avatar's images were in a cloud. In example (15), a student avatar was stuck on a table.

(15) (from audio)

S4: am I flying

IP1: ((laughing)) why are you standing on the table

S4: I don't know I actually have no clue (10.0) ok well er I'll stand on the table then er I can't move

To summarize, different types of technical problems and viewers arguably inhibited participation, and it was time-consuming to solve certain technical problems. Consequently, in terms of Nielsen's (1993) system acceptability, the reliability and compatibility of SL are not ensured.

Avoiding and Solving Technical Challenges

This section addresses research question 3, '[h]ow were technical challenges avoided or solved in this course?'. Each subsection that follows answers this research question in the order that these technical challenges were presented in the section above.

Dealing With Software Complexity

The initiation session gave the participants the opportunity to familiarize themselves with the complex environment of SL. In this session, MP emphasized the importance of mastering the basic communication functions in SL to avoid potential technical problems. In the audio data, the percentage devoted to technology was reduced from about 41% in the initiation session to about 8% in the later course sessions; however, the proportion (76%) of technology-related words in the chat is the highest of all the course sessions in the two workshops. Thus the initiation session proved insufficient to avoid all potential technical problems in SL.

Some strategies for dealing with the multiple communication modes in this course are worth mentioning. Firstly, MP emphasized that adjusting the volume was one of the basic functions the participants had to master. However, he could not help the students who did not know how to adjust volume as he used a different viewer, so he suggested that the two TFs help the students. It seemed that the two TFs provided assistance in real life. Importantly, some IPs and SL-experienced students also offered support. Example (16) shows how the SL-experienced peer S12 gave detailed guidance on adjusting the volume (see example (1)).

(16) (from audio)

S1: faintly but yes er how did you turn the=

S12: =if you if you just yeah if you go at push the local chat. erm and then you put on the red little button with the () can you see that and then you can see my name and you push that and then you can turn the volume up

S1: the local chat where

S12: erm down to your left (8.0) do you find it

[…]

S1: yes

S12: and then up in the corner of that little like gray square you have a red button. can you see that one

S1: yes

S12: push that one

S1: ok

S12: and then you scroll scroll down for my name

S1: ok found it

S12: yeah and then you turn the volume up

[…]

S1: I can hear you a lot better now thanks

Additionally, MP and the TFs reminded the participants to turn off the 'talk' button in SL when not speaking. See example (17).

(17) (from chat)

TF1: Remember to turn off the Talk button when you are not talking, just to be sure that you are not experiencing an echo

In the initiation session, MP also used audio and chat to test whether the participants' audio was working before the collaborative workshops.

(18) (from audio)

MP: [...] can everybody hear me and if you can hear me just just yeah put a little yes in there. yes exactly good good good good good good it's good to know 'cause you are not sure sometimes. so I have to say this as well in the chat of course does anyone not hear me ((laughing))

(19) (from chat)

MP: Does anyone not hear me

S8: i cant hear you

During the later sessions of this course, all the participants also tested whether their audio worked before they started the course tasks. Moreover, given the lack of body language in SL, MP suggested that the participants use backchanneling, as shown in example (20).

(20) (from audio)

MP: [...] it is a bit confusing in Second Life 'cause when you speak like I do now. I am not sure if you can hear me or not and unless you sort of erm get some sort of feedback backchanneling that's called. you can do that either by er saying aha yeah yeah I see what you mean erm er then erm you don't really know if people can you hear you or not and that's very spr- strange speaking to- to people wh- wh- who don't sort of acknowledge the fact that you are speaking so tha- that's a very special thing about Second Life in many ways actually [...]

Third, as regards the sound parcel problem mentioned in example (3), TF2 reminded the participants that they could not hear each other if they were not inside the same parcel. See example (21).

(21) (from chat)

TF2: only those inside the parcel can hear each other

TF2: so please sit on the chairs

TF2: right click and choose Sit Here

TF2: on the chairs

MP also suggested that the participants show the borderlines between the sound parcels so that they would know if they were inside or outside of a sound parcel. See example (22) and Figure 1.

(22) (from chat)

MP: If you press ctrl+alt+shift+P you can see the boxes ((sound parcels)) you have to stand in to hear

MP, one TF, and some participants also tested every sound parcel together before the two workshops to make sure that every sound parcel would work.

Participants received technical support when they could not operate the basic functions in SL. MP helped one student to teleport to another virtual island by using the search function; he found that the student had ignored letter case when typing the name of the virtual island as the student did not know that the search function in SL was case-sensitive. MP and TF2 helped the students to fix sunlight in SL, as shown in example (23).

(23) (from audio)

MP: I think you can adjust that b- by clicking ya clicking

TF2: world

MP: world

Regarding how to change display names, mentioned in example (4), the student got help from an SL-experienced peer, S6.

(24) (from chat)

S6: edit -> display name

Another example of peer-support was when S14 helped S13 to find the course program saved in a notecard. See example (25).

(25) (from chat)

S13: Can someone tell where can I get the program?

[…]

S14: The programme is in this notecard.

S13: I got it.

S14::)

Regarding the orienting of avatars, the use of clear terms by all the participants is of importance. For example, while asking all the participants to sit on 'the red chairs' via audio, MP also typed the same instruction in the chat to describe 'the red chairs' that he was referring to, as shown in example (26).

(26) (from chat)

MP: Hi all!

MP: Could you all take a seat on the red chairs

MP: where MP is sitting

MP: the chairs floating in the sky

MP: Could all sit on the red chairs floating in the sky for now

Those students sitting with their backs towards others, as mentioned in the section of *Software complexity*, managed to adjust their sitting positions after several attempts under the guidance of their peers.

Dealing With Unreliable Functionality of the Software

As illustrated in example (8), the volume of the voice-morphed avatars was very high. Consequently, the voice-morphed pedagogical facilitator had to adjust and test volume every time when leaving one sound parcel and entering another to facilitate different group discussions in the two workshops. See example (27).

(27) (from audio)

FV: hello hi can you hear me ok? 'cause I had some problems with my sound before ((microphone-adjusting sound))

S15: yeah, we can hear you

S16: yeah

[…]

FV: so my my sound is not too overwhelming 'cause I spoke earlier on and somebody said oh please switch that off 'cause it was really bad the levels were really bad

S15: it's ok

S17: it's just fine

FV: it's ok ok that sounds good […]

When the audio in the sound parcel did not work, as mentioned in the section of *unreliable functionality of the software*, the group inside that sound parcel started to use chat. In the end, to avoid typing all the time, TF1 asked the group to move to another sound parcel, in which the sound worked.

Two strategies were used when the participants were confronted by the unreliable functions in the audio and chat communication modes. The participants usually logged out SL and logged back in again or were advised to do so when the sound was distorted, when the participants could neither hear nor be heard, when the 'talk' button disappeared, or when instant messaging could not be used. In some cases, they repeated these measures until SL worked. This was also the strategy for dealing with the program crashes. The other strategy was that the participants used chat or were told to use chat to compensate for the audio problems.

When dealing with the avatar problems, peer support is important. For example, as mentioned the section of *unreliable functionality of the software*, one student could not find the avatar's hair. In this case, the peer S17 offered help, as shown in example (28).

(28) (from audio)

S17: if you go to inventory S15 there you should find your- your hair

Concerning the malfunctions of different SL viewers, the TFs provided most of the assistance as MP had Viewer 2, which had a different interface from other viewers. Usually the participants were advised to change to a different viewer when the viewer they used did not work.

To make sure that SL functioned properly, the two TFs checked regularly whether any participants experienced technical problems, in every sound parcel. Both of them reminded the participants that they could always seek help from them, as illustrated in examples (29) and (30).

(29) (from chat)

TF2: If anyone needs help who is not on campus but is here please IM me

(30) (from chat)

TF1: Everyone, call me or TF2 if you are having any trouble in the group

Dealing With Hardware and Connectivity

To facilitate student participation and avoid technical problems, the university laboratory offered computers that had the configurations required for running SL. Also, most students chose to do the course at the laboratory where the two TFs were located in real life. These students had access to good technical facilities and instant technical support from the TFs. The student mentioned in example (12), who had a computer with insufficient capability at home, could not participate due to the sound break-up, and had to run to the laboratory to finish the rest of the collaborative work with peers, using a computer at the laboratory. However, when both IPs' computers crashed, as illustrated in the section of *hardware and connectivity*, no computers with better performance could be arranged. Given the lack of IPs in certain groups, FV participated in one group as an 'IP', and one student who had more subject knowledge in another group was told to fill in the role of as an 'IP'.

The importance of using a headset was stressed in this course. The university laboratory offered headsets to every participant working at the laboratory. Participants who did not have headsets and were not physically present at the laboratory were instructed to buy or borrow headsets. Interestingly, MP and TF2 accidentally demonstrated the importance of using headsets. They commenced a conversation in SL when TF2, who was running around the laboratory helping participants while keeping his avatar logged in SL, did not have access to a headset. It was clear that there were echoes, as shown in example (31).

(31) (from audio)

MP: [...] you're in HUMlab ((the university laboratory)) yeah=

TF2: = I am here I am in HUMlab yea

MP: yeah ok fine excellent ok ok I am getting feedback off you then ((echoes while one student was talking at the same time))

TF2: ok sorry I have to use the headphones

MP: yeah I know I know. ok so there you had a practical demonstration what it sounds like when somebody does not have a headset you get this sort of echo effect and er sort of feedback [...]

With regard to the volume problem caused by the use of two microphones at the same time mentioned in example (14), TF1 joined this group to help the student S7. In order not to affect other participants' discussions, TF1 asked S7 to go out of the sound parcel and dealt with the problem privately. See example (32).

(32) (from audio)

TF1: S7 can you step out can you come with me? erm I go and we'll go and check erm what I can do so the others can start discussing [...]

S7: so I just leave the table

((after 10 minutes both of them returned to the sound parcel))

TF1: S7 is it working [...]

[...]

S7: yeah I hear you it's quite low though but I can hear you

The university laboratory also offered a fast Internet connection. Again when one was not at the laboratory, this facility was obviously not available. Regarding the Internet problems identified in the section of *hardware and connectivity*, the participants usually waited for a while for a PowerPoint and avatars in the shape of a cloud to upload. Waiting or logging out and logging back in again were also used to manage these problems, i.e. some avatars were stuck in mid-air, on a table, or on a chair, and the sound was breaking up. Moreover, speaking close to microphones was also used to cope with the sound breaking up.

In sum, to avoid and solve technical problems, the pedagogical facilitators and the TFs provided a significant amount of technical assistance. The 'newbie' students were also supported by the SL-experienced peers. Moreover, the participants were aware that technology in SL affected participation. One group in Workshop 2 used SL in their lesson plan, and in their plan they explicitly allocated time to avoiding and solving potential technical problems.

DISCUSSION

This section discusses the findings above from three different perspectives. In regard to Nielsen's (1993) model of system acceptability, whether SL can be widely applied in language education will be discussed. From an ecological perspective, how the affordances of SL can be better explored is answered. Finally, by referring to Wang's (2017a) study, when and where SL can and cannot adopted is suggested.

System Acceptability

The result section reveals that using SL in this English course has been problematic. A considerable amount of audio and chat communication dealt with technical challenges, and various minor or severe problems (in terms of hardware or software) influenced participation negatively or even prevented participants from joining in the course, although this course had been carefully planned, with initiation session to train students to use SL, SL-experienced teachers and technical assistants, laboratory support, and funding. Therefore, it is essential to ask: whether SL can be a system widely applied or used in language learning practice? This is answered by referring to Nielsen's (1993) model of usefulness, cost, compatibility, and reliability.

In terms of usefulness, for example, SL can be used to manipulate gender issues or explore the use of complex Web2.0 tools, as designed in this course under study. However, when the complexity of the technology or the unreliability of the software hindered participation as shown above, the goal of learning and teaching a foreign language and student participation are influenced negatively, which is definitely not what a collaborative language course aims for. Moreover, as the results above show, functions of SL are not easy to remember, not efficient to use, and not easy to learn. The participants also made errors when using SL although they were taught beforehand, and some of them did not feel pleased to use it. Therefore, it can be concluded that the usability of SL is challenged.

The use of SL also incurred a considerable amount of course time of training participants' technical skills or dealing with technical issues, and a large amount of funding to support the use of it. These cost, nonetheless, reduces language learning time and cannot be afforded by all language courses/institutions/

universities. With regard to compatibility, although SL is compatible with different operating systems (i.e. windows, Linux, and Mac OS), the constant updating of SL viewers, which are essentially different interfaces with different functions, makes it difficult to create useful instructional materials. Importantly, the updates do not seem to address the robustness of the software as the various technical problems in this study show. After almost a decade, SL is as unstable as it was in the early days, and this is a real problem in educational contexts when technology is expected to work smoothly to facilitate student participation.

Arguably, as a complex, unreliable, incompatible, and high-cost technology, SL may not be widely used in language education unless its special affordances are needed and there are sufficient technical support. How to explore these affordances will be discussed below.

Ecological Perspective

Technical challenges occurred throughout the English course under study. This finding corroborates Wang (2017a) in that it takes time for students to acquire skills in using different functions in SL. The results from this study indicate that 'newbies' may not be a realistic target group in this complex virtual learning environment as the affordances of SL are not easy to learn. Consequently, how could participants acquire the skills of using SL affordances is a question that course designers, teachers, institutions/universities need to consider.

Students, as active agents in perceiving and using affordances, should take initiatives in learning SL. Apart from learning a foreign langue, they should learn a technology as well. This could be realized if students have positive attitudes towards using SL, are personally interested in this technology, or are rewarded by doing so. However, this will take them more time, compared with simply learning a language or using a simply technology, e.g. a mobile app, to learn a language. If they frequently encounter difficulties in learning or using this technology, they may be reluctant to try that again. Consequently, peer-support and teacher motivation are of vital importance (cf. Hubbard, 2019).

Using peer-support is conducive to learning and using the affordances of SL. As manifested from this English course under investigation, some novices in SL not only received technical support from the pedagogical facilitators and the TFs but also from the SL-experienced peers. These are typical language learning activities in virtual collaborative environment, where students help each other to solve real problems in time, and ones where the technical complexity actually stimulates language use. For this reason, SL can potentially promote authentic collaborative learning. Although this course encouraged the participants to learn more about SL from each other in their spare time, it is unknown to what extent they did so, if at all.

From a teacher perspective, motivating students to learn more affordances of SL by themselves is also important, especially given the financial reality of running a language course at a university. In this course, extra resources that were funded by a project were present, but technical problems still occurred. Under more normal circumstances there may simply not be enough resources to deal with the complex technology. It is thus important for language teachers or course organizers to realize that motivating learners to explore SL and to develop technical skills with SL-experienced peers after class is necessary (cf. Hubbard, 2019). Furthermore, language teachers should explore and learn affordances of SL first and provide students with insightful suggestions to use the technology to achieve course goals. If teachers lack skills of operating SL, students would not get instant support when they encounter technical problems especially when there are no technical assistants. Nonetheless, even if a teacher is an expert user of SL, he/she should be aware that employing new affordances such as sound isolated parcels and voice-morphing deserves scrutiny. In this course, the sound parcels were tested before the workshops. MP also asked his colleagues who were SL-experienced users to help him to decide which voice-morphing sounded natural and what volume was suitable for both feminine and masculine voice-morphed avatars. Nevertheless, technical malfunctions still occurred. Voice-morphing is probably an affordance of SL most language courses do not employ unless a course explores gender issues using this type of environment, but isolated sound parcels may be useful in organizing parallel group discussions. As a result, it is essential for course teachers to test special affordances of SL again and again, probably in different technical situations, e.g. with different Internet connection speeds, computers, or SL viewers, to ensure that they could work normally during teaching time so that students could participate.

Using SL or Not

Based on the discussion above, it seems that there exists constraints on using SL. This section thus highlights situations where SL can be and cannot be used.

This study confirms Wang's findings (2017a). Same to what Wang (2017a) has proposed (see Figure 1a), this study demonstrates that SL can be used to introduce a complex technology in language teaching and can also trigger "authentic and unrehearsed language use" (Wang, 2017a, p. 73). In general, the exploration of special affordances of SL (voice morphing) helped achieve the goal of manipulating gender issues (cf. Wang et al., 2014), with the special task design of using sound isolated parcels and intensive technical support and resources, i.e. technical facilitators, teachers, fast Internet connection, and capable computers. However, this study also indicates that technical initiation session time is not enough to train students to have adequate technical skills to operate SL. Accordingly, when "financial support" is deficient and technology resources are scare, or participants feel frustrated of exploring or learning the technology further especially for those who do not have the knowledge of using SL, using SL can be very challenging.

CONCLUSION

The discussion above all suggest that although SL has potential added value for foreign language learning and teaching, its weaknesses in practical acceptability, together with other technical challenges, can affect its adoption for and student participation in, a language course. Stockwell (2012) argues, users' 'experience, skills, and knowledge of what the technology can do' (p. 7) largely predetermines how affordances will be realized. Albeit SL can afford potentially useful affordances, these affordances may add little value to a language course when participation is hindered. In sum, the complexity of the environment may simply not match its added benefits (cf. Rogers, 2003).

This study has provided a quantitative description of the proportions of technical issues in the two main communication modes, i.e. voice and chat, in Second Life. It has also given a qualitative analysis of the different types of technical challenges in SL. It is hoped that the technical challenges and strategies for dealing with these challenges mapped in this course can provide some insights into language courses in SL. This study also suggests that teachers and students should be aware that adopting this complex technology and acquiring appropriate technical skills may be time-consuming. Additionally, SL is not applicable to any type of language courses due to its critical technical demands. Consequently, choosing a suitable technology based on the course budget, timetable and technical resources is a pragmatic strategy to maximize student participation in a language course.

REFERENCES

Baker, S. C., Wentz, R. K., & Woods, M. M. (2009). Using virtual worlds in education: Second Life as an educational tool. *Teaching of Psychology*, *36*(1), 59–64. doi:10.1080/00986280802529079

Barr, D. (2013). Embedding technology in translation teaching: Evaluative considerations for courseware integration. *Computer Assisted Language Learning*, *26*(4), 295–310. doi:10.1080/09588221.2012.658406

Blasing, M. T. (2010). Second language in Second Life: Exploring interaction, identity and pedagogical practice in a virtual world. *SEEJ*, *54*(1), 96–117.

Chen, J. C. C. (2016). The crossroads of English language learners, task-based instruction, and 3D multi-user virtual learning in Second Life. *Computers & Education*, *102*, 125–171. doi:10.1016/j.compedu.2016.08.004

Chen, J. C. C. (2018). The interplay of tasks, strategies and negotiations in Second Life. *Computer Assisted Language Learning*, *31*(8), 960–986. doi:10.1080/09588221.2018.1466810

Cooke-Plagwitz, J. (2008). New directions in CALL: An objective introduction to Second Life. *CALICO Journal*, *25*(3), 547–557. doi:10.1558/cj.v25i3.547-557

Deutschmann, M., & Panichi, L. (2013). Towards models for designing language learning in virtual worlds. *International Journal of Virtual and Personal Learning Environments*, *4*(2), 65–84. doi:10.4018/jvple.2013040104

Deutschmann, M., Steinvall, A., & Lagerström, A. (2011). Gender-bending in virtual space: Using voice-morphing in Second Life to raise sociolinguistic gender awareness. In S. Czepielewski (Ed.), *Learning a language in virtual worlds: A review of innovation and ICT in language teaching methodology* (pp. 54–61). Warsaw, Poland: Warsaw Academy of Computer Science, Management, and Administration.

Gamage, V., Tretiakov, A., & Crump, B. (2011). Teacher perceptions of learning affordances of multi-user virtual environments. *Computers & Education*, *57*(4), 2406–2413. doi:10.1016/j.compedu.2011.06.015

Gee, J. P. (2007). *Good video games and good learning*. New York: Peter Lang. doi:10.3726/978-1-4539-1162-4

Henderson, M., Huang, H., Grant, S., & Henderson, L. (2009). Language acquisition in Second Life: Improving self-efficacy beliefs. In R. J. Atkinson, & C. McBeath (Eds.), Same places, different spaces: Proceedings ascilite Auckland 2009 (pp. 464-472). Auckland & Tugun: The University of Auckland, Auckland University of Technology, & Australasian Society for Computers in Learning in Tertiary Education (ascilite).

Hsu, L. (2015). EFL learners' implicit theory of intelligence and the application of MMORPG in EFL Learning. [IJCALLT]. *International Journal of Computer-Assisted Language Learning and Teaching*, *5*(2), 58–71. doi:10.4018/IJCALLT.2015040104

Hubbard, P. (2019). Five keys from the past to the future of CALL. [IJCALLT]. *International Journal of Computer-Assisted Language Learning and Teaching*, *9*(3), 1–13. doi:10.4018/IJCALLT.2019070101

Hutchby, I., & Wooffitt, R. (2008). *Conversational analysis* (2nd ed.). Cambridge, UK: Polity Press.

Inman, C., Wright, V. H., & Hartman, J. A. (2010). Use of Second Life in K-12 and higher education: A review of research. *Journal of Interactive Online Learning*, *9*(1), 44–63.

Liou, H. C. (2011). The roles of Second Life in a college computer-assisted language learning (CALL) course in Taiwan, ROC. *Computer Assisted Language Learning, iFirst article*, 1-18.

Liu, Q., & Chao, C.-C. (2017). CALL from an ecological perspective: How a teacher perceives affordance and fosters learner agency in a technology-mediated language classroom. *ReCALL*, *30*(1), 68–87. doi:10.1017/S0958344017000222

MacIntyre, D. P. (1995). How does anxiety affect second language learning? A reply to Sparks and Ganschow. *Modern Language Journal*, *79*(1), 90–99. doi:10.1111/j.1540-4781.1995.tb05418.x

Melchor-Couto, S. (2017). Foreign language anxiety levels in Second Life oral interaction. *ReCALL*, *29*(1), 99–119. doi:10.1017/S0958344016000185

Nielsen, J. (1993). *Usability engineering*. San Francisco, CA: Morgan Kaufmann. doi:10.1016/B978-0-08-052029-2.50007-3

Palomeque, C., & Pujolà, J.-T. (2018). Managing multimodal data in virtual world research for language learning. *ReCALL*, *30*(2), 177–195. doi:10.1017/S0958344017000374

Peterson, M. (2012). EFL learner collaborative interaction in Second Life. *ReCALL*, *24*(1), 20–39. doi:10.1017/S0958344011000279

Peterson, M., & Swier, R. (2018). 3D digital games, virtual worlds, and language learning in higher education: continuing challenges in Japan. JALT CALL Journal, *14*(3), 225-238.

Rogers, E. M. (2003). *Diffusion of innovations* (5th ed.). New York, NY: Free Press.

Salmon, G. (2009). The future for (second) life and learning. *British Journal of Educational Technology*, *40*(3), 526–538. doi:10.1111/j.1467-8535.2009.00967.x

Stockwell, G. (2012). Introduction. In G. Stockwell (Ed.), *Computer-assisted language learning: Diversity in environments* (pp. 1–13). Cambridge, UK: Cambridge University Press. doi:10.1017/CBO9781139060981.001

Thomas, M. (2013). TBLT in business English communication: An approach for evaluating Adobe Connect and Second Life in a blended language learning format. [IJCALLT]. *International Journal of Computer-Assisted Language Learning and Teaching*, *3*(1), 73–89. doi:10.4018/ijcallt.2013010105

van Lier, L. (2004). *The ecology and semiotics of language learning: A sociocultural perspective*. Boston, MA: Kluwer Academic. doi:10.1007/1-4020-7912-5

Venkatesh, V., Morris, M. G., Davis, G. B., & Davis, F. D. (2003). User acceptance of information technology: Toward a unified view. *Management Information Systems Quarterly*, *27*(3), 425–478. doi:10.2307/30036540

Wang, A. (2014). Managing student participation: Teacher strategies in a virtual English course. *The JALT CALL Journal*, *10*(2), 105–125.

Wang, A. (2015). Facilitating participation: Teacher roles in a multi-user virtual learning environment. *Language Learning & Technology*, *19*(2), 156–176.

Wang, A. (2017a). *Learning English in a multi-user virtual environment: exploring factors affecting participation (PhD dissertation)*. Sundsvall, Sweden: Mid Sweden University. Retrieved from http://urn.kb.se/resolve?urn=urn:nbn:se:miun:diva-30795

Wang, A. (2017b). Using Second Life in an English course: How does the technology affect participation? [IJCALLT]. *International Journal of Computer-Assisted Language Learning and Teaching*, *7*(1), 67–86. doi:10.4018/IJCALLT.2017010105

Wang, A., Deutschmann, M., & Steinvall, A. (2013). Towards a model for mapping participation: Exploring factors affecting participation in a telecollaborative learning scenario in Second Life. *The JALT CALL Journal*, *9*(1), 3–22.

Wang, A., Steinvall, A., & Deutschmann, M. (2014). Who owns the floor? Examining participation in a collaborative learning scenario between student teachers and active professionals in second life. *International Journal of Virtual and Personal Learning Environments*, *5*(1), 34–53. doi:10.4018/ijvple.2014010103

Wang, C. X., Song, H., Stone, D. E., & Yan, Q. (2009). Integrating SL into an EFL program in China: Research collaboration across the continents. *TechTrends*, *53*(6), 14–19. doi:10.100711528-009-0337-z

Wehner, A. K., Gump, A. W., & Downey, S. (2011). The effects of Second Life on the motivation of undergraduate students learning a foreign language. *Computer Assisted Language Learning*, *24*(3), 277–289. doi:10.1080/09588221.2010.551757

Wigham, C. R., & Chanier, T. (2013). A study of verbal and nonverbal communication in Second Life—The ARCHI21 experience. *ReCALL*, *25*(1), 63–84. doi:10.1017/S0958344012000250

Zheng, D. (2012). Caring in the dynamics of design and languaging: Exploring second language learning in 3D virtual spaces. *Language Sciences*, *34*(5), 543–558. doi:10.1016/j.langsci.2012.03.010

ENDNOTE

1. S represents student, IP invited professional, TF technical facilitator, MP the male pedagogical facilitator, FV the feminine voice-morphed pedagogical facilitator, and MV the masculine voice-morphed pedagogical facilitator. For the transcription glossary see the Appendix.

APPENDIX

Figure 3. Transcription glossary (Adapted from Hutchby & Wooffitt, 2008, p. x-xii)

(1.0)	The number in brackets indicates a time gap in tenths of a second.
a:::	The number of colons indicates the degree to which the prior syllable is prolonged.
=	The equal sign indicates latching between utterances.
[ ]	Square brackets indicate the onset and end of a spate of overlapping talk.
( )	Empty parenthesis indicates the presence of unclear fragment in the recording.
.	A full stop indicates a falling tone.
,	A comma indicates a continuous tone.
?	A question mark indicates a rising tone.
under	Underlined fragment indicates the speaker's emphasis.
yeah-	The short dash indicates a 'cut off' of the prior word or sound.

Compilation of References

Abadin, H., Fried, D., Good, G., & Surface, E. (2012). *Reliability study of the ACTFL OPI in Chinese, Portuguese, Russian, Spanish, German, and English for the ACE review*. Raleigh, NC: SWA Consulting.

Abazaoğlu, I., Yıldırım, O., & Yıldızhan, Y. (2014). Teacher profile in Turkey]. *Turkish Studies: International Periodical for the Languages, Literature, and History of Turkish or Turkic*, *9*(2), 1–20.

Abbitt, J. T. (2011). Measuring technological pedagogical content knowledge in preservice teacher education: a review of current methods and instruments. *Journal of Research on Technology in Education*, *43*(4), 281–300. doi:10.1080/15391523.2011.10782573

Abbot, M. L., Lee, K. K., & Rossiter, M. J. (2018). Evaluating the effectiveness and functionality of professional learning communities in adult ESL programs. *TESL Canada Journal*, *35*(2), 1–25. doi:10.18806/tesl.v35i2.1288

Abbott, R. (2016). *Embracing digital technologies in classroom practice: the impact of teacher identity*. 26.

Abdullah, Z., & Ghani, A., M. F. (2014). Professional learning community in secondary schools community in Malaysia. [EduLearn]. *Journal of Education and Learning*, *8*(3), 227. doi:10.11591/edulearn.v8i3.265

Abeysekera, L., & Dawson, P. (2014). Motivation and cognition load in the flipped classroom: Definition, rational and a call for research. *Higher Education Research & Development*, *34*(1), 1–14. doi:10.1080/07294360.2014.934336

Abolghasseminits, S., Jahromi, F., & Salimi, F. (2013). Exploring the human element of computer-assisted language learning: An Iranian context. *Computer Assisted Language Learning*, *26*(2), 158–176. doi:10.1080/09588221.2011.643411

Abrams, Z., & Byrd, D. R. (2017). The effects of meaning-focused pre-tasks on beginning-level L2 writing in German: An exploratory study. *Language Teaching Research*, *21*(4), 434–453. doi:10.1177/1362168815627383

Adams, R., & Nik, A. N. (2014). Prior knowledge and second language task production in text chat. In M. González-Lloret, & L. Ortega (Eds.), *Technology-mediated TBLT: Researching technology and tasks* (pp. 51–78). Amsterdam, The Netherlands: John Benjamins. doi:10.1075/tblt.6.03ada

Agca, R. K., & Özdemir, S. (2013). Foreign language vocabulary learning with mobile technologies. *Procedia: Social and Behavioral Sciences*, *83*, 781–785. doi:10.1016/j.sbspro.2013.06.147

Ahmad, K. S., Armarego, J. & Sudweeks, F. (2017). The impact of utilising mobile assisted language learning (MALL) on vocabulary acquisition among migrant women English learners. *Interdisciplinary Journal of E-Skills and Lifelong learning*, 13, 38-57.

Ai, H. (2017). Graduated corrective feedback. *ReCALL*, *29*(3), 313–334. doi:10.1017/S095834401700012X

Albin, M. L., Benton, S. L., & Khramtsova, I. (1996). Individual differences in interest and narrative writing. *Contemporary Educational Psychology*, *21*(4), 305–324. doi:10.1006/ceps.1996.0024 PMID:8979867

Ali, A. D. (2016). Effectiveness of using screencast feedback on EFL students' writing and perception. *English Language Teaching*, *9*(8), 106–121. doi:10.5539/elt.v9n8p106

Aljaloud, A., Billingsley, W., & Kwan, P. (2019). Factors that influence teachers' decisions to use smartphone clicker apps to enhance teacher-student interactions in university classrooms in Saudi Arabia. *Learning: Research and Practice*, *5*(1), 67–86. doi:10.1080/23735082.2018.1459802

Allen, C. [Karelia Kondor- Teachmeet Second Life]. (2010, May 9). *Karelia Kondor (Helen Myres) presentation at the first Teachmeet Second Life talking about learning languages using Second Life* [Video file]. Retrieved from https://www.youtube.com/watch?v=LhTAmHM34gE

Allen, J. P., & Corder, S. Pit. (1974). Techniques in applied linguistics. London, UK: Oxford University Press.

Ally, M. (2013). Mobile learning: From research to practice to impact education. *Learning and Teaching in Higher Education: Gulf Perspectives*, *10*(2), 1–10.

Almutairi, S. (2014). *Managing and analysing task-based interaction in digital tabletop environments*. Newcastle Upon Tyne, UK: Unpublished University of Newcastle Upon Tyne.

Alotumi, M. (2018). The effect of CALL-based instruction on students' score attainment on the TOEFL iBT in a Yemeni context. *International Journal of Computer-Assisted Language Learning and Teaching*, *8*(1), 50–64. doi:10.4018/IJCALLT.2018010104

Al-Qallaf, C. L., & Al-Mutairi, A. S. (2016). Digital literacy and digital content supports learning: The impact of blogs on teaching English as a foreign language. *The Electronic Library*, *34*(3), 522–547. doi:10.1108/EL-05-2015-0076

Alsubaie, A., & Madine, A. (2018). The effect of using blogs to enhance the writing skill of English language learners at a Saudi University. *Global Journal of Educational Studies*, *4*(1), 13–30. doi:10.5296/gjes.v4i1.12224

Álvarez, J. A. (2015). Language views on social networking sites for language learning: The case of Busuu. *Computer Assisted Language Learning*, *29*(5), 1–15.

Álvarez, J. A. (2016). Social networking sites for language learning: Examining learning theories in nested semiotic spaces. *Signo y Pensamiento*, *68*(68), 66–84. doi:10.11144/Javeriana.syp35-68.snsl

Amengual-Pizarro, M., & Garcia-Laborda, J. (2017). Analysing test-takers' views on a computer-based speaking test. *Profile: Issues in Teachers' Professional Development*, *19*(1), 23–38.

American Council on the Teaching of Foreign Languages. (2011). *A decade of language standards: Influence, impact and future directions*. Retrieved from https://www.actfl.org/sites/default/files/publications/standards/StandardsImpact-Survey.pdf

Andriani, G. (2014). Using Livemocha for independent language learning, a study of students' perception. Paper presented at Sriwijaya University Learning and Education-International Conference 2014, Sriwijaya University, Palembang, May 16-18.

Antonenko, P. D., Dawson, K., & Sahay, S. (2017). A framework for aligning needs, abilities, and affordances to inform design and practice of educational technologies. *British Journal of Educational Technology*, *48*(4), 916–927. doi:10.1111/bjet.12466

Araminta, L. D., & Halimi, S. S. (2015). ASEAN economic community 2015: Needs analysis of Universitas Indonesia's engineering students. *Indonesian Journal of Applied Linguistics*, *5*(1), 11–18. doi:10.17509/ijal.v5i1.841

Armstrong, K., & Retterer, O. (2008). Blogging as L2 writing: A case study. *AACE Journal*, *16*(3), 233–251.

Arnold, N., & Ducate, L. (2015). Contextualized views of practices and competencies in CALL teacher education research. *Language Learning & Technology*, *19*(1), 1–9.

Arnold, N., Ducate, L., & Kost, C. (2009). Collaborative writing in wikis: Insights from culture projects in German class. In L. Lomicka, & G. Lord (Eds.), *The next generation: Social networking and online collaboration in foreign language learning* (pp. 115–144). San Marcos, TX: CALICO.

Arnold, N., Ducate, L., & Kost, C. (2009). Collaborative writing in wikis: Insights from culture projects in German classes. In L. Lomicka, & G. Lord (Eds.), *The next generation: Social networking and online collaboration in foreign language learning* (pp. 115–144). San Marcos, TX: CALICO.

Arslan, R. Ş., & Şahin-Kızıl, A. (2010). How can the use of blog software facilitate the writing process of English language learners? *Computer Assisted Language Learning*, *23*(3), 183–197. doi:10.1080/09588221.2010.486575

Asraf, R. M., & Supian, N. (2017). Metacognition and mobile-assisted vocabulary learning. *Arab World English Journal*, *8*(2), 16–35. doi:10.24093/awej/vol8no2.2

Atkinson, J. M., & Heritage, J. (Eds.). (1984). *Structures of social action: Studies in conversational analysis*. Cambridge, UK: Cambridge University Press.

Attwell, G., & Hughes, J. (2010). Pedagogic approaches to using technology for learning: Literature review. *Lifelong Learning UK*. Retrieved from http://webarchive.nationalarchives.gov.uk/20110414152025/http:/www.lluk.org/wp-content/uploads/2011/01/Pedagogical-appraches-for-using-technology-literature-review-january-11-FINAL.pdf

Aukerman, M., & Schuldt, L. C. (2016). "The pictures can say more things": Change across time in young children's references to images and words during text discussion. *Reading Research Quarterly*, *51*(3), 267–287. doi:10.1002/rrq.138

Aulia, D., Yulastri, D., & Handayani, W. (2016). The use of e-portfolio for improving students' English skills: A pilot study in English department, the State Polytechnic of Padang. *Journal Polingua*, *5*(2), 52–59.

Aulia, D., Yulastri, D., & Sari, I. (2014). The use of portfolio to improve translation ability of English department students in State Polytechnic of Padang. *Proceedings of ISELT FBS Universitas Negeri Padang*, *2*, 100–106.

Aydin, S. (2014). The use of blogs in learning English as a foreign language. [MIJE]. *Mevlana International Journal of Education*, *4*(1), 244–259. doi:10.13054/mije.13.79.4.1

Aydin, Z., & Yildiz, S. (2014). Using wikis to promote collaborative EFL writing. *Language Learning & Technology*, *18*(1), 160–180.

Baddeley, A. (1990). *Human memory*. London, UK: Lawrence Erlbaum Associates.

Badger, R., & Write, G. (2000). A process genre approach to teaching writing. *ELT Journal*, *54*(2), 153–160. doi:10.1093/elt/54.2.153

Baek, Y. K., Jung, J. Y., & Kim, B. K. (2008). What makes teachers use technology in the classroom? Exploring the factors affecting facilitation of technology with a Korean sample. *Computers & Education*, *50*(1), 224–234. doi:10.1016/j.compedu.2006.05.002

Bai, H., & Ertmer, P. (2008). Teacher educators' beliefs and technology uses as predictors of preservice teachers' beliefs and technology attitudes. *Journal of Technology and Teacher Education*, *16*(1), 93–112.

Baker, S. C., Wentz, R. K., & Woods, M. M. (2009). Using virtual worlds in education: Second Life as an educational tool. *Teaching of Psychology*, *36*(1), 59–64. doi:10.1080/00986280802529079

Bakir, N., Devers, C., & Hug, B. (2016). Affordances and constraints of a blended course in a teacher professional development program. *Journal of Educational Multimedia and Hypermedia*, *25*(4), 323–341.

Balakrishnan, V., & Lay, G. C. (2016). Students' learning styles and their effects on the use of social media technology for learning. *Telematics and Informatics*, *33*(3), 808–821. doi:10.1016/j.tele.2015.12.004

Bandura, A. (1986). *Social foundations of thought and action*. Englewood Cliffs, NJ: Prentice-Hall.

Bandura, A. (1994). Self-efficacy. In V. S. Ramachaudran (Ed.), *Encyclopedia of human behavior* (Vol. 4, pp. 71–81).

Bao, R., & Du, X. (2015). Implementation of task-based language teaching in Chinese as a foreign language: Benefits and challenges. *Language, Culture, and Curriculum*, *28*(3), 291–310. doi:10.1080/07908318.2015.1058392

Barak, M., & Levenberg, A. (2016). Flexible thinking in learning: An individual differences measure for learning in technology-enhanced environments. *Computers & Education*, *99*, 39–52. doi:10.1016/j.compedu.2016.04.003

Barba, P., Kennedy, G., & Ainley, M. (2016). The role of students' motivation and participation in predicting performance in a MOOC motivation and participation in MOOCs. *Journal of Computer Assisted Learning*, *32*(3), 218–231. doi:10.1111/jcal.12130

Barkley, J., & Lepp, A. (2013). Cellular telephone use is associated with greater sedentary behavior independent of leisure-time physical activity. *Applied Physiology, Nutrition, and Metabolism*, *38*(S1), 1023. Retrieved from https://www.ncbi.nlm.nih.gov/pmc/articles/PMC4815203/

Barnhisel, G., Stoddard, E., & Gorman, J. (2012). Incorporating process-based writing pedagogy into first-year learning communities. *The Journal of General Education*, *61*(4), 461–487. doi:10.1353/jge.2012.0041

Barr, D. (2013). Embedding technology in translation teaching: Evaluative considerations for courseware integration. *Computer Assisted Language Learning*, *26*(4), 295–310. doi:10.1080/09588221.2012.658406

Barth, I., Spector-Cohen, E., Sitman, R., Jiang, G., Jiaotong, X., Liu, F., & Xu, Y. (2019). Beyond small chunks: Designing vocabulary OERs for mobile learning. *International Journal of Computer-Assisted Language Learning and Teaching*, *9*(2), 79–97. doi:10.4018/IJCALLT.2019040105

Barton, M. D., & Heiman, J. R. (2012). Process, product, and potential: the archaeological assessment of collaborative, wiki-based student projects in the technical communication classroom. *Technical Communication Quarterly*, *21*(1), 46–60. doi:10.1080/10572252.2012.626391

Bates, A. (2000). *Managing technological change: Strategies for college and university leaders*. San Francisco, CA: Jossey-Bass.

Bax, S. (2018). MOOCs as a new technology: approaches to normalising the MOOC experience for our learners; paper posthumously transcribed by Marina Orsini-Jones. In M. Orsini-Jones, & S. Smith (Eds.), Flipping the blend through MOOCs, MALL, and OIL – new directions in CALL (pp. 9-16). Research-publishing.net. doi:10.14705/rpnet.2018.23.785

Bax, S. (2003). CALL – Past, present and future. *System*, *31*(11), 13–28. doi:10.1016/S0346-251X(02)00071-4

Bax, S. (2011). Normalisation revisited: the effective use of technology in language education. *International Journal of Computer-Assisted Language Learning and Teaching*, *1*(2), 1–15. doi:10.4018/ijcallt.2011040101

Becker, H. (2000). Findings from the teaching, learning, and computing survey: Is Larry Cuban right? *Education Policy Analysis Archives*, *51*(8), 1–32. Retrieved from http://www.crito.uci.edu/tlc/findings/ccsso.pdf

Beechler, S., & Williams, S. (2012). Computer assisted instruction and elementary ESL students in sight word recognition. *International Journal of Business and Social Science*, *3*(4), 85–92.

Beheydt, L. (1987). The semantization of vocabulary in foreign language learning. *System, 15*(1), 55–67. doi:10.1016/0346-251X(87)90048-0

Belo, N., Belo, N., McKenney, S., Voogt, J., & Bradley, B. (2016). Teacher knowledge for using technology to foster early literacy: A literature review. *Computers in Human Behavior, 60*, 372–383. doi:10.1016/j.chb.2016.02.053

Beltran, J. (2016). The effects of visual input on scoring a speaking achievement test. *Working papers in TESOL & Applied Linguistics, 16*(2), 1-23. doi:10.7916/D8543VDT

Benson, P. (2007). Autonomy in language teaching and learning. *Language Teaching, 40*(1), 21–40. doi:10.1017/S0261444806003958

Benson, P. (2013). *Teaching and researching: Autonomy in language learning*. New York: Routledge.

Benson, S. D. (2016). Task-based language teaching: An empirical study of task transfer. *Language Teaching Research, 20*(3), 341–365. doi:10.1177/1362168815569829

Beriswill, J. E., Bracey, P. S., Sherman-Morris, K., Huang, K., & Lee, S. J. (2016). Professional development for promoting 21st century skills and common core state standards in foreign language and social studies classrooms. *TechTrends, 60*(1), 77–84. doi:10.100711528-015-0004-5

Berns, A., Gonzalez-Pardo, A., & Camacho, D. (2013). Game-like language learning in 3D virtual environments. *Computers & Education, 60*(1), 210–220. doi:10.1016/j.compedu.2012.07.001

Berry, V., Nakatsuhara, F., Inoue, C., & Galaczi, E. (2018). *Exploring the use of video-conferencing technology to deliver the IELTS speaking test: Phase 3 technical trial*. Retrieved from https://www.ielts.org/-/media/research-reports/ielts-research-partner-paper-4.ashx

Bikowski, D., & Vithanage, R. (2016). Effects of web-based collaborative writing on individual L2 writing development. *Language Learning & Technology, 20*(1), 79–99.

Blackmore-Squires, S. (2010). *An investigation into the use of s blog as a tool to improve writing in the second language classroom*. (Unpublished MA dissertation, University of Manchester, UK).

Blake, R. J. (2008). *Brave new digital classroom: Technology and foreign language learning*. Washington, DC: Georgetown University Press.

Blasing, M. T. (2010). Second language in Second Life: Exploring interaction, identity and pedagogical practice in a virtual world. *SEEJ, 54*(1), 96–117.

Blattner, G., & Lomicka, L. (2012). Facebook-ing and the social generation: A new era of language learning. *ALSIC, 15*(1). Retrieved https://journals.openedition.org/alsic/2413

Blitz, C. L., & Schulman, R. (2016). *Measurement instruments for assessing the performance of professional learning communities. REL 2016-144*. Retrieved from https://eric.ed.gov/?q=measuring+the+effectiveness+of+professional+learning+community+in+schools+&pr=on&id=ED568594

Blokzijl, W., & Naeff, R. (2004). The instructor as stagehand: Dutch student responses to PowerPoint. *Business Communication Quarterly, 67*(1), 70–77. doi:10.1177/1080569903262046

Boczkowski, P., Matassi, M., & Mitchelstein, E. (2018). How young users deal with multiple platforms: The role of meaning-making in social media repertoires. *Journal of Computer-Mediated Communication, 23*(5), 245–259. doi:10.1093/jcmc/zmy012

Boling, E. C., Holan, E., Horbatt, B., Hough, M., Jean-Louis, J., Khurana, C., ... Spiezio, C. (2014). Using online tools for communication and collaboration: Understanding educators' experiences in an online course. *Internet & Higher Education*, *23*, 48–55. doi:10.1016/j.iheduc.2014.07.002

Bond, B. J. (2009). He posted, she posted: Gender differences in self-disclosure on social networking sites. *Rocky Mountain Communication Review*, *6*(2), 29–37.

Bonzo, D. (2008). To assign topics or not: Observing fluency and complexity in intermediate foreign language writing. *Foreign Language Annals*, *41*(4), 722–735. doi:10.1111/j.1944-9720.2008.tb03327.x

Borg, S. (2015). *Teacher cognition and language education*. London, UK: Bloomsbury Academic.

Borg, S. (2003). Teacher cognition in language teaching: A review of research on what language teachers think, know, believe, and do. *Language Teaching*, *36*(2), 81–109. doi:10.1017/S0261444803001903

Borg, S. (2011). The impact of in-service teacher education on language teachers' beliefs. *System*, *39*(3), 370–380. doi:10.1016/j.system.2011.07.009

Borthwick, K. (2018). What our MOOC did next: embedding, exploiting, and extending an existing MOOC to fit strategic purposes and priorities. In M. Orsini-Jones, & S. Smith (Eds.), Flipping the blend through MOOCs, MALL and OIL – new directions in CALL (pp. 17-23). Dublin, Ireland: Research-publishing.net. doi:10.14705/rpnet.2018.23.786

Borup, J., West, R. E., & Thomas, R. (2015). The impact of text versus video communication on instructor feedback in blended courses. *Educational Technology Research and Development*, *63*(2), 161–184. doi:10.100711423-015-9367-8

Boscolo, P., & Hidi, S. (2007). The multiple meanings of motivation to write. In P. Boscolo, & S. Hidi (Eds.), *Writing and Motivation* (pp. 1–14). Bingley, UK: Emerald.

Boumosleh, J., & Jaalouk, D. (2018). Smartphone addiction among university students and its relationship with academic performance. *Global Journal of Health Science*, *10*(1), 48–59. doi:10.5539/gjhs.v10n1p48

Bourke, R., Mentis, M., & O'Neill, J. (2013). Using activity theory to evaluate a professional learning and development initiative in the use of narrative assessment. *Cambridge Journal of Education*, *43*(1), 35–50. doi:10.1080/03057 64X.2012.749214

Bower, K. (2017). Explaining motivation in language learning: A framework for evaluation and research. *Language Learning Journal*, 1–17. doi:10.1080/09571736.2017.1321035

Boyd, D., & Ellison, N.B. (2008). Social network sites: Definition, history, and scholarship. *Journal of Computer-Mediated Communication, 13*, 210-230.

Boyd, D. M. (2008). *Taken out of context: American teen sociality in networked publics. (Ph.D. Dissertation)*. Berkeley, CA: School of Information, University of California-Berkeley; Retrieved from https://www.danah.org/papers/TakenOutOfContext.pdf

Boyd, D. M., & Ellison, N. B. (2007). Social network sites: Definition, history, and scholarship. *Journal of Computer-Mediated Communication*, *13*(1), 210–230. doi:10.1111/j.1083-6101.2007.00393.x

Brady, K., Holcomb, L., & Smith, B. (2010). The use of alternative social networking sites in higher educational settings: A case study of the e-learning benefits of Ning in education. *Journal of Interactive Online Learning*, *9*(2), 151–170.

Brander, B. G. (2005). Considering culture in CALL research. In J. L. Egbert, & G. M. Petrie (Eds.), *CALL research perspectives* (pp. 141–153). Mahwah, NJ: Routledge.

Brandon, D. P., & Hollingshead, A. B. (1999). Collaborative learning and computer-supported groups. *Communication Education*, *48*(2), 109–126. doi:10.1080/03634529909379159

Brantley-Dias, L., & Ertmer, P. A. (2013). Goldilocks and TPACK: Is the construct 'Just Right?'. *Journal of Research on Technology in Education*, *46*(2), 103–128. doi:10.1080/15391523.2013.10782615

Braun, A., Maguire, M., & Ball, S. J. (2010). Policy enactments in the UK secondary school: examining policy, practice and school positioning. *Journal of Education Policy*, *25*(4), 547–560. doi:10.1080/02680931003698544

Breslow, L., Pritchard, D. E., de Boer, J., Stump, G. S., Ho, A. D., & Seaton, D. T. (2013). Studying learning in the worldwide classroom: Research into edX's first MOOC. *Research and Practice in Assessment*, *8*(1), 13–25.

Briansolis. (2010). The age of social networks. Retrieved from https://www.briansolis.com/2010/03/the-age-of-social-networks/

Brick, B. (2013). Evaluating social networking sites (SNSs) for language learning: An inquiry-based student project. Retrieved from http://coursefinder.coventry.ac.uk.public.freestyleinteractive.co.uk/Global/BES/Active%20Learning/Billy%20Brick.pdf

Brick, B. (2011a). How effective are web 2.0 language learning sites in facilitating language learning? *Compass: The Journal of Learning and Teaching at the University of Greenwich*, *3*, 57–63.

Brick, B. (2011b). Social networking sites and language learning. *International Journal of Virtual and Personal Learning Environments*, *2*(3), 18–31. doi:10.4018/jvple.2011070102

Brick, B. (2012). The role of social networking sites for language learning in UK higher education: The views of learners and practitioners. *International Journal of Computer-Assisted Language Learning and Teaching*, *2*(3), 35–53. doi:10.4018/ijcallt.2012070103

Brissenden-Smith, K., Moreno, A., Peloquin, L., Radiloff, J., & Wachtel, J. (2018). Growing opportunities: collaboration nurtures and supports early learning educators. *Learning Professional*, *39*(3), 42–46.

British Council. (2016). *Aptis general speaking test: Practice version.* Retrieved from https://www.britishcouncil.org/aptis-practice-tests/AptisSpeakingPractice/

British Council. (2018). *What is Aptis.* Retrieved from https://www.britishcouncil.my/exam/aptis/what

Brooker, J. (2019). Why banning phones from schools is a backward step for education: Instead, let's treat this as an opportunity to help young people today become productive members of society. *Podium Online*. Retrieved from https://thenextweb.com/podium/2019/03/23/why-banning-phones-from-schools-is-a-backward-step-for-education/

Brooks, L., & Swain, M. (2014). Contextualizing performances: Comparing performances during TOEFL iBT™ and real-life academic speaking activities. *Language Assessment Quarterly*, *11*(4), 353–373. doi:10.1080/15434303.2014.947532

Brophy, J. E. (2013). *Motivating students to learn.* New York: Routledge. doi:10.4324/9780203858318

Brown, A., & Campione, J. (1996). Psychological theory and the design of innovative learning environments: On procedures, principles, and systems. In L. Schauble, & R. Glaser (Eds.), *Innovations in learning: New environments for education* (pp. 289–325). Mahwah, NJ: Lawrence Erlbaum Associates.

Brown, B. D., Horn, R. S., & King, G. (2018). The effective implementation of professional learning communities. *Alabama Journal of Educational Leadership*, *5*, 53–59.

Brown, D. H. (1987). *Principles of language learning and teaching.* New Jersey: Prentice-Hall.

Brown, J. S., Collins, A., & Duguid, P. (1989). Situated cognition and the culture of learning. *Educational Researcher, 18*(1), 32–42. doi:10.3102/0013189X018001032

Brown, S., & Adler, R. P. (2008). Minds on fire. Open education, the long trail, and learning 2.0. *EDUCAUSE Review, 43*(1), 16–32.

Bruestle, P., Haubner, D., Schinzel, B., Holthaus, M., Remmele, B., Schirmer, D., & Reips, U. D. (2009). Doing E-learning/doing gender? Examining the relationship between students' gender concepts and E-learning technology. *Proceedings of the 5th European Symposium on Gender & ICT Digital Cultures: Participation - Empowerment – Diversity, University of Bremen.*

Bugueño, W. (2013). Using TPACK to promote effective language teaching in an ESL/EFL classroom. *Graduate Research Papers*. Retrieved from https://scholarworks.uni.edu/grp/150

Bukor, E. (2015). Exploring teacher identity from a holistic perspective: Reconstructing and reconnecting personal and professional selves. *Teachers and Teaching, 21*(3), 305–327. doi:10.1080/13540602.2014.953818

Bulkot, M. (2015). *Using Minecraftedu to establish common ground and increase collaboration in an American literature college course.* (Unpublished master's dissertation, State University of New York, Utica, NY).

Bündgens-Kosten, J. (2011). Blogging in the target language: Review of the 'Lang-8' online community. *Studies in Self-Access Learning Journal, 2*(2), 97–99.

Burke, A., & Hughes, J. (2018). A shifting landscape: using tablets to support learning in students with diverse abilities. *Technology, Pedagogy, and Education, 27*(2), 183–198. doi:10.1080/1475939X.2017.1396492

Burnett, C. (2011). Pre-service teachers' digital literacy practices: Exploring contingency in identity and digital literacy in and out of educational contexts. *Language and Education, 25*(5), 433–449. doi:10.1080/09500782.2011.584347

Burns, A. (2011). *Doing action research in English language teaching: A guide for practitioners.* Beijing, China: Foreign Language Teaching and Research Press.

Burston, J. (2014). The reality of MALL: Still on the fringes. *CALICO Journal, 31*(1), 103–125. doi:10.11139/cj.31.1.103-125

Busse, V., & Walter, C. (2013). Foreign language learning motivation in higher education: A longitudinal study of motivational changes and their causes. *Modern Language Journal, 97*(2), 435–456. doi:10.1111/j.1540-4781.2013.12004.x

Buysse, V., Sparkman, K. L., & Wesley, P. W. (2003). Communities of practice: connecting what we know with what we do. *Exceptional Children, 69*(3), 263–277. doi:10.1177/001440290306900301

Cain, G. (2014). The South Korean government wants to impose a curfew on smartphone use. *GlobalPost Online*. Retrieved from https://www.pri.org/stories/2014-04-14/south-korean-government-wants-impose-curfew-smartphone-use

Çakmak, F., & Erçein, G. (2018). Effects of gloss type on text recall. *ReCALL, 30*(1), 24–43. doi:10.1017/S0958344017000155

Calvani, A., Fini, A., & Ranieri, M. (2009). Assessing digital competence in secondary education. Issues, models and instruments. In M. Learning (Ed.), *Issues in information and media literacy: education, practice, and pedagogy* (pp. 153–172). Santa Rosa, CA: Information Science Press.

Cambridge English Language Assessment. (2018). *Test your English - adult learners.* Retrieved from http://www.cambridgeenglish.org/in/test-your-english/adult-learners/

Campbell, C. (1987). *Writing with others words: Native and non-native university students' use of information from a background reading text in academic compositions. (CLEAR Technical Report Series Publication No. TR4).* Los Angeles, CA: Center for Language Education and Research.

Canham, N. (2017). Comparing Web 2.0 applications for peer feedback. *Conference paper: European Association of Computer Assisted language Learning*. Southampton, UK.

Cappellini, M., & Azaoui, B. (2017). Sequences of normative evaluation in two telecollaboration projects: A comparative study of multimodal feedback through desktop videoconference. *Language Learning in Higher Education*, *7*(1), 55–80. doi:10.1515/cercles-2017-0002

Cappellini, M., Lewis, T., & Rivens Mompean, A. (2017). *Learner Autonomy and Web 2.0*. Sheffield, UK: Equinox.

Cardon, D. (2008). Le Design de la Visibilité: Un Essai de Typologie du Web 2.0. *Internet Actu*. Retrieved from http://www.internetactu.net/2008/02/01/le-Design-de-la-visibilite-un-essai-de-typologie-du-web-20/

Carless, D. R. (2003). Factors in the implementation of task-based teaching in primary schools. *System*, *31*(4), 485–500. doi:10.1016/j.system.2003.03.002

Carless, D. R. (2009). Revisiting the TBLT versus PPP debate: Voices from Hong Kong. *Asian Journal of English Language Teaching*, *19*(1), 49–66.

Carlos, A. M. F., Verónica, E. C. R., & Guerrero, J. S. (2017). BLMOOCs, a proposal for the design of Language MOOCs in a Blended context. *International Conference on Edemocracy & Egovernment* (pp.265-268). IEEE.

Caruso, M., Faschini, N., & Kuuse, S. (2019). Online tools for feedback engagement in second language learning. *International Journal of Computer-Assisted Language Learning and Teaching*, *9*(1), 58–78. doi:10.4018/IJCALLT.2019010104

Cassidy, G., & MacDonald, R. (2007). The effect of background music and background noise on the task performance of introverts and extraverts. *Psychology of Music*, *35*(3), 517–537. doi:10.1177/0305735607076444

Cavanagh, R. F., & Koehler, M. J. (2013). A turn toward specifying validity criteria in the measurement of technological pedagogical content knowledge (TPACK). *Journal of Research on Technology in Education*, *46*(2), 129–148. doi:10.1080/15391523.2013.10782616

Celik, I., Sahin, I., & Akturk, A. O. (2014). Analysis of the relations among the components of technological pedagogical and content knowledge (TPACK): A structural equation model. *Journal of Educational Computing Research*, *51*(1), 1–22. doi:10.2190/EC.51.1.a

Cequena, M. B., & Gustilo, L. (2014). Can Weblogs reduce writing anxiety and facilitate improvement in writing skills? *Asian Journal of English Language Studies*, *2*, 1–23.

Chaemchoy, S. (2017, February). An investigation of Thai Principals' Technology Leadership and Understanding of Mobile Technology in Education: Apply the TPACK Framework. *Advanced Science Letters*, *23*(2), 1134–1139.

Chang, B., Sheldon, L., Si, M., & Hand, A. (2012). Foreign language learning in immersive virtual environments, In *Proceedings of the IS&T/SPIE Electronic Imaging* (pp. 2–9). Burlingame, CA: SPIE Digital Library. 10.1117/12.909835

Chao, C. C. (2015, February). Rethinking transfer: Learning from CALL teacher education as consequential transition. *Language Learning & Technology*, *19*(1), 102–118.

Chao, Y., & Lo, H. (2009). Students perceptions of Wiki-based collaborative writing for learners of English as a foreign language. *Interactive Learning Environments*, *19*(4), 395–411. doi:10.1080/10494820903298662

Chapelle, C. A., & Sauro, S. (Eds.). (2017). The handbook of technology and second language teaching and learning. New York, NY: John Wiley & Sons.

Chapelle, C. A. (2001). *Computer applications in second language acquisition: Foundations for teaching, testing and research*. Cambridge, UK: Cambridge University Press. doi:10.1017/CBO9781139524681

Chapelle, C. A. (2003). *English language learning and technology*. Amsterdam, The Netherlands: John Benjamins. doi:10.1075/lllt.7

Chapelle, C. A. (2009). The relationship between second language acquisition theory and computer-assisted language learning. *Modern Language Journal*, *93*(1), 741–753. doi:10.1111/j.1540-4781.2009.00970.x

Cheah, Y. H., Chai, C. S., & Toh, Y. (2019). Traversing the context of professional learning communities: Development and implementation of technological pedagogical content knowledge of a primary science teacher. *Research in Science & Technological Education*, *37*(2), 147–167. doi:10.1080/02635143.2018.1504765

Chen, B., & Denoyelles, A. (2013). Exploring students' mobile learning practices in higher education. *Educause Review Online*. Retrieved from http://er.educause.edu/articles/2013/10/exploring-students-practices-inhighereducationmobile-learning-

Chen, B. (2014). MOOCs: Contributions and dilemmas. *TEFLE*, *157*, 38–43.

Chen, C.-M., Liu, H., & Huang, H.-B. (2019). Effects of a mobile game-based English vocabulary learning app on learners' perceptions learning performance: A case study of Taiwanese EFL learners. *ReCALL*, *31*(2), 170–188. doi:10.1017/S0958344018000228

Cheng, K.-H. (2017). A survey of native language teachers' technological pedagogical and content knowledge (TPACK) in Taiwan. *Computer Assisted Language Learning*, *30*(7), 692–708. doi:10.1080/09588221.2017.1349805

Chen, J. (2015). MOOCs and foreign language teaching studies in the big data era: challenges and opportunities. *TEFLE*, *1*, 3–8.

Chen, J. C. (2016). The crossroads of English language learners, task-based instruction, and 3D multi-user virtual learning in Second Life. *Computers & Education*, *102*, 152–171. doi:10.1016/j.compedu.2016.08.004

Chen, J. C. C. (2018). The interplay of tasks, strategies and negotiations in Second Life. *Computer Assisted Language Learning*, *31*(8), 960–986. doi:10.1080/09588221.2018.1466810

Chen, J. C., & Brown, K. L. (2012). The effects of authentic audience on English as a second language (ESL) writers: A task-based computer-mediated approach. *Computer Assisted Language Learning*, *25*(5), 435–454. doi:10.1080/09588221.2011.606224

Chen, K. T. (2012). Blog-based peer reviewing in EFL writing classrooms for Chinese speakers. *Computers and Composition*, *29*(4), 280–291. doi:10.1016/j.compcom.2012.09.004

Chen, M. H. (2019). Computer-assisted synonymous phrase learning: A feasible approach to lexical development. [IJCALLT]. *International Journal of Computer-Assisted Language Learning and Teaching*, *9*(2), 1–18. doi:10.4018/IJCALLT.2019040101

Chen, M. H., Huang, S. T., Chang, J. S., & Liou, H. C. (2013). Developing a corpus-based paraphrase tool to improve EFL learners' writing skills. *Computer Assisted Language Learning*, *28*(1), 22–40. doi:10.1080/09588221.2013.783873

Chen, Y., & Zhang, Y. (2019). Culture and context impact on mobile tech application in organizational learning: Case study of UK higher education institution and Chinese state-owned enterprise. In A. Forkish Baruch, & H. Meishar Tal (Eds.), *Mobile technologies in educational organizations* (pp. 142–169). Hershey, PA: IGI Global. doi:10.4018/978-1-5225-8106-2.ch008

Ching, Y.-H., Yang, D., Baek, Y., & Baldwin, S. (2016). Enhancing graduate students' reflection in e-portfolios using the TPACK framework. *Australasian Journal of Educational Technology*, *32*(5), 108–122. doi:10.14742/ajet.2830

Chinnery, G. M. (2006). Emerging technologies: Going to the MALL (Mobile Assisted Language Learning). *Language Learning & Technology, 10*, 9–16.

Chinnery, G. M. (2006). Going to the MALL: Mobile assisted language learning. *Language Learning & Technology, 10*(1), 9–16. Retrieved from https://www.learntechlib.org/p/74432/

Choi, I. (2014). The comparability of direct and semi-direct oral proficiency interviews in a foreign language context: A case study with advanced Korean learners of English. *Language Research, 50*(2), 545-568. doi:10371/93290/1/12

Chorianopoulos, K., & Giannakos, M. N. (2013). Usability design for video lectures. In *Proceedings of the 11th European Conference on Interactive TV and Video* (pp. 163-164). New York, NY: ACM. 10.1145/2465958.2465982

Christ, T., Arya, P., & Liu, Y. (2019). Technology integration in literacy lessons: challenges and successes. *Literacy Research and Instruction, 58*(1), 49–66. doi:10.1080/19388071.2018.1554732

Chun, W. S. M. (2013). An exploration of gender differences in the use of social networking and knowledge management tools. *Journal of Information Technology Management, 24*(2), 20–31.

Chuo, T. W. I. (2007). The effects of the WebQuest writing instruction program on EFL learners' writing performance, writing apprehension, and perception. *TESL-EJ, 11*(3), 1–27.

Chwo, G. S.-M., Lin, Y.-S., Chen, P.-J., Lai, G.-W., Liu, H.-C., Ho, C.-C., & Wang, Y.-P. (2012) Engagement with Livemocha® as an informal learning resource - Initial findings from a technology university reading course in central Taiwan. *ICCE 2012. The 20th International Conference on Computers in Education. Proceedings.* 609-613.

Çiftçi, H., & Aslan, E. (2019). Computer-mediated communication in the L2 writing process: A review of studies between 2000 and 2017. [IJCALLT]. *International Journal of Computer-Assisted Language Learning and Teaching, 9*(2), 19–36. doi:10.4018/IJCALLT.2019040102

Çiftçi, H., & Kocoglu, Z. (2012). Effects of peer e-feedback on Turkish EFL students' writing performance. *Journal of Educational Computing Research, 46*(1), 61–84. doi:10.2190/EC.46.1.c

Clandinin, D. J., & Connelly, F. M. (1994). Personal experience methods. In *Handbook of qualitative research* (pp. 413–427). Thousand Oaks, CA: Sage.

Clandinin, D. J., & Connelly, F. M. (2004). *Narrative inquiry: Experience and story in qualitative research.* San Francisco, CA: Jossey Bass.

Clandinin, J. D. (2013). *Engaging in narrative inquiry.* New York: Routledge.

Clark, C., & Gruba, P. (2010). The use of social networking sites for foreign language learning: An autoethnographic study of Livemocha. In C.H. Steel, M.J. Keppell, P. Gerbic, & S. Housego (Eds.), Curriculum, technology, & transformation for an unknown future. Proceedings Ascilite, 164-173.

Clark, J. L. D. (1979). Direct versus semi-direct tests of speaking proficiency. In E. J. Briere & F. B. Hinofotis (Eds.), *Concepts in language testing: Some recent studies* (pp. 35–49). Washington, DC: TESOL.

Clark, J. L. D., & Swinton, S. S. (1980). The test of spoken English as a measure of communicative ability in English-medium instructional settings. *TOEFL Research Report, 7*, 1–68. doi:10.1002/j.2333-8504.1980.tb01230.x

Clément, R., Gardner, R. C., & Smythe, P. C. (1980). Social and individual factors in second language acquisition. *Canadian Journal of Behavioural Science, 12*(4), 293–302. doi:10.1037/h0081081

Coccoli, M., Iacono, S., & Vercelli, G. (2015). Applying gamification techniques to enhance the effectiveness of video-lessons. *Journal of E-Learning and Knowledge Society, 11*(3), 73–84.

ComScore. (2011). It's a social world: Social networking leads as top online activity globally, accounting for 1 in every 5 online minutes. Retrieved from https://www.comscore.com/Insights/Press-Releases/2011/12/Social-Networking-Leads-as-Top-Online-Activity-Globally

Connelly, F. M., & Clandinin, J. D. (1990). Stories of experience and narrative inquiry. *Educational Researcher, 19*(5), 2–14. doi:10.3102/0013189X019005002

Cooke-Plagwitz, J. (2008). New directions in CALL: An objective introduction to Second Life. *CALICO Journal, 25*(3), 547–557. doi:10.1558/cj.v25i3.547-557

Cook, V. (2013). *Second language learning and language teaching, 4th Ed.* New York: Routledge.

Coxhead, A. (2000). A new academic word list. *TESOL Quarterly, 34*(2), 213–238. doi:10.2307/3587951

Craik, F. I. M., & Lockhart, R. S. (1972). Levels of processing: A framework for memory research. *Journal of Verbal Learning and Verbal Behavior, 11*(6), 671–684. doi:10.1016/S0022-5371(72)80001-X

Creswell, J. W. (2014). Educational research: Pearson New International Edition: Planning, conducting, and evaluating quantitative and qualitative research (4th ed.). Harlow, UK: Pearson.

Creswell, J. W., & Plano Clark, V. L. (2011). *Designing and conducting mixed methods research* (2nd ed.). London, UK: Sage.

Crookes, G., & Schmidt, R. (1989). Motivation: Reopening the research agenda. *University of Hawai'i working papers in English as a second language, 8*(1), 217-256.

Cross, A., Bayyapunedi, M., Cutrell, E., Agarwal, A., & Thies, W. (2013). TypeRighting: combining the benefits of handwriting and typeface in online educational videos. In *Proceedings of the SIGCHI Conference on Human Factors in Computing Systems* (pp. 793-796). New York, NY: ACM. 10.1145/2470654.2470766

Crystal, D. (2009). *Just a phrase I'm going through.* London, UK: Routledge. doi:10.4324/9780203878491

Cuadrado-García, M., Ruiz-Molina, M. E., & Montoro-Pons, J. D. (2010). Are there gender differences in e-learning use and assessment? Evidence from an interuniversity online project in Europe. *Procedia: Social and Behavioral Sciences, 2*(2), 367–371. doi:10.1016/j.sbspro.2010.03.027

Cuban, L. (2001). *Oversold and underused: Computers in the classroom.* Cambridge, MA: Harvard University Press.

Curwood, J. S. (2014). Between continuity and change: Identities and narratives within teacher professional development. *Teaching Education, 25*(2), 156–183. doi:10.1080/10476210.2012.755159

Dahlstrom, E., de Boor, T., Grunwald, P., & Vockley, M. (2011). ECAR National study of students and information technology in higer education, 2011. *EDUCAUSE Center for Applied Research.* Retrieved from http://grunwald.com/pdfs/EDUCAUSE_Grunwald_College_Student_Tech_Study.pdf

Dalton, G., & Devitt, A. (2016). Irish in a 3D world: Engaging primary school children. *Language Learning & Technology, 20*(1), 21–33.

Daly, J. A. (1978). Writing apprehension and writing competency. *The Journal of Educational Research, 72*(1), 10–14. doi:10.1080/00220671.1978.10885110

Daly, J. A., & Wilson, D. A. (1983). Writing apprehension, self-esteem, and personality. *Research in the Teaching of English, 17*(4), 327–341.

Darasawang, P., & Reinders, H. (2010). Encouraging autonomy with an online language support system. *CALL-EJ Online, 11*(2). Retrieved from http://callej.org/journal/11-2/darasawang_reinders.html

Darmi, R., & Albion, P. (2014). A review of integrating mobile phones for language learning. In *Proceedings of the 10*th *International Conference Mobile learning IADIS'14.*

Dashtestani, R. (2015). Moving bravely towards mobile learning: Iranian students' use of mobile devices for learning English as a foreign language. *Computer Assisted Language Learning*. doi:10.1080/09588221.2015.1069360

Davis, F. D. (1989). Perceived usefulness, perceived ease of use, and user acceptance of information technology. *MIS Quarterly, 13*(3), 319–340. doi:, JSTOR 249008. doi:10.2307/249008

de Andrés Martínez, C. (2012). Developing metacognition at a distance: Sharing students' learning strategies on a reflective blog. *Computer Assisted Language Learning, 25*(2), 199–212. doi:10.1080/09588221.2011.636056

De Azevedo, C. G. (2013). Livemocha: uma rede social de aprendizagem de línguas. Unpublished Masters' Dissertation, Universidade do Minho, Instituto de Educaçao. Retrieved from https://repositorium.sdum.uminho.pt/bitstream/1822/30231/1/Cristiana%20Gracinda%20de%20Azevedo%20Gon%C3%A7alves%20Cerdeira%20Lopes.pdf

de Groot, A. M. B. (2006). Effects of stimulus characteristics and background music on foreign language vocabulary learning and forgetting. *Language Learning, 56*(3), 463–506. doi:10.1111/j.1467-9922.2006.00374.x

de Jong Derrington, M. (2013). Second language acquisition by immersive and collaborative task-based learning in a virtual world. In M. Childs, & A. Peachey (Eds.), *Understanding learning in virtual worlds* (pp. 135–163). London, UK: Springer. doi:10.1007/978-1-4471-5370-2_8

Deborah, J. L., & Bodrova, E. (2001). Lev Vygotsky: Playing to learn. *Scholastic Early Childhood Today, 15*(4), 48.

Deci, E. L., & Ryan, R. M. (1985). *Intrinsic motivation and self-determination in human behavior*. London, UK: Plenum Press. doi:10.1007/978-1-4899-2271-7

Deci, E. L., & Ryan, R. M. (1985). The general causality orientations scale: Self-determination in personality. *Journal of Research in Personality, 19*(2), 109–134. doi:10.1016/0092-6566(85)90023-6

Degennaro, T. (2019). Ten most popular social media sites in China (2019 updated). Retrieved from https://www.dragonsocial.net/blog/social-media-in-china/

DELNI. (1998). Lifelong learning: A new learning culture for all, Retrieved from http://www.delni.gov.uk/acfbb7f.pdf

Demirbilek, M. (2015). Social media and peer feedback: What do students really think about using wiki and Facebook as platforms for peer feedback? *Active Learning in Higher Education*, 1–14.

Deng, L., & Tavares, N. (2013). From moodle to Facebook: Exploring students' motivation and experiences in online communities. *Computer Educ, 68*, 167–176. doi:10.1016/j.compedu.2013.04.028

Deng, L., & Yuen, H. K. (2012). Understanding student perceptions and motivation towards academic blogs: An exploratory study. *Australasian Journal of Educational Technology, 28*(1), 48–66. doi:10.14742/ajet.883

Derbel, F. (2017). Technology-capable teachers transitioning to technology-challenged schools. *The Electronic Journal of E-Learning, 15*(3), 269–280.

Deutschmann, M., & Panichi, L. (2009). Talking into empty space? Signalling involvement in a virtual language classroom in Second Life. *Language Awareness, 18*(3-4), 310–328. doi:10.1080/09658410903197306

Deutschmann, M., & Panichi, L. (2013). Towards models for designing language learning in virtual worlds. *International Journal of Virtual and Personal Learning Environments*, *4*(2), 65–84. doi:10.4018/jvple.2013040104

Deutschmann, M., Steinvall, A., & Lagerström, A. (2011). Gender-bending in virtual space: Using voice-morphing in Second Life to raise sociolinguistic gender awareness. In S. Czepielewski (Ed.), *Learning a language in virtual worlds: A review of innovation and ICT in language teaching methodology* (pp. 54–61). Warsaw, Poland: Warsaw Academy of Computer Science, Management, and Administration.

Dewey, J. (1933). *How we think: A restatement of the relation pf reflective thinking to the educative process* (Revised ed.). Boston, MA: D.C. Heath.

Dewey, J. (1938). *Experience and education*. New York: Collier Books, Macmillan.

Dickinson, L. (1987). *Self-instruction in language learning*. Cambridge, UK: Cambridge University Press.

Dickinson, P. (2014). The effect of topic-selection control on EFL writing fluency. *Journal of Niigata University of International and Information Studies*, *17*, 15–25.

Diehl, W. C., & Prins, E. (2008). Unintended outcomes in Second Life: Intercultural literacy and cultural identity in a virtual world. *Language and Intercultural Communication*, *8*(2), 101–118. doi:10.1080/14708470802139619

Dillenbourg, P. (1999). Collaborative learning: Cognitive and computational approaches. Advances in learning and instruction series. Elsevier Science, Inc., Madison Square Station, New York.

Dimmock, C. (2016). Conceptualising the research–practice–professional development nexus: Mobilising schools as 'research-engaged' professional learning communities. *Professional Development in Education*, *42*(1), 36–53. doi:10.1080/19415257.2014.963884

Ding, Y., & Jiang, X. (2016). *Exploring hot topics of MOOC research in China and abroad: a co-word analysis*. Paper presented at the International Symposium on CALL, Qingdao, China.

Dingli, A., & Seychell, D. (2015). *The new digital natives*. Berlin, Germany: Springer. doi:10.1007/978-3-662-46590-5

Dippold, D. (2009). Peer feedback through blogs: Student and teacher perceptions in an advanced German class. *ReCALL*, *21*(1), 18–36. doi:10.1017/S095834400900010X

Dixon, E., & Thomas, M. (2015). *Researching language learner interactions online: from social media to MOOCs. CALICO*. Monograph Series.

Dominguez, A., Saenz-de-Navarrete, J., de Marcos, L., Fernandez-Sanz, L., Pages, C., & Martinez-Herraiz, J.-J. (2013). Gamifying learning experiences: Practical implications and outcomes. *Computers & Education*, *63*, 380–392. doi:10.1016/j.compedu.2012.12.020

Donaghue, H. (2003). An instrument to elicit teachers' beliefs and assumptions. *ELT Journal*, *57*(4), 344–351. doi:10.1093/elt/57.4.344

Dong, Y., Chai, C. S., Sang, G.-Y., Koh, J. H. L., & Tsai, C.-C. (2015). Exploring the profiles and interplays of pre-service and in-service teachers' technological pedagogical content knowledge (TPACK) in China. *Journal of Educational Technology & Society*, *18*(1), 158–169.

Donner, J. (2008). Research approaches to mobile use in the developing world: a review of the literature. *The Information Society*, *24*(3), 140–159. doi:10.1080/01972240802019970

Dooey, P. (2008). Language testing and technology: Problems of transition to a new era. *ReCALL*, *20*(1), 21–34. doi:10.1017/S0958344008000311

Dooly, M. (2018). "I do which the question": Students' innovative use of technology resources in the language classroom. *Language Learning & Technology*, *22*(1), 184–217.

Dörnyei, Z., & Ottó, I. (1998). Motivation in action: A process model of L2 motivation. *Working papers in applied linguistics (Thames Valley University, London), 4*, 43-69.

Dörnyei, Z. (1990). Conceptualizing motivation in foreign-language learning. *Language Learning*, *40*(1), 45–78. doi:10.1111/j.1467-1770.1990.tb00954.x

Dörnyei, Z. (2001a). *Motivational strategies in the language classroom.* Cambridge, UK: Cambridge University Press. doi:10.1017/CBO9780511667343

Dörnyei, Z. (2001b). *Teaching and researching motivation.* Harlow, UK: Longman.

Dörnyei, Z. (2009). The L2 motivational self system. In Z. Dörnyei, & E. Ushioda (Eds.), *Motivation, language identity and the L2 self* (pp. 9–42). Bristol: Multilingual Matters. doi:10.21832/9781847691293-003

Doucleff, M., & Aubrey, A. (2018). Smartphone detox: How to power down in a wired world. NPR Morning Edition. Retrieved from https://www.npr.org/sections/health-shots/2018/02/12/584389201/smartphone-detox-how-to-power-down-in-a-wired-world

Drent, M., & Meelissen, M. (2008). Which factors obstruct or stimulate teacher educators to use ICT innovatively? *Computers & Education*, *51*(1), 187–199. doi:10.1016/j.compedu.2007.05.001

Ducate, L. C. I, & Lomicka, L. L. (2008). Adventures in the blogosphere: From blog readers to blog writers. *Computer Assisted Language Learning*, *21*(1), 9–28. doi:10.1080/09588220701865474

Ducate, L. C., & Lomicka, L. L. (2005). Exploring the blogosphere: Use of weblogs in the foreign language classroom. *Foreign Language Annals*, *38*(3), 410–421. doi:10.1111/j.1944-9720.2005.tb02227.x

Ducate, L., Anderson, L., & Moreno, N. (2011). Wading through the world of wikis: An analysis of three wiki projects. *Foreign Language Annals*, *44*(3), 495–524. doi:10.1111/j.1944-9720.2011.01144.x

Dudeney, G., Hockly, N., & Pegrum, M. (2013). *Digital literacies: Research and Resources in language teaching.* London, UK: Routledge.

Du, F. (2013). Student perspectives of self-directed language learning: implications for teaching and research. International Journal for the Scholarship of Teaching and Learning, 7(2). *Article*, *24*, 1–16. doi:10.20429/ijsotl.2013.070224

Duffy, P. (2011). Facebook or faceblock. Cautionary tales exploring the rise of social networking within tertiary education. In M. Lee, & C. McLoughlin (Eds.), *Web 2.0-based e-learning: Applying social informatics for tertiary teaching* (pp. 284–300). Hershey, PA: IGI Global. doi:10.4018/978-1-60566-294-7.ch015

DuFour, R., & DuFour, R. (2010). The role of professional learning communities in advancing 21st century skills. In J. A. Bellanca (Ed.), 21st century skills: rethinking how students learn (pp. 77–95). Bloomington, IN: Solution Tree Press.

Duncan, I., Miller, A., & Jiang, S. (2012). A taxonomy of virtual worlds usage in education. *British Journal of Educational Technology*, *43*(6), 949–964. doi:10.1111/j.1467-8535.2011.01263.x

Dunlea, J., Spiby, R., Nguyen, Q., Nguyen, H., Nguyen, Y., Nguyen, T., . . . Bui, S. (2018). *Aptis-VSTEP comparability study: Investigating the usage of two EFL tests in the context of higher education in Vietnam* (VS/2018/001). Retrieved from https://www.britishcouncil.org/sites/default/files/aptis-vstep_study.pdf

Dutta, S., Geiger, T., & Lanvin, B. (2015). The global information technology report 2015. Retrieved from http://www3.weforum.org/docs/WEF_Global_IT_Report_2015.pdf

East, M. (2012). *Task-based language teaching from the teachers' perspective: Insights from New Zealand* (Vol. 3). Amsterdam, The Netherlands: John Benjamins Publishing. doi:10.1075/tblt.3

Easton, L. B. (2015). The 5 habits of effective PLCs. *Journal of Staff Development, 36*(6), 24.

Educause. (2012). 7 things you should know about microlectures. Retrieved from https://library.educause.edu/resources/2012/11/7-things-you-should-know-about-microlectures

Efkledis, A. (2006). Metacognition, affect, and conceptual difficulty. In J. H. F. Meyer, & R. Land (Eds.), *Overcoming barriers to student understanding: Threshold concepts and troublesome knowledge. London, UK.* (pp. 48–69). Falmer, UK: Routledge.

Egbert, J., & Shahrokni, S. A. (2018). CALL principles and practices. *OER.* Available at https://opentext.wsu.edu/call/chapter/principles-of-call/

Egbert, J., & Abobaker, R. (2018). Opportunities for engaging young English language learners through technology use. In N. Guler (Ed.), *Optimizing elementary education for English language learners* (pp. 158–176). Hershey, PA: IGI Global. doi:10.4018/978-1-5225-3123-4.ch009

Egbert, J., Hanson-Smith, E., & Chao, C. C. (2007). Introduction: Foundations for teaching and learning. In J. Egbert, & E. Hanson-Smith (Eds.), *CALL environments: Research, practice, and critical issues* (2nd ed., pp. 1–18). Alexandria, VA: TESOL.

Egbert, J., Paulus, T., & Nakamichi, Y. (2002, September). The impact of CALL instruction on language classroom computer use: A foundation for rethinking technology in teacher education. *Language Learning & Technology, 6*(3), 108–126.

Egbert, J., Shahrokni, S., Zhang, X., Yahia, I., Borysenko, N., Mohamed, A., ... AlJarih, F. (2018). Planning for future inquiry: Gaps in the CALL research. *International Journal of Computer-Assisted Language Learning and Teaching, 8*(2), 39–59. doi:10.4018/IJCALLT.2018040103

Ellis, R. (2015). The study of second language acquisition (2nd ed.). Oxford, UK: Oxford University Press.

Ellis, N. C. (2003). Constructions, chunking, and connectionism: The emergence of second language structure. In C. J. Doughty, & M. H. Long (Eds.), *The handbook of second language acquisition* (pp. 63–103). Malden, MA: Wiley-Blackwell. doi:10.1002/9780470756492.ch4

Ellis, R. (1997). *The study of second language acquisition.* New York: Oxford University Press.

Ellis, R. (2003). *Task-based language learning and teaching.* Oxford, UK: Oxford University Press.

Ellis, R. (2009). Task-based language teaching: Sorting out the misunderstandings. *International Journal of Applied Linguistics, 19*(3), 221–246. doi:10.1111/j.1473-4192.2009.00231.x

Ellis, R. (2009a). Corrective feedback and teacher development. *Journal of Linguistics and Language Teaching, 1*(1), 3–18.

Ellis, R. (2012). *Language teaching research & language pedagogy.* West Sussex, UK: Wiley-Blackwell. doi:10.1002/9781118271643

Elola, I., & Oskoz, A. (2008). Blogging: Fostering intercultural competence development in foreign language and study abroad contexts. *Foreign Language Annals, 41*(3), 454–477. doi:10.1111/j.1944-9720.2008.tb03307.x

Elola, I., & Oskoz, A. (2010). Collaborative writing: Fostering foreign language and writing conventions development. *Language Learning & Technology, 14*(3), 51–71.

Elola, I., & Oskoz, A. (2016). Supporting second language writing using multimodal feedback. *Foreign Language Annals*, *49*(1), 58–74. doi:10.1111/flan.12183

Engeström, Y. (2001). Expansive learning at work: toward an activity theoretical reconceptualization. *Journal of Education and Work*, *14*(1), 133–156. doi:10.1080/13639080020028747

English Profile. Retrieved from (http://www.englishprofile.org/wordlists)

Enochsson, A. B., & Rizza, C. (2009). ICT in initial teacher training: Research review (38). *OECD Education Working Paper*: OECD Publishing.

Erkan, D. Y., & Saban, A. I. (2011). Writing performance relative to writing apprehension, self-efficacy in writing, and attitudes towards writing: A correlational study in Turkish tertiary-level EFL. *The Asian EFL Journal Quarterly*, *13*(1), 163–191.

Ertmer, P., & Park, S. H. (n.d.). Changing teachers' beliefs toward classroom technology use: The potential of problem-based learning. Retrieved from http://www.edci.purdue.edu/ertmer/docs/earli09_ertmer_park.pdf

Ertmer, P. A., & Ottenbreit-Leftwich, A. T. (2010). Teacher technology change: how knowledge, confidence, beliefs, and culture intersect. *Journal of Research on Technology in Education*, *42*(3), 255–284. doi:10.1080/15391523.2010.10782551

Eshet-Alkalai, Y. (2004). Digital literacy: A conceptual framework for survival skills in the digital era. *Journal of Educational Multimedia and Hypermedia*, *13*(1), 93–106.

Evans, M. A., Nino, M., Deater-Deckard, K., & Chang, M. (2015). School-wide adoption of a mathematics learning game in a middle school setting: Using the TPACK framework to analyze effects on practice. *The Asia-Pacific Education Researcher*, *24*(3), 495–504. doi:10.100740299-014-0225-y

Faigley, L., Daly, J. A., & Witte, S. P. (1981). The role of writing apprehension in writing performance and competence. *The Journal of Educational Research*, *75*(1), 16–21. doi:10.1080/00220671.1981.10885348

Fairbairn, J., & Dunlea, J. (2017). *Speaking and writing rating scales revision technical report* (TR/2017/001). Retrieved from https://www.britishcouncil.org/exam/aptis/research/publications/scale-revision

Farr, F., & Murray, L. (2016). *The Routledge handbook of language learning and technology*. New York: Routledge. doi:10.4324/9781315657899

Felix, U. (1993). The contribution of background music to the enhancement of learning in Suggestopedia: A critical review of the literature. *Journal of the Society for Accelerative Learning and Teaching*, *18*, 277–303.

Feng, S., Wong, Y. K., Wong, L. Y., & Hossain, L. (2019). The Internet and Facebook usage on academic distraction of college students. *Computers & Education*, *134*, 41–49. doi:10.1016/j.compedu.2019.02.005

Ferguson, R., Coughlan, T., & Heredotou, C. (2016). *MOOCs: what the open university research tells us. The Open University*. Milton Keynes: Institute of Educational Technology.

Ferris, D. (2012). Written corrective feedback in second language acquisition and writing studies. *Language Teaching*, *45*(04), 446–459. doi:10.1017/S0261444812000250

Ferris, D., & Roberts, B. (2001). Error feedback in L2 writing classes: How explicit does it need to be? *Journal of Second Language Writing*, *10*(3), 161–184. doi:10.1016/S1060-3743(01)00039-X

Fidaoui, D., Bahous, R., & Bacha, N. (2010). CALL in Lebanese elementary ESL writing classrooms. *Computer Assisted Language Learning*, *23*(2), 151–168. doi:10.1080/09588221003666248

Fitzgerald, J. (1987). Research on revision in writing. *Review of Educational Research, 57*(4), 481–506. doi:10.3102/00346543057004481

Flavell, J. (1979). Metacognition and cognitive monitoring: A new era cognitive-developmental inquiry. *The American Psychologist, 34*(10), 906–911. doi:10.1037/0003-066X.34.10.906

Flores, J. F. F. (2015). Using gamification to enhance second language learning. *Digital Education Review, (27)*, 32-54.

Flower, L., & Hayes, J. R. (1981). A cognitive process theory of writing. *College Composition and Communication, 32*(4), 365–387. doi:10.2307/356600

Folse, K. S. (2006). The effect of type of written exercise on l2 vocabulary retention. *TESOL Quarterly, 40*(2), 273–293. doi:10.2307/40264523

Fontana, M. V. L., & Leffa, V. L. (2018). MOOCs for language teaching: A study on CALL from the connectivist perspective. *Alfa: Revista de Linguistica, 62*(1), 73–86.

Foorman, B. R., Petscher, Y., & Bishop, M. D. (2012). The incremental variance of morphological knowledge to reading comprehension in grades 3–10 beyond prior reading comprehension, spelling, and text reading efficiency. *Learning and Individual Differences, 22*(6), 792–798. doi:10.1016/j.lindif.2012.07.009

Foster, P., Tonkyn, A., & Wigglesworth, G. (2000). Measuring spoken language: A unit for all reasons. *Applied Linguistics, 21*(3), 354–375. doi:10.1093/applin/21.3.354

Fulcher, G. (2014). *Testing second language speaking*. Oxon, UK: Routledge. doi:10.4324/9781315837376

Furlong, N. E., Lovelace, K. L., & Lovelace, E. A. (2000). *Research methods and statistics: An integrated approach.* Belmont: Wadsworth/Thomson Learning.

Furnham, A., & Strbac, L. (2002). Music is as distracting as noises: The differential distraction of background music and noise on the cognitive test performance of introverts and extraverts. *Ergonomics, 45*(3), 203–217. doi:10.1080/00140130210121932 PMID:11964204

FutureLearn. (n.d.). Retrieved from https://www.futurelearn.com

Gabrielatos, C. (2001). L1 use in ELT: Not a skeleton but a bone of contention. A response to Prodromou. *TESOL Greece Newsletter, 70*, 6–9.

Gamage, V., Tretiakov, A., & Crump, B. (2011). Teacher perceptions of learning affordances of multi-user virtual environments. *Computers & Education, 57*(4), 2406–2413. doi:10.1016/j.compedu.2011.06.015

Gardner, R. C., & Lambert, W. E. (1972). Attitudes and motivation in second-language Learning. Rowley, MA: Newbury.

Gardner, D., & Davies, M. (2014). A new academic vocabulary List. *Applied Linguistics, 35*(3), 305–327. doi:10.1093/applin/amt015

Gardner, R. C. (1985). *Social psychology and second language learning: The role of attitudes and motivation.* London, UK: Arnold.

Gardner, R. C. (2007). Motivation and second language acquisition. *Porta Linguarum, 8*, 9–20.

Gardner, R. C. (2010). *Motivation and second language acquisition: The socio-educational model.* Oxford, UK: Peter Lang.

Gardner, R. C., & Lambert, W. E. (1959). Motivational variables in second-language acquisition. *Canadian Journal of Psychology/Revue. Canadian Psychology, 13*(4), 266–272. doi:10.1037/h0083787

Gardner, R. C., & Lambert, W. E. (1972). *Attitudes and motivation in second language learning*. Massachusetts: Newbury House.

Gardner, R. C., & Smythe, P. C. (1981). On the development of the attitude/motivation test battery. *Canadian Modern Language Review*, *37*(3), 510–525. doi:10.3138/cmlr.37.3.510

Gedera, D. (2012). The dynamics of blog peer feedback in ESL classroom. *Teaching English with Technology*, *12*(4), 16–30.

Gee, J. P. (2007). *Good video games and good learning*. New York: Peter Lang. doi:10.3726/978-1-4539-1162-4

Gee, J. P., & Hayes, E. (2012). Nurturing affinity spaces and game-based learning. In *Games, learning, and society: Learning and meaning in the digital age* (pp. 129–153). Cambridge University Press; doi:10.1017/CBO9781139031127.015

Gee, J. P., & Hayes, E. R. (2011). *Language and learning in the digital age*. New York, NY: Routledge. doi:10.4324/9780203830918

Gillmor, D. (2008). *Principles for a new media literacy*. Harvard, MA: Berkman Center for Internet & Society at Harvard University. Retrieved from https://cyber.law.harvard.edu/sites/cyber.law.harvard.edu/files/Principles%20for%20a%20New%20Media%20Literacy_MR.pdf

Gilster, P. (1997). *Digital Literacy*. New York: John Wiley & Sons.

Gimeno, A. (2019) Ana Gimeno MOOC and free online courses. Retrieved from https://www.mooc-list.com/instructor/ana-gimeno

Gimeno-Sanz, A. (2017). Designing a MOOC for learners of Spanish: exploring learner usage and satisfaction. In K. Borthwick, L. Bradley & S. Thouësny (Eds), CALL in a climate of change: adapting to turbulent global conditions – short papers from EUROCALL 2017 (pp. 122-127). Research-publishing.net. https://doi.org/. eurocall2017.700 doi:10.14705/rpnet.2017

Gitsaki, C., Ya'akub, A., & Honan, E. (2010). ICT integration in second language writing: a Malay language case study. In D. L. Pullen, & D. R. Cole (Eds.), Multiliteracies and technology enhanced education: social practices and the global classroom. Hershey, PA: IGI Global. doi:10.4018/978-1-60566-673-0.ch011

GlobalWebIndex. (2015). Quarterly report on the latest trends in social networking. Retrieved March 2018 from https://www.globalwebindex.net/hs-fs/hub/304927/file-2812772150 pdf/Reports/ GWI_Social_Summary_Report_Q1_2015.pdf

Godwin-Jones, R. (2003). Blogs and wikis: Environments for on-line collaboration. *Language Learning & Technology*, *7*(2), 12–16.

Godwin-Jones, R. (2018). Second language writing online: An update. *Language Learning & Technology*, *22*(1), 1–15.

Gomez, M. V. G. (2019). Developing soft skills in higher education foreign language programs. Initial insights into telecollaboration. In M. L. Carrio-Pastor (Ed.), *Teaching language and teaching literature in virtual environments* (pp. 151–161). Singapore: Springer Nature Singapore Pte Ltd. doi:10.1007/978-981-13-1358-5_8

González-Lloret, M., & Ortega, L. (2014). Towards technology-mediated TBLT: An introduction. In M. González-Lloret, & L. Ortega (Eds.), *Technology-mediated TBLT: Researching technology and tasks* (pp. 1–22). Amsterdam, The Netherlands: John Benjamins.

Goodhue, D. L., & Thompson, R. L. (1995). Task technology fit and educational purpose. *Management Information Systems Quarterly*, *19*(2), 213–231. doi:10.2307/249689

Goodwin, A., & Ahn, S. (2010). A meta-analysis of morphological interventions: Effects on literacy achievement of children with literacy difficulties. *Annals of Dyslexia*, *60*(2), 183–208. doi:10.100711881-010-0041-x PMID:20799003

Goodwin, A., Huggins, A., Carlo, M., August, D., & Calderon, M. (2013). Minding morphology: How morphological awareness relates to reading for English language learners. *Reading and Writing*, *26*(9), 1387–1415. doi:10.100711145-012-9412-5

Gorjian, B., Moosavinia, S. R., Kavari, K. E., Asgari, P., & Hydarei, A. (2011). The impact of asynchronous computer-assisted language learning approaches on English as a foreign language high and low achievers' vocabulary retention and recall. *Computer Assisted Language Learning*, *24*(5), 383–391. doi:10.1080/09588221.2011.552186

Graham, S., & Sandmel, K. (2011). The process writing approach: A meta-analysis. *The Journal of Educational Research*, *104*(6), 396–407. doi:10.1080/00220671.2010.488703

Gray, R. (2011, Jan. 2). Facebook generation suffer information withdrawal syndrome. *The telegraph*. Retrieved from http://www.telegraph.co.uk/technology/news/8235302/Facebook-generation-suffer-information-withdrawal-syndrome.html

Greene, R. L. (1989). Spacing effects in memory: evidence for a two-process account. *Experimental psychology: Learning, Memory, & Cognition*, *15*(3), 371–377. doi:10.1037/0278-7393.15.3.371

Greenfeld, K. (2014). Faking cultural literacy. *New York Times Online*. Retrieved from https://www.nytimes.com/2014/05/25/opinion/sunday/faking-cultural-literacy.html

Greenlaw, J. (2015). Deconstructing the metanarrative of the 21st century skills movement. *Educational Philosophy and Theory*, *47*(9), 894–903. doi:10.1080/00131857.2015.1035156

Grgurovic, M., Chapelle, A., & Shelley, C. (2013). A meta-analysis of effectiveness studies on computer technology-supported language learning. *ReCALL*, *25*(2), 165–198. doi:10.1017/S0958344013000013

Griffith, S., & Liyanage, L. (2008). An introduction to the potential of social networking sitesin education. *Proceedings of the Second Emerging Technologies Conference 2008. Australia: Wollongong.*

Grohol, J. (2008). SMS addiction and texting addiction. *Psych Central*. Retrieved from http://psychcentral.com/blog/archives/2008/03/01/sms-addiction-and-texting-addiction/

Grohol, J. (2018). Internet addiction and depression. *Psych Central*. Retrieved from https://psychcentral.com/blog/internet-addiction-and-depression/

Gruba, P., & Clark, C. (2013). Formative assessment within social network sites for language learning. In M.-N. Lamy & K. Zourou (Eds.), *Social networking for language education* (pp. 177–193). Basingstoke, UK: Palgrave MacMillan. doi:10.1057/9781137023384_10

Guba, E. G., & Lincoln, Y. S. (1994). Competing paradigms in qualitative research. Handbook of qualitative research, 2(163-194), 105.

Guglielmino, L. M. (1978). Development of the self-directed learning readiness scale. (Doctoral dissertation, University of Georgia, 1977). *Dissertation Abstracts International*, *38*, 6467A.

Gui, S. (2006). A holistic view of English vocabulary learning in China. *Foreign Language World* (1), 57-65.

Guichon, N., & Cohen, C. (2016). Multimodality and CALL. In F. Farr & L. Murray (Eds.), *The Routledge handbook of language learning and technology* (pp. 509–521). London, UK: Routledge.

Guilloteaux, M. J., & Dörnyei, Z. (2008). Motivating language learners: A classroom-oriented investigation of the effects of motivational strategies on student motivation. *TESOL Quarterly*, *42*(1), 55–77. doi:10.1002/j.1545-7249.2008.tb00207.x

Gunduz, M. (2016). Promoting interaction through blogging in language classrooms. [IJRES]. *International Journal of Research in Education and Science*, *2*(2), 438–443. doi:10.21890/ijres.82857

Güneş, E., & Bahçivan, E. (2018). A mixed research-based model for pre-service science teachers' digital literacy: Responses to "which beliefs" and "how and why they interact" questions. *Computers & Education, 118*, 96–106. doi:10.1016/j.compedu.2017.11.012

Guo, P. J., Kim, J., & Rubin, R. (2014). How video production affects student engagement: an empirical study of MOOC videos. In *Proceedings of the First ACM Conference on Learning @ Scale Conference* (pp. 41-50). New York, NY: ACM. 10.1145/2556325.2566239

Gürkan, S. (2018). The effects of a mobile assisted vocabulary learning application on vocabulary learning. *Turkish Online Journal of Qualitative Inquiry*, *9*(3), 288–311. doi:10.17569/tojqi.407512

Guskey, T. R. (2014). Planning professional learning. *Educational Leadership*, *71*(8), 10–16.

Güzel, S., & Aydin, S. (2019). The effect of Second Life as a virtual language learning environment on speaking anxiety: Second Life and anxiety. In M. Kruk (Ed.), *Assessing the effectiveness of virtual technologies in foreign and second language instruction* (pp. 115–146). Hershey, PA: IGI Global. doi:10.4018/978-1-5225-7286-2.ch005

Hafner, C. A., Chik, A., & Jones, R. H. (2015). Digital literacies and language learning. *Language Learning & Technology*, *19*(3), 1–7.

Halili, S. H., & Sulaiman, H. (2018). (article in press). Factors influencing the rural students' acceptance of using ICT for educational purposes. *Kasetsart Journal of Social Sciences*, 1–6.

Hallam, S., Price, J., & Katsarou, G. (2002). The effects of background music on primary school pupils' task performance'. *Educational Studies*, *28*(2), 112–122. doi:10.1080/03055690220124551

Halliday, M. A. K. (1989). *Spoken and written language* (2nd ed.). Oxford, UK: Oxford University Press.

Halliday, M. A. K. (2003). *On language and linguistics*. London, UK: Continuum.

Hamat, A., Embi, M. A., & Abu Hassan, H. (2012). The use of social networking sites among Malaysian university students. *International Education Studies*, *5*(3), 56–66. doi:10.5539/ies.v5n3p56

Hampel, R. (2006). Rethinking task design for the digital age: A framework for language teaching and learning in a synchronous online environment. *ReCALL*, *18*(1), 105–121. doi:10.1017/S0958344006000711

Hampel, R. (2010). Task design for a virtual learning environment in a distance language course. In M. Thomas, & H. Reinders (Eds.), *Task-based language learning and teaching with technology* (pp. 131–153). London, UK: Continuum.

Hamuddin, B., Syahdan, S., & Kurniawan, K. (2018). Cyberbullying on students' blog: Exploring bully in digital era. *ELT-Lectura*, *5*(2), 189–197. doi:10.31849/elt-lectura.v5i2.1700

Hanewald, R. (2013). Learners and collaborative learning in virtual worlds: A review of the literature. *Turkish Online Journal of Distance Education*, *14*(2), 233–247.

Hannibal Jensen, S. (2019). Language learning in the wild: A young user perspective. *Language Learning & Technology*, *23*(1), 72–86.

Harris, J., Grandgenett, N., & Hofer, M. (2010, March 29). *Testing a TPACK-based technology integration assessment rubric*. 3833–3840. Retrieved from https://www.learntechlib.org/primary/p/33978/

Harris, J. B., & Hofer, M. J. (2017). "TPACK stories": Schools and school districts repurposing a theoretical construct for technology-related professional development. *Journal of Research on Technology in Education*, *49*(1–2), 1–15. doi:10.1080/15391523.2017.1295408

Harris, J., Koehler, M., & Mishra, P. (2009). What is technological pedagogical content knowledge? *Contemporary Issues in Technology & Teacher Education*, 9.

Harrison, R. (2013). Profiles in social networking sites for language learning – Livemocha R revisited. In M.-N. Lamy, & K. Zourou (Eds.), *Social networking for language education: New language learning and teaching environments* (pp. 100-116). Basingstoke, UK: Palgrave Macmillan.

Harrison, R., & Thomas, M. (2009). Identity in online communities: Social networking sites and language learning. *International Journal of Emerging Technologies & Society.*, *7*(2), 109–124.

Hasler, B. S. (2011). Intercultural collaborative learning in virtual worlds. In R. Hindrichs, & C. Wankel (Eds.), *Transforming virtual world learning* (pp. 265–304). Bingley, UK: Emerald Group Publishing. doi:10.1108/S2044-9968(2011)0000004015

Hassan, R., Ahmad, J., & Boon, Y. (2018). Professional learning community in Malaysia. *International Journal of Engineering*, 12.

Hawi, N., & Samaha, M. (2016). To excel or not to excel: Strong evidence on the adverse effect of smartphone addiction on academic performance. *Computers & Education*, *98*, 81–89. doi:10.1016/j.compedu.2016.03.007

Hedayati, M., Reynolds, B., & Bown, A. (2018). The impact of computer-assisted language learning training on teachers' practices. *Journal of Language Teaching and Research*, *9*(6), 1127–1137. doi:10.17507/jltr.0906.02

Hegelheimer, V., & Lee, J. (2013). The role of technology in teaching and researching writing. In M. Thomas, H. Reinders, & M. Warschauer (Eds.), *Contemporary computer-assisted language learning* (pp. 287–302). London, UK: Bloomsbury.

Heil, C. R., Wu, J. S., Lee, J. J., & Schmidt, T. (2016). A review of mobile language learning applications: Trends, challenges and opportunities. *The EUROCALL Review*, *24*(2), 32–50. doi:10.4995/eurocall.2016.6402

Helmke, A., & Tuyet, V. T. A. (1999). Do Asian and western students learn in different way? An empirical study on motivation, study time, and learning strategies of German and Vietnamese university students. *Asia Pacific Journal of Education*, *19*(2), 30–44. doi:10.1080/0218879990190204

Henderson, M., Huang, H., Grant, S., & Henderson, L. (2009). Language acquisition in Second Life: Improving self-efficacy beliefs. In R. J. Atkinson, & C. McBeath (Eds.), Same places, different spaces: Proceedings ascilite Auckland 2009 (pp. 464-472). Auckland & Tugun: The University of Auckland, Auckland University of Technology, & Australasian Society for Computers in Learning in Tertiary Education (ascilite).

Herman, J. M. (2012). Creating balance in the new age of technology. *Montessori Life: A Publication of the American Montessori Society, 24*(3), 36–43.

Herro, D., Quigley, C., & Cian, H. (2019). The challenges of STEAM instruction: Lessons from the field. *Action in Teacher Education*, *41*(2), 172–190. doi:10.1080/01626620.2018.1551159

Hew, K. F., & Brush, T. (2007). Integrating technology into K-12 teaching and learning: current knowledge gaps and recommendations for future research. *Educational Technology Research and Development*, *55*(3), 223–252. doi:10.100711423-006-9022-5

Hill, H. C., Blazar, D., & Lynch, K. (2015). Resources for teaching: examining personal and institutional predictors of high-quality instruction. *AERA Open, 1*(4). Retrieved from https://eric.ed.gov/?q=hill%2c+blazar+%26+lynch+2015 &pr=on&id=EJ1194657

Hindley, D., Clughen, L., & Rawden, B. (2018). Implementing blog writing as a tool for promoting student engagement and literacy development. *RAISE: Student Engagement in Higher Education Journal*, 2(2), 133–140.

Hipp, K. K., & Huffman, J. B. (2003). *Professional learning communities: Assessment--Development--Effects*. Retrieved from https://eric.ed.gov/?id=ED482255

Hirvela, A., & Du, Q. (2013). "Why am I paraphrasing?": Undergraduate ESL writers' engagement with source- based academic writing and reading. *Journal of English for Academic Purposes*, *12*(2), 87–98. doi:10.1016/j.jeap.2012.11.005

Hismanoglu, M. (2012). Integrating second life into an EFL classroom: A new dimension in foreign language learning and teaching. *International Journal on New Trends in Education and Their Implications*, *3*(4), 100–111.

Ho, B. (2006). Using the process approach to teach writing in 6 Hong Kong primary classrooms. *New Horizons in Education*. Retrieved from ERIC Database (EJ847597) from http://eric.ed.gov/?id=EJ847597

Hofer, M., & Harris, J. (2012, March 5). *TPACK research with inservice teachers: Where's the TCK?* 4704–4709. Retrieved from https://www.learntechlib.org/primary/p/40352/

Hong, K. H. (2010). CALL teacher education as an impetus for L2 teachers in integrating technology. *ReCALL*, *22*(1), 53–69. doi:10.1017/S095834400999019X

Hood, N., Littlejohn, A., & Milligan, C. (2015). Context counts: How learners' contexts influence learning in a MOOC. *Computers & Education*, *91*, 83–91. doi:10.1016/j.compedu.2015.10.019

Hord, S. M. (1997). *Professional learning communities: communities of continuous inquiry and improvement*. Retrieved from https://eric.ed.gov/?id=ED410659

Hosseini, S. J. F., Niknami, M., & Chizari, M. (2009). To determine the challenges in the application of ICTs by the agricultural extension service in Iran. *Journal of Agricultural Extension and Rural Development*, *1*(1), 292e299.

Hourigan, T., & Murray, L. (2010). Using blogs to help language students to develop reflective learning strategies: Towards a pedagogical framework. *Australasian Journal of Educational Technology*, *26*(2), 209–225. doi:10.14742/ajet.1091

Hsieh, H. F., & Shannon, S. E. (2005). Three approaches to qualitative content analysis. *Qualitative Health Research*, *15*(9), 1277–1288. doi:10.1177/1049732305276687 PMID:16204405

Hsu, H.-C., & Lo, Y.-F. (2018). Using wiki-mediated collaboration to foster L2 writing performance. *Language Learning & Technology*, *22*(3), 103–123.

Hsu, L. (2013). English as a foreign language learners perception of mobile assisted language learning: A crossnational study. *Computer Assisted Language Learning*, *26*(3), 197–213. doi:10.1080/09588221.2011.649485

Hsu, L. (2015). EFL learners' implicit theory of intelligence and the application of MMORPG in EFL Learning. [IJCALLT]. *International Journal of Computer-Assisted Language Learning and Teaching*, *5*(2), 58–71. doi:10.4018/IJCALLT.2015040104

Huang, F., Teo, T., & Zhou, M. (2019). Factors affecting Chinese English as a foreign language teachers' technology acceptance: A qualitative study. *Journal of Educational Computing Research*, *57*(1), 83–105. doi:10.1177/0735633117746168

Huang, J. (2005). A diary study of difficulties and constraints in EFL learning. *System*, *33*(4), 609–621. doi:10.1016/j.system.2005.04.001

Huang, S. A. (2016). Enhancing feedback provision through multimodal video technology. *Computers & Education*, *98*, 90–101. doi:10.1016/j.compedu.2016.03.009

Hubbard, P. (2012, August). Curation for systemization of authentic content for autonomous learning. From *EUROCALL Conference*, Gothenburg, Sweden.

Hubbard, P. (2019). Five keys from the past to the future of CALL. [IJCALLT]. *International Journal of Computer-Assisted Language Learning and Teaching*, *9*(3), 1–13. doi:10.4018/IJCALLT.2019070101

Hubbard, P., & Levy, M. (2016). Theory in computer-assisted language learning research and practice. In F. Farr, & L. Murray (Eds.), *The Routledge handbook of language learning and technology* (pp. 24–38). London, UK: Routledge.

Hudson, H. (2014). *Do your students know more about technology than you do?* Retrieved from http://www.scholastic.com/teachers/article/do-your-students-know-more-about-technology-you-do

Hudson, J. (2018). Using wikis for collaborative writing in the ELT classroom. *International Journal of Pedagogy and teacher. Education*, *2*(2), 413–426.

Huizingh, E. (2007). *Applied statistics with SPSS.* London, UK: Sage. doi:10.4135/9781446249390

Hutchby, I., & Wooffitt, R. (2008). *Conversational analysis* (2nd ed.). Cambridge, UK: Polity Press.

Hyland, K., & Hyland, F. (2006). Feedback on second language students writing. *Language Teaching*, *39*(02), 83–101. doi:10.1017/S0261444806003399

Ibáñez, M. B., García, J. J., Galán, S., Maroto, D., Morillo, D., & Kloos, C. D. (2011). Design and implementation of a 3D multi-user virtual world for language learning. *Journal of Educational Technology & Society*, *14*(4), 2–10.

Ilioudi, C., Giannakos, M. N., & Chorianopoulos, K. (2013). Investigating differences among the commonly used video lecture styles. In *Proceedings of the 2013 Workshop on Analytics on Video-based Learning* (pp. 21–26). Retrieved from http://ceur-ws.org/Vol-983/

Inman, C., Wright, V. H., & Hartman, J. A. (2010). Use of Second Life in K-12 and higher education: A review of research. *Journal of Interactive Online Learning*, *9*(1), 44–63.

Instefjord, E., & Munthe, E. (2015). Preparing pre-service teachers to integrate technology: An analysis of the emphasis on digital competence in teacher education curricula. *European Journal of Teacher Education*, *39*, 1–17.

International Center for Media & the Public Agenda (ICMPA). (2014). *The world unplugged.* Retrieved from http://theworldunplugged.wordpress.com/about/international-center-for-media-the-public-agenda/

Ishikawa, S. (2018). Composition of three kinds of alternative essay-rating methods to the ESL composition profile. [IJCALLT]. *International Journal of Computer-Assisted Language Learning and Teaching*, *8*(4), 32–44. doi:10.4018/IJCALLT.2018100103

Ismail, S. A. A. (2011). Exploring students' perceptions of ESL writing. *English Language Teaching*, *4*(2), 73–84. doi:10.5539/elt.v4n2p73

Jang, S.-J., & Tsai, M.-F. (2012). Exploring the TPACK of Taiwanese elementary mathematics and science teachers with respect to use of interactive whiteboards. *Computers & Education*, *59*(2), 327–338. doi:10.1016/j.compedu.2012.02.003

Jaska, L. (2015). *Virtual worlds in pre-service teacher education: The introduction of virtual worlds in pre- service teacher education to foster innovative teaching-learning processes* (Doctoral dissertation). Retrieved from http://epubs.scu.edu.au/theses/428/

Jauregi, K., & Bañados, E. (2008). Virtual interaction through video-web communication: A step towards enriching and internationalizing language learning programs. *ReCALL*, *20*(2), 183–207. doi:10.1017/S0958344008000529

Jee, M., & Park, M. (2009). Livemocha as an online language-learning community. *CALICO Journal*, *26*(2), 448–456. doi:10.1558/cj.v26i2.448-456

Jiang, Y., & Hu, J. S. (2018). A study on the large-scale instruction mechanism of SPOC-based college English flipped classroom. *TEFLE, 4*, 9–15.

Johns, A. M., & Mayes, P. (1990). An analysis of summary protocols of university ESL students. *Applied Linguistics, 11*(3), 253–271. doi:10.1093/applin/11.3.253

Johnson, S. (2005). *Everything bad is good for you: How today's popular culture is actually making us smarter*. New York: Penguin Group.

Joiner, R., Gavin, J., Brosnan, M., Cromby, J., Gregory, H., Guiller, J., ... Moon, A. (2012). Gender, internet experience, internet identification and internet anxiety: A ten year follow-up. *Cyberpsychology, Behavior, and Social Networking, 15*(7), 370–372. doi:10.1089/cyber.2012.0033 PMID:22690795

Jones, J. (2001). CALL and the responsibilities of teachers and administrators. *ELT Journal, 55*(4), 360–367. doi:10.1093/elt/55.4.360

Jones, R. H., & Hafner, C. A. (2012). *Understanding digital literacies: a practical introduction*. London, UK: Routledge. doi:10.4324/9780203095317

Joo, Y. J., Park, S., & Lim, E. (2018). Factors influencing preservice teachers' intention to use technology: TPACK, teacher self-efficacy, and technology acceptance model. *Journal of Educational Technology & Society, 21*(3), 48–59.

Joseph-Israel, M. (2013). Effectiveness of integrating MOOCs in traditional classrooms for undergraduate students. *IRRODL. The International Review of Open and Distributed Learning, 16*(5). doi:10.19173/irrodl.v16i5.2222

Junco, R. (2012). In-class multitasking and academic performance. *Computers in Human Behavior, 28*(6), 2236–2243. doi:10.1016/j.chb.2012.06.031

Junco, R., & Cotton, S. (2012). No A 4 U: The relationship between multitasking and academic performance. *Computers & Education, 59*(2), 505–514. doi:10.1016/j.compedu.2011.12.023

Kang, S. J. (2014). The leadership on a safe and secure cyberspace. *Korea IT Times Global New Network* (pp. 26-27). Retrieved from http://www.koreaittimes.com/pdf/2014_04.pdf

Karasavvidis, I. (2010). Wiki uses in higher education: Exploring barriers to successful implementation. *Interactive Learning Environments, 18*(3), 219–231. doi:10.1080/10494820.2010.500514

Karpinski, A., Kirschner, P., Ozer, I., Mellott, J., & Ochwo, P. (2013). An exploration of social networking site use, multitasking, and academic performance among United States and European university students. *Computers in Human Behavior, 29*(3), 1182–1192. doi:10.1016/j.chb.2012.10.011

Kassem, M. A. M. (2017). Developing business writing skills and reducing writing anxiety of EFL learners through wikis. *English Language Teaching, 10*(3), 151–163. doi:10.5539/elt.v10n3p151

Kaufman, J. H., & Schunn, C. D. (2010). Students perceptions about peer assessment for writing: Their origin and impact on revision work. *Instructional Science, 39*(3), 387–406. doi:10.100711251-010-9133-6

Keck, C. (2006). The use of paraphrase in summary writing: A comparison of L1 and L2 writers. *Journal of Second Language Writing, 15*(4), 261–278. doi:10.1016/j.jslw.2006.09.006

Keck, C. (2014). Copying, paraphrasing, and academic writing development: A re-examination of L1 and L2 summarization practices. *Journal of Second Language Writing, 25*, 4–22. doi:10.1016/j.jslw.2014.05.005

Keengwe, J., & Kang, J.-J. (2011). A review of empirical research on blended learning in teacher education programs. *Education and Information Technologies, 18*(3), 479–493. doi:10.100710639-011-9182-8

Kennedy, A. (2005). Models of continuing professional development: A framework for analysis. *Journal of In-service Education, 31*(2), 235–250. doi:10.1080/13674580500200277

Kenny, N. (2017). Developing communicative competence through task based approach. In N. Stojković, M. Tošić, & V. Nejković (Eds.), *Synergies of English for specific purposes and language learning technologies* (pp. 78–88). Cambridge Scholars Publishing.

Kenyon, D. M., & Malabonga, V. (2001). Comparing examinee attitudes toward computer-assisted and other oral proficiency assessments. *Language Learning & Technology, 5*(2), 60.

Kerin, R. (2009). Digital portraits: teacher education and multiliteracies pedagogy. In V. Carrington, & M. Robinson (Eds.), *Digital literacies: social learning and classroom practice*. London, UK: Sage. doi:10.4135/9781446288238.n9

Kessler, S. (2011, May 31). 38% of college students can't go 10 minutes without tech (STATS). *Mashable Asia*. Retrieved from https://mashable.com/video/digital-art-tablet-review/

Kessler, G. (2009). Student-initiated attention to form in wiki-based collaborative writing. *Language Learning & Technology, 13*(1), 79–95.

Kessler, G. (2018). Technology and the future of language teaching. *Foreign Language Annals, 51*(1), 205–218. doi:10.1111/flan.12318

Kessler, G., & Bikowski, D. (2010). Developing collaborative autonomous learning abilities in computer mediated language learning: Attention to meaning among students in wiki space. *Computer Assisted Language Learning, 23*(1), 41–58. doi:10.1080/09588220903467335

Kessler, G., Bikowski, D., & Boggs, J. (2012). Collaborative writing among second language learners in academic web-based projects. *Language Learning & Technology, 16*(1), 91–109.

Kessler, G., & Hubbard, P. (2017). Language teacher education and technology. In C. Chapelle, & S. Sauro (Eds.), *Handbook of technology and second language teaching and learning* (pp. 278–292). New York: John Wiley & Sons. doi:10.1002/9781118914069.ch19

Kétyi, A. (2015). Practical evaluation of a mobile language learning tool in higher education. In F. Helm, L. Bradley, M. Guarda, & S. Thouësny (Eds), *Critical CALL – Proceedings of the 2015 EUROCALL Conference*, Padova, Italy (pp. 306-311). Dublin, Ireland: Research-publishing.net. 10.14705/rpnet.2015.000350

Khalil, M., Brunner, H., & Ebner, M. (2015). Evaluation grid for xMOOCs. *International Journal of Emerging Technologies in Learning, 10*(4), 40–45. doi:10.3991/ijet.v10i4.4653

Khoii, R., & Arabsarhangi, Z. (2019). Developing young EFL learners' writing skill in wikis' collaborative environment. In M. Rahimi, & S. Rajaee (Eds.), Handbook of research on individual differences in computer-assisted language learning (pp. 345–374). Hershey, PA: IGI Global. doi:10.4018/978-1-5225-7663-1.ch067

Kiddle, T., & Kormos, J. (2011). The effect of mode of response on a semi-direct test of oral proficiency. *Language Assessment Quarterly, 8*(4), 342–360. doi:10.1080/15434303.2011.613503

Kieffer, M. J., & Lesaux, N. K. (2012). Direct and indirect roles of morphological awareness in the English reading comprehension of native English, Spanish, Filipino, and Vietnamese speakers. *Language Learning, 62*(4), 1170–1204. doi:10.1111/j.1467-9922.2012.00722.x

Kiger, D. M. (1989). Effects of music information load on a reading comprehension task. *Perceptual and Motor Skills, 69*(2), 531–534. doi:10.2466/pms.1989.69.2.531 PMID:2717361

Killion, J. P., & Todnem, G. R. (1991). A process for personal theory building. *Educational Leadership, 48*(6), 14–16.

Kim, Y. N. (2014, April 1). The power of big data, the power of Korea: Who would dare to come forward to try estimating big data technology's growth potential? Korea IT Times Global New Network (pp. 18-19). Retrieved from http://www.koreaittimes.com/pdf/2014_04.pdf

Kim, A., Tak, H., & Lee, C. (2010). The development and validation of a learning flow scale for adults. *The Korean Journal of Educational Psychology, 24*, 39–59. Retrieved from http://www.newnonmun.com/article=193913

Kim, C. M., Kim, M. K., Lee, C. J., Spector, M., & DeMeester, K. (2013). Teacher beliefs and technology integration. *Teaching and Teacher Education, 29*, 76–85. doi:10.1016/j.tate.2012.08.005

Kim, H. J., Min, J. Y., Min, K. B., Lee, T. J., & Yoo, S. H. (2018). Relationship among family environment, self-control, friendship quality, and adolescents' smartphone addiction in South Korea: Findings from nationwide data. *PLoS One, 13*(2), 1–13. doi:10.1371/journal.pone.0190896 PMID:29401496

Kim, J., & Craig, D. A. (2012). Validation of a video-conferenced speaking test. *Computer Assisted Language Learning, 25*(3), 257–275. doi:10.1080/09588221.2011.649482

Kim, J., Guo, P. J., Seaton, D. T., Mitros, P., Gajos, K. Z., & Miller, R. C. (2014). Understanding in-video dropouts and interaction peaks in online lecture videos. In *Proceedings of the First ACM Conference on Learning @ Scale Conference* (pp. 31-40). New York, NY: ACM. 10.1145/2556325.2566237

Kim, P. (Ed.). (2015). *Massive open online courses: the MOOC revolution.* New York: Routledge.

Kim, S. G., Park, J., Kim, H. T., Pan, Z., Lee, Y., & McIntyre, R. (2019). The relationship between smartphone addiction and symptoms of depression, anxiety, and attention-deficit/hyperactivity in South Korean adolescents. *Annals of General Psychiatry, 18*(1), 1–8. doi:10.118612991-019-0224-8 PMID:30899316

Kirkup, G. (2010). Academic blogging: Academic practice and academic identity. *London Review of Education, 8*(1), 75–84. doi:10.1080/14748460903557803

Kirkup, G., & von Prümmer, C. (1997). Distance education for European women: The treats and opportunities of new educational forms and media. *European Journal of Women's Studies, 4*(1), 39–62. doi:10.1177/135050689700400104

Kirkwood, A., & Price, L. (2013). Technology-enhanced learning and teaching in higher education: What is 'enhanced' and how do we know? A critical literature review. *Learning, Media, and Technology, 39*(1), 6–36. doi:10.1080/17439884.2013.770404

Kirschner, P., & Karpinski, A. (2010). Facebook and academic performance. *Computers in Human Behavior, 26*(6), 1237–1245. doi:10.1016/j.chb.2010.03.024

Kirschner, P., Wubbels, T., & Brekelmans, M. (2008). *Benchmarks for teacher education programs in the pedagogical use of ict.international handbook of information technology in primary and secondary education.* US: Springer.

Kizilcec, R. F., Piech, C., & Schneider, E. (2013). Deconstructing disengagement: Analyzing learner subpopulations in massive open online courses. In *Proceedings of the Third International Conference on Learning Analytics and Knowledge* (pp. 170-179). New York, NY: ACM. 10.1145/2460296.2460330

Kleinginna, P. R. Jr, & Kleinginna, A. M. (1981). A categorized list of emotion definitions, with suggestions for a consensual definition. *Motivation and Emotion, 5*(4), 263–291. doi:10.1007/BF00993889

Klobus, J., Mackintosh, B., & Murphy, J. (2015). The anatomy of MOOCs. In P. Kim (Ed.), *Massive open online courses: the MOOC revolution.* New York: Routledge.

Klopfer, E., Osterweil, S., Groff, J., & Haas, J. (2009). The instructional power of digital games social networking simulations and how teachers can leverage them. *Using the technology of today, in the classroom today*. Cambridge, MA: The Education Arcade, MIT, Creative Commons. Retrieved from http://education.mit.edu/papers/GamesSims-SocNets_EdArcade.pdf

Koçoğlu, Z. (2009). Exploring the technological pedagogical content knowledge of pre-service teachers in language education. *Procedia: Social and Behavioral Sciences*, *1*(1), 2734–2737. doi:10.1016/j.sbspro.2009.01.485

Kocoglu, Z. (2009). Weblog use in EFL writing class. *Ankara University Journal of Faculty of Educational Sciences*, *42*(1), 311–327.

Koh, J. H. L., Chai, C. S., & Lee, M.-H. (2015). Technological pedagogical content knowledge (TPACK) for pedagogical improvement: editorial for special issue on TPACK. *The Asia-Pacific Education Researcher*, *24*(3), 459–462. doi:10.100740299-015-0241-6

Koh, J. H. L., Chai, C. S., & Lim, W. Y. (2017). Teacher professional development for TPACK-21CL: Effects on teacher ICT integration and student outcomes. *Journal of Educational Computing Research*, *55*(2), 172–196. doi:10.1177/0735633116656848

Kohsamut, T., & Sucaromana, U. (2017). Using blog to enhance English writing skill among high school students in Thailand. *PEOPLE: International Journal of Social Sciences*, *3*(2), 1337–1348.

Kondor, K. (2016, March 5). Le Louvre in second life [Blog post]. Retrieved from https://kareliakondor.wordpress.com/2016/03/

Kondor, K. [Karelia Kondor: Language learning in second life - An introduction]. (2013, Nov. 21). *Karelia Kondor: Language learning in second life - an introduction* [Video file]. Retrieved from https://www.youtube.com/watch?v=D9ks7jOdJ88&t=2s

Kost, C. R. (2011). Investigating writing strategies and revision behavior in collaborative wiki projects. *CALICO Journal*, *28*(3), 606–620. doi:10.11139/cj.28.3.606-620

Kovacs, G. (2016). Effects of in-video quizzes on MOOC lecture viewing. In *Proceedings of the Third ACM Conference on Learning* (pp. 31-40). New York, NY: ACM. 10.1145/2876034.2876041

Kozlova, I., & Priven, D. (2015). ESL teacher training in 3D virtual worlds. *Language Learning & Technology*, *19*(1), 83–101.

Krashen, S. (1982). *Principles and practice in second language acquisition*. Oxford, UK: Pergamon.

Kress, G. (2003). *Literacy in the new media age*. London, UK: Routledge.

Krumsvik, R. J. (2014). Teacher educators' digital competence. *Scandinavian Journal of Educational Research*, *58*(3), 269–280. doi:10.1080/00313831.2012.726273

Kukulska-Hulme, A. (2013). Mobile-assisted language learning. In C. Chapelle (Ed.), *The encyclopedia of applied linguistics* (pp. 3701–3709). New York: Wiley.

Kukulska-Hulme, A. (2016). Mobile assistance in language learning: A critical appraisal. In A. Palalas, & M. Ally (Eds.), *The international handbook of mobile-assisted language learning* (pp. 138–160). Beijing, China: China Central Radio & TV University Press.

Kukulska-Hulme, A., & Bull, S. (2009). Theory-based support for mobile language learning: Noticing and recording. *International Journal of Interactive Mobile Technologies*, *3*(2), 12–18.

Kukulska-Hulme, A., & Shield, L. (2008). An overview of mobile assisted language learning: From content delivery to supported collaboration and interaction. *ReCALL, 20*(3), 271–289. doi:10.1017/S0958344008000335

Kumar, S., & Vigil, K. (2010). Pre-service teachers' perspectives on web 2.0 integration in teacher education courses. In J. Sanchez, & K. Zhang (Eds.), *Proceedings of e-learn: world conference on e-learning in corporate, government, healthcare, and higher education, 1908-1913.*

Kurt, S. (2017). Wikis in education. How wikis are being used in the classroom. *Educational Technology, 2017*(March). Retrieved from https://educationaltechnology.net/educational-technology-articles/

Kuteeva, M. (2011). Wikis and academic writing: Changing the writer–reader relationship. *English for Specific Purposes, 30*(1), 44–57. doi:10.1016/j.esp.2010.04.007

La Velle, L., & Flores, M. A. (2018). Perspectives on evidence-based knowledge for teachers: Acquisition, mobilisation and utilisation. *Journal of Education for Teaching, 44*(5), 524–538. doi:10.1080/02607476.2018.1516345

Laborda, J. G. (2010). Contextual clues in semi-direct interviews for computer-assisted language testing. *Procedia - Social and Behavioral Sciences 2*. 3591-3595. doi:10.1016/j.sbspro.2010.03.557

Lacina, J., & Griffith, R. (2012). Blogging as a means of crafting writing. *The Reading Teacher, 66*(4), 316–320. doi:10.1002/TRTR.01128

Lai, K.-W., Khaddage, F., & Knezek, G. (2013). Student technology experiences in formal and informal learning in WCCE 2013: Learning while we are connected. *Proceedings of the IFIP Computers in Education 2013 World Conference,* 290-290. Torun, Poland: Nicolaus Copernicus University Press.

Lai, C., Wang, Q., Li, X., & Hu, X. (2016). The influence of individual espoused cultural values on self-directed use of technology for language learning beyond the classroom. *Computers in Human Behavior, 63*, 676–688. doi:10.1016/j.chb.2016.04.039

Lai, C., & Zheng, D. (2018). Self-directed use of mobile devices for language learning beyond the classroom. *ReCALL, 30*(3), 299–318. doi:10.1017/S0958344017000258

Lamb, M. (2004b). 'It depends on the students themselves': Independent language learning at an Indonesian state school.

Lamb, B. (2004). Wide open spaces wikis ready or not. *EDUCAUSE Review, 39*(5), 36–48.

Lamb, J. (2018). To boldly go: Feedback as digital, multimodal dialogue. *Multimodal Technologies and Interaction, 2*(3), 49–65. doi:10.3390/mti2030049

Lamb, M. (2004a). Integrative motivation in a globalizing world. *System, 32*(1), 3–19. doi:10.1016/j.system.2003.04.002

Lamb, M. (2007). The impact of school on EFL learning motivation: An Indonesian case study. *TESOL Quarterly, 41*(4), 757–780. doi:10.1002/j.1545-7249.2007.tb00102.x

Lam, R. (2013). The relationship between assessment types and text revision. *ELT Journal, 67*(4), 446–458. doi:10.1093/elt/cct034

Lam, S. F., & Law, Y. K. (2007). The roles of instructional practices and motivation in writing performance. *Journal of Experimental Education, 75*(2), 145–164. doi:10.3200/JEXE.75.2.145-164

Lamy, M.-N., & Mangenot, F. (2013). Social media-based language learning: Insights from research and practice. In M.-N. Lamy, & K. Zourou (Eds.), *Social networking for language education: New language learning and teaching environments* (pp. 197–213). Basingstoke, UK: Palgrave MacMillan. doi:10.1057/9781137023384_11

Lamy, M.-N., & Zourou, K. (Eds.). *Social networking for language education: New language learning and teaching environments*. Basingstoke, UK: Palgrave MacMillan. doi:10.1057/9781137023384

Lantolf, J. P. (2011). The sociocultural approach to second language acquisition: Sociocultural theory, second language acquisition, and artificial L2 development. In D. Atkinson (Ed.), *Alternative approaches to second language acquisition* (pp. 24–47). New York, NY: Taylor & Francis.

Lantolf, J. P., & Thorne, S. L. (2013). *Sociocultural theory and the genesis of second language development*. Shanghai, China: Shanghai Foreign Language Education Press.

Lantolf, J., Thorne, S. L., & Poehner, M. (2015). Sociocultural theory and second language development. In B. van Patten, & J. Williams (Eds.), *Theories in second language acquisition* (pp. 207–226). New York: Routledge.

Lan, Y. J. (2019). Contextual EFL learning in a 3D virtual environment. *Language Learning & Technology*, *19*(2), 16–31.

Lan, Y. J., Hsiao, I. Y., & Shih, M. F. (2018). Effective learning design of game-based 3d virtual language learning environments for special education students. *Journal of Educational Technology & Society*, *21*(3), 213–227.

Laskaris, J. (2015). 6 Benefits of informal learning. *Talentslms.com*. Retrieved from https://www.talentlms.com/blog/6-benefits-of-informal-learning/

Lauder, A. (2010). The status and function of English in Indonesia: A review of key factors. *MAKARA of Social Sciences and Humanities Series, 12*(1).

Laufer, B. (2005). Ten best ideas for teaching vocabulary. *The Language Teacher. Special Issue: Vocabulary*, *29*(7), 3–4.

Laufer, B., & Ravenhorst-Kalovski, G. C. (2010). Lexical threshold revisited: Lexical text coverage, learner's vocabulary size and reading comprehension. *Reading in a Foreign Language*, *22*(1), 15–30.

Laurillard (2002). Rethinking University Teaching: A Framework for the Effective. Use of Learning Technologies, 2nd ed. London: Routledge Falmer.

Lave, J., & Wenger, E. (1990). *Situated learning: Legitimate peripheral participation*. Cambridge, UK: Cambridge University Press.

Lawrence, G. (2014). The role of teachers and their beliefs in implementing technology-mediated language learning: Implications for teacher development and research. *IJCALLT, 4*(4), 59-75.

Lawrence, G. (2013). A working model for intercultural learning and engagement in collaborative online language learning environments. *Intercultural Education*, *24*(4), 303–314. doi:10.1080/14675986.2013.809247

Lawrence, G., & Ahmed, F. (2018). Pedagogical insights into hyper-immersive virtual world language learning environments. *International Journal of Computer-Assisted Language Learning and Teaching*, *8*(1), 1–14. doi:10.4018/IJCALLT.2018010101

Lazaraton, A. (1996). Interlocutor support in oral proficiency interviews: The case of CASE. *Language Testing*, *13*(2), 151–172. doi:10.1177/026553229601300202

Lazaraton, A. (2002). *A qualitative approach to the validation of oral language tests. Studies in Language Testing, 14*. Cambridge, UK: Cambridge University Press.

Le Ha, P. (2014). The politics of naming: Critiquing "learner-centred" and "teacher as facilitator" in English language and humanities classrooms. *Asia-Pacific Journal of Teacher Education*, *42*(4), 392–405. doi:10.1080/1359866X.2014.956048

Leakey, J. (2011). *Evaluating computer assisted language learning: an integrated approach to effectiveness research in CALL.* Bern, Switzerland: Peter Lang. doi:10.3726/978-3-0353-0131-1

Lech, I. B., & Harris, L. N. (2019). Language learning in the virtual wild. In M. L. Carrio-Pastor (Ed.), Teaching language and teaching literature in virtual environments (pp. 39 -53). Springer, Singapore: Springer Nature Singapore Pte Ltd. doi:10.1007/978-981-13-1358-5_3

Lee, Y., & Rofe, J. S. (2016). Pedagogy and flipped assessment: experience of designing and running a MOOC on research methods. *Open Learning: The Journal of Open, Distance and e-Learning, 31*(2), 116-129, doi:10.1080/02680513.2016.1188690

Lee, C. Y., & Warren, M. (2007). Security issues within virtual worlds such as second life. *Proceedings of 5th Australian Information Security Management Conference* (pp. 151-161). Perth, Australia: Edith Cowan University.

Lee, C.-J., & Kim, C. (2014). An implementation study of a TPACK-based instructional design model in a technology integration course. *Educational Technology Research and Development, 62*(4), 437–460. doi:10.100711423-014-9335-8

Lee, D. H. (2013). Smartphones, mobile social space, and new sociality in Korea. *Mobile Media & Communication, 1*(3), 269–284. doi:10.1177/2050157913486790

Lee, J. S. (2006). Exploring the relationship between electronic literacy and heritage language maintenance. *Language Learning & Technology, 10*(2), 93–113.

Lee, J. W., Sung, M. J., Song, S. H., Lee, Y. M., Lee, J. J., Cho, S. M., ... Shin, Y. M. (2018). Psychological factors associated with smartphone addiction in South Korean adolescents. *The Journal of Early Adolescence, 38*(3), 288–302. doi:10.1177/0272431616670751

Lee, K. W., & James, C. C. (2018). Exploring a transformative teacher professional development model to engender technology integration in the 21st century ESL language classrooms. [IJCALLT]. *International Journal of Computer-Assisted Language Learning and Teaching, 8*(4), 13–31. doi:10.4018/IJCALLT.2018100102

Lee, K. W., Ng, S. I., & Tan, C. K. (2014). Developing Malaysian ESL teachers technological pedagogical content knowledge with digital materials. In S. In (Ed.), *Computer-Assisted Language Learning: Learners, Teachers & Tools* (pp. 97–121). Newcastle upon Tyne, UK: Cambridge Publishing Press.

Lee, L. (2008). Focus on form through collaborative scaffolding in expert-to-novice online interaction. *Language Learning & Technology, 12*(3), 53–72.

Lee, L. (2008). Focus-on-form through collaborative scaffolding in expert-to-novice online interaction. *Language Learning & Technology, 12*(3), 53–72.

Lee, L. (2010). Exploring wiki-mediated collaborative writing: A case study in an elementary Spanish course. *CALICO Journal, 27*(2), 260–276. doi:10.11139/cj.27.2.260-276

Lee, L. (2010). Fostering reflective writing and interactive exchange through blogging in an advanced language course. *ReCALL, 22*(2), 212–227. doi:10.1017/S095834401000008X

Lee, L. (2011a). Blogging: Promoting learner autonomy and intercultural competence through study abroad. *Language Learning & Technology, 15*(3), 87–109.

Lee, L. (2011b). Focus on form through peer feedback in a Spanish-American telecollaborative exchange. *Language Awareness, 20*(4), 343–357. doi:10.1080/09658416.2011.592589

Lee, L. (2012a). Engaging study abroad students in intercultural learning through blogging and ethnographic interviews. *Foreign Language Annals*, *45*(1), 7–21.

Lee, L. (2012b). Linguistic feedback and focus on form through expert scaffolding in L2 blog writing. In G. Kessler, A. Oskoz, & I. Elola (Eds.), *Technology use across writing contexts* (pp. 57–80). CALICO Book Series.

Lee, L. (2016). Autonomous learning through task-based instruction in fully online language courses. *Language Learning & Technology*, *20*(2), 81–97.

Lee, L. (2017). Extending the intercultural learning after study abroad through a telecollaborative exchange. In J. Jackson, & S. Oguro (Eds.), *Intercultural Interventions in Study Abroad* (pp. 137–154). London, UK: Routledge Publishing. doi:10.4324/9781315276595-9

Lee, L. (2017). Learners' perceptions of the effectiveness of blogging for L2 writing in fully online language courses. [IJCALLT]. *International Journal of Computer-Assisted Language Learning and Teaching*, *7*(1), 19–33. doi:10.4018/IJCALLT.2017010102

Lee, L., & Markey, A. (2014). A study of learners' perceptions of online intercultural exchange through Web 2.0 technologies. *ReCALL*, *26*(3), 1–20. doi:10.1017/S0958344014000111

Lee, S. H. (2006). *Korean higher education: Its emergence, development & future challenges*. Seoul, South Korea: Hakjisa Publisher.

Lee, S. Y., Kim, M. S., Mendoza, J., & McDonough, I. (2018). Addicted to cellphones: Exploring the psychometric properties between the nomophobia questionnaire and obsessiveness in college students. *Heliyon (London)*, *4*(11), 1–21. doi:10.1016/j.heliyon.2018.e00895 PMID:30426100

Lee, S. Y., Kim, M. W., McDonough, I., Mendoza, J., & Kim, M. S. (2017). The effects of mobile phone use and emotion-regulation style on college students' learning. *Applied Cognitive Psychology*, *31*(3), 360–366. doi:10.1002/acp.3323

Lee, Y. K., Chang, C. T., Lin, Y., & Cheng, Z. H. (2014). The dark side of smartphone usage: Psychological traits, compulsive behavior, and technostress. *Computers in Human Behavior*, *31*, 373–383. doi:10.1016/j.chb.2013.10.047

Lee, Y.-J. (2007). The multimedia assisted test of English speaking: The SOPI Approach. *Language Assessment Quarterly*, *4*(4), 352–366. doi:10.1080/15434300701533661

Lenhart, A., Madden, M., & Hitlin, P. (2010). Social media and mobile internet use among teens and young adults. *Washington, D.C.: Pew Internet & American Life Project*. Retrieved from https://files.eric.ed.gov/fulltext/ED525056.pdf

Lenhart, A., Purcell, K., Smith, A., & Zickuhr, K. (2010). Social media & mobile Internet use among teens and young adults. *Pew Internet & American Life Project*. Retrieved from https://files.eric.ed.gov/fulltext/ED525056.pdf

Leong, D. J., & Bodrova, E. (2007). Vygotsky's zone of proximal development. *NAECS/SDE: Of Primary Interest*, 2(4).

Lepp, A., Barkley, J., & Karpinski, A. (2015). The relationship between cell phone use and academic performance in a sample of U.S. college students. *SAGE Open*, 1–9.

Levasseur, D. G., & Sawyer, J. K. (2006). Pedagogy meets PowerPoint: A research review of the effects of computer-generated slides in the classroom. *Review of Communication*, *6*(1-2), 101–123. doi:10.1080/15358590600763383

Levin, B. (2013). To know is not enough: Research knowledge and its use. *Review of Education*, *1*(1), 2–31. doi:10.1002/rev3.3001

Levy, M., & Kennedy, C. (2004). A task-cycling pedagogy using stimulated reflection and audio-conferencing in foreign language learning. *Language Learning & Technology*, *8*(2), 50–69.

Lewis, H. (1997). The mission of Harvard College. *Harvard University*. Retrieved from http://www.harvard.edu/faqs/mission-statement

Liaw, M.-L. (2011). Review of Livemocha. *Language Learning & Technology*, *15*(1), 36–40.

Li, H., & Zhao, D. M. (2015). Teacher talk and its effects in the micro-course of College English. *Technology Enhanced Foreign Language Education*, *165*, 15–20.

Li, M. (2012). Use of wikis in second/foreign language classes: A literature review. *CALL-EJ*, *13*(1), 17–35.

Li, M., & Zhu, W. (2011). Patterns of computer-mediated interaction in small writing groups using wikis. *Computer Assisted Language Learning*, *26*, 1–22.

Limberg, L., Sundin, O., & Talja, S. (2012). Three theoretical perspectives on information literacy. *Hum. IT: J. Inf. Technol. Stud. Hum. Sci.*, *11*(2).

Lin, C.-H., Warschauer, M., & Blake, R. (2016). Language learning through social networks: Perceptions and reality. *Language Learning & Technology*, *20*(1), 124–147.

Lin, L., Cranton, P., & Bridglall, B. (2010). Psychological type and asynchronous written dialogue in adult learning. *Teachers College Record*, *107*(8), 1788–1813. doi:10.1111/j.1467-9620.2005.00542.x

Lin, M. H. (2014). Effects of classroom blogging on ESL student writers: An empirical reassessment. *The Asia-Pacific Education Researcher*, *23*(3), 577–590. doi:10.100740299-013-0131-8

Lin, M. H. (2015). Learner-centered blogging: A preliminary investigation of EFL student writers' experience. *Journal of Educational Technology & Society*, *18*(4), 446–458.

Lin, M. H., Li, J. J., Hung, P. Y., & Huang, H. W. (2014). Blogging a journal: Changing students' writing skills and perceptions. *ELT Journal*, *68*(4), 422–431. doi:10.1093/elt/ccu032

Lin, T. J., & Lan, Y. J. (2015). Language learning in virtual reality environments: Past, present, and future. *Journal of Educational Technology & Society*, *18*(4), 486–497.

Lin, W., & Yang, S. C. (2011). Exploring students' perceptions of integrating Wiki technology and peer feedback into writing courses. *English Teaching*, *10*(2), 88–103.

Liou, H. C. (2011). The roles of Second Life in a college computer-assisted language learning (CALL) course in Taiwan, ROC. *Computer Assisted Language Learning, iFirst article*, 1-18.

Liou, H. C., & Lee, S. L. (2011). How wiki-based writing influences college students' collaborative and individual composing products, processes, and learners' perceptions. *International Journal of Computer-Assisted Language Learning and Teaching*, *1*(1), 45–61. doi:10.4018/ijcallt.2011010104

List, D. (2002). *Know your audience: A practical guide to media research.* Retrieved from http://www.audiencedialogue.net/kya.html

List, A. (2019). Defining digital literacy development: An examination of pre- service teachers' beliefs. *Computers & Education*, *138*, 146–158. doi:10.1016/j.compedu.2019.03.009

Littlewood, W. (2007). Communicative and task-based language teaching in East Asian classrooms. *Language Teaching*, *40*(03), 243–249. doi:10.1017/S0261444807004363

Littlewood, W. (2014). Communication-oriented language teaching: Where are we now? where do we go from here? *Language Teaching*, *47*(3), 349–362. doi:10.1017/S0261444812000134

Liu, C. Y., & Yu, C. P. (2013). Can Facebook use induce well-being? *Cyberpsychology, Behavior, and Social Networking, 16*(9), 674–678. doi:10.1089/cyber.2012.0301 PMID:24028138

Liu, F., Ritzhaupt, A. D., Dawson, K., & Barron, A. E. (2017). Explaining technology integration in K-12 classrooms: a multilevel path analysis model. *Educational Technology Research and Development, 65*(4), 795–813. doi:10.100711423-016-9487-9

Liu, M. H. (2016). Blending a class video blog to optimize student learning outcomes in higher education. *The Internet and Higher Education, 30*, 44–53. doi:10.1016/j.iheduc.2016.03.001

Liu, M. H., & Kleinsasser, R. C. (2015). Exploring EFL teachers' CALL knowledge and competencies: In-service program perspectives. *Language Learning & Technology, 19*(1), 119–138.

Liu, Q., & Chao, C.-C. (2017). CALL from an ecological perspective: How a teacher perceives affordance and fosters learner agency in a technology-mediated language classroom. *ReCALL, 30*(1), 68–87. doi:10.1017/S0958344017000222

Liu, T. Y. (2009). A context-aware ubiquitous learning environment for language listening and speaking. *Journal of Computer Assisted Learning, 25*(6), 515–527. doi:10.1111/j.1365-2729.2009.00329.x

Livingstone, D. W. (1999). Exploring the icebergs of adult learning: Findings of the first Canadian survey of informal learning practices. *Nall Working Paper No:10.* Centre for the Study of Education and Work, OISE/UT, Toronto. Retrieved from https://tspace.library.utoronto.ca/bitstream/1807/2724/2/10

Li, X., Chu, S. K. W., & Ki, W. W. (2014). The effects of a wiki-based collaborative process writing pedagogy on writing ability and attitudes among upper primary school students in mainland China. *Computers & Education, 77*, 151–169. doi:10.1016/j.compedu.2014.04.019

Li, X., Chu, S. K. W., Ki, W. W., & Woo, M. (2012). Using a wiki-based collaborative process writing pedagogy to facilitate collaborative writing among Chinese primary school students. *Australasian Journal of Educational Technology, 28*(1), 159–181. doi:10.14742/ajet.889

Li, Y., Zhang, M., Bonk, C. J., & Guo, N. (2015). Integrating MOOC and flipped classroom practice in a traditional undergraduate course: students' experience and perceptions. [iJET]. *International Journal of Emerging Technologies in Learning, 10*(6), 4–10. doi:10.3991/ijet.v10i6.4708

Lloyd, E. (2012). Language learners' 'willingness to communicate' through Livemocha.com. *ALSIC, Apprentissage des langues et systèmes d'information et de Communication.* 15(1): *Médias sociaux et apprentissage des langues: (R) évolution?* Retrieved from http://alsic.revues.org/2415

Loh, Y. L. (2013). Errors in paraphrasing and strategies in overcoming them. *Journal of Creative Practices in Language Learning and Teaching, 1*(1), 4–17.

Lo, J., & Hyland, F. (2007). Enhancing students' engagement and motivation in writing: The case of primary students in Hong Kong. *Journal of Second Language Writing, 16*(4), 219–237. doi:10.1016/j.jslw.2007.06.002

Loke, S. K. (2015). How do virtual world experiences bring about learning? A critical review of theories. *Australasian Journal of Educational Technology, 31*(1), 112–122. doi:10.14742/ajet.2532

Lo, M., & Clarke, M. (2010). Practicing or preaching? Teacher educators and student teachers appropriating new literacies. In D. L. Pullen, & D. R. Cole (Eds.), *Multiliteracies and technology enhanced education: social practice and the global classroom.* New York: Information Science Reference. doi:10.4018/978-1-60566-673-0.ch010

Longhurst, M. L., Jones, S. H., & Campbell, T. (2017). Factors influencing teacher appropriation of professional learning focused on the use of technology in science classrooms. *Teacher Development*, *21*(3), 365–387. doi:10.1080/13664530.2016.1273848

Loranc-Paszylk, B. (2015). Videoconferencing as a tool for developing speaking skills. In M. Pawlak, & E. Waniek-Klimczak (Eds.), *Issues in teaching, learning, and testing speaking in a second language* (pp. 189–203). London, UK: Springer. doi:10.1007/978-3-642-38339-7_12

Lowry, C. M. (1989). Supporting and facilitating self-directed learning. (ERIC Digest No. 93). Retrieved from ERIC database. (ED312457)

Lu, M. (2008). Effectiveness of vocabulary learning via mobile phone. *Journal of Computer Assisted Learning*, *24*(6), 515–525. doi:10.1111/j.1365-2729.2008.00289.x

Lund, A. (2008). Wikis: A collective approach to language production. *ReCALL*, *20*(01), 35–54. doi:10.1017/S0958344008000414

Lundin, R. W. (2008). Teaching with Wikis: Toward a networked pedagogy. *Computers and Composition*, *24*(5), 432–448. doi:10.1016/j.compcom.2008.06.001

Luoma, S. (1997). *Comparability of a tape-mediated and face-to-face test of speaking: A triangulation study* (Licentiate thesis). Retrieved from http://urn.fi/URN:NBN:fi:jyu-1997698892

Luo, R. (2017). A study of autonomous foreign language learning in the Internet environment- An investigation on MOOCs in the USA and China. *Foreign Language World*, *6*, 29–36.

Luo, S. (2018). Evaluating the learning environment of MOOC-based college English flipped classrooms. *TEFLE*, *4*, 16–22.

Mabuan, R. A. (2018). Using blogs in teaching tertiary ESL writing. *English Review: Journal of English Education*, *6*(2), 1–10.

MacIntyre, D. P. (1995). How does anxiety affect second language learning? A reply to Sparks and Ganschow. *Modern Language Journal*, *79*(1), 90–99. doi:10.1111/j.1540-4781.1995.tb05418.x

MacIntyre, P. D., & Blackie, R. A. (2012). Action control, motivated strategies, and integrative motivation as predictors of language learning affect and the intention to continue learning French. *System*, *40*(4), 533–543. doi:10.1016/j.system.2012.10.014

Mackay, A., & Gass, S. M. (2000). *Stimulated recall methodology in second language Research*. Mahwah, NJ: Lawrence Erlbaum Associates.

Mackey, A. (2006). Feedback, Noticing, and Instructed Second Language Learning. *Applied Linguistics*, *27*(3), 405–530. doi:10.1093/applin/ami051

Mackey, A., & Gass, S. (2005). *Second language research: Methodology and design*. Mahwah, NJ: Erlbaum.

Mackey, A., & Gass, S. M. (2005). *Second language research: methods and design*. London, UK: Routledge.

Maclean, R., & Pavlova, M. (2013). Vocationalization of secondary and higher education: Pathways to the world of work. In UNESCO-UNEVOC, *Revisiting global trend in TVET* (pp. 42-85). Retrieved from http://www.unevoc.unesco.org/fileadmin/up/2013_epub_revisiting_global_trends_in_tvet_chapter2.pdf

Mahathir, M. (1991). Malaysia: the way forward (Vision 2020). Malaysian Business Council.

Majlesi, A. R. (2018). Instructed vision: Navigating grammatical rules by using landmarks for linguistic structures in corrective feedback sequences. *Modern Language Journal*, *102*, 11–29. doi:10.1111/modl.12452

Mak, B., & Coniam, D. (2008). Using wikis to enhance and develop writing skills among secondary school students in Hong Kong. *System*, *36*(3), 437–455. doi:10.1016/j.system.2008.02.004

Mak, B., & Pun, S.-H. (2015). Cultivating a teacher community of practice for sustainable professional development: beyond planned efforts. *Teachers and Teaching*, *21*(1), 4–21. doi:10.1080/13540602.2014.928120

Malaysian Communications and Multimedia Commission. (2017). Internet users survey 2017. Retrieved from https://www.mcmc.gov.my/skmmgovmy/media/General/pdf/MCMC-Internet-Users-Survey-2017.pdf

Malaysian Communications and Multimedia Commission. (2018). Internet users survey 2018. Retrieved from https://www.mcmc.gov.my/skmmgovmy/media/General/pdf/Internet-Users-Survey-2018.pdf

Malerba, M. L. (2011). Social networking in language learning. In M. Ciastellardi, C. Miranda de Almeida, & C.A. Scolari (Eds.), *McLuhan galaxy Conference. Understanding Media, Today. Conference Proceedings* (pp.142-153).

Malerba, M. L. (2012). L2 Learners' informal online interactions in social network communities. Conference paper. *CALL: Using, learning, knowing*. Gothenburg. Retrieved from http://www.researchgate.net/publication/269243503

Malerba, M. L. (2015). Learner's behaviours and autonomy in and Busuu online communities. Conference paper. Retrieved from http://www.researchgate.net/publication/280730772

Manago, A. M., Taylor, T., & Greenfield, P. M. (2012). Me and my 400 friends: the anatomy of college students' Facebook networks, their communication patterns, and well-being. *Developmental Psychology*, *48*(2), 369–380. doi:10.1037/a0026338 PMID:22288367

Mann, S., & Walsh, S. (2017). *Reflective practice in English language teaching: research-based principles and practices*. Abingdon, UK: Routledge. doi:10.4324/9781315733395

Ma, Q. (2019). Examining the role of inter-group peer online feedback on wiki writing in an EAP context. *Computer Assisted Language Learning*, 1–20. doi:10.1080/09588221.2018.1556703

Maretich, K. (2017). Data in the digital age: charting the way for multimedia learning. *Australian Primary Mathematics Classroom*, *22*(4), 22–26.

Margaryan, A., Littlejohn, A., & Vojt, G. (2011). Are digital natives a myth or reality? University students' use of digital technologies. *Computers & Education*, *56*(2), 429–440. doi:10.1016/j.compedu.2010.09.004

Marin, L., & Halpern, D. (2011). Pedagogy for developing critical thinking in adolescents: Explicit instruction produces greatest gains. *Thinking Skills and Creativity*, *6*(1), 1–13. doi:10.1016/j.tsc.2010.08.002

Marsick, V. J., & Watkins, K. E. (2001). Informal and incidental learning. *New Directions for Adult and Continuing Education*, *89*(89), 25–34. doi:10.1002/ace.5

Mattarima, K., & Hamdan, A. R. (2011). Learners' motivation and learning strategies in English foreign language (EFI) in Indonesian context. *Journal of Edupres*, *1*, 100–108.

Mattarima, K., & Hamdan, A. R. (2016). The teaching constraints of English as a foreign language in Indonesia: The context of school-based curriculum. *Sosiohumanika*, *4*(2), 287–300.

Matthew, K. I., & Callaway, R. A. (2009). Wiki as a collaborative learning tool in a language arts methods class. *Journal of Research on Technology in Education*, *42*(1), 51–72. doi:10.1080/15391523.2009.10782541

Matthews, T., Pierce, J., & Tang, J. (2009). No smartphone is an island: The impact of places, situations, and other devices on smartphone use. IBM Technical Report #RJ10452. Retrieved from https://domino.research.ibm.com/library/cyberdig.nsf/papers/F5FD878B5B062ACA85257635004EC3F5/$File/rj10452.pdf

Mavhunga, F., Kibirige, I., Chigonga, B., & Ramaboka, M. (2016). Smartphones in public secondary schools: Views of matric graduates. *Perspectives in Education*, *34*(3), 72–85. doi:10.18820/2519593X/pie.v34i3.6

Ma, W. L., & He, J. J. (2017). A study on characteristics of excellent micro-lectures of foreign languages. *Technology Enhanced Foreign Language Education*, *174*, 22–26.

Ma, W., & Hu, J. (2015). On the impact of international MOOCs and redesign of college English curriculum. *CAFLT*, *157*, 48–54.

Ma, W., Kuang, S., Su, X., & Liu, S. (2018). A study on college English instruction in a MOOC-based flipped classroom in China. In J. Colpaert (Ed.), pp. 260-270. *Proceedings of the 19th International CALL Research Conference CALL Your Data*, Brugge (Belgium) University of Antwerp.

Mayrath, M. C., Traphagan, T., Heikes, E. J., & Trivedi, A. (2011). Instructional design best practices for Second Life: A case study from a college-level English course. *Interactive Learning Environments*, *19*(2), 125–142. doi:10.1080/10494820802602568

Mazman, S. G., & Usluel, Y. K. (2011). Gender differences in using social networks. *The Turkish Online Journal of Educational Technology*, *10*(2), 133–139.

McGrath, A. L., Taylor, A., & Pychyl, T. A. (2011). Writing helpful feedback: the influence of feedback type on students perceptions and writing performance. *The Canadian Journal for the Scholarship of Teaching and Learning*, *2*(2), 1–14. doi:10.5206/cjsotl-rcacea.2011.2.5

McLnnis, L. (2009). *Analyzing English L1 and L2 paraphrasing strategies through concurrent verbal report and stimulated recall protocols.* (Unpublished master's thesis). University of Toronto, Toronto.

McNiff, J. (1988). *Action research: Principles and practices*. London, UK: Routledge. doi:10.4324/9780203305676

Melchor-Couto, S. (2017). Foreign language anxiety levels in Second Life oral interaction. *ReCALL*, *29*(1), 99–119. doi:10.1017/S0958344016000185

Merriam, S. B., & Tisdell, E. J. (2016). *Qualitative research: a guide to design and implementation* (4th ed.). Jossey Bass.

Milićević, J., & Tsedryk, A. (2011). Assessing and improving paraphrasing competence in FSL. In I. Boguslavsky, & L. Wanner (Eds.), *Proceedings of the 5th international conference on meaning-text theory* (pp. 175-184). Barcelona, Spain: Pompeu Fabra University.

Ministry of Education Malaysia. (2013). *Malaysia education blueprint 2013-2025 (Preschool to post-secondary education)*. Ministry of Education Malaysia.

Mishra, P., & Koehler, M. J. (2006). Technological pedagogical content knowledge: a framework for teacher knowledge. *Teachers College Record*, *108*(6), 1017–1054. doi:10.1111/j.1467-9620.2006.00684.x

Misra, N., Dangi, S., & Patel, S. (2015). Gender differences in usage of social networking sites and perceived online social support on psychological well-being of youth. *The International Journal of Indian Psychology*, *3*(1), 63–74.

Miyazoe, T., & Anderson, T. (2010). Learning outcomes and students' perceptions of online writing: Simultaneous implementation of a forum, blog, and wiki in an EFL blended learning setting. *System*, *38*(2), 185–199. doi:10.1016/j.system.2010.03.006

Mohamed, A. F. S. (2017). *Immediate feedback in a morphology software application for English vocabulary learning.* (Unpublished master's thesis). Washington State University, Pullman, WA.

Mohammadi, M., & Moradi, K. (2017). Exploring change in EFL teachers' perceptions of professional development. *Journal of Teacher Education for Sustainability, 19*(1), 22–42. doi:10.1515/jtes-2017-0002

Mollerup, P. (2014). Slide presentations, seriously. *Visible Language, 48*(1), 4–21.

Moore, M. G. (1973). Toward a theory of independent learning and teaching. *The Journal of Higher Education, 44*(9), 661–679. doi:10.2307/1980599

Morris, C., & Chikwa, G. (2014). Screencasts: How effective are they and how do students engage with them? *Active Learning in Higher Education, 15*(1), 25–37. doi:10.1177/1469787413514654

Morris, C., & Chikwa, G. (2016). Audio versus written feedback: Exploring learners' preference and the impact of feedback format on students' academic performance. *Active Learning in Higher Education, 17*(2), 125–137. doi:10.1177/1469787416637482

Motzo, A., & Proudfoot, A. (2017). MOOCs for language learning – opportunities and challenges: the case of the Open University Italian Beginners' MOOCs. In Q. Kan, & S. Bax (Eds.), Beyond the language classroom: Researching MOOCs and other innovations. (pp. 85-98). Dublin, Ireland: Research Publishing.net.

Mousavi, S. A. (2009). Multimedia as a test method facet in oral proficiency tests. *International Journal of Pedagogies & Learning, 5*(1), 37–48. doi:10.5172/ijpl.5.1.37

Mufida, A. R., Mukhyaiyar, M., & Radjab, D. (2013). The effect of content-based instruction and task-based language teaching on the second semester students' speaking skill and students' speaking motivation of English Department Islamic University Indragiri. [ELT]. *English Language Teaching, 1*(3).

Muhaimin, M., Habibi, A., Mukminin, A., Saudagar, F., Pratama, R., Wahyuni, S., ... Indrayana, B. (2019). A sequential explanatory investigation of TPACK: Indonesian science teachers' survey and perspective. *Journal of Technology and Science Education, 9*(3), 269–281. doi:10.3926/jotse.662

Muncie, J. (2002). Process writing and vocabulary development: Comparing lexical frequency profiles across drafts. *System, 30*(2), 225–235. doi:10.1016/S0346-251X(02)00006-4

Murphy, K., DePasquale, R., & McNamara, E. (2003). Meaningful connections: Using technology in primary classrooms. *The National Association for the Education of Young Children (NAEYC).* Retrieved from http://www.naeyc.org/files/yc/file/200311/TechInPrimaryClassrooms.pdf

Murray, J. (2011, Nov. 11). Do students know more about technology than their teachers? *The Guardian* (online edition). Retrieved from http://www.theguardian.com/education/2011/nov/21/multiple-choice-students-teachers-technology

Murray, L., & Hourigan, T. (2008). Blogs for specific purposes: Expressivist or socio-cognitivist approach? *ReCALL, 20*(1), 82–97. doi:10.1017/S0958344008000719

Murthy, S., Warriem, J., & Iyer, S. (2017). Technology integration for student-centered learning; A model for teacher professional development programs. In S. Kong, T. Wong, M. Yang, C. Chow, & K. Tse (Eds.), *Emerging practices in scholarship of learning and teaching in a digital era* (pp. 55–74). Singapore: Springer. doi:10.1007/978-981-10-3344-5_4

Mustafa, Z. (2010). Teachers' levels of use in the adoption of task-based language teaching in Malaysian classrooms. *The International Journal of Interdisciplinary Social Sciences: Annual Review, 5*(3), 127–138. doi:10.18848/1833-1882/CGP/v05i03/51621

Musthafa, B. (2015). Communicative language teaching in Indonesia: Issues of theoretical assumptions and challenges in the classroom practice. *TEFLIN Journal*, *12*(2), 184–193.

Nagy, W. E. (1995). The role of context in first- and second-language vocabulary learning. *Technical Report No. 627*, Center for the Study of Reading, Urbana, IL.

Naidorf, J. (2014). Knowledge utility: from social relevance to knowledge mobilization. *Education Policy Analysis Archives*, *22*(89). Retrieved from https://eric.ed.gov/?q=Naidorf%2c+J.+2014.+%e2%80%9cKnowledge+Utility%3a+From+Social+Relevance+to+Knowledge+Mobilization.%e2%80%9d+Education+Policy+Analysis+Archives+22+(89)%3a+1%e2%80%9331.&pr=on&id=EJ1050049

Nair, S. S., Tay, L. Y., & Koh, J. H. L. (2013). Students' motivation and teachers' teaching practices towards the use of blogs for writing of online journals. *Educational Media International*, *50*(2), 108–119. doi:10.1080/09523987.2013.795351

Nakatsuhara, F., Inoue, C., & Taylor, L. (2017b). *An investigation into double-marking methods: comparing live, audio and video rating of performance on the IELTS speaking test*. Retrieved from https://www.ielts.org/teaching-and-research/research-reports/ielts_online_rr_2017-1

Nakatsuhara, F., Inoue, C., Berry, V., & Galaczi, E. (2017a). Exploring the use of video-conferencing technology in the assessment of spoken language: A mixed-methods study. *Language Assessment Quarterly*, *14*(1), 1–18. doi:10.1080/15434303.2016.1263637

Nam, I. S. (2013, July 23). A rising addiction among youths: Smartphones. *The Wall Street Journal* (online edition). Retrieved from http://online.wsj.com/news/articles/SB10001424127887324263404578615162292157222

Nami, F., & Marandi, S. S. (2013). Wikis as discussion forums: Exploring students' contribution and their attention to form. *Computer Assisted Language Learning*, *27*(6), 483–508. doi:10.1080/09588221.2013.770036

Nascimento, A. K., & Knobel, M. (2017). What's to be learned? A review of sociocultural digital literacies research within pre-service teacher education. *Nordic Journal of Digital Literacy*, *12*(3), 67–88. doi:10.18261/issn.1891-943x-2017-03-03

Nation, I. S. P. (2005). Ten best ideas for teaching vocabulary. The Japan Association for Language Teaching, 29(7), 5-6.

Nation, I. S. P. (2001). *Learning vocabulary in another language*. Cambridge, UK: Cambridge University Press. doi:10.1017/CBO9781139524759

Nation, I. S. P. (2006). How large a vocabulary is needed for reading and listening? *Canadian Modern Language Review*, *63*(1), 59–82. doi:10.3138/cmlr.63.1.59

Nation, I. S. P., & Newton, J. (2008). *Teaching ESL/EFL listening and speaking*. New York: Routledge. doi:10.4324/9780203891704

Nerbonne, J., Dokter, D., & Smit, P. (1998). Morphological processing and computer-assisted language learning. *Computer Assisted Language Learning*, *11*(5), 543–559. doi:10.1076/call.11.5.543.5660

Ng, L. S., Thang, S. M., & Mohd, N. N. (2018). The usage of social networking sites for informal learning: a comparative study between Malaysia students of different gender and age group. [IJCALLT]. *International Journal of Computer-Assisted Language Learning and Teaching*, *8*(4), 76–88. doi:10.4018/IJCALLT.2018100106

Nguyen, P. T. (2012). Peer feedback on second language writing through blogs: The case of a Vietnamese EFL classroom. [IJCALLT]. *International Journal of Computer-Assisted Language Learning and Teaching*, *2*(1), 13–23. doi:10.4018/ijcallt.2012010102

Nielsen, J. (1993). *Usability engineering.* San Francisco, CA: Morgan Kaufmann. doi:10.1016/B978-0-08-052029-2.50007-3

Nielson, K. B. (2011). Self-study with language learning software in the workplace: What happens? *Language Learning & Technology, 15*(3), 110–129.

Nielson, K. B. (2014). Evaluation of an online, task-based Chinese course. In M. González-Lloret, & L. Ortega (Eds.), *Technology-mediated TBLT: Researching technology and tasks* (pp. 295–322). Amsterdam, The Netherlands: John Benjamins.

Nightingale, P. (1988). Understanding processes and problems in student writing. *Studies in Higher Education, 13*(3), 263–283. doi:10.1080/03075078812331377720

Nikian, S., Nor, F. M., & Aziz, M. A. (2013). Malaysian teachers' perception of applying technology in the classroom. *Procedia: Social and Behavioral Sciences, 103*, 621–627. doi:10.1016/j.sbspro.2013.10.380

Nimrod, G. (2013). Applying gerontographics in the study of older Internet users. *Journal of Audience & Perception Study, 10*(2), 46–64.

Norton, B. (2013). *Identity and language learning: Extending the conversation* (2nd ed.). Bristol, UK: Multilingual Matters. doi:10.21832/9781783090563

Noytim, U. (2010). Weblogs enhancing EFL students' English language learning. *Procedia: Social and Behavioral Sciences, 2*(2), 1127–1132. doi:10.1016/j.sbspro.2010.03.159

Numrich, C. (1996). On becoming a language teacher: Insights from diary studies. *TESOL Quarterly, 30*(1), 131–153. doi:10.2307/3587610

Nunan, D. (1997). Designing and adapting materials to encourage learner autonomy. In P. Benson, & P. Voller (Eds.), *Autonomy and independence in language learning* (pp. 192–203). Harlow, UK: Longman.

Nunan, D. (2004). *Task-based language teaching* (Rev. ed.). Cambridge, UK: Cambridge University Press. doi:10.1017/CBO9780511667336

Nunan, D. (2015). *Teaching English to speakers of other languages: an introduction.* London, UK: Routledge. doi:10.4324/9781315740553

O' Dwyer, A. (2018). An insight into how a constructivist professional development program can influence practice in six high school chemistry classrooms. *Journal of Science Teacher Education, 29*(5), 353–377. doi:10.1080/1046560X.2018.1457348

O'Donnell, S., & Epstein, L. (2019). Smartphones are more reinforcing than food for students. *Addictive Behaviors, 90*, 124–133. doi:10.1016/j.addbeh.2018.10.018 PMID:30390436

O'Loughlin. (2001). *The equivalence of direct and semi-direct speaking tests. Studies in Language Testing, 13.* Cambridge, UK: Cambridge University Press.

O'Sullivan, B., & Dunlea, J. (2015). *Aptis general technical manual: Version 1* (TR/2015/005). Retrieved from https://www.britishcouncil.org/aptis-general-technical-manual-version-10

O'Sullivan, B. (2000). Exploring gender and oral proficiency interview performance. *System, 28*(3), 373–386. doi:10.1016/S0346-251X(00)00018-X

Ockey, G., Koyama, D., Setoguchi, E., & Sun, A. (2015). The extent to which TOEFL iBT speaking scores are associated with performance on oral language tasks and oral ability components for Japanese university students. *Language Testing, 32*(1), 39–62. doi:10.1177/0265532214538014

Okan, Z. (2008). Computing laboratory classes as language learning environments. *Learning Environments Research, 11*(1), 31–48. doi:10.100710984-007-9035-y

Oksman, V., & Turtianinen, J. (2004). Mobile communication as a social stage: Meanings of mobile communication in everyday life among teenagers in Finland. *New Media & Society, 6*(3), 319–339. doi:10.1177/1461444804042518

Onguko, B. B. (2014). JiFUNzeni: A blended learning approach for sustainable teachers' professional development. *Electronic Journal of E-Learning, 12*(1), 77–88.

Orsini-Jones, M. (2015). Integrating a MOOC into the MA in English Language Teaching at Coventry University. York, UK: Higher Education Academy. Retrieved from https://www.heacademy.ac.uk/sites/default/files/marina_orsini_jones_final.pdf

Orsini-Jones, M. (2018) Chinese English teachers' perspectives on "distributed flip MOOC blends": From BMELTT to BMELTE'. Coventry, UK: Coventry University. Retrieved from https://vilte.warwick.ac.uk/items/show/49?

Orsini-Jones, M., & Cerveró Carrascosa, A. (2019). BMELTET – Blending MOOCs into English language teacher education with telecollaboration. In A. Plutino, K. Borthwick, & E. Corradini (Eds.), *New educational landscapes: innovative perspectives in language learning and technology* (pp. 1-7). Research-publishing.net.

Orsini-Jones, M., Altamimi, S., & Conde, B. (2017). Integrating a MOOC into the postgraduate ELT curriculum: Reflecting on students' beliefs with a MOOC blend. In Q. Kan, & S. Bax (Eds.), *Beyond the language classroom: researching MOOCS and other innovations* (pp. 71-83). Dublin, Ireland: Researchpublishing.net. doi:10.14705/rpnet.2017.mooc2016.672

Orsini-Jones, M., Pibworth-Dolinski, L., Cribb, M., Brick, B., Gazeley-Eke, Z., Leinster, H., & Lloyd, E. (2015). Learning about language learning on a MOOC: how massive, open, online and "course"? In F. Helm, L. Bradley, M. Guarda, & S. Thouësny (Eds.), *Critical CALL – Proceedings of the 2015 EUROCALL Conference,* Padova, Italy (pp. 450-457). Dublin, Ireland: Research-publishing.net. doi:10.14705/rpnet.2015.000374

Orsini-Jones, M., Zou, B., Borthwick, K., & Conde, B. (2017). BMELTT (Blending MOOCs for English language teacher training): a 'distributed MOOC flip' to explore local and global ELT contexts and beliefs (pp. 608-625). In R. Kern, J. Colpaert, A. Aerts, & M. Kaiser, *Proceedings of the XVIIIth International CALL Conference: CALL in Context,* UC Berkeley. Retrieved from http://call2017.language.berkeley.edu/wpcontent/uploads/2017/07/CALL2017_proceedings.pdf

Orsini-Jones, M., Zou, B., Hu, Y., & Li, W. (2017). Chinese English teachers' perspectives on "distributed flip MOOC blends": From BMELTT to BMELTE, special issue of IJCALLT, 7(4), pp. 1-14.

Orsini-Jones, M., Brick, B., & Pibworth, L. (2013). Practising language interaction via social networking sites: The expert student's perspective on personalized language learning. In B. Zou, M. Xing, Y. Wang, M. Sun, & C. H. Xiang (Eds.), *Computer-assisted foreign language teaching and learning: Technological advances* (pp. 40–53). Hershey, PA: IGI Global. doi:10.4018/978-1-4666-2821-2.ch003

Orsini-Jones, M., & Lee, F. (2018). *Intercultural communicative competence for global citizenship: identifying rules of engagement in telecollaboration.* Basingstoke, UK: Palgrave MacMillan. doi:10.1057/978-1-137-58103-7

Ortega, L. (2012). Task-based language teaching in foreign language contexts: One pragmatist's view. Paper presented at the *Plenary delivered at JASELE Conference*, Nagoya, Japan.

Ortega, L. (2009). *Understanding second language acquisition.* London, UK: Hodder Education.

Oskaz, A., & Elola, I. (2014). Promoting foreign language collaborative writing through the use of Web 2.0 tools and tasks. In M. González-Lloret, & L. Ortega (Eds.), *Technology-mediated TBLT: Researching technology and tasks*. Amsterdam, The Netherlands: John Benjamins Publishing. doi:10.1075/tblt.6.05osk

Owston, R. D., & Wideman, H. H. (1997). Word processors and children's writing in a high-computer-access setting. *Journal of Research on Computing in Education, 30*(2), 202–220. doi:10.1080/08886504.1997.10782223

Oxford, R. L. (2006). Task-based language teaching and learning: An overview. *Asian EFL Journal, 8*(3), 94–121.

Oxford, R., & Shearin, J. (1994). Language learning motivation: Expanding the theoretical framework. *Modern Language Journal, 78*(1), 12–28. doi:10.1111/j.1540-4781.1994.tb02011.x

Pajares, F. (2003). Self-efficacy beliefs, motivation, and achievement in writing: A review of the literature. *Reading & Writing Quarterly, 19*(2), 139–158. doi:10.1080/10573560308222

Palfrey, J., & Gasser, U. (2008). *Born digital: Understanding the first generation of digital natives*. New York: Basic Books.

Palfreyman, D. (2003). The representation of learner autonomy and learner independence in organizational culture. In D. Palfreyman, & R. C. Smith (Eds.), *Learner autonomy across cultures: Language education perspectives* (pp. 183–200). Basingstoke, UK: Palgrave Macmillan. doi:10.1057/9780230504684_11

Palmer, S. D. (2010). *Second language pragmatic socialization in World of Warcraft*. (Unpublished doctoral dissertation, Office of Graduate Studies, University of California, Davis).

Palomeque, C., & Pujolà, J.-T. (2018). Managing multimodal data in virtual world research for language learning. *ReCALL, 30*(2), 177–195. doi:10.1017/S0958344017000374

Pammu, A., Amir, Z., & Maasum, T. N. R. T. M. (2014). Metacognitive reading strategies of less proficient tertiary learners: A case study of EFL learners at a public university in Makassar, Indonesia. *Procedia: Social and Behavioral Sciences, 118*, 357–364. doi:10.1016/j.sbspro.2014.02.049

Panichi, L. (2015). A critical analysis of learner participation in virtual worlds: How can virtual worlds inform our pedagogy? In F. Helm, L. Bradley, M. Guarda, & S. Thouesny (Eds.), *Critical CALL–Proceedings of the 2015 EUROCALL Conference,* Padova, Italy (pp. 464-469). Dublin, Ireland: Research-publishing.net.

Pappano, L. (2014, Nov. 12). The year of the MOOC. *The New York Times*. Retrieved from https://www.nytimes.com/2012/11/04/education/edlife/massive-open-online-courses-are-multiplying-at-a-rapid-pace.html

Park, C. N., & Son, J.-B. (2009). Implementing computer-assisted language learning in the EFL classroom: Teachers' perceptions and perspectives. *International Journal of Pedagogies and Learning, 5*(2), 80–101. doi:10.5172/ijpl.5.2.80

Park, M., & So, K. (2014). Opportunities and challenges for teacher professional development: a case of collaborative learning community in South Korea. *International Education Studies, 7*(7), 96–108. doi:10.5539/ies.v7n7p96

Park, S. H., & Ertmer, P. (2007). Impact of problem-based learning (PBL) on teachers' beliefs regarding technology use. *Journal of Research on Technology in Education, 40*(2), 247–267. doi:10.1080/15391523.2007.10782507

Payne, A. R. (2012). *Development of the academic writing motivation questionnaire*. (Doctoral Dissertation, University of Georgia).

Pecorari, D. (2003). Good and original: Plagiarism and patchwriting in academic second-language writing. *Journal of Second Language Writing, 12*(4), 317–345. doi:10.1016/j.jslw.2003.08.004

Pecorari, D., & Petrić, B. (2014). Plagiarism in second-language writing. *Language Teaching, 47*(3), 269–302. doi:10.1017/S0261444814000056

Pegrum, M. (2011). Modified, multiplied, and (re-) mixed: Social media and digital literacies. In M. Thomas (Ed.), *Digital Education: opportunities for social collaboration* (pp. 9–35). Basingstoke, UK: Palgrave Macmillan. doi:10.1057/9780230118003_2

Peled, Y., Shalom, O., & Sharon, R. (2014). Characterization of pre-service teachers' attitude to feedback in a wiki-environment framework. *Interactive Learning Environments, 22*(5), 578–593. doi:10.1080/10494820.2012.731002

Pempek, T. A., Yermolayeva, Y. A., & Calvert, S. L. (2009). College students'social networking experiences on Facebook. *Journal of Applied Developmental Psychology, 30*(3), 227–238. doi:10.1016/j.appdev.2008.12.010

Pennycook, A. (2001). *Critical applied linguistics: A critical introduction.* Routledge. doi:10.4324/9781410600790

Perifanou, M. (2016). Designing strategies for an efficient language MOOC. In S. Papadima-Sophocleous, L. Bradley, & S. Thouësny (Eds.), CALL communities and culture – short papers from EUROCALL 2016 (pp. 380-385). Research-publishing.net. doi:10.14705/rpnet.2016.eurocall2016.592

Peterson, M., & Swier, R. (2018). 3D digital games, virtual worlds, and language learning in higher education: continuing challenges in Japan. JALT CALL Journal, *14*(3), 225-238.

Peterson, M. (2010). Learner participation patterns and strategy use in Second Life: An exploratory case study. *ReCALL, 22*(3), 273–292. doi:10.1017/S0958344010000169

Peterson, M. (2011). Towards a research agenda for the use of three-dimensional virtual worlds in language learning. *CALICO Journal, 29*(1), 67–80. doi:10.11139/cj.29.1.67-80

Peterson, M. (2012). EFL learner collaborative interaction in Second Life. *ReCALL, 24*(1), 20–39. doi:10.1017/S0958344011000279

Pettes Guikema, J. (2013). Software review: WeSpeke. *CALICO Journal, 30*(3), 465–471. doi:10.11139/cj.30.3.465-471

Pew Research Center. (2018). Social media use in 2018. Retrieved from http://www.pewinternet.org/2018/03/01/social-media-use-in-2018/

Pew Research. (2018). *Social media use continues to rise in developing countries but plateaus across developed ones.* Retrieved from http://www.pewglobal.org/2018/06/19/social-media-use-continues-to-rise-in-developing-countries-but-plateaus-across-developed-ones/#table

Pham, V. P. H., & Usaha, S. (2016). Blog-based peer response for L2 writing revision. *Computer Assisted Language Learning, 29*(4), 724–748. doi:10.1080/09588221.2015.1026355

Piccardo, E. (2014). *From communicative to action-oriented: A research pathway.* Retrieved from https://www.coe.int/t/dg4/linguistic/Source/CSC605_Research_Guide_English.pdf

Pinkman, K. (2005). Using blogs in the foreign classroom: Encouraging learner independence. *JALT CALL Journal, 1*(1), 12–24.

Pitarch, R. C. (2018). An approach to digital game-based learning: Video-games principles and applications in foreign language teaching. *Journal of Language Teaching Research, 9*(6), 1147–1159. doi:10.17507/jltr.0906.04

Policy on ICT in education. (2010). (p. 104).

Poushter, J., Bishop, C., & Chwe, H. (2019). Social media use continues to rise in developing countries but plateaus across developed ones: Digital divides remain, both within and across countries. Pew Research Center: Global Attitudes & Trends. Retrieved from https://www.pewglobal.org/2018/06/19/social-media-use-continues-to-rise-in-developing-countries-but-plateaus-across-developed-ones/#table

Pozzi, F. (2008). Teaching dimension in web-based learning communities. *International Journal of Web-Based Learning and Teaching Technologies*, *3*(3), 34–43. doi:10.4018/jwltt.2008070103

Prabhu, N. S. (1987). *Second language pedagogy*. Oxford University Press Oxford.

Prensky, M. (2009). H. sapiens digital: from digital immigrants and digital natives to digital wisdom. *Innovate: Journal of Online Education, 5*(3).

Prensky, M. (2001). Digital natives, digital immigrants Part 1. *On the Horizon*, *9*(5), 1–6. doi:10.1108/10748120110424816

Prensky, M. (2005). *What can you learn from a cell phone? Almost anything! The Innovate Gateway 1*. June/July.

Pullen, D. L., & Cole, D. R. (2010). *Multiliteracies and technology enhanced education: social practice and the global classroom*. New York: Information Science Reference. doi:10.4018/978-1-60566-673-0

Qian, D. (2009). Comparing direct and semi-direct modes for speaking assessment: Affective effects on test takers. *Language Assessment Quarterly*, *6*(2), 113–125. doi:10.1080/15434300902800059

Qian, K., & Tang, J. (2018). Researching mobile-assisted English language learning among adult distance learners in China: Emerging practices and learner perception of teacher role. *International Journal of Computer-Assisted Language Learning and Teaching*, *8*(3), 1–28. doi:10.4018/IJCALLT.2018070101

Quaid, E. D. (2018). Output register parallelism in an identical direct and semi-direct speaking test: A case study. *International Journal of Computer-Assisted Language Learning and Teaching*, *8*(2), 75–91. doi:10.4018/IJCALLT.2018040105

Raimes, A. (1991). Out of the woods: Emerging traditions in the teaching of writing. *TESOL Quarterly*, *25*(3), 407–429. doi:10.2307/3586978

Raith, T., & Hegelheimer, V. (2010). Teacher development, TBLT and technology. In M. Thomas, & H. Reinders (Eds.), *Task-based language learning and teaching with technology*. London, UK: Continuum International Publishing Group.

Ramsey, V., & Fitzgibbons, D. (2005). Being in the classroom. *Journal of Management Education, 29*(2), 333–356. doi:10.1177/1052562904271144

Rass, R. A. (2011). Cultural transfer as an obstacle for writing well in English: The case of Arabic speakers writing in English. *English Language Teaching*, *4*(2), 206. doi:10.5539/elt.v4n2p206

Ravizza, S., Hambrick, D., & Fenn, K. (2014). Non-academic Internet use in the classroom is negatively related to classroom learning regardless of intellectual ability. *Computers & Education*, *78*, 109–114. doi:10.1016/j.compedu.2014.05.007

Reemann, E., Alas, E., & Liiv, S. (2013). Interviewer behaviour during oral proficiency interviews: A gender perspective. *Eesti Rakenduslingvistika Uhingu Aastaraamat*, (9), 209-226. doi:10.5128/ERYa9.14

Reeves, T. C., & McKenney, S. (2012). 7 things you should know about educational design research. Web publication/site, EDUCAUSE. Retrieved from http://www.educause.edu/library/resources/7-things-you-should-know-about-educational-design-research

Reeves, B., & Nass, C. (1996). *The media equation: How people treat computers, television, and new media like real people and places*. Cambridge, UK: Cambridge University Press.

Reeves, T. C., & Hedberg, J. G. (2003). *Interactive learning systems evaluation*. Englewood Cliffs, NJ: Educational Technology Publications.

Regan, K., Evmenova, A. S., Sacco, D., Schwartzer, J., Chirinos, D. S., & Hughes, M. D. (2019). Teacher perceptions of integrating technology in writing. *Technology, Pedagogy, and Education*, *28*(1), 1–19. doi:10.1080/1475939X.2018.1561507

Reinders, H., & Hubbard, P. (2013). CALL and learner autonomy: Affordances and constraints. In M. Thomas, H. Reinders, & M. Warschauer (Eds.), *Contemporary Computer Assisted Language Learning* (pp. 359–375). London, UK: Continuum Books.

Reinders, H., & Pegrum, M. (2015). Supporting language learning on the move. An evaluative framework for mobile language learning resources. In B. Tomlinson (Ed.), *Second language acquisition research and materials development for language learning* (pp. 116–141). London, UK: Taylor & Francis.

Reisoğlu, I., Topu, F., Yılmaz, R., Yılmaz, T., & Göktaş, Y. (2017). 3D virtual learning environments in education: A meta-review. *Asia Pacific Education Review*, *18*(1), 81–100. doi:10.100712564-016-9467-0

Resnick, L. B. (1989). *Knowing, learning, and instruction: Essays in honor of Robert Glaser*. New Jersey: Lawrence Erlbaum Associates.

Reynolds, B. L., Wu, W. H., Liu, H. W., Kuo, S. Y., & Yeh, C. H. (2015). Towards a model of advanced learners' vocabulary acquisition: an investigation of l2 vocabulary acquisition and retention by Taiwanese English majors. *Applied Linguistics Review*, *6*(1), 121–144. doi:10.1515/applirev-2015-0006

Reynolds, G. (2008). *Presentation Zen: Simple ideas on presentation design and delivery*. Upper Saddle River, NJ: New Riders Press.

Richards, J. C., & Rodgers, T. S. (2001). Approaches and methods in language teaching (2nd ed.). Cambridge, UK: Cambridge University Press. doi:10.1017/CBO9780511667305

Richards, J. C., & Rodgers, T. S. (2001). Communicative language teaching. *Approaches and methods in language teaching, 2*, 153-177.

Richards, J., & Rogers, T. (2014). *Approaches and methods in language teaching* (3rd ed.). Cambridge, UK: Cambridge University Press.

Richardson, W. (2006). *Blogs, wikis, podcasts, and other powerful web tools for classrooms*. Thousand Oaks, CA: Corwin Press.

Richardson, W. (2011). *Blogs, wikis, podcasts, and other powerful Web tools for classrooms* (3rd ed.). Thousand Oaks, CA: Corwin Press.

Robinson, P. (2005). Cognitive complexity and task sequencing: Studies in a componential framework for second language task design. *International Journal of Applied Linguistics*, *43*(1), 1–32. doi:10.1515/iral.2005.43.1.1

Robson, D. (2016). Our IQs have never been higher – but it hasn't made us smarter. *BBC Online*. Retrieved from http://www.bbc.com/future/story/20160929-our-iqs-have-never-been-higher-but-it-hasnt-made-us-smart

Rogers, E. M. (2003). *Diffusion of innovations* (5th ed.). New York, NY: Free Press.

Rogerson, A. M., & McCarthy, G. (2017). Using Internet based paraphrasing tools: Original work, patchwriting or facilitated plagiarism? *International Journal for Educational Integrity*, *13*(1), 2. doi:10.100740979-016-0013-y

Røkenes, F. M., & Krumsvik, R. J. (2014). Development of student teachers' digital competence in teacher education: A literature review. *Nordic Journal of Digital Literacy*, *9*(4), 250–280.

Rollinson, P. (2005). Using peer feedback in the ESL writing class. *ELT Journal*, *59*(1), 23–30. doi:10.1093/elt/cci003

Rosell-Aguilar, F. (2005). Task design for audiographic conferencing: Promoting beginner oral interaction in distance language learning. *Computer Assisted Language Learning*, *18*(5), 417–442. doi:10.1080/09588220500442772

Rosell-Aguilar, F. (2017). State of the app: A taxonomy and framework for evaluating language learning mobile applications. *CALICO Journal*, *34*(2), 243–258.

Rosenfeld, E., Bernstein, J., & Balogh, J. (2005). Validation of an automatic measurement of Spanish speaking proficiency. *The Journal of the Acoustical Society of America*, *117*(4), 2428–2428. doi:10.1121/1.4786630

Rourke, L., & Kanuka, H. (2009). Learning in communities of inquiry: A review of the literature. *Journal of Distance Education*, *23*(1), 19–48.

Rudd, A., & Tyldesley, A. (2006). *Literacy and ICT in the primary school*. London, UK: David Fulton Publishers.

Russell, T. L. (1999). *The no significant difference phenomenon*. Raleigh, NC: North Carolina State University.

Saad, K. A., Walsh, B., Mallaburn, A., & Brundrett, M. (2017). Exploring the implementation of professional learning communities in Malaysian schools. *International Journal of Education. Psychology and Counselling*, *2*(5), 1–18.

Sadler, R., & Dooly, M. (2014). Language learning in virtual worlds: Research and practice. In M. Thomas, H. Reinders, & M. Warschauer (Eds.), *Contemporary computer-assisted language learning* (pp. 159–182). New York, NY: Bloomsbury.

Salkind, N. (2010). *Encyclopedia of Research Design*. doi:10.4135/9781412961288

Salmond, R., & Smith, D. T. (2011). Cheating death-by-PowerPoint: Effective use of visual aids at professional conferences. *PS, Political Science & Politics*, *44*(3), 589–596. doi:10.1017/S1049096511000813

Salmon, G. (2009). The future for (second) life and learning. *British Journal of Educational Technology*, *40*(3), 526–538. doi:10.1111/j.1467-8535.2009.00967.x

Salvucci, D., & Taatgen, N. (2008). Threaded cognition: An integrated theory of concurrent multitasking. *Psychological Review*, *115*(1), 101–130. doi:10.1037/0033-295X.115.1.101 PMID:18211187

Sama, C. M., & Wu, Y. (2019). Integrating "Talk Abroad" into the intermediate foreign language course: Building learner autonomy and engagement through video conversations with native speakers. In M. L. Carrio-Pastor (Ed.), *Teaching language and teaching literature in virtual environments* (pp. 73–94). Singapore: Springer Nature Singapore Pte Ltd. doi:10.1007/978-981-13-1358-5_5

Samuda, V. (2001). Guiding relationships between form and meaning during task performance: The role of the teacher. In M. Bygate, P. Skehan, & M. Swain (Eds.), *Researching pedagogic tasks: Second language learning, teaching and testing* (pp. 119–140). Harlow, UK: Longman.

Sánchez, R. A., Cortijo, V., & Javed, U. (2014). Students' perceptions of Facebook for academic purposes. *Computers & Education*, *70*, 138–149. doi:10.1016/j.compedu.2013.08.012

Sandberg, J., Maris, M., & de Geus, K. (2011). Mobile English learning: An evidence-based study with fifth graders. *Computers & Education*, *57*(1), 1334–1347. doi:10.1016/j.compedu.2011.01.015

Sandeen, C. (2013). Integrating MOOCs into traditional higher education: the emerging "MOOC 3.0" Era. *Change*, *45*(6), 34–39. doi:10.1080/00091383.2013.842103

Sang, G., Valcke, M., Braak, J. V., & Tondeur, J. (2010). Student teachers' thinking processes and ict integration: Predictors of prospective teaching behaviors with educational technology. *Computers & Education*, *54*(1), 103–112. doi:10.1016/j.compedu.2009.07.010

Sardegna, V. G., & Dugartsyrenova, V. A. (2014). Pre-service foreign language teachers' perspectives on learning with technology. *Foreign Language Annals*, *47*(1), 147–167. doi:10.1111/flan.12078

Sattar, S. (2015). Learning via blogging: The ESL/EFL perspective. [JEd]. *GSTF Journal on Education, 3*(1), 7–12.

Sauro, S. (2009). Computer-mediated corrective feedback and the development of L2 grammar. *Language Learning & Technology, 13*, 96–120.

Schmidgall, J. E. (2017). *The consistency of TOEIC speaking scores across ratings and tasks* (Research Report No. RR-17-46). Princeton, NJ: Educational Testing Service. doi:10.1002/ets2.12178

Schmid, R., Bernard, R., Borokhovski, E., Tamim, R., Abrami, P., Surkes, M., ... Woods, J. (2014). The effects of technology use in postsecondary education: A meta-analysis of classroom applications. *Computers & Education, 72*, 271–291. doi:10.1016/j.compedu.2013.11.002

Schmidt, R. (1995). Consciousness and foreign language learning: A tutorial on the role of attention and awareness in learning. In R. Schmidt (Ed.), Attention and awareness in foreign language learning (Tech. Rep. No. 9, pp. 1–63). University of Hawaii at Manoa: Second Language Teaching and Curriculum Center.

Schmidt, R. (1990). The role of consciousness in second language learning. *Applied Linguistics, 11*(2), 129–158. doi:10.1093/applin/11.2.129

Schmidt, R. (1995). Consciousness and foreign language learning: A tutorial on the role of attention and awareness in learning. In R. Schmidt (Ed.), *Attention and awareness in foreign language learning* (pp. 1–63). Honolulu, HI: University of Hawaii, Second Language Teaching & Curriculum Center.

Schmidt, R., & Frota, S. N. (1986). Developing basic conversational ability in a second language: A case study of an adult learner of Portuguese. In R. R. Day (Ed.), *Talking to learn: Conversation in second language acquisition* (pp. 237–326). Rowley, MA: Newbury House.

Schmitt, N. (2008). Instructed second language vocabulary learning. *Language Teaching Research, 12*(3), 329–363. doi:10.1177/1362168808089921

Schmitt, N., Jiang, X., & Grabe, W. (2011). The percentage of words known in a text and reading comprehension. *Modern Language Journal, 95*(i), 26–43. doi:10.1111/j.1540-4781.2011.01146.x

Schmitt, N., & Schmitt, D. (2014). A reassessment of frequency and vocabulary size in L2 vocabulary teaching. *Language Teaching, 47*(4), 484–503. doi:10.1017/S0261444812000018

Schoepp, K. (2005). Barriers to technology integration in a technology-rich environment. *Learning and Teaching in Higher Education: Gulf Perspectives, 2*(1), 1–24.

Schön, D. (1983). *The reflective practitioner: how professionals think in action.* New York: Basic Books.

Schroeder, R. (2008, July). Defining virtual worlds and virtual environments. *Journal of Virtual Worlds Research: Past, Present, & Future, 1*(1), 2–3.

Schunk, D. H., Meece, J. R., & Pintrich, P. R. (2008). *Motivation in education: Theory, research, and applications* (3rd ed.). Harlow, UK: Pearson Education Ltd.

Schunk, D. H., & Zimmerman, B. J. (Eds.). (2008). *Motivation and self-regulated Learning: Theory, research, and applications.* New York, NY: Lawrence Erlbaum.

Scrivner, O., Madewell, J., Buckley, C., & Perez, N. (2019). Best practices in the use of augmented and virtual reality technologies for SLA: Design, implementation and feedback. In M. L. Carrio-Pastor (Ed.), Teaching language and teaching literature in virtual environments (pp. 55-70). Springer, Singapore: Springer Nature Singapore Pte Ltd.

Sedhu, D., Lee, M., & Choy, S. (2013). The influence of teaching strategies on students' paraphrasing strategies: A case study. *International Journal of Independent Research and Studies*, *2*(3), 130–137.

Seedhouse, P., & Morales, S. (2017). *Candidates questioning examiners in the IELTS speaking test: An intervention study*. Retrieved from https://www.ielts.org/-/media/research-reports/ielts_online_rr_2017-5.ashx

Seedhouse, P., & Almutairi, S. (2009). A holistic approach to task-based interaction. *International Journal of Applied Linguistics*, *19*(3), 311–338. doi:10.1111/j.1473-4192.2009.00243.x

Selwyn, N. (2003). Apart from technology: Understanding people's non-use of information and communication technologies in everyday life. *Technology in Society*, *25*(1), 99–116. doi:10.1016/S0160-791X(02)00062-3

Selwyn, N. (2007). An investigation in undergraduates' academic use of the Internet. *Active Learning in Higher Education*, *9*(1), 11–22. doi:10.1177/1469787407086744

Selwyn, N. (2009). Faceworking: Exploring students' education-related use of "Facebook". *Learning, Media, and Technology*, *34*(2), 157–174. doi:10.1080/17439880902923622

Séror, J. (2013). Show me! Enhanced feedback through screencasting technology. *TESL Canada Journal*, *30*(1), 104–116. doi:10.18806/tesl.v30i1.1128

Shao, Y., & Crook, C. (2015). The potential of a mobile group blog to support cultural learning among overseas students. *Journal of Studies in International Education*, *19*(5), 1–14. doi:10.1177/1028315315574101

Sharp, S. K. (2017). *iPads in the second language classroom: An examination of iPad use by teachers through TPACK and teacher perception lenses* (Unpublished doctoral dissertation). University of Maryland, College Park.

Sharples, M., Goodlet, J. S., Beck, E. E., Wood, C. C., Easterbrook, S. M., & Plowman, L. (1993). *Research issues in the study of computer supported collaborative writing*. London, UK: Springer. doi:10.1007/978-1-4471-2007-0

Sharples, M., Taylor, J., & Vavoula, G. (2007). A theory of learning for the mobile age. In R. Andrews, & C. Haythornthwaite (Eds.), *The Sage handbook of e-learning research* (pp. 221–247). London, UK: Sage. doi:10.4135/9781848607859.n10

Shelton, C. (2018). "You have to teach to your personality": Caring, sharing, and teaching with technology. *Australasian Journal of Educational Technology*, *34*(4). doi:10.14742/ajet.3557

Shih, R. C. (2011). Can Web 2.0 technology assist college students in learning English writing? Integrating Facebook and peer assessment with blended learning. *Australasian Journal of Educational Technology*, *27*(5), 829–845. doi:10.14742/ajet.934

Shih, Y. C., & Yang, M. T. (2008). A collaborative virtual environment for situated language learning using VEC3D. *Journal of Educational Technology & Society*, *11*(1), 56–68.

Shi, L. (2004). Textual borrowing in second-language writing. *Written Communication*, *21*(2), 171–200. doi:10.1177/0741088303262846

Shi, L. (2012). Rewriting and paraphrasing source texts in second language writing. *Journal of Second Language Writing*, *21*(2), 134–148. doi:10.1016/j.jslw.2012.03.003

Shohamy, E., Donitsa-Schmidt, S., & Waizer, R. (1993). *The effect of the elicitation mode on the language samples obtained in oral tests*. Paper presented at the 15th Language Testing Research Colloquium, Cambridge, UK.

Shohamy, E. (1994). The validity of direct versus semi-direct oral tests. *Language Testing*, *11*(2), 99–123. doi:10.1177/026553229401100202

Shrestha, S., & Harrison, T. (2019). Using machinima as teaching and learning materials: A Nepalese case study. *International Journal of Computer-Assisted Language Learning and Teaching*, *9*(2), 37–52. doi:10.4018/IJCALLT.2019040103

Shulman, L. S. (1986). Those who understand: knowledge growth in teaching. *Educational Researcher*, *15*(2), 4–14. doi:10.3102/0013189X015002004

Siemens, G. (2005). Connectivism: A learning theory for the digital age. *International Journal of Instructional Technology & Distance Learning*, *2*(1). Retrieved from http://itdl.org/Journal/Jan_05/article01.htm

Silverman, D. (2014). *Interpreting qualitative data* (5th ed.). London, UK: Sage.

Simin, G., & Sani, I. M. (2015). *Effectiveness of ICT integration in Malaysian schools: a quantitative analysis. 2*, 12.

Skehan, P. (1998). *A cognitive approach to language learning*. Oxford University Press.

Smith, A., Rainie, L., & Zickuhr, K. (2011). College students and technology. Pew Research Center. Retrieved from https://www.pewinternet.org/2011/07/19/college-students-and-technology/

Smith, B. V. (2009). *Use of online educational social networking in a school environment.* (Unpublished master's thesis). North Carolina State University, Raleigh, NC. Retrieved from http://www.ncolr.org/jiol/issues/pdf/9.2.4.pdf

Social Media Today. (2016). Gender-specific behaviors on social media and what they mean for online communications. Retrieved from https://www.socialmediatoday.com/social-networks/gender-specific-behaviors-social-media-and-what-they-mean-online-communications

Sokolik, M. (2003). Writing. In D. Nunan (Ed.), *Practical English language teaching* (pp. 87–88). New York: McGraw-Hill.

Sokolik, M. (2014). What constitutes an effective language MOOC? In E. Martin-Monje, & E. Bárcena (Eds.), *Language MOOCs: Providing learning, transcending boundaries* (pp. 16–32). Berlin, Germany: Walter de Gruyter.

Sole, R. C., Calic, J., & Neijmann, D. (2010). A social and self-reflective approach to MALL. *ReCALL*, *22*(1), 39–52. doi:10.1017/S0958344009990188

Solikhah, I. (2015). KKNI dalam kurikulum berbasis learning outcomes. (Indonesian National Framework in learning outcome Curriculum) *LINGUA: Journal of Language. Literature and Teaching*, *12*(1), 1–22. doi:10.30957/lingua.v12i1.68

Somekh, B. (2008). Factors affecting teachers' pedagogical adoption of ICT. In J. Voogt, & G. Knezek (Eds.), *International handbook of information technology in primary and secondary education* (pp. 449–460). doi:10.1007/978-0-387-73315-9_27

Song, K.-O., & Choi, J. (2017). Structural analysis of factors that influence professional learning communities in Korean elementary schools. *International Electronic Journal of Elementary Education*, *10*(1), 1–9.

Sotoudehnamah, E., & Pilehvari, A. (2016). The impact of peer review on EFL learners' writing proficiency: Global and local aspects. *Porta Linguarum*, *25*, 35–47.

Souppouris, A., & Jang, H. J. (2014, March 20). South Korean schools are remotely disabling students' smartphones. *The Verge*. Retrieved from http://www.theverge.com/2014/3/20/5528842/korean-schools-block-smartphones-in-class-ismartkeeper

Spencer, E. J. (2016). Professional learning communities: keeping the focus on instructional practice. *Kappa Delta Pi Record*, *52*(2), 83–85. doi:10.1080/00228958.2016.1156544

Spillane, M., & Shapiro, B. (1992). A small circle of friends. *Nation (New York, N.Y.)*, *25*(8), 279–281.

Spires, H., Hervey, L., & Watson, T. (2013). Scaffolding the TPACK framework in reading and language arts: new literacies, new minds. In *Research on Technology in English Education*. Information Age Publishing.

Sproutsocial. (2017). The Q1 2017 Sprout social index-The social generations: Millennials ask, Gen X buys & Baby Boomers observe. Retrieved from https://sproutsocial.com/insights/data/q1-2017/

Staer, L. S. (2008). Vocabulary size and the skills of listening, reading and writing. *Language Learning Journal*, *36*(2), 139–152. doi:10.1080/09571730802389975

Stake, R. (1988). Case study methods in educational research: Seeking sweet water. In R. M. Jaeger (Ed.), *Complementary methods for research in education*. Washington, DC: American Educational Research Association.

Stansfield, C. W. (1991). A comparative analysis of simulated and direct oral interviews. Anivan, S. (Ed.), Current developments in language testing (pp. 199–209). Singapore: SEAMEO RELC.

Stansfield, C. W., & Kenyon, D. (1992a). The development and validation of a simulated oral proficiency interview. *Modern Language Journal*, *72*(2), 129–141. doi:10.1111/j.1540-4781.1992.tb01093.x

Stansfield, C. W., & Kenyon, D. (1992b). Research on the comparability of the oral proficiency interview and the simulated oral proficiency interview. *System*, *20*(3), 347–364. doi:10.1016/0346-251X(92)90045-5

Starr, A., Al-Najjar, B., Holmberg, K., Jantunen, E., Bellew, J., & Albarbar, A. (2010). Maintenance today and future trends. In K. Holmberg, A. Adgar, A. Arnaiz, E. Jantunen, J. Mascolo, & S. Mekid (Eds.), *E-maintenance* (pp. 5–37). London, UK: Springer-Verlag. doi:10.1007/978-1-84996-205-6_2

Statista.com. (2019) Retrieved from https://www.statista.com/statistics/883712/malaysia-social-media-penetration/

Steel, C. (2012). Fitting learning into life: Language students' perspectives on benefits of using mobile apps. In M. Brown, M. Hartnett, & T. Stewart (Eds.), *ASCILITE 2012 Conference Proceedings* (pp. 875–880). Wellington, New Zealand.

Sternberg, R. J. (1987). Most vocabulary is learned from context. In M. G. McKeown, & M. E. Curtis (Eds.), *The nature of vocabulary acquisition* (pp. 89–105). Hillsdale, NJ: Erlbaum.

Stevenson, M. P., & Liu, M. (2010). Learning a language with Web 2.0: Exploring the use of social networking features of foreign language learning websites. *CALICO Journal*, *27*(2), 233–259. doi:10.11139/cj.27.2.233-259

Stickler, U., & Hampel, R. (2010). Cyber Deutsch: Language production and user preferences in a Moodle VLE. *CALICO Journal*, *28*(1), 49–73. doi:10.11139/cj.28.1.49-73

Stockwell, G. (2007). Vocabulary on the move: Investigating an intelligent mobile phone-based vocabulary tutor. *Computer Assisted Language Learning*, *20*(4), 365–383. doi:10.1080/09588220701745817

Stockwell, G. (2008). Investigating learner preparedness for and usage patterns of mobile learning. *ReCALL*, *20*(3), 253–270. doi:10.1017/S0958344008000232

Stockwell, G. (2010). Using mobile phones for vocabulary activities: Examining the effect of the platform. *Language Learning & Technology*, *14*(2), 95–110.

Stockwell, G. (2012). Introduction. In G. Stockwell (Ed.), *Computer-assisted language learning: Diversity in environments* (pp. 1–13). Cambridge, UK: Cambridge University Press. doi:10.1017/CBO9781139060981.001

Stockwell, G. (2013). Tracking learner usage of mobile phones for language learning outside of the classroom. *CALICO Journal*, *30*, 118–136.

Stockwell, G., & Hubbard, P. (2013). *Some emerging principles for mobile-assisted language learning*. Monterey, CA: The International Research Foundation for English Language.

Stollak, M., Vanderberg, A., Burklund, A., & Weiss, S. (2011). Getting social: The impact of social networking usage on grades among college students. In *Proceedings from ASBBS Annual Conference* (pp. 859-865). Retrieved from http://asbs.org/files/2011/ASBBS2011v1/PDF/S/StollakM.pdf

Storch, N. (2005). Collaborative writing: Product, process, and students' reflections. *Journal of Second Language Writing*, *14*(3), 153–173. doi:10.1016/j.jslw.2005.05.002

Stricker, L. J., & Attali, Y. (2010). *Test takers' attitudes about the TOEFL iBT™*. ETS TOEFL iBT Report No. iBT-13. Retrieved from https://onlinelibrary.wiley.com/doi/pdf/10.1002/j.2333-8504.2010.tb02209.x

Strijbos, J. W., Narciss, S., & Dünnebier, K. (2010). Peer feedback content and senders competence level in academic writing revision tasks: Are they critical for feedback perceptions and efficiency? *Learning and Instruction*, *20*(4), 291–303. doi:10.1016/j.learninstruc.2009.08.008

Sukandi, S. S., & Syafar, D. N. (2018). EFL students' responses to learning basic reading and writing skills. *Studies in English Language and Education*, *5*(1), 40–53. doi:10.24815iele.v5i1.8419

Sulistiyo, U. (2016). Learning English as a foreign language in an Indonesian university: A study of non-English department students' preferred activities inside and outside the classroom. [Indonesian Journal of English Teaching]. *IJET*, *5*(1), 1–26. doi:10.15642/ijet2.2016.5.1.1-26

Sulistyo, T., Mukminatien, N., Cahyono, B. Y., & Saukah, A. (2019). Enhancing learners' writing performance through blog-assisted language Learning. *International Journal of Emerging Technologies in Learning*, *14*(9), 61–73. doi:10.3991/ijet.v14i09.9535

Sullivan, N., & Pratt, E. (1996). A comparative study of two ESL writing environments: A computer-assisted classroom and a traditional oral classroom. *System*, *24*(4), 491–501. doi:10.1016/S0346-251X(96)00044-9

Sundari, H., Febriyanti, R., & Saragih, G. (2018). Using task-based materials in teaching writing for EFL classes in Indonesia. *International Journal of Applied Linguistics and English Literature*, *7*(3), 119–124. doi:10.7575/aiac.ijalel.v.7n.3p.119

Sung, W. J. (2016). A study of the digital divide in the current phrase of the information age: The moderating effect of smartphones. *Information Policy*, *21*(3), 291–306. doi:10.3233/IP-160398

Sung, Y. T., Chang, K. E., & Liu, T. C. (2016). The effects of integrating mobile devices with teaching and learning on students' learning performance. A meta-analysis and research synthesis. *Computers & Education*, *94*, 252–275. doi:10.1016/j.compedu.2015.11.008

Sun, Y. C. (2010). Extensive writing in foreign-language classrooms: A blogging approach. *Innovations in Education and Teaching International*, *47*(3), 327–339. doi:10.1080/14703297.2010.498184

Sun, Y. C. (2012). Does text readability matter? A study of paraphrasing and plagiarism in English as a foreign language writing context. [De La Salle University Manila]. *The Asia-Pacific Education Researcher*, *21*(2), 296–306.

Sun, Y. C., & Chang, Y. J. (2012). Blogging to learn: Becoming EFL academic writers through collaborative dialogues. *Language Learning & Technology*, *16*(1), 43–61.

Suo, G. F., & Chi, R. B. (2018). Blended learning in intercultural foreign language teaching based on MOOCs. *Foreign Language World*, *3*, 89–96.

Surface, E. A., Harman, R. P., Watson, A. M., & Thompson, L. F. (2009). *Are human and computer-administered interviews comparable?* Paper presented at the 24th annual meeting of the Society for Industrial and Organizational Psychology, New Orleans, LA.

Surface, E. A., Poncheri, R. M., & Bhavsar, K. S. (2008). *Two studies investigating the reliability and validity of the English ACTFL OPIc with Korean test takers.* Retrieved from https://www.languagetesting.com/research

Swain, M. (2000). The output hypothesis and beyond. In J. Lantolf (Ed.), *Sociocultural theory and second language acquisition* (pp. 97–114). Oxford, UK: Oxford University Press.

Swain, M. (2013). The inseparability of cognition and emotion in second language learning. *Language Teaching*, *46*(2), 195–207. doi:10.1017/S0261444811000486

Swallow, M. J. C., & Olofson, M. W. (2017). Contextual understandings in the TPACK framework. *Journal of Research on Technology in Education*, *49*(3-4), 228–244. doi:10.1080/15391523.2017.1347537

Swarts, J. (2012). New modes of help: Best practices for instructional video. *Technical Communication (Washington)*, *59*(3), 195–206.

Sweeney, P., & Moore, C. (2012). Mobile apps for learning vocabulary: Categories, evaluation and design criteria for teachers and developers. *International Journal of Computer-Assisted Language Learning and Teaching*, *2*(2), 45–60.

Sweller, J. (1988). Cognitive load during problem solving: Effects on learning. *Cognitive Science*, *12*(2), 257–285. doi:10.120715516709cog1202_4

Sweller, J. (1994). Cognitive load theory, learning difficulty, and instructional design. *Learning and Instruction*, *4*(4), 295–312. doi:10.1016/0959-4752(94)90003-5

Swier, R. (2014). Tasks for easily modifiable virtual environments. *JALT CALL Journal*, *10*(3), 203–219.

Sykes, J. M., Oskoz, A., & Thorne, S. L. (2016). Web 2.0, synthetic immersive environments, and mobile resources for language education. In G. Kessler (Ed.), *Landmarks in CALL research* (pp. 160–183). Bristol, CT: Equinox.

Tagg, C. (2015). *Exploring digital communication: Language in action*. London, UK: Routledge. doi:10.4324/9781315727165

Tahir, L. M., Said, M. N. H. M., Ali, M. F., Samah, N. A., Daud, K., & Mohtar, T. H. (2013). Examining the professional learning community practices: an empirical comparison from Malaysian universities clusters. *Procedia: Social and Behavioral Sciences*, *97*, 105–113. doi:10.1016/j.sbspro.2013.10.210

Tai, S.-J. D. (2015). From TPACK-in-action workshops to classrooms: CALL competency developed and integrated. *Language Learning & Technology*, *19*(1), 139–164.

Talebi, Z., Aidinlou, N. A., & Farhadi, S. (2015). Form-based approaches vs. task-based approaches. *International Journal of Applied Linguistics and English Literature*, *4*(4), 137–143.

Tan, A. (2011). Why write with wikis? In C. M. L. Ho, K. T. Anderson, & A. P. Leong (Eds.), *Transforming literacies and language: multimodality and literacy in the new media age.* London, UK: Continuum.

Tan, K. E. (2017). Using online discussion forums to support learning of paraphrasing. *British Journal of Educational Technology*, *48*(6), 1239–1249. doi:10.1111/bjet.12491

Tapscott, D., & Williams, A. D. (2010). Innovating the 21st-century university: It's time. *EDUCAUSE Review*, *45*(1), 16–29.

Tavakol, M., & Dennick, R. (2011). Making sense of Cronbach's alpha. *International Journal of Medical Education*, *2*, 53–55. doi:10.5116/ijme.4dfb.8dfd PMID:28029643

Taylor, K., & Silver, L. (2019). Smartphone ownership is growing rapidly around the world, but not always equally: In emerging economies, technology use still much more common among young people and the well-educated. Pew Research Center. Retrieved from https://www.pewglobal.org/2019/02/05/smartphone-ownership-is-growing-rapidly-around-the-world-but-not-always-equally/

Teixeira, A. M., & Mota, J. (2014). A proposal for the methodological design of collaborative language MOOCs. In E. Martin-Monje, & E. Bárcena (Eds.), *Language MOOCs: Providing learning, transcending boundaries* (pp. 33–47). Berlin, Germany: Walter de Gruyter. doi:10.2478/9783110420067.3

Thanasoulas, D. (2000). What is learner autonomy and how can it be fostered. *The Internet TESL Journal*, *6*(11), 37–48.

Thang, S. M., Lin, L. K., Mahmud, N., Ismail, K., & Zabidi, N. A. (2014). Technology integration in the form of digital storytelling: Mapping the concerns of four Malaysian ESL instructors. *Computer Assisted Language Learning*, *27*(4), 311–329. doi:10.1080/09588221.2014.903979

The United Nations Educational, Scientific and Cultural Organization (UNESCO). (2004). The plurality of literacy and its implications for policies and programmes. UNESCO Education Sector Position Paper. Retrieved from http://unesdoc.unesco.org/images/0013/001362/136246e.pdf

Thoma, J., Hutchison, A., Johnson, D., Johnson, K., & Stromer, E. (2017). Planning for technology integration in a professional learning community. *The Reading Teacher*, *71*(2), 167–175. doi:10.1002/trtr.1604

Thomas, M. (2013). TBLT in business English communication: An approach for evaluating Adobe Connect and Second Life in a blended language learning format. [IJCALLT]. *International Journal of Computer-Assisted Language Learning and Teaching*, *3*(1), 73–89. doi:10.4018/ijcallt.2013010105

Thomas, M., & Reinders, H. (Eds.). (2010). *Task-based language learning and teaching with technology*. London, UK: Continuum.

Thomas, M., & Schneider, C. (2018). Language teaching in 3D virtual worlds with machinima: Reflecting on an online machinima teacher training course. *International Journal of Computer-Assisted Language Learning and Teaching*, *8*(2), 20–38. doi:10.4018/IJCALLT.2018040102

Thompson, G. L., Cox, T. L., & Knapp, N. (2016). Comparing the OPI and OPIc: The effect of test method on oral proficiency scores and student preference. *Foreign Language Annals*, *49*(1), 75–92. doi:10.1111/flan.12178

Thompson, S. C., Gregg, L., & Niska, J. M. (2004). Professional learning communities, leadership, and student learning. *RMLE Online: Research in Middle Level Education*, *28*(1), 1–15. doi:10.1080/19404476.2004.11658173

Thompson, W. F., Schellenberg, E. G., & Letnic, A. K. (2012). Fast and loud background music disrupts reading comprehension. *Psychology of Music*, *40*(6), 700–708. doi:10.1177/0305735611400173

Thornbury, S. (2004). *How to teach vocabulary*. Longman: Pearson Education Limited.

Thorne, S. (2013). Digital literacies. In M. Hawkins (Ed.), *Framing languages and literacies: socially situated views and perspectives* (pp. 192–218). New York: Routledge.

Thornton, K. (2010). Supporting self-directed learning: A framework for teachers. *Language*.

Thornton, P., & Houser, C. (2005). Using mobile phones in English education in Japan. *Journal of Computer Assisted Learning*, *21*(3), 217–228. doi:10.1111/j.1365-2729.2005.00129.x

Tiene, C. D. (2000). Online discussions: A survey of advantages and disadvantages compared to face-to-face discussions. *Journal of Educational Multimedia and Hypermedia*, *9*(4), 371–384.

Tondeur, J., van Braak, J., Sang, G., Voogt, J., Fisser, P., & Ottenbreit-Leftwich, A. (2012). Preparing pre-service teachers to integrate technology in education: A synthesis of qualitative evidence. *Computers & Education, 59*(1), 134–144. doi:10.1016/j.compedu.2011.10.009

Tondeur, J., van Keer, H., van Braak, J., & Valcke, M. (2008). ICT integration in the classroom: Challenging the potential of a school policy. *Computers & Education, 51*(1), 212–223. doi:10.1016/j.compedu.2007.05.003

Topping, K. J. (1998). Peer assessment between students in colleges and universities. *Review of Educational Research, 68*(3), 249–276. doi:10.3102/00346543068003249

Tossell, C. (2012). An empirical analysis of internet use on smartphones: Characterizing visit patterns and user differences. (Unpublished Doctoral Dissertation, Rice University). Retrieved from https://scholarship.rice.edu/bitstream/handle/1911/64626/TOSSELL-THESIS.pdf?sequence=1&isAllowed=y

Tossell, C., Kortum, P., Shepard, C., Rahmati, A., & Zhong, L. (2015). You can lead a horse to water but you can't make him learn: Smartphone use in higher education. *British Journal of Educational Technology, 46*(4), 713–724. doi:10.1111/bjet.12176

Trajtemberg, C., & Yiakoumetti, A. (2011). Weblogs: A tool for EFL interaction, expression, and self-evaluation. *ELT Journal, 65*(4), 437–445. doi:10.1093/elt/ccr015

Truscott, J. (1998). Noticing in second language acquisition: a critical review. *Second Language Research, 14*(2), 103–135. doi:10.1191/026765898674803209

Tseng, J.-J., Lien, Y.-J., & Chen, H.-J. (2016). Using a teacher support group to develop teacher knowledge of mandarin teaching via web conferencing technology. *Computer Assisted Language Learning, 29*(1), 127–147. doi:10.1080/09588221.2014.903978

Tsutsui, M. (2004). Multimedia as a means to enhance feedback. *Computer Assisted Language Learning, 17*(3-4), 377–402.

Turkish Ministry of Development. (2015). *Public investments of information and communication technologies*. Department of Information Society. Retrieved from http://www.bilgitoplumu.gov.tr/wp-content/uploads/2015/04/2015_Kamu_BIT_Yatirimlari_Raporu.pdf

Turkle, S. (2011). *Alone together: Why we expect more from technology and less from each other*. New York: Basic Books.

Uemlianin, I. A. (2000). Engaging text: Assessing paraphrase and understanding. *Studies in Higher Education, 25*(3), 347–358. doi:10.1080/713696160

Umar, I. N., & Hassan, A. S. A. (2015). Malaysian teachers' levels of ICT integration and its perceived impact on teaching and learning. *Procedia: Social and Behavioral Sciences, 197*, 2015–2021. doi:10.1016/j.sbspro.2015.07.586

Umar, I. N., & Jalil, N. A. (2012). ICT skills, practices, and barriers of its use among secondary school students. *Procedia: Social and Behavioral Sciences, 46*, 5672–5676. doi:10.1016/j.sbspro.2012.06.494

Umar, I., & Rathakrishnan, M. (2012). The effects of online teachers' social role and learning style on students' essay writing performance and critical thinking in a wiki environment. *Procedia: Social and Behavioral Sciences, 46*, 5730–5735. doi:10.1016/j.sbspro.2012.06.506

United Nations Educational, Scientific and Cultural Organization (UNESCO). (2008). *ICT competency standards for teachers – competency standard modules*. Retrieved from http://unesdoc.unesco.org/images/0015/001562/156207e.pdf

Ushioda, E. (2013). Motivation matters in mobile language learning: A brief commentary. *Language Learning & Technology, 17*(3), 1–5.

van den Berg, R. (2002). Teacher's meanings regarding educational practice. *Review of Educational Research, 72*(4), 577–625. doi:10.3102/00346543072004577

Van den Branden, K. (2016). Task-based language teaching. In G. Hall (Ed.), *The Routledge handbook of English language teaching* (pp. 238–252). Routledge.

Van der Pol, J., Van den Berg, B. A. M., Admiraal, W. F., & Simons, P. R. J. (2008). The nature, reception, and use of online peer feedback in higher education. *Computers & Education, 51*(4), 1804–1817. doi:10.1016/j.compedu.2008.06.001

Van Dixhoorn, L., Loiseau, M., Mangenot, F., Potolia, A., & Zourou, K. (2010). Language learning: Resources and networks. Study operated by the network 'language learning and social media'. Retrieved http://www.elearningeuropa.info/files/LS6/Language_learning-resources_and_networks.pdf

Van Duzor, A. (2011). Capitalizing on teacher expertise: motivations for contemplating transfer from professional development to the classroom. *Journal of Science Education and Technology, 20*(4), 363–374. doi:10.100710956-010-9258-z

van Gelder, T. (2005). Teaching critical thinking: Some lessons from cognitive science. *College Teaching, 53*(1), 41–46. doi:10.3200/CTCH.53.1.41-48

van Laar, E., van Deursen, A. J., van Dijk, J. A., & de Haan, J. (2017). The relation between 21st-century skills and digital skills: A systematic literature review. *Computers in Human Behavior, 72*, 577–588. doi:10.1016/j.chb.2017.03.010

van Lier, L. (2004). *The ecology and semiotics of language learning: A sociocultural perspective.* Boston, MA: Kluwer Academic. doi:10.1007/1-4020-7912-5

Varidesk, (2017, Nov. 2). Minecraft can transform your world language classroom. *EdTech.* Retrieved from https://edtechmagazine.com/k12/article/2017/11/minecraft-can-transform-your-world-language-classroom

Vasinda, S., Ryter, D. A., Hathcock, S., & Wang, Q. (2017). Access is not enough: a collaborative autoethnographic study of affordances and challenges of teacher educators' iPad integration in elementary education methods courses. [CITE Journal]. *Contemporary Issues in Technology & Teacher Education, 17*(3).

Vavik, L., & Salomon, G. (2015). Twenty First Century skills vs. disciplinary studies. In Handbook of research on technology tools for real-world skill development (pp. 1-12). Hershey, PA: IGI Global.

Venkatesh, V., Morris, M. G., Davis, G. B., & Davis, F. D. (2003). User acceptance of information technology: Toward a unified view. *Management Information Systems Quarterly, 27*(3), 425–478. doi:10.2307/30036540

Vescio, V., Ross, D., & Adams, A. (2008). A review of research on the impact of professional learning communities on teaching practice and student learning. *Teaching and Teacher Education, 24*(1), 80–91. doi:10.1016/j.tate.2007.01.004

Vesselinov, R., & Grego, J. (2016). *The Busuu efficacy study.* Retrieved from https://www.busuu.com/en/it-works/university-study

Vinagre, M., & Lera, M. (2008). The role of error correction in online exchanges. In F. Zhang, & B. Barber (Eds.), *Handbook of research on computer-enhanced language acquisition and learning* (pp. 326–341). Hershey, PA: IGI Global. doi:10.4018/978-1-59904-895-6.ch019

Vinagre, M., & Munoz, B. (2011). Computer-mediated corrective feedback and language accuracy in telecollaborative exchanges. *Language Learning & Technology, 15*(1), 72–103.

Vivian, R., & Barnes, A. (2010). Social networking: From living technology to learning technology? In C.H. Steel, M. J. Keppell, P. Gerbic, & S. Housego (Eds.), Curriculum, Technology, & Transformation for an unknown Future. Proceedings of Ascilite Sydney 2010, 1007–1019.

Vserv. (2015). Smartphone user Persona report (SUPR) 2015. Retrieved from https://www.vserv.com/vserv-unveils-first-smartphone-user-persona-report-supr-malaysia/

Vurdien, R. (2013). Enhancing writing skills through blogging in an advanced English as a foreign Language class in Spain. *Computer Assisted Language Learning*, *26*(2), 126–143. doi:10.1080/09588221.2011.639784

Vygotsky, L. S. (1978). *Mind in society: The development of higher psychological processes*. Cambridge, MA: Harvard University Press.

Wang, S., & Vasquez, C. (2012). Web 2.0 and second language learning: What does the research tell us? *CALICO Journal, 29*(3), pp. 412-430.

Wang, A. (2014). Managing student participation: Teacher strategies in a virtual English course. *The JALT CALL Journal*, *10*(2), 105–125.

Wang, A. (2015). Facilitating participation: Teacher roles in a multiuser virtual learning environment. *Language Learning & Technology*, *19*(2), 156–176.

Wang, A. (2015). Facilitating participation: Teacher roles in a multi-user virtual learning environment. *Language Learning & Technology*, *19*(2), 156–176.

Wang, A. (2017). Using Second Life in an English course: How does the technology affect participation? *International Journal of Computer-Assisted Language Learning and Teaching*, *7*(1), 66–85. doi:10.4018/IJCALLT.2017010105

Wang, A. (2017a). *Learning English in a multi-user virtual environment: exploring factors affecting participation (PhD dissertation)*. Sundsvall, Sweden: Mid Sweden University. Retrieved from http://urn.kb.se/resolve?urn=urn:nbn:se:miun:diva-30795

Wang, A., Deutschmann, M., & Steinvall, A. (2013). Towards a model for mapping participation: Exploring factors affecting participation in a telecollaborative learning scenario in Second Life. *The JALT CALL Journal*, *9*(1), 3–22.

Wang, A., Steinvall, A., & Deutschmann, M. (2014). Who owns the floor? Examining participation in a collaborative learning scenario between student teachers and active professionals in second life. *International Journal of Virtual and Personal Learning Environments*, *5*(1), 34–53. doi:10.4018/ijvple.2014010103

Wang, C. P., Lan, Y. J., Tseng, W. T., Lin, Y. T. R., & Gupta, K. C. L. (2019). On the effects of 3D virtual worlds in language learning–a meta-analysis. *Computer Assisted Language Learning*, *32*, 1–25.

Wang, C. X., Lefaiver, M. L. M., Wang, Q., & Hunt, C. (2011). Teaching in an EFL program in second life: Student teachers' perspectives and implications. *Journal of Educational Technology Development and Exchange*, *4*(1), 27–40. doi:10.18785/jetde.0401.03

Wang, C. X., Song, H., Stone, D. E., & Yan, Q. (2009). Integrating SL into an EFL program in China: Research collaboration across the continents. *TechTrends*, *53*(6), 14–19. doi:10.100711528-009-0337-z

Wang, D., Zou, B., & Xing, M. (2012). Interactive learning between Chinese students learning English and English students leaning Chinese on the platform of wiki. [IJCALLT]. *International Journal of Computer-Assisted Language Learning and Teaching*, *1*(3), 70–85. doi:10.4018/ijcallt.2011070105

Wang, D., Zou, B., & Xing, M. (2014). Vocabulary learning and consolidation with mobile application. *International Journal of Computer-Assisted Language Learning and Teaching*, *4*(31), 101–112. doi:10.4018/ijcallt.2014010106

Wang, F., & Hannafin, J. (2005). Design-based research and technology-enhanced learning environments. *ETR&D*, *53*(4), 5–23. doi:10.1007/BF02504682

Wang, J., Hao, Y. H., & Lu, J. L. (2014). The effect of the presentation styles of videos on the effectiveness of autonomous learning. *Curriculum and Teaching*, (03): 93–99.

Wang, Y., & Baker, R. (2018). Grit and intention: Why do learners complete MOOCs? *International Review of Research in Open and Distributed Learning*, *19*(3). doi:10.19173/irrodl.v19i3.3393

Wang, Y.-C. (2015). Promoting collaborative writing through wikis: A new approach for advancing innovative and active learning in an ESP context. *Computer Assisted Language Learning*, *28*(6), 499–512. doi:10.1080/09588221.2014.881386

Ware, P. (2011). Computer-generated feedback on student writing. *TESOL Quarterly*, *45*(4), 769–775. doi:10.5054/tq.2011.272525

Ware, P., & Kessler, G. (2013). CALL and digital feedback. In M. Thomas, H. Reinders, & M. Warschauer (Eds.), *Contemporary Computer-Assisted Language Learning* (pp. 323–339). London, UK: Continuum.

Ware, P., & Kessler, G. (2016). Telecollaboration in the secondary language classroom: Case study of adolescent interaction and pedagogical integration. *Computer Assisted Language Learning*, *29*(3), 427–450. doi:10.1080/09588221.2014.961481

Ware, P., & O'Dowd, R. (2008). Peer feedback on language form in telecollaboration. *Language Learning & Technology*, *12*(1), 43–63.

Warr, M., Mishra, P., & Scragg, B. (2019, March). Beyond TPACK: Expanding technology and teacher education to systems and culture. In K. Graziano (Ed.), *Society for Information Technology & Teacher Education International Conference* (pp. 2558-2562). Las Vegas, NV: Association for the Advancement of Computing in Education (AACE). Retrieved from https://www.learntechlib.org/primary/p/208009

Warschauer, M. (2000). The changing global economy and the future of English teaching. *TESOL Quarterly*, *34*(3), 511–535. doi:10.2307/3587741

Warschauer, M. (2000). The death of cyberspace and the rebirth of CALL. *English Teachers Journal*, *1*, 61–67.

Warschauer, M. (2000). The death of cyberspace and the rebirth of CALL. *English Teachers'. Journal*, *53*, 61–67.

Warschauer, M. (2010). Invited commentary: new tools for teaching writing. *Language Learning & Technology*, *14*(1), 3–8.

Warschauer, M., & Healey, D. (1998). Computers and language learning: An overview. *Language Teaching*, *31*(2), 57–71. doi:10.1017/S0261444800012970

Webster, T. (2011). *Doing what works: A substantive grounded theory of teachers' perceptions and uses of technology in a Korean university general English department.* (Unpublished doctoral dissertation). Toowoomba, Australia: The University of Southern Queensland. Retrieved from http://eprints.usq.edu.au/19651/2/Webster_2011_whole.pdf

Webster, T. E., & Son, J.-B. (2015). Doing what works: A grounded theory case study of technology use by teachers of English at a Korean university. *Computers & Education*, *80*, 84–94. doi:10.1016/j.compedu.2014.08.012

Webster, T., & Son, J.-B. (2012). Implementing proactive maintenance policies to address problems with access to technology at Korean universities. *International Journal of Pedagogies and Learning*, *7*(2), 109–121. doi:10.5172/ijpl.2012.7.2.109

Wehner, A. K., Gump, A. W., & Downey, S. (2011). The effects of Second Life on the motivation of undergraduate students learning a foreign language. *Computer Assisted Language Learning*, *24*(3), 277–289. doi:10.1080/09588221.2010.551757

Weir, C. J. (2005). *Language testing and validation: An evidenced-based approach.* London, UK: Palgrave Macmillan. doi:10.1057/9780230514577

Wenger, E. (1998). *Communities of practice: Learning, meaning, and identity*. New York, NY: Cambridge University Press. doi:10.1017/CBO9780511803932

Wenger-Trayner, E., & Wenger-Trayner, B. (2015). Introduction to communities of practice: a brief overview of the concept and its uses. Retrieved from https://wenger-trayner.com/introduction-to-communities-of-practice/

Wertz, F. J., Charmaz, K., McMullen, L. M., Josselson, R., Anderson, R., & McSpadden, E. (2011). *Five ways of doing qualitative analysis*. New York, NY: Guilford.

West, J. A., & West, M. L. (2009). *Using wikis for online collaboration: The power of the read-write web*. San Francisco, CA: Jossey-Bass.

Wichadee, S. (2013). Improving students' writing ability through collaboration: A comparison between online wiki group and conventional face- to- face group. *TOJET: The Turkish Online Journal of Educational Technology*, *12*(3), 107–116.

Wigham, C. R., & Chanier, T. (2013). A study of verbal and nonverbal communication in Second Life— The ARCHI21 experience. *ReCALL*, *25*(1), 63–84. doi:10.1017/S0958344012000250

Wik, P., & Hjalmarsson, A. (2009). Embodied conversational agents in computer assisted language learning. *Speech Communication*, *51*(10), 1024–1037. doi:10.1016/j.specom.2009.05.006

Willis, J. (1996). *A framework for task-based learning*. Harlow, UK: Longman.

Wilson, K. B., & Acheampong, B. (2014). Implications of computer technology in language teaching: Accessing CALL in teacher education. *US-China Education Review*, *4*(9), 651–661.

Wok, S., & Mohamed, S. (2017). Internet and social media in Malaysia: Development, challenges and potentials. *The Evolution of Media Communication*, 45-64.

Woo, M., Chu, S., Ho, A., & Li, X. (2010). Collaborative writing with a wiki in a primary five English classroom. *Managing knowledge for global and collaborative innovations*. 193-206.

Wozney, L., Vivek, V., & Abrami, P. (2006). Implementing computer technologies: Teachers' perceptions and practices. *Journal of Technology and Teacher Education*, *14*(1), 173–207. Retrieved from https://www.learntechlib.org/primary/p/5437/

Wu, H. (2015). *The effects of blog-supported collaborative writing on writing performance, writing anxiety and perceptions of EFL college students in Taiwan*. (Doctoral Dissertation, University of South Florida).

Wu, Y.-L. (2014). The impact of technology on language learning. In J. H. Park, Y. Pan, C.-S. Kim, & Y. Yang (Eds.), Future Information Technology (pp. 727–731). Springer Berlin. doi:10.1007/978-3-642-55038-6_112

Xu, Q., & Yu, S. (2018). An action research on computer-mediated communication (CMC) peer feedback in EFL writing context. *The Asia-Pacific Education Researcher*, *27*(3), 207–216. doi:10.100740299-018-0379-0

Yakut, A. D., & Aydın, S. (2015). An experimental study on the effects of the use of blogs on EFL reading comprehension. *Innovation in Language Learning and Teaching*, *11*(1), 1–16. doi:10.1080/17501229.2015.1006634

Yaman, H. (2009). Teachers' views on the applicability of the Turkish course curriculum in crowded primary classrooms. *Educational Sciences: Theory and Practice*, *9*(1), 349–359.

Yang, S. C., & Chen, Y. J. (2007). Technology-enhanced language learning: A case study. *Computers in Human Behavior*, *23*(1), 860–879. doi:10.1016/j.chb.2006.02.015

Yang, Y. F., & Meng, W. T. (2013). The effects of online feedback training on students' text revision. *Language Learning & Technology*, *17*(2), 220–238.

Yao, C. (2019, March). How peer review affects Chinese adult college students' English writing acquisition in a computer assisted online learning environment? [IOP Publishing]. *Journal of Physics: Conference Series*, *1176*(2), 022044. doi:10.1088/1742-6596/1176/2/022044

Yasuda, S. (2017). Toward a framework for linking linguistic knowledge and writing expertise: Interplay between SFL-based genre pedagogy and task-based language teaching. *TESOL Quarterly*, *51*(3), 576–606. doi:10.1002/tesq.383

Yeboah, J., & Ewur, G. (2014). The impact of Whatsapp Messenger usage on students' performance in tertiary institutions in Ghana. *Journal of Education and Practice*, *5*(6), 157–164.

Yin, R. K. (2014). *Case study research: Design and methods* (5th ed.). London, UK: Sage.

Yonezaki, M. (2016). A comparative analysis of semi-direct speaking testing and direct speaking testing for Japanese EFL learners. *International Journal of Curriculum Development and Practice*, *18*(1), 27–38. doi:10.18993/jcrdaen.18.1_27

Young, P. T. (1961). Motivation and emotion: A survey of the determinants of human and animal activity.

Younie, S., Audain, J., Eloff, I., Leask, M., Procter, R., & Shelton, C. (2018). Mobilising knowledge through global partnerships to support research-informed teaching: Five models for translational research. *Journal of Education for Teaching*, *44*(5), 574–589. doi:10.1080/02607476.2018.1516348

Yuksel, D., & Inan, B. (2014). The effects of communication mode on negotiation of meaning and its noticing. *ReCALL*, *26*(3), 333–354. doi:10.1017/S0958344014000147

Yulastri, D. (2015b). Enriching students' vocabulary by using charade game. Proceeding Research Interchange between Politeknik Negeri Padang, Indonesia and Leyte Normal University, Philippines, 1, 57-62.

Yulastri, D. (2015a). Building students' writing skill by using Edmodo. *Journal Polingua*, *4*(2), 47–51.

Yulastri, D., Aulia, D., & Saptopramono, H. (2016). The use of Edmodo to improve the writing ability of English department students of State Polytechnic of Padang. *Journal Polingua*, *5*(2), 67–72.

Yu, S., & Lee, I. (2016). Exploring Chinese students' strategy use in a cooperative peer feedback writing group. *System*, *58*, 1–11. doi:10.1016/j.system.2016.02.005

Yusop, F. D., & Sumari, M. (2013). The use of social media technologies among Malaysian youth. *Procedia: Social and Behavioral Sciences*, *103*, 1204–1209.

Zhang, P., & Aikman, S. (2007, July 22-27). *Attitudes in ICT acceptance and use.* Paper presented at the International Conference on Human Computer Interaction, Beijing, China.

Zhang, X. (2017). Researching into a MOOC embedded flipped classroom model for college English reading and writing course. In Q. Kan, & S. Bax (Eds.), Beyond the language classroom: researching MOOCs and other innovations (pp. 15-27). Dublin, Ireland: Research-publishing.net. doi:10.14705/rpnet.2017.mooc2016.668

Zhang, E., Zhang, W., & Jin, C. (2018). SPOC-based flipped classroom of college English: Construction of an effective learning model. [iJET]. *International Journal of Emerging Technology*, *13*(01), 37–45. doi:10.3991/ijet.v13i01.7513

Zhang, Y., & Guo, H. (2012). A study of English writing and domain-specific motivation and self-efficacy of Chinese EFL learners. *Journal of Pan-Pacific Association of Applied Linguistics*, *16*(2), 101–121.

Zhan, Y., & Wan, Z. H. (2016). Test takers' beliefs and experiences of a high-stakes computer-based English listening and speaking test. *RELC Journal*, *47*(3), 363–376. doi:10.1177/0033688216631174

Zheng, J., Wang, Y. N., Wang, K. L., & Bai, Y. (2012). A study into the design of micro-lecturing videos. *China Educational Technology,* (04), 21-24.

Zheng, Y., & Zhang, Y. (2017). *Aptis in China: Exploring test-taker perceptions of its test validity and practicality* (AR-G/2017/6). Retrieved from https://www.britishcouncil.org/sites/default/files/ying_layout.pdf

Zheng, D. (2012). Caring in the dynamics of design and languaging: Exploring second language learning in 3D virtual spaces. *Language Sciences*, *34*(5), 543–558. doi:10.1016/j.langsci.2012.03.010

Zheng, D., Young, M. F., Brewer, R. A., & Wagner, M. (2013). Attitude and self-efficacy change: English language learning in virtual worlds. *CALICO Journal*, *27*(1), 205–231. doi:10.11139/cj.27.1.205-231

Zheng, Y., & Cheng, L. (2008). Test review: college English test (CET) in China. *Language Testing*, *25*(3), 408–417. doi:10.1177/0265532208092433

Zhou, Y. J. (2008). A comparison of speech samples of monologic tasks in speaking tests between computer-delivered and face-to-face modes. *Japan Language Testing Association Journal*, *11*, 189–208. doi:10.20622/jltaj.11.0_189

Zhou, Y. J. (2015). Computer-delivered or face-to-face: Effects of delivery mode on the testing of second language speaking. *Language Testing in Asia*, *5*(2), 1–16. doi:10.118640468-014-0012-y

Zhu, Y., Mark Shum, S. K., Brian Tse, S. K., & Liu, J. J. (2015). Word-processor or pencil-and-paper? A comparison of students' writing in Chinese as a foreign language. *Computer Assisted Language Learning*, (ahead-of-print), 1-22.

Zhukova, O. (2018). Novice teachers' concerns, early professional experiences and development: implications for theory and practice. *Discourse and Communication for Sustainable Education*, *9*(1), 100–114. doi:10.2478/dcse-2018-0008

Zhu, Y., Pei, L., & Shang, J. (2017). Improving video engagement by gamification: A proposed design of MOOC videos. In *Proceedings of the International Conference on Blended Learning* (pp. 433-444). New York, NY: Springer. 10.1007/978-3-319-59360-9_38

Ziegler, N. (2016). Taking technology to task: Technology-mediated TBLT, performance, and production. *Annual Review of Applied Linguistics*, *36*, 136–163. doi:10.1017/S0267190516000039

Zimmerman, B. J., & Kitsantas, A. (2007). A writer's discipline: The development of self-regulatory skill. In P. Boscolo, & S. Hidi (Eds.), *Writing and motivation* (pp. 51–69). Oxford, UK: Elsevier.

Zou, B., Li, H., & Li, J. (2018). Exploring a curriculum app and a social communication app for EFL learning. *Computer Assisted Language Learning*, *31*(7), 694–713. doi:10.1080/09588221.2018.1438474

Zou, B., & Yan, X. (2014). Chinese students' perceptions of using mobile devices for English learning. *International Journal of Computer-Assisted Language Learning and Teaching*, *4*(3), 20–33. doi:10.4018/ijcallt.2014070102

Zourou, K., & Loiseau, M. (2013). Bridging design and language interaction and reuse in Livemocha's culture section. In M.-N. Lamy, & K. Zourou (Eds.), *Social networking for language education* (pp. 77–99). Basingstoke, UK: Palgrave Macmillan. doi:10.1057/9781137023384_5

Zulkhairi, M. D., Azizah, A., Abdul Razak, A., & Rafidah, A. R. (2010, November). Community informatics: Success factors at a rural community telecentre. *Proceedings of rural ICT development 3rd national conference on rural ICT development,* UUM Sintok, Malaysia. Retrieved from http:// www.moe.gov.my/userfiles/file/PPP/Preliminary-Blueprint-Eng.pdf

About the Contributors

Michael Thomas is Professor of Higher Education at the University of Central Lancashire and Principal Fellow of the HEA. He holds two PhDs from Newcastle University and Lancaster University respectively and has research interests in the postgraduate research student experience and widening participation. He has worked in universities in the UK, Germany and Japan over 24 years and his latest book series is Global Policy and Critical Futures in Education with Palgrave Macmillan. He is a REF unit of assessment lead and serves as Projects Director at the Graduate School of Education at UCLan.

* * *

Farhana Ahmed has a Ph.D. in Applied Linguistics from York University. Dr. Farhana Ahmed has specialized in the teaching of ESL, EFL, EAP and Business English in countries including Canada, Bahrain, Singapore and Bangladesh. Her research experience and interests include EAP, technology-mediated English language teaching/learning, language learner beliefs, teacher beliefs, and virtual reality environments for the teaching of English.

Faraj Aljarih is a faculty member at the University of Benghazi English Department, Suluq campus in Libya. He holds an M.A. degree from Washington State University, Pullman, in the USA, in English Language Learners and Bilingual Education. Aljarih also holds a Graduate Certificate in Educational Technology across the Curriculum and a second Graduate Certificate in Teaching English Language Learners from Washington State University. His research interests include computer-assisted language learning (CALL) and student engagement, as well as culture and its role in teaching and learning.

Selami Aydın is a professor in the Department of English Language Teaching at Istanbul Medeniyet University, Istanbul, Turkey. He researches on EFL writing, testing, affective states, technology use and social media effects on language learning and teaching processes. Currently, he teaches ELT courses for pre-service EFL teachers.

Baetty Baetty is a researcher and Lecturer in EFL at Politeknik Negeri Padang in Indonesia. Her research interests are in language learning motivation, the use of technology in language learning, and sociolingustics in the language learning context. Baetty has taught in universities and colleges in Indonesia since 2004 and currently works as an EAP tutor for a Summer Pre-sessional Programme at the University of Nottingham. She completed her first degree at the Andalas University, Indonesia, majoring in English (Literature and Linguistics) in 2003 and graduated from the University of Melbourne,

Australia, majoring in Applied Linguistics in TESOL (Teaching English to Other Speakers). Her PhD in Applied Linguistics at the University of Central Lancashire, UK, focused on technology-mediated task-based learning.

Alex Barrett has worked in the assessment of spoken and written discourse throughout his career and across several countries, including the U.S.A., Honduras, Japan, Uzbekistan and China. His current research is in technology-mediated pedagogy, including the application of virtual reality learning environments to written and spoken assessment in English for Academic Purposes. He is also interested in research on language in diplomacy and language teacher training.

Ingrid Barth is head of research projects in the Division of Languages at Tel Aviv University. She has an M.A. in Curriculum Design and a PhD in Educational Technology from Bar-Ilan University. She specializes in providing technology-based solutions for EMI courses and professional development for EMI lecturers. Her research interests focus on digital reading support tools, effective utilization of vocabulary OERs to close high-school – university gaps and design features for overcoming potential barriers to online learning.

Nataliia Borysenko is an Assistant Professor at Higher Colleges of Technology, UAE. She has earned two PhDs: in Linguistics (Kyiv National Linguistic University, Ukraine) and in Language, Literacy, and Technology (Washington State University, USA). A former Fulbright scholar, her research interests are in pragmatics, intercultural communication, and language pedagogy (the use of technology for student engagement and language learning).

Yan Ding is Lecturer in School of Languages and Communication Studies at Beijing Jiaotong University. She holds a PhD in linguistics from the University of Hong Kong. Her research interests include the learning and teaching of EFL vocabulary and writing, design of English MOOCs, and learner emotions.

Joy Egbert is Professor of ELL and education technology at Washington State University, Pullman, in the US. Her research and teaching interests center around learner engagement and technology use. She has published and presented widely on these and other topics and currently serves as a co-editor for IJCALLT.

Chioma Ezeh is a doctoral student in the program in Language, Literacy, and Technology at WSU. She is originally from Nigeria and serves as Vice President of the Nigerian Students and Scholars Association.

Pengpeng Feng is an associate professor in School of Foreign Languages, Sun Yat-sen University. Her research interests are EFL eductaion studies, English-language literature and film studies, gender studies.

David Herman, PhD, is a recent graduate of Washington State University's doctoral program in Language, Literacy, and Technology program. His research focused on online ESL/EFL teacher education. He is currently working as an EFL teacher in a public junior high school in New Taipei City, Taiwan. David's research interests include computer-assisted language learning, online teaching and learning, and language teacher education.

Cynthia C. James has over 15 years of experience in the field of ELT as a teacher, published author, website manager, conference speaker and ELT supervisor at district level. Her research interests include ELT methodology, computer-assisted language learning (CALL), creativity in the language classroom and teacher professional development.

Geoff Lawrence is an Associate Professor in English language teaching/learning and Applied Linguistics at York University, Toronto, Canada. His research explores the potential of online, blended and web-enhanced English language teaching and teacher education programs. His publications and research projects have examined teacher beliefs towards educational innovation, online/blended language teaching methodology and curriculum design in community-based and EAP contexts, along with the integration of plurilingual and intercultural learning in language and teacher education.

Lina Lee is a Professor of Spanish in the Department of Languages, Literatures and Cultures at the University of New Hampshire where she teaches courses in second language acquisition, foreign language methodology and applied linguistics. She has conducted research and published articles on language pedagogy, computer-mediated communication, telecollaborative exchange for intercultural learning, study abroad, peer feedback and discourse analysis. Her articles have appeared in refereed journals, including Foreign Language Annals, Hispania, Language Learning & Technology, CALICO, CALL, ReCALL, System and more.

Wah Lee (PhD) is the Director of Undergraduate Studies at the School of Education, University of Nottingham Malaysia. He has more than 30 years of teaching experience, teaching English and TESL at all levels of basic and higher education in Malaysia. His main research interests are in teacher professional development, TELL, CALL, e-learning, and TESL methodology. He has published extensively in these areas in both international and local journals, books and book chapters.

Sonia Lopez is originally from Colombia and teaches Spanish in the Department of Foreign Languages and Cultures at WSU. She is interested in the use of CALL to teach heritage languages. She is a doctoral candidate in the College of Education at WSU.

Yi Luo is a Ph.D. candidate at Tianjin Foreign Studies University. His research interests include cognitive linguistics and translation studies.

Adnan F. Saad Mohamed is a Ph.D. candidate in Language, Literacy, and Technology at Washington State University, Pullman, WA. His research interests are computer-assisted language learning (CALL) and morphology. He has presented widely around this topic.

Marina Orsini-Jones is Associate Head of School International and Course Director for the MA in English Language Teaching and Applied Linguistics in the School of Humanities at Coventry University. Marina is a Principal Fellow and a National Teaching Fellow of the Higher Education Academy and has been involved in CALL since 1985. Marina has published work on intercultural communicative competence, e-learning innovation, language awareness, CALL, digital literacies and e-portfolio-supported personal development planning. She has delivered numerous papers (including plenaries) at national and international conferences and has been invited to run pedagogical innovation workshops by various

HEIs. Recent publications include: Intercultural Communicative Competence for Global Citizenship with Fiona Lee in 2018 and a British Council ELT research report in 2018 on the re-purposing of existing MOOCs for teacher education in collaboration with Zou, Ma, Conde and Borthwick: https://www.teachingenglish.org.uk/article/b-meltt-blending-moocs-english-language-teacher-training

Emrah Özdemir has an MA degree in the field of English language teaching. He is currently doing PhD in the field of English language teaching. He also teaches English at the School of Foreign Languages at Balikesir University, Turkey. His main research interests are computer assisted language learning, intercultural communication, affective factors and language learning strategies.

Ethan Douglas Quaid is actively involved, both academically and professionally, in the field of language testing and assessment, with his current research being primarily focused on the equivalence of test taker spoken output in face-to-face and computer-based speaking tests, and natural language processing and automated scoring. His research interests also extend to encompass the productive language use skills of speaking and writing in test events more generally.

Miguel Saona-Vallejos is a researcher at the University of Central Lancashire in the UK. He holds a master's degree in Spanish as a Foreign Language and qualified teacher status from Manchester Metropolitan University. His research interests are in social networking and blended language learning.

Seyed Abdollah Shahrokni received his PhD in the Language, Literacy, and Technology Education program at Washington State University, Pullman. His research interests include computer-assisted language learning (CALL) environments, second language socialization (SLS) in online social spaces, and task engagement.

Ng Lay Shi is an experienced lecturer in teaching Chinese Mandarin as Second Language. She obtained her PhD in Linguistics and Applied Linguistics from Beijing Normal University, China. Her area of expertise is in Chinese syntax. Her current research interests include Chinese grammaticalization, CALL and MALL.

Rosalie Sitman holds a doctorate in Latin American History from Tel Aviv University and an M.A. in Modern Languages from Oxford University. She is the Head of the Division of Languages and a researcher of Latin American cultural and intellectual history at the Sverdlin Institute for Latin American History and Culture, both at Tel Aviv University. She has published extensively on the application of new technologies to language teaching, as well as on Latin American cultural history.

Elana Spector-Cohen is the Head of English Programs in the Division of Languages and Director of the International MA TESOL program at Tel Aviv University. Her main areas of interest are virtual exchange in higher education, internationalization in higher education, curriculum and materials design, and educational technology.

Siew Ming Thang is a Professor at the Department of Education at HELP University, Kuala Lumpur. Previously she was a Professor at the School of Language Studies and Linguistics, UKM. Her areas of interest are CALL, Learner Autonomy, Motivation, and Eye-tracking research. She is President of Pac-CALL and Co-chair of GLoCALL series of conferences.

Ruby Vurdien is the director of White Rose Language School in Spain. She holds an MEd and EdD from the University of Sheffield and has been involved with EFL teaching for more than thirty years. She is also a Teacher Trainer, Speaking Examiner for Cambridge English examinations, and the Materials Reviews Editor for Voices, the IATEFL magazine. Her research area focuses on CALL and intercultural learning via telecollaboration. She has published several articles and book chapters.

Airong Wang is now a Lecturer at Xi'an Jiaotong-Liverpool University, China. She obtained Doctor of Philosophy in English from Mid-Sweden University, Sweden. Airong has taught university English courses, ranging from Linguistics, Translation to EAP, in both Chinese and Swedish cultures. Her research interest lies in language learning and teaching in virtual environments, particularly in formal credit English courses taught in 3D virtual worlds, using mobile phones or VR. During the past few years, Airong has been publishing in reputable journals, including SCI-indexed journals.

Le Wang is currently an assistant professor in school of foreign languages, Qingdao University. His research interests include applied linguistics and ecolinguistics.

Thomas E. Webster is the College English Curriculum Committee Chair in the Global Language Education Office (GLEO) of Ewha Womans University. He has a PhD in education, an MEd in teaching second languages, and an MFA in photography. His research focuses on perceptions and uses of technology, and in particular how they relate to curriculum development, student achievement, and teacher training. He has published in international journals such as Computers & Education and The International Journal of Pedagogies and Learning, as well as contributed to book publications such as the Routledge Education series: The Role of Participants in Education Research Ethics, Epistemologies, and Methods.

Intissar Yahia is ABD in Language, Literacy and Technology Education at Washington State University. Her research interests include computer-assisted language learning, second language writing, teaching methods, culture and learning, and universal design for learning.

Xue Zhang, PhD, is a Senior Research Assistant at the University of Hong Kong. Her research interests revolve around English learners (ELs) and center on contributions of individual differences to second language development, CALL, and language task engagement. She has published her work in English for Specific Purposes and The Asia-Pacific Education Researcher. She is currently a Co-PI on a grant project investigating an evidence-based model of ELL task engagement.

Bin Zou is associate professor at the Department of English, Xi'an Jiaotong-Liverpool University. He received his PhD in TESOL and computer technology from the University of Bristol, UK. His research interests include Computer-Assisted Language Learning (CALL), EAP ELT and AI. He has published more than 40 papers including in SSCI and CSSCI journals and chapter books. He is currently the executive committee member of China Computer-Assisted Language Learning Association, committee member of China Foreign Language Education and Technology Association and China ESP Association and the vice chair of China EAP Association.

Index

www.ingramcontent.com/pod-product-compliance
Lightning Source LLC
LaVergne TN
LVHW062108300926
849161LV00010B/2394